RECOGNIZING ABORIGINAL TITLE

Eddie Koiki Mabo

Recognizing Aboriginal Title

The *Mabo* Case and
Indigenous Resistance to
English-Settler Colonialism

PETER H. RUSSELL

UNIVERSITY OF TORONTO PRESS
Toronto Buffalo London

© University of Toronto Press Incorporated 2005
Toronto Buffalo London
Printed in Canada

ISBN 0-8020-3863-8

∞

Printed on acid-free paper

Library and Archives Canada Cataloguing in Publication

Russell, Peter H.
  Recognizing Aboriginal title : the Mabo case and indigenous
resistance to English-settler colonialism / Peter H. Russell.

  Includes bibliographical references and index.
  ISBN 0-8020-3863-8

  1. Native title (Australia)   2. Mabo, Eddie – Trials, litigations, etc.
I. Title.

GN666.R88 2004   346.9404'32'0899915   C2004-906932-2

This book has been published with the help of a grant from the
Canadian Federation for the Humanities and Social Sciences, through
the Aid to Scholarly Publications Programme, using funds provided by
the Social Sciences and Humanities Research Council of Canada.

University of Toronto Press acknowledges the financial assistance to
its publishing program of the Canada Council for the Arts and the
Ontario Arts Council.

University of Toronto Press acknowledges the financial support for
its publishing activities of the Government of Canada through the
Book Publishing Industry Development Program (BPIDP).

In memory of Eddie Koiki Mabo, a shit-disturber *par excellence*

Contents

Acknowledgments

Authors always need a good deal of help in bringing a major scholarly project to fruition. But this author never needed so much help as in the writing of this book.

In the introduction I explain how Jillian Evans at the Australian National University was instrumental in getting me interested in the Mabo story. The two colleagues I contacted soon after going through Jillian's press clipping files were Peter Jull and Garth Nettheim. They both encouraged me to undertake the project and were wonderfully helpful throughout. They are, of course, not responsible for the result, but they are totally responsible for leaving me with no doubt that the project was worth doing.

In researching the book, I was fortunate in the cooperation and assistance I received from a group of people who, like myself, do not draw a sharp line between their professional work and their political advocacy. They were all key players in the story of the *Mabo* case. On the legal side, Barbara Hocking, the late Ron Casten, Ron's daughter Melissa, Bryan Keon-Cohen, and Greg McIntyre were all generous with the time they gave me and the knowledge of the conduct of the litigation they shared with me. On the academic side, historians Noel Loos and Henry Reynolds, Eddie Mabo's friends and colleagues at James Cook University, could not have been more helpful and encouraging, as was anthropologist Nonie Sharp. Besides their help on details of the Mabo story, I learned much from the books they have written. The friendship of Senator Margaret Reynolds, who was involved all the way through the Mabo story and beyond, helped me connect with Australian parliamentary life.

No person could have been more involved in the Mabo story than Bonita 'Netta' Mabo, Eddie Mabo's wife. On my first research trip to

Townsville, I phoned Netta to introduce myself and get her advice on a person to serve as research assistant to guide me to the people and places that were significant in her late husband's life. She surprised me by immediately offering to be that person. I am deeply grateful for Netta's help and kindness. My conversations with Netta and visits to the Mabo home at 23 Hibiscus Street gave me a sense of Eddie Mabo's character and the love that sustained him.

In researching the book, I travelled extensively in Australia. These journeys gave me an opportunity to meet and discuss the implications of the *Mabo* decision with some of Indigenous Australia's political leaders and to visit a number of Aboriginal communities and the Meriam people on Eddie Mabo's island home in the Torres Strait. Among the leaders who took time out of busy lives to talk with me, I want to give particular thanks to both of the Dodsons, Mick and Patrick, Peter Yu of the Kimberly Land Council, David Ross of the Indigenous Land Corporation, Tracker Tilmouth of the Central Land Council, John Abednego of the Torres Strait Regional Authority, Getano Lui of the Island Co-ordinating Council, Ron Day of the Murray Island Council, and Olga Havnen of the National Indigenous Working Group on Native Title. My wife, Sue, and I are most grateful for the gracious hospitality shown to us by the people of two communities where we enjoyed extended stays: Warburton, in the 'red centre' part of Western Australia, and Mer Island in the Torres Strait. Both communities provided a living confirmation of the central thesis of this book that Indigenous recovery of control over their societies and their country is the key to improving their well-being. On Mer we were particularly fortunate in having James Rice, one of the two surviving litigants in the *Mabo* case, as our friend and guide.

I also received much help and encouragement from Australian colleagues and friends, new and old, in the non-Indigenous academic community who, though not players in the Mabo story, are very knowledgeable about their country's politics and law. Among these I owe special thanks to Brian Galligan, Christine Fletcher, Helen Nelson, Jennifer Clark, Mary Edmunds, Barbara Ann Hocking, and Richard Mulgan. I should also acknowledge a special debt to two other 'professional' helpers – the Jesuit scholar Frank Brennan (another beneficiary of Jillian Evans's newspaper files at the ANU) and the filmmaker Trevor Graham. Their conversations and works (in the one case, books, and in the other, documentary films) were for me both instructive and inspirational.

My sense of how *Mabo* was affecting the Australian body politic was enriched by conversations with Australians from all walks of life whom I met in the course of my travels. Just about everyone I talked to had an opinion – usually a strong opinion – about *Mabo* and *Wik* and native title. I thank all these Australians for their candour, goodwill, and patience with a Canadian probing into a subject that goes to the heart of what their country is all about. I owe very special thanks to my friends Tricia and Jim Davey for making their home in Melbourne my home away from home in Australia.

To carry out the comparative framework of my study, it was important also to travel and research in New Zealand. I am particularly grateful to Professor Andrew Sharp at the University of Auckland, for giving generously of his own time and for helping me make so many valuable contacts in the Maori and Pakeha communities, and to Daniel Arsenault, a young Canadian scholar who took time out from his doctoral studies to be a superb guide to leading participants in Maori affairs in the Wellington area.

In Canada it was the Dene Nation in Canada's Northwest Territories that, thirty years ago, first sparked my interest in the political aspirations of Aboriginal peoples. During the writing of this book I had the opportunity to serve as Canada's 'envoy' to the Deh Cho Dene in a process that identified sufficient common ground of principle and interest for Canada and the Deh Cho to enter into treaty negotiations on land and self-government issues. Though this activity delayed the completion of the book, it gave me a first-hand experience in the building of mutual trust that is the necessary prelude to ordering settler-indigenous relations through consensual agreements. I am grateful to the Deh Cho people and the Government of Canada for entrusting me with such a mandate.

In the years immediately preceding my work on this book, my close involvement with Canada's Royal Commission on Aboriginal Peoples gave me exceptional exposure to the history of Aboriginal-state relations and the prospects for a more just and mutually beneficial relationship. I thank the members of the commission, especially the co-chairs, George Erasmus and René Dussault, for this opportunity, and the co-directors of research, Marlene Brent-Castelano and David Hawkes, for the rich streams of scholarship and humane ingenuity they opened up for me. Over the years, and often through the work of the royal commission, many Canadian colleagues have contributed to my education in the law, politics, and philosophy of relations with Indigenous peoples. On the Aboriginal side, I am particularly grateful to Paul Chartrand, Gordon Peters, Taiaiki Alfred, and John Borrows for their insights and knowledge. On the non-Aboriginal side, Michael Asche, Kent McNeil, Brian Slattery and Jim

Tully have been real mentors. I would also like to thank the University of Toronto Press's anonymous readers and Michael Murphy of Queen's University for their helpful comments on the book manuscript.

Throughout this project I have benefited from the support and encouragement of Virgil Duff at the University of Toronto Press, which manages to be highly professional and, at the same time, friendly and personal. And once again I am the fortunate beneficiary of Rosemary Shipton's skilful and intelligent editing.

In researching and thinking through the issues and events discussed in the book, I was helped not only by established scholars but also by student research assistants. The first year of working on this book was my last year of undergraduate teaching at the University of Toronto. This was also the first year for a new program at the university through which students could earn a course credit by participating in a professor's research project. Eleven students signed up to work with me on the Mabo project. Each chose a dimension of particular interest, ranging from the mining industry in Australia, through the history of Indian treaties in the United States, to the beginning of the international Indigenous movement. The binders of background documents and analysis that each of the students created provided a great launch to my research. I drew heavily from this material all the way through the writing of the book. To Rafael Cashman, Julian Davis, Maria Gallo, Greg Gannett, Amanda Keenan, Victoria Lam, Elizabeth Lundy, Nathan Ross, Maria Sciarrettea, Shawna Sklar, and Helen Smetana I owe a vote of thanks for their work, their ideas, and the tonic of their enthusiasm. And I must thank Damian O'Leary, an Australian doing his PhD at the University of Toronto (and now a scholar at the Australian National University), for coordinating the work of this small army of student researchers and bringing us together for meetings and conversation. Damian also began to organize and build my bibliography. Another University of Toronto student who was a tremendous help to me in preparing the manuscript for publication was Amanda Bittner. I am most grateful, too, for the help I was given by Kevin Dolman, a graduate student at the University of New South Wales, in keeping in touch with Indigenous politics and opinion in the wake of the *Wik* decision.

I could not have written this book without the material support of the Social Sciences and Humanities Research Council of Canada. The three-year research grant I received from SSHRC supported my travels in Australia and other research expenses. Nor would I have completed this book without the moral support and companionship of my wife, Sue, who made sure, as she always does, that I did not lose my way.

RECOGNIZING ABORIGINAL TITLE

Introduction

The genesis of this book occurred on a visit to the Australian National University in 1994. More precisely, it occurred in the press-clippings room maintained by the political science program in ANU's Research School of Social Sciences.

Since the mid-1980s I had been visiting Australia researching various aspects of Australia's Constitution and efforts to reform the Constitution. My aim was to add a comparative dimension to my inquiry into the politics of constitutional change.[1] On these visits, like many other foreign scholars, I found the newspaper files at the ANU of enormous help in bringing me up to date on what had been happening in the country since my previous visit. The clipping service was in the care of a most capable and helpful custodian, Jillian Evans, who was knowledgeable about Australian politics and knew her regular foreign visitors well. If Jillian Evans knew you were coming, she would have all the files she anticipated you would need ready for inspection.

On the day I arrived in March 1994 a pile of files was waiting for me, with news magazines and cuttings from Australia's major national and regional newspapers on my usual topics of interest – reform of the federal system, talk of restructuring Parliament, arguments about an Australian bill of rights and the republic, judicial reform, appointments to the High Court, and various constitutional centenary celebrations. By tea time I had read them all through and returned the files to the desk. 'Well,' I said, 'there's not much brewing on the constitutional front these days.' Evans, looking at me quizzically, replied, 'I didn't show you the *Mabo* files.' I knew that a year or so earlier the High Court had rendered a decision having something to do with common law land rights on a tiny island at the outer edge of Australia, but I had not considered it of major constitutional significance. On that point, Jillian Evans was far more insightful than I. She suggested that if I had time, I had better look at her collection of *Mabo* clippings.

When I returned the next day and Jillian came to my office pushing a trolley load of files, I was astonished. The press cuttings covered the twenty months since the High Court's *Mabo* decision on 3 June 1992 to March 1994. After an initial explosion of excited coverage in the days immediately following the decision, reporting in the next eight months, including the election in March 1993, was moderately heavy but not intense. However, after the election, as the Keating government pushed ahead with its plan 'to legislate native title,' I could see that *Mabo* and native title was Australia's top political news story. The intensity and passion of Australia's nine-month struggle over legislating native title reminded me of one of Canada's big constitutional rounds when all the country's major political players were preoccupied with proposals for constitutional change. The clincher was the cartoons. Scarcely a day went by without a political cartoon on the latest turn in the native title debate. Cartoonists must deal with issues, personalities, and events with which the body politic is so engaged that they are readily recognized by the newspapers' mass audience. Clearly the Australian body politic was more engaged in *Mabo* and native title than it had been in any of the other constitutional issues or events I had been studying. By the end of that day (and I wasn't nearly through reading all the files) I had decided to write a book about *Mabo*.

The project had the attraction of bringing together all three of my research interests – judicial politics, constitutional politics, and Aboriginal politics.[2] When I began my political science career in 1958, judicial politics was recognized as an important field of political science study only in the United States. Elsewhere – and this was certainly the case in Australia and Canada – because judges exercised little political power or, more likely, because the dominant intellectual paradigms were blind to judicial power, the judiciary was not a subject of political science inquiry. Over the next few decades, however, the reality of judicial power and the inescapably creative nature of adjudication began to be recognized in Canada. My political science colleagues became less puzzled by my interest in the courts, and lawyers and judges less dubious about a layman encroaching on their domain. In Australia the advent of judicial realism came much later. To this day, most Australian barristers are almost physically ill when I explain that I study 'judicial politics.' The High Court's decision in *Mabo* was certainly a landmark event in Australia's judicial politics. It arrived like a tidal wave on the beaches of a country whose legal profession was still dominated by the myth that judges are – or at least ought to be – apolitical eunuchs who spin their judgments entirely out of legal whole cloth.

I decided to take the measure of this case from the perspective of judicial politics. By rejecting the idea that Australia was a *terra nullius* (literally, a land of no one) when the white man arrived, an idea that had been the foundation of Australian law and policy for over two centuries, *Mabo* appeared to be a judicial revolution. But revolutions never come out of the blue. If it was a revolution, what were the forces, local and international, that produced it? How revolutionary were the judges? What were the assumptions and arguments that led to their earth-shaking conclusion that Indigenous peoples formed and operated societies in Australia before the arrival of British settlers, and that the laws of these societies could survive the imposition of British sovereignty? And was this decision really as revolutionary as the first rush of journalistic reaction proclaimed? Students of judicial politics have come to appreciate the wisdom of Alexander Bickel in calling the judiciary 'the least dangerous branch.'[3] Judges have no power to enforce their decisions. However revolutionary a judicial decision may be on paper, the changes it effects in the real world depend on how the political system as a whole responds to it. It is essential to look at the political consequences of the High Court's decision in *Mabo* and assess the extent to which the decision is leading to a fundamental transformation of the position of Indigenous peoples in Australia.

As a decision on common law native title, the *Mabo* case did not, on its face, seem to be of constitutional significance. If I did not include it among the Australian constitutional developments I needed to examine, however, I would be perpetuating the narrow understanding of constitutional politics that had characterized my earlier work in this field. Since the mid-1960s, Canada has been engaged in a seemingly endless series of constitutional crises all having to do with attempts at major restructuring of its formal 'written' Constitution. The politics of these constitutional efforts to rewrite the country's Constitution had been the focus of my interest in constitutional politics. When I came to Australia to do comparative work, it was similar efforts to overhaul the formal Constitution – the Constitutional Convention, the Constitutional Commission, and the Constitutional Centenary Foundation – that captured my attention. As I watched the political elites in both countries flail away at these grandiose projects of constitutional renewal, the futility of their efforts became increasingly apparent. I had come to the conclusion that, in highly democratic countries like Australia and Canada which take their Constitutions seriously, in the absence of an undeniable crisis such as imminent civil war or break-up, massive overhauls of the Constitution are politically impossible.[4] This conclusion led me to appreciate that the formal, written Constitution is only one of the components of a constitutional system. The other components are political practices and conventions – organic statues that, even though they are not formally part of the 'written' Constitution, define some of a country's governing institutions – and, finally but by no means least, judicial decisions interpreting and developing the Constitution. I had come to appreciate that it is through these various components of the constitutional system, including the occasional amendment of the formal Constitution, that constitutional systems adapt and evolve. Seen in this light, *Mabo* might well have constitutional significance.

As I read about *Mabo* and the debate it aroused – and looked at those cartoons – I could see that this case raised what I had come to believe is the most fundamental issue in constitutional politics: the nature of the political community on which the Constitution is based. In Canada it was conflicting 'visions' of the country – whether it was based on two (or three) founding peoples, or ten equal provinces, or the majority will of a single people – that, at rock bottom, prevented Canadians from agreeing on how to renew their constitution. Similarly, *Mabo* challenged the vision of their country held by many Australians – that it is a political society formed by British settlers which non-British immigrants and native people have been allowed to join. *Mabo* raised the need to recognize the existence of ancient societies pre-dating by many centuries the Britons' arrival – societies that continue to be the primary civic identity of many of their modern-day descendants. Such recognition would be necessary if an Australian political community that includes these peoples is to be built on freedom rather than force. It would require the forging of a more complex and pluralist Australia than the one-nation Australia that has been the dominant vision of the country up to now. The debate over *Mabo* had the potential to stir a deep ideological struggle over the Constitution of the Australian nation.

There could be no doubt that the *Mabo* case was a major development in what I call Indigenous politics – the political forces and ideas that shape the relations of Indigenous peoples[5] with the larger societies in which they find themselves embedded. My exposure to this sphere of politics began in 1974 when leaders of the Dene people in Canada's

Northwest Territories invited me to meet with them to consider the constitutional implications of a 'new model' for their relationship with Canada. This model was the basis of the submission they were planning to make to Canada for permitting major resource development in their traditional lands and waters.[6] On that first meeting with Aboriginal political thinkers, a woman elder asked me two questions: What was sovereignty? And how did the Queen get it over us? I had no difficulty with the first question – trotting out my learning about Bodin and Hobbes. But the second question stopped me in my tracks. I had no idea how the Dene – or any other Indigenous people – came to be under British or Canadian sovereignty.[7]

After that first encounter, I began to work on filling this gap in my knowledge of constitutional history. The *Mabo* case made me aware that I still had much to learn. While I had become reasonably familiar with the stages through which Indigenous-settler relations had passed on the North American continent – from initial warfare, through a period of military and commercial alliances, followed by colonial domination – I had no idea why British settlement in Australia had proceeded on a different basis. There, the country was considered to be a *terra nullius* when the Europeans arrived. Nor did I know how this apparent difference in the legal assumptions underpinning British settlement had influenced the actual relations that unfolded between Indigenous peoples and settlers in Australia. How would this legacy of non-recognition affect the prospects of Indigenous decolonization in Australia? By the 1990s Indigenous peoples in Canada had made considerable headway in recovering recognition of their right to govern their own societies and their traditional lands. Could judicial recognition of Indigenous societies in the *Mabo* case be a catalyst in propelling Indigenous resistance to colonialism in Australia?

Pursuing these questions would lead me back to the roots of Western imperialism and the foundations of the British Empire. Britain's colonization of Australia must be understood in the context of the expansion of European power that began half a millennium ago and was the basis of the first truly global political order. What were the ideological and legal justifications of that order, and how were they expressed in the relationships that developed with native peoples in the colonies of British settlement? After the Second World War, the founding of the United Nations and the adoption of the Universal Declaration of Human Rights challenged the premises of that imperial order and led to the constitutional decolonization of the Third World. By the 1960s, Third World decolonization was beginning to stir the colonized peoples – the Fourth World – within the states of the First World. These international developments had certainly played a role in providing Indigenous peoples in Canada with new political resources. An international movement of Indigenous peoples was emerging as part of a new kind of global politics. Australia was obviously not immune to these international developments. In assessing the factors that led to *Mabo* and the ideological underpinnings of the High Court judges' reasoning, it would be important to look at the international context of the decision.

I could also see that writing about *Mabo* not as an Australian but as a descendant of English settlers in Canada should give my study a particular comparative cast. It would make sense to place the law and policies governing relations with Torres Strait Islanders and Aborigines in Australia alongside those of other states in which descendants of English-speaking settlers had become the dominant population. Britain had colonies in many parts of the world, but in only four places did English-speaking settlers become the dominant population both in numbers and in the influence of their legal and political traditions. These four are Australia, Canada, New Zealand, and the United States. The legal foundations of all four of these countries derive primarily from English common law. One of the puzzling features of the *Mabo* case is why common law recognition of Indigenous peoples came so late in Australia. In all four of these countries it was the policies and practices of the same imperial state, Great Britain, which shaped relations with native peoples in the early years of settlement. And yet, so far as I knew, *terra nullius* – the denial of the very existence of Indigenous peoples as human societies – had not been the governing assumption of settler-Indigenous relations in British North America or New Zealand. Why had things been so different in Australia? And how significant was this difference in imperial practice and in the actual relations with Indigenous peoples that developed over time?

There was also a forward-looking rationale for this comparative framework. These four countries, three by evolution and one by revolution, have all become modern liberal democracies. Though there are important differences in their constitutions, they had all been built on a strong respect for political liberty, civil rights, and the rule of law. The democratic foundations of these English-settler states are much stronger than states founded and dominated by other European settlers – for example, the Portuguese and Spanish settler states of Latin America. The liberal democratic political culture of the English-settler states generated a political climate in which there was greater opportunity for Indigenous peoples to resist their subjugation and advance their political objectives. Even so, the ideology of liberal constitutionalism that came to prevail in the English-settler democracies gives supreme value to the equal rights of the individual citizen and is unfriendly to claims of special rights for particular groups of citizens. Historical memories of the coerced nature of Indigenous peoples' subjugation to the settler society's domination are weak to non-existent.

In endeavouring to reclaim their collective right to govern their own societies and to enjoy economic security in their traditional country, Indigenous peoples in all four of the English-settler states challenge the dominant constitutional ideology of the liberal democracies as well as the economic acquisitiveness of the majorities in these states. Despite these formidable obstacles, Aboriginal peoples in Canada, Indian tribes in the United States, and the Maori in New Zealand experienced some success in securing their political and economic interests – considerably more than their counterparts in Australia or virtually anywhere else in the world. Would *Mabo* enable Aborigines and Torres Strait Islanders to come closer to enjoying the recognition and rights secured by Indigenous peoples in other English-settler states? And could the struggle and successes of Indigenous peoples within the English-settler liberal democracies of the New World, including the Meriam people's judicial victory in *Mabo*, contribute to a general advance in the just treatment of Indigenous peoples worldwide?

These, then, are the theoretical interests and comparative framework that have guided my inquiry and the writing of this book. But there is one other crucial ingredient here – the personal contribution of Eddie Koiki Mabo. When I began to think about the *Mabo* case, it struck me that it must have taken an extraordinary individual to instigate and sustain this litigation. The case challenged legal thinking and political attitudes that had prevailed in Australia for over two centuries. It took ten years for the case to work its way through the judicial process. Eddie Mabo, whose name it bore, died in January 1992, a few months before its final resolution in June that same year. Who was this man? What led him to push this seemingly impossible lawsuit so hard? How essential was he to bringing the case forward and seeing it through? I have always had the general idea that historical change comes about through the interaction of the thoughts and deeds of exceptional individuals with great societal forces. It seemed to me that Mabo might well be such an individual. Without the *Mabo* case, it is certainly possible that the Australian state might eventually have abandoned the *terra nullius* doctrine and recognized in its laws the Indigenous societies that predate European settlement. But the fact that this happened in the 1980s and early 1990s, when a particularly favourable constellation of judicial minds and political leadership was in place, and through a law case based on a community of islanders with a tradition of property ownership not unlike that of Europeans, must surely have had a lot to do with Eddie Mabo.

And so the book interweaves two narratives: one is the story of Eddie Mabo, the islander legal warrior; the other is the story of imperialism, colonization, and the efforts of Indigenous peoples in the contemporary period to get out from under the colonialism imposed on them by the English-settler democracies. The first three chapters, forming Part One of the book, set the stage. Chapter 1 introduces the reader to Eddie Koiki Mabo, giving a brief account of his upbringing on Mer Island in the Torres Strait and the societal forces that shaped his character and circumstances. The chapter follows Mabo's story through his exile from Mer, his move to mainland Australia, his marriage to Netta and the beginning of their family, and his radicalization on the Townsville docks. In chapter 2 I shift to the global themes, first the legal and philosophical foundations of Western imperialism, and then the laws and policies Great Britain developed in its relations with Indigenous peoples in North America before the arrival of the First Fleet at Port Jackson. In chapter 3 I return to Eddie Mabo – his early involvement in aboriginal politics and the shaping of his bold political-legal project as he interacted with forces stirring Australian politics in the late 1960s and 1970s. This chapter concludes with a glimpse of the formidable obstacles that confronted Mabo as he began to assert his people's ownership of their island home.

The two chapters of Part Two set out the historical foundations of the obstacles Mabo faced and the turning of the tide of history in the direction of decolonization. Chapter 4 is the key comparative chapter of the book, showing how, at the beginning of British settlement in Australia, Indigenous policy on the ground differed sharply from the treaty relationships that Britain had entered into with Indian nations in North America and would enter into with the Maori in New Zealand. But the chapter goes on to track the convergence of policy as British colonial rule over its colonies of white settlement receded and new settler democracies, by the end of the nineteenth century, imposed their colonial rule over Indigenous peoples in the four English-settler states. Chapter 5 is the hinge chapter of the book. It begins with the stark exclusion of

Indigenous people from the founding of the Australian federation at the beginning of the twentieth century, when European imperialism was still at its zenith and the Australian-settler population was saturated with white racism. But it then traces the way Aborigines and Torres Strait Islanders begin to make some progress in being heard by the settler democracy when they shift to using the settler society's political techniques of organization and advocacy. In the latter part of this chapter we see how the interaction of domestic and international politics, in the dawning of a new post-imperial era after the Second World War, pave the way for removing the starkest incidents of Indigenous subjugation in Australia. The chapter ends with the Australian democracy's offer of full citizenship to Aborigines and Torres Strait Islanders, culminating in the 1967 referendum.

In Part Three, Eddie Mabo returns to the stage as we follow the events – personal, national, and international – that led to the High Court decision in the *Mabo* case. Aborigines and Torres Strait Islanders welcomed the end of constitutional discrimination against them, but access to the civil rights available to all Australians did not address their dispossession or recognize their historical societies. This limitation of the gains made by Indigenous Australians in the 1960s soon became evident in the land rights movement that followed in the 1970s. Chapter 6 looks at that movement – its failure in the courts, its dramatic symbol of protest in the national capital, its first legislative breakthrough under the Whitlam and Fraser governments, its stimulation by an emerging international Indigenous political network – and the beginning of political interest in a treaty with Australia's Indigenous peoples. We see Eddie Mabo, now a leader of 'black Australia' in his own community and in the country, as he interacts with these events, becoming acutely aware of the inadequacy of legislated land rights in recognizing the inherent rights of Indigenous peoples. By the end of the decade, Mabo's determination and maturation as a political leader are combining with national and international forces to build the momentum that will launch the *Mabo* case early in the 1980s. Chapter 7 follows the ten long years of litigation: from the decision of participants at a student anti-discrimination conference in Townsville to take a case to the High Court; the emergence of the Mer Islanders as the claimants; the formation of their legal team; the arguments, strategies, and manoeuvres of the lawyers; the lengthy fact-finding stage before Judge Moynihan; and Queensland's unsuccessful move to abort the case, resulting in the first *Mabo* case before the High Court, the case that had to be won to get the fundamental *Mabo* challenge to *terra nullius* before the High Court. Eddie Mabo is kept in view through this decade of litigation, a constant presence and inspiration in the law case until his death shortly after the final arguments were made to the High Court. As a backdrop to the litigation, I sketch in key developments in the recognition of Indigenous peoples' rights that were occurring internationally during this period, especially in Canada and New Zealand, as well as political reforms in Indigenous relations introduced by the Hawke Labor government in Australia.

Part Four, the final section of the book, deals with the High Court's decision in the fundamental *Mabo* case, *Mabo (No. 2)*, its aftermath, and its consequences. Chapter 8 is devoted to the High Court judgment itself in *Mabo (No. 2)*. I examine the reasons of the justices for deciding, six to one, that all along the Australian courts should have been following the common law's recognition of native title, and that the Meriam people have title to their island home except for the bits that have been taken from them by the Crown for the use of others. I show that however revolutionary such a finding may have been in Australia, from a comparative perspective it was a relatively conservative judgment. The three chapters that follow are about the consequences of the High Court's decision as they played out during the period I was writing the book. I chose to end my account with the end of the century, the date when the mandates of both the Council for Aboriginal Reconciliation and the Constitutional Centenary Foundation ran out. At the beginning of the 1990s there was a widespread expectation among Australia's political and intellectual elites that the country would launch its second century with the healing of relations with its Indigenous peoples and a renewed constitutional order. Not surprisingly, that did not happen: history does not follow such a tidy and celebratory schedule. But these years at least gave me a chance to follow the immediate responses to *Mabo* in law and legislation, as well as to measure its potential for longer-term effects on the body politic.

My account of the political fallout from *Mabo* is divided into two chapters. Chapter 9 recounts the political struggle over the *Native Title Act*, the Keating Labor government's attempt to give legislative effect to *Mabo*. Chapter 10 tells the story of the political response to the High Court's decision in *Wik* (a second coming of *Mabo*), and the final but futile efforts to complete the Reconciliation project. As I worked on these chapters, I found I was writing about the mainstream of Australian political life during the 1990s. That fact in itself is testimony to how profoundly the Indigenous issue had penetrated Australian political life. In no other settler country were questions about the rights and conditions of Indigenous peoples so prominent in national politics and such a source of partisan controversy. Though *Mabo* was not solely responsible for this development, it has done more than anything else to plunge the country into a continuing debate about the way to establish just relations with Aborigines and Torres Strait Islanders. That, I believe, is the most important consequence of the *Mabo* case. The international context of Australia's engagement in Indigenous politics and the abortive effort to have a grand reconciliation of aboriginal/settler differences are the subject matter of chapter 11.

In chapter 12, the final chapter of the book, I turn from the larger political consequences of *Mabo* to its more tangible results in recovering *terra nullius*. An examination of the legislation designed to 'implement' *Mabo*, as well as the leading High Court decisions on native title that followed, shows that the gains made by Aborigines and Torres Strait Islanders in recovering control of their traditional lands and waters, and directly attributed to *Mabo*, are very limited. The *Native Title Act* and its amendments, far from giving full legislative expression to the decision, validated massive dispossession and severely restricted the meaning and value of native title. By the time my book ends, the High Court is in full retreat from the cutting edge of protecting Indigenous peoples' rights. Does this mean that Eddie Mabo's judicial triumph was just a flash in the pan, with no enduring long-term significance? No, not at all. The real legacy of the *Mabo* case for non-Indigenous Australia is to make the building of fair, mutually beneficial, and consensual relations with Indigenous peoples the country's defining question of political justice. The strongest legacy of Eddie Koiki Mabo for Indigenous Australia is his example of personal agency, of rejecting the circumstances that oppressed him but accepting his personal responsibility for changing those circumstances. At the end of chapter 12 I point to a number of initiatives that Indigenous leaders are now taking in the spirit of Eddie Mabo – none of them court related, but with native title, in its broadest sense, as their ideological backdrop. These initiatives are also in tune with the advance of Indigenous internationalism. Just where these efforts will take Aborigines and Torres Strait Islanders, and Australia itself, is impossible to say. We can only be sure that it will not be back to a condition of *terra nullius*, in which the very existence of Indigenous peoples as ongoing human societies and a defining part of Australia is denied by the majority. We can only hope that the new relationships that emerge will, like Eddie Mabo, combine much of what is best in both white and black Australia.

Part One

SETTING THE STAGE

CHAPTER 1

Preparation of an Indigenous Challenger

This book focuses on a man and a law case: Edward Koiki Mabo and the decision of the High Court of Australia, rendered in 1992, known as *Mabo v. Queensland (No. 2)*. It also describes the broad historical process to which Mabo and his legal action made their distinctive contribution: the colonization and decolonization that began when European states sponsored voyages of discovery to the 'New World,' five hundred years ago. This process, in turn, committed human beings to membership in a global political community.

Eddie Mabo and his case make their distinctive mark on this process as it reaches the final stages of decolonization. The first phase of decolonization occurred for the most part in the decades immediately following the Second World War, when the European states terminated their direct rule over countries in Asia, Africa, and the Caribbean where European settlers were never more than a small minority. The second and later phase of decolonization happened in countries where descendants of the European settlers became the majority, while the descendants of the peoples the Europeans encountered in the lands they 'discovered' and colonized became small and marginalized minorities. These are the peoples of the Fourth World – the Indigenous peoples living in Third World conditions within First World countries, dominated by the descendants of the European settlers and other relative newcomers.

Mabo devoted his life to the struggle of Fourth World peoples to overcome their colonized condition of subjugation and dispossession, and the law case he inspired made a notable contribution to this cause. Though decolonization of the Fourth World is nourished by the principle of self-determination and the spirit of nationalism that fostered decolonization of the Third World, the outcomes of the two stages of decolonization must be markedly different. Simply expressed, the heirs of the colonizers in the settler countries are not about to pack their bags and go home. The only home the settlers' descendants know are the New World countries they now inhabit and on which they base their collective identities. The challenge of decolonization in this context is to work out ways in which descendants of the original occupants and descendants of the settlers can share these countries on a basis of mutual respect and consent, rather than on the force of the majority.

The great irony in decolonization struggles is that the colonizeds' success in overcoming their subjugation depends on their becoming adept in the use of the colonizers' political instruments. This is as true of Fourth World peoples as it was of Third World peoples. The very vocabulary through which Indigenous leaders have come to articulate their aspirations – referring to their societies as 'nations,' asserting an original 'sovereignty,' and claiming 'title' to their lands and waters – is the vocabulary of the dominant society. Thus, Fourth World peoples, especially their leaders, find themselves becoming less distinct from the dominant society as they adopt that society's political culture to resist its domination. Such are the ironic wages of success in the decolonizing struggle. Such also is the limit of anything Eddie Mabo could achieve through success in the colonizers' law courts.

A Fateful Conversation

As is so often the case in the interplay of personal events and the tide of history, a conversation was the seminal event in propelling Eddie Mabo towards his legal action. The conversation took place in 1974 in historian Henry Reynolds's study at James Cook University of North Queensland in the city of Townsville. The room was one in which members of the history faculty often met for a sandwich lunch. On the day in question two faculty members, Noel Loos and Henry Reynolds, were having lunch with a recently hired research assistant, Eddie Mabo.

Mabo was no ordinary research assistant. His principal paid employment at the university was as a member of the grounds crew.[1] In 1967 he had given up a job on the Townsville docks after the Harbour Board transferred him from work as a tugboat deckhand to lower-paid work with a sledge-hammer gang on the wharf. Mabo was convinced that his involvement in radical politics had prompted his transfer.

Earlier in 1967, Mabo had initiated the organization of an Inter-Racial

Conference in Townsville to consider what should follow Australia's referendum that year. In the referendum, Australians approved, by the largest majority in their history (just over 90 per cent), the removal of clauses from their Constitution that had very negative connotations for Australia's Indigenous peoples. One of these clauses stipulated that 'aboriginal natives' must not be counted in reckoning the number of people in Australia or any of its states. The other barred the Commonwealth Parliament from making special laws for people of 'the aboriginal race.'

Mabo had also developed close ties with Communist leaders who were active in union organizing on the docks and who, more than any other white politicians in Townsville, were active in encouraging blacks like him to pursue issues of racial justice. A news bite showing him attending a Communist Party conference appeared on local television. At this time Australia was engaged as the United States's keenest ally in the Vietnam War. Indeed, someone at the Harbour Board had even labelled Mabo 'a Viet Cong.'

Mabo's reasons for moving from the docks to the university were not all negative. The James Cook campus was much closer to the house at 23 Hibiscus Street which he and his wife had purchased earlier in the decade and where they were raising a family of seven children. Even more important for Mabo were the opportunities the campus would provide for pursuing the deepest passion of his life – the history, the culture, and the rights of the land of his birth, Mer Island in the Torres Strait.

Growing Up on Mer

Edward Koiki Mabo was born on Mer Island in the Torres Strait on 29 June 1936, the son of Robert and Poipe Sambo. Mer is the largest in a cluster of three islands – known in English as the Murray Islands – at the eastern end of the 170-kilometre-wide strait that separates Australia from Papua New Guinea. The Murray Islands are at the eastern end of a group of more than a hundred small islands scattered through the 225-kilometre length of the strait. Most of these islands are even smaller than Mer, which itself is only 2.8 kilometres in length and just over 1.5 kilometres at its widest point. Only seventeen of the islands are populated. Collectively, the people of these islands are known as the Torres Strait Islanders.[2]

When Mabo's mother died shortly after his birth, he was adopted by his mother's brother, Benny Mabo, and his aunt, Maiga. Though adop-

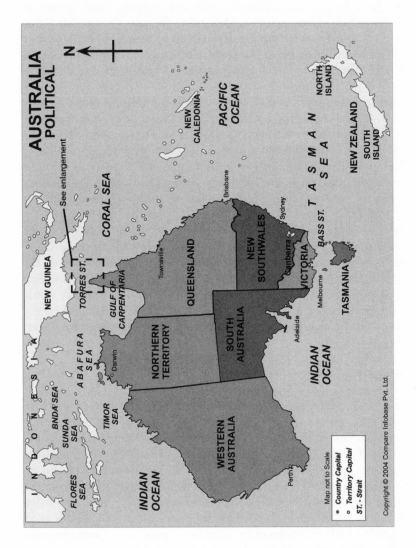

AUSTRALIA
POLITICAL

N

See enlargement

INDONESIA

NEW GUINEA

FLORES SEA

SUNDA SEA

BNDA SEA

TIMOR SEA

ARAFURA SEA

INDIAN OCEAN

WESTERN AUSTRALIA

Perth

NORTHERN TERRITORY

Darwin

GULF OF CARPENTARIA

TORRES ST.

CORAL SEA

Townsville

QUEENSLAND

Brisbane

NEW CALEDONIA

PACIFIC OCEAN

SOUTH AUSTRALIA

Adelaide

NEW SOUTH WALES

Sydney

Canberra

VICTORIA

Melbourne

INDIAN OCEAN

BASS ST.

TASMANIA

T A S M A N   S E A

NEW ZEALAND

NORTH ISLAND

SOUTH ISLAND

Map not to Scale

• Country Capital
○ Territory Capital

ST. - Strait

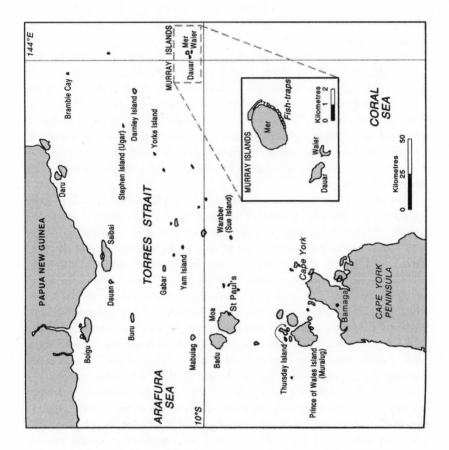

PAPUA NEW GUINEA

Bramble Cay •

Daru

Saibai

Boigu

Dauan

Buru

Stephen Island (Ugar)

Darnley Island

Yorke Island

MURRAY ISLANDS

Mer
Dauar ○ Waier

144°E

TORRES STRAIT

ARAFURA SEA

Mabuiag

Gabar

Yam Island

Waraber
(Sue Island)

10°S

Badu

Moa

St Paul's

Thursday Island

Prince of Wales Island
(Muralug)

Cape York

Bamaga

CAPE YORK PENINSULA

Kilometres
0   25   50

MURRAY ISLANDS

Dauar

Mer

Fish-traps

Waier

Kilometres
0   1   2

CORAL SEA

tion by close relatives in this manner was customary among the Meriam people, many years later it would be viewed as problematic by a Queensland judge, M.P. Moynihan, who had been appointed by the High Court as its 'fact-finder' in the *Mabo* case. Moynihan said he could not uphold Mabo's rights to plots of land he claimed were passed down to him by Benny Mabo. One of the great ironies of the *Mabo* litigation is that, while it led to the recognition of native title for all Australia's Indigenous peoples, it did not recognize Eddie Mabo's rights to his own ancestral lands.

Mabo grew up in the village of Las, on the northeast corner of Mer, where the Mabos and other families of the Piadram clan had their garden plots and fishing weirs – walled areas of the foreshore trapping sea foods washed in on the tide. He would describe these years as 'the best time of my life.'[3] There he was nurtured by a society in which Indigenous tradition and Western influences were intricately intertwined, whether in their economy or their religion. Indeed, it is through this interaction – this accommodation of cultures – that the Islanders' identity has been forged.

The Melanesian peoples who, centuries earlier, had migrated from Papua to the islands of the Torres Strait had always been a sea-faring people. Traditionally they had derived most of their protein from the sea, harvesting numerous varieties of fish, molluscs, turtles, and dugong. By the early 1900s this traditional maritime life was giving way to wage labour on boats owned mostly by Europeans. These boats harvested products for overseas markets – principally trochus pearl shell, the material from which most buttons were fashioned in the pre-plastic age, and beche-de-mer, a large sea-slug much prized in Chinese cuisine as a delicacy and aphrodisiac. It was on one of these boats that Benny Mabo went to work soon after adopting his nephew. Eddie himself would begin working on trochus fishing luggers when he reached his late teens.

By the time Eddie was born, the full force of globalization and Westernization was transforming the political economy of his island home. In the 1930s the Torres Strait felt the impact of the Great Depression. The garment industry in the West cut back on the price it would pay for trochus pearl shell. The wages paid to Islanders working on the pearling luggers fell below the £8 a month they had been earning in 1930. In 1936, the year Eddie was born, Islanders working on boats owned and operated by an agency of the Queensland protector, Australia's governing authority in the Torres Strait, went on strike. The strike was instigated by Murray Islanders – 'the Irish of the Torres Strait.'[4]

Historian Jeremy Beckett refers to the strike as 'the first organized Islander challenge to European authority.'[5] It would be more accurate to say that it was the first organized Islander resistance using the European's political technology – an industrial strike. Nearly a century and a half earlier, in 1792, Island warriors in a flotilla of canoes had put up a stiff resistance to the *Providence* and the *Assistant*, British ships led by Captain William Bligh (of *Mutiny on the Bounty* fame) charting a course through the strait. But the Islanders' arrows and spears were no match for British guns. Nor could they deter Bligh from claiming the Torres Strait Islands as 'new jewels for Britannia's crown.'[6] Two hundred years after this military defeat, the High Court of Australia's decision in the *Mabo* case would demonstrate that the Islanders might better secure their interests through another European political activity – vindicating rights in courts of law.

Growing up on Mer, Mabo participated in the dances and ceremonies through which the Meriam people traditionally marked the seasons and observed the rites of passage. From elders, especially his grandfather, he learned the myths and stories about the creation of the islands and the spiritual power of *zogo*, embodied in *Bomai* – 'the pinnacle of sacred power'[7] and the source of Malo's Law. In a spiritual sense, this law regulated the Islanders' relations with nature and with one another. At the same time, he was exposed to the distinctive amalgam of Christianity and traditional religion so integral to Islander identity.

To the Torres Strait Islanders, July 1 is as much a national founding day as July 4 is to Americans. The event that is celebrated on that day throughout the Torres Strait is the arrival of the Reverend A.W. Murray and Samuel MacFarlane, two members of the London Missionary Society, on Darnley Island in 1871.[8] That event is known as 'the Coming of the Light.' The English missionaries arrived at a time of deep distress, when there was no effective European political authority to counter the devastating intrusion of well-armed fishing boats manned by adventurous South Sea islanders and captained by ruthless and avaricious Europeans. In these circumstances, the Christian missionaries, with a supporting cast of evangelical assistants from the South Pacific, were welcomed as a way of restoring a structure of moral order.

The Islanders quickly became and remained devoutly Christian – and none more so than the people of Mer. Rather than leading to the abandonment of traditional Indigenous beliefs, acceptance of Christianity confirmed the fundamentally religious nature of Islander culture – the fusion of the sacred and the secular. Though some traditional practices were banned by the missionaries and had to go underground, Islander theologians were able to integrate Christian doctrine into a traditional frame of reference. In a conversation with historian Noel Loos that took place just before the end of his life, Eddie Mabo pointed out how Island priests, including Joseph Lui who had baptised him, participated emotionally in traditional ceremonies.[9] One of Mabo's co-litigants, the Reverend David Passi (the senior Anglican priest on Mer), expounded on Christianity as the fulfilment of the Bomai-Malo story, both in his preaching and in the evidence he submitted to Judge Moynihan.[10]

Both traditional and Western cultures interacted in Eddie's education on Mer. In the large family house at Las, he went through a process of traditional education. Much of this learning was imbibed through listening to the discussions of property, marriage, and ceremonial issues that people would bring to his father, Benny Mabo, who was regarded as *Aet*, an authoritative custodian of sacred tradition. He also attended the state-operated school, though he made little progress until the arrival of Robert Victor Miles. Unlike previous teachers, Miles spoke fluent Meriam Mir, and he excelled in teaching the Meriam children English. In 1949, when his adoptive mother became ill, Eddie lived with Miles for about two years. He flourished under this tutelage – so much so that when Miles was transferred to the Yorke Island school in 1951, Eddie went with him as an assistant to teach Grades 1 and 2. The next year, his linguistic skills earned him the opportunity to travel through the Torres Strait and to Aboriginal communities on Cape York as an interpreter for a medical team investigating a serious outbreak of malaria in the area.

Mabo Becomes an Exile

As Mabo approached manhood, he was unable to follow his scholastic bent or build a life for himself in his homeland. In 1953, after a drinking spree with other frustrated young people on Mer, he found himself charged not only with being drunk on a reserve (at that time, Mer and other islands populated by Islanders were treated by Queensland as native reserves) but also with being with a woman.[11] The strict moralism of Mer's official Christianized culture meant that this second offence attracted a heavy penalty – a year of exile from Murray.

Eddie was sent to Thursday Island to serve his sentence. Thursday Island was then, as it is now, the administrative headquarters of the Torres Strait – though at that time the central administration was entirely white and the island, under the prevailing regime of strict racial segregation, was reserved for white residents. Paddy Killoran, who headed up the Torres Strait branch of Queensland's Department of Native Affairs and acted, effectively, as the czar of the island communities, gave Mabo a choice for his year of exile: he could do unpaid labour on one of Killoran's 'green trucks,' which picked up garbage and kept the island up to spiffy European standards, or he could work – for wages – on a local pearling lugger. Mabo would have preferred to go south to earn the higher wages available on luggers working out of ports in northern Queensland. But even in the early 1950s the Islanders, despite the wartime service of many of their men, were subjects but not full citizens of the Australian state and needed official permission to migrate to the Australian mainland. So Mabo went to work on a pearling lugger in the Torres Strait.

Two years after his exile he came home to Mer and, for the next two years, worked mostly on Murray-based luggers, with occasional stints on boats operating from Thursday Island. He became a skilled diver, able to reach depths of 50 feet just with goggles. Towards the end of 1957 Mabo succumbed to the lure of higher wages and freedom from the restrictions of Queensland's Torres Strait colony and decided to try his luck on the Australian mainland. He gravitated to Townsville, a major port on Queensland's north coast. From there he went west looking for opportunities in the expanding frontier of the Queensland interior. Though he found employment cutting cane and with railway construction gangs, he kept coming back to Townsville to do marine work on fishing boats and Harbour Board tugs.

Eddie Mabo's move to the mainland was part of a general pattern of emigration out of the Torres Strait that began in the mid-1950s and escalated towards the end of the decade. Again we can see how his biography interacts with outside forces that shape the circumstances of Indigenous peoples. Through the nineteenth and early twentieth centuries, European guns and European-induced disease drastically reduced the Islander population. By the time Mabo reached working age, however, this trend had spectacularly reversed. Beckett estimates that, by 1960, 536 Meriam lived on the small island of Mer, and almost 50 per cent of them were under twenty.[12] With Western medicine came a taste for Western goods and the wages needed to purchase them – a trend reinforced by Island men returning from wartime service. The rise of the plastics industry knocked the bottom out of the value of trochus pearl shell – the main source of wage employment for Islanders. Meantime, the labour requirements of a booming postwar Australian economy were overcoming restrictions on black migration. Islanders were sought for the sweaty manual work – cutting cane, building roads, and maintaining rail lines – that the white labour force in a full-employment economy eschewed.

Most of the migrant Islanders came to northern Queensland, forming sizable communities in a number of coastal towns and cities – the largest in Townsville and Cairns. By 1979 the Torres Strait Islanders resident in Townsville alone were estimated at between 4500 and 8000 – a number considerably greater, probably, than the entire population in the strait itself.[13] In 1995 the Torres Strait Regional Authority reported that 5600 Islanders lived in island communities and two communities at the top of Cape York, while 21,000 Torres Strait Islanders were living outside the Torres Strait.[14]

For the first year or so after leaving Mer, Mabo worked mostly on luggers along the Queensland coast between Townsville and Cairns. He met his wife, Bonita, or 'Netta' as he always called her, in a community of South Sea Islanders near the coastal town of Halifax. The close-knit character of village life in this community reminded Mabo of his own village on Mer. He kept coming back to Netta's home. In 1959 Bonita and Eddie were married. After several years of moving between work on the coast and in the interior – he on the railway, she cooking on a cattle station – they decided it was time for them and their two small children to move permanently to Townsville.

Townsville and Mabo's Initiation in Aboriginal Politics

In Townsville, Mabo wasted no time getting involved in aboriginal politics. By the early 1960s Indigenous Australians, particularly those who had moved into cities and towns, were beginning to be stirred by a more militant sense of aboriginal nationalism.[15] Part of this stirring came via the television screens on which urban Australian aboriginals could witness the freedom marches and the rise of the Black Power movement in the United States. Mabo became the secretary of the Aboriginal Advancement League in Townsville. By distributing leaflets, staging fundraising events, and organizing the 1967 Inter-Racial Conference, the league's few members had an influence far beyond their numbers. They heightened political consciousness among the aboriginal communities and raised enough money to send delegates to the national meetings that were beginning to form a pan-Australian aboriginal movement.

Making common cause in political action with mainland Aborigines was problematic for Mabo. Torres Strait Islanders have a strong sense of their own identity as a distinct people. Their spiritual beliefs, history, and culture are very different from those of the Indigenous peoples on the Australian continent. The pattern of life that has evolved in island communities has been exposed to Western influence for a much longer period of time. The Islanders' culture, in many respects – not least of all in the highly individualized tradition of land ownership – has more similarity with Western culture than is the case with Australian Aborigines, whose ancient civilization was formed tens of thousands of years before contact with the West. Their relatively greater degree of Westernization has, on occasion, prompted Islanders to adopt a condescending attitude to Aboriginals. Indeed, Eddie Mabo was eventually forced to leave the Council for Aboriginal Rights (which the league had become) because of pressure from colleagues who, as he put it, 'thought it was not necessary for Islanders to be involved in Aboriginal Affairs.'[16]

Though Mabo remained deeply proud of his distinct Islander heritage, the experience of working and living with Aboriginal Australians in northern Queensland made him acutely aware that Islanders and Aborigines shared a fundamentally common position as colonized peoples. In the end, the law case that he did so much to promote would be a victory for all of Australia's Indigenous peoples in gaining some recognition of their rights to their ancestral lands. And the breadth of that victory was very much what Mabo wished to achieve. But, as we shall see, the success of the *Mabo* case can in part be attributed to the fact that the Islanders' relationship to their land was more congenial to the Western legal minds who would adjudicate his case.

Mabo had an exceptional appetite for learning and culture. His shift of employment to James Cook University enabled him to pursue these interests as never before. The fact that his formal education had not gone beyond primary school did not deter him from making full use of the university's resources. In the library he found the results of Western scholars' research on the Islanders' history and culture, in particular the six volumes of the Cambridge Anthropological Expedition.[17] Through his studies, Mabo expanded his knowledge of his own people and, in the words of his biographer, Noel Loos, 'grafted on new insights to his old understanding.'[18] Years later the very sophistication of his testimony about Islander culture and history would cause the fact-finding judge to question its authenticity.

On the James Cook campus, Mabo made friends with faculty members and became a regular speaker in a course on race relations. He also spoke to education classes and attended seminars and conferences. At one such conference in 1973, held as a training session for white teachers in schools with mostly Aborigine and Torres Strait Islander students, Eddie raised a storm. He thumped the floor, shouting, 'Who the hell's going to send their kids to be taught by racist people like these bastards?'[19]

It is typical of Mabo's energy and determination that, within a few weeks of this incident, with some assistance from sympathetic university educators, he had established the Townsville Black Community School. He aimed to give Indigenous students an education that combined the best that both cultures – traditional and Western – had to offer. For the next ten years the school was at the centre of the Mabos' life: their children were among the thirty or so Islander and Aborigine pupils; Bonita worked there as a teachers' assistant; and Eddie, as chairman of the community council that ran the school, became its chief fundraiser and leader in managing its often tense relationships with municipal and educational authorities. During these years his involvement in education and culture gained him national recognition, with appointments to Australia's Aboriginal Arts Council and the National Aboriginal Education Committee.

In 1973 Mabo planned a visit to the Murray Islands to do oral history research and to introduce his family to their Meriam relations. He had not been back to Mer since 1957 and was keen to bring his wife and children to the place that would always be his home. However, when the Mabo family reached Thursday Island, Mabo received a telegram from the chairman of the Murray Council refusing him permission to come to the island. The message curtly stated: 'Such visit or research will create problems to people.' It ended: 'Do not question further the authority of myself and Council.'[20] The island's elected council in this period was still in a highly colonized condition and had no desire to welcome back someone with Mabo's reputation as a political 'trouble-maker.' The white administrators on Thursday Island were happy to stand behind this decision. The Mabos had to return to Townsville without seeing Mer.

Perhaps it was the frustration engendered by this abortive effort to return to Mer that prompted the conversation that took place in Henry Reynolds office 'some time around 1974.'[21] Mabo talked about land that still belonged to him on Murray Island and his determination to return to it. At this point, Loos and Reynolds exchanged glances and tried to explain gently to Mabo that, because the land belonged to the Crown, he was probably mistaken about his land ownership. To demonstrate the point, they took down an old Queensland map and showed him that his island, like all the Torres Strait Islands, was marked 'Aboriginal Reserve.' Loos recalls that Mabo exploded at this explanation. 'I'd like to see someone take my land away from me,' he screamed at them. By this time, Mabo knew about mainland Aborigines having land rights problems, but he had no idea that his own people's possession of their island home could be in question. Like so many aboriginal people, Mabo had not reckoned with the presumptions of European imperialism. To these presumptions we must now turn.

CHAPTER 2

Western Imperialism and Its Legal Magic

A half-millennium ago, when Europeans set out on the voyages of discovery that launched the modern age of imperialism, they knew nothing about the human societies they would encounter in this New World. Their total ignorance, however, did not prevent them from holding fast to what they regarded as a moral truth about the relative worth of these societies: that these peoples, to the extent they were fundamentally different from the Europeans, were inferior. Although the European empires had their economic and military rationales, Edward Said provides a compelling perspective when he writes that 'over and above profit,' the 'commitment that allowed decent men and women to accept the notion that distant territories and their native peoples *should* be subjugated' was 'the almost metaphysical obligation to rule subordinate, inferior, less-advanced peoples.'[1]

European understandings of what makes Indigenous peoples not just different but inferior have gone through several transformations. At first, the assumption of Western European superiority was based on religion. The inhabitants of the New World were infidels, and, as such, were a proper target for conquest and conversion by Christian states. Though the Christian rationale for subjugation never vanished, after the Reformation and during the Age of the Enlightenment it gave way to more secular and technological theories that denied the rationality of Indigenous peoples – especially those who did not cultivate the land. From the early nineteenth century, Aboriginal peoples were increasingly seen as belonging to an inferior race. As that century wore on, evolutionary 'science' fostered the belief that this inferior race was biologically determined and fated for extinction. Today, the major source of prejudice is the perceived inability or disinclination of Aboriginal people to adapt to the lifestyle needed for success in western capitalist societies. Whatever the sources of prejudice, the result is the same: a belief in the inherent inferiority of the Aboriginal peoples as peoples. That belief is the bed-rock presumption of imperial rule.

In dwelling on this basic presumption of imperialism, the point is not to judge the past by the standards of today. Rather, it is to understand how, despite the moral and legal evolution that has gone on since the dawn of the imperial age and particularly through the period of decolonization that followed the Second World War, this fundamental presumption continues to permeate the treatment of Indigenous peoples in countries where the descendants of the Europeans have become dominant. The lingering strength of this presumption of cultural superiority remains the major barrier in moving towards a truly post-colonial position for Indigenous peoples in these countries. The essence of a post-colonial relationship is the principle of the equality of peoples – the opposite of the fundamental presumption of imperialism.

Imperialism as a Legal Enterprise

We are most likely to look to the law for manifestations of the principles that govern relationships with Aboriginal peoples. Europeans have always regarded the rule of law as a defining feature of their civilization. From the very beginning of the age of exploration, the European states expressed in legal terms their right to rule in the New World and their relationship with the peoples they encountered there. As Robert Williams put it, 'Europe's conquest of the New World was a legal enterprise.'[2] Law has provided the justifying discourse in taking over other peoples' lands. Aboriginal thinkers have often been struck by the way law has served as a kind of magic, so devoutly and reverently have European authorities and their legal cadres believed in its self-redeeming powers.

During the centuries of the colonial experience, there have been many laws and many changes in the laws relating to Indigenous peoples. The legal action that Eddie Mabo led was a landmark in this process of change. Throughout all these changes in the law, including the most recent and most progressive ones, there has, however, been one constant factor that has never changed: it is the Europeans – their authorities, their judges, their jurists – who get to make the law that counts. It counts because it is backed up by superior military power.

To be sure, all along Indigenous peoples have had their laws and their law-makers. Mabo's people, as we have seen, have Malo's Law. Occasion-

ally, this Aboriginal law has received some recognition in the courts of
the settler states. But the scope of this legal pluralism – the extent to
which the laws of Indigenous peoples are accepted as a legitimate way of
regulating their societies – is entirely subject to decision-making by non-
Indigenous judges.

It is important not to lose sight of this crucial fact about the politics of
law. In so-called civilized countries, people are apt to get misty-eyed
about how great it is to live under the 'rule of law' rather than the 'rule
of men.' While there is much to be said for ordering social and political
relations by a settled legal order, it must not be forgotten that it is men
and women who identify and interpret the laws that are binding and
that, in the case of laws governing Aboriginal peoples – laws backed up
by overwhelming coercive force – it is non-Aboriginals who have mo-
nopolized the making of the law.

This primary feature of the colonizing legal order stems, of course,
from the European states' success in asserting legal and political sovereignty over Indigenous peoples. As Kent McNeil notes, however debat-
able the juristic theories used to justify the annexation of new lands by
European powers may have been, 'in practical terms ... might made
right, so that a sovereign who succeeded in exercising a sufficient degree
of exclusive control was generally regarded as having acquired sovereignty.'[3] The initial assertion of sovereignty by the European power or its
successor state is regarded by the judges of these states as an 'act of state'
(a nice piece of legal magic!) whose legitimacy they will not question.
John Marshall, chief justice of the United States Supreme Court, could
not have put the point more bluntly when, in 1823, in the first of his
path-breaking trilogy of cases on the rights of Aboriginal peoples, he
wrote that 'conquest gives a title which the courts of the conqueror
cannot deny.'[4] The unchallengeable sovereign authority of the states in
which Indigenous peoples find themselves marks the limits of the
decolonization these peoples can achieve through legal actions such as
Mabo's.

In thinking about where the *Mabo* case fits into the larger scheme of
things, it is useful to recognize three dominant phases through which
laws concerning the status and rights of Aboriginal peoples have evolved
– and a possible fourth whose day may now be dawning. The first was
fundamentally Christian and papal. The second was the emergence of a
secular international law – a Law of Nations – developed by the colonizing European imperial states. The third has been the domestic laws –
constitutions, agreements, and treaties,[5] statutes and judicial decisions –

of the nation-states, the successor states of the colonizing empires. The fourth is the effort now under way through the United Nations to establish worldwide standards on the rights of Aboriginal peoples which are acceptable to those peoples. Though the first three phases had their periods of dominance, each ran into the next and continued to influence later legal developments.

The Search for a Moral Justification in Christian and Natural Law

The first phase, that of the papal 'donations,' need not detain us long. During this period at the end of the Middle Ages and the very beginning of the Age of Discovery, the Catholic rulers of Europe still looked to the Pope to legitimize their colonizing activities. In 1492, Columbus, whose voyage in search of a short route to the Indies had been sponsored by King Ferdinand and Queen Isabella of Spain, was detained for a while in the Azores, on his return trip, by the Portuguese, who had also been colonizing in the Atlantic. The two Iberian Christian kingdoms called on Pope Alexander VI to settle their New World claims. In 1493 the Pope issued a papal bull that drew a line of demarcation from the top to the bottom of the world, about three hundred miles west of the Azores. He literally donated to Spain all territory to the west of this line not already possessed by a Christian prince, and, similarly, to Portugal, all territory to the east of the line.[6]

Papal authority to dispose of New World territories was short lived. It was soon challenged even by Catholic France, which could not accept its exclusion from the rights of discovery. And, of course, after the Reformation, Protestant states like England and the Netherlands would not be bound by papal bulls. Of much more enduring importance was the rationale behind the claims of papal authority and the debates among Europeans to which it gave rise. The justification of papal authority was that, as Christ's earthly vicar, the Pope had care of all human souls. The monarchs of Portugal and Spain were licensed to colonize and civilize the New World so that its inhabitants might embrace the Christian faith and their souls become eligible for eternal salvation. To today's ears, this medieval Catholic claim will sound arrogant and ethnocentric. Nonetheless, lurking within it was a concern and an aspiration that germinated more secular efforts to establish a universal moral order among Christian Europeans and other peoples. As the Age of Discovery unfolded, Europeans were faced with a serious question of justice. Acquiring new territory that was uninhabited – *territorium nullius*, to use a term from

Roman law – presented no problem.[7] But the territories in the New World which the Portuguese and Spaniards claimed through acts of discovery were most certainly inhabited. How could the annexation of already inhabited territories be justified by 'discovering' states?

The methods of annexing such territories – of bringing them under the aegis of the discovering imperial power – were clear enough. 'Conquest or cession' was the answer that European jurists presiding over an emerging international law soon gave to the question of how European states could acquire other peoples' territory.[8] In effect, conquest and cession were most often two sides of the same coin, since a people will not consciously cede its land to another people unless it has been conquered, or fears it might soon be, by a foreign power. 'Conquest,' as we shall see, did not always take the form of the clear-cut military victory that this word conjures up. Much more often European sovereign authority, in particular the sovereignty of the English Crown, was insinuated into existence through a clever process that depended more on cunning and guile – and heavy doses of Western legal magic – than military victory. Nonetheless, even if the conquest or cession formula provided Europeans with a satisfactory explanation of how they could take over territories inhabited and possessed by others, it did not address the issue of justification.

How could a war of conquest over a newly discovered country and people be justified? In Spain, in the first fifty to sixty years following Columbus's discoveries, that question became a major intellectual preoccupation. One line of justification based on the Christian imperialism of the Crusades was readily at hand: the belief that because authority on this earth must be commissioned by God through his earthly representative, the Pope, infidels could not form legitimate political societies. According to this doctrine, the natives – or 'savages'– of the New World, being infidels who had never heard of the Christian God, were incapable of exercising *dominium* – they could neither exercise political jurisdiction over their lands nor possess the territory they inhabited. War could be justly waged on natives who, on first contact, did not acknowledge 'the Church as the Ruler and Superior of the whole world and the high priest called the Pope and who refused to allow the faith to be preached to them.'[9]

This line of Christian thinking, denying human rights to savage peoples, was fortified by more secular theories and popular prejudices. As Renaissance Europe emerged from the Middle Ages, there was a revival of interest in the pre-Christian thought of classical Greece and Rome. No piece of classical philosophy 'had a more dramatic impact' on Amerindians than Aristotle's theory of natural servitude: 'that one part of mankind is set aside by nature to be slaves in the service of masters born for a life of virtue free of manual labour.'[10] Most Europeans did not need Aristotle to justify their sense of superiority and their right to rule the savages of the New World. They were totally shocked by reports of people who lived 'in the manner of beasts in the woods,' apparently lacking the essential marks of a civilized society, practising polygamy and cannibalism, and, worst of all, not wearing clothes. Their infidelity and savage nature 'combined to convince Europeans that Amerindians could not possess the same rights as those whose natures had been refined by Christianity, and who had attained the maturity of civility.'[11]

The prevailing tide of opinion did not go unchallenged. The voice of Christian humanists building on St Thomas Aquinas's thirteenth-century reconciliation of faith and reason, of the natural and the super-natural, began to be heard in Renaissance universities. Philosopher priests drawing on the Thomistic tradition and a revival of interest in Roman law were beginning to lay the intellectual foundations for a Law of Nations. Their underlying vision was one of all human kind belonging to a universal civil society bound together by laws based ultimately on natural law and justice.

The most influential proponent of this universal humanism and the most systematic expositor of its application to the native peoples of the New World was the Spanish Dominican Franciscus de Vitoria. As the leading theologian at the University of Salamanca, Renaissance Spain's most important seat of learning, Vitoria was asked to advise the Spanish Crown on the rights of the Amerindians. This he did in a series of lectures in 1532 entitled 'On the Indians Lately Discovered.'[12] Vitoria cut the ground out from under the Pope's claim to temporal authority over the Indians. As free and rational peoples, the Americans 'undoubt-edly had true *dominium* in both public and private matters, just like Christians, and ... neither their princes nor private persons could be despoiled of their property on the grounds of them not being true owners.'[13] Vitoria insisted on a distinction between political authority and title to property. European sovereigns, through discovery, might make political claims in the New World to ensure a beneficial order and to exclude the intervention of other European powers, but discovery gave 'no right to occupy the lands of the Aboriginal population.'[14] However, while this emerging Law of Nations recognized the natural rights of Aboriginal peoples, it also imposed obligations on them to recognize the natural rights of others. These rights, supposedly based on pure reason, included the right to trade and participate in commerce and the right to travel freely through alien lands. If the Spanish could not safely exercise these rights in the Indians' countries 'save by seizing their cities and reducing them to subjection, they may lawfully proceed to these extremities.'[15]

The most vigorous and controversial attack on Spanish conquest in the Indies was launched by Bartolomé de Las Casas. Las Casas, whose father had sailed with Columbus on his second voyage to America, became a land-owner and slave-owner in Cuba. After participating for a few years as a typical gentleman adventurer in Spain's conquest and exploitation of the Indians, in 1514, under the influence of Dominican preaching, he experienced a decisive conversion. The 'scales fell from his eyes' and he became convinced 'that everything done to the Indians thus far was unjust and tyrannical.'[16] Las Casas became a Dominican and devoted his life to attacking the cruelties and injustice inflicted on the native peoples of America by the Spanish conquistadors. The fiery friar took his crusade to Europe, where he agitated at the imperial court for a change in law and policy. He published a number of treatises, including *Very Brief Account of the Destruction of the Indes*, which was illustrated with gruesome pictures of atrocities and translated into all the principal European languages. By the time he became bishop of Chiapa, Las Casas 'was perhaps the most abused man of his time in America and Spain.'[17]

The controversy stirred up by Las Casas, Vitoria, and other Dominicans became so intense that, in 1550, King Charles I of Spain, who as Charles V also occupied the position of Holy Roman Emperor, suspended all conquests in the New World. Charles summoned a special council of judges to Valladolid to adjudicate a debate on whether the current practice of carrying on conquests in America was just or unjust. The two debaters were Bishop Las Casas and Ginés de Sepúlveda, the leading Spanish legal scholar of the day and the royal historiographer. The 'great debate' went on for over a month. Sepúlveda argued that the sins of the Indians, especially their idolatries, justified waging war against them. Moreover, the 'rudeness of their natures' meant that Indians were obliged to serve those of elevated natures, such as Spaniards. Their subjugation was a necessary condition for their conversion to Christianity and for protecting them from cruelties within their own societies. Against these propositions, Las Casas insisted on the fundamental unity of mankind: 'All the peoples of the world are men ... all have understanding and volition ... No nation exists today, nor could exist, no matter how barbarous, fierce, or depraved its customs may be, which may not be attracted and converted to all political virtues and to all the humanity of domestic, political and rational man.'[18] As a devout Christian, Las Casas believed in the religious conversion of the Indians – indeed, that was the only justification for the Europeans' presence in the New World. That conversion was to be achieved not by conquest but through 'a method which persuades their understanding and which moves, exhorts and gently attracts the will.'[19]

The judges on the imperial council agonized for months over the debaters' submissions but never did render a clear verdict. However, well before the debate, official Catholic policy had moved in the direction advocated by the Dominicans, with the issuing of a bull in 1537 by Pope Paul III declaring that the Indians were not to be treated as 'dumb brutes created for our services' but 'as truly men ... capable of understanding the Christian faith,' and recognizing their natural rights to property.[20] The publication of Sepúlveda's works was prohibited. Las Casas might be said, then, to have won the intellectual debate. However, the Dominicans' ideas did not triumph on the ground in the practical field of imperial policy. Spanish conquests in the New World did not stop. Nor did the conscience of Christian humanism deter other European states from attempting to secure their share of the New World.

The debate at Valladolid was significant: it was the fullest debate Europeans ever had about the justice of their subjugation of the peoples of the New World. Even on the 'pro-native' side, the presumption of the Europeans' superiority and their right to rule others is evident. Though Vitoria's *Law of Nations* did not justify papal licensing of European rule in the New World, his ethnocentric conception of natural law provided a convenient moral rationalization for subjugating the Amerindians. Though Las Casas insisted on the full human potential of New World natives, his measure of that potential was their capacity for conversion to his religion and the political virtues of his society. Still, the very fact that this debate took place shows a sense of moral unease at the summit of Western political authority about denying other human beings rights that Europeans would, by this time in history, insist on claiming for themselves. For the next four centuries, this moral sense would compete, ineptly, with ignorance, arrogance, and the bloody pursuit of economic self-interest in shaping the laws and policies that European powers and their successor states imposed on the Indigenous peoples of the New World. Yet it is always there – with greater force at some times than others – challenging more brutal and inhumane treatments of

Indigenous peoples. But not until Eddie Mabo's time does this moral aspiration begin to show signs of transcending its cramped Eurocentrism and recognizing the equal rights of Indigenous peoples.

European Powers Adopt Rules of International Law for the Acquisition of Colonies

Over the next two centuries or so, from the mid-1500s until the latter part of the 1700s, the emerging nation-states of Europe – Spain, Portugal, France, the Netherlands, and Great Britain – struggled to assert their sense of self-determination in the New World. Law had little regulatory influence on this European scramble for empire, but its very lawlessness inspired European jurists to fashion a body of international law on the rights of discovering states and discovered peoples. Though this emerging body of international 'law' would become thoroughly secular, it built on the work of the Spanish Dominicans and, at least in its mainstream, had a highly normative intent. Law to be valid must be just. The modern version of a Law of Nations must be consistent with natural law – the dictates of 'right reason.' Hugo Grotius, the Dutch lawyer and Swedish diplomat who is often referred to as the 'Father of International Law' and whose classic work, *The Law of War and Peace*, was published in 1625, believed that underlying the civil societies into which humanity was dividing was 'the universal human society' based on an immutable 'law of nature,' which should be the standard for the voluntary Law of Nations.[21]

The efforts of Grotius and his successors were limited in both their practical impact and the scope of their universalism. These legal scholars provided legal doctrine, rather than an agreed upon body of law, which colonizing states complied with. This doctrine applied, theoretically, to a state system whose members were confined to political communities with structures of authority meeting European standards of governance. The doctrinal apparatus of these pioneering international jurists established a legacy of concepts which, though confused and confusing, have had a long-term effect on the way European-dominated nation-states have defined their relationship with Indigenous peoples. We will meet this legacy in the Australian High Court's response to Mabo's claim. At this point, it is important to understand the doctrine's underlying premises and political utility for the imperial powers and their colonists.

The European powers were certainly not shy about asserting their unilateral right to take possession and assert sovereignty over territories in the Americas. Henry VII of England, for example, in 1496 commissioned

John Cabot and sons 'to subdue, occupy and possess' such lands as they might discover in North America.[22] French monarchs gave similar instructions to their explorers in the Americas. The European states imposed only one restriction on this right of discovery: it could not be applied to a territory that had already been acquired by another Christian power.

As a legal doctrine, the right of discovery regulated the relations of the imperial European states to one another. States claimed the right of first discovery in order to establish an exclusive sphere of influence over a particular territory. A claim of discovery did not in itself define the rights of the people already occupying the discovered territory. The extent to which the discovered peoples retained ownership of their lands or freedom to govern their own societies would depend on the relationships established – through force, fraud, or consent – with the discovering European state. However, European states all aimed to establish one crucial element of sovereignty over the discovered people and their lands: the discovering state had the exclusive right to deal with the people native to the territory. Discovery created 'some form of priority for the discovering state vis-à-vis other potential colonizers.'[23] All European states claiming territory in the New World insisted on one fundamental diminution of the rights of the Indigenous peoples: the sovereign rights these people had at the time of discovery could no longer be freely exercised in the world community.

Discovering European states did not hesitate to lay claim to much more territory than their agents had actually seen or explored. Spanish, French, and English navigator-explorers all stuck up crosses or cairns and ran their country's flag up transient flag poles, claiming for their sovereigns possession of vast stretches of country they had never seen and only surmised lay beyond the coasts they had sailed past. Thus, in 1770, Captain James Cook on his first voyage of discovery, after anchoring for a few days in Botany Bay (on the southern side of present-day Sydney), sailed up the east coast of Australia, rounded Cape York, and, on a wee 'nubbin of rock' now called Possession Island, hoisted a Union Jack, naming all the land he had sailed past 'New South Wales' and claimed it in the name of George III as part of the British Empire.[24] These pretensions of acquiring land, simply by 'passing by and discovering with the eye,' were mere puffery unless followed up by effective occupation. Emmerich de Vattel, the Swiss jurist and successor to Grotius, whose *Law of Nations* became the leading international law text in the eighteenth century, denied that a state could 'claim possession or appropriate to itself land which it does not really occupy.'[25]

Since effective occupation, not mere discovery, was a necessary condition for acquiring new territory, the crucial question became by what means could effective occupation be accomplished. The answer developed by international lawyers, as noted above, depended on whether the territory was regarded as inhabited or uninhabited at the time of annexation. Inhabited territories could be acquired either by conquering the inhabitants or through the inhabitants ceding their land to the acquiring state. If, in contrast, a territory was uninhabited – was in effect a *terra nullius*, a land of no one – then it could be acquired by establishing a settlement of the state's own people on the empty territory. According to this theory, colonies could be divided into two categories: inhabited territories acquired through conquest or cession and uninhabited territories acquired through settlement.

On paper, this distinction between colonies acquired through conquest or cession of native peoples and those acquired through settlement of one's own people seems tidy and clear-cut. The reality on the ground, however, never corresponded with these simple legal categories. The insistence on using categories that did not fit the actual facts of the colonization process incorporated a major source of confusion not only into international law but also, as we shall see when we examine the Australian High Court's decision in the *Mabo* case, into the legal discourse and judicial decisions of the colonizing states.[26]

In reality, in those parts of the world that the European states were interested in colonizing, there simply were no uninhabited lands. Aside from Antarctic ice and a few island atolls, there was no *terra nullius*. Effective occupation and colonization always involved some combination of European settlement and imposition by force or fraud of European rule over native peoples. The purpose of maintaining the false distinction and insisting that there were colonies of pure settlement was to provide legal justification for ignoring the rights and interests of the people who were indigenous to the area. If the settlers and their political leaders came to believe in the truth of this legal fiction, it could be potent. And that is what happened in the Australian case – at least up until Eddie Mabo's time.

This tendency to insist on the totally unreal idea that land invaded and taken over by Europeans could be considered to be unoccupied *terra nullius* did not emerge until the later stages of colonization. Up until the nineteenth century, conquest and cession were regarded as the normal ways of acquiring territory already in the possession of native tribes.[27] By these means, Europeans understood they had established their dominion in the Americas as well as in Africa and Asia. Conquest or cession could certainly result in the Indigenous people losing or ceding some of their lands and in a diminution of their right to carry on with their own laws and system of government. However – and this is the key point – forcing or inducing native peoples to succumb to the sovereignty of a European state by conquest or treaty never meant denying that the native peoples had been organized societies with their own laws and system of government before the Europeans arrived.

In a colony considered to be acquired by settlement, the presumption was that, though native people were present on the land when the Europeans settlers arrived, the Indigenous peoples' political economy was so underdeveloped that their very existence as self-governing societies in possession of their lands could be denied. On the political side, what Europeans found missing among natives regarded as living in a *terra nullius* was an effective sovereign authority. The centuries of imperial European expansion were also the centuries in which the nation-state, with its well-defined structure of sovereign political authority, was emerging as the primary unit of politics in Western Europe. This obsession with sovereignty could make Europeans blind to political authority in native societies – one that was much more diffused and less differentiated from religious authority.

There was an even more pervasive bias on the economic side – the idea that ownership of land could be established only through its cultivation. Those who held this view could not regard a hunting and gathering people as possessing or having title to the lands on which they lived. Among the European thinkers who advanced this view, none was more influential than the seventeenth-century English philosopher John Locke. A right to property, according to Locke, could be established only through mixing one's labour with the land. 'As much land as a man tills, plants, improves, cultivates and can use the product of,' he wrote, 'so much is his property.'[28] For Locke, the untilled lands of America were 'vacant places' – in effect, a *terra nullius*.

Locke, like the English Board of Trade and Plantations on which he served, had little knowledge of Aboriginal agriculture or how hunting and gathering peoples used their lands. *Terra nullius* was not a reality of the New World but a state of mind about the New World based on ignorance and arrogance. Though this state of mind about 'backward territories' has always had its influential European adherents, it never became the prevailing doctrine either in international law or in domestic law with regard to the native peoples of America – or the Indigenous peoples of Africa, Asia, or the Pacific. It is the unhappy distinction of Australia's Indigenous peoples alone to live in a land that came to be considered as 'properly *territorium nullius* upon its acquisition.'[29] The official European view of Australia's colonization that came to prevail, from the early days of settlement until Eddie Mabo instigated his court challenge in the 1980s, held that it was a colony acquired entirely through peaceful occupation and settlement, not conquest or cession.

The Early Reliance on Treaties in Relations with Indigenous Peoples

How and why *terra nullius* became the dominant settler view in Australia – and the consequences it had for its Indigenous peoples – is something to be explored in the chapters that follow. But here we should note that British imperialism in Australasia was, in its beginnings, in no way predicated on the *terra nullius* doctrine. In 1768 James Cook set out on his first great voyage to discover Terra Australia, that vast and rich southern continent which, since the Dutch navigator Abel Tasman's voyage in 1642, had been thought by Europeans to occupy the high latitudes of the Pacific south of New Zealand. When Cook cleared Plymouth Sound and opened his secret instructions from the Admiralty, he read that, among other things, he was 'with the Consent of the Natives to take possession of Convenient Situations in the Country in the Name of the King of Great Britain; or, if you find the Country uninhabited take Possession for His Majesty by setting up Proper Marks and Inscriptions, as first discoverers and possessors.'[30]

Cook, of course, never found the fabled southern continent. He did, however, encounter native peoples when he circumnavigated New Zealand and again when he sailed west and anchored in Botany Bay on what we now know was the east coast of Australia. These encounters were much too fleeting and shocking – on both sides – to enable Captain Cook, in the optimistic phrase of his Admiralty instructions, 'to cultivate a Friendship and Alliance' with these peoples. Though Cook's instructions contemplated the possibility of discovering and claiming uninhabited lands, nowhere did they suggest that natives, if they were encountered, could be ignored and their land occupied and possessed as if their societies did not exist. Indeed, the vision of the 'second British Empire' that inspired Cook's voyages to the South Pacific was not one of colonization and settlement but of securing 'amicable intercourse for mutual benefit' with newfound peoples.[31]

In North America, the New World of the first British Empire, it was never an option to ignore native societies as if, for practical purposes, they did not exist. English settlement in America, from the very first efforts in the early 1600s, depended on a successful 'intercourse' with Amerindian nations. Such intercourse was occasionally amicable and often mutually beneficial. The interaction of settler and native peoples through most of the first two centuries of English colonization in North America ran through a cycle of peaceful, though wary, coexistence, broken by outbreaks of violence and warfare, and with peace restored at least for a while through treaty-like agreements.

The cycle is exemplified by Virginia, the first English colony established in America under a royal charter. The 145 English settlers who landed at Jamestown in 1607 were vastly outnumbered by the Algonkian-speaking peoples of the Tidewater region, who at that time may have included as many as 9000 people.[32] When the supplies they brought from England ran out and they were too sick and incompetent to provide for themselves, the native people provided them with food.[33] In December 1607, when the Englishman John Smith was brought before Powhatan, the great 'emperor'of the confederated tribes in the area, Powhatan could have easily wiped the settlement out had Smith told him that the English intended to occupy his peoples' lands and rule over them. Instead, peaceful relations were soon established through a formal ceremony, 'the first-ever formal treaty ceremony between the English and an Indian confederacy in North America.'[34] To Powhatan, the English, 'with their trade goods and novel but deadly weaponry,' looked like useful allies in maintaining and expanding his own empire. As for the English, though Powhatan's friendship was at this stage crucial for their very survival, in their own legal discourse Powhatan had become a loyal vassal submitting to the authority of their sovereign.

In 1622, in retaliation for a number of incidents in which settlers encroached on the Indians and tried to extort food from them, Openchancanough, Powhatan's much less accommodating successor, attacked the English colonies along the James River, killing several hundred settlers. This 'massacre' provided the justification for the Virginia Company, whose settler population in a decade and a half had grown to over 3000, to conduct an all-out war against Openchancanough's people. In the warfare that followed, the native people were overcome by European guns – their villages were destroyed, their cultivated fields set ablaze, and many of their younger people taken as slaves. Eventually, Openchancanough's successor, Necotowance, signed a treaty with the English ceding to them most of the confederacy's lands and reserving a small area north of the River York for his people's use.[35]

In North America the favoured instrument of the British Crown and the English colonies in regularizing relations with native peoples was the treaty.[36] Treaties were used to secure friendly relations, to establish trading partnerships and military alliances, to delineate the boundaries of European settlement, to settle the terms on which Europeans could enter Indian territory, and, sometimes, to arrange for the purchase of Indian lands for European settlement. Under circumstances in which there was a rough equality of power between settlers and natives, treaties were a natural way of ordering the relationship between their societies. A tradition of diplomacy and international agreements among nations indigenous to North America pre-dated the arrival of the Europeans by many centuries. By the eighteenth century the emerging nation-states of Europe turned increasingly to treaties to order their relations not only with one another but also with the Indigenous peoples they encountered in Africa, Asia, and North America. North American Indian nations and confederacies were never more actively involved in this extended worldwide treaty system than in the period between the end of the Seven Years' War and the beginning of the American Revolution. Between 1763 and 1774, North American Indians were signatories to thirty treaties.[37]

Treaty relationships between Europeans and native peoples had a Janus-like, two-faced quality. On one face, the treaties reflected mutual recognition of each nation by the other. By entering into formal treaty relationships with native peoples, European states and their colonists implicitly recognized these peoples as organized political societies with a proprietorial interest in the lands they used and occupied. There is no room for the *terra nullius* presumption to operate in a treaty relationship. But the other face of the treaty relationship – the hidden face – was a conflict in the underlying objectives of the parties to these treaties. By entering into these formal agreements, especially those that dealt with land rights, Indigenous nations aimed to obtain long-term security for themselves from European encroachment by establishing permanent boundaries and a nation-to-nation political relationship. For the Europeans, in contrast, the treaties were more often conceived as temporary instruments of pacification to protect the foothold their people had established in the New World before advancing farther and increasing the area of their occupation.

The political assumptions underlying the treaties were also profoundly different. While the native peoples might agree to conceding parts of their territory to white settlement, their leaders did not intend to surrender their peoples' freedom or accept their subjugation to the Europeans' political authorities. From the outset, however, the Europeans assumed an overarching political sovereignty over the native peoples and their lands. It was only when the rough equilibrium of power between settlers and natives broke down that the conflicting objectives and assumptions underlying treaties came plainly to the surface. Once the Europeans, through the combination of superior military fire-power and predominant numbers, could clearly have their way without being obliged to observe previous agreements or enter into new ones, treaties ceased to be an honourable and effective way of regulating settler-native relations. In the English settler colonies of North America and later in New Zealand, treaty relationships in the nineteenth century would degenerate into a sad story of shattered hopes and broken promises.

The Liberal Phase in Britain's Relations with Indigenous Peoples

In the 1770s, when Cook first claimed Australasian territory for Great Britain and the first boatloads of English settlers arrived at Botany Bay on the eastern shore of 'New Holland,' this tragic story lay ahead. In the latter half of the eighteenth century, British imperial policy was taking on a more self-conscious liberal air. English monarchs had always been relatively parsimonious in their support of colonial ventures and had not attempted direct rule over the peoples in the territories they claimed. As Trevor Lloyd puts it:

> The English colonies looked rather like colonies of the Greek type, where emigrants set out from their native city to launch a new city and, while often cherishing a deep affection for the city that they had left, did not acknowledge a political obligation to obey it. The other European countries acted much more like Romans: they had conquered large existing populations in the territories to which they had gone, and had established substantial colonies that were ruled by the sovereign power at home much more directly than was the case in English colonies.[38]

As the British moved towards becoming the pre-eminent European imperial power and their empire became more integral to their own sense of identity, they began to justify it on the moral ground that, compared with other Europeans, they were better imperial rulers.

The liberal spirit that animated England's Glorious Revolution of 1688 began, in the latter part of the eighteenth century, to find some reflection in the laws and policies the British applied to the Indigenous peoples of the New World. An important decision by Lord Mansfield in the case of *Campbell v. Hall* in 1774 repudiated as absurd crusading 'madness' the position taken by Lord Coke in the early 1600s that the laws of infidels whose territory was acquired by conquest were automatically terminated upon conquest. Lord Mansfield's decision aimed to bring English common law into line with the more universal principles of the Roman *ius gentium*.[39] This meant that the laws of Indigenous peoples in territories regarded as acquired by conquest continued in force until they were altered by the conqueror. Indigenous peoples in British-held territories would continue to be seen as legitimately subject to the Crown's overall political sovereignty. Nonetheless, the branch of English common law being fashioned for the constitution of the British Empire was now, in principle, open to accommodating the continuity of Indigenous peoples' laws and customs.

Blackstone, whose *Commentaries on the Laws of England*, first published in 1765, rapidly became the most influential digest of English law, did not apply to America the Lockean notion that its uncultivated lands were, in effect, a *terra nullius* and, therefore, acquired by settlement. Blackstone regarded the American plantations as having been obtained 'by right of conquest and driving out the natives (with what natural justice I shall not at present enquire) or by treaties.'[40] He concluded that, because of this origin, the common law of England did not apply in America.

In fact, and in law, the situation in America was considerably more complicated than Blackstone suggested. The American colonies combined features of conquered and settled colonies. As Brian Slattery explains:

> Regarded initially as conquests by the Crown, they eventually in most instances assumed the characteristics of settled colonies, with English law and representative institutions, at least so far as the settler communities were concerned. However the Indians stood in a different position. Generally speaking, they retained an autonomous status living under their own laws and political structures and dealing directly with the Crown and its emissaries on a communal basis.[41]

Thus, at the time Captain Cook came into contact with native peoples in New Zealand and Australia, Indigenous peoples in North America living outside areas of European settlement enjoyed full powers of internal self-government and dealt with Europeans on a nation-to-nation basis.

Such a relationship was a central feature of the policy set out in the Royal Proclamation that George III issued in 1763 at the conclusion of the Seven Years' War with France. In the Peace of Paris of that year, France ceded to Great Britain its remaining North American possessions with the exception of a small area around New Orleans. Much of what is now New Brunswick and Nova Scotia, as well as territory claimed by France in the Canadian northwest, had already been ceded to Great Britain by the Treaty of Utrecht in 1713. Nearly all of North America was now regarded by European nations as under British sovereignty. The Royal Proclamation established the boundaries of Britain's new colonies and set out British policy with respect to Indian lands beyond the settled colonies.

The second part of this proclamation began by referring to the Indigenous peoples as 'the several Nations or Tribes with whom We are connected' and acknowledged that these nations and tribes were 'in the Possession of such Parts of our Dominions and Territories as, not having been ceded to or purchased by Us, are reserved to them.'[42] It went on to explain that this document aimed to put an end to the 'great Frauds and Abuses' committed in purchasing Indian lands so that 'the Indians may be convinced of our Justice and determined Resolution to remove all reasonable Cause of Discontent.' To this end, the King, with the advice of his Privy Council (Cabinet), did 'strictly enjoin and require, that no private Person do presume to make any purchase from the said Indians of any Lands reserved to the said Indians, within those parts of our Colonies where, We have thought proper to allow Settlement; but that, if at any Time any of the Said Indians should be inclined to dispose of the said Lands, the same shall be Purchased only for Us, in our Name, at some public Meeting or Assembly of the said Indians.' Thus, the proclamation informed all the King's subjects in the colonies along the Atlantic seaboard, as well as in the new colonies (Quebec and Florida) acquired from the French, that they were not to expand their settlements beyond existing borders until such time as additional lands were obtained by the Imperial government through treaty-like agreements with Indian nations.

The Royal Proclamation of 1763 was undoubtedly a major landmark in Aboriginal-European relations. It was a landmark, however, whose essential purpose and meaning resonated quite differently with the three parties whose relationships it purported to regulate: the imperial government, the Indian nations, and the North American settlers.

For the British government, the proclamation was, first and foremost, an instrument of imperial management. The Board of Trade, the King's advisers on North American policy, proposed that, instead of annexing to Canada the vast Indian territory acquired from France and giving Canada a huge advantage in the Indian trade, the unsettled interior should be put under the military governance of the British commander-in-chief of North America. By banning private purchase of these lands, the British aimed to encourage new English settlement in the Floridas and Nova Scotia and to prevent an uncontrolled influx of land-hungry American colonists into the lands west of the Alleghenies, now, in their view, securely under British rule. The British, having just finished a lengthy imperial conflict with France and being the parsimonious and prudent managers of empire they were, wanted to avoid fighting a costly war with the Indian tribes that were still very much in control of the entire continent west of the eastern line of settlements. A war with the Cherokees in South Carolina was just over. Further north, an Indian uprising led by Pontiac, an Ottawa war chief, had broken out and was reported in the London press. Between May 16 and June 20, 1763, nine British forts fell.[43] In these circumstances, publicly recognizing Aboriginal rights on unsettled lands and pledging to keep colonists from settling on unceded Indian lands reflected established English law as well as the imperatives of maintaining peace on the frontier of settlement.

For the Aboriginal nations, the Proclamation of 1763 presented an opportunity to restore and reorganize their treaty relationship with Europeans now that France had been eliminated from the North American scene. During the winter of 1763–4, a printed copy of the proclamation was circulated among the nations of the northeast, mideast, and midwest of North America, with an invitation to send representatives to a peace council at Niagara.[44] In the summer of 1764, approximately two thousand chiefs representing over twenty-four nations gathered at Niagara to meet with William Johnson, the northern superintendent of Indian affairs. Gifts and wampum were exchanged. Johnson read the terms of the Royal Proclamation, and the Aboriginal representatives gave a promise of peace. The treaty of alliance was sealed with the presentation of the two-row wampum belt, whose symbolism of two distinct vessels travelling together along the same river depicted the interaction and separation of settler and Aboriginal societies.[45]

The Indians at Niagara considered themselves free peoples, and Johnson did not dare attempt a real meeting of minds with the Indians on Great Britain's presumption of sovereignty over them and their lands. Thus, Aboriginal peoples in North America often look back on the 1763 proclamation and the Treaty of Niagara as their 'Magna Carta.'

This attitude prevails in Canada, where the continuity of British law has been maintained and the proclamation has been incorporated into its contemporary Constitution.[46] Canada's *Charter of Rights and Freedoms* stipulates that its rights and freedoms are not 'to abrogate or derogate' from the Aboriginal and treaty rights of the Aboriginal peoples of Canada, including 'any rights or freedoms that have been recognized by the Royal Proclamation of October 7, 1763.'[47] However, what those 'recognized' rights and freedoms might mean has come to depend much more on the settler society and its courts than on the kind of negotiation that took place between British and Aboriginal representatives on the banks of the Niagara over two hundred years ago.

The colonial settlers were the third party affected by the proclamation. The irony here is that it is this third party, the English and French settler societies, who were not themselves represented at Niagara, who would soon have the dominant say in shaping the actual rights and freedoms that Aboriginal peoples in North America would enjoy. For them, the Royal Proclamation of 1763 was no Magna Carta. Indeed, for the American colonists, it was a red flag, for it denied them the right to make their own deals with the Indians and gain access to the rich lands of the interior. Their radical leaders 'rejected flatly the proposition that an English king could deny them their right to purchase lands from the frontier Indians.'[48] And, of course, it is as participants in the democratic states that would be built by the descendants of these colonial settlers that Amerindians would ultimately have to claim their rights.

The same would also be true for those other English-settler societies that achieved democracy and independence along an evolutionary rather than a revolutionary path – Australia, Canada, and New Zealand. In all three, as in the United States of America, the rights of Aboriginal peoples would soon be at the mercy of settler majorities. In all four of these countries, settler interests and outlooks would quickly prevail over any doctrines of divine, international, or English common law in determining the conditions of Indigenous peoples. For more than a century and a half, despite significant differences in the constitutions and laws of these countries, their native peoples experienced a common fate. Rather than being partners in the democratic nation-building projects that the descendants of the colonists and other newcomers took on, the more ancient Aboriginal nations resident on their territories, very simply, were 'a problem.'

Though the four English-settler countries tackled the native people problem with different laws and policies, the results in all four were basically the same: massive dispossession and political oppression of the Indigenous peoples. Australia differed only in being more extreme – both in the extent to which it denied aboriginal peoples any recognition in building a modern democratic nation and in its lateness in moving to overcome this moral flaw in its national development. This comparative analysis of Aboriginal-settler relations in the four English-settler countries will be taken up in chapter 4. Before considering these national biographies, however, we must return to Eddie Mabo's personal biography to see how the politics and law of his day moved him to challenge the conditions of his colonization.

CHAPTER 3

Eddie Mabo's Project and Its Obstacles

By the 1970s the rights and status of Indigenous peoples had become important issues in Australian politics. Even though Aborigines and Torres Strait Islanders at this time constituted little more than 1 per cent of Australia's population, the issues they raised were becoming as prominent in Australia's politics as those of Afro-Americans in U.S. politics. And, as with the American response to black political issues, the Australian debate about the position of Indigenous peoples tended to be conceptualized in terms of race relations. Much more than in Canada, New Zealand, or the United States, the other three countries dominated by the descendants of English-speaking settlers, the descendants of the original occupants of Australia tend to be spoken of as a distinct race rather than as distinct peoples or nations.

Election of the Whitlam Government

The election of Gough Whitlam's Labor government in December 1972, after twenty-three years of Liberal/Country Party (right-of-centre) government in Canberra, was a stimulating event for aboriginal politics in Australia. For the first time in the country's history, a Commonwealth government took power with a strong commitment in its platform to reform relations with Indigenous peoples. In February 1972, before the election, Whitlam met Aboriginal leaders at the Aboriginal Tent Embassy facing the entrance of the Commonwealth Parliament Building in Canberra. The Tent Embassy had become, and remains to this day, the symbolic centre of Indigenous peoples' protest in Australia. On this occasion, Whitlam committed his party to moving beyond 'assimilation' and 'integration,' as the objectives of reform in aboriginal relations, to a policy of 'self-determination.' After becoming prime minister, Whitlam talked of restoring to Aborigines 'their lost power of self-determination in economic, social and political affairs.'[1]

The Whitlam government could not, of course, come even close to meeting the expectations aroused by its rhetoric. However, in its three short and turbulent years in office, it delivered two tangible and significant benefits to Indigenous Australians. First, it introduced Australia's first national human rights legislation, the *Racial Discrimination Act* (*RDA*), which declared it 'unlawful for a person to do any act involving a distinction, exclusion, restriction or preference based on race, colour, descent or national or ethnic origin which has the purpose or effect of nullifying or impairing the recognition, enjoyment or exercise, on an equal footing, of any human right or fundamental freedom in the political, economic, social, cultural or any other field of public life.'[2] The *RDA* embodies the liberal, egalitarian principle of extending equal civic rights to all citizens, regardless of their race, colour, ethnic, or national background. This same ideal animated the civil rights movement in the United States. That both sides of politics in Australia could now embrace this principle marked how far the country's dominant population had moved from its commitment to a 'white Australia.'

While the *RDA* was undoubtedly a major milestone in the ethical evolution of Australia, the liberal principle of individual equality on which it is based, as I will argue throughout this book, cannot provide an adequate basis for establishing just relations with Indigenous peoples. Nonetheless, the *Racial Discrimination Act* turned out, in quite unanticipated ways, to be an essential vehicle for protecting rights of more fundamental importance to aboriginal peoples. Without it, Eddie Mabo's effort to obtain recognition of his people's ownership of their ancestral lands and waters could not have reached the High Court.

The second tangible benefit from the Whitlam administration was the establishment of a commission of inquiry into aboriginal land rights. The commission was chaired by Mr Justice A.E. Woodward, who was directed to inquire into 'appropriate means to recognize and establish the traditional rights and interests of the Aborigines in and in relation to land.'[3] The Woodward inquiry led to the introduction of a statutory scheme of land rights for the Northern Territory. This legislation, with some narrowing modifications, was passed by the Fraser Liberal government, which came to power in 1976. Aboriginal land rights defined and created by the Australian Parliament, in both a legal and a philosophical sense, were not the kind of rights Eddie Mabo would strive to have recognized in his litigation. Still, legislation creating positive rights to be enjoyed by aboriginal *communities* did represent a significant move in Australian aboriginal policy. It was the first recognition in national law that building a just relationship with Indigenous peoples would require more than the removal of discriminatory barriers. Moreover, although it was little appreciated at the time, the fact that a Labor government introduced the legislation, and a Liberal Coalition government steered it through Parliament, represented a high-water mark for bipartisan cooperation in reforming aboriginal relations.

Eddie Mabo's Political Activism

The momentum the Whitlam government gave to reforming aboriginal relations soon began to quicken the pace of Eddie Mabo's activism. Though Mabo, in his own words, was 'eliminated' from the Aboriginal Advancement League (the local branch of the Australia-wide Federal Council for the Advancement of Aborigines and Torres Strait Islanders) just as it was receiving its first government grant, he found plenty of other outlets for his activism.[4] Soon after leaving the league, he became the president of the Council for the Rights of Indigenous Peoples, an organization that supported a number of all-black activities in the Townsville area. These groups included the Aboriginal Legal Aid Service and the Aboriginal Medical Service. He was also active in developing cooperative housing for Townsville's growing black population. From 1975 to 1980 he was president of the Yumba Meta Housing Association.[5] And, of course, he was deeply and continually involved with the Black Community School in Townsville, which he had been instrumental in founding.

Through his leadership and the range of his activities in Townsville, Mabo became 'a national figure in black Australian circles.'[6] For a time he represented Torres Strait Islanders on the Aboriginal Arts Board. He worked with Aboriginal organizations 'down south' in recruiting Indigenous students for advanced educational opportunities and in raising money for their support. Through his work for the Black Community School, he became involved with the National Aboriginal Education Committee, which had been set up to provide government with advice on the educational needs of Indigenous peoples. This school, along with Mabo's views on education policy, featured prominently in national conferences on aboriginal education.[7]

Mabo was a natural social and political activist. He was self-confident, energetic, and articulate. He could also be abrasive. He was never one to back away from a tough political battle, whether winning recognition for his school, evicting non-paying residents from the housing cooperative, or dealing with factional conflicts within the Townsville black community. And sometimes, as Netta lovingly relates, he brought this anger home with him.[8] The intensive pace of his activism and its frustrations, even for a man with his spirit and energy, could be almost overwhelming. In Trevor Graham's film documentary *Life of an Island Man*, Bonita Mabo tells how, some days during these years, Mabo would come home exhausted and 'just say that he didn't know what to do.'[9]

Most of the activities that Mabo took up represented the approach to reforming aboriginal relations premised on classical liberal egalitarianism – the philosophy that inspired the *Racial Discrimination Act*. Providing better access to legal and medical services, to decent urban housing, to social services, and to mainstream education – all these activities were designed to make it easier for the individual of aboriginal background to enjoy the full benefits of Australian citizenship. Given the dreadful hardships that aboriginal people had suffered in the past through exclusion from virtually all the basic rights of Australian citizenship, reforms of this kind were liberal, progressive, and greatly valued by most Indigenous Australians. But this approach on its own would never be enough to establish a just relationship with aboriginal peoples, a relationship based on mutual consent which could be truly post-colonial.

When the liberal, egalitarian, but fundamentally integrationist approach is the only one on offer, it becomes illiberal – a softer form of forced assimilation. In effect, aboriginal peoples are offered full membership in the dominant society on condition that they abandon their aboriginality – that they give up any effective means of continuing the historical societies from which they derive so much of their own sense of identity and self-worth. The challenge of decolonization, in the context of relations with Indigenous peoples who have become small, marginalized minorities within First World nation-states, is to establish a mutually acceptable balance between the integrationist and autonomist approaches to reform.[10]

Within the whirlpool of reform activities into which Eddie Mabo was swept, only the Black Community School, the project that, more than any other, was of his own making, held some possibility of working at this balance. Mabo hoped that the education offered in that school would give students a strong grounding and pride in their own distinct heritage while at the same time preparing them well for effective participation in

Australian life. In his own words: 'One may argue that we need to survive as a race as Australians, but again the actual thing is that the kids are themselves first, before they are Australians ... For instance, I am Piadram first and secondly I am a Murray Islander and then a Torres Strait Islander and then an Australian afterwards.'[11] Mabo knew from his own personal struggle to establish a decent life for himself and his family that it was necessary, first, to master the language, acquire the skills of the dominant society, and overcome the barriers to full participation in that society. At the same time, he was determined to nurture knowledge of the traditional culture, which he saw as the source of his own inner strength and sense of purpose.

The Conference on the Torres Strait Border

It was through his engaging in activities at colleges and universities that we can best see Eddie Mabo's political project maturing. One such event was a conference at the Townsville College of Advanced Education from 29 to 31 October 1976 on the Torres Strait border issue.

The issue before the conference had been brought on by Papua New Guinea, which had gained its independence from Great Britain in 1975 and was now pressing for a redrawing of its border with Australia in the Torres Strait. The original border was drawn by Britain in the 1870s and came within 'less than a bowshot' of the Papuan coast.[12] So nearly all the Torres Strait Islands, including Saibu, Boigu, and Dauan, three of the larger inhabited islands just a few kilometres off New Guinea, had been incorporated into the colony of Queensland and subsequently became part of Australia. By being so generous with Queensland's border, Britain had hoped to dampen any fervour in the eastern colonies of Australia for annexation of Eastern New Guinea. Now political leaders of an independent Papua New Guinea were agitating for a readjustment of the border, and the Whitlam government, sympathetic to Third World decolonization and despite protests from Sir Joh Bjelke-Petersen's Queensland government, had shown some signs of being willing to shift the border southward. The Liberal government of Malcolm Fraser was proceeding more cautiously.

The Townsville conference was attended by academics, diplomats, and a few Torres Strait Islanders. The latter included George Mye from Darnley Island, the senior and best-known Islander political leader; Getano Lui from Yam Island, the chairman of the Torres Strait Islands Advisory Council; and Eddie Koiki Mabo. Though Mabo had lived in

Townsville for many years, he still identified strongly with his island home and, along with all his other activities, was chairman of the Torres Strait Border Action Committee in Townsville. The participation of Islanders at the conference was in itself a breakthrough. Never before had the British or Australians sought the inhabitants' views on such matters of state. Third World decolonization was stimulating Fourth World decolonization.

In this case, representatives of the Indigenous Fourth World people, the Torres Strait Islanders, showed not the slightest interest in becoming part of a Third World country. Indeed, Getano Lui declared that 'there is not one Islander who would wish to become a Papuan if our islands were to be taken over by Papua New Guinea.'[13] He and other Islanders said that though they wanted to maintain friendly relations with Papua New Guinea, there had always been an acknowledged, though undocumented, boundary between the Islanders and their 'Papuan brothers,' one they were strongly opposed to changing. Nor, according to Lui, did the Islanders have any interest in leaving Australia: 'While being proud to be Australians and Queenslanders, we are most proud to be called Torres Strait Islanders.'[14]

When Eddie Mabo's turn to speak came, the Islander-in-exile struck a more radical note:

> We Islanders ought to look closely at Australian laws and Australia's attitude towards us. Are we prepared to go on for the next hundred years being regarded as second-class citizens? Are we going to live in the slums of big cities? Brothers and Sisters, it's time to decide. I know several people have stated to me that independence for the Torres Strait Islands is not necessary. However, I think independence should be accepted as a long-term policy. We are people of unique identity and we should work towards an ultimate goal of independence.[15]

Mabo went on to suggest that the federal government take over all the Torres Strait Islands from Queensland and negotiate with the Islanders themselves an arrangement under which the Islanders would administer the area as an autonomous region of Australia. In this autonomous region, 'all fishing rights and all seabed rights would be reserved exclusively for the use of the Islanders, with heavy penalties imposed on intruders who infringe our rights.'[16]

Though the conference did not adopt Mabo's radical proposal, its chief organizer, James Griffin, concluded: 'It should now be clear from the testimony of the Islanders ... that any redrawing of the boundary will be perceived as a betrayal by the federal Government and the white liberals of Australia.'[17] The Australian government did not commit such a betrayal. In 1978 Australia signed a treaty with Papua New Guinea that did not transfer any of the Torres Strait Islands to Papuan jurisdiction.[18] The treaty did, however, move the line demarcating the seabed and fisheries slightly further south into the Torres Strait and out into the Coral Sea to the limit of the continental shelf.[19] It created a Protected Zone in which Islanders and residents of the adjacent coast of Papua New Guinea could enjoy 'traditional customary rights of access to and usage of areas of land, seabed seas, estuaries and coastal tidal areas.'[20] Moreover, it made a move towards a co-management regime by providing for the representation of traditional inhabitants on the Torres Strait Joint Advisory Council, established to assist the two countries in the implementation of the treaty.

Eddie Mabo may have been well ahead of his time and his people, but we can see from this 1976 Townsville conference on the Torres Strait that the times were changing. Traditional owners and inhabitants of at least one part of Australia now had some voice in decisions about their lands and waters. Granted this voice would be heard only in an advisory process, but consultation is typically the first step in a decolonizing process. The conference also indicated that the colonized people in this context were not likely to share Mabo's long-term goal of complete independence. There was probably more truth than Islanders cared to admit in Papuan innuendos that the only reason the Islanders refused to join Papua New Guinea was that they had been bought off by Australian welfare. The very tangible benefits (in terms of both welfare and defence) of being Australian citizens, as compared with being Papuans, combined with some political and social identification with Australia (albeit subordinate to their Islander identity), meant that the autonomist thrust of Islander nationalism could likely be satisfied within Australia.

By the mid-1970s, Indigenous peoples, in pressing for their rights, were finding a more receptive and a wider audience in white Australia. In the passage from Griffin's conclusions to the Townsville conference quoted above, it is 'the white liberals of Australia' who would betray the Torres Strait Islanders if their wishes about the boundary were ignored. At the 1967 Inter-Racial Conference in Townsville where Eddie Mabo had his first indoctrination into aboriginal politics, it was mostly Communists, trade unionists, and the more radical end of the white political spectrum who were rallying to the support of Indigenous peoples. Now the support was broadening out to the liberal mainstream, and, on occasion, even beyond. In 1973 Premier Bjelke-Petersen, the rising star of conservative politics in Australia, presented a petition of the Torres Strait Islanders to the Queensland Parliament. The petition, brought on by the impending Papua New Guinea border issue, asked for Queensland's help in enabling the Islanders to 'retain their rights to their islands, their ancestral homes for generations before the discovery of Australia.'[21] On this occasion, when the Islanders' interests in retaining the existing boundary with Papua New Guinea coincided with Queensland's interests, Sir Joh was on their side. A decade later, as we shall see, when the Murray Islanders' court action challenged his government's power over them, Sir Joh's government became their major adversary.

Progress in gaining Australian recognition of Indigenous peoples' rights came more easily in the islands of the Torres Strait than on the Australian mainland. The vast majority of the Torres Strait Islands population have family ties to the traditional inhabitants. While Australia has a major defence interest in the area and some economic interests (a commercial fishery and some oil and gas potential), these islands off the far northeast tip of the continent, unlike the rural 'outback,' the homeland of most Aboriginal Australians, are not central to white Australia's sense of identity. Even so, recognition of the Islanders' status and rights at this stage of Australian history was modest and tentative. The treaty established a mechanism through which the traditional inhabitants could be heard in decisions affecting their interests, but it gave them no share in decision-making itself. While it recognized 'customary rights of access to and usage of' their lands and waters, it fell far short of recognizing Islander ownership of these traditional resources. Although no one knew it at the time, progress in that direction would depend on Eddie Mabo.

Eddie Mabo Begins to Fight for His Land Rights

It was not until February 1977 that Eddie Mabo was finally able to return to Mer Island. When he did, it was not with anyone's permission. He simply hired a boat at Thursday Island and went out to Mer with his family.

In 1974, when he heard that his father, Benny Mabo, was seriously ill, Mabo had applied to the Murray Island Council for permission to visit. The council granted permission on condition that he would 'never undertake political affairs.'[22] This condition infuriated Mabo and was absolutely unacceptable to him. He could no more abandon his political objectives than he could shed his skin. Arriving on Mer in 1977 without any official permission, he was apprehensive and expected to be arrested by the Queensland police.[23] Although he was not actually arrested, he did encounter a great deal of suspicion and opposition to his political activism. As his widow recalls: 'When Koiki went home to Murray Island, they told him they didn't want his "ideas from the south." They put him out of meetings, offered to take him outside to fight, and called the police.'[24] Mabo's difficulties with his fellow Islanders would continue all through his struggle to achieve recognition of their ownership of their homeland. Though the Murray Islanders were a proud people with a strong sense of identity, their political style in relation to colonial authorities was much quieter, less aggressive, and less ideological than Mabo's. They could accept, much more than Mabo ever could, what Jeremy Beckett terms 'welfare colonialism' as the primary means of advancing their collective interests.[25]

Many Islanders had come to rely on a relationship of welfare dependency with outside authorities (increasingly, in the 1970s, the federal government in Canberra) as the principal means of improving living standards. And it was through a framework of local government established by the state government of Queensland that leaders sought to achieve the Meriam people's political development. In a political environment dominated by welfare colonialism, Mabo's focus on recognition of the Islanders' pre-colonial proprietorship of their lands and waters did not receive a ready, warm welcome. His fiery temperament and the personal disputes with litigious neighbours in which he became embroiled, once he began asserting claims to garden plots inherited from his father, added to his difficulties. In the end he would be acclaimed on Mer as a popular hero, but it would not be until after his death and after his great legal victory.

It was on this first visit back to Murray Island, beside his father's grave, that Eddie Mabo committed himself to 'the great battle of his life.'[26] After this visit he would return often to his island home,[27] renewing his ties with his extended family and caring for the family property in the village of Las. But until their children completed their education, Eddie and Netta's permanent residence would remain 23 Hibiscus Street in Townsville. But 'home' for Mabo never ceased to be Murray Island. The depth of his love and yearning for his island home can be heard in the songs he taught his children. It can be seen in his drawings and paintings of it that still adorn the walls of his house. And we can feel it in this poem that he left with his papers:

Oh Murray my sweet home
I'm so badly missing you
Living down south is like
Motherless children at large
I know you're watching my way
Waiting for me to return to you
When I do it will be for good
For ever neaiem.[28]

While the passion and affection for his island home would gird him
for the great battle on which he was about to embark, that battle would
be fought in an arena as alien to Mabo's artistic inclinations as it was to
his political temperament. It would be fought in the law courts – more
precisely, in the 'white man's law courts.' It was part of Mabo's political
genius to recognize that the decolonization struggle of Indigenous peoples
had entered a new era. As he described it in a report he made halfway
through his decade of litigation in Australia's courts: 'This is a new era
for us. We are struggling 200 years after the initial invasion fighting the
white man's law makers in their own legal game where our fathers and
our ancestors before us were not able to do.'[29] In this new era, Indigenous peoples with access to the most accomplished practitioners in the
white man's law would try to obtain recognition of their rights in the
white man's courts. Eddie Mabo's case would test the limits of that
strategy.

A Forbidding Legal Landscape

The legal regime under which Eddie Mabo would attempt to vindicate
his people's rights could scarcely have been less promising. This was true
with respect to the general constitutional and legal culture prevailing in
Australia up to this time, as well as the precedents pertaining to aboriginal rights.

The Constitution that founded the Australian federation on 1 January
1901 was not a rights constitution. It was – and is – a document that deals
primarily with the structure of government and the federal system, and
on these matters it was modelled closely on the American Constitution.
It did not include a constitutional bill of rights. Scattered through the
Australian Constitution are a few very specific rights – notably to trial by

jury, to 'just terms' for government acquisition of private property, and to freedom of religion – but these rights bind only the Commonwealth, not the states, and have not given rise to a tradition of vindicating constitutional rights in the courts.[30] As for aboriginal rights, they were totally unrecognized in the Constitution. Indigenous peoples were treated entirely in the negative: the Commonwealth Parliament was denied any power to legislate in relation to them, and they were not to be counted in the census. Though these negative provisions were removed by referendum in 1967, they were not replaced by any positive constitutional recognition of Indigenous peoples or their rights.[31]

Australia's supreme court,[32] the High Court, has played an anomalous role in the country's history. From the beginning, the High Court has had a major influence in shaping the laws and Constitution of Australia, yet the country has been slow to comprehend its political power. The justices of Australia's High Court have never been shy about vetoing legislation that, in their view, exceeds the powers accorded by the Constitution to the states and the Commonwealth. In the 1940s the High Court read freedom of enterprise and freedom of contract into the Constitution, and it struck down Labor government legislation nationalizing the banking system and interstate airlines, along with two attempts by Labor to provide for free medicine.[33] In the 1950s, High Court activism cut in a different direction when it ruled unconstitutional the Menzies government's attempt to ban the Communist Party.[34] The High Court did all this, and much more, behind a veil of legalism – an insistence that adjudicating disputes about legal rights and powers, including those set out in the Constitution, is a technical exercise driven entirely by legal logic, and not at all by the social or political beliefs of the judges.

Legal realism has come very late to Australia. Both within the legal establishment and at the level of popular opinion, Australia lagged far behind the United States, and even behind Canada and the United Kingdom, in acknowledging the discretionary role of judges in interpreting and applying the law. Far from reducing judicial power, this denial of judicial discretion sustained a 'legal mystique' that encouraged the assignment of contentious social issues, including labour relations, to adjudication by technically proficient and (in theory) politically neutral lawyer/judges.[35]

By the time Eddie Mabo was beginning to look for justice in the courts, cracks were appearing in the veneer of legalism. In the academy, the controversial appointment of Julius Stone to the Law School at the University of Sydney in 1945 challenged the intellectual hegemony of traditional formalists. In 1975 one of the first imbibers of Stone's legal pluralism and realism, Lionel Murphy, was appointed to the High Court. Murphy, as attorney general in the first Labor government since 1949, was the architect of the *Racial Discrimination Act* and numerous other liberal reforms.[36] With his appointment to the High Court, the politicization of the Australian judiciary was well under way. Murphy's open avowal of the radical premises of his decisions advertised the implicit conservatism of his positivist colleagues.

The judicial and legal system confronting Mabo as he turned to the courts was still relatively unpenetrated by these new currents of legal thought and judicial politics. In contrast to common law courts in North America, no Australian court had ever recognized any kind of aboriginal right. Indeed, the first and only attempt by Indigenous peoples in Australia to have ownership of their lands recognized in Australian courts had produced the negative decision of the Federal Court's Justice Blackburn in the *Milirrpum* decision of 1970.[37]

Milirrpum was an unprecedented case in Australian history. On a number of occasions in the past, court decisions had dealt with the legal status of native peoples in Australia, but these previous cases had been instigated by settlers and their governments. In *Milirrpum*, for the first time an aboriginal community took the initiative and tried to gain recognition of its rights in an Australian court. The case was initiated by Milirrpum and other Yolngu people from Cape Gove in the northeastern tip of the Northern Territory's Arnhem Land. In 1963 the Yolngu people sent a petition in the form of a traditional bark painting to the House of Representatives, protesting the government's decision to take part of their ancestral land for a bauxite mine. The bark petition, though an important symbolic event in signalling the determination of Indigenous peoples to secure their rights and interests through the institutions of Australian government, had little practical effect. It hangs now in the new Parliament House in Canberra, in Galarrwuy Yunupingu's words, 'a proud but sad symbol of my people's fight for their land.'[38]

Having failed in the political arena, the Yolngu resorted to the courts. Their submission to the Federal Court did not challenge the assertion of Crown sovereignty over their land. Their main contention was that 'at common law the rights, under native law or custom, of native communities to land within territory acquired by the Crown, provided that these rights were intelligible and capable of recognition by the common law, were rights that persisted, and must be respected by the Crown itself and

by its colonizing subjects, unless and until they were validly terminated.'
Valid termination required the consent of the native people and perhaps
explicit legislation.[39]

Justice Blackburn rejected this argument. He did not do so lightly. It
took him 150 pages to explain and justify his decision – up to this point,
by far the longest opinion on aboriginal rights (or the absence thereof)
written by an Australian judge. The crux of Blackburn's decision is his
acceptance of the idea that Australia was a colony acquired entirely by
peaceful settlement. As we saw in chapter 2, according to the international law doctrine developed by legal theorists of the European imperial states, the territory of a colony considered to be acquired by
settlement, rather than by conquest or cession, was regarded as being
unoccupied by any organized society at the time European settlers
arrived. There might well have been some human inhabitants, but
European jurists regarded them as at such a low level of social and
political development as not to warrant any recognition of their political
authorities or laws. That Australia was such a colony was settled for
Blackburn by a 'binding' decision made by the Judicial Committee of
the Privy Council in the case of *Cooper v. Stuart* in 1889.[40] In settling this
dispute over a grant of Crown land to settlers, Lord Watson, speaking for
the supreme court of the British Empire, found that New South Wales
was 'a Colony which consisted of a tract of territory practically unoccupied, without settled inhabitants or settled law, at the time it was peacefully annexed to the British dominions.'[41]

Blackburn heard a good deal of evidence from anthropologists and
(through a translator) Aboriginal witnesses about the organization and
laws of the Yolngu. This evidence flew in the face of Lord Watson's
finding. In Blackburn's own words, the evidence shows

> that the social rules and customs of the plaintiffs cannot possibly be dis-
> missed as lying on the other side of an unbridgeable gulf. The evidence
> shows a subtle and elaborate system highly adapted to the country in which
> the people led their lives, which provided a stable order of society and was
> remarkably free from the vagaries of personal whim or influence. If ever a
> system could be called 'a government of laws, and not of men,' it is that
> shown in the evidence before me.[42]

And yet, despite this evidence, Blackburn concluded that the argument
by the Yolngu's lawyer, A.E. Woodward, that the Judicial Committee's
finding should be dismissed as inaccurate was 'hopeless.' Why? Because

'the question is not one of fact but of law.'[43] Justice Blackburn was a firm believer in the overriding power of legal magic.

Woodward placed before Blackburn many international precedents for recognizing the communal land ownership of native peoples. In Blackburn's view, however, when such recognition occurred in a settled colony, it was not because a right of collective ownership was considered to inhere in those who first occupied the land but solely as the result of a policy decision of the imperial or settler authorities. He was particularly at pains to explain, in this way, precedents from settler countries with common law roots. Thus, he went out of his way to diminish the significance of decisions of Chief Justice Marshall of the United States, decisions we will look at more closely in chapter 4, which, among other things, held that the Indian tribes of North America, as the original inhabitants, 'were acknowledged to be the rightful occupants of the soil, with a legal as well as just claim to retain possession of it.'[44] However, Blackburn contended that a right of possession does not amount to a property right, and he fastened on a decision of the modern U.S. Supreme Court, some 135 years after Marshall's decisions,[45] that original Indian title did not give rise to a property right protected by the American Constitution.

In considering Canadian precedents, Blackburn had before him a case virtually coterminous with his own. In 1967 the Nisga'a people had gone to court to claim Aboriginal title to their ancestral lands in the Nass River valley in northwest British Columbia. Having failed at trial, Frank Calder and other Nisga'a leaders appealed to the Court of Appeal of British Columbia. The British Columbia Court of Appeal's decision in *Calder*,[46] dismissing the Nisga'a appeal, was decided just in time for Blackburn to receive copies of the judgment. In it he found strong confirmation for the position he was taking, in particular the proposition put forward by Justice Davey: 'Whether aboriginal rights ought to be confirmed or recognized depends entirely upon the Crown's or legislature's view of the policy required to deal properly with each situation.'[47] The timing here was most unfortunate. Three years later the Supreme Court of Canada would overturn Davey's (and Blackburn's) position on the common law doctrine of native title. The legal obstacles confronting Mabo would have been significantly reduced had Justice Blackburn rendered his decision after the Supreme Court of Canada's decision in *Calder*.

It is time now to look back at the laws and policies through which the settler society in Australia established its hegemony over the Aborigines and Torres Strait Islanders. Though, as we shall see, relations with Indigenous peoples in Australia differed in important ways from the other countries that came to be dominated by English-speaking settlers – Canada, New Zealand, and the United States – the overall result of settler domination was basically the same. In all four countries the Indigenous peoples were reduced to small, massively dispossessed, and politically oppressed minorities. In all four countries the overall aim of the new democracies built by the descendants of the settlers and other newcomers became the elimination of the native peoples as distinct political communities.

This legacy of New World imperialism was firmly in place at the end of the Second World War, and it was just beginning to be challenged in the years leading up to Mabo's court case. Although in a broad sense Australia was no different in its treatment of Indigenous peoples from other New World countries resulting from British expansion, the distinctive qualities of its aboriginal relations produced a structure of attitude and practice that would make the possibility of decolonization considerably more difficult than in other English-settler countries. A comparative examination of the foundations of Australian colonialism will help us to appreciate just how formidable was the challenge Eddie Mabo faced as he launched his project.

Part Two

INDIGENOUS COLONIZATION
AND ITS CONTESTATION

CHAPTER 4

The Distinctive Foundations of Australian Colonialism

When Captain James Cook set out in 1768 on the voyage of discovery that led to the first official British contact with Aboriginal people in Australia, his instructions, as we saw in chapter 2, contemplated that if he encountered local 'Natives,' he was to obtain their consent to take possession of 'Convenient Situations, in the King's name.' Natives Cook certainly did encounter. In April 1770, when he attempted to land at Botany Bay, native warriors shied stones at his longboat to resist the invasion. Though Cook's fleeting encounters with Aborigines in Botany Bay did not result in any coherent connection or settled agreement, they were fateful for aboriginal peoples' relationship with Europeans in Australia. Robert Hughes goes so far as to aver that those few days of sparse contact on the coast of New South Wales 'sealed the doom of the Aborigine.'[1]

Hughes's pronouncement is unduly apocalyptic. What the Indigenous peoples of Australia can achieve as they struggle to overcome two centuries of colonization is far from settled. But Cook's brief encounter and the reports he brought back to England were a major contributing factor to dooming Aborigines to a particularly oppressive brand of British imperialism.

Though Cook himself had a relatively positive 'noble savage' view of the natives he encountered, far more influential was the report of Joseph Banks, the gentleman botanist who accompanied Cook as the Royal Society's official scientific observer. On the basis of a few observations along the coast of New South Wales, Banks reported that the continent was sparsely populated by a very timid, ill-armed, and backwards people.[2] After the American Revolution, when Britain began to look for a new destination for the transportation of its swelling convict population, Banks's impressions had much to do with the choice of New Holland (as Australia was then known) as, in effect, an empty land – a *terra nullius* – where such a project would encounter no serious resistance from the local population.

Thus, the option in Cook's instructions of taking possession of some land in Australia with the consent of the native people was never taken up. When the First Fleet deposited its first load of convicts at Port Jackson (present-day Sydney) on 26 January 1788, Arthur Phillip, captain of the fleet and the first British governor, though instructed to establish friendly relations with the natives, was not directed to negotiate the terms on which the settlers would occupy their land. From the very beginning, the British colonies in Australia were treated as 'colonies of settlement' established on uninhabited waste lands.

It hardly needs to be said that the hundreds of thousands of Aboriginal peoples who actually inhabited these lands when the British settlers arrived, and who had been their custodians for many thousands of years, never for a moment accepted the official British view of the situation.[3] Nevertheless, it was not until Eddie Mabo took up his law case that the *terra nullius* doctrine was effectively challenged in the courts of the settler society. Years after Mabo's court triumph, the continuing strength of *terra nullius* as political myth is evident in an Australian prime minister's refusal to acknowledge the Aborigines and Torres Strait Islanders as the original custodians of Australia's land and waters.

In this chapter we survey the main contours of the relationship that developed in Australia between settlers and Indigenous peoples from the beginning of colonization in the seventeenth century to the birth of the Australian Commonwealth at the beginning of the twentieth century. Such a survey cannot capture all the important shifts and variations in such a complex relationship. Its aim is to illuminate those features of colonialism within Australia that have given the decolonization struggle of Indigenous peoples in Australia its distinctive shape and character.

A Settler Colony from the Outset

The arrival in Port Jackson, on 26 January 1788, of eleven ships carrying over a thousand British subjects, most of them convicts, followed in the immediately ensuing years by thousands more,[4] meant that, right from the beginning, the Australian colonies were developed as colonies of settlement. This is very different from North America and New Zealand –

the other New World territories in which English-speaking settlers and their descendants ultimately became the dominant populations. In these areas, lengthy periods of coexistence preceded the time when the English-speaking settlers became the dominant population. During these periods of coexistence, though there was plenty of friction and considerable violence, Europeans were in no position to treat the country as *terra nullius*. From both an economic and a military perspective, they depended on establishing working relationships with native peoples. No such extended period of mutual recognition and interdependence preceded major British settlement in Australia. It is this difference in the pattern and timing of colonization, more than philosophical or legal theories, that accounts for the grip of the *terra nullius* outlook on the settlers' treatment of Aborigines in Australia.

English settlement in North America began much more tentatively than in Australia. In chapter 2 we saw how the first English settlements in America depended on a successful 'intercourse' with Amerindian nations. From the first small settlements in Virginia and New England in the early 1600s until the late 1700s, Britain and its colonists relied on treaties with Indian nations to secure friendly relations, military alliances, and trading partnerships, as well as to delineate the boundaries of settlement and fix the terms on which settlers and soldiers could move through Indian territory. In this context there was no room for the doctrine of *terra nullius*. These treaty relationships necessitated the recognition of Aboriginal societies as political communities, along with their collective ownership of the lands and waters on which they lived.

Once the balance of power between the Amerindians and the European settlers changed decisively, the reciprocity and mutual recognition implicit in these treaty relationships gave way to colonial domination and subjugation. The turning points were Great Britain's victory over France in the Seven Years' War and the American Revolution. The first left Britain without rivals as the dominant European power in North America, no longer in need of Indian allies, while the second released American colonists from the constraints of British Aboriginal policy as set out in the Royal Proclamation of 1763.

At the end of the Revolutionary War, land-hungry American settlers flooded westward into Indian territory, ignoring treaties and the principles of law and policy embedded in the proclamation. Though the proclamation has remained part of the Constitution of British North America and of Canada until this day, the thousands of Loyalists who moved north to Canada scarcely paid lip-service to its precepts in rapidly taking over large stretches of what is now Ontario and the Maritime provinces.

This decisive shift in North American Indigenous relations coincided with the beginning of colonization in Australia. But during this same period – the late 1700s and early 1800s – a very different situation existed in New Zealand. Though James Cook visited New Zealand three times in the 1770s, his visits did not inaugurate the beginning of European settlement. Organized colonization did not begin in New Zealand until the 1830s. For nearly seventy years after Cook's fleeting contacts with the Maori along the New Zealand coastline, the European presence consisted of isolated whaling and trading stations – predominantly English, but also French and American – and, beginning in 1814, some Christian missions.[5] These isolated bands of Europeans were never in any doubt that they were on Maori land. The culture and societal structure of the Maori, descendants of the migrating Polynesians who settled Aotearoa (their name for the lands the English call New Zealand) a few centuries before Cook's arrival, bore a closer resemblance to European ways than those of the Australian Aborigines.[6] In these circumstances, there was no inclination to treat New Zealand as a *terra nullius*.

Indeed, British rule in New Zealand was inaugurated in 1840 by a treaty with Maori leaders – the 1840 Treaty of Waitangi. Britain saw the treaty as a necessary step in international law to exclude other European powers from New Zealand.[7] Five years before the treaty, James Busby, the official British 'resident' in New Zealand, encouraged Maori chiefs to declare the independence of New Zealand. If Maori national unity had been more developed at that time, an independent New Zealand under Maori rule might have remained Britain's plan for securing political stability and protecting its economic interests in the country. But by the 1830s the Colonial Office had become interested in the kind of self-sustaining settler colony proposed by Edward Gibbon Wakefield as a means of relieving population pressures in Britain.[8] By 1837, preparation for planting a major Wakefield-type colony in New Zealand was under way in London. Two years later, William Hobson, who was to become the first British governor of New Zealand, was dispatched from London with instructions to acquire sovereignty over either 'the whole or any parts' of New Zealand that the Maori were willing to cede. Britain's plans for New Zealand had fundamentally changed. As Claudia Orange puts it: 'No longer were they considering a Maori New Zealand in which a place had to be found for British intruders, but a settler New Zealand in which a place had to be found for the Maori.'[9]

The Treaty of Waitangi was drafted when liberal approaches to colonial policy were much in vogue in London. The treaty is a short document containing just three articles and a preamble. Its second article very neatly encapsulates the policy embedded in the Royal Proclamation of 1763 – recognition of collective Indigenous land ownership and the exclusive right of the Crown to purchase land from the native people. It is worth quoting in full:

> Her Majesty the Queen of England confirms and guarantees to the Chiefs and Tribes of New Zealand and to the respective families and individuals thereof the full exclusive and undisturbed possession of their Lands and Estates Forests Fisheries and other properties which they may collectively or individually possess so long as it is their wish and desire to maintain the same in their possession: but the Chiefs of the United Tribes and the individual Chiefs yield to Her Majesty the exclusive right of Preemption over such lands as the proprietors thereof may be disposed to alienate at such prices as may be agreed upon between the respective Proprietors and persons appointed by Her Majesty to treat with them.[10]

A key difference between English and Maori versions of the treaty's first article neatly captures the difference between British and Indian understandings of the 1763 proclamation's political meaning. According to the English version, the Maori chiefs 'cede to Her Majesty the Queen of England absolutely and without reservation all the rights and powers of Sovereignty ...' But the word used to translate 'sovereignty,' *kawanatanga*, does not convey the sweeping authority of the English word, and there remains to this day a fundamental difference of perspective between Pakeha and Maori on this point.[11] In the treaty's third article, the Queen 'extends to the Natives of New Zealand her royal protection and imparts to them all the Rights and Privileges of British Subjects.'

The Treaty of Waitangi paved the way for a massive influx of settlers. Within twenty years of its signing, the European population surpassed that of the Maori. The Crown used its power of 'pre-emptive purchase' under the treaty to extinguish native title. By 1860, two-thirds of the country had passed out of Maori hands, including virtually all the South Island.[12] The Treaty of Waitangi, far from being recognized by the white majority and its courts as a foundation for Maori rights for the next hundred years, was treated as a 'legal nullity.'[13]

In New Zealand, as in North America, once the settlers had the upper hand militarily and demographically, treaty-like relations with Indigenous peoples gave way to colonial domination. Nonetheless, the lengthy early periods of contact and conflict, in which there was considerable reciprocity and mutual recognition in Indigenous-settler relations, has left its mark on the laws and, more important, the historical conscious-ness of these societies. In Canada, New Zealand, and the United States, moving away from imperial relations of domination to a more consensual relationship with Indigenous peoples is, to be sure, still very problematic for the settler majorities. But moving in this direction is less of a jolt to the historical conscience, less of a break with the past, than in Australia, where oppression, dispossession, and non-recognition dominated the first years of contact.

Colonization of the Native Peoples

Following the arrival of the first boatloads of settlers, Great Britain wasted little time in laying claim to the entire Australian continent and the offshore island of Van Diemen's Land. The British declared the boundaries of the original colony of New South Wales, out of which Queensland, Victoria, Tasmania, the eastern parts of South Australia, and the Northern Territory were carved, as extending all the way from Cape York (the northern tip of Queensland) to its southern extremity, South Cape (of what is now Tasmania). All the islands adjacent in the Pacific Ocean within these latitudes were included. Originally, New South Wales was deemed to extend westward to the 129th parallel of longitude, which cuts right through Arnhem Land just to the west of the Yolngu people's land on Cape Gove. An 1825 proclamation extended this boundary farther west to the 135th parallel, the boundary of what is now Western Australia. Four years later, on the founding of the Swan River settlement at present-day Perth, Captain Fremantle was instructed to take possession of 'the whole of the West Coast of New Holland' in the King's name.[14]

All these decisions were made unilaterally by representatives of the British Crown, with neither the knowledge nor the consent of the native population. To ensure that other European powers respected these claims of British sovereignty, it was essential that settlement followed. And it did, quite quickly, at least at the outer edges of the continent and in Van Diemen's Land. Though by 1800 the European population of New South Wales had not quite reached 5000,[15] it spurted ahead through the first half of the nineteenth century with a steadily swelling stream of free migrants. The European population doubled in the 1820s and nearly trebled in the 1830s.[16] By mid-century it was over 400,000, and by 1861 it was over a million. By this time the Aboriginal population, estimated to have been 314,000 and 99.7 per cent of Australia's population in 1788, had declined to 180,400 – just 15.7 per cent of the overall population.[17]

Right from the beginning the relationship between the British settlers and native Australians was a tragic one, steeped in mutual misunderstanding. The British did not come to Australia with the intention of conquering or suppressing its native people. On the contrary, the government's instructions to Arthur Phillip, commodore of the First Fleet and first governor of New South Wales, like those of Captain Cook, directed him to 'open an intercourse with the natives, and to conciliate their affections, enjoining all subjects to live in amity and kindness with them ... and to report in what manner intercourse with them might be turned to the advantage of the colony.'[18] So they did come to stay, convinced that their permanent presence could be only of benefit to the Aborigines. As Manning Clark so poignantly puts it, 'The white man came bearing his civilization as his offering, expecting the aborigine to perceive the great benefits he would receive at its hands.'[19]

When British settlement in Australia began, the period of the Enlightenment was reaching its apex among European peoples. The Europeans' sense of certitude about the universal validity of their civilization would never be stronger. In their initial offer of 'amity and kindness,' they were 'enfolding the Aborigines within an embrace, from which in principle, there could be no escape.'[20] Their intention was to make it possible for these people, perceived as 'uncivilized' and 'savage,' to become civilized by adopting the culture of the Europeans. The commitment that Edward Said refers to as the moral imperative of European imperialism – 'the almost metaphysical obligation to rule subordinate, inferior, less-advanced peoples' – was alive and well in Sydney Cove in 1788.

It is this very commitment, this overpowering sense of the fundamental goodness and universal validity of their own culture and the need for all of human kind to embrace it, that blinded these early British colonists to the genius of the Aborigines' culture. It was not that they were lacking in curiosity or scientific interest in the native people they encountered. They were consumed with curiosity and had many able chroniclers in their ranks. What fascinated and amazed these early witnesses of the native Australians were their differences from the Europeans.[21] They could not comprehend or respect that these people, so different from themselves, had an ancient and valuable civilization of their own with its own law, its own political economy, and its own permeating sense of spirituality. This blindness has endured and remains to this day the most fundamental barrier to developing a decolonized relationship with Indigenous peoples in Australia.

On the Aboriginal side there was also, at first, a fundamental incomprehension of what the arrival of European settlers portended for them. In these early encounters there could have been no understanding that these strange beings were 'settlers' who intended to stay permanently, and that their political authorities claimed sovereignty over all their land. Nor was there any understanding that these human-like forms came laden with diseases that would prove to be much more dangerous than their frightening firearms. Indeed, the Aborigines initially thought that these strange creatures with the colour of ghosts were spirits of their own people returning. 'All over the continent in areas of early settlement,' writes Henry Reynolds, 'the Aborigines applied to Europeans traditional terms meaning variously, ghost, spirit, eternal, departed, the dead.'[22] The arrival of these peculiar beings on their shores must have seemed like an encounter with visitors from another planet.

The experience of the Eora who lived around the harbour and along the beaches of Sydney Cove where the British first decided to settle was a harbinger of the tragedy that would begin to unfold. Within a few weeks, black corpses became 'a common sight' as the cholera and influenza germs from the newcomers' ships began to take effect.[23] While some of the Eora frequented the arrivals' encampment, partaking of their foods and medicines, others stayed back and resisted encroachments on their lands. The first serious outbreak of violence occurred in December 1790, when Governor Phillip's gamekeeper was speared by an Aborigine man from Botany Bay. Phillip retaliated by ordering the first official punitive expedition against the native people, instructing 'that ten adult males be killed and their heads hacked off and returned to Sydney.'[24] Though the expedition failed, its rationale embodies the fundamental political conflict in settler-native relations. As one of Phillip's officers, David Collins, explained, conflict was inevitable so long as the Aborigines 'entertained the idea of our having dispossessed them of their residences, they must always consider us as enemies.'[25] Most Aborigines did indeed entertain precisely that idea, and for decades to come it would inspire their resistance to the Europeans.

Resistance did not become intense and continuous until the line of settlement advanced beyond the immediate environs of Sydney Cove – first northward in 1794 up the coast to the banks of the Hawkesbury

River, then in the early 1800s to Van Dieman's Land, and, after the European crossing of the Blue Mountains in 1813, on into the vast Australian 'outback.' The economic base of the white man's advance into the interior of Australia was not agriculture, the cultivation of the soil, but the grazing of domesticated animals. Sheep and cattle were 'the shock troups of empire.'[26] Though the pastoral industry was destructive of the Aborigines' traditional economy and they often resisted its encroachment with force, they themselves came to be major participants in it.

The Australian Aborigines, over tens of thousands of years, in isolation from any other civilization, had built a complex civilization of their own. Their economic pursuits were those of hunters, fishers, and gatherers. They moved about in small bands over their ancestral territory, carrying their few material possessions on their backs, not aimlessly 'but to a purpose, and in tune with the seasonal food supply.'[27] Occasionally they congregated in larger tribal gatherings of a few hundred for ceremonial, social, or trade purposes.[28]

The material simplicity of the Aboriginal lifestyle blinded the Europeans to its ecological, spiritual, and social complexity. They did not appreciate that the grasslands that awaited their sheep and cattle in the arid interior had been cultivated by fires set by Aboriginal clans 'in the hope of producing lush grass for the game when the next showers fell.'[29] Nor could the Europeans understand the relationship the Aborigine bands and clans had with their lands and waters. It was a relationship 'rooted in the sacred and in revered family histories of attachment to particular places.'[30] The Aboriginal relationship to country or territory was 'expressed not through absolute control of a distinct area, but rather through responsibility for sections of Dreaming tracks representing the travels of the ancestral beings.'[31] It is a relationship that then, and now, cannot easily – perhaps not at all – be fitted into the categories of Western land ownership, including, as we shall see, the common law concept of aboriginal title.

Aboriginal Australians could not but see the arrival of the Europeans as an invasion of their country. It was not, as Reynolds observes, the original trespass of the Europeans that the Aborigines resisted but 'the ruthless assertion by Europeans of exclusive proprietorial rights often from the very first day of occupation.'[32] This political challenge combined with a devastating economic challenge, as the settlers' herds drove out the indigenous animals and took over the watering places so central to Aboriginal society. The Aborigines fought back fiercely all along the advancing frontier – occasionally in large pitched battles, more often through small, stealthy revenge expeditions. An early pioneer in the outback wrote that 'every acre of land in these districts was won from the Aborigines by bloodshed and warfare.'[33] Historians estimate that, over more than a century, as many as 20,000 Aboriginals may have been killed in defending their country.[34]

The settlers' early relations with the Aboriginals were not driven or controlled by law. Later on – much later on – British and Australian courts would render decisions justifying the colonization and dispossession of the native people. And when they did so, their justifications would draw on the common law's version of *terra nullius* and treat Australia as a pure colony of settlement established on land that was 'practically unoccupied' – in Blackstone's terms, land found to be 'desert and uncultivated.' But these judicial pronouncements would come as *ex post facto* rationalizations after settler domination was clearly established. The denial of Aboriginal peoples' common law land rights in Australia, as David Ritter has shown, originated not in a discourse of law but through a 'discourse of power.'[35]

In fact, there were moments in the early period of colonization when there was some inclination for settlers and natives to regulate their relations through treaty-like agreements. In 1804 Governor King tried to overcome Aboriginal resistance to new settlements along the Hawkesbury by assuring the Aborigines that lands would be reserved for them on the lower part of the river. Though this undertaking did not ripen into a permanent agreement, it clearly demonstrates that the highest colonial authority in New South Wales at that time recognized 'the Aborigines as parties who were actually in possession' of their land.[36] However, three decades later when John Batman from Van Dieman's Land crossed the Bass Strait and, on behalf of a Hobart syndicate, negotiated an agreement with the Kulin people to access the grasslands on the site of present-day Melbourne, Richard Bourke, the governor of New South Wales, declared the agreement null and void. This decision was backed up by the colonial secretary in London, who informed Batman that his 'treaty' would 'subvert the foundation on which all proprietory rights in New South Wales rest.'[37]

Until Eddie Mabo's case, the standard interpretation of the British government's refusal to recognize Batman's 'treaty' was that it 'virtually concluded, once and for all, any lingering doubts which may have existed on the status of the Australian colonies. The attitude of the British authorities confirmed that Australia was not to be treated as a conquest either through cession or forceful acquisition.'[38] But more recent research by Henry Reynolds, the historian at James Cook University who was stimulated by Mabo's determination to re-examine the standard interpretation, shows that there is another side to the story.

Reynolds focuses on Aboriginal policy in the imperial capital. By the 1830s, political opinion in London on the rights of native peoples was being influenced by the same currents of liberalism that successfully challenged the slave trade. This trend became evident in Australian affairs when the Colonial Office and the British Parliament became engaged in defining the conditions under which a private land company could establish a settlement in what is now South Australia. Though the act establishing the colony (an act that was drawn up by the company promoting the venture) declared the large area of southern Australia to be 'waste and unoccupied lands,' this view was immediately challenged by a Select Committee of Parliament established to review the treatment of native peoples throughout the empire. The committee took the view that because the act ignored the rights of native people, it was out of step with British policy. The Colonial Office, it appears, shared this view and attached to the Letters Patent authorizing the departure of settlers for South Australia a clause recognizing 'the rights of any Aboriginal natives of said Province to the actual occupation or employment in their persons or in the persons of their descendants of any lands now occupied or enjoyed by such Natives.'[39] The Letters Patent called for appointment of a 'protector' to ensure fair treatment of Aboriginal natives. The land commissioners of the new colony agreed that land found by the protector to be occupied by Aborigines would not be declared open for sale, 'unless the natives shall surrender their right of occupation or enjoyment by voluntary sale.'[40]

Though eventually reserves of land were set aside for Aboriginal people in South Australia (and in other parts of Australia), the policy of purchasing land occupied by Aborigines was never put into effect. It was subverted by the first local commissioner of lands in Adelaide, who was responsive to settler sentiment and brushed aside the feeble efforts of protectors to secure Aboriginal interests. Reynolds doubts that the commissioners ever had any intention of respecting Aboriginal land rights. The ability of British settlers in their dealings with native peoples to resist relatively liberal policies emanating from the distant imperial capital derived not from the imperatives of common law but from the freedom and power they had to secure their own material interests in their own way.[41]

The fictitious nature of the *terra nullius* doctrine was most blatantly and tragically evident in Van Dieman's Land (which the colonists renamed Tasmania in 1855). Following the introduction of sheep-farming and an influx of thousands of settlers in the 1820s, conflict with Aborigines intensified. The colony's governor, George Arthur, aimed to follow the policy being applied to British colonies in Canada and South Africa and concentrate the native population on a reserve in the northeast corner of the island. When violence continued in the settled areas, Arthur declared martial law against Aborigines, authorizing the capture and imprisonment of any found in the settled districts. In effect, 'Aborigines were to be considered enemy aliens in their own country.'[42] In October 1830, Arthur attempted to drive the Aborigines into a remote corner of the island by organizing a moving 'Black Line' along a 120-mile front composed of 2200 soldiers, convicts, and civilians. This manoeuvre was a total failure. In the words of the government's Aborigines Committee, the Aborigines' 'cunning, celerity of Movement and knowledge of the Country defied the United Civil and Military Power of the Colony.'[43]

Military measures having failed, Arthur resorted to diplomacy. He recruited George Augustus Robinson, described by Reynolds as a 'building contractor and religious enthusiast,'[44] to conduct a 'friendly mission' to the Aborigines. From 1830 to 1834, Robinson, assisted by Aboriginal guides and emissaries, journeyed along the coastline and into the interior meeting with representatives of most of the Aboriginal families who had survived the years of warfare. By this time the native Tasmanian population had been reduced from a few thousand to two or three hundred. Robinson proposed that these survivors now leave their homeland – at least temporarily – and live in a mission settlement on an island where they would be safe from settler violence. The Aborigines agreed to this plan 'only on the firm condition that their needs would be fully met, including their requirement to make regular journeys to the mainland.'[45] By 1834 'all but one small family group' had been moved to Wybalenna settlement on Flinders Island in Bass Strait.[46]

The agreement with the Tasmanian Aborigines was undoubtedly a treaty-like arrangement. George Arthur came away from his Tasmanian experience a firm believer in treaties as the just and prudent way of regulating relations with Aboriginal peoples in British colonies, including Australia. Reynolds thinks that Arthur's advocacy of treaties may well have been a factor in the Colonial Office's decision to negotiate a treaty with the Maori as a basis for settlement in New Zealand.[47]

Sadly, the colonial government failed to honour Robinson's promise that the Aborigines would be able to maintain association with their traditional lands by making return visits. In 1847 they were transferred to a disused penal station near Hobart. By this time, disease and depression had reduced their numbers from over two hundred to forty-four. In 1876, when Truganini, the Aboriginal woman who played a lead role in Robinson's 'friendly mission,' died, the legend arose that she was the last Tasmanian Aborigine. But in truth the Tasmanian Aborigines were not extinguished. Some married whalers and sealers and settled in the Cape Barren Islands, while a significant number of Pallawah lived on in various locations on the Tasmanian mainland.[48] Today, following the *Mabo* decision, the descendants of these Indigenous Tasmanians, numbering some 8000, are able to reclaim their association with lands they never surrendered.

The Uncertainty of Settler Law

The Tasmania story demonstrates that force, not law, determined the fate of Indigenous Australians. In Australia, as in the other English-settler countries, the settlers' courts came along later to provide legal rationalizations for the reality of colonization and dispossession. As we noted in chapter 3, the legal hurdle that Eddie Mabo had to clear to gain recognition for his people's land rights was set in 1889, when the highest court in the British Empire, the Judicial Committee of the Privy Council, declared that when Britain 'peacefully annexed' New South Wales to its dominions, it 'consisted of a tract of territory practically unoccupied, without settled inhabitants or settled law.'[49] Though this legal fiction was stated with conviction and authority by the imperial Law Lords, for much of the preceding century the Australian colonists displayed uncertainty and ambivalence about the legal existence and status of the native peoples.

For a long time there was uncertainty even on the fundamental question of whether the Aborigines were British subjects. If the Australian colonies were pure colonies of settlement, then all their inhabitants, including those who were native born, should have been treated as the King's subjects enjoying the protection of the King's laws. But this was far from the case. In the early days of settlement (Alex Castles suggests the first fifty years),[50] settlers who hunted down and shot Aborigines were rarely subjected to the colonial justice system. On the few occasions when whites were brought before colonial courts for murdering Aborigines, there was considerable debate among members of the court over whether Aborigines were entitled to the full protection of the law.[51] In 1838 at Myall Creek in northern New South Wales, after an Aborigine killed a shepherd, twelve stockmen attacked a camp of Aborigines, brutally killing at least twenty-eight of them – mostly old men, women, and children. By this time the Colonial Office, reflecting the liberal sentiment now stirring in London, was urging that the Aborigines be treated as British subjects. The New South Wales governor, Sir George Gipps, responding to this pressure, had eleven men (those with convict backgrounds) put on trial for murder. Local landowners and stockmen were enraged. At the first trial, all eleven accused were acquitted. Subsequently, seven of the men were put on trial for murdering an Aboriginal child. They were convicted and hanged. Historian Manning Clark comments that the executions 'only served to make the blacks so outrageous that great numbers of them fell victim in 1839 to the vindictive spirit kindled in the hearts of white men.'[52]

On those very few occasions when conflicts within Aboriginal communities were brought before settler courts, considerable doubt was expressed about the applicability of British law. In 1835, when two Aborigines, Jack Congo Murrell and George Bummary, in retaliation of an earlier murder of a kinsman, murdered two countrymen on the Parramatta Road near Sydney, they were charged with murder. Their lawyer, Sydney Stephen, submitted that as 'the Aborigines had manners and customs of their own and as the country had been neither conquered nor ceded,' they were not subject to the settlers' laws.[53] Justice Burton, writing for a full bench of the New South Wales Supreme Court, rejected Stephen's argument. He did so not on the basis of New South Wales being a pure colony of settlement but largely in policy terms, emphasizing the 'inconvenience and scandal to this Community' if his court had no jurisdiction to deal with crimes of this kind. The murder had taken place 'very near the centre of White settlement.'[54] In the course of his opinion, Justice Burton had this to say about the rights and status of the Aborigines:

Although it be granted that the Aboriginal natives of New Holland are entitled to be regarded by Civilised nations as a free and independent people, and are entitled to the possession of those rights which as such are valuable to them, yet the various tribes had not attained at the first settlement of the English people amongst them to such a position in point of numbers and civilisation and to such a form of Government and laws, as to be entitled to be recognized as so many sovereign states governed by laws of their own.[55]

In this decision of the New South Wales Supreme Court, we can see a glimmer of recognition that the Aborigines are entitled to be recognized 'as a free and independent people' and that some of their rights – those that are valuable to them – survive the imposition of British sovereignty. But we should also note that the *Murrell* case relegated Aborigines to an even more subordinate constitutional position than the contemporaneous jurisdiction of US Chief Justice John Marshall consigned American Indian nations. In the 1831 *Cherokee Nation* case, Marshall defined the Indians' status as 'domestic dependent nations,' a status he likened to 'that of a ward to his guardian' and falling short of foreign nations, which have the right to sue.[56] Though Marshall's definition stripped Indian nations of their own sovereignty, a further decision of his acknowledged that the sovereignty that Great Britain and now the United States claims over the Indian nations 'furnishes no example ... of any attempt ... to interfere with the internal affairs of the Indians.'[57] Marshall recognized that 'the Indian nations had always been considered as distinct, independent, political communities, retaining their original natural rights, as the undisputed possessors of the soil, from time immemorial.'[58]

Lawyers in colonial Australia were familiar with the Marshallian doctrine, and a number of them considered that it applied to the Aborigines. In a case decided five years after *Murrell*, one member of the New South Wales judiciary, Justice Willis, accepted such a submission and refused to proceed with the trial of Bon Jon, an Aborigine accused of murdering another Aborigine.[59] Justice Willis viewed the Aborigines as a domestic dependent nation that had retained the right to govern itself by its own customary law. That right could only be taken from it by an express statute or by treaty, neither of which existed. Willis's judgment was too much for the colonial authorities to swallow. He was sternly rebuked by Chief Justice Dowling and the governor, Sir George Gipps, and he received no support when he appealed to the Law Officers of the Crown in London. In June 1843 Willis was removed from office.

Even though Marshall's concept of 'domestic dependent nation' never caught on in Australia as legal dogma, official thinking fifty years after the first settlement was still some way from the stark terms of the English Law Lords' 'practically unoccupied' *terra nullius*. The managers and emissaries of British sovereignty in Australia did not conceive of British sovereignty as obliterating all the rights or autonomy of its native peoples.

Reynolds's research unearthed an internal memo written in 1835 by James Stephen, the senior official in the Colonial Office, expressing concern about trying to set the boundaries of the new colony of South Australia in what Stephens refers to as a '*terra incognito*' (unknown land) and with 'due regard to the present Proprietors of the Soil or rulers of the country.'[60]

Colonial officials on the ground in Australia shared Stephen's recognition that much of the continent over which Britain declared its sovereignty was in fact a '*terra incognito*' inhabited by self-governing native peoples. In 1836 Colonel F.C. Irwin, the military commandant at Swan River in Western Australia, urged that dealings with Aborigines in the vast hinterland beyond the infant colony should be governed 'by treaties negotiated between the two parties.'[61] While the second governor of South Australia, George Gawler, did not go as far as the colony's Justice Cooper, who believed that British law could not apply to 'a people towards a political union with whom no approach has been made,'[62] he dismissed the idea of treating 'distant tribes inhabiting a territory beyond the limits of our territory' as British subjects. These tribes, 'however savage and barbarous their manners,' must be treated 'as a *separate state or nation*, not acknowledging but acting independently of, and in opposition to, British interests and authority.'[63]

In New South Wales that same governor, George Gipps, who had dismissed Justice Willis implicitly acknowledged some kind of Aboriginal proprietorship of land when he chastised a local landowner for attempting to buy a large tract of land from the Maori in New Zealand. In Gipps's view, such a private purchase of native land violated the principle of the Crown's exclusive right of pre-emption over native land, a principle of English law which Gipps maintained applied in Australia and New Zealand as much as in America. In one sense the principle of exclusive Crown pre-emption was a limit on the sovereignty of native peoples, for it meant they could alienate or sell their land only to the Crown and not to private purchasers. But it also meant that native people were recognized as owners. As Hookey observes, 'it was irrelevant to talk of a right of pre-emption if Aborigines and Maoris had no title recognized by law.'[64]

Conditions of Rural Coexistence

Throughout much of the interior of the Australian continent, and in the north along the beaches and on the off-shore islands, Indigenous Australians, despite the imposition of British sovereignty and considerable violence, generally remained on or connected to their traditional country and subject to their own laws and traditions. In North America, in contrast, as European settlement advanced across the continent, Aboriginal peoples – by treaties in Canada and through warfare in the United States – were pushed off most of the land to small reserves in areas that were of least economic interest to the Europeans. That Australia did not experience this same clearing of the continent by the Europeans had more to do with economics than law.

The main economic motive that lured British settlers (initially, emancipated convicts) into the interior of Australia was cheap pasturage for the grazing of sheep and cattle. This 'settler capitalism' was initiated by squatters occupying land without authorization from British authorities or native custodians.[65] Moreover, it was a use of land that did not fit easily with the moral and economic rationale by which the governing class and intelligentsia justified Europeans taking possession of land in places like Australia. That rationale, as John Locke and other natural law theorists advanced it and as we saw in chapter 2, held that man acquires a right to land only when, by his labour, he cultivates and improves it.[66] In point of fact, the intensive grazing of the arid Australian interior by exogenous mammals was destructive of the land, and much of the labour in the pastoral industry was provided by the Aborigines, the traditional owners of the land.

After a period of terror and violence, squatter pastoralists began to appreciate that native people had knowledge and skills that could be of great benefit to their industry. Instead of trying to exclude them from the grazing lands, it made much more sense to engage their knowledge and cheap supply of labour in the service of the pastoral enterprize. Family-related members of Aboriginal clans formed camps on cattle stations – the men working as shepherds, stockmen, horse-breakers, property managers, and guides; the women providing child care and domestic help where there were white families, but more often servicing the sexual needs of that 'nomadic tribe of single (white) men' who dominated the pastoral industry.[67] The departure of many white pastoral workers for the newly discovered gold-fields of New South Wales and Victoria created an acute labour shortage in the 1850s. The services of Aborigines for a while became 'indispensable' to the settlers.[68] Though pastoralism's dependence on native labour soon declined in the southeast, by the end of the century Aboriginal workers from resident camps still accounted for 30 per cent of pastoral labour in northwest New South

Wales.[69] Throughout the nineteenth century and well on into the twentieth, as the pastoral industry extended into northern and central Australia, Aborigines played a crucial role as diplomats, guides, stockmen, and managers of the land.[70]

The ecology of pastoralism in Australia provided the conditions for a distinctive pattern of 'dual occupation'[71] of the range-lands. In the dry Australian 'outback,' with its thin layer of topsoil, a very large tract of land is required to support the number of animals needed for a profitable settler enterprise. As Justice Kirby observed in the *Wik* case, 'pastoral leases covered huge areas as extensive as many a county in England and bigger than some nations.'[72] The Wik and Thayorre peoples, who would eventually use Eddie Mabo's victory to defend their own land rights, inhabited country in northern Queensland on which pastoral leases had been issued over areas covering 1119 and 535 square miles, respectively.[73] Though the intrusion of pastoralism was often destructive of the Aborigines' traditional foods and gathering places, many of them continued to inhabit and access range-lands for their own spiritual, recreational, and economic purposes. Those who lived in station camps and worked in the pastoral industry could make the accommodation with the settlers' culture necessary to maintain their position without abandoning their own customs and laws.

The collaboration of white settlers and native Australians in the pastoral industry resembles the early partnership of Europeans and Amerindians in the fur trade. In both cases the Indigenous peoples were valued by the Europeans for their knowledge of their native country and their ability to live in it. And in both cases, while Indigenous participation in European economic activity meant adopting some European skills and behaviours and led to a growing dependence on the Europeans' material products, food staples, and intoxicants, it left the Indigenous people on or in close touch with their homelands and under the primary sway of their traditional culture.[74] There is one major difference between the two continents, however: whereas the fur trade – except for the Canadian North and Alaska – had pretty well died out early in the nineteenth century, Aboriginal participation in the pastoral industry continued to be a major feature of Australian rural life. Right into the 1960s, Aborigines were by far the majority of labourers in the cattle industry of northern Australia and, as Ann McGrath notes, 'they still comprise a large proportion of people living in rural or pastoral Australia.'[75]

The legal regime colonial authorities designed for pastoralism provided for dual occupancy of Australia's grazing lands. Settler squatters were anxious to secure title over their station properties, but the Crown's advisers thought it unwise and inhumane to allow a single landowner exclusive title over such vast stretches of land on which large numbers of Aborigines continued to live. In 1846 George Augustus Robinson, then serving as Chief Protector of Aborigines in the Port Philip district, observed that if nothing was done to secure the 'claims of Aborigines to a reasonable share of their fatherland,' against the claims of the pastoralists, Aboriginal people would soon have 'no place for the soles of their feet.'[76] Responding to this concern, Earl Grey, the colonial secretary in London, insisted that the leases issued to pastoralists under the *Imperial Waste Land Act* of 1842 and 1846 gave 'the grantees only an exclusive right to pasturage for their cattle and of cultivating such land as they may require within the larger limits of this assigned to them, but that these leases are not intended to deprive the natives of their former right to hunt over these districts or to wander over them in search of subsistence in the manner to which they have been hithertofore accustomed, from the spontaneous production of the soil, except over land actually cultivated or fenced in for that purpose.'[77] Unfortunately, Grey left the implementation of this policy to the newly appointed governor of New South Wales, C.A. Fitzroy. Though local land commissioners proposed that Aborigines be guaranteed access, Governor Fitzroy, who, as Heather Goodall puts it, 'was not known for his deep interest in Aboriginal matters,'[78] succumbed to the pressure of the dominant pastoralists in the colony's Legislative Council and did not have aboriginal rights written in as a condition of pastoral leases.

However, colonial officials in other parts of Australia showed more backbone in standing up to pastoralist pressure. In South Australia, for example, the lieutenant governor, Sir Henry Young, had clauses written into the long-term leases being issued to pastoralists which reserved to the Aboriginal inhabitants and their descendants during the continuance of the lease 'full and free right of ingress, egress, and regress into, upon, and over' the lands demised, and provided further that 'the said Aboriginal inhabitants and their descendants shall and may at all times during this demise use occupy, dwell on, and obtain food and water thereon and every part thereof unobstructed by the said [lessee].'[79] Reynolds's research shows that in Queensland and Western Australia, as well as in the part of South Australia which in 1911 became the Northern Territory, pastoral leases contained similar clauses providing for Aboriginal rights to use and occupy the land.[80]

Failure to explicitly recognize Aboriginal rights of use and occupancy in the terms of leases, as was usually the case in New South Wales, did not mean that such rights ceased to exist. The Aboriginal peoples themselves never conceded their connection to these lands, and the British authorities showed no intention of extinguishing the rights of Aboriginal people to use and inhabit these lands. When one bears in mind how much of Australia – an estimated 52.6 per cent of its total area[81] – eventually came under leasehold tenure, the extent of continuing Aboriginal rights on pastoral lands can be appreciated. But in the circumstances of settler colonialism, possessing rights in your own law and having that right recognized by authorities in the distant capital of empire provided no protection to Aborigines on pastoral lands. Even where the Aboriginal people's rights were inscribed in pastoral leases, they 'were almost universally ignored.' Reynolds records the sad fact that 'thousands of Aborigines were shot in northern Australia because they tried to stay on their land and pursue their normal manner of living.'[82]

More than a century would go by before Aboriginal peoples turned to the white man's courts to vindicate their rights. And when at first they did, as we have seen in Justice Blackburn's 1970 decision in *Milirrpum*, they found the ideology of *terra nullius* entrenched in the judicial mind. It was not until Eddie Mabo had instigated his judicial revolution that Aboriginals on pastoral lands finally had some success in the settlers' courts, but then they faced an even tougher struggle to defend their rights in the political arena of contemporary Australian democracy.

At the very time that imperial policy was making room for one kind of Aboriginal reservation – a reserved right of natives to continue their traditional use and habitation of pastoral lands – it was endorsing the establishment of a very different kind of reservation. That was the reserving of small parcels of land on which Aborigines could be confined, protected, supervised, and assimilated into the settlers' culture. Earl Grey, the same colonial secretary who wanted to reserve Aborigines' rights 'to wander over' lands leased to grazers, also proposed that small tracts of land be set aside for Aborigines 'to be cultivated either by them, or for their advantage.'[83] Grey, like so many of the liberal humanitarian reformers, had no appreciation of the spiritual and economic values that underlay what, to European eyes, was the aimless 'wandering' of Aborigines over the land. On small reserves there would be some prospect of 'civilizing' Aborigines. In Heather Goodall's words, reserves of this kind were seen as 'tools for forcing social and cultural change, to transform Aboriginal landowners into the mythologized agrarian ideal of yeoman farmers.'[84]

So long as Aborigines could maintain a traditional lifestyle on ancestral lands, they showed little interest in settling down on the small plots of land set aside for them. In South Australia by 1860, most of the 8000 acres of land reserved for Aborigines had been leased out to non-Aboriginal farmers.[85] In New South Wales, lines drawn by land commissioners marking off reserves around Aboriginal camps on pastoral stations had no real meaning 'as long as the greater extent of their lands still seemed to be within reach of their Aboriginal owners.'[86] However, as pastoralism made traditional use of their lands increasingly difficult, Aborigines began to seek security and sustenance on lands Europeans were willing to set aside for them. During the second half of the nineteenth century, reserves were set aside for Aborigines all over Australia.[87] Sometimes Aborigines selected their own 'reserve,' and often they settled around Christian missions. In these enclaves many took up agriculture as their main economic activity, and all were encouraged to partake of the two other core elements of the white man's 'civilization' – Christianity and a taste for the acquisition of material goods.

Natives and settlers did not share a common understanding of the legal status of the land they settled on as reserves. To the Aborigines, these small parcels of land were a part of their ancestral country for which they sought some security of collective tenure in the white man's law. This idea resonates in a letter written in 1887 by a Cumeragunja man, William Cooper, to a colonial politician, seeking a secure inalienable title for land his people wished to farm along the Murray River. Cooper referred to the land as 'this small portion of a vast territory which is ours by Divine right.'[88] Reynolds points out that it would have been logical to think of reservations or reserves as lands kept in the possession of their original owners, and that European doctrines of natural law recognized the obligation of imperial states to leave natives enough land for their sustenance.[89] But this was neither the logic nor the legal thinking of the authorities on the ground in Australia, men who were increasingly responsive to the emerging settler democracy in the colonies rather than to liberal-minded officials and politicians in London. Settler political leaders saw the setting aside of lands for Aborigines as stemming from a sense of Christian charity and prudent public policy, not from a legal or moral obligation to recognize the rights of Aboriginal peoples. By 1847 Australian settlers had the authority of New South Wales' highest court for the proposition that all the land of the colony (the so-called waste lands the first settlers discovered) were 'the patrimony of the nation,' of which the Sovereign is 'the representative and executive authority.'[90]

Settler Democracy and a New Kind of Colonialism

By the middle of the nineteenth century, Britain was handing over self-government powers to its Australian colonists. Parliamentary institutions had been introduced in New South Wales, Queensland, South Australia, Tasmania, and Victoria by the end of the 1850s, and by 1875 in Western Australia.[91] During the same period, the British were also granting control over local affairs to their colonists in Canada and New Zealand. How would this important move in the liberalization of the British Empire affect relations with native peoples in these colonies?

In imperial relationships with Aboriginal peoples, an iron law is at work that goes roughly like this: the further policy-making authority is from the native peoples, the more liberal (or less oppressive) it will be. We have already seen how in Australia, from Cook's and Phillip's instructions, on through the direction of subsequent governors and the founding of South Australia, imperial policy-makers in London appeared anxious to protect the interests of native peoples from settler encroachments. This humanitarian sentiment in the imperial capital was directed to the treatment of natives in other British colonies. It was never so evident as in 1837, when the British House of Commons, moved by the same surge of liberalism that had inspired the abolition of slavery, established a Select Committee on Aborigines. The committee was extremely critical of the treatment of native peoples in Australia and Canada (and in other British colonies). Its first recommendation was to keep Aboriginal relations under the exclusive control of the executive government in the colonies. It warned against giving local legislatures any responsibility in this area because 'the settlers in almost every colony, having either disputes to adjust with native tribes, or claims to urge against them, the representative body is virtually a party, and therefore ought not to be the judge in such controversies.'[92]

Though this liberal, humanitarian impulse lingered on in the capital of the empire through the nineteenth century, its locus was mainly philanthropic organizations such as the Aborigines' Protection Society and the London Missionary Society – what a later-day Australian liberal would snidely refer to as 'honorary prickers of conscience.'[93] By mid-century it was losing any leverage it might have had on government policy. The first call on British liberals in relation to those colonies where their own kith and kin were becoming the dominant population was settler self-government. As Niall Ferguson points out, this was the essence of Britain's imperial dilemma: 'How could an empire that claimed to be founded on liberty justify overruling the wishes of colonists when they clashed with those of a very distant legislature?'[94] The lesson of the American Revolution was clear: if English colonies were to remain associated with the mother country, they must be given self-government over their internal affairs. No imperial government would be zealous enough about protecting the interests of native people to interrupt that process. And so in Australia, Canada, and New Zealand, over a period of about twenty-five years – from the late 1830s to the early 1860s – a system in which the British Crown and its direct representatives tried to function as a buffer and mediator between weakened native societies and land-hungry colonists[95] gave way to a system of local home rule for the white people.

Though the transfer of power to the settlers had some ominous implications for native peoples, it would be a mistake to read too much into it. Even in its heyday, London's liberalism so far as Indigenous peoples were concerned was thoroughly imperial. Policy-makers, parliamentarians, and liberal thinkers in London were not imbued with any deep philosophical or natural law doctrine of Aboriginal rights. There is a telling passage in a memorandum written by Sir James Stephen, who served as the permanent undersecretary in the Colonial Office from 1836 to 1846, a period when Aboriginal policy in the head office of the empire was in its most liberal phase. In the course of a memorandum dismissing the relevance to New Zealand of American Chief Justice John Marshall's first major decision on native rights, Stephen expressed a broad scepticism about the possibility of international jurists rendering justice to native peoples: 'Whatever may be the ground occupied by international jurists, they never forget the policy and interests of their own Country. Their business is to give to rapacity and injustice the most decorous veil which legal ingenuity can weave.'[96] Stephen and his colleagues at the centre of empire never forgot that their first priority was to serve the interests of their country. At its best their liberalism was a charitable, Christian concern for treating vulnerable people decently. Pride in seeing that this policy was done, so far as possible, throughout the far-flung reaches of the empire was – and still is – a central element of English nationalism. But there was never any doubt in English liberal minds that native peoples in colonies of settlement were, in John Stuart Mill's words, 'backward populations' whose right to enjoy the fruits of liberty would depend entirely on their capacity to adopt the white man's civilization.[97]

Colonization in the United States under John Marshall's Jurisprudence

The fate of Indigenous peoples in the democracies built by English-speaking settlers in the New World was presaged by the experience of Amerindians in the United States. If ever there was a society whose founders and leaders were imbued with the spirit of English liberalism and Protestant religiosity, it is surely the American republic. The British practice of acquiring lands for settlement by means of treaties with Indian nations survived the revolutionary war. But the liberal element of this policy would soon be subsumed by the confident and acquisitive nationalism of the new American democracy.[98] We can hear both the liberal and the nationalist overtones in the Northwest Ordinance of 1787, in which the Continental Congress set out the principles that would govern its conduct in areas beyond the frontier of settlement: 'The utmost good faith shall always be observed towards the Indians; their land and property shall never be taken away from them without their consent; and in their property, rights and liberty, they shall never be invaded or disturbed, unless in just and lawful wars authorized by Congress.'[99] Native peoples had rights which were to be respected until such time as they stood in the way of the 'just and lawful' aspirations of the American people.

The American people who, according to the opening words of the Constitution of the United States, are its authors did not include the Indian nations. The Constitution's sole reference to native people is its grant to Congress of the power 'to regulate commerce' with 'the Indian tribes' as well as with foreign nations and the several states. While some of the Indian nations supported the Americans in the revolutionary war, others fought on the British side. An alliance of Iroquois and Shawnee continued to resist the new republic's encroachments on their lands. They did so with considerable success until 1794, when the British signed Jay's Treaty with the United States and withdrew support for their Aboriginal allies.[100]

The jurisprudence of the United States' most renowned chief justice, John Marshall, worked out a distinctive status for the Amerindian nations in American constitutional law. Marshall's treatment of the rights of Indian nations was creative and political. His initial treatment of Aboriginal rights in the 1810 case of *Fletcher v. Peck*[101] shows that the chief justice was just beginning to think about these issues. The case is notable as the first time the United States Supreme Court struck down a major state law for violating the Constitution. The law in question was a Georgia statute revoking a patent of land it had made to four land companies. The land in question was still occupied by Indians. Marshall found Georgia's rescinding of its land grant a violation of the constitutional clause respecting the sanctity of contracts. But he dealt very casually with the fact that the land in question was occupied by Indians, denying neither Georgia's right to dispose of Indian lands it had not purchased from the Indians nor the Indians' right to continue to occupy the land until they agreed to sell it.[102]

It was not until the 1823 case of *Johnson v. McIntosh* that Marshall gave his first considered opinion on the rights and status of Indian nations in American law. The case concerned the validity of title to land purchased by speculators directly from Indians in the Illinois territory. The chief justice recognized that the original inhabitants 'were admitted to be the rightful occupants of the soil, with a legal as well as just claim to retain possession of it, and use it according to their own discretion; but their rights to complete sovereignty, as independent nations, were necessarily diminished, and their power to dispose of the soil, at their own will, to whomsoever they pleased, was denied by the original fundamental principle, that discovery gave exclusive title to those who made it.'[103] He saw the United States as taking over from the British Crown 'the exclusive right of the discoverer to appropriate the lands occupied by the Indians.'[104] This right could be exercised only by the government of the United States. The Illinois land-speculators' title was invalid because Indians could sell land only to the United States government.

Marshall's position incorporates into republican America the British imperial concept of the Crown's pre-emptive right of acquiring lands from natives. We have seen representatives of the British Crown asserting this principle in the Australian colonies and in New Zealand. But Marshall went beyond English common law or British imperial policy in his conception of the European discoverer's rights. According to Marshall, the United States took over from Britain not only its exclusive right to acquire land from Indians but 'a clear title to all the lands' within its boundaries, 'subject only to the Indian right of occupancy.'[105] In other words, with one stroke of the pen – or one should say, with one foot on the shore – the discovering power had political sovereignty over all the discovered lands, both seen and unseen and no matter how much they might be occupied by native inhabitants, as well as ownership and title over all the lands, leaving native dwellers as mere occupants.

Marshall performed this wondrous feat of legal magic by equating discovery with conquest. 'Conquest,' he wrote, 'gives a title which the

Courts of the conqueror cannot deny, whatever the private and speculative opinions of individuals may be respecting the original justice of the claim which has been successfully asserted.'[106] Knowing how little this notion of conquest fitted the facts of American history – above all in relation to Indian tribes to the west, who had scarcely been encountered let alone conquered by the Americans or any European power – Marshall must have blushed a little at this point in his opinion. We can sense both his moral embarrassment and his political determination in the following lines:

> However extravagant the pretension of converting the discovery of an inhabited country into conquest may appear; if the principle has been asserted in the first instance, and afterwards sustained; if a country has been acquired and held under it; if the property of the great mass of the community originates in it, it becomes the law of the land, and cannot be questioned. So, too, with the concomitant principle, that the Indian inhabitants are to be considered merely as occupants, to be protected, indeed, while in peace, in the possession of their lands, but to be deemed incapable of transferring the absolute title to others.

Marshall concluded with a frankly utilitarian justification for this restriction on Indian land rights: 'However this restriction may be opposed to natural right, and to the usages of civilized nations, yet, if it be indispensable to that system under which the country has been settled, and be adapted to the actual condition of the two people, it may be supported by reason, and certainly cannot be rejected by courts of justice.'[107] We can see in the great American chief justice's treatment of Indigenous peoples' rights the truth of Sir James Stephen's observation about the primacy of national interest in this branch of imperial jurisprudence.

When Congress delayed exercising the exclusive power of settling Indian land issues that Marshall had conferred on it, some of the states took matters into their own hands. One of these was Georgia, whose assembly passed laws taking control of the lands of the Cherokee nation, imposing state law on the Cherokee, annulling all tribal law, and imprisoning tribal officials. This situation called on Marshall to make two more major decisions about the status of Indian peoples in American law.

The first of these decisions, *Cherokee Nation v. State of Georgia*,[108] was brought to the Supreme Court by the Cherokee nation itself. This was the first time in world history that an Indigenous nation had attempted to obtain justice in the white man's courts. Marshall's decision seemed bent on making it the last such attempt. He denied that the Cherokee or any other nation had the right to bring suits in American courts. The framers of the Constitution must have thought that 'the idea of appealing to an American court of justice for an assertion of right or a redress of wrong, had perhaps never entered the mind of an Indian or of his tribe. Their appeal was to the tomahawk, or to the government.'[109] Foreign nations had the right to use American courts, but though the Cherokee and other Indian tribes were nations, Marshall regarded them as domesticated nations lacking the full international status of nation-states. Again the chief justice was inventive, fashioning a new piece of constitutional doctrine on the relationship of the Indian nations to the United States – a relationship, he opined, that 'is, perhaps, unlike that of any other two people in existence.'[110] At this point, Marshall rendered his famous dictum on the Indians' status as 'domestic sovereign nations,' a status he likened to 'that of a ward to his guardian.'

The following year, in *Worcester v. Georgia*,[111] Marshall was able to give the Cherokee some protection – in law – from land-hungry Georgia. The case had been brought by a northern missionary who challenged Georgia laws punishing him for being on Cherokee lands. In this, Marshall's final contribution to the jurisprudence concerning Indigenous peoples, he gave his most generous interpretation of their rights. Through the submissions of counsel and the influence of other members of the court, he was now more conversant with British policy and law in relation to Amerindian nations during the colonial period. This history showed him that the sovereignty Great Britain, and now the United States, claimed over the Indian nations 'furnishes no example ... of any attempt ... to interfere with the internal affairs of the Indians.'[112] He continued: 'The Indians had always been considered as distinct, independent, political communities, retaining their original natural rights, as the undisputed possessors of the soil, from time immemorial, with the single exception of that imposed by irresistible power, which excluded them from intercourse with any other European potentate than the first discoverer of the coast of the particular region claimed.'[113] The chief justice now appeared to repudiate the very subordinate, wardship-like, status he had given Indian nations the previous year. He admitted that the Indian nations 'rank among those powers who are capable of making treaties.' When the English word 'treaty' was used in relations with Indians, it had the same meaning as in relations with 'other nations of the earth.' Thus the treaty that the United States had made with the

Cherokee nation 'explicitly recognizing their national character ... and their right to self-government; thus guarantying [*sic*] their lands' was now 'in full force,' and, like all other treaties entered into by the United States, was 'the supreme law of the land.'[114]

In the *Worcester* case, the American chief justice also gave a stronger interpretation of Aboriginal land rights than he had ever given before. The political sovereignty claimed by the discovering European power was now seen as strictly a right to exclude other foreign powers from dealing with the native inhabitants of the discovered lands. Marshall held that this right of discovery 'could not affect the rights of those already in possession, either as aboriginal occupants, or as occupants by virtue of discovery made before the memory of man.' As inheritor of the discoverer's right, the United States government had the exclusive 'right of acquiring the soil and making settlements on it.' While this right 'shut out' the right of other competitor nations who had agreed to it, it was 'not one which could annul the previous rights of those who had not agreed to it.'[115] Indians were not mere occupants of their lands but were owners and rulers of all their lands they had not ceded or sold to the United States or its imperial predecessors.

Marshall concluded his judgment by lowering the boom on the state of Georgia. Georgia's laws purporting to destroy the Cherokee's political community and take over their lands were null and void.

Marshall's decision did not save the Cherokee. On hearing of the decision, Andrew Jackson, the president of the United States, is reported to have said, 'John Marshall has made his decision: now let him enforce it!' Whether or not Jackson uttered these words, it is clear that 'he never intended to enforce the decision of the court against an unwilling Georgia.'[116] President Jackson was committed to a policy of opening up land for American settlers by removing Indians to west of the Mississippi. This policy was backed not only by Georgia and other frontier states but also by a majority in Congress, which in 1830 passed the *Indian Removal Act*.[117] In 1835, just three years after the *Worcester* decision, a breakaway faction of Cherokee signed away the last 20,000 square miles of Cherokee lands in return for $5 million and the promise of land in 'Indian Territory.'[118] In the forced removal that followed, 4000 Cherokee (a quarter of the nation), in the modern world's first experience of 'ethnic cleansing,'[119] died along the tragic 'trail of tears' to Oklahoma.

At this point in our story it is worth reflecting on the long-term significance of Chief Justice's Marshall's decisions on the rights of native peoples. These decisions were the work of the leading jurist of the liberal democracy that has led the world in enabling its citizens, and all within its borders, to challenge state authority in the courts. At the time Marshall was rendering these decisions, and for a long time afterwards, it was extremely difficult both in Britain and in those of its colonies that remained under its aegis, for anyone, native or non-native, to bring suit against the Crown in the courts.[120] So Marshall's treatment of native peoples' rights was as good as it could get for native people who might try to secure their rights and interests in the courts of the colonizing power. We have seen lawyers in colonial Australia, as well as at the headquarters of the British Empire, referring to Marshall's decisions as setting a benchmark in this area of law. Not only was Marshall's jurisprudence as good as it could get for his own time, but, for nearly a century and a half, it set a higher standard of justice than was obtainable through the colonizers' courts anywhere else on earth.

The most positive feature of Marshall's decisions for Indian nations in the United States is the protection he wanted them to have from state governments. Given the tendency of colonial authority to be less liberal to Indigenous people the closer its locus of power is to them, this concentration of power over Aboriginal affairs in the central government of the American federation, if backed up politically as well as juridically, could be a considerable benefit. However, Marshall left the Indian nations with no *constitutional* protection against the United States government's sovereign authority. As Barsh and Henderson put it, Marshall's conception of 'tribal sovereignty' recognized that 'tribes are so far foreign as to be immune from the internal sovereignty of the states, but so far domestic as to be limited by the internal sovereignty of the United States.'[121] On property rights, though he finally recognized Indians as not mere occupants but owners of their lands, he offered no protection against the taking of their lands by the federal government. The leading text on common law Aboriginal title states: 'It may just be that this federal power to take Indian lands by any means, including conquest, is the price the American tribes have paid for their semi-autonomous status.'[122] Indeed, it is this negative implication of Marshall's decisions that will be given most emphasis by Australia's High Court – in both the main majority and the dissenting opinions – when it rules on the rights of Eddie Mabo's people.[123]

What is striking about Marshall's judicial decisions is not that they were so political but that they were so *transparently* political. Indeed, the great merit of Marshall's jurisprudence is that he had the intellectual honesty and courage to articulate and defend the first premises of his judgments – which in the field of Aboriginal rights, as in so many other areas of adjudication, are bound to involve beliefs about political justice and prudence. We will find a similar honesty and courage in the opinions the justices of the Australian High Court render in the *Mabo* case, but we will also see how badly this quality is received by a legal and political community that continues to believe that judicial decisions, even on great issues of constitutional justice, should float down from an apolitical legal heaven. The very transparency of Marshall's thinking shows, however, the fundamental injustice of subjecting the fate of Aboriginal peoples to the reasoning of non-Aboriginal judges, even if they are as enlightened and liberal as John Marshall. Though he came to recognize the rights of Indian nations to govern themselves on their lands, there was no doubt in his mind that if these rights conflicted with the will of the American people, as expressed through their national government, that will must prevail.

Even so, Marshall was willing to test that will and render a decision in the *Worcester* case that he hoped would persuade the national government to protect the rights of the Cherokee nation. But, as we know, his decision failed to do so. This is the other lesson to be taken from the Marshall court's decisions on Aboriginal rights: decisions of high courts upholding Aboriginal rights in settler democracies will be ineffective if they go against the tide of opinion and outlook in the dominant society.[124] At this formative stage in American history, the tide of opinion was running in the direction of excluding the Indian nations from the new democracy the Americans were building. This policy of exclusion applied not only to the Cherokee but to the other Indian nations in the south and to those further north who occupied land wanted by the settlers. All were to be moved to 'Indian country' west of the Mississippi, where they could govern themselves on lands not yet needed by the American people.

Exclusion of the Cherokee was particularly ironic. In the 1790s the Cherokee leaders adopted a new strategy for coexistence with the Americans. In order to remain in their homeland, they would adopt many of the white man's ways and become 'civilized.'[125] While this strategy encountered some internal resistance, it was largely carried out. The Cherokee adopted a written constitution modelled on that of the United States, turned to small homestead farming, produced a written form of their language, and established their own school system. In 1821 they founded the first native American newspaper, with parallel columns in Cherokee and English.[126] But it was all of no avail. There was no room for the Cherokee in the American nation, however assimilated they might become. Martin Van Buren expressed the governing ethos when he wrote in 1837: 'No State can achieve proper culture, civilization and progress ... as long as Indians are permitted to remain.'[127]

Settler Colonialism in New Zealand and Canada

In the other English-settler societies of the New World, the transfer of control over Aboriginal affairs to settler democracies came more than a half-century later than in the United States and was a more gradual process. But though variations in circumstances and cultures produced different policies,[128] there was a similar blindness to the colonial relationship these heirs of imperial Britain were building into their own societies. As the Australian, Canadian, and New Zealand colonists moved from being imperial subjects to citizens of new democratic states, they, no more than the Americans, could view themselves as becoming colonizing powers in relation to the Indigenous peoples they could now dominate. This new kind of colonialism was largely blocked out of the historical consciousness of these settler peoples as they built their own democracies.

It was in New Zealand that Indigenous relations were most intertwined with the establishment of settler self-government. In the 1850s, when the settler community in New Zealand was achieving responsible parliamentary government, Maori-settler relations were the central issue of politics on both islands of Aetearoa, analogous to French-English relations in colonial Canada. Land-hungry settlers who were flooding in and just beginning to equal the Maori in numbers felt blocked by recognition of native land rights in the Treaty of Waitangi and the unavailability of native lands that had not been purchased by the Crown.[129] The Maori tribes, or iwi,[130] in response to this threat, became increasingly united, with a growing sense of Maori national identity, which in the 1850s found institutional expression in the establishment of a Maori kingship.[131] The British governor formally retained control of Maori relations but was soon on a collision course with the settler assembly, where the dominant mood favoured speeding up land sales by ignoring the Treaty of Waitangi and collective tribal ownership, and by allowing settlers to purchase land directly from individual Maori 'owners.' The result was a policy deadlock that helped bring on full-scale war between Maori and Pakeha (or European, in the Maori language).

The Pakeha wars broke out in 1860 in areas of the North Island where the king movement was strongest. Though the largest battles were fought in the first five years, the Maori king did not submit until 1881.[132] In the end, the combination of British troops, colonial militia, and volunteers prevailed militarily. In the settlers' eyes, this military victory marked the end of any ambiguity about the sovereignty of their government over the Maori. The Maori, though defeated militarily, came out of the war with an enhanced sense of their collective identity and of the Pakeha's unwillingness to respect their sovereignty, or *mana*. Many of them continued to think of their relationship with the British as being governed primarily by the treaty their representatives had signed with representatives of the Queen. Tragically, as Claudia Orange writes, 'It was inconceivable to them that both the Queen and her parliament had washed their hands of the Waitangi covenant. But they had.'[133]

By the time the Australian and Canadian colonists were achieving self-government, not only did they have the numbers and the military strength to dominate Indigenous peoples near their centres of settlement but they were confident they could maintain that domination as they extended the frontier of settlement and economic development over the continents to which they laid claim. Native peoples were a 'problem' they would have to tackle as they took over responsibilities from Britain, but the Aborigines' and Indians' conflict with settler interests and aspirations was not the central issue in politics that Maori relations were in New Zealand. For both the Australian and the Canadian settlers, like the new Americans, the Indigenous peoples at this formative stage of national development were no more than 'problems.' They were certainly not seen as partners in the new societies they were developing, nor even as enduring, identifiable components of their national populations.

Thus, despite major differences in their early colonial relations with native peoples – the treaty relations and recognition of native land rights in British North America versus the *terra nullius* practices in Australia – by mid-century these burgeoning settler democracies were adopting much the same policies for dealing with the 'native problem.' These policies had two, seemingly contradictory, branches – assimilation and segregation. Assimilation was the long-term objective for individual natives who could overcome what the settlers regarded as the regressive features of their native background. Segregation was needed in the short term to protect native and non-native societies from each other. The final solution to the 'native problem' was the disappearance of native communities as distinct parts of society and the absorption of individual 'civilized' natives into the mainstream society. The newly self-governing Australian and Canadian societies' plans for dealing with the 'native problem' were essentially a somewhat less brutal version of the American plan: native peoples, as peoples, were slated to disappear.

In New Zealand the Maori presence was just too great for disappearance to be envisioned as a solution to the native problem. After 1840, there was some wavering between a strategy of separate Maori development and a policy of 'amalgamation.' In both the 1846 and the 1852 constitutions, imperial authorities made provision for separate native districts in which the Maori could live according to their own laws and customs.[134] Though this provision was never implemented and the policy of rapid Europeanization won out, the strength of Maori resistance in the Pakeha wars won them a place in the settlers' system of government. In 1867 the *Maori Representation Act* created four Maori seats in the New Zealand House of Representatives. This act was imposed in a thoroughly colonial matter. It followed the confiscation of millions of acres of Maori land and the introduction of a *Native Land Act* that severed Crown protection of Maori lands and, in effect, nullified the second article of the Waitangi Treaty.[135] As Augie Fleras points out, the provision of these Maori seats was 'seen as a temporary concession' and was consistent with an assimilationist philosophy.[136] Nonetheless, it meant that the Maori people had a recognized place in the most important institution of settler democracy and kept open the possibility of the emergence of a bicultural or even a binational Aotearoa New Zealand.[137] The Maori, in marked contrast to native peoples in Australia, Canada, and the United States, were invited to share citizenship with the settler population without having to surrender their national identity.

No such place was provided for native peoples in the institutions of the new Canadian federation that came into existence in 1867. The only explicit reference to Indigenous peoples in the *British North America Act*, Canada's founding Constitution, is in the section setting out the exclusive powers of the federal Parliament. The twenty-fourth in this list of exclusive federal powers is legislation relating to 'Indians, and Lands reserved for the Indians.'[138] Canada's constitution-makers saw Aboriginal peoples not as 'partners in Confederation'[139] but simply as a subject matter of the new federation's central legislature.

But Canada's Constitution did not obliterate the recognition of the Indian nations or the Crown's obligation to protect them from settler encroachments on lands they had not ceded or sold to the Crown. Quite to the contrary, a section of the Constitution provided for the continuation of all laws in force in Canada at the time of Confederation until such time as they were repealed or altered by the appropriate Canadian legislature.[140] These continuing laws included the Royal Proclamation of 1763 and the rights of Aboriginal peoples that it recognized.

Canada continued the British practice of acquiring land for settlement by making treaties with Indian peoples. In 1871, the very year in which the US Congress was terminating the treaty process, Canada embarked on an extensive treaty process which, over the next half-century, would deal with Indian lands in northern Ontario, across the western prairies, and up into the Northwest Territories. But by now treaties had been subverted into colonizing instruments. Earlier in the century, the treaty process had become primarily a vehicle for legalizing dispossession rather than forging partnerships with Indigenous nations. The printed versions of the treaties (available in English only) bore little resemblance to what was communicated in oral negotiations. Typically they included clauses in which the Aboriginal signatories were purported to have agreed to 'CEDE, RELEASE, SURRENDER AND YIELD UP to the Government of the Dominion of Canada, for her Majesty the Queen and Her successors forever, all their rights, titles and privileges whatsoever' over vast tracts of lands.'[141] In return, the Indians were granted tiny postage-stamp reserves, small annual annuities, and a few tools and trinkets. Whereas the Americans won their west through brutal warfare with the Indian nations, the Canadians won theirs primarily through duplicitous treaties.

Well before Confederation, treaties had given way to legislation as the Canadian settler state's principal means for regulating Aboriginal affairs. The objective of this legislation is clear from the title of the statute enacted by the united colony of Canada in 1857 – the *Gradual Civilization Act*. Under this legislation, an adult Indian male (Indian women were ineligible) who could read and write and pass a morals test could become 'enfranchised.' An enfranchised Indian would be allotted 50 acres of reserve land for his individual use, but would no longer be considered an Indian and his land would cease to be Indian land.[142] Enfranchisement was to work on a voluntary basis and, though only one Indian took up the option under the act, the 1857 legislation served as a blueprint for the 1876 *Indian Act*, the Canadian Parliament's major legislation governing Indian peoples.

Canada's *Indian Act* is the most comprehensive effort of any settler state to regulate native peoples' lives. It fairly bristles with the moral imperative of European imperialism to rule peoples regarded as subordinate and inferior.[143] Canada's first prime minister, Sir John A. Macdonald, spoke of Canada's benevolent duty 'to do away with the tribal system and assimilate the Indian people in all respects with the inhabitants of the Dominion, as speedily as they are fit to change.'[144] An excerpt from the 1876 report of the Department of the Interior, charged with responsibility for administering the act, captures its spirit:

> Our Indian legislation generally rests on the principle, that the aborigines are to be kept in a condition of tutelage and treated as wards or children of the State ... the true interests of the aborigines and of the State alike require that every effort should be made to aid the Red man in lifting himself out of his condition of tutelage and dependence, and that is clearly our wisdom and our duty, through education and every other means, to prepare him for a higher civilization by encouraging him to assume the privileges and responsibilities of full citizenship.[145]

The choice for Indians was to be children or white men.

The *Indian Act*, with its many amendments, empowered federal officials in Ottawa and their agents across the country to regulate virtually every aspect of Indian life, including the definition of Indianness itself. As it came into effect in all the provinces, it broke up the historical Indian nations into small 'bands,' confining them to bits of marginal land reserved under the treaties or set aside for their use by government. Amendments to the act made it increasingly subversive of Aboriginal self-government. A system of elected band councils could be imposed, and the authority of traditional leaders and governmental practices denied. The superintendent general could override decisions of elected bands and annul the election of chiefs. In its most authoritarian phase, the act prohibited sacred ceremonies such as potlatch feasts and sun dances integral to Aboriginal cultures and provided for the compulsory education of Indian children by 'arrest and conveyance to school, and detention there.'[146] This latter power, introduced in 1894, provided the legal foundation for removing Indian children to church-run residential schools – a program that proved to be very destructive of Aboriginal families and communities.[147]

Not all Canadian peoples with native heritage came under the *Indian Act* regime. This is certainly true of the Métis, a people of mixed Aboriginal and European backgrounds in the southern part of what is now Manitoba, who had developed a unique and distinctive culture in the early decades of the nineteenth century.[148] In 1869, when the British

Government transferred authority over the Hudson's Bay Company lands to Canada, the Métis, led by Louis Riel, formed a provisional government to negotiate the terms on which they would join the new Canadian federation. Though this effort and a second Métis 'rebellion' further west in 1885 were put down by Canadian troops, the Métis retained a strong sense of national identity. Their land claims having been dissolved in nearly worthless scrip certificates, the Métis formed isolated communities across the Prairie provinces on lands ceded by Indian nations through the treaty process. For over a hundred years the Metis were not recognized as an Aboriginal people.

After the High Arctic came under Canadian jurisdiction in the 1880, Canada, right up to the late twentieth century, carried on the British practice of treating the Inuit people who had lived in that region in effect as a non-people without land rights or political rights.[149] The Inuit lived too far from the frontier of settlement to be brought under the tight regulatory regime of the *Indian Act*. But the spirit of the *Indian Act* infused Canadian governments' treatment of Inuit populations in the Arctic as well as in northern Quebec and Labrador. Inuit people were treated as childlike wards of the state and, although never confined to reserves, were on occasion subjected to a tragic and deceitful relocation.[150]

There were also many Indians who fell outside the *Indian Act* regime because federal officials did not consider they had a sufficient quotient of Indian blood or because the officials had no contact with them when lists of band members or treaty beneficiaries were drawn up. These people became Canada's 'non-status' Indians and were denied any benefits available under the treaties or the *Indian Act*. A major contributor to the growth of the non-status Indian population were the Indian women considered by government officials to have married non-Indian men. From the beginning, the act provided that such women and their children would lose their Indian status and band membership. No such provision applied to Indian men who married non-Indian women. Many of the women affected by this provision were deserted by the white men who fathered their children. They often ended up living in a 'no man's land' between a city or town and the reserve from which they had been evicted but with whose people they still identified.[151] This sexist provision of the *Indian Act* remained in effect until 1985, when Canada, prodded by a decision of the United Nation's Human Rights Committee, removed it.[152]

Racism and Decentralized Control in Australia

In Australia, the segregation dimension of settler colonialism was more marked than the assimilation objective. Though white Australians continued to see 'civilization' as the only conceivable future for the individual native person, they were becoming increasingly doubtful about the capacity of Aborigines to become 'civilized.' In his book on 'Black Australians,' a young Paul Hasluck, who would later become a leading Australian politician and governor general, cited this view by the 'dominant race' in explaining the deterioration of the civilizing efforts of 'native administration' in Western Australia. In Hasluck's view, this attitude, already discernible in the 1830s and becoming stronger in the 1850s, was based on two beliefs: one, 'that the natives were declining and must inevitably die out,' and the other, 'a contempt for their capacity and their persons.'[153] Though white North Americans and New Zealanders came to think about native peoples in racist terms – particularly at the high tide of Social Darwinism – racist thinking was more deeply rooted and enduring in Australian settler society.

Another distinctive feature of settler colonialism in Australia was its decentralization. In contrast to the central control over native policy maintained by settler administrations in Canada, New Zealand, and the United States, the Australian colonies retained their own separate native administrations. Even the pace of British withdrawal from native affairs varied substantially. The imperial government and its representatives were never much of a restraint on Queensland's colonists in their treatment of Aborigines, and by 1856 had withdrawn from native administration in the eastern colonies. Western Australia, in contrast, did not take over full control of native affairs until the end of the 1890s.[154] The decentralized nature of native policy in Australia, as we shall see, continued well after federal union of the Australian colonies in 1901.

Leaving control over native policy in the hands of the individual colonies, and later in the hands of the states, exposed Aborigines and Torres Strait Islanders to the harsher treatment of governments responsive to settlers in close contact and conflict with native populations. But relative differences during this period fade into insignificance. During the last three decades of the nineteenth century and through most of the first half of the twentieth century, native policy in all four of the English-settler democracies was heavily authoritarian and racist. For Australia's Indigenous peoples, decentralization at least had the benefit of saving them from exposure to military forces as strong as those that the settler democracies of New Zealand and North America could direct at their native peoples.

Some of the Australian colonies, for quite some time after attaining self-government, took little official notice of native peoples. This is certainly true of Tasmania's colonists, who had come to believe that the only native Tasmanians left were descendants of those who had married whalers and sealers and lived in the islands of the Bass Strait. In South Australia, after the withdrawal of imperial direction, it was mainly philanthropic and religious organizations that played the lead role in native affairs. These 'private' efforts combined the hallmarks of settler colonialism – segregation (in South Australia on a voluntary basis) with intense efforts to Christianize and 'civilize.' Not until 1911, when the Northern Territory was split off from South Australia and brought under federal government control, did South Australia enact a full regulatory regime – an *Aboriginal Protection Act* modelled on legislation in Queensland and Western Australia but implemented in a less 'draconian' way.[155]

Victoria was the first colony to impose a thorough Canadian-style regulatory scheme on the Aborigines. It began in 1860 by creating a Central Board of Aborigines to set up reserves and oversee their management by local protection committees.[156] In 1869 the *Aborigines Act* gave the board (now called the Board for the Protection of Aborigines) extraordinary powers over native peoples. It could control where Aborigines lived, the conditions under which they could be employed, and their earnings. Most draconian of all was the board's power to remove children from parents if the youngsters were deemed in need of care and to place them on a reserve or in an industrial or reformatory school. Like Canada's *Indian Act*, Victoria's *Aborigines Act* led to an increasingly authoritarian effort to regulate every aspect of the Aboriginal person's life. An 1880 regulation gives the flavor of the regime: 'Every Aboriginal male under 14 years of age, and all unmarried females under the age of 18 years, shall, when so required by the person in charge of any station ... reside and take their meals, and sleep in any building set apart for such purpose.'[157]

In 1886 Victoria took the next step dictated by the racist thinking that had come to have such a strong grip on its governing elite. The policy now was to merge the mixed bloods, or 'half-castes,' with the general population by removing them from the reserves. Full-blood Aborigines were to remain on reserves, where they were expected to die out over a generation or two, in isolation but under the benevolent care of their minders.[158] By no means did Victorian Aborigines simply comply with this scheme of things. Richard Broome reports that an 1877 police census revealed that fewer than half of the 1067 Aborigines listed as living in Victoria at that time were on reserves. For those who did move to reserves, the forceful removal of the younger half-castes had tragic consequences, breaking up families and depriving Aboriginal farming communities of much of their able-bodied labour.

In New South Wales, thousands more Aborigines survived the disease and frontier violence than in Victoria. Intensive occupation of the land by settlers proceeded more slowly in the later decades of the nineteenth century and the early 1900s. This delay meant that Aborigines in many parts of New South Wales who were interested in taking up farming could secure land for themselves by having parcels of land, usually on or near their traditional country, recognized as reserves. Some South Australian reserves developed in a similar fashion.[159] Also like South Australia, New South Wales was much slower to impose a full regulatory scheme on its Aboriginal peoples. It set up an Aboriginal Protection Board in the 1880s but did not arm it with regulatory powers until 1909. Once the board had these powers, it moved quickly to make use of them. Heather Goodall records that between 1912 and 1938, when the Aboriginal population of New South Wales was somewhere between 6000 and 10,000, 1500 children were taken from their families.[160] Again, the aim was to remove the children of mixed blood from Aboriginal camps and reserves – particularly those classed as 'quadroon' (one Aboriginal grandparent) or 'octoroon' (one Aboriginal great-grandparent).[161]

The Aboriginal Protection Board turned out to be a very poor protector of Aboriginal interests. It applied itself energetically to the dismantling of Aboriginal reserves. It sold reserve lands both to finance its own administrative costs and to clear Aboriginal people out of good farm land wanted by the expanding settler population. In effect, Aborigines suffered a second dispossession. By 1927 half of the land on the 115 reserves that existed in 1911 was lost in this way.[162] Most of these reserves were along the fertile southeast coast. Two-thirds of them had been created through Aboriginal initiative. Though the Aboriginal people believed strongly that their title to this land was recognized by the Queen, settler society and its authority, as we have seen, had no understanding of native title. Aboriginal farmers not only lost their land – without compensation – but in some cases even the crops they had planted on it.

The breaking up of reserves did not mean that Aborigines were simply absorbed into the general population. They remained living mostly in fringe communities just outside country towns, still in touch with their own country but relying increasingly for their livelihood on low-paid labour for the residents of the determinedly all-white towns. Though visible to the European population, these Aborigines were virtually invisible in an official sense. For these fringe-dwellers, colonial officials in New South Wales did not record even such vital statistics as births and deaths. Their absence from official records, as Marilyn Wood points out, supported the official theory that Aborigines were a disappearing race and made it difficult for subsequent generations to establish their links with their people and their country.[163] As with American tribes such as the Cherokee and the Canadian Indians and Métis, no matter how 'civilized' they might become, there was no place for them in the democracy the Australian settlers were building.

Warfare and Indigenous Labour on the Northern Frontier

Settler economic activities began to penetrate northern Australia in the latter decades of the nineteenth century. On this second Australian frontier, settler relations with native peoples were directed entirely by the colonists themselves. In Western Australia, the British government did not relinquish formal control over Aboriginal affairs until 1898, and it bound the colony in its Constitution to commit a minimal amount of its annual revenues to Aboriginal welfare.[164] But well before this time, economic development of the colony's vast northern reaches – pastoralism, gold-mining, and pearling – was controlled and directed by Perth politicians. And the constitutional requirement of spending funds on 'Aboriginal welfare' did nothing to soften the brutality or eliminate the violence on Western Australia's northern frontier.

Indeed, during these closing years of the nineteenth century and on into the early years of the twentieth, from northern Queensland in the east through what became the Northern Territory and across to the Kimberley region of Western Australia, this part of the Australian continent was virtually a war zone. On this second frontier the Australian colonists encountered large Aboriginal populations, for they were entering a region 'most favourable to the aboriginal system of economy.'[165] Noel Loos estimates, for example, that the Aborigines of northern Queensland at the time of this invasion numbered between 61,000 and 76,000.[166] In fact, despite the ravages of warfare and disease, much of northern Australia and the central interior has remained to this day country in which its principal population is its Indigenous people.

In this respect this vast northern Australian hinterland resembles the Canadian North – with one major difference. These later generations of Australian settlers, freed from the liberal conscience of imperial London, entered ancient Aboriginal lands and coastal waters unburdened by any sense of native title or ownership. Unlike their Canadian counterparts, they did not go through the pretense of having the natives surrender their country through treaties. The Australians acted openly as invaders. They relied not on treaties but on warfare, killing, and imprisonment, followed by administrative controls, to establish order on this, their last frontier.

The warfare was sporadic, but deadly, and went on for over half a century. It did not take the form of the pitched battles fought between the U.S. cavalry and Indian nations in the American West or the military engagements of New Zealand's Pakeha wars or Canada's Riel rebellions. Though the individual episodes of violence between settlers and natives in Australia were on a smaller scale, over time they may well have engaged more ordinary people and left a deeper legacy of hate and fear – on both sides of the frontier. Most often the conflict was provoked by a small band of Aboriginal clansmen stealing livestock or taking action against an isolated settler family or a few stockmen for not respecting their country or sharing things with them or for assaulting their women.[167] The Aborigines' action – or in settler parlance, 'outrage' – would provoke a stern retaliation on the settler side. Often, especially in Queensland, the colonists' attack was carried out by mounted native police, recruited from distant clans and armed with lethal breach-loading rifles.[168] Retaliation sometimes resulted in massacres of all the men, women, and children in a native camp, such as took place earlier at Myall Creek. The difference now was that there was no pressure from an imperial-instructed governor to put the killers on trial for murdering British subjects. Waging war against the Aborigines had become the policy of the settler state.

Though the number of native persons killed through this frontier violence was only a small fraction of the numbers killed by diseases spread through contact with the settlers, it was still a significant number. Henry Reynolds estimates that the 'recurrent skirmishing' in Queensland took the lives of 1000 Europeans and 10,000 Aborigines.[169] Robert Murray projects a figure of 5000 for the Aborigines killed through violent conflict in the Northern Territory and Western Australia.[170] These figures point to an Aboriginal death toll in the North three times that resulting from earlier conflicts in southern Australia. To appreciate the challenge this warfare and killing poses to reconciliation in contemporary Australia, it is important to bear in mind that they are not ancient history. The last major massacres – at Forrest River in Western Australia and Coniston in the Northern Territory – took place in 1926 and 1928, respectively.[171]

As the Europeans' invasion northward and into the interior disrupted or destroyed the Aborigines' traditional economy, Aborigines became increasingly involved in the settlers' economy. Aboriginal participation in pastoralism and pearling was essential for these mainstays of the settlers' northern economy. But the Aborigines did not participate in this economy on free-market terms. For the pastoral industry, they formed a pool of cheap labour, being paid in station rations rather than earning wages. The large number of Aborigines associated with pastoral stations was particularly marked in the Northern Territory.[172] Though these 'station blackfellows' in the off season would 'go walkabout' in their traditional country, they sometimes came into conflict with those of their people who remained 'in the bush.'

Aborigines and Torres Strait Islanders were much sought after as divers for the pearling and beche-de-mer industries, which began to flourish in the later decades of the nineteenth century. In northwestern Australia, which became the world's largest supplier of pearlshell for buttons, the pearling industry depended 'almost entirely on the enslavement of Aboriginal divers.'[173] Their enslavement was often the result of close collaboration between sheep grazers and pearlers. Noel Loos observes that some of the participation of Aboriginal communities along the Queensland coast in the pearling and beche-de-mer industries was voluntary, but he also records many instances where men were duped into serving on ships for long voyages and prevented from returning to their traditional land.[174]

When Aborigines entered the wage economy, they did not do so on equal terms with whites. Their contracts of employment were tightly administered, wages were kept below the remuneration of white workers, and, under Queensland's tough protection regime, were usually taken over by their 'protectors' and used to offset the upkeep of Aborigines on reserves.[175]

By the beginning of the twentieth century in Queensland, the Northern Territory, and Western Australia, the gun was giving way to administrative control as the settler state's principal means of ordering relations with Indigenous peoples. In all three areas, the controls were administered under 'protection' legislation similar to that which Victoria had pioneered. Queensland led the way with the passage of its *Aboriginals*

Protection and Restriction of the Sale of Opium Act in 1897.[176] Western Australia followed in 1905 with its *Aborigines Protection Act*, heavily influenced by the findings of a royal commission conducted by Queensland's chief protector, W.E. Roth.[177] The commonwealth government, in the same year it assumed responsibility for governing the Northern Territory, brought in an *Aboriginal Ordinance* to establish a protection regime for the territory.[178]

Protection continued to be two dimensional: white townspeople needed protection from Aborigines, and Aborigines needed protection from the darker side of 'civilization.' Aboriginal access to towns and cities was strictly controlled. Racial segregation did not preclude an assimilative objective, but now that racial theory was gospel in Australian settler society, civilizing efforts focused almost entirely on mixed bloods. The protection regimes armed their administrators with the power to remove 'part-Aboriginal children' from their natural parents to homes, missions or institutions where they could be 'civilized' and to establish reserves or missions, where Aboriginals could be confined, in the words of the Queensland legislation, 'entirely isolated from contact with other races.'[179] Settler control of the places where Aborigines could live was administered most vigorously and harshly in Queensland. Aborigines were relocated to reserves far from their traditional country. Nowhere were the bonds of family and country more cruelly severed than in that state.

Queensland Colonialism in Torres Strait

It was to the colony of Queensland that Britain, in the 1870s, annexed the islands of the Torres Strait, including Eddie Mabo's ancestral island, Mer. But the Torres Strait Islanders did not feel the full weight of the harsh colonial regime Queensland imposed on its Aboriginal population, partly because, as C.S. Rowley dryly observed, 'they occupied no land required for cattle runs.'[180] The only significant European settlement was on Thursday Island, where the headquarters of the islands' colonial administration was located. The Islanders continued to cultivate family garden plots and harvest fish from their shore-line weirs. They had always been a maritime people, deriving most of their protein from the sea. From the 1860s on, Islander men in increasing numbers participated in the pearling and beche-de-mer industries that began to flourish in the strait. The presence of Christian missionaries, both before annexation and, through their continuing influence, after, contributed to the softening of colonial rule in the Torres Strait. On the Queensland mainland, Aborigines were spared the worst brutalities of settler domination in places where Christian missions at least for a time were the main European presence.[181] As we saw in chapter 1, the Torres Strait Islanders celebrate the anniversary of the arrival of the first missionaries as a national holiday and have evolved a faith that melds traditional beliefs with Christianity.

This syncreticism of the Torres Strait Islanders extends far beyond religion. Islander custom and language, as Anna Shnukal observes, 'have always been syncretic ... receptive to difference and outside influences and ready to accept and transform them.'[182] Two decades before annexation, the pearl rush had brought hundreds of foreign seamen to the Torres Strait from all parts of the world – from the Pacific islands, the Philippines and Indonesia, and also from the British Isles and North and Central America. Many of these migrant seamen married Islander women and settled permanently on various islands in the Strait. The Torres Strait Islanders had become, in Jeremy Beckett's words, 'a society of such extraordinary racial diversity' that Thursday Island was known as the 'Sink of the Pacific.'[183] Though cultural syncreticism and racial diversity reduced the distance that Queensland's colonizers saw between themselves and the Islanders, it did not stop them from maintaining an economic and political hierarchy built along racial lines, with white Anglo-Australians at the top, black-skinned peoples at the bottom, and 'the rest distributed according to their position along the colour spectrum.'[184]

John Douglas, a former Queensland premier and Queensland's first 'government resident' in the Torres Strait, established a system of 'indirect rule' there similar to that which Frederick Lugard had introduced into Britain's African colonies. Under this system, management of an island's internal affairs was put in the hands of a native chief, or 'Mamoose,' appointed or recognized by the resident, assisted by an elected island council and a native police force.[185] The system included native courts, which the missionaries had encouraged for settling disputes within the island communities. On several islands, a resident European teacher functioned as a supervisor of the island council and clerk of its court. When the Cambridge anthropological expedition visited Mer in 1898, it reported that Queensland 'had not affected native land tenure which is upheld in the Court of the Island.'[186] Decisions of the Mamoose's court dealing with disputes over the boundaries of privately owned garden lots would turn out to be of great importance when Eddie Mabo brought his case before Australia's High Court.

When Queensland introduced its *Aborigines Protection Act* in 1897, Douglas insisted that the Islanders, because of 'their marked mental superiority over the mainland native,' should be exempt from its provisions.[187] But this situation changed in 1904, when Douglas's seventeen-year regime as resident ended with his death, and the Islanders, at least on paper, became subject to the same controls as applied to Aborigines. The Islanders' desire to be distinguished from Aborigines was not met in statutory terms until the passage of the *Torres Srait Islanders Act* in 1939.[188] However, the Islanders who remained in the islands enjoyed much more autonomy and de facto recognition of their land rights and economic interests than mainland Aborigines. Indeed, the Torres Strait Islanders had elected councils half a century before the colonial regime introduced them in Papua and New Guinea.[189] It is not surprising – though deeply ironic – that the effective assault on the *terra nullius* legal underpinnings of Australia's colonization of its Indigenous peoples was eventually led by an Islander who, though resident most of his life on the Australian mainland, never lost his spiritual or political root in his island home.

The High Tide of Empire

The five decades preceding the First World War are referred to as the Age of Empire.[190] During this period, nearly the entire world was under the formal rule or political domination of a handful of European nation-states and the United States of America. Never before – and never since – did such a few states and peoples have such a technological, economic, and military advantage over all the rest of human kind. Empire was not new, but imperialism as a political process to be celebrated and to be resisted was quite new. To the classic economic, strategic, and civilizing motives of empire were now added the popularizing energies of nationalism and racism. Accumulating imperial possessions was sold to new democratic electorates as a badge of national prowess. Pseudo-scientific racism and Social Darwinism provided a potent ideology for justifying the white man's domination of 'lesser breeds without the law.' All these notions were wonderfully encapsulated in the appeal to British people to celebrate the coronation of their new monarch in 1902 'as a symbol of the world-wide domination of their race.'[191]

For those parts of the New World where English-speaking settlers had become the dominant population and were turning British colonies into self-governing democratic nations, imperialists envisioned virtual disappearance, not simply domination, as the fate of native populations. In 1883 Sir John Seeley, Regius Professor of History in the University of Cambridge, gave a course of lectures celebrating the 'the Expansion of England.' He contrasted the situation of European settlements in Central and South America, where 'the European, though supreme, yet lived in the midst of a population of native Indians,' with the European in North America, who 'supplanted the native race entirely, pushed it even further back as he advanced, and did not blend with it at all.'[192] Then, casting his eye southwards to the Antipodes, Seeley referred to 'the Australian race' as being 'so low in the ethnological scale that it can never give the least trouble.' He acknowledged that the situation in New Zealand was not so clear, for there 'the Maori tribe occupy the Northern Island in some force, much as in the last century the Highland clans gave us trouble in the northern part of our own island.' But Sir John found consolation in observing that 'the Maori is by no means a contemptible type of man.' The elimination of native peoples from these new English nations was, for him, a matter for some self-congratulation, for it meant that 'the English Empire is on the whole free from that weakness which has brought down most empires, the weakness of being mechanical forced unions of alien nationalities.'[193]

Six years after Seeley's lectures, Lord Watson, speaking for the Judicial Committee of the Privy Council, the highest court of the British Empire, pronounced that the Colony of New South Wales 'consisted of a tract of territory practically unoccupied, without settled inhabitants or settled law, at the time when it was peacefully annexed to the British dominions.'[194] *Cooper v. Stuart*, the case in which Lord Watson made this assertion and which, as we earlier noted, would prove to be a formidable legal obstacle to Eddie Mabo, was not one brought by native litigants. The issue in the case involved a dispute between Australian settlers about the extent to which English common law applied to them. Watson now affixed the empire's legal seal of approval to the belief that the Australian colonies were pure colonies of settlement, 'discovered and planted by English subjects' in 'an uninhabited country.' To such a colony, English subjects brought so much of the laws of England – 'the birthright of every English subject' – as is applicable 'to the conditions of an infant Colony.' The belief being honoured in this bold bit of legal reasoning did not go so far as to deny that Australia had any inhabitants before the English colonists arrived. It simply consigned the native inhabitants to such a low place on the evolutionary scale that their existence had no practical or legal significance.

It remained for a later panel of English Law Lords to do the fine-tuning of Lord Watson's dictum. That came in the Privy Council's 1919 decision in *Re Southern Rhodesia*. Though the case dealt with native peoples in southern Africa, the Privy Council, which continued to function as the highest court of appeal for the settler dominions, used the occasion to make some general pronouncements on the rights of Indigenous peoples. Acknowledging that 'estimation of the rights of aboriginal tribes is always inherently difficult,' their Lordships went on to make the following pronouncement: 'Some tribes are so low in the scale of social organization that their usages and conceptions of rights and duties are not to be reconciled with the institutions or legal ideas of civilized society. Such a gulf cannot be bridged. It would be idle to impute to such people some shadow of the rights known to our law and then to transmute it into the substance of transferable rights of property as we know them.'[195] For other Indigenous peoples whose legal conceptions 'are hardly less precise than our own,' it might be possible for the new imperial sovereign to acknowledge their rights. In the eyes of the colonizers, Australia's Indigenous peoples – Aborigines and Torres Strait Islanders alike – would not qualify for this elite category of native people. Belief in an evolutionary hierarchy of human societies had as firm a grip on the Australian settlers' mind as on the thinking of the empire's highest judges.[196]

The law of other English-settler countries during this imperialist period was almost as hostile as Australia's to the rights of Indigenous peoples. In Canada, as the frontier of settlement and industrial development moved northward and westward, the practice prescribed by the Royal Proclamation of 1763 of acquiring land through treaties with the Indians continued. Though this process implicitly recognized the Indians as owners of the vast territories 'surrendered' through the treaties, the goal was to extinguish all the signatories' Aboriginal rights. In 1889, the same year that the Privy Council decided *Cooper v. Stuart*, the English Law Lords rendered a decision that greatly diminished the significance of native land rights in Canada. This case, *St. Catherine's Milling and Lumbering Company v. The Queen*, dealt only indirectly with Indian land rights. The main issue was whether 50,000 square miles of land 'surrendered' to the Crown by the Ojibwa people in northern Ontario through Treaty 3 in 1873 were now owned by the provincial or the federal Crown. The Privy Council decided in favour of the province, but in the course of reaching that conclusion referred to the Ojibwa people's prior 'possession' of their lands, 'such as it was,' as having its legal source in the Royal

Proclamation. Watson, much like US Chief Justice Marshall in *Johnson v. McIntosh*, reduced Indian 'possession' of land from a property right to a 'tenure' that 'was a personal and usufructury right, dependent upon the good will of the Sovereign.'[197]

When British Columbia became a province of Canada in 1871, its government rejected the federal government's proposal to use the treaty process to acquire lands for railway building and settlement in the province. Except for a wedge of its northeast corner covered by Treaty 8 in 1899 and some colonial treaties on Vancouver Island, British Columbia was developed Australian style, as a *terra nullius*.[198] Settlement and resource development took place on Indian lands without treaties (but not without conflict),[199] as if the Aboriginal rights recognized by the 1763 proclamation did not exist in this part of Canada. Later on, the opportunity for native leaders who learned about the proclamation in the settlers' schools to test the assumptions underlying BC policy in the courts was foreclosed, when the *Indian Act* was amended to impede Indians from obtaining legal assistance to litigate land claims.[200]

In the United States, native policy continued to have a tougher and more ideological edge than in Canada. After the Civil War, a Republican-dominated Congress became impatient with the bother and expense of pacifying the Indians by making treaties with them. In 1871 it voted to repudiate the president's power to make treaties with Indian tribes.[201] Tribes retained the status Chief Justice Marshall had bestowed on them as 'domestic dependent nations,' but control over their internal affairs was now thoroughly subject to Congressional intervention. When the Supreme Court in 1883 ruled that the federal courts could not try Crow Dog, an Indian leader, for murdering Spotted Tail, a noted Sioux chief, in Indian country because the United States, through treaties, had recognized the Indian tribes as semi-independent nations,[202] Congress quickly replied by passing the *Major Crimes Act*. The act made it a federal offence for an Indian to commit murder, manslaughter, rape, assault with intent to kill, arson, burglary, or larceny against another Indian on an Indian reservation.[203]

Increasingly, the main aim of Congress was not to respect the Indian tribes but to break them up and destroy their land base. The ideological drive of the 'First New Nation' could not tolerate nations within. Moreover, the Indians' system of 'tribal communism' prevented them from becoming true Americans. Merrill Gates urged a gathering of American anthropologists in the 1870s to awaken acquisitive desires in the Indian: 'In his dull savagery he must be touched by the wings of the divine angel of discontent.'[204] To move up the evolutionary ladder of human development, Indians would have to become possessive individualists. This ideological vision was expressed legislatively in the *Allotment Act of 1887*, sponsored by Senator Henry Dawes. The *Dawes Act* permitted members of tribes considered to be sufficiently advanced to select individual allotments of land (generally 160 acres per family), and the remainder of the reserve to be sold off. During the forty-year period of allotment, more than 86 million acres, over 60 per cent of the Amerindians' remaining land base, passed into non-native hands.[205] Three years after passage of the *Allotment Act*, US troops chased down 250 women, children, and the remaining Sioux warriors on the Pine Ridge Reserve in South Dakota, killing most of them and ending the Indians' military resistance on the western plains of America.[206]

The Indians were now, in effect, subject peoples of the United States. In 1884, when John Elk, an Omaha farmer who had given up his tribal membership and farmed his own land, was denied the right to vote, the Supreme Court upheld the denial on the grounds that he was an Indian and therefore not a citizen.[207] Even though the Fourteenth Amendment of the US Constitution states that 'all persons born or naturalized in the United States and subject to the jurisdiction thereof, are citizens of the United States and of the State in which they reside,' native Americans were deemed to be non-citizens unless Congress ruled differently.[208] It was not until 1924 that Congress granted citizenship to all Indians born in the United States. In the meantime, the Supreme Court vindicated paternalist rule over Indians who remained on reserves. In a 1913 case, in justifying application of the federal Bureau of Indian Affairs' regulations on Pueblo lands in New Mexico, the court described the Pueblos as 'a simple, uninformed and inferior people.' It concluded that the United States, 'as a superior and civilized nation,' had 'the power and duty of exercising a fostering care and protection over all dependent Indian tribes within its borders.'[209] The assumptions of evolutionary racism were as firmly rooted in the thinking of American political and legal leaders of this era as among their counterparts in the British dominions.

From a comparative perspective, among the four English-settler countries in this century of massive dispossession and colonization, relations with native peoples were the least oppressive and discriminatory in New Zealand. The flood of settler emigration had reduced the Maori demographically to a minority status in Aotearoa. From constituting half of New Zealand's population in 1860, the 40,000 Maori by the 1890s made up only 10 per cent of the population.[210] Though this number represents a tremendous change, it is not nearly as dramatic a relative decline as native peoples in the other English-settler countries experienced. By the end of the nineteenth century, though the native populations of New Zealand's sister dominions, Australia and Canada, were considerably larger – 94,000 in Australia and 127,000 in Canada – they constituted only 2.5 per cent of the overall population.[211] In the United States, at the official end of the 'Indian Wars' in 1890, the federal government determined that only 248,253 identifiable Indians remained within its borders.[212] This total represented considerably less than 1 per cent of the American population.

At the turn of the century, more than 95 per cent of the Maori lived in rural locations apart from settler communities. This segregation was driven not by settler law or policy, but rested on the Maori's continued attachment to at least a portion of their traditional lands and to their local communities. The Native Land Court established in 1865 – a unique feature of the New Zealand settler regime – though insensitive to the Maori tradition of collective, tribal ownership and in violation of the principle of Crown pre-emption in the Waitangi Treaty – nevertheless enabled Maori who used the system to secure private ownership of parcels of land on the white man's terms. It was not until land reforms in the early part of the twentieth century broke up much of the Maori estate on the North Island and made it much easier to acquire Maori land[213] that substantial numbers of landless Maori began to form a black urban proletariat, particularly in and around Auckland.

The settler regime in New Zealand aimed at amalgamation, not separation of the country's Indigenous people. Certainly the colonists wanted the Maori to become Christians and adopt the 'civilized' political and economic ways of the Europeans. In this sense their policy was assimilationist. But unlike their counterparts in Australia, Canada, and the United States, they were not counting on the disappearance of the Maori. The Maori had a distinct and permanent place in New Zealanders' vision of their civic future. Maori seats in their legislature, and a system of courts to deal with Maori land issues, were institutional expressions of that place. To be sure, this vision was not the same as that harboured by many of the Maori people and much of the Maori leadership. The Maori made several attempts to set up their own parliament. Some of the more urbanized Maori in the Young Maori Party began to use their education in settler institutions to inculcate a sense of Maori nationalism. At the same time, a strong sense of tribal pride and identity was being nurtured in rural locations, where leaders were intent on strengthening the resources of their communities so that the intake of Western elements could be regulated 'in a manner that strengthened Maori values and institutions.'[214] By the turn of the century, Pakeha and Maori were a long way from striking a mutually satisfactory balance between integration and autonomy, but still, compared with their counterparts in the other English-settler countries, they were far closer to recognizing that integration and autonomy would be the essential ingredients of a successful accommodation.

In Australia, at century's end, settler-native relations were at the other end of the spectrum. On the European side, the Indigenous peoples were seen not as partners in building a new society but as a problem whose long-term solution was their disappearance as distinct societies. The hold of the 'doomed-race theory' on the colonists' thinking is evident in the idea advanced in an 1880 issue of the *Bulletin*, a popular magazine, that 'all we can do now is to give an opiate to the dying man, and when he dies bury him respectfully.'[215] From being a *terra nullius*, a land of no one, Australia had become in law and in politics, even more than Canada, the United States, or New Zealand, a land of white Europeans. By the 1890s the Chinese who had come to Australia in search of gold, and whose numbers by the 1890s were roughly half those of Indigenous Australians, were seen as a more serious threat to white hegemony than the Aborigines.[216] For their part, the Indigenous peoples over whom the Australian colonies claimed sovereign authority were much less united and politically equipped to resist and assert their rights than the Amerindians, whose tribal structures and identities in large measure survived the settlers' incursions.

CHAPTER 5

Colonialism Contested and the Winds of Change

On 1 January 1901, the Commonwealth of Australia was born. The federal union of the six colonies to form the Australian state was an act of exceptional statecraft and popular participation. The Constitution of Australia that the British Parliament formally enacted into law was the product of a decade of intense political discussion and debate among the Australian colonists.[1] Beginning in 1891, political leaders from the different colonies, including at first New Zealand, met in a series of conventions to identify shared principles and find a way of accommodating their interests in a common scheme of government.

For their time, and by world standards, the leaders who drafted the Australian Constitution and the people who ratified it were remarkably progressive. Two of the founding states, South Australia and Western Australia, had enfranchised women before federation – among the first jurisdictions in the world to do so. The new Commonwealth itself would extend the vote to women in its 1902 *Franchise Act*. Though few representatives of the working class participated in the drafting conventions, organized labour was rapidly gathering political power. The Australian Labor Party would come to power nationally a few years after federation. Nor was there ever any doubt among Australia's founding fathers that the legitimacy of the Constitution they drafted would depend on its approval by the people. No other state established by Europeans had a more democratic founding than Australia.

The founders of Australia were clearly a progressive people – but they were also a white people. They saw themselves as a white British society on the edge of Asia, and through their combined strength they were determined to keep it that way. The marks of this determination are found less in the federation's founding Constitution than in its first batch of national legislation.[2] Indeed, the Commonwealth Parliament's very first act was the *Immigration Restriction Act, 1901,* which was designed to prevent the entry of non-European immigrants.[3] The *Commonwealth Franchise Act, 1902,* though it enfranchised women, denied the vote not only to 'aboriginal natives' of Australia but to 'aboriginal natives' of Asia, Africa, and the Pacific Islands. This category of alien aboriginal natives would come to be interpreted broadly and racially as including all those who belonged to the peoples occupying these places when the Europeans arrived. Except for New Zealand Maori (there was still a hope that New Zealand might join the federation), alien aboriginal natives were excluded from the *Naturalization Act, 1903.* And to make it easier for any aboriginal person to leave, the *Emigration Act, 1910* relieved them of the necessity of obtaining an exit permit. The White Australia policy aimed not only at keeping non-Europeans out but also at reducing the numbers of those already in Australia 'at the earliest time, by reasonable and just means.'[4]

While the founding generation of Australians was self-consciously white – through the lens of historical hindsight, painfully so – they did not see themselves as colonizers of peoples within. The black people indigenous to their country were expected to die out. The Aborigines and Torres Strait Islanders defied this expectation. Not only did they survive but they grew in numbers, in their own sense of identity, and in political strength. Before the end of Australia's first century, their challenge to the law and politics of *terra nullius* had become the most difficult issue in the country's political life. This chapter will examine the national and international conditions – the winds of change – that brought the aboriginal issue to the centre of Australian politics and laid the foundations for Eddie Mabo's successful challenge.

Constitutional Negatives

Australia's founding Constitution did not recognize the Aborigines or Torres Strait Islanders as having any enduring, positive place in Australian society or governance. The Constitution contained only two explicit references to indigenous Australians, and both of them were negative.

The first came in the Commonwealth Parliament's 'race power.' This power is stated in Section 51 of the Constitution, which lists the legislative powers assigned to the Commonwealth. (The Australian Constitution, like the American, specified the powers of the new federal legislature it was creating, leaving the state legislatures with the residue.) Section 51

(xxvi) stated the following as a subject on which the Commonwealth could make laws: 'The people of any race, other than the aboriginal race in any State, for whom it is deemed necessary to make special laws.' The purpose of this section was to arm the Commonwealth with the power to keep alien races from entering Australia.[5] There was particular concern about Kanakas (South Sea Islanders) coming into Queensland as indentured labour, in addition to people who the state's Samuel Griffith (later Australia's first chief justice) loosely referred to as 'coolies from British India.' Given this purpose, it was logical to exclude Australian 'aboriginal natives' from the clause. Indeed, when the clause was put forward at the 1891 Convention, Captain William Russell, then representing New Zealand, insisted that it should not cover the Maori.[6] Though at first the race power was proposed as an exclusive Commonwealth power, in the end it was treated as an area of concurrent jurisdiction in which both the Commonwealth and the state legislatures could make laws.

The significance of this section of the founding Constitution is twofold. In the first place, it perpetuated the decentralization of native policy in Australia. Until the 1967 referendum removed the constitutional prohibition against Commonwealth legislation in relation to Australians of the 'aboriginal race,' there could be no nationwide legislation with respect to Aborigines or Torres Strait Islanders. This gap left Indigenous peoples in Australia at the mercy of state legislatures whose regulatory regimes, especially in Queensland and New South Wales (the states with the largest aboriginal populations), could be extremely harsh. Not only that, but it ruled out any possibility of the nation-to-nation or people-to-people relations that Indigenous peoples in all the English-settler countries have always preferred. The power the Commonwealth acquired in 1967 to legislate with respect to aboriginal peoples was concurrent, not exclusive. The states can still legislate in this field, although, under the rule of federal paramountcy, their laws, in case of a conflict, must give way to the Commonwealth's. After the High Court's 1992 decision in *Mabo* swept away *terra nullius*, the Commonwealth government encountered a great deal of resistance from the states in trying to legislate a nationwide system of native land rights. Federal governments in Canada and the United States have not had an easy time securing provincial or state compliance with national policies concerning native peoples, especially on matters pertaining to land and resources, but federalism remains an even bigger constraint on national efforts to restructure relations with aboriginal peoples in Australia.[7]

The other major implication of the race power in the Australian

Constitution is the way it entrenched racial thinking in the country's public life. In Canada, New Zealand, and the United States, there has been plenty of racial thinking in the settler societies' treatment of native peoples. That was especially so during the period – roughly from the mid-nineteenth century up to the 1930s – when pseudo-scientific racism was in vogue among Europeans. But only in Australia did this way of thinking get encrusted in the country's founding Constitution. Today Section 51 (xxvi), the section of the Constitution that empowers the federal government to pass special laws applying to Indigenous peoples, is referred to as the 'race power.' In 1997 the High Court of Australia ruled that this power need not be exercised to benefit the 'aboriginal race,' but may also be used in a negative way against them.[8] The Australian Constitution also contains a clause that recognizes the states' power to disenfranchise citizens on the basis of race. Section 25 provides that all persons of any race who have been disqualified from voting for elections to a state's lower house should be excluded in reckoning the state's population for purposes of representation in the federal lower house. Though Australian states no longer deny the franchise on racial grounds – and if they did, they might run afoul of the Commonwealth's *Racial Discrimination Act* – Section 25 has not been removed from the Constitution. Among the world's constitutional democracies, Australia may well be unique in constitutionally enshrining a power to enact racially discriminatory legislation.

The comparative point is not that white Australians are more racist than their counterparts in other countries but that the tendency to conceptualize diverse native peoples as a race is more deeply ingrained in Australia. The thinking that underlay the idea, promulgated by Australia policy-makers in the 1920s and 1930s, of 'bleaching' out the Aboriginal population by promoting the 'breeding' of half-castes with whites,[9] finds its counterpart in contemporary Australia in the difficulty many Australians have in accepting that persons with white physical features and achievements such as university degrees can have an aboriginal identity. Constructing aboriginality in biological terms – in terms of blood and colour – makes it difficult to appreciate either the diversity or the malleability of aboriginal societies. Sadly, the centrality of race in the Australian discourse about Indigenous peoples, including their constitutional discourse, may have encouraged Indigenous people themselves to cling to a fixed racial distinctiveness as fundamental to their identity. Thinking of natives and non-natives as racial categories has done much to impede the progress in Australia to a restructuring of relationships that can, in Geoffrey Stokes' words, 'accommodate the diverse Aboriginal identities associated with place or region.'[10] Defining one another primarily in fixed biological terms prevents a mutual recognition of and enrichment from each other's cultures. Racial thinking remains a formidable barrier to true reconciliation.

The other negative constitutional provision explicitly aimed at Australians of the 'aboriginal race' was Section 127, which read as follows: 'In reckoning the numbers of the people of the Commonwealth, or of a State or other part of the Commonwealth, aboriginal natives shall not be counted.' According to constitutional historians, the main purpose of this clause was to exclude aboriginal people in calculating the states' or the Commonwealth's fiscal obligations – in particular, the transitional obligation of the states to provide funds for Commonwealth expenditures. The provision had special appeal to Queensland and Western Australia, with their large aboriginal populations. Chesterman and Galligan observe that this explanation suggests 'that Aborigines were considered marginal or insignificant for public expenditure purposes.'[11] More broadly, Section 127 added to the sense of exclusion of the Aborigines and Torres Strait Islanders from civic participation in the new federation.

The Constitution itself did not extend that exclusion to participation in elections. In fact, one constitutional provision – Section 41 – barred the Commonwealth from denying the vote in federal elections to persons who could vote in state elections. Only two states, Queensland and Western Australia, explicitly denied the vote to aboriginal persons (except those who owned freehold property). In the other states, at least in theory, aboriginal men, and in South Australia aboriginal men and women, appeared to have the right to vote. Though Section 41 was put in the Constitution to protect women's voting rights in states where women had been enfranchised, it looked as if it might secure an aboriginal franchise in states where aboriginal persons had not been disenfranchised. But this section turned out to be of little value in enabling aboriginal Australians to overcome their exclusion from the Commonwealth's 1902 *Franchise Act*. States that did not explicitly prohibit aboriginal natives from voting had indirect ways of doing so. Both New South Wales and Victoria, for instance, denied the vote to persons in receipt of charitable aid. This exclusion prevented most Aborigines from voting, because so many of those who were recognized as Aborigines in those states were associated with missions, confined to reserves, or otherwise subjected to protection regimes. When the Northern Territory was severed from South Australia and brought under the Commonwealth government's authority in 1911, its aboriginal population, by this time second in size only to Queensland's, was disenfranchised. The final blow to even a very limited aboriginal franchise was delivered by administrators who simply struck off the Commonwealth voting roll the names of Aborigines who were registered to vote in South Australia.[12]

Exclusion from Citizenship and Its Unintended Consequences

Strictly speaking, aboriginal Australians cannot be said to have been excluded from citizenship at the beginning of the Australian federation's history. Australia's founding fathers considered the concept of Australian citizenship either too republican or as creating too much confusion with state citizenship to embrace it in their Constitution. In Section 110, which was first introduced as an American-style privileges and immunities clause, the word 'citizen' was replaced in the final draft by 'subject of the Queen.' Australian citizenship was not formally established until passage of the *Naturalization and Citizenship Act* in 1948. Aboriginal Australians were then considered by Commonwealth officials to be Australian citizens.[13]

But this is simply the formal, legal story. In reality, from the very beginning non-aboriginal Australians thought of themselves as citizens, and the governments they elected treated them as citizens. The denial of citizenship to aboriginal Australians was equally real from the beginning, and, before the tide of opinion moved against it, the deprivation of rights actually intensified. The rights that citizen-members of a shared political community expect to enjoy, but which were denied to Aborigines and Torres Strait Islanders, were more fundamental to people's lives than the right to vote. They included the freedom to choose where to live and travel in their own country; the freedom to choose a marriage partner and to be responsible for the raising of children and for their education; the right to keep and the freedom to spend wages and to buy alcohol; equal access to the social services provided by the state; and, perhaps most important right of all, the right to determine their own identity. These were among the dimensions of citizenship denied for many decades to Aborigines and Torres Strait Islanders. By no means were all these deprivations automatically removed on the formal attainment of citizenship in 1948. Indeed, for quite some time, aboriginal Australians continued, in Chesterman and Galligan's words, to be 'citizens without rights.'

The vehicles for this systematic denial of the everyday rights of citizenship were the protection regimes established in the different colonies before federation. The states and the Commonwealth (in its administration of the Northern Territory) carried forward these instruments of colonization with increasing vigour.

Nowhere in the federation did control over aboriginal people become more vehement than in Queensland, the state with the largest Indigenous population. In the early decades of the twentieth century, Queensland's administration of aboriginal affairs was, unfortunately, regarded as a model by other jurisdictions.[14] In Queensland, protectors continually tried to bring as many Aborigines as possible under the control of missions or reserves, even in the most remote parts of the state. On government-run reserves and settlements, not only were the aboriginal inmates subjected to rigorous surveillance by unaccountable local protectors but they also suffered appalling health conditions and severe malnutrition.[15] Amendments to the protection legislation required aboriginal men's wages to be paid to protectors, with a portion taken for the relief of 'indigent natives.' A fund created by compulsory savings deducted from wages was managed by protectors, who had to approve any significant purchases by persons under their control. Further amendments in the 1930s greatly extended the sweep of this legislation by defining half-castes as aboriginal.

Eddie Mabo's birthplace, Mer, and the other Torres Strait Islands, though a very remote part of Queensland, did not escape the tight protection regime. The islands were treated as reserves, with much of the control on individual islands administered by teacher-supervisors. Controls on consumption were relaxed in 1913 to encourage Islanders to keep working on the pearling boats. But the government maintained tight control over wage levels and much of the money earned on the boats. Indeed, the government used its control of Islanders' money to purchase boats on their behalf. For many years, a nine o'clock curfew was enforced throughout the strait. The mobility of Islanders was tightly controlled. As we noted in chapter 1, when Eddie Mabo was growing up, Islanders were not free to move on their own accord to mainland Australia. Sexual relations between Islanders and others was a criminal offence, and intermarriage was possible only with the chief protector's express consent. At the height of the protection regime, segregation of the Islanders not only from white Australia but from Aboriginal Australia seemed to have become a long-term strategy. Chief protector J.W. Bleakley referred to the Islanders as a 'race apart' who had 'nothing to gain by deserting their own people.' Their future, he said, was that of 'a self-dependent community life in the islands that are their birthright, as an integral part of our great Commonwealth.'[16]

On the Australian mainland, white Australians, especially in country towns, increasingly pushed for segregation of Aborigines. They pressed to keep children from black camps on the edge of town out of their schools, and the black fringe-dwellers off their streets and out of their pubs. Protectors in the southern states came under increasing pressure to confine the black population to a few reserve settlements. This pressure came to a head in the Depression. Discriminatory employment policies and ineligibility for unemployment relief forced the Aboriginal unemployed onto reserves. Amendments to New South Wales legislation in 1934 gave its Protection Board draconian powers. Rumours that a contagious eye disease was rampant among Aborigines garnered support in the white community for the board's confinement policy. Aboriginal people referred to the legislation as the 'Dog Act' because it meant they could be rounded up and carted off in cattle trucks to reserves where living conditions were appalling. Entire communities were moved in this way. In 1936 the scope of the legislation was expanded to include all those of 'light caste' who had previously been told they were not Aboriginal.[17]

Native peoples in Canada, New Zealand, and the United States at this time were also encountering barriers that prevented them from enjoying full and equal citizenship, but nothing as systematically exclusionary as the Australian protection regimes. In the early decades of the twentieth century, Maori and Pakeha in New Zealand were becoming increasingly integrated. While Maori who came to live in the towns and cities had to put up with constant racial slurs on the street and in the press, the discrimination they experienced was not backed by public policies. In the United States, even though American Indians had been granted the status of United States citizens in 1924, the federal government continued to treat them as wards of the state. But during the New Deal years, the United States became the first settler state to grapple seriously with an approach to the reform of native policy that was not entirely assimilationist. In legislating the 1934 *Indian Reorganization Act*, Congress was at least struggling to somehow balance its deep assimilationist inclinations with a system of tribal self-government.[18] Canada continued to administer an oppressive system of controls over Indians on reserves, but remained strongly committed to 'emancipation' of those who were sufficiently assimilated to become full citizens (provided, of course, they gave up their Indian status). As its frontier began to move northward, it did not try to corral the Indians and Inuit in the Yukon or the Northwest Territories onto reserves.

By the end of the 1930s, Australia was showing signs of moving in the North American direction of extending citizenship to assimilated natives. In February 1939 John McEwan, the Commonwealth minister of the interior, made a landmark statement on aboriginal affairs. The Aborigine, he declared, 'irrespective of his race or colour, was entitled by right to eventual full citizenship.'[19] Though aimed primarily at the Northern Territory, it was heralded as a New Deal for Aborigines throughout Australia. It followed the first premiers' conference on aboriginal issues in Canberra in 1937. The premiers had been more tentative, declaring that 'ultimate absorption by the people of the Commonwealth' was the destiny of at least those natives of aboriginal origin who were not full-blood.[20]

What is notable about McEwan's statement is that, while it was entirely assimilationist in objective, it nonetheless discarded race and blood as criteria of citizenship. In that sense it marks the point where the white-settler society in Australia began to move its program of colonization from separation to assimilation. The doomed-race theory was not dead, but it was dying. Within the country's white governing class a consensus was now developing that the Australian Aborigines were neither a doomed race fated to simply die out nor biologically incapable of becoming 'civilized.' This shift of opinion, this wind of change within the settler society elite, would surely not be a sufficient foundation for decolonization, but it was a necessary condition.

The intellectual architect of this shift in position was A.P. Elkin, an Anglican clergyman and professor of anthropology at the University of Sydney, who from the mid-1930s to the 1960s was a highly respected adviser to government on aboriginal policy. As the country's first professor of anthropology, he spoke and wrote with the authority of an expert who had a scientific understanding of Aborigines. While Elkin used this claim of scientific expertise effectively to attack the doomed-race theory and to argue for the eventual absorption of all Aborigines into the mainstream of Australian society, racial categorization remained an important element in his thinking.[21] He believed that only mixed-bloods were ready for full citizenship. Full-bloods would likely require several generations of nurturing before they were ready to move from 'nomadism to citizenship.' Thus, Geoffrey Gray writes, he 'conflated blood and culture to explain individual behaviour and potentiality.'[22]

Elkin was fully committed to an evolutionist vision of the Aborigines' final destiny. They could survive and flourish only by becoming fully 'civilized.' It was the duty of his own race to serve as a 'trustee race' and take on the task of raising primitive races in the cultural scale.[23] And yet his outlook was not entirely assimilationist. Some features of traditional aboriginal culture he admired – especially their spirituality – and these, he thought, should be a significant part of the base for aboriginal advancement. Becoming 'civilized' did not mean totally adopting the European way of life. There was no reason to believe that 'our civilization' in all its developments would be most suited to the Aborigines. He acknowledged that 'there are other types of civilized environment, and any race must ultimately develop its own from within.'[24] Thus, Elkin's vision of the Australian society in which aboriginal peoples should ultimately enjoy full citizenship was not entirely monocultural. There was a touch of integration rather than total assimilation in it. In this view, Elkin was considerably ahead of most of the politicians whom he advised.

The policy shift from segregation and protection to assimilation was also prompted by demographic realities. The 1939 census showed that the section of the population officially recognized as aboriginal had increased by nearly 10 per cent since 1921 to 77,269.[25] This increase was entirely accounted for by growth in the 'half-caste' population. The number of 'full-bloods' had actually declined by a few thousand, and the 'full-blood' percentage of the overall aboriginal population had fallen from 82 per cent to 67 per cent. Although this trend did not decisively contradict the doomed-race theory, it also failed to encourage the leaders of white Australia to cling to the belief that the final solution to the native problem would be for the Aborigines to disappear. If the pure-bloods were dying out they were doing so very slowly, and a great many of the mixed-bloods, whose numbers were rapidly rising despite decades of trying to separate them from full-bloods, were not severing their connections with aboriginal communities. The sudden reversal of the separation policy in the 1930s was in part an acknowledgment of this reality.

The Australian settlers' strenuous effort over such a long stretch of time to segregate and marginalize the Aborigines had the effect of strengthening the Aborigines' sense of identity – one distinct from that of the Europeans. That, indeed, was the unintended consequence of the exclusionary practices and policies of the Australian federation in its formative decades. No doubt the first peoples of Australia would have retained and developed identities different from those of their European colonizers even in the absence of forced separation. The Maori of

Aotearoa–New Zealand are evidence of that. But the ideological emphasis on *innate* differences between whites and blacks in Australia created a formidable barrier for later generations of Australians to overcome in finding a consensual basis for sharing citizenship. Domination by a society that regards your own people as inherently inferior can be suffocating and humiliating, but it is also the stuff from which political cultures of opposition are fashioned. In the interwar years, Australians were beginning to get some sense of this possibility.

A New Kind of Aboriginal Political Resistance Begins

From the time Eora men shied stones at Captain Cook's longboat in Botany Bay and a flotilla of Islander war canoes confronted Captain Bligh in Torres Strait, Aborigines and Torres Strait Islanders had resisted the English-speaking settlers. By the end of the 1920s, that kind of violent, military resistance was over in Australia. Though the native peoples' methods had been military, their purposes were always political: to keep possession of their lands and waters and control over their lives. As settler-native politics evolved through the twentieth century, what changed among Indigenous people – the wind of change on their side – was not abandonment of the objective of securing territory and autonomy, but the use of many of the white man's political methods to secure their ends. This change in political technology occurred at roughly the same time among Aboriginal peoples in Canada,[26] the United States,[27] and Australia. In New Zealand, the Maori had a head start, their participation in settler politics having been well under way in the previous century.

Indigenous peoples' use of European political technologies began modestly with petitions in the settlers' language to the colonists' political authorities, initially the Crown (in the British dominions) and later to premiers and parliaments. Then various forms of collective protest action were organized, including strikes, demonstrations, walking off reserves, and mass refusals to comply with regulations. A few disgruntled Aboriginal activists began to consider framing protests so they could be litigated in the colonizers' courts, but they went no further than seeking legal advice.[28] The idea of endeavouring to vindicate the rights of Indigenous peoples in the colonizers' courts (as Eddie Mabo would do) was not yet a component of aboriginal political strategy in Australia. At this stage, more direct forms of political action were favoured. By the 1920s, Indigenous leaders were establishing formal political organizations to espouse their various peoples' cause in the country's mainstream political arena. These organizations built networks linking together formerly isolated aboriginal communities. They linked up too with political parties, politicians, and supportive organizations engaged in white politics. Political activity of this kind began to get a hearing for aboriginal peoples in the popular press. Natives and settlers begin to share the same political space.

Adopting the white man's political means to achieve Aboriginal ends is a deeply ironic process. It means that colonized peoples' greatest success in reducing, if not completely overcoming, their subjugation is achieved by adopting much of the colonizers' political methods and culture. Such are 'the ironic wages of success in the decolonizing struggle.'[29] This has been as true of the struggle of Third World peoples as it turns out to be for the 'Fourth World' – the colonized peoples within the 'First' world. The very vocabulary through which Indigenous leaders come to articulate their aspirations – referring to their societies as 'nations,' asserting an original 'sovereignty,' and claiming 'title' to their lands and waters – is the vocabulary of the dominant society.

Something deeper is going on here than just a choice of new symbols or techniques of resistance. Using the dominant society's language and politics, and becoming good at it – as many Aboriginal leaders do – entails a significant integration into that society. As this occurs, 'Fourth World' peoples, like 'Third World' peoples – particularly at the level of leadership – find themselves becoming less distinct from the dominant society. Moreover, in the case of Indigenous peoples who become resigned to the fact that they are fated to constitute a permanent and small numerical minority inside the state in which they are located, participation in a political process established by the settler society becomes a permanent imperative. That is bound to have a moderating influence on the objectives that native groups pursue through such participation. But this integrative process can be a two-way street. Over time, the dominant society's recognition of Indigenous peoples and interaction with them in the pursuit and enjoyment of common political, legal, economic, and cultural ends leads to the enrichment of the dominant society by the perspectives, knowledge, and achievements of the Indigenous communities.[30] Initially, this Indigenous influence on the settler society is felt much more in the artistic than the political realm.

Organized political activity is by no means the only way in which Indigenous Australians continued to resist settler domination and oppression. There was, and is, a whole realm of informal, private resistance

– personal and unorganized in form, but political in spirit. This kind of resistance by a family might simply be a matter of moving about to keep out of the reach of protection regimes. Or, as happened at Cumeragunja on the New South Wales side of the Murray River in the 1920s, Aboriginal parents resisted the removal of their children by escaping from reserves and moving across the river into Victoria, where protection surveillance was much lighter.[31] A more pervasive form of private resistance is what Gillian Cowlishaw calls 'the rebellious display of disreputable behaviour.'[32] Drunkenness is the most common form of this type of resistance. Being frequently convicted and imprisoned for drunkenness, rather than being a source of shame, could be a way of displaying contempt for an unjust regime. Important as these private forms of resistance have been in fuelling an oppositional political culture among aboriginal Australians, they could not persuade the dominant society to change its laws or policies. On the contrary, they have done much – especially public drunkenness – to incur contempt towards Aborigines among white Australians. It is the organized political efforts led by aboriginal persons who conform with white standards of propriety and whose aboriginal identity may thereby be called into question that begin to get demands for structural change on the agenda of mainstream politics.

Goodall identifies the Australian Aboriginal Progressive Association (AAPA), formed in New South Wales in the early 1920s, as the first Aboriginal organization linking together communities over a wide area.[33] The AAPA's leading spokesperson was Fred Maynard, a Hunter Valley Koori. Maynard's upbringing and political education has parallels with Eddie Mabo's. His mother died in childbirth when he was only five years old and, when his father abandoned the surviving children, Fred went to live for a few years with a local Presbyterian minister – a time for him that was similar to Mabo's apprenticeship with the schoolteacher Robert Miles. Just as coming to live in the industrial port of Townsville raised Mabo's political consciousness, so Maynard began to turn to political organizing after coming to live with his sisters in Sydney. The black émigré communities in cities like Townsville, Melbourne, and Sydney were producing leaders who, instead of merging into white politics, re-established connections with their traditional communities and began organizing them politically. And, again like Mabo, Maynard's first lessons in political agitation came through working on the docks and taking an active part in radical trade unionism – in Maynard's case, the Waterside Workers' Union on the wharves of Sydney.

The AAPA held its first country conference in Kempsey in 1925. The actions it called for, as reported in the local press, embrace what became and would remain the two main branches of aboriginal aspiration. One motion called for granting to aboriginal Australians 'the full rights and privileges of citizenship as are enjoyed by all other sections of the community.'[34] But along with this motion pointing in the direction of integration were others claiming land rights. Many of the Koori had suffered through two waves of dispossession. The land claim they made was not recognition of title to their traditional country from which they had been cut off for several generations but individual family farms, to be owned under settler law in fee simple near where they were now living. They expressed their demand for land in Aboriginal language, framed so as to stress that their right to land arose from their traditional ownership. When the AAPA's petition to the Protection Board and the state premier was rebuffed, Maynard's response again shows that it was a combination of integration and autonomy that he was after. In his opening lines, Maynard said he wanted to make it perfectly clear 'on behalf of our people that we accept no condition of inferiority as compared with European people. Two distinct civilizations are represented by the distinctive races.' He went on to ask for recognition of Aboriginal people 'as the original owners of this land' and to argue for the right 'to supervise our own affairs.'[35]

After 1927 the AAPA 'disappeared from white public view.'[36] But in the late 1930s there was a resurgence of organized political activity among Aborigines in the earliest settled parts of the country. Three separate organizations emerged, each with a different regional base. Two sprang from networks built by the AAPA – one in the western communities of New South Wales, whose most prominent spokespersons were Bill Ferguson and Pearl Gibbs, and the other based on coastal communities, whose chief spokesman was Jack Patten. The third, the Australian Aboriginal League (AAL), though originating from a challenge to the New South Wales Protection Board's oppressive administration of the Cumeragunja settlement, was led by exiles from Cumeragunja, many of whom had gone to live in Melbourne. The best known of the AAL leaders – in Goodall's words its 'motivating force' – was its honorary secretary, William Cooper. He is the same man who, in chapter 4, we saw petitioning politicians in the 1880s to secure rights to reserve lands at Cumerganuja. Cooper was a tireless correspondent who wrote at least seventy-seven letters to various politicians.[37] He began to promulgate the idea of peopling Australia's unsettled areas with 'civilized Aborigines' –

the best way, he thought to 'close Australia's back door.'[38] Dr Cecil Cook, the chief protector of the Northern Territory at the time, dismissed this suggestion by stating that 'politically, the Northern Territory must always be governed as a white man's country, by the white man for the white man.'[39]

These Aboriginal political organizations found supporters at both the left and the right edges of white politics. On the left the strongest support came from unions, feminists, left-leaning Christians, and the Communist Party of Australia (CPA). For these white supporters on the left, and this certainly was true of the CPA, the integrationist goals – equal political and economic rights for Aborigines – were the appealing part of the Aboriginal political agenda. Bill Ferguson's relations with the CPA became strained when party members complained that in demanding rights recognizing the Aborigines as Australia's first peoples, the APA was making the error of 'separatism.' It would take another generation for white liberals in Australia (and elsewhere) to become warm to the autonomist part of the Aboriginal political agenda – the desire of Indigenous peoples, as James Anaya, puts it, 'to flourish as distinct communities on their ancestral lands.'[40] There was more support for separate Aboriginal development from white nationalists on the political far right. But the rationale for support from this quarter was deeply racist, and the apartheid ideal it entertained was one of 'segregation under benevolent expert control' – in other words, an extension of the protection regime. Still, one white nativist, J.J. Maloney, was sufficiently interested in what Aboriginal leaders were saying to give considerable coverage to their speeches in *Voice of the North*, a leading white nationalist publication.[41]

The climatic event of this early period of Aboriginal political activity came in 1938, the year white Australians celebrated 150 years of settlement. Cooper, Ferguson, and Patten, and the organizations they led, responded by holding a protest meeting in Sydney on January 26 – Australia Day. They declared it the 'Day of Mourning' and issued the following manifesto:

> You are the New Australians but we are the Old Australians. We have in our arteries the blood of the Original Australians, who have lived in this land for many thousands of years. You came here only recently, and you took our land away from us by force. You have almost exterminated our people, but there are enough of us remaining to expose the humbug of your claim, as white Australians, to be a civilised, progressive, kindly and humane nation.

By your cruelty and callousness towards the Aborigines you stand condemned in the eyes of the world.[42]

This declaration coming on white Australia's day of national celebration
was the most dramatic, and probably the most widely heard, political
challenge to settler domination aboriginal Australians had ever made. In
rejecting Australian nationalism – as it was then understood – it affirmed
an emerging aboriginal nationalism.

The sense of aboriginal identity – of aboriginality – underlying this
nationalism, was an identity that had evolved largely through the condition of being colonized.[43] Its adoption means defining one's self as 'the
other,' as the colonizers have defined you. At century's end, the sense of
aboriginality expressed in the Day of Mourning manifesto was firmly
Australian. The people the authors of this manifesto wished to speak for
were the Old Australians. The capacity of Indigenous leaders to speak in
terms of a continent-wide, aboriginal community of interest had come
about through learning of the common struggle to resist settler invasion
and domination. Fourth World nationalism, like Third World nationalism, is forged through resistance to colonialism.[44] But blood and a spirit
of opposition also course through the veins of this aboriginal nationalism. It will not be easy for these Fourth World nationalists to share a civic
identity with the 'New Australians.'

The pan-Australian aboriginal identity functions primarily as an ethnic political identity. It is an identity embraced by persons of Indigenous
background who wish to make common cause with others of the same
background to get a better deal for all Indigenous peoples in the nation-
state in which they reside. Many Indigenous persons, including many of
those who participate in country-wide aboriginal politics, have other
collective identities that are more local in character and more essential
to their understanding of who they are.

Some of these other identities are non-traditional. They stem from a
generation or more of living or being closely associated with an aboriginal diaspora in a big city, or an Aboriginal camp on the edge of a country
town, or a reserve, or a mission, or a pastoral station, or perhaps several
of these. But nearly all persons who identify themselves as an Aborigine
or a Torres Strait Islander identify also with a particular traditional
community, a historical society that pre-dates European settlement. We
can see this with Eddie Mabo. Though absent from Mer for most of his
adult life and deeply involved in the black urban politics of Townsville

and of Australia and, in his later years, an advocate of Torres Strait Island nationalism, Edward Koiki Mabo never lost his sense of being a Meriam man of the Piaderem clan from the village of Las in the Murray Islands. For Mabo, these ties to island culture and tradition, and to the place where his ancestors had lived for so long, were at the very core of his sense of who he was.

The role of tradition in decolonizing movements of native resistance to European domination is bound to be problematic. Tensions surrounding tradition arise among the colonized and perplex the colonizers. The bona fides of Aboriginal leaders whose political style and whose personal lifestyle appear highly Westernized are questioned by more traditionalist sections of Aboriginal communities and by political opponents in the non-Aboriginal community. The Aboriginal claim for recognition of special status as the country's 'first peoples' – as historic and ancient peoples – prompts some, on both sides of the struggle, to regard only what is authentically, entirely, and uniquely Aboriginal as a valid claim.

What James Tully calls a 'frozen-culture' understanding of Aboriginal identity and Aboriginal rights is a major barrier to the mutual understanding and reciprocity required for establishing a more just relationship with Indigenous peoples everywhere.[45] We will find sad evidence of this tendency in Australia in the legislation that follows Mabo's judicial victory – legislation that requires exacting demonstrations of historical connections for Indigenous claimants to enjoy their native title. Non-native leaders and intellectuals have come full circle: instead of denying the value of historical Aboriginal cultures, they now want to deny any benefits the state might bestow on Indigenous peoples to those whom earlier generations of settlers removed from their homelands. This unfortunate and unjust tendency is captured well by Jeremy Beckett, when he concludes his book on aboriginality by writing that 'Aborigines, like native Americans and others, face the unending task of resisting attempts, on the one hand to cut them off from their "heritage," and on the other to bury them within it as a "thing of the past."'[46]

Questions of aboriginal identity are of more than theoretical interest. As the Aborigines and Torres Strait Islanders begin to make progress in advancing their cause, it becomes important for them to identify the communities that are to enjoy and exercise the collective political rights they ask the dominant society to recognize. Determining communal, ethnic identity then becomes a practical question of political reform. It is, after all, the principle of the self-determination of peoples that finally provides the normative basis for Indigenous decolonization. If that is so, then it becomes essential, once there is a will to give this principle real effect, for the Indigenous peoples who are to self-determine their future to identify their operative political communities.

But, at this stage, that challenge is still a long way off. On the eve of the Second World War, the Western states that dominated the world and controlled its system of international law were a long way from recognizing a universal collective right of peoples to determine their own political futures. The principle of self-determination of peoples lay tarnished in the ashes of Woodrow Wilson's naïve idealism and the efforts of enclaves of Germanic peoples in Czechoslovakia and Poland to invoke the principle as a pretext for Nazi invasion. Before decolonization can take place anywhere, there must be a change internationally in the philosophy and principles of the European powers and the settler states. It is to the beginning of this wind of change that we must turn next.

Founding a New International Order

Just as the Western imperialism that began with Christopher Columbus's voyages five centuries ago was a process with enormous globalizing effects, so also the process of dismantling that imperialism – of decolonization – must be a global affair. The worldwide political system constructed through Western imperialism was not a just political order. As we saw in chapter 2, judged even by the Christian principles of Columbus's day, the imposition of European rule over the peoples of the New World was found wanting in a moral or ethical sense. As European states consolidated their colonial rule, spreading it to cover virtually all the known world, they abandoned any pretext of their imperial projects being accountable even to the standards of ecclesiastical humanism that inspired Bartolome de Las Casas's denunciation of Spanish rule in America.[47] The moral imperative of empire, to the extent that European imperialists felt the need for moral justification, was the presumption of European superiority – that 'almost metaphysical obligation,' as Edward Said put it, 'to rule subordinate, inferior, less-advanced people.'[48] Until there is some movement away from that presumption among the Western powers, decolonization cannot begin.

Such a movement began at the end of the Second World War. This movement has two sides to it: one is a wavering of belief among Europeans in their cultural and racial superiority and a search for less ethnocentric, more universal principles on which a system of world order can be based; the other is the increased political strength of colonized peoples in challenging imperial rule. An important part of this increase in the colonized peoples' political power is the international alliances they formed in the decolonization struggle. These two sides of the decolonizing process worked together. The weakening of racism and the interest in universal human rights among Europeans made them less inclined to respond to the colonized peoples' challenge simply by putting them down with military force. New international political forums such as the United Nations and a worldwide system of telecommunications created a global political space. In this space the actions of European and settler states could be assessed by a global jury applying international human rights standards. Sovereign nation-states, like Australia, became increasingly vulnerable to the politics of shame, which is often the only effective way of sanctioning breaches by states of universal standards of justice.

The movement towards a new international order that began after the Second World War was only a beginning, and even now, over fifty years later, it is far from complete. We are still far from living in a global political community based on respect for the equality of peoples, rather than a political order based on the force of the strongest states. The first stage of decolonization, the independence of Third World nations, may be achieved in formal law but is far from a reality in terms of political economy. As for the subjects of the second stage of decolonization, the Indigenous peoples colonized within member-states of the UN, the harvest of freedom for them in the first half-century of the movement towards a new world order has, thus far, been even leaner.

The grandeloquent words of the many declarations, covenants, treaties, and protocols that litter the landscape of the emerging international order so often seem like empty promises. These instruments of a new international system of human rights law, even when liberally interpreted, lack any reliable system of securing compliance.[49] International shameing remains the chief enforcement process. And, although it may be true, as Robert Williams says, 'that few governments actively desire pariah status in the international community,'[50] there are still too many governments that are willing to risk becoming pariahs – and too many situations in which governments are oppressing Indigenous peoples and other national minorities. There is the further problem that when states with an even worse record of human rights abuse than the country being condemned by a UN committee join in the shameing, the exercise may turn out to be quite counter-productive.

It is easy, then, to be cynical. But abject cynicism misses the real value of the little progress that has been made. Without the humanizing, decolonizing changes taking place in the international system when Eddie Mabo went to court, it is most unlikely that he would have won his case. And without some of these same international influences, the benefits for aboriginal Australians flowing from his victory would have been even slighter. Winds of change in the international environment are an important part of the Mabo story.

At the end of the Second World War, the countries that united to defeat the Axis powers were determined not to revert to an international order in which states were unaccountable to any moral standards. Standards of civic justice capable of acceptance worldwide – and that was the hope – should, in principle, be ones that all humankind, regardless of race, creed, or culture, can embrace. The horrors of the Holocaust demonstrated where political power premised on belief in a superior race and the worthlessness of inferior races could lead. There was a desire among leaders of the victorious nations to work out some definition of universal human rights. Given the ideological and cultural differences among these states, that would be no easy task. Nevertheless, it was undertaken, and we find its initial products in the Charter that founded the United Nations in 1945 and the Universal Declaration of Human Rights adopted by the UN General Assembly in 1948.

The Charter of the United Nations, signed by its fifty-one founding members in June 1945, begins by affirming 'a faith in fundamental human rights, in the dignity and worth of the human person, in the equal rights of men and women and of nations large and small.' The first Article of the Charter sets out as one of the United Nations' purposes: 'To develop friendly relations among nations based on respect for the principle of equal rights and self-determination of peoples, and to take other appropriate measures to strengthen universal peace.'[51] The reference here to the equal rights of peoples and to the principle of self-determination of nations looks, on its face, to be promising for Indigenous peoples. After all, are they not peoples who should enjoy equal rights with others, including the right to control their own political destinies? The UN's founders would have been very reluctant to answer this question in the affirmative had representatives of Indigenous peoples been allowed into their forum to ask the question. In drafting this part of Article 1, a number of states had expressed the fear that it might be used to legitimate secession movements. The UN Charter also affirms the 'sovereign equality' and 'territorial integrity' of member states.[52] Article 1(2) was adopted on the understanding of the drafting committee's report that it did not confer 'the right of secession.'[53]

This nervousness about secession remains a major obstacle for Aboriginal peoples in obtaining recognition in the international legal system for their right to self-determination. International law is made by established nation-states whose governments give priority to the sanctity of existing state boundaries. Even though few Indigenous peoples' movements aim for secession, the possibility that some might gives governments of existing states (and much of their population) the jitters.

Equally important is the concern of UN member-states to maintain the absolute sovereign authority of their governments over their citizens and territory. Concern over state sovereignty prompted the UN's founders to stipulate that, with the exception of one circumstance, nothing in the Charter authorized even the United Nations to intervene in matters within the domestic jurisdiction of any state. The one exception was a finding of the Security Council that a matter within a state was a 'threat to peace, breach of peace or act of aggression.'[54] Several of the UN's founding states were federations in which sovereignty is shared between central and state or provincial governments, but the possibility that sovereignty might be further shared with Indigenous peoples was, at this point in history, beyond the constitutional imagination of the most liberal of states. Delegates sent by the Haudenosaunnee (Iroquois) Confederacy to the international conference at San Francisco that drafted the UN Charter, and to subsequent international meetings, were told that 'their problem was domestic and that it must be resolved within the political institutions of the state.'[55]

From this time until the early 1970s, the doors of the United Nations remained firmly shut to Indigenous peoples. It was not simply statist concerns that closed these doors. A residue of racism likely remained in the minds of those who represented the European and settler states that constituted most of the 'family of nations' that controlled the pre-war system of international law. Here is how one of this family's most respected international legal theorists, the British writer John Westlake, spoke at the end of the nineteenth century in his text on international law of Indigenous peoples:

> When people of European race come into contact with American or African tribes, the prime necessity is that the former may carry on the complex life to which they have been accustomed in their homes ... and which may

protect the natives in the enjoyment of a security and well-being at least not less than they enjoyed before the arrival of the strangers. Can the natives furnish such a government, or can it be looked for from the Europeans alone? In the answer to that question lies, for international law, the difference between civilisation and want of it ... The inflow of the white race cannot be stopped where there is land to cultivate, ore to be mined, commerce to be developed, sport to enjoy, curiosity to be satisfied ... Accordingly, international law has to treat such natives as uncivilised.[56]

As Robert Williams observes, for Westlake and his colleagues, all territories occupied by Indigenous peoples, not just Australia, were *terra nullius*. So long as this kind of bias permeated respectable international legal thinking, there would be no hope for the recovery of *terra nullius* through the agency of the United Nations.

But lingering racism among Europeans could not impede the process of granting independence to overseas colonies of the Western powers. Even at its founding, countries that were neither European nor settler states had a majority in the General Assembly, and once decolonization got under way, that majority grew. Chapter XI of the UN Charter affirmed an obligation to dismantle colonial rule over Non-Self-Governing Territories. It committed member-states 'to develop self-government, to take due account of the political aspirations of the peoples, and to assist them in the progressive development of their free political institutions.'[57] There was a continuing political struggle against occupying European powers in the 'Third World,' particularly in Africa and Asia. By 1960 the decolonization process had accelerated enough for the General Assembly to adopt a Declaration on the Granting of Independence to Colonial Countries and Peoples. It stated that 'immediate steps shall be taken, in ... Non-Self-Governing Territories ... to transfer all powers to the peoples of those territories.'[58] It would take many more years for this declaration to be fully implemented in even a formal sense. Nonetheless, its adoption firmly marks the end of any legitimacy in world opinion and international law for overseas colonies of European states. Moreover, the 1960 UN declaration against colonialism is considered by most scholars 'as the point at which the principle of self-determination became a recognized right in international law.'[59]

This commitment of the UN to decolonization and self-determination had no immediate benefits for Indigenous peoples. During the 1950s there was a debate at the UN on whether national minorities and Indigenous peoples within states should be recognized as having the right of self-determination. At one point, Belgian delegates proposed that the principle should apply to Indigenous peoples. But fear that this right would endanger the territorial integrity of states meant that the 'Belgian thesis' got nowhere.[60] The peoples to which the 1960 UN declaration on decolonization applied were the entire populations of countries in which European colonizers had never been more than a small minority of the population. These peoples would not revert to the situation they were in before colonialism but would get their independence with their colonial boundaries intact. The governments of these newly independent states, often with very diverse populations, were not interested in having the principle of self-determination apply to peoples within their own boundaries. They, too, were jittery about the danger of secession if the principle were recognized as applying to distinct historical communities within their territories. National unity, not respect for diversity, was their priority.

Thus, new states joined with old states in adopting what came to be referred to as the 'blue water' thesis, limiting decolonization to overseas territories ruled by European states. The UN-backed decolonization regime would not apply to 'enclaves of Indigenous or tribal peoples living within the external boundaries of independent states.'[61] Certainly the English-settler states of Australia, Canada, New Zealand, and the United States would not have recognized that the UN's commitment to decolonization (which they strongly endorsed) could apply to the colonized Indigenous peoples in their own countries.

The position of the world's states that Indigenous peoples are ineligible for decolonization endured for many years. It is a position that did not begin to weaken until about the time that Eddie Mabo and his fellow colonized Torres Strait Islanders were arguing their case in the Australian courts. By then, what Franke Wilmer refers to as the 'Indigenous voice in world politics' had become strong enough to persuade some within and some outside the United Nations that Indigenous peoples were indeed 'internal colonies' within nation-states who should be supported in their efforts to move to a post-colonial situation.[62]

Equating decolonization with becoming an independent sovereign state made it difficult to appreciate that there could be post-colonial arrangements for Indigenous peoples that are less drastic than secession and yet more in line with the aspirations of at least a great many of these peoples. The key to decolonization and self-determination for any people is living under political arrangements to which they have consented. Professor Erica-Irene Daes, the scholar-stateswoman who has been a great leader in turning the United Nations around on these issues, put it well when she defined self-determination in the context of the decolonization of Indigenous peoples as a process 'through which Indigenous peoples are able to join with all other peoples that make up the State on mutually agreed upon and just terms, after many years of isolation and exclusion.'[63] The condition that is crucial to self-determination and to decolonization in this formulation is not becoming a separate sovereign state but *mutual agreement* of Indigenous peoples with the descendants of settlers and other newcomer peoples on how they can all be part of the same state.

The other foundational human rights document of the United Nations, the Universal Declaration of Human Rights, adopted without dissent by the General Assembly on 10 December 1948, did not include the right of peoples to self-determination. Clearly the questions of who had this right (i.e., what is a 'people') and what does the right entail were too controversial for the founders to include in this litany of political, legal, social, and economic rights. The first attempt at the UN to address the problems of Indigenous peoples, not in the context of their political rights but in terms of their general well being, was not propitious. In 1949 the General Assembly mandated a study of the 'social problem of aboriginal populations and other under-developed social groups of the American continent.' But the United States opposed this motion vigorously, viewing it as inspired by Cold War politics. This opposition resulted not only in termination of the inquiry but also in the temporary suspension of the UN body that was to carry it out – the Sub-Commission on Prevention of Discrimination and Protection of Minorities.[64]

The first international organization to take an active interest in the rights of Aboriginal peoples was the International Labour Organization.[65] The ILO was established by the Treaty of Versailles at the end of the First World War and carried on under UN auspices after the Second World War. As far back as 1921 the ILO had shown concern about the working conditions of Indigenous peoples – as well it might, given what we have seen about the discriminatory conditions imposed on aboriginal workers in Australia. In the 1950s the ILO returned to this concern and drafted ILO Convention 107 on the Protection and Integration of Indigenous and Other Tribal and Semi-Tribal Populations in Independent Countries.

The title of Convention 107 spells out clearly enough the ILO's limited perspective on Aboriginal objectives. The convention's drafters took care not to bestow the badge of 'people-hood' on its targets and referred to them only as populations. Its focus was entirely on the integration of these 'less-advanced' sections of the national society into the mainstream economy.[66] Needless to say, Indigenous representatives played no part in its drafting. Nevertheless, as Russel Barsh points out, ILO Convention 107 contained the first international standards on Indigenous land rights.[67] It recognized 'the right of ownership, collective or individual, of the members of the populations concerned over the lands which these populations traditionally occupy.' Further, it recognized Indigenous peoples' customary laws regarding land use and inheritance, and their right to be compensated for lands appropriated by national governments for development purposes. If the Australian government had been willing to ratify and comply with Convention 107 – which in 1957 and right up through Eddie Mabo's time it certainly was not – there might have been no need for the *Mabo* case. Still, the inclusion of recognition of Aboriginal land rights in this addition to formal international law shows which way the wind was blowing.

In 1966, the year before Australia had its referendum on removing those negative provisions about 'aboriginal natives' from its Constitution, the UN took an important step in giving a more concrete expression to the standards broadly set out in the Universal Declaration of Human Rights. It adopted two covenants, one on civil and political rights and the other on economic, social, and cultural rights. Both covenants in their first article recognize the right of 'all peoples' to self-determination. The conventions give some content to this right. By virtue of the right to self-determination, peoples have the right 'to freely determine their political status and freely pursue their economic, cultural and social development.'[68] But, other than that, both covenants are written in terms that confer rights on individuals rather than groups. Even so, many so-called individual rights are only meaningful when they can be enjoyed in groups – freedom of religion and freedom of association are obvious examples.[69] In these UN covenants the one section that could clearly be helpful to the group rights of Indigenous peoples is Article 27 on minority rights. It provides that 'in those States in which ethnic, religious or linguistic minorities exist, persons belonging to such minorities shall not be denied the right, in community with the other members of the group, to enjoy their own culture, to profess and practise their own religion, or to use their language.' Though Aboriginal peoples are adverse to being lumped in with all other ethnic or cultural minorities in a state, this article turns out later on to be of some value to them. Similarly, numerous references to the principle of non-discrimination in the covenants are also relevant to Indigenous peoples, who, as we have seen, suffered gross discrimination in the settler democracies, as is the Convention on Elimination of All Forms of Racial Discrimination adopted at the UN a year before the covenants.

Mere adoption of these documents by the United Nations General Assembly does not give their fine-sounding principles any immediate application. UN covenants and conventions, unlike UN declarations, are considered by international lawyers to have the status of treaties for countries that agree to ratify them. According to international lawyers, human rights principles in these documents 'may acquire the status of customary law and become binding on States, even where a State is not a party to a particular treaty.'[70] But in this international context, legal magic loses much of its potency even for states strongly committed to 'the rule of law.' The 'binding' quality of international human rights norms within any state will depend on whether they are in tune with powerful currents of opinion in the country. When Australia ratified the UN Convention on the Elimination of Racial Discrimination in 1975, the Commonwealth Parliament passed the *Racial Discrimination Act, 1975*. We have already had a glimpse in chapter 3 of how crucial this legislation turned out to be for Eddie Mabo's judicial victory. The point is not that, by 1975, all Australians were united in firmly rejecting all forms of racial discrimination. Human rights issues in democratic societies are always contentious.[71] But by 1975 enough opinion leaders and politicians on both sides of politics in Australia were strongly enough committed to the elimination of racial discrimination to use the UN convention as an occasion for enacting national legislation giving effect to its principle.

The same situation did not pertain with the other UN convention that has particular relevance for Indigenous peoples – the Convention on Civil and Political Rights (CCPR). Although the convention had been open for signing since 1966, not enough states had signed on for it to come into force until 1976. The Whitlam Labor government – which, as we saw in chapter 2, had sponsored the *Racial Discrimination Act* – also introduced a Human Rights Bill to prepare Australia for ratification of CCPR at the UN. But when the Liberal/Country Party led by Malcolm Fraser defeated Gough Whitlam and took power in Canberra at the end of 1975, it proceeded more cautiously. The Liberal/Country (now Liberal/National) Coalition traditionally has been much more attached than Labor to states' rights and maintaining federalism. Moreover, in Australia there was certainly no national consensus on the desirability of codifying fundamental rights in a constitutional bill of rights.[72] While the Fraser government was prepared to introduce legislation as a prelude to Australia's signing CCPR, its Human Rights Commission Bill, unlike the *Racial Discrimination Act* and Labor's proposed Human Rights Bill, did not establish enforceable rights and would not be binding on the states.[73] For this reason it ran into difficulty in the Senate, where the government did not have a majority, and failed to pass. The Fraser government went ahead anyway and ratified the Covenant on Political and Civil Rights in August 1980 – without enacting any corresponding domestic legislation.

Neither the Fraser government nor Labor when it came back into power in 1983 was willing to take the further step of signing CCPR's Optional Protocol. It is only when a state signs this protocol that its citizens are allowed to bring complaints about their government's violation of the convention before the UN's Human Rights Committee. When this committee finds that a country is guilty of a violation, it can only issue an adverse report and recommend remedial action. So this is by no means a strong or reliable kind of international sanctioning. Still, in the right circumstances, it may have some effect. After the Supreme Court of Canada rejected a challenge to the discriminatory provisions in Canada's *Indian Act* that denied Indian status to native women who married non-native men, Sandra Lovelace took her case to Geneva for a hearing before Human Rights Committee. The committee's finding that Canada's legislation was a breech of its obligations under the Covenant on Civil and Political Rights was a key factor in Canada's removing this discriminatory provision.[74] Not until 1991, when Australia finally signed the Optional Protocol, did its Indigenous citizens have access to this international form of redress.[75]

In an increasingly globalized world, it remains to be seen how effective these formal instruments of international human rights law can become for individuals or groups who suffer gross injustice at the hands of their governments. But back in 1960, when Australia was at the turning point in finally admitting Aborigines and Torres Strait Islanders to full citizenship, it was international influence of a much more informal nature that really counted. By the 1960s a popular political consensus was developing that, in the postwar international environment, Australia could not make its way in the world as White Australia. That much of its founding myth had to go.

The 1967 Referendum and the Limits of Civil Rights

On 27 May 1967, the Australian people voted overwhelmingly to remove those two negative clauses about aboriginal natives that were in their founding Constitution. The vote in favour of removing the words in Section 51 (xxvi) that barred the Commonwealth from making laws in relation to 'the aboriginal race' and repealing altogether Section 127, which excluded 'aboriginal natives' from the census, was 90.77 per cent. There were huge majorities in every state, ranging from 94.68 per cent in Victoria to 80.95 per cent in Western Australia.[76] This vote was an extraordinary outcome. The Australian Constitution can only be amended by popular referendum in which all qualified voters must vote and in which a positive result requires a national majority in favour as well as majorities in a majority (i.e., four of six) of states. The Australian people have been very conservative in exercising their power over formal constitutional change. Over the century since the Commonwealth's founding, they have rejected all but eight of the thirty-four referendums presented to them – including, most recently, a 1999 proposal to make Australia a republic. Of those few that have carried, none has come close to the approval level of 1967.[77] Never before or since has there appeared to be such accord among Australians on a constitutional matter as in removing these negative references to Indigenous Australians.

The 1967 referendum was unquestionably a symbolic event of major importance in Australian history. But there is no consensus in understanding the event's meaning to match that recorded in the bare result of the referendum. For many non-native Australians, the 1967 referendum marks the time when Aborigines and Torres Strait Islanders were granted full citizenship. And for many who view it this way, it was the one and only reform that need be made to render justice to Australian natives – aboriginal Australians would now have the right to be Australians like everyone else. But for many, perhaps most, Aborigines and Torres Strait Islanders and for a growing number of non-natives on the left side of politics, it was only the culmination of the first stage in the political struggle to obtain justice in settler-native relations.[78] These conflicting understandings of the 1967 referendum remain a barrier to genuine reconciliation in Australia.

The official pamphlet put out by the 'yes' side in the referendum campaign emphasized Australia's concern for its 'international reputation in a world in which racial issues are being highlighted every day.'[79] By the 1960s a global audience made possible by television could view the latest developments in the struggle against Apartheid in South Africa and the campaign in the United States for the civil rights of black Americans. In such a world, exposure of the racist provisions in Australia's Constitution was bad international public relations. So was Australia's racially discriminatory immigration policy. The year before the referendum, when Robert Menzies was succeeded as prime minister by the more liberal Harold Holt, the 'White Australia' immigration policy was overhauled.[80] Selected non-European immigrants with skills needed for the Australian economy could now become Australians. However, the government was careful to explain that 'the basic aim of preserving a homogeneous population will be maintained.'[81] Mainstream opinion in Australia was far from embracing the vision of a pluralist, multicultural, or multiracial society. It is one thing to support the removal of barriers preventing any group of citizens from enjoying the same rights as all Australians. It is quite another to conceive of a group of citizens – even one that has been there for more than 50,000 years – permanently forming a distinct part of the country with its own rights and identity.

Assimilation was the basic domestic policy objective of the Liberal/ Country Coalition government in sponsoring the referendum proposal. In 1964, when Arthur Calwell, leader of the opposition Labor Party, proposed a constitutional amendment identical to the one that was later adopted, Prime Minister Menzies agreed to support only the removal of Section 127, which excluded aboriginal natives from the census. For Menzies, full assimilation of Indigenous Australians meant dropping any reference to them as a group for whom special legislation could be passed. 'The best protection for Aborigines,' he argued, 'is to treat them, for all purposes, as Australian citizens.'[82] He and his government had no desire to take over from the states responsibility for aboriginal affairs. On the contrary, aboriginal Australians should simply disappear as a special category of the population. Thus, Menzies's proposal for amending the Constitution would remove Section 127, the census clause, but would leave Section 51 (xxvi) as is. However, once Holt took over, the Cabinet was persuaded to support the broader proposal favoured by the Labor Party. So the referendum proposal that the Holt government finally put to Parliament in 1967 included removal of the ban against Commonwealth legislation relating to 'the aboriginal race.'

The Holt government's aim in removing these words from Section 51 (xxvi) was not to empower the Commonwealth to take a lead role in aboriginal affairs. Quite to the contrary, the government's decision was based on 'a Cabinet agreement that the administration of Aboriginal affairs would remain in the hands of the States.'[83] But the government could see that a popular civil rights movement was painting exclusion of aboriginals from the Commonwealth's 'race power' as racially discrimi- natory. It was essentially to avoid accusations of race discrimination and build a stronger base of political support for its constitutional initiative that the Holt government adopted the full proposal favoured by Labor. Holt's change was crucial in improving the prospects of the constitutional proposal: in Australian constitutional politics, a proposal supported by only one side of politics has virtually no hope of carrying.[84]

The public sentiment that the Holt government had to take seriously was mobilized by a strong grassroots political campaign centred in the eastern part of the country. The central organization spear-heading this campaign was the Federal Council for the Advancement of Aborigines and Torres Strait Islanders. FCAATSI was broader and more representative than the Aboriginal 'advancement' organizations that preceded it. It was the first political organization to bring Aborigines and Torres Strait Islanders together in a common political cause. It was through a local branch of FCAATSI that Eddie Mabo first became involved in aboriginal politics. Unlike the Federal Council for the Advancement of Aborigines (FCAA), which FCAATSI replaced in 1964, it was not dominated by Europeans.[85]

FCAATSI and the organizations folded into it helped develop a new generation of aboriginal political activists and linked them to an array of influential white organizations, including unions, churches, and civil liberties associations. The political techniques employed by organizations working under the FCAASTI umbrella reached a new level of sophistication, especially in the use of the media. On occasion, the Australian campaign adopted tactics of the civil rights campaign that was going on simultaneously in the United States. In 1965 a young Charles Perkins, on his way to becoming one of Australia's most prominent aboriginal leaders, set out on a Freedom Ride in a bus with '29 nervous white students aboard.'[86] The Freedom Ride made its way up through the country towns of northwest New South Wales, where an informal system of racial segregation had been in place for generations.

The message, as well as the methods, of the 'yes' side in the referendum was similar to that of the American Civil Rights movement. Equal rights for all was its clarion call. Here, for instance, is the jingle the Vote Yes Committee prepared for broadcast on commercial radio a week before the vote:

Vote 'Yes' for Aborigines, they want to be Australians too,
Vote 'Yes' for Aborigines to give them rights and freedoms just like me and you,
Vote 'Yes' for Aborigines, all parties say they think you should,
Vote 'Yes' and show the world the true Australian brotherhood.[87]

This focus on the fundamentally assimilationist ideal of aboriginal Australians enjoying exactly the same rights – and no more – as all other Australians undoubtedly accounted for the 'yes' campaign's broad popular appeal. It invited white Australians, at just the right time in their history, to extend the strong egalitarian streak in their social and political culture to black Australians. But the very success of this appeal was misleading in two senses.

First, the campaign's civil rights focus suggested that equal rights with other Australians was all that Indigenous Australians were seeking. This impression was very much in error. All along, from their earliest forms of organized political action, aboriginal Australians, like Indigenous peoples almost everywhere, had made it clear that they did not want to be discriminated against in their own country. They wanted, and still want, removal of formal and structural barriers that prevent them from enjoying the political freedoms, social benefits, and economic opportunities available to other citizens. But that is not all they want. Removal of these discriminatory barriers is a very large part of the integrationist part of the aboriginal political agenda. But if this is the only reform on offer to Indigenous peoples, and the non-native population is unwilling to address the autonomy side of the Indigenous agenda, then what could be conditions for integration become, in effect, instruments of assimilation. Aboriginal people are then being told that 'yes, you can enjoy the full rights of citizens, providing you give up any rights to what you deem necessary to maintaining the historical societies with which you identify.' Such an offer may well be satisfactory for some individuals of aboriginal ancestry, but it is not enough for a great many Indigenous people, including those who represent them in politics. Certainly, those Aborigines and Torres Strait Islanders who were actively involved in the referendum campaign, including – most emphatically – Eddie Mabo, were not interested in such a Faustian bargain.

All through this period, land rights were central to the autonomy part of the aboriginal agenda. One of Heather Goodall's major achievements as a historian of aboriginal politics in Australia is to show how, even in New South Wales, where most Aborigines had been pushed away from their traditional country, Aboriginal leaders continued to claim an aboriginal right to land. Pearl Gibbs, Bert Grove, and other Aboriginal leaders insisted that the constitution of the Federal Council for Aboriginal Advancement drop any mention of assimilation and give as much emphasis to 'the retention of all remaining native reserves, with native communal title or individual ownership,' as to equality and full citizen's rights.[88] Addressing a National Aborigines Day rally in Sydney in 1964, Joyce Mercy, an Aboriginal woman from the Bandjalang area, emphasized land rights. Reminding the crowd of Australia's attachment to the doctrine of *terra nullius*, she told the crowd that 'Australia is the only country in the world which does not recognize that its Indigenous people have a right to land.'[89]

If land rights were integral to the aspirations of Aborigines in the more developed parts of Australia, they surely were the central concern of Indigenous peoples in the northern and central parts of Australia, so many of whom were still living in their traditional country. This point was brought dramatically to the attention of Australians in 1963, when the Yolngu people of Arnhem's Land sent their petition in the form of a traditional bark painting to the Commonwealth Parliament.[90] The importance of land to aboriginal peoples extends much beyond its economic value. Their attachment and responsibility to land is fundamental to their spiritual life. That is why recognition of that connection in the civic culture of their country is crucial to their collective survival as peoples. The focus on equal rights by the broad-based alliance that conducted the 1967 referendum campaign meant that much of non-native Australia was ill-prepared for the land rights campaign that followed.

The referendum campaign's civil liberties focus was misleading in a second way. It created the impression that the constitutional changes being voted on, in and of themselves, extended full citizen's rights to aboriginal Australians. The reality was very different. The constitutional changes approved in the referendum had little direct impact on the rights of Aborigines and Torres Strait Islanders. They merely meant that these Australians would now be included in the census and that the Commonwealth could pass laws relating to them. The latter change did not transfer responsibility for aboriginal affairs to the federal government. The states retained jurisdiction in the field and, until a Commonwealth government came to power with the will to take a lead in aboriginal policy, the states would remain the primary policy-makers. And as for civil rights, while, by the time of the referendum, some important rights of citizenship had been extended to all aboriginal Australians, many discriminatory racist practices remained in place.

One of the most widespread misconceptions about the 1967 referendum is that it gave aboriginal Australians the right to vote. In truth, by 1965 all legal barriers excluding Aborigines and Torres Strait from the right to vote – that quintessential right of citizenship in a democracy – had been removed. In 1962, after a lengthy parliamentary inquiry and amid fear that the disenfranchisement of native Australians was about to be raised in the United Nations General Assembly, the Commonwealth Parliament finally passed legislation enfranchising all aboriginal Australians at the federal level.[91] Later in the same year, Western Australia, one of the two states that banned Aborigines from voting at the state level, gave Aborigines the right to vote in state elections. In 1962 restrictions against aboriginal voters in the Northern Territory were also removed. Queensland was the last jurisdiction to extend the franchise to its aboriginal peoples. It finally made the move in 1965. Up to then, the only Indigenous 'citizens' who could vote in state elections were 'half-castes' not covered by Queensland's protection legislation. That meant that all the full-blood Aborigines and all of the Torres Strait Islanders, including those who served in the defence force in the Second World War, were denied the vote until 1965.

The other important civil rights objective achieved before the referendum was the granting of Commonwealth social welfare benefits to Indigenous Australians. The last discriminatory exclusions from social security legislation were not removed until 1965. Before this, in states that maintained protection regimes, aboriginal citizens' eligibility for national social security programs depended on their being exempted from protection and certified by the state as citizens, even though, according to Australian law, all aboriginal people were already citizens! Qualifying for state-recognized citizenship meant meeting an assimilationist standard. The criteria for a Certificate of Citizenship in Western Australia, for instance, were 'the dissolution of tribal associations, the adoption of the habits of 'civilized life' and the non-existence of certain diseases.'[92] In Victoria and Tasmania, states without exemptions from protection regimes, a director general would ascertain whether an aboriginal person's character, intelligence, and social development warranted a pension.

By the late 1960s, liberalizing winds of change were blowing away instruments of colonial oppression that had denied individual Aborigines and Torres Strait Islanders the rights and opportunities of Australian citizenship. But the decolonizing process had not yet come to grips with the more challenging part of the aboriginal political agenda – the collective right to equality of Australia's Indigenous peoples. It remained now for a vigorous land rights movement to push these issues to the fore and pave the way for Eddie Mabo's resort to the courts.

Part Three

BUILD-UP TO THE *MABO* CASE

CHAPTER 6

The Land Rights Movement

The quest for recognition of land rights is at the centre of the modern Indigenous peoples' movement. The denial by occupying states of Indigenous peoples' ownership of the lands and waters that supported them for generations is the root cause of the injustice these peoples have suffered. Endeavouring to overcome this injustice is what distinguishes the political movement of Indigenous peoples from that of any other group or minority within the world's nation-states. For Indigenous peoples, land rights subsume their right to self-determination. The collective self whose future they wish to determine derives its identity from a historical relationship with a particular place on the earth. Their right to self-determination, therefore, can be realized only when their right to decide how to live in that part of the earth and their responsibility to care for it are recognized.

Recognition of a people's proprietorship of the land they occupy and to which they have long had a sense of belonging has been understood as a principle of human justice since ancient times. It was a fundamental principle of Roman law,[1] and, as we saw earlier, it was drawn on by Christian theologians at the beginning of the Age of Discovery to advise European rulers, in the words of Franciscus de Vitoria, that as free and rational peoples, natives of the New World could not 'be despoiled of their properties on the grounds of them not being true owners.'[2] Similarly, the very first move by the community of nation-states after the Second World War to deal with justice for Indigenous peoples, the International Labour Organization's Convention 107, recognized 'the right of ownership, collective or individual, of the members of the populations concerned over the lands which these populations traditionally occupy.'[3] Though an Indigenous people's ownership of traditional country has important economic implications, it is also profoundly political. For the land they own as original occupants is their homeland – not a 'homeland' imposed on them by their colonial oppressors, as was done by the apartheid regime in South Africa, but that unique place on earth which gave birth to their society. Maintaining some control over what happens on a people's homeland is essential to those who continue to identify with that people no matter how far they may move or be removed from it. For Eddie Mabo, Mer remained the only place that was truly home.

For Torres Strait Islanders and Australian Aborigines, as for other Indigenous peoples around the world, asserting ownership of their lands and waters was nothing new. What was new in the land rights movement that got under way towards the end of the 1960s was the method used by Indigenous people to assert that ownership – to assert it as a 'right' and to seek recognition of this right by the colonizers' legal institutions. Indigenous peoples would now see whether they could use the white man's legal magic to begin to reverse their dispossession. Adoption of such a strategy had an ironic implication for Indigenous peoples. Implicitly, it meant conceding some legitimacy to the courts and legislatures established by the settler society. In a context where full citizenship in the political communities developed by the newcomers was at least formally available to native peoples and was accepted by many, such a concession was not an illogical development.

First Moves to Recognize Aboriginal Land Rights

Land rights were always front and centre in the political agenda of aboriginal Australians. That was evident in 1963, when the Yolngu people from the Yirrkala area of Cape Gove in 1963 submitted their 'bark petition' to the Australian Parliament in an effort to protect their land from development of a bauxite mine. When the Yolngu failed to achieve recognition of their land rights through direct political action, Milirrpum and others resorted to the courts, instigating Australia's first land rights case. Again, in 1966, when Aboriginal stockmen walked off the Wave Hill pastoral station in the Northern Territory, it was their land claim that quickly took precedence over their demand for equal pay.[4]

In claiming land and demanding recognition of land rights, aboriginal Australians were seeking more than permission to occupy parts of their traditional country. They already occupied significant tracts of land set aside by settler governments and reserved for native peoples – particularly in the Northern Territory, South Australia, Western Australia, and Queensland. Indeed, Australia compared rather well with other English-settler countries in terms of the amount of land that was reserved for the use and benefit of native peoples.[5] Also, most pastoral leases contained clauses granting Aborigines access to pastoral lands so long as they did not interfere with the grazers' activities. These vast areas of Australia were available to Aborigines and Torres Strait Islanders not because they were recognized as having rights to these lands but because the settlers did not yet have any use for them that was at odds with native occupancy. Indigenous inhabitants had no security that they could continue to live on these lands according to their own lights. The Aboriginal peoples of Cape Gove and Eddie Mabo's Murray Island people lived on 'reserves.' What they totally lacked was recognition of their unique relationship with these lands and any political or legal power to protect their interests in them.

Recognition of Indigenous Australians' original proprietorship of the land and the special rights which flow from that recognition was not on the agenda of the popular aboriginal reform movement that had swept to victory in the 1967 referendum campaign. Nor was it a policy objective of the Liberal/Country Party Coalition governments that were the first to have the opportunity of using the legislative power in aboriginal affairs that the Commonwealth had acquired as a result of the 1967 referendum. The Holt, Gorton, and McMahon governments did not view the 1967 referendum as creating a strong mandate for the Commonwealth to take a leadership role in aboriginal policy. Rather than establishing a new government department to take charge of aboriginal affairs, they set up a small secretariat, the Council for Aboriginal Affairs (CAA), to provide a central source of policy advice to the prime minister and to departments whose activities affected Indigenous Australians. Direct relations with native peoples, and management of the rural lands on which many of them still lived, would continue to be primarily the responsibility of the states.

The strong inclination of the politicians who led these Coalition governments was that any new initiatives in aboriginal affairs should be directed towards easing the integration of Aborigines and Torres Strait Islanders into the mainstream of Australian life and society. It was the persistence of Aborigines in pressing land rights, particularly in the Northern Territory where the Commonwealth had primary responsibility for both Aboriginal and resource development policy, that forced the central government to address the land rights issue. The Council for

Aboriginal Affairs, as the government's main source of policy advice, soon found itself deeply involved in responding to the Gurundji people, who had walked off the Vesteys pastoral station and who now claimed traditional land at Wattie Creek,[6] and the Yirrkala people as they argued their case before Justice Blackburn in the Federal Court in Darwin.

Blackburn rendered his decision on 27 April 1971, and, though its denial of native title and affirmation of *terra nullius* were a grave legal loss for the claimants, the decision had catalytic force in increasing attention to native land rights in mainstream politics. Much of the media coverage expressed shock and outrage at the brutal exposure of colonial doctrine in the *Milirrpum* decision. Opposition politicians became more vocal in their support for aboriginal land rights.[7] Building on this apparent shift in public sentiment, the government's in-house advisers, the Council for Aboriginal Affairs, was able to place before McMahon's Cabinet a number of proposals for responding positively to concerns raised by the *Milirrpum* decision.

The CAA was no ordinary collection of public officials. It was headed by Dr H.C. Coombs. 'Nugget' Coombs, as he was known to Australians – and Australians had come to know him well – was the outstanding public servant of Australia's first century. He had held major positions in economic and social policy, including serving as director general of postwar reconstruction from 1943 to 1948 and as governor of the Commonwealth Bank, Australia's chief central banker, from 1949 to 1968. During the time he chaired the Council for Aboriginal Affairs, he also chaired the Australian Council for the Arts and was pro-chancellor and chancellor of the Australian National University. Coombs's two principal colleagues at CAA were also remarkable individuals. Barrie Dexter was a career diplomat with a great deal of Third World experience in the decolonization era and a firm understanding of the international human rights standards emerging under the auspices of the United Nations. William Stanner was an anthropologist and public administrator with much first-hand exposure to the circumstances of colonized peoples in Africa, the South Pacific, and Australia's Northern Territory. From 1968 until the disbandonment of the CAA in 1976, this formidable troika, often assisted by Charles Rowley, up to that time Australia's leading scholar of the colonization of Indigenous peoples, had an influence on Australian aboriginal policy that went far beyond their numbers or legal status.

Coombs and his CAA colleagues spent as much time interacting with

Indigenous communities as they did in Canberra. In effect, they were functioning as mediators between an emerging movement of aboriginal peoples and the Australian government. Though they did not have a single or fixed theory of how relations with Indigenous peoples should develop, they were much more open than their political masters to the possibility that integration should not and need not require the extinction of distinct Indigenous societies. When Stanner, in his 'After the Dreaming' Boyer lectures delivered on ABC radio in 1968, said that he found in Aboriginal actions 'an implicit offer of some sort of union of lives with us, and an implicit appeal for a new identity within the union,'[8] he summarized as succinctly as possible the common vision of Coombs and company. Even such a modest accommodation of the Indigenous desire for collective survival was highly contentious in Australia at this time. Prime Minister McMahon told the state ministers of aboriginal affairs assembled at Cairns in April 1971 that he believed Indigenous Australians should be assisted either as individuals or as groups 'to preserve and develop their culture – their languages, traditions and arts.' When Dexter repeated this theme in a public address, editorialists claimed it meant that the Commonwealth government 'did not believe in the integration or assimilation of Aborigines into the rest of the community.'[9]

So far as land rights were concerned, the furthest the Coalition government could be pushed by the CAA was to permit Aboriginal groups to lease portions of reserve lands. Coombs pressed hard for making traditional association with land a ground for granting a lease. For Peter Howson, who had replaced Billy Wentworth as minister in charge of aboriginal affairs in May 1971, this policy smacked too much of separate development. Thus, when McMahon announced the government's 'land rights' policy in his 26 January 1972 Australia Day statement, he made it clear that leases would be available to Northern Territory Aborigines not as a right, nor on the basis of traditional association, but where a group could show the intention and ability to make reasonable economic and social use of the land.[10] The Yolngu people would receive royalties from bauxite mining, but only at a trivial rate, and a small fund would be available to purchase land as it became available.

McMahon's statement, coming as it did on the anniversary of Britain's claim of sovereignty over Australia, was a red flag to Indigenous activists. On the night of January 25, a group of Sydney-based Aborigines, in a car organized by Communist Party supporters, drove to Canberra and, with a beach umbrella and some plastic, erected an 'Aboriginal Embassy' on the lawns of Parliament House. The Tent Embassy, as it came to be called, was and is a remarkable symbol of the determination of Indigenous Australians to assert their identity as distinct peoples. Land rights were very much at the centre of this symbolic protest. The placards held by protestors as dawn broke on January 26 read:

Land Rights Now or Else

Legally This Land Is Our Land

We Shall Take It if Need Be

Land Now Not Lease Tomorrow[11]

The small band of protestors from Sydney and Canberra who erected the Tent Embassy were soon joined by Aborigines from other parts of the country.[12] A group from the Australian National University rallied to its support. Within a day or two, the demonstrators had virtually taken over the lawns of Parliament House. The Tent Embassy was a brilliant piece of political theatre. It had the colour, the element of surprise, and the threat of violence that are tailor-made for the age of television. It quickly attracted national and international attention to land and other issues being raised by aboriginal Australians. Tourists, foreign correspondents, and diplomats began to drop in. So did many non-Indigenous Australians, including members of the opposition Australian Labor Party. A number of ALP members signed a petition promising to physically defend the tents.

CAA staff also spent time with embassy members. When Nugget Coombs visited the tents, he was reported as expressing 'complete sympathy' with the demands of the protestors. These demands, though vague in detail, called for a stronger form of Indigenous tenure than McMahon's Australia Day statement offered. The Tent Embassy was also a vivid demonstration that recovering *terra nullius* is a common cause both of urban-based aboriginal activists and members of more traditional Indigenous societies. Coombs and his colleagues had seriously underestimated the importance of land rights to the descendants of Aborigines who had suffered massive dispossession in the southeast part of the country. The embassy activists, as Tim Rowse observes, 'were showing that they wanted from government something more than programs that eased and accelerated their urbanization.'[13]

The McMahon government was flummoxed. It was not prepared to develop a stronger land rights policy, but feared the violence likely to result from any attempt to forcibly remove the Tent Embassy. Finally, after six months of continuous demonstration, the government threatened to bring in a new ordinance empowering police to remove the embassy. On July 18, when a phalanx of 150 police marching as a paramilitary force advanced towards the tents, they were confronted by a wall of protestors linking arms and singing the protest anthem 'We shall overcome.'[14] A violent brawl ensued. The Tent Embassy came down. Five days later protestors marched through Canberra and put it up once more. Another violent brawl ensued as the police tore it down again. On July 30 the largest crowd yet, estimated at 2000 Aboriginal people and supporters, marched through the city and formed a circle around a re-erected tent. This time, through the intervention of Professor Hal Wootten, the embassy came down peacefully, but not before a day of powerful non-violent protest. On September 12 the Tent Embassy was erected once more, this fourth time for good, after Justice Blackburn – the very judge who had decided the provocative *Milirrpum* case – found technical legal difficulties in the government's removal ordinance.

Erection of the Tent Embassy on the lawns of Parliament House was more than a symbolic victory. After a meeting with Aboriginal representatives in the embassy, opposition leader Gough Whitlam committed his party to a policy of 'self-determination.'[15] During the ensuing parliamentary debate, Whitlam called for the establishment of a commission to consider land rights 'for the whole Commonwealth ... not just the Northern Territory.'[16] Two months after the final re-erection of the embassy, Whitlam's Labor Party defeated the Coalition in a general election. Though Indigenous land rights were not a central issue in the election, the McMahon government's ineptitude in responding to the Tent Embassy likely contributed to its defeat. Whitlam would soon move to establish a land rights commission. Although its terms of reference were not as broad as promised and the legislatively created land rights resulting from it were a far cry from the recognition of original proprietorship sought by Eddie Mabo and others, the Whitlam government's initiative demonstrated the influence that Indigenous Australians were coming to have on democratic politics in Australia. Though less than 2 per cent of the population, they could, through dramatic and inventive political action, capture sufficient national and international attention to get their drive to recover *terra nullius* on the country's political agenda.

Some progress by Aborigines in recovering land had been made through changes in state policies even before the Whitlam government launched its land rights initiatives. Australia's first land rights legislation was introduced in 1966 in South Australia – the only Australian colony which, in its founding, had been committed to the principle that had guided British practice in North America: that land occupied and possessed by Indigenous natives should not be sold to settlers until ceded to the Crown. Moreover, a portion of ceded lands was to be reserved for the use of Aborigines. Don Dunston, the Labor minister of aboriginal affairs who was soon to become state premier, acknowledged that these commitments had never been honoured.[17] His government's *Aboriginal Lands Trust Act, 1966* would provide 'some form of possible compensation' and recognition that Aborigines had 'come to know, understand, and in many cases to accept the attitudes of the European community as to proprietory rights in land.'[18] Under the act, a trust composed of Aboriginal persons working with a non-Aboriginal adviser would assume control over unoccupied reserve lands and occupied reserves whose residents wanted their lands to be held by the trust. The trust, with a minister's consent, could sell or lease lands and use funds to make loans to Aborigines for developing trust lands. In 1970 Victoria's *Aboriginal Lands Act* went a little further in granting communal freehold title over reserves at Lake Tyers and Framlingham to trusts made up of Aboriginal residents. Under this title, while individual members held trust shares, no shares could be sold if any one member objected.[19] This policy followed a dramatic march a few years earlier by Lake Tyers residents to the state Parliament in Melbourne demanding the right to keep their reserve. In New South Wales a much larger statewide Aboriginal organization had, by 1970, formed a Land and Rights Council. The Tent Embassy, which had its organizational roots in this council, at least moved the New South Wales government to rename the state's Aboriginal Advisory Council the 'Lands Trust,' although without giving that body more powers or land.[20]

Even these very modest developments in the south and east went beyond what state governments could contemplate in the north and west, where the majority of Indigenous Australians lived and where the largest areas of land were still occupied by their original owners. In 1972 Western Australia established an Aboriginal Affairs Planning Authority to administer reserve lands held in trust for Aborigines, but it made no move towards devolving control or ownership to the residents themselves. As for Queensland, the state where Eddie Mabo would have to

subject to treaty. This plan led to the resumption of the treaty process and Canada's first modern treaty, the James Bay and Northern Quebec Agreement of 1975.

All these situations involved a profound clash of civilizations. The relentless drive of Western European societies for energy to fuel their appetite for ever higher levels of material comfort and prosperity brought their industrial and governmental emissaries into conflict with peoples whose natural environment was still understood as part of their own identity and not a commodity to be exploited dangerously for their own benefit or the benefit of faraway peoples. In days gone by – during the high tide of Western imperialism – the conflict would have been swiftly resolved. The industrialized Europeans would quickly have their way, making few, if any, concessions to the natives. Now the situation was somewhat different – not in terms of raw power but in moral outlook and political capacity. On the European side, by the 1970s there was enough acknowledgment of universal human rights among elites in these liberal democracies to challenge industrial projects that totally ignored rights claimed by native peoples. It was a liberally minded secretary of the interior in the Johnson administration in the United States, Stewart Udall, who froze Alaskan land concessions to the oil companies until native claims were settled. Udall was supported by a growing body of opinion among legislators in Alaska and Washington that Congress had a moral obligation to settle native claims. That view led to the 1971 Alaska settlement.[28] In Canada a small social democratic party used its bargaining power in the Canadian Parliament to have Thomas Berger, one of its former provincial leaders and the lawyer who had represented the Nisga'a Indians in the *Calder* case, appointed to conduct the Commission of Inquiry into the Mackenzie Valley pipeline proposal.[29] The groundwork for the James Bay and Northern Quebec Agreement was laid by the decision of a centrist Liberal government in Ottawa, supported by opposition parties on both the right and the left, to set up a comprehensive land claims process in response to the recognition of unextinguished Aboriginal title by three Supreme Court judges in *Calder*.[30]

On the Aboriginal side, important changes were occurring in political techniques and capabilities. By the 1960s, Indigenous peoples in North America, as in Australia, were showing an increasing inclination to defend their interests through the white man's courts and European-style political organizations. Following the US Supreme Court's rejection of Alaskan natives' claim to proprietory land rights in the 1955 *Tee-Hot-*

Ton Indians case, a federation of Alaskan natives lobbied at the state and national levels for the resolution of land claims as a pre-condition for further development of petroleum resources.[31] Through their response to the Berger Inquiry, the native communities scattered over a huge area in the Mackenzie Valley came together to represent themselves as the Dene Nation. In Quebec, the James Bay Cree and the Northern Quebec Inuit Association went to court to stop the province's hydroelectric project.[32] Although their court action obtained only a temporary injunction, the highly visible court proceedings, theatrical evenings, and demonstrations in Montreal, Quebec City, and Ottawa built significant public support for negotiating a settlement with Quebec's northern natives.[33]

These changes in moral sentiment on the European side and in political capacity on the Aboriginal side have meant that energy megaprojects in North America must make some accommodation with claims of the traditional owners of the lands affected. These accommodations implicitly recognize, if not native title, at least a special native interest in the lands and waters on which the projects are to take place. But the very process of reaching an accommodation has the effect of increasing the integration of the native peoples concerned into the predominant culture of the nation-states in which they find themselves embedded. And the settlements themselves have resulted in the extinguishment or ignoring of Aboriginal title. This outcome was most evident in the United States, where the ideology of individualistic capitalism is a defining feature of the national culture. The *Alaska Native Claims Settlement*, with its grant to natives of 44 million acres of land (about 10 per cent of Alaska's territory) and just under a billion dollars, was the largest settlement in settler history. In return, Indigenous Alaskans gave up Aboriginal title to land and Aboriginal rights to hunt and fish on their lands. Under the settlement, they became individual shareholders in village and regional corporations in which ownership of these acres was vested.[34]

In Canada, integration was becoming less assimilationist. Through the Berger Inquiry, Canadians became aware that development of the vast northern hinterland of their country could proceed only in partnership with the native peoples who were its dominant population. Berger proposed no quick fix. His report focused on the need for an approach to economic development in the North that concentrated on non-renewable resources and the long-term economic security of its permanent residents.[35] The Canadian government accepted his recommendation for a ten-year moratorium on building a Mackenzie Valley pipeline to give time to settle native claims and establish 'the new institutions and programs that will form the basis for native self-determination.'[36] The Inuvialuit and Dene peoples began to organize for negotiating land claims agreements with the government, albeit a government that was still insisting on extinguishment of native title as a condition of settlement. The James Bay and Northern Quebec Agreement did exactly that – it extinguished the Cree's and the Inuit's Aboriginal rights in return for statutory rights to small parcels of land, limited hunting and fishing rights, and an income support system for trappers.[37] Nonetheless, the recognition the Grand Council of the Crees and the Northern Quebec Inuit Association gained through their engagement in these negotiations enabled them to emerge as the dominant political organizations in their regions of Quebec.

In Australia, Justice Woodward, like his Canadian counterpart Thomas Berger, was determined that his inquiry should be informed by the concerns and aspirations of the Aboriginal people. Like Berger, who had represented the Nisga'a in the *Calder* case, Woodward, as legal counsel for Milirrpum and other Yolngu people in the Cape Gove case, had learned a good deal about the traditional relationship of native people to their land and the impact of industrial development on native societies. He knew how difficult it would be to find the instruments through which the views of traditional land owners could be authentically expressed. The very concept of 'owning land' was alien to the culture of Aboriginal peoples in the Northern Territory.[38] Moreover, there were no counterparts to the organizations built by the Dene, Métis, and Inuvialuit peoples in Canada's Northwest Territories to make their submissions to the Berger Inquiry.[39] Accordingly, Woodward proposed that the state create the institutions through which Aboriginal interests would be heard. His First Report, submitted in July 1973 just five months after his appointment, called for the immediate establishment of land councils through which Aboriginal people could make their views known. The Commonwealth government complied by setting up two councils, the Northern Land Council, based in Darwin, to represent communities in the northern half of the territory, and the Central Land Council, based in Alice Springs, to represent the remainder.

The two land councils became the instruments through which Woodward consulted with Aboriginal people in the Northern Territory on how best to recognize and establish their traditional rights and interests in relation to land. The councils received funds from the Commonwealth to hire administrative staff, lawyers, and anthropologists. In principle, the councils were to be composed of Aborigines chosen by communities across each region. But in practice, particularly at the beginning, it was difficult to locate, and then recruit, individuals who could represent their people. As with land ownership, the very idea of representative government had no place in the organization of Aboriginal society. The land councils came in for a great deal of criticism, especially from missionaries and anthropologists with long periods of residency in the Northern Territory, as being overly centralized and inauthentic.[40] Woodward himself admitted that he had underestimated the importance of clan and dialect affiliations within communities.[41] But the critics offered no alternative means of enabling Aborigines to be effective in engaging politically with the large governmental and industrial forces that had both the will and the power to determine the fate of the Aborigines' country. In any event, Woodward relied heavily on the councils to inform him of the Aboriginal viewpoint, not just through the council membership but also by their visiting 'some fifty different communities.'[42] The land councils had a central role both in the legislative scheme that he recommended to government and in the legislation that eventually resulted from his recommendations.

Woodward's Second Report, containing his substantive proposals on land rights, came less than a year after his First Report. Rather than recording views about land actually held by Aborigines across the Territory, the report reflected more the work of the land councils' non-native staff who, in effect, were acting as mediators between the state and the Aborigines. Even so, as Kenneth Maddock observes, this does not mean that the product was 'a travesty of Aboriginal wishes.'[43] In terms of giving Aborigines – or, more accurately, institutions designed to represent Aborigines' interests – control over land, the report's principal recommendations were revolutionary in the Australian context, and extremely generous by any international comparison. Ownership of all reserve lands in the Northern Territory – except for those within Darwin's municipal boundaries, some cattle stations already owned by Aboriginal corporations, and some wildlife sanctuaries – was to be vested in Aboriginal land trusts. In addition, Woodward recommended establishing a land commission to hear claims based on traditional ownership to unalienated Crown lands and to recommend other measures to 'satisfy the land needs of Aboriginal people.'[44]

The general principles set out in Woodward's report – principles that applied to Indigenous relations throughout the country – were as important as its detailed proposals on land rights in the Northern Territory. These principles stemmed, in part, from his critical appraisal of the treatment of land rights in North America, rights he learned about in a brief visit to Canada and the United States in late 1973. He was particularly critical of the U.S. Indian Claims Commission, which was designed to get rid of land claims by paying Indians cash for past dispossession.[45] A paragraph of his report written in italics to underline its importance stated: 'Cash compensation in the pockets of this generation of Aborigines is no answer to the legitimate land claims of a people with a distinct past who want to maintain their separate identity in the future.'[46] The most appropriate recompense for those who have lost their traditional land was other land, and funds to use that land for the native society's purposes. Woodward was opposed to an aboriginal policy that had as its overriding goal the disappearance of native peoples as distinct societies. At the same time, he opposed 'non-Aboriginal enthusiasts' who wanted to freeze aboriginal societies in the past. Aborigines, he wrote, 'should be free to choose their own manner of living.'[47] Choice and consent were touchstones of his report. He stressed the importance of affording Aboriginal communities as much autonomy as possible and not forcing them to adopt forms of political organizations alien to their tradition. In the summary, which he addressed to the Aboriginal people, he said there should be no new mining on Aboriginal land for over two years and, even then, only if the owners of the land and other Aborigines want it. But then, cognizant of the looming issue of uranium mining, he added the telling words 'or if the Government says it is very important for Australia.'[48] Clearly, the new energy frontier set limits even to Woodward's support for Indigenous autonomy.

The Commonwealth's First Land Rights Legislation

Woodward's Second Report was well received by the Whitlam government, which had won a second election in 1974. The governor general's speech opening the parliamentary session that followed the election accepted Woodward's recommendations and promised to give legislative effect to them. Second reading of the Aboriginal Land Rights (Northern Territory) Bill began in the House of Representatives on 16 October 1975. But Labor's bill was not enacted. In November 1975 a crisis arose over the opposition's blockage of supply in the Senate, and Governor General Kerr decided to resolve the crisis by replacing Prime Minister Whitlam with the opposition leader, Malcolm Fraser. Fraser's Liberal/National Country Party Coalition won the ensuing election and introduced its own version of the Northern Territory land rights legislation. It was this bill that was passed into law at the end of 1976.

The fact that the Commonwealth's first land rights legislation was enacted by a Coalition government meant that, by this time, even the right side of politics in Australia had moved away from a total commitment to assimilation and could support at least a limited recognition of the unique rights of Indigenous peoples. Indeed, earlier in 1975, all parties had accepted a motion by Neville Bonner, a Liberal senator and the first Indigenous person to be elected to the Australian Parliament, to the effect that Aborigines and Torres Strait Islanders 'were in possession of this entire nation prior to the 1788 First Fleet landing at Botany Bay.'[49] *Terra nullius* was beginning to be nudged in the Australian mainstream. Still, the Fraser government's legislation departed in significant ways from Labor's bill and was bitterly attacked by Labor. Les Johnson, who had introduced Labor's bill and was now opposition spokesman on aboriginal affairs, called the Coalition's bill 'a cynical sell-out to the National Country Party and other vested interests in the Northern Territory.'[50]

Labor's attack on the revised bill focused on three points. First, the legislation now gave the Northern Territory the lead role in protecting sacred sites and controlling access to Aboriginal lands and to the sea adjoining these lands. The fact that territorial ordinances would have to be consistent with any Commonwealth legislation on these subjects[51] was little consolation to Labor or others who took aboriginal rights seriously. The non-native majority in the Northern Territory Assembly was hardly a credible first line of defence for protecting native interests. Second, there was some reduction in the functions of the land councils, especially with respect to making representations on expenditure priorities. Third, and somewhat ironically, the Fraser government's legislation did not provide for the consideration of land claims based on need. One might have thought that politicians who had been the keenest assimilationists would not have been so insistent that claims must be based on traditional connections with the land. The omission of claims based on need was a serious blow to the thousand or so Aborigines from different parts of the territory who had come to live on the outskirts of Alice Springs. These fringe-dwellers, with the help of the Central Land Council, were in the process of submitting a needs-based claim to Justice Ward, who had been appointed interim land commissioner when Labor's legislation was still before Parliament.[52]

Despite Labor's criticisms, the Northern Territory land rights legislation that emerged from the Commonwealth Parliament in 1976 must be seen as a major step forward in recovering *terra nullius*. To enact it, Prime Minister Fraser and his aboriginal affairs minister, Ian Viner, had to override resistance in their own caucus and a national campaign led by Dr Goff Letts, the majority leader in the Northern Territory Assembly, which aimed to gut Labor's bill. The act enabled Aborigines to secure recognition, in terms of the white man's law, of their ownership of much of the Territory. It did so in two ways. First, as Woodward had recommended, it provided for the immediate transfer to Aboriginal ownership of the lands set aside under past protection policy for the use and benefit of Aborigines. Under this provision, reserves and mission leases adding up to 256,680 square kilometres of land would soon be owned by Aboriginal trusts.[53] Second, again following Woodward, the act established a process through which 'traditional Aboriginal owners' could try to recover traditional lands by submitting claims to a land commissioner. Such claims could not apply to lands within town boundaries but only to unalienated Crown lands, unless it was land – for instance, a pastoral property – that had been purchased by or on behalf of Aborigines. By 1982, through these two processes, Aborigines were recognized as the owners of 28.32 per cent of the Northern Territory. Another 18.35 per cent was under pending claims.[54]

The legislation was much less respectful of Woodward's commitment to Aboriginal autonomy than to his proposals for land ownership. To take advantage of the procedures for recovering some security of ownership over their lands, Aborigines had to operate within a convoluted and alien institutional structure. At the top of this structure was the government in Canberra, acting through its minister of aboriginal affairs. It was this minister who would decide whether a recommendation of the land commissioner to return land to its traditional owners should be honoured and who established and appointed the members of the land trusts in which Aboriginal ownership was vested. Again, it was the minister who had the power to establish the land councils, which in turn controlled what the land trusts (i.e., the Aboriginal owners) could do with their land. Land council members, like members of land trusts, had to be Aborigines, but the minister would have to approve their method of selection. The Central and Northern land councils that had been created before the act came into effect continued. A third was added in 1978, when the Tiwi Land Council was created for Bathurst and Melville Islands. It was the function of the councils 'to ascertain and express the wishes and the opinion of Aborigines' living in the council's area on both the management and the protection of their lands.[55] It was also their function to assist traditional owners in making land claims.

On the hot topic of mining developments, the act went about as far as

Woodward in accommodating Aboriginal interests. Though Aboriginal ownership did not include mineral rights, a request to explore and recover minerals on Aboriginal lands required the consent of the land council for the area – unless the government issued a proclamation declaring that 'the national interest' required that the grant be made.[56] Here, again, the land council had the key role of negotiating on behalf of the owners the terms on which permission for new mining ventures might be given. In the event that the land council and the mining venture did not reach agreement on the terms for a grant, the minister was empowered to appoint an arbitrator whose decision was binding on the council.[57] In the view of Nuggett Coombs, whose Council for Aboriginal Affairs had, by the end of 1976, given way to a full-fledged government department, the Fraser government's legislation 'could as accurately be described as an Act to facilitate mining as an Act to give effect to Aboriginal title to land.'[58] Royalties for mining on Aboriginal lands would be paid into a trust fund for the benefit of all Northern Territory Aboriginal people.[59] The Commonwealth was clearly counting on mining revenues as a means of funding the land councils and other Aboriginal services.

The handling of uranium mining left no doubt that, when push came to shove, the rights and interests of Aborigines and Torres Strait Islanders would have to give way to the economic imperatives of Australia's non-aboriginal majority. The final report of the Ranger Uranium Environment Inquiry, presided over by Justice Fox, contained this passage:

> There can be no compromise with the Aboriginal position; either it is treated as conclusive, or it is set aside. We are a tribunal of white men and any attempt on our part to state what is a reasonable accommodation of the various claims and interests can be regarded as white man's arrogance, or paternalism. ... That our values are different is not to be denied, but we have nevertheless striven to understand as well as can be done their values and their viewpoint. We have given careful attention to all that has been put before us by them or on their behalf. In the end, we form the conclusion that their opposition [to uranium mining] should not be allowed to prevail.[60]

The inquiry recommended that land claims made to the commission by traditional owners in the area be granted and that Aborigines be co-managers of the new national Kakadu National Park. But uranium mining was to proceed in the area – though on a sequential basis and with strict environmental controls. The land rights legislation had already ensured that even if Aborigines secured ownership of lands in the Ranger Project, the consent of the land council for the area would not be required for uranium mining.[61] Still, the terms under which uranium mining would proceed were to be worked out through an agreement between the Northern Land Council and the Commonwealth government, which owned 72.5 per cent of the Ranger Project. The government applied high-pressure tactics, which resulted in the council's approving an agreement that could hardly be regarded as honoring the council's statutory obligation to act only when the traditional owners 'understand the nature and purpose of the proposed action and, as a group, consent to it.'[62]

The Commonwealth Parliament's first effort at legislating Indigenous land rights certainly had its limitations. To begin with, it applied only to the Northern Territory and was designed as much to pave the way for new industrial development on the northern frontier as to recognize the rights of the traditional owners of that country. Confining the legislation to the Northern Territory was not the result of the Coalition's taking over the bill. By the time Les Johnson introduced Labor's bill, it appeared that the Whitlam government had backed down from its earlier position that the 1967 referendum had given the Commonwealth a plenary power over aboriginal affairs. It is, he said, 'a matter of regret' that the Australian Parliament 'may only legislate' on native land rights in the Northern Territory.[63] Though the Coalition was happy to live with such a limited view of the Commonwealth's power, it was a position that Labor, in order to give effect to Eddie Mabo's judicial victory, would eventually have to repudiate.

A more fundamental limitation was that the legislation made Aboriginal ownership contingent on the discretion of the settlers' government. It did not recognize, as British North America had centuries earlier, that native occupation before the Europeans' arrival gave rise to land rights that were a 'burden' on the sovereignty the Crown claimed over these lands. Nor was it an approach to land rights that could satisfy Eddie Mabo. He was enraged at the idea that 'whiteman's legislation' could establish his people's ownership of their ancestral island homes.[64] And yet, this 'whiteman's legislation' did recognize 'traditional Aboriginal owners' if not *of* the land, at least 'in relation to land.' It defined traditional owners as 'a local descent group of Aborigines' who have 'common spiritual affiliations to a site on the land ... that place the group under a primary spiritual responsibility for that site and for the land.'[65] The act's drafters, it seemed, could not quite bring themselves to move past Justice Blackburn's position in *Milirrpum* and concede that traditional owners actually had a proprietary right to their land. Instead, it recognized only that traditional owners 'are entitled by Aboriginal tradition to forage as of right' over the land for which they were spiritually responsible. Nonetheless, as Barbara Hocking points out, the logic of the act's express recognition of traditional ownership was that the proprietory rights of Aborigines were still in existence.[66] This observation would be important in building momentum for Mabo's frontal attack on *terra nullius*.

Despite its limitations, the 1976 *Aboriginal Land Rights (NT) Act* was a significant advance for the land rights movement. Its most practical achievement was to give Aborigines in the Northern Territory a process through which they could secure the Australian state's recognition of their land interests. The Northern Territory government for many years fought virtually every claim brought forward by the land councils. Nonetheless, as Galarrwuy Yunupingu (a former chairman of the Northern Council) observed, many victories were won. These victories included the recovery of the Gurindji lands twenty years after the walk-off at Wave Hill, and handing back Uluru (Ayer's Rock), Kakadu, and Nitmiluk (Katherine Gorge) to their Aboriginal owners.[67] The very struggle to secure recognition of their ownership through the act's procedures strengthened the political sinews of the Aboriginal groups involved. The institutions through which Aborigines in the Territory expressed their collective interest were not of their own making. Participation in these structures was no doubt transformative and often divisive. But such are the ironic wages of success in the struggle to overcome colonization: success is won through effective use of the colonizers' instrumentalities of governance. For the Aborigines, the resulting accommodation – or integration – with the dominant society was economic as well as political. The act has served as the basis for brokering a number of agreements between native title holders and the mining industry, and these accords have given traditional owners a stake in exploiting the mineral wealth of their land along with some influence on how that exploitation affects their land. For Aboriginal leaders of Galarrwuy Yunupingu's practical persuasion, recognition of Indigenous land rights and economic development need not be in conflict with each other. The essential point is that Aboriginal people should be able to choose how to live on their traditional land, and, while some might wish to continue a 'traditional lifestyle,' others want to use the resources of their country 'to develop a more secure economic base for their family and community.'[68]

The Northern Territory land rights act was not the only Commonwealth effort at this time to recover land for Indigenous Australians. Another national legislative product responding to Woodward's recommendations was the *Aboriginal Land Fund Act, 1974*. The act established a commission that could use Commonwealth funds to purchase land for Aboriginal groups anywhere in the country. Though set up under Whitlam, the commission had to rely on an unenthusiastic Fraser government for funding. As Charles Rowley, who chaired the commission through its five years of existence explained, 'as the Commission's general expertise increased, so did its funds decrease.'[69] The commission's efforts to buy land on the open market would seem a relatively unobtrusive way for the Commonwealth to assist Indigenous peoples in the states. But it led to a great deal of tension with Queensland, the state that claimed ownership of Eddie Mabo's homeland.

Comparative Perspectives

In the other English-settler countries, where native ownership of land had been recognized from the early days of settlement, there was nothing to match these modern Australian statutory responses to the native land rights movement. Across the Tasman Sea in New Zealand, the increasingly urbanized Maori were beginning to take vigorous political action to recover land. Despite recognition of their land ownership in the Treaty of Waitangi, the Maori, through war and settler law, had lost 95 per cent of their land.[70] By the 1970s the Maori were organizing political action aimed both at stopping the dispossession process and at recovering land. In 1975 Whina Cooper, first president of the Maori Women's Welfare League, led a march of 5000 Maori from the north to the Parliament Building in Wellington. The marchers presented a petition to the prime minister signed by over 60,000 people, calling for the preservation of Maori lands in Maori hands. In 1977 a group of Maori occupied Bastion Point near Auckland to protest a proposed subdivision of their land designed to afford wealthy Aucklanders undisturbed harbour views. The protestors spurned an offer of a few hectares of land and $200,000 in cash. After seventeen months of occupation, they were forcibly removed by the largest police operation in the country's history up to that time.[71] During the same period, another protest resulted in the return of the Raglan Golf Course to Maori ownership. The only legislative response to these Maori efforts to recover land was the 1975 *Treaty of Waitangi Act* establishing a Treaty of Waitangi Tribunal. At this stage the tribunal was not empowered to deal with past violations of the treaty. It could only make recommendations on the future application of the treaty's principles. Though a feeble response to the land rights movement, it was a harbinger of greater things to come.[72]

In Canada, as we have seen, the Supreme Court's 1973 decision in *Calder* resuscitated the common law doctrine of native title. This judicial decision received a positive response at the political level. The government of Pierre Trudeau, the same Trudeau who had told a Vancouver audience in 1969 that 'we won't recognize aboriginal rights,'[73] launched a new policy of negotiating 'comprehensive' land claims agreements with Aboriginal groups whose 'rights of traditional use and occupancy had been neither extinguished by treaty nor superseded by law.'[74] From an Aboriginal perspective, the new federal policy left much to be desired. The comprehensive land claims process would be controlled unilaterally by the federal government. The policy was defined not in a statute but in a glossy government pamphlet bearing the pretentious title *In All Fairness*. Even though the policy was in response to a Supreme Court decision recognizing common law native title, the policy statement was careful to say that, in accepting a claim for negotiation, the government was not admitting any legal liability.[75] The government would decide who would have access to the claims process and when access would be granted.

In agreeing to negotiate land claims with native peoples on unceded lands, the Canadian government's primary motivation was not to recognize Indigenous ownership or provide a secure land base on which Indigenous peoples could recover their economic self-sufficiency, but to extinguish native title and remove any legal uncertainties that might impede economic development. Thus, Canada's first comprehensive land claims settlement, with the Cree and Inuit of northern Quebec, was designed to pave the way for Quebec's massive James Bay hydroelectric project. Similarly, the motivation for the 1984 agreement with the Inuvialuit in the Northwest Territories was to facilitate the extraction of oil and gas from the western Arctic. In these agreements, as in others to follow, the native side was pressured to surrender all its Aboriginal land rights in return for secure ownership in settler law of a very small parcel of traditional lands, with limited access to traditional harvesting in the remainder, plus some cash.

The federal government's comprehensive land claims program promised neither a quick resolution of Indigenous claims nor one that was acceptable to most of Canada's Indigenous peoples. As in Australia, it was easier for the federal government to implement its land rights policy in the northern territories, where it retained total control of land and resources. Even though Canada's Constitution, in contrast to Australia's, gave the federal Parliament exclusive jurisdiction over 'Indians, and Lands reserved for the Indians,' the federal government would not enter into comprehensive land settlements with Indigenous peoples in a province without the provincial government of that province being a cosignatory. The need for provincial participation in comprehensive land settlements was more of a political than a legal imperative. The strength of the federal ethic in the Canadian political structure is such that Canadian governments of all political persuasions are very cautious about infringing 'provincial rights,' and no provincial right is more jealously guarded than the province's control over its lands and resources. After the 1975 James Bay and Northern Quebec Agreement and the 1978 Northeastern Quebec Agreement, though agreements were reached in Yukon and the Northwest Territories, there were no more comprehensive settlements in any of the provinces until the agreement between Canada, British Columbia, and the Nisga'a was finally signed and ratified in 2000.

In 1973, besides launching its program to negotiate comprehensive land settlements with Indigenous peoples living on unceded lands, the federal government inaugurated a 'specific claims' process to deal with claims of failure to comply with treaty obligations, improper sale of reserve lands or assets, or failure to discharge other lawful obligations.[76] The 'specific claims' policy was most pertinent to Indian nations south of the sixtieth parallel in the provinces where most of the land cession treaties had been made – Alberta, Saskatchewan, Manitoba, and Ontario – and in British Columbia, which had eschewed the treaty process but had set aside a few small reserves for native peoples. The 'specific claims' policy, however, was extraordinarily weak. Though designed to deal with breaches of the law by the federal government, the process had no legal teeth. The government itself would play a major role in advising the commission investigating 'specific claims' on the validity of claims and could ignore commissions recommendations on the settlement of claims.[77] For Indigenous peoples in Canada's provinces whose dispossession was more severe than in any of the other English-settler countries – lands acknowledged as Aboriginal made up less than one-half of 1 per cent of the Canadian land mass[78] – the 'specific claims' process was a cruel hoax.

The white man's courts in Canada may have recognized the native title that their Australian counterparts denied, but the white man's legal magic was not yet delivering remarkably better outcomes in terms of overcoming the massive dispossession experienced by Canada's Indigenous peoples. That legal magic works only when it is backed by the political will of the settlers' government, and, in Canada, the political will to assist Indigenous peoples in recovering economic security in their homelands was no stronger than in Australia – or, for that matter, in New Zealand.

In the United States, the political climate and legal regime were even less promising. Interest in the rights of native peoples was by now markedly weaker in the American mainstream than in the settler countries of the British Commonwealth. Legal recognition of native land rights was moving in the opposite direction of legal developments in Australia, Canada, and New Zealand. As we saw earlier, Chief Justice John Marshall, in working out a set of principles on the legal status of Amerindian nations, finally came to recognize that Indians owned the lands they had traditionally occupied. But he did not provide the foundations for a firm or coherent conception of native title in American law.[79] The weakness of the legal underpinning of native title in the American 'whiteman's law' became fully evident in 1954, when the United States Supreme Court drained any proprietary significance out of native occupancy of traditional lands. The decision arose from an action brought by the Tee-Hit-Tons, a clan of the Tlingit tribe in Alaska, for compensation for timber taken from lands to which they claimed original native title. Justice Reed, writing for the majority, did not deny the existence of native title but equated 'original Indian title' with 'permission from the whites to occupy.'[80] Performing a wonderous feat of legal reasoning, Reed transformed the United States' purchase of Alaska from Russia in 1867 into a 'conquest,' after which the Tee-Hit-Tons 'were permitted to occupy portions of the territory.' But such permission, Reed insisted, 'is not a property right but amounts to a right of occupancy which the sovereign grants and protects against intrusion by third parties but which may be terminated and such lands fully disposed of by the sovereign itself without any legally enforceable obligation to compensate the Indians.'[81] Thus, the world's wealthiest state and leading democracy, in giving constitutional protection to property rights, denied that protection to lands owned by its Indigenous peoples. The requirement in the Fifth Amendment of the US Constitution – that citizens receive 'just compensation' for property taken from them by the state – would not apply to lands to which American natives had 'original Indian title.' According to the Supreme Court, Indians in the past may have received 'generous' compensation from the sovereign US Congress for lands and resources taken from them, but that was 'as a matter of grace, not because of legal liability.'[82]

Amerindian nations' ownership of lands would now depend entirely on the good will of Congress. This dependence on the benevolence of Congress applied to lands reserved for Indian nations under the historical treaties they had made with the United States. Many Indigenous peoples, especially in the western states, lived on reserves set aside for them in the treaties through which the United States, up until 1871, had acquired Indian lands for non-native settlement and development. The native peoples' ownership of these reserve lands was no more secure than Alaska's Indigenous peoples' original title to unceded lands. Early in the twentieth century, in *Lone Wolf v. Hitchcock*,[83] the US Supreme Court held that Congress had the power to unilaterally abrogate or terminate treaties with Indian nations. John R. Wunder refers to *Lone Wolf* as 'the key to the alienation of Indian homelands.'[84]

The abrogation of treaties was the focal point for mobilizing Native American activism in the United States in the 1970s. The occupation of Alcatraz in 1969 was followed by a series of incidents all over the United States in which 'Indian activists seized and occupied – for varying lengths of time – lands and buildings in nearly every part of the country.'[85] By far the most spectacular of these events was the occupation of the Bureau of Indian Affairs offices in Washington, D.C., in 1972. The occupation was the culmination of a caravan of cars and trucks that began in San Francisco and kept growing as it wound its way across the western states. By the time it reached Washington, it was four miles long. The caravan was organized by the American Indian Movement (AIM), an organization springing from the radicalism of the 1960s and led by young, more urbanized Indian leaders such as Dennis Banks and Russell Means. Their methods were contemporary, but their objective was traditional: to revive the treaty process. The march on Washington was called the 'Trail of Broken Treaties Caravan.' At the top of its Twenty Points program were demands for Congress to restore the treaty-making process and a commission to review treaty commitments and violations.[86] After six days of occupation, at the height of a presidential election, the demonstrators left the BIA building with a vague promise that the White House would 'consider' the Twenty Points and a brown paper bag containing $66,650, handed over by two of President Nixon's aides, to cover the Indians' expenses for returning home. Two facts – that no government official of Cabinet rank would meet with the AIM leaders and that their request to address the US Congress went nowhere – are indicative of how little response the Trail of Broken Treaties elicited from non-Native American leaders. Even though the caravan and the occupation were every bit as spectacular as the Tent Embassy in Australia, the Maori march to the New Zealand Parliament, and the gathering of Aboriginal leaders in Ottawa in 1969 to receive (and reject) the Trudeau government's White Paper, these Amerindian events were far less effective in securing a place for Aboriginal issues on the country's political agenda.

The caravan's tragic aftermath at Wounded Knee revealed just how empty the American government's response to the treaty caravan was and how deeply frustrated it left American Natives who were trying to recover historical rights. After the events in Washington, Dennis Banks, Russell Means, and other AIM leaders went to the Pine Ridge reservation in South Dakota in response to requests from 'traditionals' on the reservation for assistance in resisting a corrupt and federally installed tribal council.[87] The Pine Ridge reservation was a small part of the vast stretch of land west of the Missouri River reserved for the Sioux Nation in the 1868 Fort Laramie Treaty following military victories of the Cheyenne, Arapaho, and Sioux in the Red Cloud War of 1866–8. Very little of the 'Great Sioux Reservation' remained, despite a clause in the treaty that required the signatures of at least three-quarters of adult male Indians for the cession of any portion of the reservation. Now the Oglala Sioux at Pine Ridge faced the prospect of losing yet another eighth of their land, which the Department of the Interior wanted to incorporate into the Badlands National Museum. The tribal council on the reserve outlawed AIM activities and called in National Guardsmen and US marshals, who encircled AIM leaders, joined by hundreds of Sioux and members of sixty-four other nations, at a small reserve village on a hillside called Wounded Knee. The siege lasted for ten weeks and ended in May 1973 with two Indians dead, 185 charged with criminal offences, and yet another broken pledge. After promising to send emissaries to discuss the Sioux's treaty, the White House, through a presidential aide, sent a curt note saying: 'The days of treaty making with the American Indians ended in 1871.'[88]

Wounded Knee was the high-water mark of Indian activism in the United States. James Wilson's statement that the American Indian Movement 'was never again able to attain the same level of public awareness and support' seems a fair verdict for at least the remainder of the twentieth century.[89] The dramatic events of the early 1970s which made for riveting television stimulated a romantic, Hollywood interest in the Native American past. But it did not translate into public support in the American mainstream for native Americans' quest for recognition of their inherent right to self-government or their ownership of traditional lands.

Here and there across the United States, Indian tribes continued to chisel away in the courts, seeking recognition of their rights in the white man's law. A leading example were the Passamaquoddies, who had fought against the British in the revolutionary war but whose very existence as a tribe was subsequently denied by Maine's highest court. In 1975 the Federal Court of Appeals found that decision was wrong – the Passamaquaddy people were indeed a tribe. The court also found that the sale of their lands by Massachusetts and Maine violated a 1790 Act of Congress prohibiting the sale of Indian lands where a treaty had not been made with the United States.[90] As compensation, Congress set aside funds totaling $81 million, which the Passamaquoddies could use to acquire lands near where they lived. Their success enabled other similarly situated tribes to buy back tracks of their traditional territories in New England. In the same year as the Passamaquoddies' success, Congress passed the *Indian Self-Determination and Education Assistance Act*, giving Native American communities the option of running their own schools and administering other federal programs. This act and other government moves demonstrated that Termination, as an official program, was now over. But there was no interest among Democrats or Republicans to go further and recognize native peoples as 'nations within,' peoples whose rights to land and self-government do not depend – 100 per cent – on the benevolence of the national majority.

The American Indian Movement now looked more to the international arena to challenge the United States' denial of Indian sovereignty. In 1974 AIM established the International Treaty Council, which became a leading force in gaining recognition of Indigenous peoples at the United Nations.[91] In the 1970s, progress began to be made at the United Nations in recognizing the rights of Indigenous peoples, and American Indian leaders played an important role in this international process. But, ironically – and it is surely a cruel irony – Indigenous peoples within the United States may be among the last to benefit from recognition of their rights at the UN. The great republic that has colonized them has become the world's most powerful state, and the least inclined of the Western democracies to feel bound by human rights standards established at the United Nations. As Anthony Hall observes, the American people and their government have a propensity 'to turn away from any approaches to global governance that might render the United States as a subject as well as a maker of international law.'[92]

Gathering Momentum

By the latter half of the 1970s, currents of thought and action – both international and national – were gathering momentum that would lead to the launching of the *Mabo* case. Internationally, the globalization of the Indigenous peoples' decolonization struggle was now under way. The meeting of the Arctic Peoples' Conference at Copenhagen in 1973 – a meeting that brought together the Inuit of Greenland; the Sami peoples of Scandinavia; and the Dene, Métis, and Inuvialuit of Northern Canada – is often regarded as the beginning of Indigenous internationalism. There in Christiansborg, the home of Denmark's *Folketing* (the people's assembly), to quote eye-witness Peter Jull, 'the international Indigenous peoples movement was born.'[93]

It was also in Copenhagen, one year earlier, that George Manuel, the president of Canada's National Indian Brotherhood, announced his intention to establish a worldwide organization of Indigenous peoples. In 1975 the World Council of Indigenous Peoples had its founding meeting on Vancouver Island in British Columbia. Indigenous delegates from nineteen countries, including Australia and New Zealand, attended.[94] In 1981 the World Council would hold its fourth General Assembly in Australia. Through their participation in these international meetings, Indigenous men and women with very different cultural backgrounds learned that they shared a common political experience of massive dispossession and unrelenting assimilationist pressure from larger societies in which they had become embedded. The most immediate product of these international Indigenous meetings was a boost in the morale of Indigenous leadership – a lessening of their sense of isolation and a strengthening of resolve to improve their peoples' circumstances. Some participants, and none more than those from Australia, had their sights raised by learning about what other Aboriginal peoples had achieved – for instance, in Greenland, Canada, and parts of the United States – in recovering more control over their own lives and a better stake in their traditional lands and waters.

International contacts among Indigenous peoples were not confined to formal meetings. Much of the interaction and much of the consciousness-raising occurred informally at a personal level through foreign travel and exposure to world events. Manuel, the Canadian Indian leader, is a good example. In the early 1970s, through meetings in Ottawa with Tanzania's high commissioner to Canada, he learned about the Africans' independence struggle, and a visit to Tanzania was arranged. It was an African diplomat who told Manuel: 'When native peoples come into their own, on the basis of their own cultures and traditions, that will be the Fourth World.'[95] Manuel explains that he did not take this to mean 'that we would create nation-states like his own,' but that 'the nation-state would learn to contain within itself many different cultures and life-ways, some highly tribal and traditional, some highly urban and individual.'[96] From his travels in the Third World, Manuel concluded that the Fourth World's greatest challenge would be 'to produce a new reality that reconstructs a tradition in which people can hold a common belief, and which uses all the benefits of global technology.'[97] Subsequently, Manuel visited the Maori in New Zealand and Aborigines in Australia. He saw these peoples as 'at almost opposite poles' in their relations with government. Whereas the Maori, like Canadian native peoples, had made some progress in overcoming colonial subjugation, in Australia he found it impossible to meet with aboriginal people without a white official being present – a condition he compared with Canadian Indian reserves eighty years earlier.[98] When we remember the problem Eddie Mabo was having at this time in getting permission to return to his birthplace, we can appreciate the reality underlying Manuel's perception and the impact a visit from an articulate leader like him could have on the political determination of Indigenous Australians.

It was not only Indigenous people who participated in the international movement to overcome Indigenous colonization. A growing band of non-native scholars and activists in Australia, Canada, Latin America, New Zealand, Scandinavia, and the United States became active in Indigenous internationalism. Like the clerics of Las Casa's day, members of this group were pressing the moral conscience of the powerful states of their day to recognize the fundamental human rights of Indigenous peoples. Two non-governmental organizations (NGOs) formed by non-aboriginals, which focused on the oppression of Indigenous peoples in South America – the International Work Group for Indigenous Affairs (based in Copenhagen) and Survival International (based in London) –

were instrumental in pushing Aboriginal peoples' issues onto the agenda of the United Nations.[99]

The first UN activity dealing directly with Indigenous peoples was a study on the 'Problem of Discrimination against Indigenous Populations,' launched in 1971 by the UN's Sub-commission on Prevention of Discrimination and Protection of Minorities. The UN still could not bring itself to recognize Indigenous 'peoples,' only Indigenous 'populations,' and the focus was still on overcoming discrimination that might prevent Indigenous persons, as individuals, from participating in the dominant societies of member states. Indigenous peoples gained entry to the UN system through the back door of NGOs. In 1977 an international organization of NGOs organized a conference at Geneva on Discrimination Against Indigenous Peoples in the Americas, and a number of Indigenous peoples' representatives from North and South America attended. This UN-based network soon 'expanded to embrace Indigenous peoples from other parts of the world.'[100] Indigenous representatives began to appear at Geneva on a regular basis, with some groups achieving official consultative status with UNESCO, the parent body of the UN's human rights machinery. The Indigenous peoples whose representatives came together at Geneva obtained a formal structure in 1982, when the UN's Human Rights Committee and its Economic and Social Council approved the establishment of the UN Working Group on Indigenous Populations (WGIP).[101] It is from this group that the impetus would come for developing a United Nations Declaration on the Rights of Indigenous Peoples.

Australia would now more than ever feel the gaze of an international human rights jury on its treatment of Indigenous peoples. Censorious foreign judgment of Australian affairs, particularly when it comes from UN bodies, many of whose member-states have atrocious human rights records, does not go down well with many Australians. At the same time, Australians like to hold their heads high as citizens of a humane and progressive country. And, as the country began to look increasingly to its Asian neighbours for economic trade, its government could not afford to thumb its nose at international disapproval of how it treated the country's most disadvantaged and oppressed non-European minority.

The Commonwealth government's first report to the UN Committee on the Elimination of Racial Discrimination in 1976 was very upbeat about how well Australia was doing in implementing its new *Racial Discrimination Act*. It noted that its Department of Aboriginal Affairs 'is concerned with the rights of Aboriginals to retain their own languages, cultures and tradition, their right to manage their own affairs and their rights in land.'[102] This complacent report glossed over the ugly reality, noted by the Australian official responsible for implementing the *Racial Discrimination Act*, the commissioner for community relations, that 'in practice, such rights are daily neglected on the Queensland Aboriginal Reserves, which are managed by white staff appointed by the Queensland Government, and where the land is owned, not by Aboriginal communities, but by the State Government.'[103] Nevertheless, the fact that Australia's report to a UN body speaks of being 'concerned with' Aboriginal land and self-government rights shows that its national government had come to feel under some international pressure to make progress in recognizing these rights. In August 1980 a delegation of Australian Aboriginals travelled to Geneva to address the UN Sub-commission on the Prevention of Discrimination and the Protection of Minorities. Their aim was to draw international attention to Western Australia's imposition of a mining project on pastoral lands whose traditional owners were the Noonkanbah people. Indigenous Australians were learning to use the politics of international shameing.[104]

Aboriginal politics in Australia in the latter part of the 1970s was marked by rising expectations giving way to bitter disappointment. Exposure to the burgeoning international Indigenous movement gave Australian Indigenous leaders and their white supporters the confidence of knowing that their cause was part of a worldwide movement. Real gains had been made in the Whitlam years through the Woodward Commission and Labor's commitment to its recommendations. At least in the Northern Territory, Aborigines were beginning to recover *terra nullius*. Some comfort could be taken from the fact that Malcolm Fraser's Liberal/National government went ahead with Labor's Northern Territory land rights legislation – albeit in a weaker form. Fraser's aboriginal affairs ministers, Ian Viner and Fred Chaney, unlike their Coalition predecessors, did not speak of assimilation as the only objective of the government's aboriginal policy. Fraser, who was establishing himself as a Commonwealth statesman committed to advancing the democratic rights of the black majority in southern Africa, did not want to be seen as adverse to the rights of the black minority in his own country. But when his government was put to the test on some concrete issues of aboriginal rights, it soon became clear that its commitment to defend and advance these rights was severely constrained – above all, by Australia's federal structure. A series of setbacks and losses for Indigenous peoples in the Fraser years advertised the weakness of the legal/constitutional foundation of Indigenous rights in Australia.

No event better exemplified the interweaving of the international with the national in Australian aboriginal affairs than an imaginative escapade organized by Paul Coe. In 1976 Coe, a young Aboriginal lawyer, one of the principal organizers of the Tent Embassy and chairman of the Aboriginal Legal Service based in Sydney's Redfern community, journeyed with his friend Cecil Patten to England. On November 2 Coe and Patten got into a small boat in the English Channel and headed for the beach at Dover. The boat sank, but Coe and Patten scrambled ashore and planted the Aboriginal flag, claiming possession on behalf of their people to the United Kingdom. It was, of course, a dramatic reversal of what the British had done on their people's land two centuries earlier, designed to show the absurdity of the concept that Australia was a *terra nullius* when the British arrived and that it had been settled rather than conquered.[105]

When Coe returned to Australia, he began an action in the High Court against the United Kingdom and Australia, seeking a declaration of the illegality of the assertion of British and, subsequently, Australian sovereignty over his people and their lands. Coe's lengthy statement of claim combined an assertion of Aboriginal sovereignty with the more modest claim that the Aborigines' proprietary rights on lands not explicitly taken away by Crown prerogative had survived the British conquest. In the High Court, Justice Anthony Mason ruled that Coe's application was too incoherent and lacking in merit to be amended for consideration by the full court.[106] Coe's appeal from Mason's ruling elicited a fuller opinion from four High Court justices.

The four justices – Aickin, Gibbs, Jacob, and Murphy – like Mason, refused to review the legitimacy of British or Australian sovereignty. Here the Australian judges followed in the footsteps of American Chief Justice John Marshall, who, as we saw in chapter 4, regarded – not without some moral embarrassment – the declaration of sovereignty by the British Crown and its successor governments as an act of state beyond judicial scrutiny. This refusal to question the legitimacy of the sovereign power that has appointed them has been the position of the judiciary in all the English settler countries.[107] It is not until the end of the century, and then only in Canada, that a 'white fella's' court would uphold a treaty in which sovereignty within a settler state is shared with an Indigenous people.[108] In the *Coe* case, Justice Gibbs rejected even the possibility of transferring to Australia US Chief Justice Marshall's subor-dinating idea of recognizing Indigenous peoples as 'domestic depen-dent nations.' 'The contention that there is in Australia an aboriginal nation exercising sovereignty, even of a limited kind,' he thundered, 'is quite impossible to maintain.'[109] Nevertheless, Gibbs and the other three justices all indicated that the High Court was open to hearing a claim of aboriginal title that challenged Justice Blackburn's decision in *Milirrpum*. Justices Jacobs and Murphy would have allowed Coe to amend his claim to more moderate dimensions. Lionel Murphy , the reforming Labor attorney general whom Whitlam had appointed to the High Court in 1975, referred in scathing terms to the Privy Council's finding in *Cooper v. Stuart* that Australia was acquired as a colony of settlement through peaceful annexation as 'having been made in ignorance or as a convenient falsehood to justify the taking of aborigines' land.'[110] He also noted a recent advisory opinion of the International Court of Justice repudiating the idea that the traditional lands of the nomadic people of the Western Sahara could be treated as *terra nullius*. Though *Coe* was viewed at the time as a rude setback for aboriginal peoples in Australia, with hindsight we can now see in it important seeds of change.

While Coe was launching his constitutional attack on *terra nullius* as the basis for European governance over Australia's Indigenous peoples, Aboriginal communities in northern Australia were engaging in a more grounded campaign to recover control over their lives and lands. In part it was a matter of groups trying to obtain more autonomy on mission and reserve lands to which colonial protection policy had confined them. There was also, from 1967 on, a continual 'returning to country' by Aborigines who had lost their positions on stations operated by pastoralists unwilling to pay them fair wages, and by others who hoped to find a lifestyle more respectful of their identity and accommodating of their culture than the alienating conditions of white-dominated towns.[111]

Across the north of Australia, wherever Aboriginal groups attempted to use Commonwealth legislation to regain possession of land, they encountered stiff resistance from territorial and state governments. We have already noted how the Northern Territory government fought every land claim brought forward under the Commonwealth's Northern Territory land rights legislation. After the Commonwealth's Aboriginal Land Funds Commission purchased a cattle station for two groups of Aborigines in the Kimberleys, the Government of Western Australia 'made a special effort to disrupt the attempts by the Aborigines to restore the station to working order.'[112] It was this opposition that led to the Noonkanbah people's 1980 appeal to the UN Sub-commission in Geneva.

Nowhere was resistance to Indigenous peoples, and Commonwealth intervention to assist them, stronger than in Queensland – Eddie Mabo's state, and the Australian state with the largest native population. Though its total Aboriginal and Torres Strait Islander population of 70,130, as reported in 1991, exceeded New South Wales' total by just over a hundred, far more of Queensland's Aboriginal and Islander communities were still living on or near their traditional land.[113] Under governments led by Premier Joh Bjelke-Petersen, Queensland's refusal to recognize Indigenous peoples was ideologically driven. Aboriginal and Islander populations were to be treated as simply part of the general population. Writing in 1981, on the eve of the launching of the *Mabo* case, Garth Nettheim observed that Queensland remained the only state that had not given some legislative recognition to aboriginal land rights.[114] Conflict over recognition came to a head in 1978, when Aboriginal communities at the Aurukun and Morningside Island reserves turned to Canberra for help in taking charge of their own affairs on reserves formerly administered by the Uniting Church. The Commonwealth introduced 'self-management' legislation that would allow reserve communities to control their affairs without being subject to the power of state officials.[115] Queensland countered with legislation that converted reserves into shires, subject to the state's local government regime. When councils elected by the Aboriginal peoples resisted, the state dismissed them, appointed an administrator, and threatened to send in the police. Eventually, the Commonwealth's aboriginal affairs minister negotiated an 'accommodation' that backed away from a Commonwealth takeover of the reserves, leaving them subject to state authorities.[116]

Queensland was equally vigorous in combating the Commonwealth's Aboriginal Land Fund. It viewed unfavourably 'proposals to acquire large areas of additional freehold or leasehold land for development by Aborigines or Aboriginal groups in isolation.'[117] When the Land Fund Commission allocated funds to purchase lands subject to a pastoral lease for its traditional owners at Archer River Bend in Cape York, the Queensland government refused to transfer the lease 'because cabinet thought Aborigines already had too much land.'[118] John Koowarta, one of the traditional owners of the land in question, challenged Queensland's refusal as a breach of the Commonwealth's *Racial Discrimination Act* (*RDA*). Queensland countered by challenging the constitutional validity of the Commonwealth act. The High Court, in *Koowarta v. Bjelke-Petersen*, held that the relevant provisions of the *Racial Discrimination Act* were constitutional.[119] John Koowarta never did get his land, but the High Court's decision in his case established a constitutional foundation for *RDA* that would be of crucial importance in Eddie Mabo's litigation. As we noted in chapter 5, the Commonwealth Parliament enacted *RDA* in 1975 in the wake of Australia's ratification of the UN Convention on the Elimination of Racial Discrimination. Accordingly, the Commonwealth defended *RDA* as implementing an international treaty and, therefore, as an exercise of its exclusive authority over Australia's foreign affairs. In the absence of a constitutional bill of rights, it would be Australia's international obligations that prevented a racist state government like Bjelke-Petersen's in Queensland from legislating to deny recognition of Aboriginal peoples' rights. *Koowarta*, decided in 1982, the same year that Eddie Mabo was launching his case, also signalled that the stuffy positivism that, as we noted in chapter 3, had dominated Australian jurisprudence in the past was being challenged in the High Court by judges of a more activist and human rights persuasion. Two of the justices who made up the majority in *Koowarta*, Mason and Brennan, would be leaders of the High Court majority that, ten years later, upheld Eddie Mabo's claim.

The defeats and setbacks of aboriginal nationalism spawned more than a localized resistance. In the late 1970s a pan-Australian movement brought forward the idea of a treaty between Indigenous peoples and the Australian state. The treaty movement had two branches: the Aboriginal Treaty Committee (ATC) and the National Aboriginal Conference (NAC). The ATC was a group of 'white' Australians who had become prominent advocates of aboriginal land and self-government rights. Stewart Harris, a London *Times* journalist, first proposed a 'Treaty of Commitment' in 1976 in the *Canberra Times*.[120] The original idea was for Australia to make a commitment to pay aboriginal Australians a percentage of royalties on natural resources extracted from the Australian territory. Nugget Coombs took up the treaty idea and expanded its scope. In 1978 he brought together a group that included Charles Rowley, William Stanner, and the well-known poet Judith Wright to form the ATC. The committee aimed to develop public pressure for a treaty, 'providing a kind of constitutional basis for the relationship of Aboriginal Australians to the Commonwealth and Australian society generally.'[121] The broad objectives of the treaty proposal were to secure recognition of aboriginal identity and the protection of culture, language, and land rights (including compensation for loss of traditional ways of living as well as the land itself); and to guarantee aboriginal societies control of their own affairs.[122]

Just as Coombs's Committee began to publicize the treaty idea through newspaper advertisements, radio broadcasts, and public meetings, the National Aboriginal Conference, a consultative Aboriginal organization set up by the Commonwealth government, came out in favour of negotiating a fundamental agreement between the government and the Aboriginal people. The NAC called such an agreement not a treaty but a 'makarrata.' *Makarrata* was a Yolngu word referring to 'a dispute settlement ceremony at which the aggrieved party would thrust a spear through the thigh of an offender to end a dispute.'[123] Makarrata had an advantage over talking of the agreement as a treaty, as it had the potential to alleviate confusion over how a nation can make a treaty with itself – a question posed by many querulous Australians. But because it was a concept derived from one society's culture and because it did not assert aboriginal sovereignty, a makarrata proposal could not easily unite the aboriginal nationalist movement in Australia. Coombs was concerned about NAC as a 'creation of the white Australian government' legitimately speaking for more traditional Aboriginal peoples.[124] By this time, new Aboriginal organizations, such as the Kimberley Land Council and the North Queensland Land Council, were springing up. There would have to be a place for these grassroot bodies in any effort at a grand pan-Australian agreement with Indigenous peoples.

Nonetheless, the ATC and the NAC worked together and were able to generate enough political strength to have the Makarrata placed on the agenda of the Senate's Standing Committee on Constitutional and Legal Affairs in 1981. Over the next year and a half, the committee held a number of hearings at which representatives of several Aboriginal communities and organizations, as well as the NAC and ATC, made submissions.[125] By 1983, with the ATC disbanding and the NAC in its final year of effective operation, the first push for a treaty fizzled out without any concrete achievement. But the treaty movement did show the strengthening of political forces in Australia for a fundamental restructuring of Indigenous peoples' relationship with the Australian state. The experience also demonstrated just how difficult it would be to achieve this restructuring through an Australia-wide agreement or treaty. Despite its failure to achieve its grand objective, the treaty effort had a by-product that is crucial for our story: it mobilized support for seeking, in the courts, the recognition of aboriginal rights – rights that, at this time, could not be won through direct political action.

The Townsville Conference: The Launching Pad for the *Mabo* Case

On 28 August 1981, a remarkable group of men and women came together at James Cook University in Townsville for a conference on 'Land rights and the future of Australian race relations.' The conference was sponsored by the university's Students Union and the Townsville branch of the Aboriginal Treaty Committee. The broad aims of the conference were to resist Queensland's aggressive denial of aboriginal rights and to increase public support for restructuring the relationship of Indigenous peoples with the Australian state. While the conference undoubtedly contributed to those political ends, its most tangible result was the decision to shift the political struggle for aboriginal rights to the courts and to launch what was to become the *Mabo* case.

The group that assembled at Townsville included the Aboriginal Treaty Committee's most prominent national leaders, Nugget Coombs and Judith Wright, and some of the country's outstanding Indigenous leaders. Among the latter were Marcia Langton from the Australian Institute of Aboriginal Studies in Canberra, Les Collins from the North Queensland Land Council, and Flo Kennedy and Ben Mills from Thursday Island in the Torres Strait. Politicians and intellectuals who had taken a leading role in the land rights movements were also in attendance. The politicians, all of them from the Labor Party, included Al Grassby, who as immigration minister in the Whitlam government had formulated the *Racial Discrimination Act*; Jim Keefe, a Queensland senator and former president of the Australian Labor Party; and Bob Collins, the leader of the opposition in the Northern Territory. Among the academic leaders were Eddie Mabo's mentors, Noel Loos and Henry Reynolds; Nonie Sharp, a social anthropologist who had worked extensively in the Torres Strait; and Garth Nettheim, Australia's leading scholar of the law relating to aboriginal people. Two practising lawyers, barrister Barbara Hocking and solicitor Greg McIntyre, were also present. As we shall see, their contributions to the conference were to play a crucial role in launching the *Mabo* case. And, of course, also in attendance was the one person who was indispensable to the *Mabo* case – that most distinguished of university gardeners, Eddie Koiki Mabo.

The August 1981 conference was the third Townsville Conference attended by Mabo. The three conferences marked defining moments both in the development of aboriginal politics in Australia as well as in Mabo's personal development as a nationalist aboriginal leader. At the 1967 conference, Indigenous peoples issues were framed in a Civil Rights context.[126] That conference, organized by 'white' Australians from the radical left, was animated by the spirit of the American Civil Rights movement. Its participants called for an end to discrimination against 'black' Australians so they could enjoy the same legal and political rights as all Australian citizens. That same idealism inspired the great majority of Australians in the 1967 referendum to vote for ending Aborigines' and Torres Strait Islanders' exclusion from the Constitution. It was an ideal which, at that time, left no room in the country's prevailing public ethic for recognizing the collective and distinctive rights of Australia's Indigenous peoples. Though the conference did not respond to Eddie Mabo's island identity or his resentment of his people's colonized status, it was the crucial experience in making him a political activist.

Eight years later, at the James Cook University Conference on the Torres Strait Treaty, Mabo had found his political voice and focus.[127] He had founded a Black Community School in Townsville and become immersed in a wide range of activities aimed at advancing the interests of aboriginal Australians. His deepest political yearning was now the emancipation of the Torres Strait Islanders from their colonized condition. In this, he had become considerably more radical than most of his own people – both in Townsville and in the Torres Strait. Mabo's radicalism struck a jarring note at a conference dominated by diplomats. By 1975 Aboriginal land rights were just emerging as a national issue and were only dimly evident in the delegates' concern for protecting Islander interests in the management of the resources of the Torres Strait. But the strength and clarity of Mabo's convictions make it clear that Australia, in managing its 'possessions' in the Torres Strait, would be no more able to ignore the sentiments of the Islanders than it could the wishes of the people of its former colony, Papua New Guinea.

By 1981, when the third Townsville conference took place, the aboriginal land rights movement had scored its first breakthrough in the 1976 Northern Territory Land Rights legislation. But this victory preceded a series of disappointments and defeats, as attempts to build on this achievement were thwarted elsewhere (and nowhere more than in Queensland) and a Liberal/National Coalition government in Canberra failed to become a sturdy national defender of the cause. Still, the success and the setbacks had mobilized a significant segment of the country's political and intellectual leaders, who were prepared to move beyond extending the equal rights of Australian citizens to Aborigines and Torres Strait Islanders and to recognize Indigenous peoples' claims to land and self-government. Aborigines and Islanders had begun to build their own political organizations, centred mostly on regional land councils, and to coalesce for securing their rights through political and legal action at the Australian national level. The 1981 Townsville Conference was the most effective coming together of these political forces that had occurred up to this time. Although the participants brought to the conference a sense of unstoppable forward momentum, they all felt that recognition of Indigenous peoples and their rights must have a stronger foundation in Australian law. The ease with which Bjelke-Petersen's government denied aboriginal rights made this imperative abundantly clear. It was no accident that the conference was taking place in Queensland.

To take the next step forward, the movement that assembled at James Cook University in August 1981 needed more than the provocation of a determined opponent. It needed Eddie Mabo to provide the personal energy and to articulate the vision that would convince enough of those in attendance that a law case challenging the *terra nullius* doctrine was the essential next step. Mabo was now, as they say, 'at the top of his game.' His involvement in black organizations in Townsville extended well beyond the Black Community School. From 1975 to 1980 he served as president of the Yumba Meta Housing Service, and from 1978 to 1981 he was a vocational officer at the Commonwealth government's Aboriginal Employment and Training Branch in Townsville. Mabo was also active in the Aboriginal Legal Aid Service and the Aboriginal Medical Service. The range and intensity of these local activities made him 'a national figure in black Australian circles.'[128] He had been recruited to a number of national advisory bodies, including the Aboriginal Arts Council, the National Aboriginal Education Committee, and the Australian Institute of Aboriginal Studies Education Advisory Committee. Though Mabo was already teaching informally about his people and their cause at university classes and community events, he had decided to obtain formal accreditation and, earlier in 1981, had enrolled in the Diploma of Teaching Program at the College of Advanced Education (soon to be amalgamated with James Cook University).[129]

In 1977 Mabo had finally been able to return to Mer Island. From then on he returned frequently to his birthplace.[130] His efforts to assert his rights to the land at Las Village which he had inherited from Benny Mabo and to fire up the Islanders' resistance to their colonized circumstances made him a controversial figure on the island. As his wife, Bonita, was later to explain: 'When Koiki went home to Murray Island, they told him they didn't want his "ideas from the south."' They put him out of meetings, offered to take him outside to fight, and called the police.'[131] But it would take a lot more than some scuffling with conservative clansmen to deter Eddie Koiki Mabo. He had become an articulate spokesman of the Islanders' right to self-determination, and it was from that perspective that he addressed the 1981 Townsville Conference. The immediate threat was Queensland's plan to repeal the 1971 *Torres Strait Islanders Act* and remove ('de-gazette') the reserve status of the islands, including Mer. Bjelke-Petersen was determined to treat the islands as lands totally at the disposal of the Queensland government.[132] At most, he was willing to consult the Islanders about the possibility of their communities having fifty-year leases. This attitude was anathema to Mabo. He gave a detailed account of the Islander's complex system of family ownership of land, comparing it to that of the English, Welsh, and Scots. 'What we actually want,' he told the conference, 'is real help, not patronizing colonial rule anymore.'[133] He said Queensland should transfer the area to the Commonwealth, with the status of an autonomous region of Australia – similar to Norfolk Island's.'[134] The 'consultation' carried out by the Torres Strait Advisory Council was now delivering much the same message to the Queensland government. Ben Mills reported that 'the Islanders agreed unanimously that they should have inalienable freehold title to the land and that also they should be given control of their own affairs.'[135] Flo Kennedy and others who attended a preparatory meeting on Thursday Island came to Townsville with a strong sense that the time had come for the Islanders to 'take the Governments to court' and challenge the applicability of Justice Blackburn's verdict to their lands and waters.[136]

If Eddie Mabo and the Islanders provided the essential political spark, Barbara Hocking and Greg McIntyre provided the essential intellectual spark for launching the law case that would blow away the cement blocks of *terra nullius*. Hocking was a remarkable legal scholar who, after raising a family and completing an LLB at the University of Melbourne, enrolled for a master's degree at Monash University. Much against the advice of her supervisor, she wrote her thesis on the recognition of original native title by the colonial powers of Europe.[137] She was the first Australian scholar to explore this legal terrain. Although Hocking's work made no impression on Justice Blackburn in the *Milirrpum* case, it was not for lack of trying – her findings had been given to Edward Woodward, the Aboriginal people's lawyer in that case. With *Milirrpum* as the prevailing law denying the original title of Indigenous people, it was not easy for Hocking to find barrister's work in her field of expertise. She wrote an article in a leading legal journal, the *Federal Law Review*, entitled 'Does Aboriginal Law Now Run in Australia?'[138] in which she showed how leading decisions of the highest courts of Canada, the United States, and the British Empire had all recognized the original property rights of Indigenous peoples, though subjecting them to the overriding sovereignty of imperial and settler states. It was time, she said, that Australia's courts came to terms with this jurisprudence – and in a manner that would 'accord ethical arguments their proper place and influence.'[139] This argument was the core of her presentation to the 1981 Townsville Conference. Much of Hocking's scholarship and analysis reappear in the High Court's 1992 decision in the *Mabo* case.[140] Indeed, Hocking was very much the intellectual architect of the *Mabo* case.

Greg McIntyre, the other lawyer whose attendance at Townsville in August 1981 was crucial, was considerably younger than Hocking and a solicitor rather than a barrister. In 1972, when he was studying law at the University of Western Australia, McIntyre was struck by the difficult circumstances of Aborigines he encountered on a student trip to the southwest corner of the state.[141] The outcome of *Milirrpum* shocked him and provoked him to apply for a grant to study aboriginal land rights at the Australian National University. His graduate work there became the basis for his submission to the Townsville Conference: that 'Aboriginal land rights' have their genesis at common law as 'customary rights.'[142] McIntyre would soon become the organizing solicitor for the *Mabo* litigation.

After some plenary meetings, the conference broke up into different workshops. History-making chemistry took place in one of these sessions attended by Eddie Mabo and other Torres Strait Islanders, Barbara Hocking, Greg McIntyre, and key scholars and activists Nugget Coombs, Garth Nettheim, Henry Reynolds, and Nonie Sharp. After the workshops, when the delegates were reassembling, Sharp spotted Noel Loos, who had been at another workshop, and exclaimed, 'Guess where we are going!' 'Where?' asked Loos. 'We are going to the High Court,' replied Nonie.[143] And so they did.

CHAPTER 7

Ten Long Years of Litigation

For Aboriginal peoples everywhere, seeking justice in the 'white fella's courts' is a problem. It is not simply that the judges are white fellas – men and women of the dominant setter society – but that, as judges, they have a limited mandate. Judges hear the Aboriginal claim for justice not as plenipotentiaries invested with full authority to fashion a response that satisfies their own sense of what is fair and politic, but as adjudicators bound to give due consideration to the legal process, precedents, and rules of the dominant society. The judges who have received their commissions from the settler state do not (and, some would argue, logically cannot) question the fundamental legitimacy of that state. Yet, for Indigenous peoples, it is the legitimacy of the authority that the settler state asserts *over* them that is at the core of their quest for justice. For Aboriginal claimants who score some 'success' in their litigious venture, their very acceptance of the court's decision, however much it falls short of what they claimed, reduces their moral capacity to challenge the legitimacy of the settler state. Having their rights recognized and defined in the white fella's courts means that Aboriginal peoples are coming to share a legal system with their colonizers.

All these problematic elements were present in the *Mabo* case, yet the case demonstrates, and herein lies in true importance, that Aboriginal peoples' resort to the highest courts in settler societies can be an opening to a new and worthwhile form of justice. That is possible because the law and the legal process that judges as adjudicators are bound to respect are not the fixed, carved-in-stone entities that conservative legal professionals (especially in Australia) are wont to talk about. There is a lot of leeway in the law – and no more so than in legal cultures based on the common law. Were it not for that leeway, the *Mabo* litigation would have made little sense – so stark were the precedents against the rights the plaintiffs claimed. In the end, the High Court of Australia responded to the *Mabo* litigants with a recognition of aboriginal rights that was timid by international standards and fell far short of what most aboriginal people, including Eddie Mabo, would regard as a full and just understanding of their rights. Yet, by incorporating into Australian law recognition of Aborigines and Torres Strait Islanders as forming societies with their own autonomous legal orders, the High Court's decision in *Mabo* opens up a new way of thinking about Australia – a way of thinking that could enable Indigenous and non-Indigenous Australians to move beyond the settler state and share participation in a common but deeply pluralist political community.[1]

There is nothing new about groups pursuing political objectives through the courts. Litigation often is – and not only in the common law world – 'politics by other means.'[2] Private economic interests and governments in Australia and throughout the liberal democratic world have long used the courts to defend and advance their interests. Nor is resort to the courts by Indigenous peoples a novel development. Earlier we saw how the Cherokees attempted to vindicate their rights in the Supreme Court of the United States.[3] We also saw how the limited judicial success of the Cherokees was virtually useless to them when the most powerful democratic authorities did not support the jurisprudence of the country's highest court.[4] In the Australian context, it was relatively novel for individuals or groups to attempt to vindicate fundamental human rights in the courts. Among the constitutional democracies, Australia has been in the rear-guard of the movement towards codifying fundamental rights and assigning the judiciary the central role in interpreting these rights.[5] But as we noted earlier, by the late 1970s Australia's political and legal cultures were beginning to respond to these international influences. We saw in the *Coe* case some signs that the High Court was open to these influences with respect to Aboriginal rights.[6]

The thinking of judges as they perform their adjudicative role is shaped by the movements of opinion and power in the world around them. Though this influence is surely obvious to any normal person, it is in fact repudiated by the high priests of strict legal positivism who view the judicial mind as more celestial than cerebral. Australia is one of the last outposts of legal positivism, and some of its adherents will lead the political attack on the High Court's succumbing to earthly influences in the *Mabo* case. But we cannot ignore the background developments that were occurring domestically and internationally while the *Mabo* case was wending its way through the judicial labyrinth. Without these changes in the judges' political and intellectual environment, we can understand neither their decision nor its prospects for having more impact on the Australian body politic than Chief Justice Marshall's decisions had on Aboriginal relations in the United States.

The Action and the Players

It is not easy to describe the legal action and the players involved in the *Mabo* case because so much changed over the ten years it took for the case to reach a conclusion. When the High Court finally rendered judgment in 1992, neither the parties nor the plaintiffs' statement of claim were the same as they had been when the litigation began in 1982. At many stages, the parties and their lawyers, and indeed the judges, really had no idea where the case was going. All the way along there was improvisation on all sides. That should not surprise us. The fundamental objective of the plaintiffs was revolutionary in the Australian context: to secure from the country's highest court recognition of an Indigenous legal order that preceded and survived the assertion of British sovereignty. To achieve such an objective – and to resist its achievement – would call for some very fancy and unprecedented legal footwork.

Under the Australian Constitution, the High Court has an original jurisdiction to hear suits in which the Commonwealth government is a party.[7] This jurisdiction is an unusual and seldom-used part of the High Court's jurisdiction. As with the highest courts in other common law countries, the High Court functions primarily as the country's highest court of appeal, reviewing the judgments of the most important cases decided in the lower courts. But the Indigenous litigants in *Mabo* were anxious to avoid the lower courts and to have their claim heard directly by the High Court. They were aware of what had happened to the Yolngu people in *Milirrpum*, when Justice Blackburn in the Federal Court rejected their claim. Going directly to the High Court could save years of costly litigation in the lower courts, and it was only the High Court that could give a definitive ruling overturning earlier precedents. In effect, *Mabo* was the delayed appeal of *Milirrpum*.

The claim to native title by Indigenous Australians could not be brought to the High Court as an abstract proposition of legal theory. It had to be embedded in a concrete lawsuit – and a suit in which the Commonwealth was a party. For a short time after the Townsville Conference, two cases were contemplated – one to be brought by Murray

Islanders, the other by the Yarrabah Aboriginal community in northern Queensland.[8] But the people involved in the latter case encountered difficulties that made it impossible for them to continue. By March 1982 it was clear that only one case would proceed, and this case would be brought by a group of Murray Islanders. Given Eddie Koiki Mabo's passionate commitment and political drive, he would certainly be one member of this group. He was joined by four others: Celuia Salee, his aunt who lived at Mer; Sam Passi from the other side of Mer that faces Dauar[9] (Sam was the nameholder for Passi land on Dauar); Sam's younger brother, the Reverend David Passi, an Anglican priest with a deep spiritual interest in the case; and James Rice, chairman of the Murray Island Council, who claimed land on both Dauar and Mer.[10] These five made their claims as nameholders on plots of land and water-based fishing places. From the beginning until almost the very end, the case was not explicitly based on a claim of communal ownership.[11] The plaintiffs sought a declaration recognizing their individual or family ownership of the places listed and an injunction to stop Queensland from proceeding with legislation that, in effect, denied their ownership.[12]

Basing the case on the Murray Islanders' claims had the advantage of presenting the judges with a practice of individualized ownership that could readily be assimilated to European conceptions of ownership. The Islanders were horticulturalists growing fruit and vegetables on well-defined clan or family plots. They harvested seafood from shoreline traps and reefs belonging to particular families. Land rights on and around the Murray Islands were regulated by 'Malo's Law,' based on a long-established oral tradition. Ownership claims based on such a tradition might be easy for Australian judges to accept precisely because they resembled their own tradition of ownership. But the danger was that the Islanders' judicial victory might do nothing for mainland Aborigines, who did not cultivate and establish residences on specific plots of land. Indeed, a judicial decision in the Islanders' favour based on the European-like nature of their economy and ownership practices might perpetuate the bias against the Aborigines as hunter-gatherer 'nomads' with no recognizable 'ownership' of land. Even for the Islanders there was the risk that a court ruling might uphold their individual ownership, but on terms that denied or ignored the underlying social and spiritual significance of land ownership in Meriam culture.[13] A judicial victory that homogenized Meriam law into Anglo-Australian law would be a pyrrhic victory indeed.

Nominally, there were two defendants in the lawsuit – the Queensland government and the Commonwealth government – though Queensland was the Islanders' real opponent. Premier Joh Bjelke-Petersen's ideological commitment to *terra nullius* was as strong as Koiki Mabo's opposition to that idea. It was Bjelke-Petersen's government that was engineering a legislative campaign denying the land rights of Aborigines and Torres Strait Islanders. The injunctive relief sought by the claimants was directed entirely against Queensland legislation. And it was the Queensland government that invested massive legal resources in fighting the Murray Islanders' and, all the way through, did everything it could in the courts and in the legislature to defeat the native title claim. The Commonwealth's participation in the lawsuit was at a very different level. The plaintiffs named the Commonwealth in their statement of claim, but, unlike Coe, did not question the legitimacy of British or Australian sovereignty over their lands. They sought no relief from the Commonwealth other than a declaration recognizing their ownership. With the return of Labor to power under Bob Hawke in 1983, they hoped for more support in Canberra and tried to convince Gareth Evans, Hawke's attorney general and a strong proponent of human rights, to support their claim 'logistically and substantially.'[14] Eddie Mabo's claim to harvesting and fishing rights in the outer seas on and around the Great Barrier Reef was the one specific part of the case that uniquely concerned Commonwealth interests. When this part of the claim was dropped in 1989 and the Commonwealth withdrew as a defendant, there was some question as to whether the case could still be brought under the High Court's original jurisdiction. Up until then, Commonwealth lawyers participated fully in the proceedings, generally weighing in against the Islanders' native title claims. But the Commonwealth's opposition, in contrast to Queensland's, was driven more by legal professionalism than ideological zeal.

In a lawsuit such as *Mabo*, which pits a party of very limited means and unfamiliar with litigation in the courts against parties such as the governments of Queensland and Australia that are constantly litigating in the courts and have vast resources at their disposal to commit to a case, the odds very much favour the latter. There is a body of social science literature on why, in the Anglo-European form of contesting law cases, the 'haves' usually defeat the 'have-nots.'[15] But this unevenness in the scales of justice can be overcome by the quality of the underdogs' legal team. That was certainly so in the *Mabo* litigation.

The assembling of the Islanders' team began with Barbara Hocking and Greg McIntyre, the two lawyers who had spoken so persuasively about native title at the Townsville Conference. As their solicitor, the

Islanders retained McIntyre, who was with the Aboriginal and Torres Strait Islanders Legal Service in Cairns. He had been the instructing solicitor in the *Koowarta* case, and his first job now was to secure legal aid funding for the Islanders' case. Soon after returning to Melbourne, Hocking began to work on a statement of the plaintiffs' legal arguments. She went out to the quiet of Sorrento on Port Phillip Bay to begin the drafting. For some hours she stared at a blank pad of paper, but then the words began to flow. The key was the 'time immemorial' of the native owners' possession of their lands.[16] Hocking's research and early drafts were crucial intellectual ingredients of the case. But she and others at Townsville realized that because the case was to be argued in the High Court, the elitist traditions of the Australian bar would require retaining a Queen's Council – not just any old QC but one with the brilliance and professional standing needed for the successful pleading of such a revolutionary argument in Australia's highest court. The organizers quickly settled on Ron Castan, a Melbourne-based QC, to be the plaintiffs' leading counsel. Castan was one of the country's most respected barristers, at the peak of his career, with a strong personal commitment to the human rights of Aboriginal and Torres Strait Islander peoples.[17] He was a founder of the Victorian Aboriginal Legal Services and the Koori Heritage Trust. Just as the Mabo litigation was getting under way, Castan, as counsel representing another aboriginal plaintiff, was registering a victory that would turn out to be crucial for his success in *Mabo* – defeating Queensland's challenge to the constitutional validity of the *Racial Discrimination Act* in the *Koowarta* case.[18] Castan was soon joined by a younger barrister, Bryan Keon-Cohen, who was well versed in the legal issues underlying the plaintiffs' arguments and would serve as junior counsel in the case. While Castan would argue the fine points of law before the High Court, Keon-Cohen would lead the production of evidence and cross-examination of witnesses in the 'trial' phase of the case. Keon-Cohen comments that when he looked at the legal team Queensland and the Commonwealth had assembled, he felt that 'the bar table was a little unevenly stacked from the beginning of hostilities – and it got worse.'[19] The other side certainly had its eminent 'silks': initially, John Bryne, QC, led for Queensland and, later on, G.L. Davies, QC, with Margaret White and Greg Koppenol as junior counsel, while the Commonwealth would be represented by its very experienced solicitor general, Gavin Griffith, at one point assisted by M.W. Gummow, who would later be appointed to the High Court. The barristers were supported by a team of Queensland solicitors headed by Paul Smith, as well as by officials and advisers from various departments of the Queensland government. Impressive as these legal resources of the defendant governments were, they were more than matched in intellectual brilliance and moral commitment by the much smaller legal team on the other side.

The plaintiffs' team was considerably more than its professional lawyers. At every stage of the case, right up to his death a few months before the final judgment, Eddie Mabo was vitally involved. He travelled – tirelessly – back and forth from Townsville to the Torres Strait and to court proceedings in Brisbane and Canberra, generating support for the case on Mer, organizing witnesses and evidence, and conferring with the lawyers about tactics and strategy. Castan said that he regarded Mabo as the real leader who 'had carriage of the case.'[20] Other Islanders too, including Flo Kennedy and the Reverend Dave Passi, were important in gathering evidence and knowledge about Islanders' land ownership. Anthropologist Nonie Sharp's ability to mediate between the legal worlds of the Islanders and the professional lawyers was instrumental in making effective use of Murray Island land records. Additional academic support was provided by Garth Nettheim and his Indigenous rights students at the University of New South Wales, who wrote research papers on selected topics for the barristers. The lawyers also received help and support from their families. The most remarkable example occurred when there was a hiatus in legal-aid funding at a crucial stage of the fact-finding and Castan's daughter Melissa (at the time a second-year, deferred law student) and her partner, Robert Lehrer, moved up from Melbourne to Brisbane to do the solicitors' work of organizing witnesses and preparing documents. Able as the legal team of Hocking, McIntyre, Castan, and Keon-Cohen were, their side might well not have prevailed without the help of their mostly unpaid volunteer colleagues.

Four Years of Skirmishing

The case of *Mabo and Others v. the State of Queensland and Another* officially began on 30 May 1982, when the plaintiffs' Statement of Claim was filed in the High Court's Brisbane registry. From then until early 1987, the Murray Islanders and their legal gladiators engaged with Queensland through a tangle of legal manoeuvres. Like two prize-fighters, they tested one another with jabs and feints while gathering strength for serious combat in the later rounds.

Queensland's first response to the filing of the suit was more like an attempted knock out punch. On August 18 Queensland issued a summons requesting that the court 'strike out' the plaintiffs' claim as frivolous, vexatious, and based on no reasonable cause of action. This application was supported by a lengthy affadavit sworn by P.J. Killoran, the veteran director of Queensland's Department of Aboriginal and Islanders Advancement, the same Paddy Killoran who had disciplined Eddie Mabo in 1953 and who was viewed in the press and among the Islanders as 'at the very heart of Queensland's resistance to the Islanders' aspirations.'[21] Killoran's statement argued that the Murray Islanders rapid conversion to Christianity meant they had abandoned their traditions. 'Dangerous and savage as the people of these Islands were,' he averred, 'they are now perfectly harmless and friendly.'[22]

Queensland's move led to the first of many meetings of the parties with a High Court judge. On 28 October 1982, a gaggle of lawyers and Eddie Mabo crowded into chambers in the High Court to make their case to Justice William Deane, who had recently been appointed to the High Court. Deane did not rule formerly on Queensland's application but instead persuaded the state's lawyers to withdraw it and await a fuller statement of facts by the plaintiffs. If eventually the parties could agree on a statement of facts, then the whole action could proceed directly to the High Court, without the need for any 'trial' of factual issues.[23]

The plaintiffs' lawyers would like to have been able to take their case directly to the High Court for determination by its full bench. That would be the quickest and least expensive way of obtaining a judgment. But the High Court, like most courts of appeal, is not equipped to be a tryer of facts. If important factual issues must be determined before it can decide the issues in a case, the *Judiciary Act, 1903*, provides that the matters in dispute can be 'remitted' to a trial court judge. Under this procedure, the trial judge is directed to be a finder of facts for the High Court. A fact-finding stage before a remitter judge could be a long-drawn-out process, quite beyond the $50,000 Greg McIntyre was requesting from the Aboriginal Legal Aid fund. But the alternatives to a fact-finding stage were not promising. The case might be argued simply on points of law without any reference to the history and practice of the Murray Islanders land-holding, but this, as Keon-Cohen observes, would have stripped away all the colour, context, and detail that Murray Island offered.[24] The other alternative – a statement of facts agreed to by the parties – was, from the start, most unlikely. At the heart of the so-called factual issues were fundamental differences of ideology and historical understanding. As the lawyers on both sides began to assemble their 'facts,' this conflict became increasingly evident.

The fact-finding of the Islanders' legal team got under way when Castan, Hocking, Keon-Cohen, and McIntyre, accompanied by Eddie Koiki Mabo and Flo Kennedy from Thursday Island, made their first visit to Mer in June 1982. The lawyers quickly became immersed in the history and details of the Islanders' landownership. They visited the garden plots and fish traps of their clients, and they heard from many Islanders about the ancient Malo Law on property and respect for boundaries. Kennedy helped bridge the cultural gap between the lawyers and their clients, putting them in touch with Islanders who could articulate Meriam knowledge of the law and explaining to the Islanders the lawyers' role and the aims of the project. The lawyers began to sense the depth and strength of the communal tradition of Meriam landownership. As Castan was to put it on several occasions, Meriam knowledge transmitted orally through the generations created an 'Oral Register of Title.'[25] Faced with this reality, it would surely be difficult for judges to accept that this bit of Australia was a *terra nullius* when the white man arrived. The lawyers also obtained written records of Meriam land law. Earlier in 1982, before the lawyers' visit, Sharp had gone through the Court Book, the record of cases heard by the Murray Island Native Court established by Queensland as part of its 'indirect' colonial rule of the Torres Strait Islands. She found records of cases recording Queensland government purchases of land from traditional owners. With the Island Council's permission and Kennedy's assistance, she got these documents to the lawyers in Melbourne.[26] On Mer, the lawyers 'discovered' the entire Court Book, recording many cases over a period of eighty years in which the Island Court, authorized by Queensland law, settled disputes according to the traditional system of land tenure.[27]

The Mabo legal team returned to Mer in 1983, and all through that year and most of 1984 continued to amplify the original Statement of Claim with additional material garnered from interviewing witnesses and from the Court Book. Eventually, following directions of Chief Justice Gibbs, the Islanders' lawyers added four bound volumes to the Statement of Claim.[28] All through this period, Queensland was actively resisting the plaintiffs' fact-finding. Government officials objected to the Islanders' using the records of the Island Court, claiming that the plaintiffs had no interest in them or entitlement to them.[29] Queensland's legal team raised a continual series of objections about the plaintiffs' evidence, objecting to the oral part as mere hearsay and questioning the relevance of island court records to claims of original title. At the same time, the defendants' lawyers were interviewing Islanders who challenged the particulars of Eddie Mabo's and other plaintiffs' claims. The state's lawyers did not seem troubled by the fact that this counter-evidence was itself based on knowledge of the traditional land tenure system. According to their legal ideology, any force that Meriam peoples' land law might have would depend on its recognition by Queensland authorities. Such was their faith in the white man's legal magic.

By early 1985 it was abundantly clear that there would be no agreed upon statement of facts. It was also 'palpably evident' that the Meriam people wished to have the opportunity that a hearing would afford to tell their story and explain their legal system.[30] The High Court was going to use the remitter procedure and submit the 'factual matters' at issue to a judge of a lower court. The only issue now was whether the remitter judge would be from the Federal Court or the Queensland Supreme Court. The Murray Islanders were wary of giving their evidence to a Queensland judge in Brisbane, the city they associated with 'the Depart-ment' that for so long had dominated their lives.[31] At a meeting on Mer in January 1986, they expressed by a show of hands their strong prefer-ence for a hearing in Canberra, not Brisbane. The plaintiffs' out-of-state lawyers feared they might be barred from representing their clients in a Queensland court.[32] On 26 February 1986, Chief Justice Gibbs disap-pointed the Islanders and ruled that the case would be remitted to the Queensland Supreme Court.[33] He noted that if the case had not been brought to the High Court, it would have been initiated in the Queensland court, the only other court with jurisdiction to hear it. He also remarked that the Commonwealth's interest in the case 'appears to be minor compared with that of Queensland.'[34] To assuage the concerns of the Islanders' lawyers, Gibbs said that the Queensland court, when serving as a remitter for the High Court, would be exercising 'federal jurisdiction,' so that any lawyer entitled to practise in a federal court could participate in the proceedings. The remitter would deal with 'all issues of fact raised by the pleadings.' Disputes about whether an issue was a question of fact or law would be determined by the High Court. Rather optimistically, the chief justice expressed the hope that such disputes would not arise.

Justice M.P. Moynihan was the Queensland Supreme Court judge appointed to be the High Court's fact-finder. Before being appointed to the court by the Queensland government, Moynihan, as a QC, with Daryl Dawson, a Victoria QC who would be the Fraser government's last appointment to the High Court, had represented the state in the *Koowarta* case. The hearing opened before him in Brisbane on 13 October 1986. It was expected to last at most four weeks. In the end, this stage of the *Mabo* case took up sixty-seven hearing days and produced 3489 pages of transcript. It did not conclude until September 1989. One reason it took so long were the number of objections counsel for Queensland raised to the plaintiffs' testimony. In the first month alone there were 289 separate objections – most of them to the oral nature of the evidence.[35] Altogether, 80 per cent of the Meriam witnesses' evidence was oral recollections of what they had been told about their own property, lines of inheritance, and Island traditions.[36] What the Islanders regarded as the very essence of legal knowledge, Queensland attacked as mere hearsay and therefore inadmissible. When this issue was brought before Justice Deane in the High Court, he refused to rule on it, leaving it to Justice Moynihan to resolve. Moynihan found himself in a quandary: 'We are talking about two parallel systems of law and their effect on each other,' he said. 'Ultimate questions revolve around how far I enter from one into the other in order to determine matters of evidence.'[37] Justice Moynihan let the oral evidence in, saying he would leave the question of admissibility to be decided at the end of the hearing. Though the judge never gave a formal decision on the admissibility of oral evidence or the weight to be given it, in his final determination he simply found that there were some witnesses he could not believe. Above all, it was Eddie Koiki Mabo whose testimony he chose not to believe.

Mabo was the first witness, the one who gave by far the most evidence about his own claims and the whole Meriam tradition of land ownership. At this point in the Mabo litigation, only two of the original five plaintiffs were participating in the case. Celuia Salee had died in 1985, and just two days after the hearing before Judge Moynihan began, the Reverend Dave Passi and his elder brother Sam Passi withdrew from the action. This was a real bombshell to the Mabo team, and it remains to this day 'something of a mystery.'[38] Dave Passi, as we shall see, resumed his participation in the case in 1989.

Despite constant interruptions by Queensland's lawyers, Mabo confidently related in great detail what his father many years earlier had told him about the land he would inherit and about Malo's Law. It never occurred to him that the judge would not believe him. Mabo had been a teacher in his youth and, later on, he had returned to teaching at his own school and at James Cook University. He was anxious to share his knowledge of Meriam law with the court. Mabo's evidence-in-chief took most of the first phase of the hearing. He had not completed his evidence when the hearing adjourned on November 17, to await the further availability of court time.[39] But more than two years would pass before the hearings before Justice Moynihan could resume. In 1985 Queensland had launched a legislative torpedo that, if allowed to hit its target, would sink the good ship *Mabo* and terminate any further proceedings in the case. By early 1987 it was clear that, for the case to proceed, the validity of this legislation would have to be successfully challenged in the High Court.

Queensland's Legislative Torpedo and *Mabo* (No. 1)

While the *Mabo* case was winding its way through the judicial process, Queensland had opened up a second front in the legislature. In May 1984 the Bjelke-Petersen government followed through with its threat to repeal the *Torres Strait Islanders Act*. The act that, for many years, had recognized the Islanders' identity and designated their island homes as reserves was replaced by the *Community Services (Torres Strait) Act, 1984.* This legislation treated the islands like other 'waste lands of the Crown.' Under the act, elected Community Councils had more restricted powers than any other local councils in Queensland. Community Councils could manage lands issued under a Deed of Grant in Trust granted by the Governor-in-Council.[40] On 24 April 1985 the Queensland Parliament passed the *Torres Islanders (Land Holding) Act*, which allowed island councils to surrender small pieces of land to 'qualified persons' approved by the Governor-in-Council.[41] Bjelke-Petersen's determination to deny native title and assimilate the Torres Strait Islanders into Queensland's system of land law was manifest in this legislation. But the *pièce de résistance* in this legislative assault came on 2 April 1985, when *The Queensland Coast Islands Declaratory Act* was introduced into the Queensland Parliament. This legislation went straight for the jugular vein of the Murray Islanders by purporting to extinguish – without compensation – any and all traditional land rights that might exist in the Torres Strait.

The *Declaratory Act*, like the parliamentary debate on it, was, in Keon-Cohen's words, 'nasty, brutish and short.'[42] Its key clause simply stated that 'the islands were vested in the Crown in the right of Queensland freed from all other rights and claims of any kind whatsoever and became waste lands of the Crown.'[43] The fifth and final clause made it clear that no payment was to be made to any person on whom the act might inflict any loss. But there was no sense on the government's part that the Islanders had anything by way of land rights to lose. Deputy Premier Bill Gunn explained that the legislation would 'prevent interminable arguments in the courts' in an action instigated by a small group of

Murray Islanders 'led by two Melbourne University do-gooders.'[44] The bill became law on 9 April 1985, after only two-and-a-half hours of debate.

With the *Declaratory Act* added to its defence, the Queensland government appeared to be in an unbeatable position. Even if the unexpected happened and the High Court was to give some credence to the Murray Islanders' claim that the Crown's sovereignty over the islands was encumbered by its traditional owners' native title, it really wouldn't matter because the *Declaratory Act* washed away any native title rights that might have existed. The white man's legal manoeuvrings could, with a stroke of the pen, obliterate centuries of the Indigenous peoples' law – so long as the *Queensland Declaratory Act* was valid.

Clearly, the Islanders' lawyers would have to challenge the constitutional validity of the *Declaratory Act*. This they did in June 1985, filing an objection, or 'demurrer' as it was called, which asked the High Court to strike down the law as beyond the powers of the Queensland Parliament. For a while they continued to press ahead with the hearing on factual issues before the trial court judge. Finally, in April 1987, months after the first stage of the remitter hearing had been completed before Justice Moynihan, the High Court's Justice Toohey, following a discussion among the lawyers for all the parties, directed that the demurrer – the Islanders' challenge to Queensland's *Declaratory Act* – would be heard by the full bench of the High Court. At this point the fact-finding trial was suspended, not to be resumed again until 1989, and the lawyers prepared for constitutional battle before the High Court.

The fate of the Mabo litigants case now depended entirely on the outcome of their challenge to Queensland's extinguishing act. The parties agreed that if the challenge failed, the Murray Islanders' case would be abandoned. This challenge had a surreal, catch-22 quality to it. For the parties also agreed that in hearing the challenge, the High Court should assume 'that the traditional legal rights specified in the statement of claim are in existence unless they have been extinguished by the 1985 Act.'[45] In other words, the rights that the Murray Islanders claimed would be assumed to exist, but would be totally extinguished if Queensland's *Declaratory Act* were upheld. What is more, the Mabo plaintiffs' key argument against the act was that it violated the Commonweath's *Racial Discrimination Act* by discriminating against the Meriam people's property rights and that this argument depended on the nature of those rights – the very issue to be determined in the suspended hearing before the remitter judge Moynihan.

The racial discrimination argument was by no means the only basis for challenging the *Queensland Declaratory Act*.[46] The Islanders' legal team pulled out virtually every piece of ammunition they could find in their jurisprudential armoury to throw at the state's extinguishing act. They contended, among other things, that imperial legislation had not given Queensland the power to extinguish native title and that Queensland's act encroached on the Commonwealth's exclusive power over the off-shore. They also urged the High Court to consider how Queensland's legislation, by purporting to obliterate the very rights at issue in a case lodged with the High Court, was interfering with the judicial power of the Commonwealth. But, in the end, it was the argument about racial discrimination that the High Court justices took most seriously and that determined the outcome of *Mabo (No. 1)*. Queensland's defence of its act was straightforward: the state had full power over its lands, including the power to extinguish any native rights that might have survived the annexation of the Torres Strait Islands. Since the act does not purport to take away rights that others (i.e., non-natives) have, it is not discriminatory. The Commonwealth supported Queensland by rejecting the argument that the act interfered with the judicial power. Interestingly, the Northern Territory, that bastion of white resistance to native rights, intervened to support Queensland by citing U.S. cases, such as *Tee-Hit-Ton Indians*, denying that American Indians had proprietary rights.[47]

During the five years that the Mabo litigation had been running, the composition of the High Court of Australia had been transformed. Only three of the seven justices who had decided *Koowarta* in 1982 were on the High Court bench that heard *Mabo (No. 1)*. In *Koowarta*, it was Queensland that was challenging the validity of the Commonwealth's *Racial Discrimination Act (RDA)*. The act – which was to prove crucial to the *Mabo* litigants' success – survived that challenge by the barest of margins, four judges to three. Two of the four members of the High Court who had supported *RDA* (under the Commonwealth's foreign affairs power) were no longer on the court – Sir Ninian Stephen moving to the governor generalship in 1982 and Lionel Murphy hounded to his grave in 1986 by his political opponents. Two of the three dissenting judges who had ruled against the validity of *RDA* had also departed – Aicken dying in office in 1982 and Chief Justice Gibbs retiring in 1987. So, in terms of friendliness to *RDA*, these changes looked like a draw. The same is true in terms of the governments that filled the vacancies. Malcohm Fraser's Coalition government appointed Daryl Dawson and William Deane in 1982; Bob Hawke's Labor government appointed Mary Gaudron and

John Toohey in 1987. Dawson and Deane both came to the bench with reputations of being conservative-minded barristers. Gaudron and Toohey looked much more promising for the Indigenous plaintiffs. Gaudron, the first woman to serve on Australia's highest court, had been solicitor general in a New South Wales Labor government and a member of the federal Arbitration Commission. Toohey had worked as a lawyer for Aboriginal Legal Aid in his home state, Western Australia, and served as aboriginal land commissioner in the Northern Territory from 1977 to 1982, where he was fully exposed to the reality of traditional Aboriginal land ownership.[48] The three veteran members of the court were a mixed bag: Anthony Mason, the new chief justice, and Gerard Brennan had been members of the pro-*RDA* majority in *Koowarta*, while Ronald Wilson had dissented. Of these three, Brennan was the most encouraging from the plaintiffs' perspective. Two years earlier, in *Gerhardy v. Brown*, in a unanimous High Court decision upholding a South Australian act giving the Pitjantjatjara people the right to control who came on their land as a 'special measure' under *RDA*, Brennan had stated his concurrence in these words: 'In Australia, the phenomenon of landless, rootless Aboriginal peoples is sadly familiar. Many of them are incapable of enjoying and exercising on an equal footing the human rights and fundamental freedoms that are the birthright of all Australian citizens.'[49] But even if Brennan could be marked down with Gaudron and Toohey as a good prospect for the plaintiffs' side, it was still going to be close.

And a very close thing it was. The High Court heard the arguments on March 15–17, 1988, and rendered its decision on December 8, 1988. It found – four judges to three – that Queensland's *Declaratory Act* violated the Commonwealth's *Racial Discrimination Act* and therefore failed to extinguish the traditional legal rights of the Meriam people. Brennan, Deane, Gaudron, and Toohey formed the majority. The key to their position is the broad view they took of the rights protected by the *RDA*. Section 10 of that act stipulated that no law of a state, territory, or the Commonwealth could deny persons of a particular race, colour, or national or ethnic origin 'a right that is enjoyed by persons of another race, colour or national or ethnic origin.' If the 'rights' that cannot be denied in a discriminatory fashion are construed very narrowly, then discrimination against Indigenous rights claimants would be difficult, if not impossible, to find. In this case the dissenting judges (Mason, Wilson, and Dawson) interpreted the right at issue as the right to hold property in an unusual Indigenous way according to traditional law that pre-dated British annexation. Since non-Indigenous Australians had no such right, then the Meriam people, in being denied that right, were not being denied a right enjoyed by others. But the majority took the view that the *RDA* had been enacted to give effect to the International Convention on the Elimination of All Forms of Racial Discrimination, which Australia had ratified in 1975.[50] Indeed, it was because of its linkage to the international convention that the act had been upheld in *Koowarta* under the Commonwealth's foreign affairs power. Accordingly, in interpreting the act, the majority were guided by the act's reference to universal human rights in the International Convention. Brennan, Toohey, and Gaudron, who wrote a joint opinion, observed that these rights are calculated to preserve and enhance 'the dignity and equality inherent in all human beings.'[51] In Deane's view, the equality right enshrined in Section 10 of the *RDA* was 'a moral entitlement to be treated in accordance with standards dictated by the fundamental notions of human dignity and essential equality which underlie the international recognition of human rights.'[52] The majority judges pointed to sections of the Universal Declaration of Human Rights enshrining the right of 'everyone ... to own property alone as well as in association with others' and to immunity from being 'arbitrarily deprived' of property. It is these human rights that the Meriam people would be deprived of if their traditional property rights were extinguished, and that would be discriminatory because, at the same time, non-Indigenous Australians whose property rights did not depend on traditional pre-annexation sources of law would suffer no impairment in the enjoyment of their human rights in relation to property.

The dissenting justices adhered to a narrow conception of the equality right in Section 10 of the *RDA*. In their view it was a right to 'formal equality' which would be breached only if the right being extinguished by Queensland was a right – the very same right – enjoyed by other Australians. But, by definition, a traditional right that adhered uniquely in the Meriam people was not a right possessed by other Australians. Though the Murray Islanders, as Australian citizens, enjoy the same rights to hold and inherit property as other Australians, and therefore enjoy 'equality before the law,' still, Justice Wilson observed with a sigh, 'a deep sense of injustice may remain. This is because formal equality before the law does not always achieve effective and genuine equality.'[53] Chief Justice Mason and Justice Dawson were troubled by being asked to make a judgment as to whether the rights claimed by the Meriam were equivalent to the property rights of other Australians without benefit of the remitter judge's fact-finding conclusions. Mason seemed more open than Dawson to being satisfied by an equivalence based on a broad human rights understanding of the right to own property, but neither were inclined to give the plaintiffs the benefit of the doubt.

The division in the High Court in *Mabo (No. 1)* over the principle of equality goes to the heart of the ideological cleavage that continues to bedevil the Australian debate over the rights of Indigenous peoples. Since the 1967 referendum, most Australians have been willing to extend the kind of formal equality before the law endorsed by Justice Wilson to Aboriginal peoples and Torres Strait Islanders. There is no opposition to the ideal that Aborigines and Torres Strait Islanders should enjoy the same rights as other Australians. This ideal is totally in keeping with the popular Australian ideal – a 'fair go for everyone.' Controversy, political division – indeed, deep division – arise when Aborigines and Torres Strait Islanders, like Indigenous peoples elsewhere, seek more than formal equality and demand recognition of being not just like everyone else but recognition of their special, unique identity as the country's first peoples. For peoples recovering from colonial suppression, recognition of that identity *and the rights attaching to it* are vital to their sense of self-worth. But the assimilationist implications of the formal equality ideal were not understood or not seen to be a problem by Justice Wilson – or probably by most Australians at this time. Australians will not readily buy into the 'rights revolution,' heralded by philosophers like Michael Ignatieff, in which the right to be equal is understood to require protection of the right to be different.[54] Indeed, the ideal of equality as requiring identical rights for all citizens has been an ideological barrier to recognizing the distinctive rights of Indigenous peoples in all the English-settler countries. So it is significant that the majority in *Mabo (No. 1)* evinced an approach to equality more amenable to recognizing Indigenous difference. This attitude was most evident in Justice Deane's comment that, at the time of annexation, the Murray Islanders, 'whether they wanted it or not,' were included among the people of the Colony of Qeensland, and although on federation they became citizens 'albeit initially unenfranchised,' it would 'appear to be common ground between the parties that the Murray Islanders have retained their identity as a distinct people.'[55]

So *Mabo (No. 1)* was a victory for the Islanders, but a narrow one. Queensland's crude effort at a blanket extinquishment of native title rights had failed by a single judicial vote. Though the majority judges seemed open to the possibility of Indigenous Australians having a human right to the ownership of their traditional lands which did not have its source in the sovereignty of the settler state, their opinions acknowledged the vulnerability of any such rights to the power of the sovereign authority of the Australian state. The Commonwealth, like the states, is subject to the *Racial Discrimination Act*, but unlike the states, the Commonwealth Parliament could, if it wished, set aside or qualify the *RDA* in order to extinguish native land rights.

The success of the plaintiffs' demurrer did more than save the Mabo litigation from Queensland's legislative torpedo. It also exposed the High Court judges to much of the evidence that the Islanders' legal team had been amassing in the fact-finding process. This evidence showed just how extensively and continually the Meriam peoples' customary land law had been recognized by the Queensland government.[56] Among other things, Queensland had purchased land on the islands for governmental facilities from traditional owners and had recognized the authority of a Murray Island Native Court to settle property disputes according to traditional law. The High Court justices were too committed to the white man's legal system to be swayed by the argument that Queensland could not by the stroke of a pen erase these historical events. Still, the evidence put before them in *Mabo (No. 1)* must have impressed them with the strength of the case that could be made, and would be made in *Mabo (No. 2)*, for finding that an Indigenous legal order pre-dating colonial annexation could have some standing in Australian law – and that was the nub of the Islanders' case. However, the court was committed to postponing its own deliberations on that issue until the remitter judge Moynihan had completed his fact-finding. It was now time for that process to resume.

The Fact-Finding Concludes

The resumption of the fact-finding process began early in 1989 with the lawyers skirmishing before remitter judge Moynihan and single justices of the High Court over the admissibility of oral evidence. Moynihan had already heard a good deal of oral evidence about Meriam law and tradition from Eddie Koiki Mabo in Brisbane. He was bound to hear a lot more if he acceded to the plaintiffs' request that he visit Mer Island to take evidence from frail and elderly witnesses who would have difficulty travelling to Brisbane. But the High Court left this matter to Moynihan and he, without any definitive ruling on the issue, agreed to reconvene the hearing process on Mer. And so, in May, the entire legal entourage – judge, court staff, barristers and solicitors, with their gowns, wigs, and tropical sportswear – along with filmmakers and a few journalists, arrived in the Murray Islands.

The Queensland court's visit to the Murray Islands was quite a show. For a few days it totally absorbed the Islanders' life. The importance of the court sitting on Mer was the exposure it gave the trial process and the Meriam people to each other. Judge Moynihan put it well when he said: 'Sitting here helps me to understand the evidence concerning Murray Island, its people, and its culture. And perhaps most importantly it, to a degree, enables the people of Murray Island to participate in the process of justice that is being worked out in these proceedings.'[57]

On Mer, the Queensland legal team let go of the admissibility issues and seriously engaged in the process of collecting and examining evidence. They looked for and began to find Murray Islanders who would contest testimony given by the Mabo plaintiffs. Against Mabo himself, twenty-three contrary claims were lodged.[58] Mabo remained in the thick of things. With vigour and confidence, he took the judge and the lawyers to the family plots that he claimed to have inherited – all thirty-six of them. He pointed to piles of rock in the bush that served as boundary markers, and he explained how, over many generations going well back before written records, fathers, in the presence of the neighbouring clan, passed on to their sons knowledge of their inheritance. Mabo was also active in organizing and preparing witnesses. His side received a big boost when the Passi brothers re-entered the case. Elder brother Sam did not rejoin as a plaintiff but gave important evidence when the court visited Mer. In June 1989 the Reverend Dave Passi rejoined Eddie Mabo and James Rice as a plaintiff and gave his evidence in Brisbane. Among the claims of the individual plaintiffs, it was Dave Passi's whose authenticity, in the end, most impressed Judge Moynihan. The two Passi brothers were also highly knowledgeable and articulate about the Meriam legal tradition and its integration with Meriam spiritual life.

The many disputes over claims to particular land areas on Mer, Dauar, and Waier, though they consumed much of the fact-finding process, turned out to be largely irrelevant. For the High Court the central issue was not the correctness of any of the plaintiffs' individual claims but whether the Meriam people *collectively* had a legal system of land ownership pre-dating annexation by the British Crown that had survived annexation and the interventions of the imperial, Queensland, and Australian governments since annexation. Of course, the lawyers and litigants at the time could not be sure that collective ownership would be the key issue for the High Court – though Koiki Mabo had a strong sense that it really did matter. In Trevor Graham's brilliant documentary *Mabo: Life of an Island Man*,[59] where he interviews Eddie at the time the fact-finding trial was hearing witnesses on Mer, Mabo tells him that he isn't worried about the disputed claims because all the Islanders – including those attacking his own claims – say they own their lands according to their people's law, which 'demonstrates to me and to anyone listening that there is a system in existence.' The fact that there was a system of land ownership in place before the Europeans came was the crucial fact that would give the lie to the *terra nullius* doctrine.

As Nonie Sharp explains, the focus of the fact-finding at this stage in the case was beginning to shift from challenging individual claims to the legal status of the Meriam's property system.[60] Queensland could hardly deny that the Meriam had a system of rule-governed practices concerning property ownership. But their lawyers and some of their 'expert' witnesses maintained that any legal status this Meriam system possessed flowed from its recognition by the colonial and Queensland authorities. On its own, the Islanders' traditional property system amounted to no more than common-sense practical rules for keeping peace among the inhabitants of a crowded island community. Queensland's star expert witness, Patrick Killorian, took this line. When he stood on a boundary between two allotments and stretched out his arms indicating the division between two traditional landowners, he was just 'making things fair and square according to their principles of balance and symmetry.' Killoran did not conceive of himself as recognizing or enforcing an Indigenous legal system but simply as using 'good common sense.'[61] Treating the difference between Mabo and Killorian on the legal status of the rules and practices of Meriam land ownership as a difference about 'facts' is absurd. Killorian and Mabo witnessed the same facts, but understood them or, as 'postmodern deconstructionists' would have it, constructed the facts through entirely different cultural lenses.

Nevertheless, the fact-finding process went on – and on. Three days on Mer, 23–25 May, were followed by two days on Thursday Island, where Judge Moynihan heard evidence about the culture and history of the Torres Strait Islands, as well as some opposition to Eddie Mabo's claims.[62] After that the court returned to Brisbane, where Justice Moynihan took evidence through June and July. It was in this final stage of the 'trial' process that the plaintiffs' resources were most severely taxed. Originally it had been estimated that the remitter would take only four weeks to do his fact-finding. Legal Aid funds (which required approval from the Commonwealth Attorney General's Department) had long been exhausted and not yet renewed. Greg McIntyre, the Islanders' solicitor, had to return to his home in Perth. At this time the services of Melissa Castan and her partner Ron Lehrer became essential – arranging travel and lodging, preparing witnesses from Murray Island and Townsville, and attending at court to provide solicitor support to Keon-Cohen, who was then doing most of the barrister's work in examining and cross-examining witnesses. And, of course, working along with the legal team, day in and day out, was the indefatigable Eddie Koiki Mabo. He got to know all too well the bus ride from his Townsville home to Brisbane.

Early in September the lawyers made their final addresses to Justice Moynihan. The judge then went off to examine the 3849 pages of evidence he had collected. Over a year later, on 16 November, 1990, Moynihan delivered his *Determination of Facts.*

Though Moynihan's report contained a general account of the history and culture of the Murray Islanders, his detailed determination of facts focused on the claims of the individual plaintiffs. For Eddie Koiki Mabo, his findings were devastating. The judge simply did not find Mabo to be a credible witness. He did not accept that he was the adopted son of Benny and Maiga Mabo. He may have lived with his aunt and uncle after his mother's death, but the judge could find no evidence that this was anything more than an informal arrangement. He could find no evidence of formal adoption under any system of law. In reaching this conclusion, Judge Moynihan rejected not only Mabo's evidence but that of other Islanders, including Marwer Depoma, one of the fiercest challengers of some of Mabo's boundary claims, who said they believed Eddie was the adopted son of Benny Mabo.[63] Nor, on his view of the evidence, was he 'prepared to conclude that Benny Mabo during his lifetime disposed of any lands to which he may have been entitled to Eddie Mabo.'[64] Justice Moynihan also rejected Mabo's claims to fish-traps on the foreshore at the village of Las and to offshore reef flats. In his view of the evidence, the walls of heavy rocks forming the fish-traps had been built for the benefit of larger groups than families, and the Islanders regarded themselves as free to use the outer waters as they wished without asking the permission of particular families.[65]

James Rice's claims did not fare much better than Mabo's. The judge wrote that he was 'sceptical about the chain of title' said to sustain Rice's claim to a block of land on Mer, and as for his claim to land on Dauar, he found the evidence unsatisfactory, characterizing it as 'part memory, part fabrication, perhaps confabulation and part opportunistic reconstruction.'[66] The judge's only unequivocal positive finding was in relation to 'Passi lands' on Mer claimed by Dave Passi as a representative of his family. This block of land, he found, was 'held' by the Passi family pursuant to property 'arrangements, which depend essentially upon acceptance of those affected, reflect an aspect of Murray Island social organizations for generations – probably antedating European contact.'[67] The words quoted are important, for they indicate that even though the 'fact-finder' came to a clear, affirmative conclusion on only one of the individual claims, he found on the evidence that there probably was a collective, operational system for ordering property relations in the Murray Islands before the arrival of the Europeans. That probability does not rest easily with the doctrine of *terra nullius*.

Justice Moynihan had a lot to say about the Meriam people's traditional system of recognizing property ownership. His characterization of the system leaned very much in the direction urged upon him by Queensland's lawyers. He described Meriam property arrangements simply as 'good manners' or an informal and flexible way of maintaining 'social harmony.'[68] He rejected the emphasis in Eddie Mabo's and David Passi's testimony on the spiritual nature of the Meriam people's relations with their island and its waters and instead adopted the secular, economic account advanced by Jeremy Beckett, the defendants' anthropological expert witness.[69] But the judge could not reach a finding of fact on whether traditional Meriam property arrangements constituted a system of law. That issue was, at least in part, a question of law, and he acknowledged, with regret, that such issues were beyond the terms of reference of a fact-finding remitter judge.[70] Given his leanings, that was probably a very happy circumstance for the plaintiffs. From the Meriam people's perspective, surely the most important fact Justice Moynihan did find is his statement: 'They [the Islanders] have no doubt that the Murray Islands are theirs.'[71]

However, Justice Moynihan's *Determination of Facts* was, on the whole, a depressing conclusion to the fact-finding stage of the litigation for the plaintiffs and, above all, for Eddie Mabo. Nonie Sharpe was with Mabo in Townsville on November 16 and shared the news with him. She says that when the decision sank in that all his claims and even his adoption had been rejected, 'the anguish of disbelief was visible in him.'[72] Moynihan's findings, as Keon-Cohen puts it, attacked Mabo's very sense of self.[73] His wife recounts how he 'just swore and carried on,' exclaiming 'I'm a Mabo, and nobody's going to change that!'[74] It took considerable courage and self-discipline for Mabo to agree with co-plaintiffs David Passi and James Rice to accept their lawyers' advice not to challenge Moynihan's finding of facts. The case would now proceed to the High Court on the basis of the fact-finders' mostly negative, or as Keon-Cohen puts it, 'somewhat ambivalent' report.[75] Because Mabo's personal claims had been so totally rejected, Castan and Keon-Cohen would make submissions to the High Court only on behalf of James Rice and Dave Passi. Eddie Mabo would be separately represented by Greg McIntyre.

One other change in the parties to the litigation had already taken place. On 26 June 1989 the Commonwealth government agreed to withdraw from the case. The reason for this decision was the plaintiffs' decision to defer their claims to outer seas and reefs. On returning from the hearing on Mer in May, the legal team concluded that the evidence to support these claims, as it stood, was very thin and it might be a considerable time before more was available, so their advice to drop these claims from the present proceedings was followed. Since these offshore claims were the only ones that uniquely concerned its interests, the Commonwealth no longer had any pressing reason for being a defendant. Moreover, as we shall now see, fighting claims to native title before the High Court was out of line with the posture Bob Hawke's Labor government was trying to maintain as a progressive force in aboriginal affairs.

A Wavering Hawke

The March 1983 election of a Labor government led by Bob Hawke and its re-election in November 1984 held out great promise for Aborigines and Torres Strait Islanders. Under Hawke's leadership, Labor seemed to recover its nerve about the Commonwealth having a plenary power in aboriginal affairs. In both the 1983 and 1984 elections, the ALP promised to introduce uniform national land rights legislation.[76] The Labor government also renewed its commitment to Indigenous self-determination. Clyde Holding became Minister of Aboriginal Affairs – the eighth person to hold the position since its establishment in 1972. As opposition leader in Victoria, Holding had earned a reputation for being a staunch foe of racism, and seemed he an ideal choice for championing the aboriginal cause.[77]

The Hawke government, once in office, soon found that it did not have the political will to follow through and implement its campaign commitments on aboriginal affairs. First on land rights, and later on a treaty of reconciliation – the big-ticket items – after initial fluries of action, its efforts fizzled out and its undertakings were abandoned. The main reason advanced by observers for Labor's failure to follow through is a sense of declining public support for policies recognizing the special rights and status of Aborigines and Torres Strait Islanders. In January 1985 the Hawke government commissioned a survey of public attitudes on aboriginal issues. The poll – which was never published – indicated that only 18 per cent of Australians were in favour of aboriginal land rights, 52 per cent were softly opposed, and 24 per cent were strongly opposed.[78] In interpreting the results of such a simple survey, there is no way of knowing what respondents understood 'aboriginal land rights' to mean. If a sustained political effort were made to explain aboriginal property concerns in the terms that the High Court majority understood them in *Mabo (No. 1)* – as based on the same fundamental human right to protection against arbitrary dispossession as other Australians enjoyed – then the result of such a poll might be quite different. But no such effort was undertaken by the Hawke government. With the economy in decline and economic rationalism on the rise, the times did not seem ripe for bold political leadership to assist the most disadvantaged section of the community. As Christine Jennett explains: 'This climate led to spending on Aboriginal affairs being viewed critically and with increasing hostility, by a growing number of Australians. Measures such as funding Aboriginal-controlled services, and especially land rights, came to be portrayed by some politicians and some elements of the media as preferential treatment for Aborigines.'[79] A few years later, when the High Court rendered its final decision in the *Mabo* case, the political climate was not markedly different. The litigation could only succeed if the High Court was well in front of Australian public opinion.

It is important to recognize that the national land rights legislation which the Hawke Labor government initially proposed had a feature that made it more radical than anything the Keating Labor government would contemplate after the High Court's decision in *Mabo (No. 2)*. Labor proposed to base its uniform national legislation on the 1976 *Aboriginal Land Rights Act (Northern Territory)*. That legislation, as we have seen, gave Aboriginal owners a veto over mineral development on their lands.[80] This feature of Labor's proposal aroused bitter opposition from the mining industry – especially in Western Australia. In 1984 a well-financed campaign by the Western Australian Chamber of Mines had forced Labor premier Brian Burke to abandon a relatively soft land rights bill.[81] Popular opposition to land rights stirred up by that campaign was now directed at the Commonwealth's proposal. Resentment of Canberra's interference in the state's control over land and economic development added fuel to the fire. Prime Minister Hawke found his government under tremendous pressure from Premier Burke as well as from the parliamentary opposition to abandon the project. For a while, Holding hoped he could persuade the Northern Territory land councils to abandon the veto secured for them in the 1976 act so that national uniform legislation would be easier to sell. But neither the Northern Territory land councils nor Aboriginal organizations elsewhere would support such an emasculated model. In March 1986 Holding admitted defeat, withdrew the Commonwealth's model legislation (giving lack of Aboriginal support as the reason), and fell back on a policy of seeking 'to advance the interest of Aboriginal people through cooperation with the States where that is possible.'[82]

Cooperation with the states would severely limit the progress that could be made in advancing aboriginal interests. Queensland and Western Australia, the states where Aborigines and Torres Strait Islanders constituted the highest percentages of the population and where large concentrations of traditional owners were pressing for recognition, actively opposed aboriginal land rights. Victoria and Tasmania, with small Aboriginal populations, were content to do nothing. South Australia continued to be the most progressive state. In 1981 the *Pitjantjatjara Land Rights Act* returned 100,000 square kilometres of the state's North-West reserve to its traditional owners. The land would be controlled by a corporate board elected by and accountable to the Pitjantjatjara people. This act was a major advance on earlier South Australian legislation, but it did not go as far as the Northern Territory's' land rights in giving the Aboriginal owners a veto power over mineral developments – an arbitrator appointed by the minister could override the will of the Aboriginal people.[83] Similar legislation passed in 1984 turned over 76,420 square kilometres to the Maralinga people, much of whose lands had been made uninhabitable by British nuclear weapons testing from 1953 to 1963.[84] In New South Wales, where Aboriginal communities in the 1970s had established their own land councils, a *Land Rights Act* was finally passed by the Wran Labor government in 1983. This legislation was a major disappointment in its failure to recognize claims to traditional lands or enable NSW Aborigines to regain possession of the 'old reserves' – the lands they had farmed and developed after removal from their traditional country.[85] The thrust of the act was to enable Aboriginal communities to acquire land for investment and development. For fifteen years, land acquisition would be funded by turning over 7.5 per cent of the revenues from the state's land tax to the NSW Aboriginal

Land Council. Instead of centralizing power in a statewide land council, the legislation left a good deal of power in the hands of more accountable local and regional land councils.

It was in the Northern Territory where, freed from the inhibitions of federalism, Labor governments in Canberra continued to make their most progressive moves on land rights. During this period the most dramatic action was undoubtedly 1985 legislation – passed against the strenuous opposition of the Liberal/National Party opposition and the Northern Territory government – returning Uluru (Ayers Rock) and Kata Tjuta (the Olgas) to Aboriginal ownership. These magnificent sites had been turned into a national park in 1958 without compensation or the consent of their traditional owners, for whom they were of great spiritual significance. Now the sites would be leased back by the Aboriginal owners for park use, but under a system of joint management that could protect the heritage value of the land and the interests of the local Mutitjulu community.[86] Heritage protection was a subject on which the Hawke government was prepared to move nationally. It introduced the *Aboriginal and Torres Strait Islander Heritage Protection Act* in 1984 on an interim basis and, in 1986, made the act permanent.[87] Even though the act left the decision as to sites that merit protection in the hands of the minister, and in that sense was weaker than the equivalent Northern Territory law, it was at least a small step in the direction of recognizing the special status of Australia's Indigenous peoples.

On the possibility of making a treaty with Aborigines and Torres Strait Islanders, Hawke did have one little flutter. His actions on this subject are best described in this way, for they were little more than ill-prepared personal musings. His government had come to office committed 'to investigate the principle of a Treaty of Commitment' setting out the relationship of Aborigines and Torres Strait Islanders with 'the wider Australian community.'[88] But when the Senate's Standing Committee on Constitutional and Legal Affairs began to look at this possibility, the 'one nation' nationalism of white Australia soon surfaced. Making a 'treaty' with Indigenous peoples had an international connotation that implied recognizing the sovereignty of these peoples – an idea that was anathema to senators on both sides of the chamber. Attorney General Gareth Evans, Labor's leader on the Senate Committee, could not even accept the word 'compact' for the understanding that might be reached with Indigenous Australians. After Labor's re-election for a third term in 1987, Hawke ruminated about how nice it would be if the celebration of the bicentenary of the settlers' arrival in 1988 could be preceded 'by some sort of understanding, compact if you like,' with 'the Aboriginal people.'[89] At the end of 1987 Gerry Hand, Hawke's new minister of aboriginal affairs, issued a statement committing the government to working on an agreement that could build 'a new and lasting era of understanding and co-operation with our Aboriginal and Torres Strait Island fellow citizens.'[90]

What happened next is an indication of how far 'white' and 'black' Australia were from the common understanding necessary for a true rapprochement. Aborigines and Torres Strait Islanders wanted no part of an agreement aimed at making everyone feel good about the arrival of the First Fleet in 1788. On 26 January 1988, Aboriginal people from many parts of the country, following the example of William Cooper and the Aboriginal leaders who, fifty years earlier, had declared Australia Day a 'day of mourning,' boycotted the big celebration in Sydney and staged their own protest rally in Hyde Park.[91] That same week in Torres Strait, an independence movement in which Eddie Mabo was very much involved held meetings on Thursday Island. On 20 January 1988, 400 delegates voted unanimously for negotiating the Torres Strait Islands' independence from Australia.[92] While Aboriginals and Islanders were demonstrating how irrelevant Hawke's vague gestures were for their political aspirations, the opposition Coalition leaders were whipping themselves into a frenzy over the dangers of Hawke's musings for Australia's unity.[93] Opposition leader John Howard, giving a foretaste of the approach he would later take as prime minister, denounced the idea of a treaty with the Indigenous peoples of Australia as 'utterly repugnant to the ideal of one Australia.'[94] The opposition could not even support a relatively mild resolution developed by church leaders and put before Parliament by the government which affirmed 'the entitlement of Aborigines to self-management and self-determination subject to the Constitution and the laws of the Commonwealth of Australia.'[95]

During 1988 Hawke continued to show interest in the treaty project. In June of that year, after obtaining support from an ALP conference for renewing Labor's commitment to finding 'a more mature and lasting relationship' with aboriginal people,[96] Hawke and his wife, Hazel, attended the annual cultural and sporting festival held at Barunga in the Northern Territory. There he was presented by the Central and Northern land councils with a statement of aboriginal aspirations set out on a piece of bark. The lengthy list of requests contained in the Barunga Statement[97] included one that Labor had at least temporarily abandoned – a national system of land rights. It also contained a proposal that Labor was about to take up – a national elected Aboriginal and

Islander organization to oversee Aboriginal and Islander affairs. But the statement's concluding call for a treaty was far more specific and fundamental than anything that Hawke had in mind: 'We call on the Commonwealth Parliament to negotiate with us a Treaty or Compact recognizing our prior ownership, continued occupation and sovereignty and affirming our human rights.'

In his very last act as prime minister before handing over power to Paul Keating at the end of 1991, Hawke had the Barunga Statement on its original bark hung in the new Parliament House where, along with the 1963 Bark Petition, it can be viewed today. But the wavering Hawke had no stomach for pressing ahead with the kind of treaty the aboriginal people had in mind. When the Constitutional Commission his government had appointed in 1986 tabled its mammoth two-volume report later in 1988, it stated that the Commonwealth had sufficient powers to promote reconciliation with Aboriginal and Torres Strait Island citizens, but concluded: 'Whether an agreement, or a number of agreements, is an appropriate way of working to that objective has yet to be determined.'[98] The commission's committee which had considered the question reported that there was not sufficient agreement between the Commonwealth and the aboriginal community to proceed with a treaty or compact.[99] That was surely an accurate conclusion.

The Hawke government's interest in finding 'an instrument of reconciliation' with Indigenous peoples shifted to establishing a new method of administering aboriginal affairs. From 1988 to 1990, while the *Mabo* case was taking the final steps on its way to a hearing in the High Court, policy and politics in aboriginal affairs focused on the creation of ATSIC – the Aboriginal and Torres Strait Islanders Commission. ATSIC was an innovation in settler-state management of relations with Indigenous peoples. It replaced the Department of Aboriginal Affairs with a commission constituted largely by representatives of regional councils elected by Indigenous peoples.[100] The commission was to be much more than an advisory body – it took over responsibility for administering most of the special programs the Commonwealth operated for Aborigines and Torres Strait Islanders. ATSIC's budget in 1992–3, the year the *Mabo* case was finally decided, was over $800 million.[101] Accountability upwards to the Commonwealth government was provided through the minister of aboriginal affairs appointing the commission's chairperson and two commissioners. Accountability downwards would be through the other seventeen commissioners, who were chosen by sixty regional councils grouped together in zones.

The creation of ATSIC was essentially a project in Indigenous 'self-management' rather than an effort to recognize Indigenous peoples' right to self-determination. The statement of ATSIC's objectives referred not to self-determination but to promoting 'the development of self-management and self-sufficiency.' That would be done by ensuring 'maximum participation of Aboriginal persons and Torres Strait Islanders in the formulation and implementation of government policies that affect them.'[102] ATSIC provided more direct Indigenous participation in administering aboriginal policy in Canberra than was present in either the gargantuan Department of Indian Affairs and Northern Development in Ottawa or the imperious Bureau of Indian Affairs in Washington.[103] In New Zealand the administration of Maori affairs was moving in the direction of devolution and cooperative arrangements with Maori communities and iwi (tribal structures) rather than the building of a large bureaucracy in the national capital. In the same year that ATSIC was introduced in Australia, the *Maori Affairs Restructuring Act* was passed, devolving Maori policy and administration to traditional iwi. Under the Ministry of Maori Development that replaced the Department of Maori Affairs in 1991, though Maori services are to be mainstreamed to Maori through general departments, the emphasis is on the 'regional delivery of services with the co-operation of iwi who can choose to form legal entities and contract with government to deliver services to Maori people in their region.'[104] With the revivification of the Treaty of Waitangi, Maori-settler relations in New Zealand were showing potential for developing along the lines of a genuine partnership – far more so than could be envisaged at this time in either Australia or the United States.[105] In Canada the revival of a modern treaty process had a similar potential, though it was still far from clear that Canadian governments were willing to give up the colonial control they exercised over Indigenous peoples through the *Indian Act*.

ATSIC was the Australian state's somewhat clumsy way of overcoming the absence of tribal structures among Aborigines by creating a whole new institutional apparatus through which it could try to make *its policies* more responsive to Indigenous peoples. Aboriginals and Torres Strait Islanders who knew about ATSIC – and there was extensive consultation in its development[106] – did not oppose it. As we have seen, a request for something like it was included in the Barunga Statement. But ATSIC was primarily a vehicle for legitimating the Commonwealth government's policies for Indigenous peoples. It was not directed at supporting Aboriginal communities and the Torres Strait Islanders in pursuing their objectives of recovering control over traditional lands and waters and recognition of their own societies. Even on its own terms, it was badly designed to facilitate the input of Indigenous people into policy-making. Decision-making on key questions of budgetary allocation and program design was highly centralized in ATSIC. Patrick Sullivan concludes a study of the commission in its early years by observing that, behind a façade of Indigenous involvement, it 'functioned as nothing but a government department with an advisory arm.'[107] Nor did its bureaucratic regional divisions connect well with Indigenous grassroots. As Nugget Coombs pointed out, ATSIC's regional councils did not interlock with the 'well established, existing network of local incorporated Aboriginal organizations.'[108]

But ATSIC, despite its shortcomings, should not be written off as simply another instrument of colonization. Robert Tickner, the minister who succeeded Gerry Hand and shepherded ATSIC through its early days, writes that ATSIC may have the 'capacity to evolve further to advance self-determination.'[109] He may well be right. One of the first steps in this direction was the establishment of the Torres Strait Island Regional Authority in 1994. Transferring the commission's powers to an Island authority established by Canberra was a far cry from the self-government and independence to which Eddie Mabo and other Islanders aspired. Nonetheless, this development recognized 'the separate and distinct nature of Torres Strait Islanders' and their island homes as more than simply one of ATSIC's electoral regions. This kind of recognition was welcomed by Islanders.[110] Though ATSIC's regional councils (reduced from sixty to thirty-five in 1993) were not founded on traditional identities, Aboriginal people would, by participating in them, forge new identities.[111] ATSIC-elected positions have been 'fairly keenly sought,' and voter turnout, though low compared with federal and state elections, compares well with voluntary elections in which political parties are not involved.[112]

An immediate impact of ATSIC was to create a 'peak organization' that could, with strong leadership, add an independent aboriginal voice to national policy-making. The first person appointed to chair the commission, Lois O'Donoghue, demonstrated the potential of this position when the Royal Commission on Aboriginal Deaths in Custody issued its report in 1991. This commission documented the extraordinary extent to which aboriginal people were targeted and incarcerated by Australia's criminal justice system, related that situation to their disadvantaged condition in Australian society, and made 339 recommendations on how that disadvantage might be reduced.[113] When the Hawke government was considering its response to the commission's report, O'Donoghue addressed the Cabinet – the first time an Indigenous person had attended a Cabinet meeting since the founding of the Commonwealth.[114] Though her presentation was powerful, the Commonwealth's leverage on the criminal justice system is slight, and state and territorial implementation of the report's recommendations has been extremely disappointing. The coming of ATSIC created a new base for Indigenous leadership in the nation's capital which would prove to be an important part of the political response to the judicial victory in *Mabo (No. 2)*.

The creation of ATSIC demonstrated just how partisan aboriginal policy had become in Australia. While ATSIC fell well short of meeting Aboriginal and Torres Strait Islander aspirations, it was too much for the Liberal/National Coalition to support. By the late 1980s the Liberal Party, which was always more sympathetic than the National Party to the aboriginal cause, was backing away even from 'self-management' and returning to an unvarnished assimilationist approach.[115] Much of the parliamentary struggle over the ATSIC bill focused on a lengthy preamble that, among other things, referred to Aborigines and Torres Strait Islanders as 'the prior occupiers and original owners of this land.' Even though the Labor government's draft added that they 'have no recognized rights over land other than those granted by the Crown,' that much recognition of Indigenous land rights went too far for the Coalition opposition. In the end, the preamble was dropped altogether. On the eve of the final decision in the *Mabo* case, aboriginal politics had become more polarized and partisan in Australia than had ever been the case in the past – or ever has been true of Aboriginal politics in Canada, New Zealand, or the United States.

The objective of building a broader Australian consensus on Indigenous issues was the principal motivation behind one of the last aboriginal policy initiatives of Hawke-led Labor governments – the creation of the Council for Aboriginal Reconciliation in 1991. The reconciliation sought for was as much among non-Indigenous Australians as between Indigenous and non-Indigenous people. The council was first and foremost directed at 'building a community-based movement for reconciliation and Indigenous social justice.'[116] The twenty-five-person council would be chaired by an aboriginal person and draw its Indigenous and non-Indigenous members from all sectors of society, including business, labour, religion, the media, and ethnic communities. The opposition parties would be consulted in the appointing process. The council would encourage the formation of locally based groups committed to shaping better relationships with Indigenous peoples. It was given a ten-year mandate to build a base of public support broad and strong enough to enable some significant 'reconciliation' with Aboriginals and Torres Strait Islanders to take place in 2001, Australia's centenary year.

The act establishing the Council for Reconciliation was supported by both parties in the Senate and was passed unanimously by the House of Representatives on 31 May 1991. But this bipartisan support was obtained only by stepping gingerly around the question of a treaty. The act stated that the purpose of the reconciliation process was 'to address Aboriginal and Torres Strait Islander disadvantage.'[117] The only reference to an agreement or treaty with Indigenous peoples was a vague mandate 'to consult Aborigines and Torres Strait Islanders and the wider Australian community on whether reconciliation would be advanced by a formal document or formal documents of reconciliation.'[118] Robert Tickner gave an undertaking to ATSIC – and his promise was essential to securing the ATSIC commissioners' support for the legislation – that the act's failure to explicitly mention the possibility of a treaty-like instrument of reconciliation did not mean that a treaty would be excluded from the council's consideration of Indigenous aspirations.[119] Despite the council's mandate being watered down to terms that the conservative opposition could support, Hawke and Tickner were able to persuade some of the most respected Aboriginal leaders in Australia to accept appointments. Patrick Dodson, a former Catholic priest, director of the Central Land Council and of the Kimberly Land Council, became council chairman, while Lois O'Donaghue and Galarrwuy Yunupingu also agreed to join. The council also included politicians from all sides of politics – Labor senator Margaret Reynolds, Australian Democrats senator Cheryl Kernot, and Liberal MP Peter Nugent – as well as prominent business, labour, and farm leaders. Sir Ronald Wilson, who had retired from the High Court in 1989 to become moderator of the Uniting Church, became deputy chairman.

'Reconciliation' was the way in which growing numbers of generous and decent white Australians conceived of reforming relations with Indigenous peoples. For most Aborigines and Torres Strait Islanders, however, if 'reconciliation' means no more than acquiescing in their colonized condition in return for help in being able to enjoy the social, economic, and political opportunities open to all Australians, it will not be enough. Making reconciliation mean more will depend increasingly on the efforts of the Indigenous peoples themselves. Soon they would receive a boost from Eddie Mabo's victory in the High Court. But even before that, they were beginning to obtain some significant international backing for their cause.

International Developments

In chapter 5 we noted how new international institutions established after the Second World War and an ever-expanding worldwide system of air travel and telecommunications were creating a global political space for Indigenous peoples. It was during the Hawke government years that Indigenous peoples became a significant presence in that new global political space. The focal point of Indigenous internationalism was now the Working Group on Indigenous Populations (WGIP), established in 1982 under the auspices of the United Nations.[120] The WGIP is no ordinary UN body. Formally, on paper, it was constituted by five members of the Sub-Commission on Prevention of Discrimination and Protection of Minorities, whose members are elected by the UN's Human Rights Committee.[121] These five individuals, like all the subcommission's members, are, at least in theory, independent human rights experts, not political representatives of states. There was a member from each of the UN's five regions – Africa, Asia, Eastern Europe, Latin America, and 'Western Europe and Others' (WEO). Interestingly, the four English-settler countries – Australia, Canada, New Zealand, and the United States, all belong to the WEO region.

Aboriginal participation in the work of the WGIP was facilitated by the very liberal rules of procedure that the group adopted. Not only could any Indigenous person speak, but Indigenous organizations were accepted as participants even when they did not meet the UN's normal criteria for accrediting NGOs (non-government organizations). The General Assembly made it possible for many impecunious Indigenous organizations to send delegates by establishing a voluntary fund to pay for their travel expenses. The Human Rights Committee, the principal sponsoring body of the WGIP, also funded Aboriginal delegations. As a result of these arrangements, the working group became 'the most open body in the UN system.'[122]

Indigenous peoples' organizations were quick to take advantage of this UN-created forum. The WGIP's annual meetings in Geneva, usually in October, were soon attracting hundreds of Indigenous representatives from all over the world. Coverage of Indigenous peoples became truly worldwide as the WGIP moved away from Cold War concentration on the 'blue-water imperialism' of Western European states to acknowledge that peoples whose lands had been invaded and taken over by more powerful societies from a contiguous area could qualify as Indigenous peoples with a capital 'I.' The definition of Indigenous peoples or populations used in a 1982 UN study and adopted as a working definition by the WGIP is as follows:

> Indigenous communities, peoples and nations are those which, having a historical continuity with pre-invasion and pre-colonial societies that developed on their territories, consider themselves distinct from other sectors of the societies now prevailing in those territories, or parts of them. They form at present non-dominant sectors of society and are determined to preserve, develop, and transmit to future generations their ancestral territories, and their ethnic identity, as the basis of their continued existence as peoples, in accordance with their own cultural patterns, social institutions and legal systems.[123]

By 1990 World Bank data indicated that approximately 264 million people distributed over six continents and in more than eighty-five countries came within the bounds of this definition.[124]

In its first few years the feature attraction at WGIP meetings was the 'Review of Developments' – which enabled Indigenous representatives to air grievances that, in some circumstances, were suppressed at home. In 1985 the group took on a mandate to draft a UN Declaration on the Rights of Indigenous Peoples for eventual adoption by the General Assembly. For the next eight years the draft declaration was the centrepiece of the WGIP's work. Indigenous representatives played a central role in the drafting sessions, as did 'observer delegations' from governments of countries in which the status and rights of Indigenous peoples had become important political issues. The political dynamics of these meetings often revolved around the interaction of Indigenous leaders and diplomat-experts from these countries. Of the countries involved in this way, Australia, Canada, and the Scandinavian countries have been most prominent.[125] But the drafting of the UN declaration was not yet a negotiation with UN member-states – that would come later when the WGIP's draft went to the UN's Human Rights Committee, a body on which member-states are politically represented. The draft that emerged from this first stage would be primarily a statement of the aspirations of Indigenous peoples around the world.

As work on the draft declaration proceeded, it soon became clear what the main sticking point would be. Clauses aimed at protecting Indigenous people from discrimination by the states in which they lived, as well as protecting their traditional cultures, were not likely to be troublesome to member-states. Repudiation of overt racism and respect for cultural pluralism had, by this time, advanced that far in the world. Even a clause recognizing the right of Indigenous peoples to own and control traditional lands and waters might eventually be accepted, providing it did not stipulate the source or precise scope of such a right. A much more fundamental concern of the states that make up the UN – including those which are relatively progressive and liberal in their approach to Indigenous issues – is the insistence of Indigenous peoples that they have the right of self-determination. The principle of equal rights and self-determination of peoples is inscribed in Article 1 of the UN's founding Charter. But, as we have seen, the admission of many new states, many of them formed by peoples once colonized themselves, had not made the UN any more receptive to the idea of extending the principle of self-determination to Indigenous peoples within member-states. The concern, of course, was that conceding this right to Indigenous peoples would be an authorization of secession. Nervousness about this possibility was evident in not permitting the 'P' in WGIP to stand for 'peoples' – WGIP remained the Working Group on Indigenous Populations.

Indigenous peoples have tried to overcome the jitters of UN member-states by denying any interest in secession. At a 1988 session of the International Labour Conference in Geneva, a coalition of Australian Aboriginal organizations put it this way: '[We] define our rights in terms of self-determination. We are not looking to dismember your States and you know it. But we do insist on the right to control our territories, our resources, the organization of our societies, our own decision-making institutions, and the maintenance of our own cultures and ways of life.'[126] Indigenous peoples have been unwilling, as a matter of principle, to settle for a diminished right to self-determination, even though most aspire to no more than autonomy or self-government for their societies within the states in which they live.[127] Few Indigenous peoples have the numbers, the economic strength, or the will to become independent states. In the Torres Strait, an independence movement that Eddie Mabo strongly supported was building as the *Mabo* case was proceeding in the courts, but it is by no means certain that, even if Australia had been willing to negotiate secession (which it surely was not), the independence movement would have had the support of a majority of Islanders – particularly if Islanders resident in mainland Australia had a say in the decision. But what Mabo and so many other Indigenous leaders insist upon is that their people must be free to choose how far they want to press their right to self-determine their political future. They see no principled reason for their peoples being denied that right. Conceding that they have no more than a right to 'internal self-determination' would be to accept being assigned a subordinate, inferior status among the world's peoples. And to accept that would be to acquiesce in the racism that, all along, has been their colonizers' justification for their subjugation. The first reason given in the preamble of the draft declaration on the Rights of Indigenous Peoples for adopting such a declaration is 'rejection of the view that some people are better than others as racist and wrong.'[128]

In 1988 the WGIP chair, Professor Erica-Irene Daes, a Greek academic, brought forward the first full draft of the declaration. It substantially reflected submissions made by Indigenous peoples' organizations. Subsequent sessions of the WGIP up until 1993 would largely be devoted to discussions of this draft. More rapid progress was made on revising the first attempt at an international codification of Indigenous peoples' rights, the International Labour Organization's Convention 107 on the Protection and Integration of Indigenous and Other Tribal and Semi-Tribal Populations in Independent Countries. That convention, adopted in 1957, was, as we noted earlier, highly assimilationist in its thrust.[129] In 1989 the ILO replaced Convention 107 with Convention 169, Concerning Indigenous and Tribal Peoples in Independent Countries. An earlier meeting of 'experts' in 1986, at which the World Council of Indigenous Peoples played a prominent role, did much of the spadework on the revision. Instead of a preoccupation with protecting the individual Indigenous person from discrimination, there were now provisions respecting the right of Indigenous peoples as collectivities to survive and flourish. The change marks an important development in the normative imagination of at least a section of the intellectual elite and political leadership in colonizing countries. There was now a greater capacity for understanding that Indigenous people, while welcoming the removal of barriers preventing them from participating as individuals in the economy and other institutions of the dominant society, do not see such liberal, civil rights reforms as an alternative to recognizing their collective right to survive and flourish as peoples. This point even today is still not appreciated by many leaders and influential commentators in settler countries. But adoption of ILO Convention 169 by the full Labour Conference at Geneva in 1989 marks some progress towards a less doctrinaire, single-minded understanding of the aspirations of Indigenous peoples. The ILO brought itself to refer to Indigenous 'peoples,' rather than populations, in the title of its new convention, but watered this down by including an explanation that use of the term 'peoples' shall not be construed as implying recognition that Indigenous peoples have the rights attaching to peoples under international law.[130] Indeed, the convention is replete with language accepting the sovereign authority of 'independent states' over Indigenous peoples. Even with this modification, only Norway and a handful of Latin American states have been willing to ratify it.[131]

The forum for Indigenous politics that UN agencies have provided at Geneva was a very distinctive political space.[132] It was largely removed from the give-and-take and the complexities of politics back home. Contention revolved around issues that are abstract and ideological, and on which Indigenous and settler state delegations tend to take polarized positions. It was hard to discern any difference between the Hawke government and the Howard-led opposition in Australia's response to drafts of the proposed UN Declaration on the Rights of Indigenous Peoples. The Australia government's fear that a reference to using agreements or treaties to settle land issues was incompatible with Australian unity was very much in line with Howard's criticism of Hawke's treaty flutter, as was its insistence that land claims were a state issue.[133] On the aboriginal side, it is articulate ideologues and intellectuals well versed in the argot of Western law and politics who are most effective at Geneva. The Aboriginal lawyer Paul Coe, who in the 1970s so dramatically challenged the assumptions of British and Australian sovereignty over his people, was the strongest Australian advocate for participation in the drafting work of the WGIP.[134]

Though the UN and other international forums may tend to be somewhat ethereal arenas of political combat for Indigenous peoples, they should not be written off as an indulgence in irrelevant wordgames. Granted, the conventions and declarations they produce cannot be directly enforced against offending states, but they can and do shape an 'emergent customary international law'[135] that establishes at least minimum standards for respecting the human rights of Indigenous peoples. We have already seen how awareness of such an international standard entered into the thinking of some members of Australia's High Court in *Mabo (No. 1)*, and we will see this again as an important element of judicial thinking in *Mabo (No. 2)*. The high-sounding phrases of international conventions are of course no substitute for concrete domestic reforms, but as Mick Dodson, perhaps Australia's most experienced Aboriginal participant at Geneva, has argued in reference to international human rights conventions, 'We're fools if we don't get on with making use of what are potentially very powerful tools.'[136]

In 1991 Indigenous peoples in Australia acquired an additional tool when the Commonwealth government agreed to adhere to the First Optional Protocol under the International Convention on Civil and Political Rights (ICCPR). The protocol enables individuals or groups who have reason to believe they have been denied rights enshrined in the ICCPR to have an international hearing. Though the Human Rights Committee at Geneva has refused to hear complaints from Indigenous peoples of violations of 'the right of all peoples to self-determination' in the ICCPR's Article 1, it has accepted numerous complaints brought by members of Indigenous communities concerning violations of their right under Article 27 to use their own language and enjoy their own culture and religion 'in community with other members of the group.'[137]

Participating together in the international political space at Geneva has also strengthened the resolve of Indigenous leaders not to abandon political goals that, though distant, are fundamental to their peoples. Aboriginal leaders who attend these international meetings help their people understand that, to secure and enjoy practical material improvements in their living conditions, it is neither necessary nor desirable for Indigenous peoples to surrender their own sense of sovereign responsibility for their lives and lands. We may be many decades away from the time when the member-states of the UN will have the moral courage and honesty to recognize the equality of Indigenous peoples. The leaders of Indigenous peoples who together press for that recognition internationally are no less concerned in narrowing the huge gap between the living standards of their peoples and those of the non-Indigenous populations in their home countries. In all four of the English-settler countries, Indigenous peoples by this time were mobilizing to secure both of these objectives: recognition of their collective rights as peoples and improvement in living standards.

This was certainly the case across the Tasman Sea in New Zealand, where the 1980s was a decade of considerable progress for the Maori. The political mobilization of the Maori was now paying off with increasing recognition of the Maori as partners with the Pakeha, the settler majority, in the founding of New Zealand. The Maori-Pakeha relationship was coming to resemble French-English relations in Canada more closely than Indigenous–non-Indigenous relations in Australia, the United States, or Canada. Maori leaders and a growing section of the Pakeha could share a fundamentally bicultural vision of New Zealand.[138] Of course, as with Canada, such a conception of New Zealand is open to challenge by other non-Indigenous minorities who feel excluded from such a vision as well as by many among the non-Indigenous majority who are uneasy about its implications for 'national unity.' Nonetheless, the approach taken to reforming Maori relations by political and judicial elites was now moving in the direction of a dualistic, bicultural New Zealand.

Most reform measures, in one way or another, were related to the Treaty of Waitangi. In 1985 a Labor government brought in legislation that enhanced the importance of the Treaty of Waitangi Tribunal, which had been established ten years earlier.[139] The tribunal could now investigate alleged violations of the treaty all the way back to 1840. Its membership was increased from three to seven, with the requirement that four of its members be Maori, and its chairman would continue to be E.T.J. (Eddie) Durie, chief justice of the Maori Land Court. In 1988, to deal with the flood of new claims, the tribunal was enlarged to a full membership of sixteen. Members are appointed by the governor general, on the recommendation of the minister of Maori affairs. Though there is no requirement for an equal number of Maori and Pakeha members, appointments are 'to recognize the spirit of partnership.'[140] This is the first time anywhere in the world that a tribunal dealing with Indigenous peoples' rights was constructed on a basis of partnership between Indigenous and non-Indigenous peoples. The 1988 legislation did more than add numbers to the tribunal. It also added power – instead of simply being able to make recommendations to the government, tribunal decisions with respect to Crown lands that have been passed to state-owned enterprises would now be binding on government.

The fact that, aside from the state-owned enterprises exception, the Waitangi Tribunal does not issue legally binding decisions has no doubt made it easier for the Pakeha to accept its dualistic structure. The tribunal functions much more like a continuing commission of inquiry than a court. Many of its inquiries excite great public interest. Often the tribunal conducts its hearing on the ancestral lands where the violation of treaty principles is alleged to have occurred. It aims at producing reports that provide a comprehensive account of the historical, economic, cultural, and environmental dimensions of the issue which 'will satisfy government, the Maori and Pakeha publics that everything has been looked at and that there is a basis for a lasting settlement.'[141] Tribunal recommendations, as befits a body dealing with a very short, three-clause, 160-year-old treaty, are not legalistic. While recording past injustices, the recommendations have tended to be more pragmatic and forward-looking – more concerned with working out an effective way of restoring the Maori's economic and cultural security than with reparations for past wrongs. In its later period, the tribunal has become more of an advocate for particular policy solutions designed to secure and enhance Maori identity.[142] The tribunal's recommendations are not without influence: Mason Durie reports that, by 1995, 43 per cent of the recommendations in the forty-five reports issued by the tribunal to that date (on average, reports contain five recommendations) had been fully implemented.[143] Perhaps more important is the extent to which the tribunal's work has become a prominent part of the country's discourse on political justice. Whatever might be said about the tribunal – and certainly it has its Maori and Pakeha critics[144] – it is one of the world's leading exercises in restorative justice.

There was more to revivifying the Treaty of Waitangi than the increased prominence and influence of the tribunal. The treaty has never been treated on its own as a source of court-enforceable rights. It is only when the Parliament of New Zealand writes the treaty into legislation or when judges can be persuaded to use it as an aid to interpreting legislation that it enters into judicial decisions. In the 1980s, Parliament created more of these adjudicative opportunities, and the judiciary, especially at the highest level, showed surprising enthusiasm for taking them on.

The most celebrated case concerned the *State-Owned Enterprises Act* decided by the Court of Appeal in 1987.[145] The policy of handing over government-operated commercial activities with their assets to profit-seeking state-owned corporations had the potential of removing Crown lands from Maori claimants. To guard against such a possibilty, a section of the act stipulated that '[n]othing in this Act shall permit the Crown to act in a manner that is inconsistent with the principles of the Treaty of Waitangi.'[146] The Maori Council brought the case to the Court of Appeal to seek clarification of this clause. The court rendered a decision that came close to conferring constitutional status on the Treaty of Waitangi. Indeed, one judge, Sir Ivor Richardson, referred to the treaty as 'a basic constitutional document'[147] Sir Robin Cooke, the president of the court, stated that 'the Treaty signified a partnership between races' and that, as a partner, the Crown was under the obligation of 'acting towards the Maori partner with the utmost good faith.'[148] He indicated that the New Zealand government's failure to comply with a Waitangi Tribunal recommendation that lost lands be returned might constitute a violation of the principles of the treaty. Cooke concluded that, as a result of the court's decision in this case, 'there will now be an effective legal remedy by which grievous wrongs suffered by one of the Treaty partners ... can be righted.'[149]

Clearly, the New Zealand judiciary had come a long way from Chief Justice Prendergast's 1877 declaration that the Treaty of Waitangi was a 'simple nullity.'[150] The Court of Appeal was now probably out in front of majority mainstream opinion in giving the treaty nearly constitutional status. In Andrew Sharp's view, the court's decision in the *Maori Council* case 'took from Parliament more than Parliament had wished to concede.'[151] After this judgment, there were signs of an anti-Maori backlash developing. Geoffrey Palmer, who had become Labor prime minister, formed a Crown Task Force on treaty issues 'to make it clear that the Government claimed for itself the right to make the final decisions on treaty policy.'[152] There were limits on the Maori/Pakeha partnership. In the mind of the dominant partner, sovereignty over New Zealand, including the Treaty rights of the Maori, rested with New Zealand's democratic Parliament. Though shared sovereignty remained beyond the Pakeha's constitutional imagination, practical sharing of resources was advancing impressively in New Zealand. Claims for a share of commercial fishing quotas is a prime example. By the early 1990s, through a combination of tribunals decisions, legislation, and treaty-like political negotiations, 37 per cent of New Zealand's commercial fishery was owned or controlled by the Maori.[153] Indigenous peoples' rights in New Zealand were being more successfully asserted in areas connected to the modern economy than in more traditional pursuits.

In the two English-settler countries of North America, the politics of reforming Indigenous relations were at this time on very different tracks. In Canada, Indigenous peoples were able to take advantage of the country's preoccupation with constitutional reform. The main arena of political action was high-level and high-profile constitutional negotiations between leaders of pan-Canadian Aboriginal organizations and the leaders of the federal and provincial governments. In the United States, by the 1980s, Indian efforts to obtain reform through national politics had cooled down. 'Today Indian affairs are only an eddy within national policy,' wrote Charles F. Wilkinson, a leading scholar of the native American scene, in 1987.[154] Wilkinson's book was about developments in the one arena where there was a lot more action in adjusting Indigenous relations – the Supreme Court of the United States. He reports that between 1970 and 1987, the US Supreme Court decided sixty-seven cases involving the rights of native Americans.[155] In Canada, as in Australia and New Zealand, Indigenous peoples were struggling to gain recognition of their rights, through a variety of channels, including the courts. But in the United States, the most sustained attention to Indigenous issues at the national level occurred in the judicial branch of government, where the Supreme Court continued to adjust to the circumstances of the late twentieth century the rights of Indian peoples recognized by Chief Justice Marshall in the early nineteenth century.

For virtually an entire generation, from the late 1960s to the early 1990s, Canadian political life was dominated by the constitutional question. It began with responses to nationalist mobilization in Quebec, but, as it continued, virtually every source of constitutional discontent – including the demand of Indigenous peoples for recognition of their rights – obtained a hearing in the debate.[156] If obtaining a significant place on the mainstream political agenda is an advantage to Indigenous peoples, then Canada's Indigenous peoples were clearly beneficiaries of Québécois nationalism. Both Quebec and Aboriginal nationalists drew upon the principle of the self-determination of peoples for their moral justification. Once Canada's political leadership decided not to use force to suppress Quebec nationalism, it could hardly deny the need to accommodate peacefully the collective aspirations of the Aboriginal peoples. Neither the Québécois nor Canada's Aboriginal peoples won recognition of their right to self-determine their political future, but they were able to participate in a debate about the nature of Canada as a political community which was far more fundamental than anything going on in the solidly 'one nation' mainstream politics of Australia and the United States.

Ironically, though Quebec was primarily responsible for opening up Canada's constitutional agenda, it is the Aboriginal peoples who made the most tangible constitutional gains. Canada's twenty-five years of constitutional turmoil produced only one set of constitutional changes. These came in 1982, when Prime Minister Trudeau, a staunch opponent of Quebec nationalism, pushed through his 'people's package' of constitutional reforms with the support of all Canada's provinces – except Quebec. Trudeau's package, with the approval of the British Parliament, 'patriated' Canada's Constitution, so that never again would constitutional amendments require approval by the Westminster Parliament.[157] The new formula for amending the Constitution in Canada required that seven of Canada's ten provinces (representing at least 50 per cent of the Canadian population), as well as the Canadian Parliament, consent to most amendments. This formula denied special status to Quebec as the homeland of one of Canada's founding peoples. Not only did the patriation package not give Quebec any additional powers but it meant that the powers that Quebec had secured at the time of Canada's founding could now be reduced without its consent. The other principal component of the 1982 changes in Canada's Constitution was a new *Canadian Charter of Rights and Freedoms*. Entirely outside of that *Charter*, section 35 of the amending act stated: 'The existing aboriginal and treaty rights of the aboriginal peoples of Canada are hereby recognized and affirmed.'[158] A section of the *Charter of Rights* stipulated that none of the rights and freedoms in the *Charter* should 'abrogate or derogate' from the rights and freedoms of Canada's Aboriginal peoples, including those recognized by the Royal Proclamation of 1763, the historical treaties, and the modern land-claims agreements.[159] A further section required that 'representatives of the aboriginal peoples of Canada' participate in any governmental discussions of amendments affecting their constitutional status or rights.[160]

These 1982 changes to the Constitution of Canada meant that Canada was the first of the English-settler countries to formally recognize the rights of Indigenous peoples in its written Constitution. In New Zealand the Maori had long enjoyed the right to Maori seats in the New Zealand Parliament, but the Treaty of Waitangi, which concerned more fundamental political and land rights, had not yet been accorded constitutional status. The American Constitution recognized Congress's power to regulate commerce with the Indian tribes, but it did not speak to the rights of Indigenous peoples. In Australia – until the breakthrough in the *Mabo* case – the rights of aboriginal peoples were not recognized in common law, let alone in the Constitution. After the 1967 constitutional amendments, the only reference to Indigenous peoples in Australia's Constitution was embedded in the Commonwealth's power to make laws for 'the people of any race for whom it is necessary to make special laws.'[161]

Aboriginal leaders in Canada were by no means thrilled with the recognition of 'existing aboriginal and treaty rights' in the Constitution. The qualifying word 'existing' was a last-minute insertion designed to win the support of recalcitrant provincial premiers, who hoped it would reduce the protected rights to those rights actually being enjoyed and recognized in 1982. More fundamentally, many Aboriginal people were opposed to the implication that their constitutional rights, which pre-dated the founding of Canada and were specific to particular nations, were being absorbed into Canada's Constitution. Three of the four pan-Canadian Aboriginal organizations rejected the treatment of Aboriginal rights in Section 35 of the *Constitution Act, 1982.*[162]

In the years immediately following 1982, Canadian Aboriginal leaders continued the effort to secure stronger recognition of their rights through constitutional negotiations. Leaders of organizations representing the four main groupings of Aboriginal peoples – status Indians (Indians recognized by the administrators of the *Indian Act*), non-status Indians, Inuit, and Métis – met with the federal prime minister and provincial premiers in 1983, 1984, 1985, and 1987.[163] Negotiating sessions were covered live on national television. While they were in progress, these constitutional negotiations with Aboriginal peoples were at the top of Canada's political agenda. The common aim of Aboriginal representatives was to secure explicit constitutional recognition of what they understood to be their most fundamental right – the inherent right to govern their own societies. Some contended that this right was already included in the 'existing aboriginal rights' recognized in the Constitution. In essence, this is the same pre-constitutional right of Aboriginal sovereignty that Chief Justice Marshall had acknowledged in the trilogy of cases he decided a century and a half earlier in the United States – except that Aboriginal leaders did not accept Marshall's domestication of that sovereignty or the tendency of the US Supreme Court in subsequent decisions to make Indian sovereignty subject to the plenary authority of Congress.[164] In insisting on the inherent nature of their self-government right, Canada's Indigenous leaders sought recognition of the fact that they had never surrendered responsibility for the governance of their own societies. In their view, relations between the governments of First Nations or first peoples[165] and the other governments of Canada should be based on consensual treaty-like agreements rather than the superior force of settler-state authorities.

Though the constitutional conferences failed to produce an agreement on recognition of the inherent right of Aboriginal peoples to self-government, it is still remarkable how close the two sides came to agreement. A Conservative federal government led by Brian Mulroney and backed by recommendations of an all-party parliamentary committee[166] was willing to support a *contingent* constitutional right to Aboriginal self-government, which would take legal effect on a nation-by-nation basis as the terms of self-government were negotiated with the federal government and the relevant provincial government. In the end the federal government and Aboriginal organizations could not secure the

seven-province support needed for such a constitutional amendment –
but they came close. It is impossible to conceive of such a high-level
constitutional negotiation on Aboriginal self-government taking place at
this time in Australia or in the United States. In the United States, the
time when the dominant society was deeply engaged in such issues was
long past, while in Australia it was only now on the horizon. By way of
contrast, recognition of the political rights of Indigenous peoples was
then – and now – much further advanced in Canada and in New Zealand.

The Canadian Aboriginal–First Ministers meetings did produce one
constitutional amendment – the first use by Canada of its patriated
amending process. A 1983 constitutional amendment clarified that rights
contained in modern land claim agreements had the status of constitutionally protected treaty rights. It also brought Aboriginal rights into line
with the normative imperatives of modernity by making it clear that
these rights 'are guaranteed equally to male and female persons.'[167] The
first part of the 1983 amendment meant that the comprehensive land
claim process the Canadian government had embarked upon, after the
Supreme Court's decision in the 1973 *Calder* case revived Aboriginal
title,[168] now had the potential to produce constitutionally binding treaties. The trouble was that the federal government continued to treat the
comprehensive claims process essentially as real estate transactions in
which an Aboriginal people surrender their lands to the Crown, extinguishing all native title, in return for ownership 'in fee simple' of a small
parcel of land and some economic benefits. This policy offered the
Indigenous party limited local government powers and the opportunity
to participate in regional co-management of resource and environmental matters, but did not recognize the Aboriginal people's right to govern their own society. Few Aboriginal peoples in Canada were willing to
enter into agreements with Canada on these terms. After the two northern Quebec agreements of 1975 and 1978 noted above,[169] only one
more agreement was reached in the 1980s – with the Inuvialuit in the
Western Arctic.[170] In Canada, government policy and constitutional law
opened the way for Indigenous land rights issues to be settled through
out-of-court political negotiations. But the aspirations and objective of
the parties were still too far apart for the modern treaty process to
produce very much by way of concrete results.

In 1871, Congress had terminated the treaty process and, despite the
desire of Amerindian nations to order their relations with the United
States by treaty-like agreements, there was no inclination on the part of
federal politicians to revive the treaty process. Indigenous peoples in the

United States continued to struggle for their land rights primarily in the courts and, to a lesser extent, through legislative lobbying. A leading example of the latter is the effort of native owners in Hawaii to obtain a legislative remedy that would compensate them for the loss of land and restore their ownership of a portion of it.[171] The pursuit of land claims through the courts was based not on native title rights but on breaches of earlier treaties, or on land rights that flow from the domestic dependent sovereignty of Indian tribes recognized by Marshall's landmark decisions. After the Second World War, Congress had attempted to establish a less litigious process for settling Indian land claims by establishing the quasi-judicial Indian Claims Commission. But the commission was a miserable failure. In its fifteen years of operation, it settled only eighty of the 600 cases submitted to it and awarded a total of $17.1 million.[172] Tribal communities were now resorting to courts – primarily federal courts – all over the country to obtain justice by way of recovery or compensation for lands they believed to have been stolen from them by state or federal authorities.[173]

Given that there was little interest in accommodating Indigenous peoples' nationalism anywhere on the mainstream political agenda, Indigenous peoples saw the courts as the most promising means of advancing their interests, though they face the usual risks and uncertainty whenever they seek justice in the 'white fella's courts.'[174] There certainly were some important wins. A notable victory in the 1980s was a 5-to-4 decision of the Supreme Court in 1989 upholding the power of a tribe to regulate land use on its reserve, including parts which, through the *Allotment Act*, had come to be owned by non-Indians.[175] The principal majority opinion held that the territorial nature of tribal sovereignty survived except where it was inconsistent with overriding national interests. But this was a narrow victory, and the four dissenting justices, with Chief Justice Rehnquist among them, showed no interest in protecting the integrity of tribal sovereignty. The following year the justices least understanding of the political rights of Indian tribes formed the majority in a 5-to-4 Supreme Court decision upholding the firing of Indians under Oregon law for using peyote in religious ceremonies of the Native American Church.[176] By this time, Australian political leaders were showing more sensitivity than leaders of the American judiciary to the value of protecting Indigenous heritage. Here the US Supreme Court hardly lived up to Philip Frickey's modest expectation that the court at its best, can make practical judgments 'that soften the harshness of colonization.'[177]

In Canada, as Aboriginal issues continued to take a prominent position in national affairs, there was now an intertwining of action both in the political arena and in the courts. The 1990s began with the most dramatic Aboriginal resort to direct action in modern Canadian history. This was the so-called Oka affair, which centred on Mohawk communities at Kanesatake, near the town of Oka, a few miles outside of Montreal, and Kahnawake, at the south end of Montreal's Mercier Bridge.[178] These two branches of the Mohawk nation resisted plans to expand Oka'a golf course onto a sacred Mohawk burial ground. For the entire summer of 1990, fortified by a steady stream of arrivals from Aboriginal communities across North America, Mohawk Warriors maintained an armed stand-off against the Quebec police and the Canadian Army. In the end the army dismantled the barricades, but Oka golfers have had to rest content with a nine-hole course. The federal government, sensing the extent of Aboriginal discontent throughout the country, asked the recently retired Chief Justice of Canada, Brian Dickson, to draw up the terms of reference and select the members of a wide-ranging royal commission on Aboriginal issues. The terms of reference of Canada's Royal Commission on Aboriginal Peoples were more comprehensive than those of Australia's Inquiry into Aboriginal Deaths in Custody. A majority of the commissioners (four out of seven) were Aboriginal persons. This was the first time in any country dominated by the descendants of settlers that a group of prominent Indigenous and non-Indigenous persons joined together to assess past relationships and consider how they could be improved in the future.

Just before retiring, Chief Justice Dickson co-authored the Supreme Court's decision in *Sparrow*, its first decision on the recognition and affirmation of 'existing aboriginal and treaty rights' inserted in the Canadian Constitution, in 1982. The court was unanimous in adopting the position that 'a generous, liberal interpretation of the words in the constitutional provision is demanded.'[179] It rejected the argument that 'the existing aboriginal right' of Sparrow and other Musqueam people to fish in a traditional way on British Columbia's Fraser River had been cut down by long-standing federal fishing regulations. Federal (or provincial) laws infringing constitutionally protected Aboriginal rights would be valid only if they could meet a tough test of justification, in which it would have to be shown that there was no other way of serving a significant competing public interest. Even then, the Aboriginal people involved would have to be consulted on how to minimize the infringement. If the justices of Australia's highest court were as open as Canada's had become to forging a strong place for Indigenous peoples' rights in their country's legal system, Eddie Mabo and his fellow Islanders might have a chance of success after all.

Death before Victory

Eddie Mabo had no doubts that the justices of Australia's High Court would respond positively to the case that was, at last, being brought before them. In late May 1991 he travelled by bus to Canberra to hear the Islanders' and Queensland's lawyers make their arguments before the High Court. It was nearly ten years since that day at James Cook University in Townsville when, with a group of Islander activists and academic supporters, he emerged from the race relations conference with a commitment to challenge *terra nullius* before the High Court. Henry Reynolds, who with Noel Loos had been close to Mabo since the dawn of his determination to have Australia abandon *terra nullius*, sat with Mabo through the three days of hearing, from May 28 to 31, before the seven justices of the High Court. While the *Mabo* case had been winding its way through the legal labyrinth, Reynolds researched, then published, his book *The Law of the Land*, showing how incompatible the *terra nullius* doctrine was with the precepts of British imperialism at the time of Australian settlement.[180] Much of Reynolds's argument would be found in the judgment the High Court judges were about to write. Of course, neither he nor Mabo knew that, as they sat behind the long row of wigged counsel listening to them make their submissions to the High Court judges. But Reynolds reports that Mabo was 'glowing with a sense of achievement.'[181] He sensed that his long quest for justice was over.

Ron Castan and Bryan Keon-Cohen, the Meriam Islanders' lawyers, could not share Mabo's optimism. They were faced with findings of the High Court's fact-finder, Judge Moynihan, that were far from positive for their clients. Indeed, in Mabo's case they were so negative that his personal claims had been abandoned.[182] In March 1991 Chief Justice Mason had ordered that the full court should hear only the personal claims of David Passi and James Rice. On Rice's claim, Moynihan's findings were at best equivocal, and though they more firmly supported Passi's claim, it related to only one block of land. But a remarkable change occurred in the plaintiffs' statement of claim during the final stage of the hearing. Justice William Deane (soon to become Australia's governor general) asked Castan to clarify whether the relief sought by the plaintiffs concerned just the individual plaintiffs or related to the whole island community. The Islanders' legal team conferred overnight and decided to amend their statement of claim to seek a declaration from the High Court that the Meriam people *collectively* had title to their island home.[183] This change, as we shall see, proved to be crucial – not only for the Murray Islanders but for all Australia's Indigenous peoples.

Eddie Koiki Mabo would not live to see the triumph of his cause. After the hearing, he returned to Townsville to await the High Court's verdict. During the long months of waiting he busied himself by working away at the side of his house on the 21-foot outboard motor boat he planned to take to Mer. It was to be used by the Meriam Trading Company he had been organizing with fellow islanders on recent trips to the island. But before this plan could come to fruition, Mabo's health began to fail. In a 6 September 1991 diary entry, he wrote: 'I was feeling my back start to ache.'[184] The pain soon became unbearable. On November 28 he was unable to stand and could speak only in a hoarse whisper.[185] The next day he was examined by a specialist, who said he had cancer. He was admitted to Townsville General Hospital, where he made his final diary entries. These last entries in January 1992 record his undying commitment to 'Black Australia's' struggle for justice, the cause of his life, and his deep love for his wife, Netta, 'the most important person in my life.'[186] Later in January he was transferred to a hospital in Brisbane. He died there on January 21 in Netta's arms.[187]

Part Four

THE *MABO* CASE AND ITS CONSEQUENCES

CHAPTER 8

The High Court's Decision

On 3 June 1992, the High Court of Australia released its decision in *Mabo and Others v. the State of Queensland (No. 2)*. It was, without a doubt, a victory for the plaintiffs. Six of the court's seven judges found that the Meriam people, subject to a few exceptions and some important qualifications, were the traditional owners of the Murray Islands. The key words in the majority's declaration were these: 'That the Meriam people are entitled as against the whole world to possession, occupation use and enjoyment of the island of Mer.'[1] That proposition would surely have gratified Eddie Mabo and justified his faith in the undeniable truth of his cause. The Meriam people were now recognized as having native title under Australian law to their island home.

A judicial decision of this kind on a controversial subject of major national importance – one that amounts, in the view of many, to a 'judicial revolution' – lives at two levels. There is the decision itself – what the judges said and the significance of their words; and there is the decision's reception by the country – the meanings it is given in public discourse and debate. *Mabo* is one of those judicial decisions whose political life has been and will continue to be enormous and far more important than its strictly legal significance. But in this chapter I wish to concentrate on the High Court justices' opinions – the arguments of law, philosophy, history, and politics filling 217 pages of the *Commonwealth Law Reports* in which they endeavoured to justify and craft their conclusions. The chapters that follows will be concerned with the political fallout of the decision and its impact on relations with Indigenous peoples in Australia.

A Difficult Compromise

The judges of Australia's High Court, as with justices of the highest courts in other English-settler countries, however sympathetic they may be to claims of Indigenous peoples' rights, accepted the legitimacy of the sovereign authority that Great Britain and its successor states claimed over Indigenous societies. On this issue – and for Indigenous peoples the legitimacy of that sovereignty has always been the fundamental issue of political justice – members of 'the white fella's courts' are not independent and impartial. They see themselves as members of the judicial branch of government bound to accept the sovereignty of the settler state which they serve. It was easy for the justices in *Mabo* to do this, as, unlike Paul Coe in his 1970s High Court action, the Murray Islanders did not challenge British or Australian sovereignty. Thus, Sir Gerard Brennan, whose opinion was concurred in by Chief Justice Sir Anthony Mason and Michael McHugh, accepted the principle stated in 1975 by Justice Harry Gibbs that 'the acquisition of territory by a sovereign state for the first time is an act of state which cannot be challenged, controlled or interfered with by the courts of that state.'[2] The other two majority opinions, one co-authored by Sir William Deane and Mary Gaudron and the other by John Toohey, as well as Sir Daryl Dawson's dissenting opinion, all accepted this proposition.

With the first premise of colonization accepted as a given by the judges, any recognition they were prepared to give to the rights of Indigenous peoples, as Richard Bartlett observes, was bound to be 'a compromise between the rights of settlers and aboriginal people.'[3] The majority in *Mabo (No. 2)* recognized rights of the Meriam people that have their source in the laws of a society that pre-dates the imposition of British sovereignty. In doing so, they jettisoned entirely the idea that Australia was a *terra nullius* when the Europeans arrived. Not only were the Meriam an organized society before the imposition of British sovereignty but so were the mainland Aborigines. The majority dismissed the racist evolutionary doctrine that relegated non-agricultural Aborigines to too low a point in human development to have rights emanating from their pre-colonial existence. But having honoured the claim of Torres Strait Islanders and Aborigines to be recognized as distinct self-governing human societies at the time of annexation, Australia's High Court justices then made the continuation of their societal rights dependent on their recognition by the law of the annexing state. More than that, they held that any rights so recognized were totally at the mercy – at the unilateral mercy – of the constitutional authorities of the settler state, authorities in which the Meriam and all other Indigenous peoples within Australia have, as yet, no collective representation.

The moral structure of the High Court's decision in *Mabo (No. 2)* is reminiscent of the jurisprudence of Chief Justice John Marshall, the first English-settler high court justice who tried to square recognition of Indigenous peoples' rights with acceptance of their colonization. Marshall, it will be recalled,[4] recognized that Indian tribes were 'the rightful occupants of the soil, with a legal as well as a just claim to retain possession of it, and use it according to their own discretion.' But he then went on to assert, somewhat euphemistically, that 'their rights to full sovereignty must be diminished.' This restriction, he admitted, may be opposed to 'natural right,' and yet 'if it be indispensable to that system under which the country has been settled ... it may be supported by reason, and certainly cannot be rejected by the courts.'[5] The same utilitarian subordination of the fundamental human rights of Indigenous peoples to the interests of the settler majority is evident in the majority's position in *Mabo (No. 2)*. Brennan used the language of classical literature to expose the political vulnerability of the legal entitlement he was willing to recognize in Indigenous communities. 'The native titles claimed by the Merian people ... escape the Scylla of the 1879 annexation of the Murray Islands to Queensland,' but they are highly vulnerable – and, in his view, validly vulnerable – to the 'Charybdis of subsequent extinction' by Queensland or Australia.[6] An academic commentator, Ian Hunter, put the point even more bluntly when he said that the majority's decision created 'the paradoxical situation of an apparently indefeasible absolute right being invested in a comparatively weak legal entitlement.'[7]

The judicial decision in the *Mabo* case has the trademark bitter-sweet quality of an Indigenous people's win in the white fella's courts.[8] Recognition of Indigenous peoples' rights is accompanied by affirmation of their political subordination. The justice rendered by the judges cannot follow Captain Cook's sailing instructions and be 'with the consent of the natives.'[9] Nor can the judges challenge the sovereignty of the state that appointed them. High court jurisprudence cannot on its own accomplish decolonization. Whether it can be a catalytic force for Indigenous decolonization depends on how it is received and acted upon by the political forces of the country. The arguments of the judges – their persuasive force and rhetorical value – may play a limited role in the political struggle that follows in the wake of their decision. But the crude short-hand references to the decision – the argot of media and political discourse about judicial decisions – are bound to be far more influential in shaping public opinion than anything the judges wrote.

Cleansing the Common Law

All the judges in *Mabo* – the majority as much as the dissenting judge – were determined that their judgment should be constructed within the common law. To use Justice Brennan's phrase, the 'skeletal principle of our legal system' must not be 'fractured' by the court's recognition of native title.[10] The difference between the majority and Justice Dawson comes down to whether or not the common law can be interpreted as developing in a normatively evolutionary fashion. The majority were willing to infuse the common law with what they understood to be contemporary international norms and what they hoped were also contemporary Australian values. Justice Dawson, in dissent, refused to do so. He admitted that in past relations with Indigenous peoples, 'there may not be a great deal to be proud about,' but 'a change in view does not of itself mean a change in the law.' The 'implementation of a new policy,' he insisted, 'is a matter for government rather than the courts.' An attempt 'to revise history or to fail to recognize its legal impact,' was, he said, 'to impugn the foundations of the very legal system under which this case must be decided.'[11]

Dawson's charge reflects a blindness to his own selective treatment of the relevant legal precedents and historical events. There was and there is no politically neutral way of 'finding' or interpreting the common law. There is always some 'leeway in the precedents'[12] – and never more so than when, as in a case like *Mabo (No. 2)*, the relevant precedents are not just from one country or era but from an empire and its successor states and different periods of history. The common law will be interpreted liberally by reform-minded judges and conservatively by judges who wish to leave law reform to the legislature. It is the great good fortune of the plaintiffs in *Mabo* that they brought their case before the High Court just as it was becoming a less conservative, more activist institution.[13] As a result, its decisions, and none more than its decision in *Mabo*, attract much more political scrutiny and debate. But the charge that these decisions undermine the country's legal system should be seen as nothing more than a rhetorical move in this political debate.

The key point of difference between the majority and Dawson concerns whether land rights that derive from Indigenous societies survived Britain's annexation of their territories. The six majority justices, giving three somewhat different rationales, found that, according to English law, native rights to land could and did survive the establishment of British sovereignty in Australia. At the core of their analysis is a distinction in English land law between the radical title of the Crown and the Crown's ownership of land. The Crown's 'radical title' refers to its sovereign political authority, or to use the ancient language of the English law of tenures, its paramount lordship over all the territory in its realm, including its colonial possessions. But this radical title is not to be equated with the Crown's having an absolute 'beneficial ownership' of all the land under its rule. Brennan cited numerous texts to distinguish the 'rule in England that all land is *held* of the Crown from the notion that all land is *owned* by the Crown.'[14] In feudal times in England the legal fiction developed – another instance of the English proclivity for legal magic – that the king was the original proprietor of all the land, so that anyone who 'owned' land received it as a grant of tenure from the Crown. But when Britain took possession of Australia, it was not a corollary of the Crown's acquisition of radical title – of sovereignty – over the territory that the Crown acquired absolute beneficial ownership of all the land to the exclusion of Indigenous owners. In Australia, said Brennan, 'the doctrine of tenure applies to every Crown grant of an interest in land, but not to rights and interests which do not owe their existence to a Crown grant.'[15] The rights and interests in the land occupied by Indigenous inhabitants when British sovereignty was established may be recognized by the common law but do not owe their existence to Crown grants. In Justice Brennan's view, it is the 'fallacy of equating sovereignty and beneficial ownership of land'[16] that accounts for the assumption so prevalent in Australian history and policy that native title was automatically extinguished by the acquisition of sovereignty.

In support of the view that native land rights survived the establishment of British sovereignty, the three majority opinions drew upon a series of decisions by the Judicial Committee of the Privy Council, the court that declared the common constitutional law of the British Empire. The Privy Council decisions they considered to be most authoritative came during a time in the twentieth century when British imperial policy was moving in a liberal direction, and these decisions dealt with African colonies acquired by conquest or cession rather than by settlement. In a 1919 case concerning Southern Rhodesia, the Privy Council stated that there are 'rights of private property' that, upon conquest, 'it is presumed, in the absence of express confiscation or of subsequent expropriatory legislation, that the conqueror has respected them.'[17] Two years later in a southern Nigerian case, Viscount Haldane stated: 'A mere change in sovereignty is not to be presumed as meant to disturb rights of private owners.'[18] In 1957 Lord Denning, in a judgment summarizing previous cases, identified as a 'guiding principle' of colonial constitutional law that pre-existing property rights of the inhabitants are to be 'fully respected.'[19] The seminal work of Kent McNeil on *Common Law Aboriginal Title* was cited in all three majority judgments as providing strong scholarly backing for the fundamental notion that, under the constitution of the British Empire, as declared by its highest judicial authorities, the Crown's acquisition of sovereignty over a territory did not necessarily involve acquisition of Crown ownership or title to all land in the territory.[20]

Dawson, in dissent, did not deny that Britain's annexation of colonial territory could accommodate native property rights. But, in his view, 'whether, in any particular case, a change of sovereignty is accompanied by a recognition or acceptance by the new sovereign of pre-exiting rights is a matter of fact.'[21] For Dawson, it was the fact of recognition by imperial and colonial authorities, not any legal obligation stemming from British imperial law, that accounted for the survival of any Indigenous land ownership in Britain's colonies. Recognition of native property rights could be explicit, as in the terms of a treaty of cession, or implicit in policies and actions that allowed continuing Indigenous occupation of lands. In either case the source of native property rights was not their existence in the society that preceded British rule but their recognition by the new sovereign. Much of Dawson's judgment is devoted to reviewing the course of early colonial history in Australia and to showing that, on the whole, the colonial authorities, in their policies and laws, as well as the leading Australian judicial decisions on the subject, showed no recognition of native rights in the land. He acknowledged some of the examples to the contrary discussed by Henry Reynolds in his *Law of the Land*, but saw them as aberrant deviations from the dominant policy – that 'the Crown considered itself to be the owner of the land, unencumbered by any form of native title.'[22]

The majority found that imperial case law as well as decisions in other English-settler countries do not, on balance, support Dawson's position that native title rights exist in law only when recognised by the colonial sovereign. A 1924 decision by Lord Dunedin, much relied upon by Dawson, said Brennan, 'is not in accord with the weight of authority.'[23] Many imperial cases could be cited, outside Australia, where there was a presumption that native ownership continued after annexation, so that native people did not automatically become trespassers, legally speaking, on their own land immediately after annexation. Much of the difference between Dawson and the majority comes down to his determination to favour precedents from the most illiberal period of British imperialism against the majority's inclination to take into account more recent decisions reflecting a softening of imperial assumptions. For instance, Dawson gave great weight to the 1889 Judicial Committee decision, rendered as we noted in chapter 4 at the high tide of empire, in which Lord Watson declared that native title in Canada had no other basis than 'the good will of the Sovereign.'[24] Brennan, in contrast, in rejecting precedents from the high court of 'an Empire then concerned with the development of its colonies,' asserted the modern independence of Australia's High Court. 'Here,' he said, 'rests the ultimate responsibility of declaring the law of the nation.'[25]

The majority opinions took into account the treatment of Privy Council precedents by the Supreme Court of Canada. In particular, Brennan cited the Canadian Supreme Court justice Emmett Hall's renunciation of Lord Watson's position in the 1973 *Calder* case. 'The proposition that after conquest or discovery the native peoples have no rights at all except those subsequently granted or recognized by the conqueror or discoverer,' Hall declared, 'was wholly wrong.'[26] Hall arrived at this position by recovering legal doctrines that pre-date the high tide of empire and were the source of Chief Justice Marshall's jurisprudence. That jurisprudence (which we reviewed in chapter 4), whatever its inconsistencies and limitations, acknowledged that the rights of Indian nations to live on their lands and govern their own internal affairs pre-dated the imposition of European sovereignty. In 1970, when Judge Blackburn was deciding *Milirrpum*, the *Calder* case had not yet reached the Canadian Supreme Court, and the lower courts in Canada were still being faithful to the late nineteenth-century Judicial Committee precedents. Now, in effecting Australia's judicial revolution, the High Court justices could absorb Canada's judicial revolution. In *Calder*, Hall wrote for only three of the six judges who dealt with the native title issue, but Justice Judson, who wrote for the other three judges, did not disagree with Hall's rejection of the Privy Council's recognition doctrine. Subsequently, in the 1984 *Guerin*[27] case, the Supreme Court of Canada clearly supported the position that native title has its source in pre-contact native society. The High Court of Australia was influenced by these Canadian developments.

The difference between the majority and the dissenting judge in *Mabo (No. 2)* on whether native title owes its very existence to recognition by the new imperial sovereign or to the Indigenous society that existed before annexation may seem to be an abstract, philosophical point. But it is a point that goes to the heart of the most profound issue at stake in relations with Indigenous peoples – the issue that was debated by Bartolome de Las Casas in the court of the Holy Roman Emperor four-and-a-half centuries earlier.[28] If, as Las Casas contended, the native peoples discovered by the Europeans are truly part of humankind, then they deserve to be respected as full, rational human beings. This means that certain fundamental rights, including the right to the land in which one lives, inhere in Indigenous peoples as part of their common humanity. Justices Deane and Gaudron acknowledged this point when they observed the support for the 'guiding principle' of common law native title in the classical natural law writings of Hugo Grotius and other philosophical founders of European international law.[29] Under the majority's understanding of the common law, native peoples coming under British rule retain land rights that they enjoyed as human societies and, whether the imperial sovereign likes it or not, these rights become a 'burden' on its sovereignty. This burden, as we shall see, though a legal one and based on morality, is not a very heavy burden on the new sovereign who, according to these Australian judges, has the legal power to extinguish it relatively easily – unless the immorality of doing so gets in the way. Justice Dawson, in dissent, acknowledged the immorality of Indigenous dispossession, but he did not see that immorality as constituting the basis for any legal burden, however slight, on the Crown.

The cleansing of the common law in *Mabo* came in the majority's critical review of how British imperial law had been applied by the courts to and in Australia. Up until *Mabo (No. 2)*, the cornerstone of judicially declared law on land ownership in Australia was the audacious statement Lord Watson made in 1889 in the case of *Cooper v. Stuart*: that the Colony of New South Wales 'consisted of a tract of territory practically unoccupied, without settled inhabitants or settled law, at the time when it was peacefully annexed to the British Dominions.'[30] Watson's dictum meant that, on annexation, there were no native inhabitants with land rights, so that the Crown had not only political sovereignty over the territory but absolute ownership of all the land. Though Watson did not use the term, in effect he gave the 'blessing' of the empire's highest court to the idea that Australia was a *terra nullius* when the British began to settle there. Watson's position was consistent with an 1847 judgment of the Supreme Court of New South Wales, in *Attorney General (N.S.W) v. Brown*,[31] and was followed by the High Court in two twentieth-century cases, *Williams v. Attorney General (N.S.W)*[32] and *Randwick Corporation v. Rutledge*.[33] These cases were the precedents that confronted Blackburn in *Milirrpum* and that he had felt bound to follow, even though, as he admitted, the premise on which they rested – that at the time of annexation Australia was without settled inhabitants or settled law – did not accord with the facts set before him by the Aboriginal people of Cape Gove. Now, in *Mabo*, six judges of the High Court were no longer willing to accept a construction of the facts based on assumptions drawn from European imperialism's most triumphal epoch.

The Privy Council and Australian precedents that the High Court majority overturned in *Mabo (No. 2)* were premised on the idea that Australia was a colony acquired entirely by settlement. As we saw in chapter 2, the doctrinal distinction in imperial legal writing between colonies acquired by conquest or cession and colonies of settlement never fitted the facts of colonization – that is, the facts as seen through a non-racist prism. A pure colony of settlement would be one planted in an entirely unoccupied land. The Australian colonies could be classified as pure colonies of settlement only if the native inhabitants were considered not to be fully human – and that is exactly what the judges and legal theorists who regarded Australia as a colony of settlement believed. Aborigines were not high enough in the scale of human evolution to count as societies with legal rights meriting recognition by their new European sovereign. That idea was still alive and well in British imperial law in 1919, when in *In re Southern Rhodesia*, Lord Sumner wrote:

> Some tribes are so low in the scale of social organization that their usages and conceptions of rights and duties are not to be reconciled with the institutions of civilized society. Such a gulf cannot be bridged. It would be idle to impute to such people some shadow of the rights known to our law and then to transmute it into the substance of transferable rights of property as we know them.[34]

In Australia, and elsewhere, many Europeans fortified this view with the idea attributed to English philosophers that an essential mark of being civilized, and therefore fully human, was cultivating the land. By that standard, the 'nomadic' Aborigines did not qualify for recognition as rights-bearing humans. Because the Murray Islanders, with their cultivated garden plots, did not suffer from that alleged disqualification for full membership in humankind, the High Court justices might have restricted themselves to finding that the Murray Islands were not *terra nullius* at the time of annexation and left the mainland Aborigines confined to a lower category of being. Many of the High Court's critics would subsequently attack the majority for their refusal to follow this line of racist thinking. But the majority threw out the racist undergirding of the notion of a pure colony of settlement – in every respect.

Justice Brennan, whose opinion attracted the most support in the court, did the cleansing with the strongest, most politically self-conscious language. 'The facts as we know them today,' he said, 'do not fit the "absence of law" or "barbarian" theory underpininng' the earlier decisions. He then injected into the decision recent post-imperial developments in international law, citing the International Court of Justice's 1975 *Advisory Opinion on Western Sahara*[35] in which the doctrine of *terra nullius* was rejected as an acceptable explanation of the colonization of lands occupied by nomadic peoples. He concluded this part of his judgment with a bold rhetorical flourish:

> Whatever the justification advanced in earlier days for refusing to recognize the rights and interests in land of the Indigenous inhabitants of settled colonies, an unjust and discriminatory doctrine of that kind can no longer be accepted. The expectations of the international community accord in this respect with the contemporary values of the Australian people.[36]

While Brennan's view certainly reflected the emerging norms of the international legal order, he was, as we shall see in chapter 9, somewhat sanguine about mainstream Australian opinion being in tune with those norms.

Taking the view that, from the beginning of British settlement, common law native title existed in Australia requires quite a stretch of the historical imagination. An essay on the *Mabo* decision entitled '204 Years of Invisible Title,'[37] by Noel Pearson, a leading Aboriginal legal scholar, speaks poignantly to how little real value Indigenous owners had derived from the common law's recognition of their rights of ownership. To accommodate his finding within the traditional categories of colonization, Justice Brennan had to construct a new kind of colony of settlement – one with a modicum of legal pluralism. On the effective assertion of British sovereignty over them, the communal holders of common law native title retained their own systems of land law but, at the same time, their members 'became British subjects owing allegiance to the Imperial Sovereign entitled to such rights and privileges and subject to such liabilities as the common law and applicable statutes provided.'[38] The historical evidence of violence and conflict in the years immediately following the arrival of the First Fleet is, to say the least, hard to square with the legal theory that the Aboriginal peoples who were literally under constant siege by the newcomers were in fact British subjects with the rights and privileges Brennan claims they possessed. Law, as was shown earlier in this book, had little bearing on relations with Aboriginal peoples in the early years of settlement. New South Wales was a penal colony and was unlike any other British colony in the New World. Blackstone's simple taxonomy of three ways of acquiring colonies – settlement, cession, and conquest – did not fit the facts of colonization in Australia any more than it conformed with the realities of North American colonization. Peter Bayne suggests that the more plausible way of applying Blackstone in Australia would be to treat New South Wales as a colony acquired by conquest.[39] But this view also seems a big stretch. Did more than a century of frontier skirmishing on the Australian continent really amount to a 'conquest'? And just when and by whom were the Torres Strait Islanders 'conquered'?

A Very Light Burden on the Crown

The majority's effort to cleanse the common law in Australia and bring it into line with contemporary international norms, while at the same time maintaining that common law native title in some mysterious theoretical sense had existed in colonial Australia right from the beginning of settlement, may not be very convincing. But still, when we bear in mind the challenge of persuading a society that has difficulty accepting the law-making role of judges, this effort to square the circle and show that native title, which seemed to have been so blatantly denied, had been there all along is understandable. What is much less understandable is the very diminished value the High Court majority attributed to common law native title. The rights and interests in the land that the Indigenous inhabitants enjoyed under the customs of their community when sovereignty was acquired by the Crown, in the words of Justice Brennan, 'are seen to be a burden on the radical title which the Crown acquires.'[40] But these rights and interests turn out to be an extremely light burden, a burden that the law of the settler society permits its government all too easily to remove.

Unfortunately for Australia's Indigenous peoples, Justice Brennan's conception of native title imposed the lightest of legal burdens on settler sovereignty, and it was his opinion that attracted the most support within the court. As Richard Bartlett succinctly puts it: 'Brennan J's judgment assumes that native title may be extinguished at common law without the consent of the Aboriginal people and without compensation.'[41] Brennan adopted the standard set in other common law jurisdictions that the power to extinguish native title 'must reveal a clear and plain intention to do so.'[42] However, his application of this standard makes it much easier to meet in Australia than in other settler states. Unlike other property rights under common law, native title, according to Brennan, can be validly extinguished by an act of the executive without any authorizing legislation. For Brennan, the 'clear and plain intention test' can be met simply by the executive doing something to or with the land 'that is wholly or partially inconsistent with a continuing right to enjoy native title.'[43] Under Brennan's theory, common law native title is wiped out – 'extinguished' – to the extent that anything government (be it federal, state, or territorial) does lawfully is inconsistent with a native people's continued occupation and use of the land. The existence of native title itself and the absence of native consent are in no way legal impediments to such acts of extinguishment.

According to Brennan, it is the exercise of this easy power of extinguishment, not the initial imposition of British sovereignty, that accounts for the dispossession of Australia's Indigenous peoples. It was by granting lands to private owners and appropriating parcels of land for its own public purposes that the settler state removed land from native ownership:

> To treat the dispossession of Australian Aborigines as the working out of the Crown's acquisition of ownership of all land on first settlement is contrary to history. Aborigines were dispossessed of their land parcel by parcel, to make way for expanding colonial settlement. Their dispossession underwrote the development of the nation.[44]

Brennan admits that through this process of extinguishment, many Aborigines have lost their native title. In the Murray Islands, however, 'the Crown has alienated only part of the land and has not acquired for itself the beneficial ownership of any substantial part.' Then, turning his attention to the Australian mainland, he speculates that 'there may be other areas of Australia where native title has not been extinguished and where an Aboriginal people, maintaining their identity and their customs, are entitled to enjoy their native title.'[45]

Given that Murray Islanders were the plaintiffs in the case, Brennan had to deal in detail with the extent to which the native title rights of the Murray Islanders may have been extinguished. On the bright side, he rejected any argument that the legislation under which Queensland in 1882 had made the Murray Islands a reserve for its native inhabitants extinguished the inhabitants' native title. But Queensland's subsequent lease of two acres on Mer to the London Missionary Society did extinguish native title to that small parcel of land. Similarly, a twenty-year lease over all of Dauer and Waier granted in 1931 to non-Meriam persons for the purpose of operating a sardine factory may have extinguished native title to those islands. There were some unresolved technical issues about whether the lease had been validly issued, but if it was, there was no doubt in Brennan's mind that it extinguished the Meriam people's native title on both islands – even though the lease had been issued on condition that the sardine factory not interfere with the natives' gardening and fishing on and around the islands, and the factory was closed down in 1938. In Brennan's view, native title, once extinguished by a lease, could not be revived. Merely by granting such a lease, the Crown indicated (according to him, in clear and plain terms) that it expected the reversion of ownership to itself following termination of the lease.[46] Public works erected on Mer for administrative purposes, such as a school, a teacher's residence, a jail house, a hospital, and even 'a village square,' may also have extinguished the Meriam people's native title. It all depends on whether these activities had been properly authorized by law – a matter that Brennan found could not be determined in the case at hand.

Unlike Justices Deane, Gaudron, and Toohey, who recognized that extinguishment of native title without consent of the rights holders was wrongful and could give rise to a right to compensation, Justice Brennan did not deal explicitly with the question of compensation. But Chief Justice Mason and Justice McHugh, the two judges who agreed with Brennan's judgment, identified the compensation issue as the 'main difference' between Brennan and the other three judges who recognized native title. The only point Mason and McHugh made in their short three-paragraph concurring opinion was that 'neither of us, nor Brennan J. agrees with the conclusion to be drawn from the judgments of Deane, Toohey and Gaudron JJ. that, at least in the absence of clear and unambiguous statutory provision to the contrary, extinguishment of native title by the Crown is wrongful and gives rise to a claim for compensatory damages.'[47] Of course, to those members of the court rejecting compensation for the extinguishment of native title, they could add Justice Dawson, who viewed any native title that might exist as dependent on recognition and permission of the imperial sovereign.

Mason and McHugh stated that they were 'authorized' by the other members of the court to say that a majority of the judges supported their position on compensation.

Though Brennan, Mason, and McHugh took the position that settler governments could unilaterally extinguish common law native title without incurring any obligation to compensate the dispossessed, they did so subject to one important caveat – the operation of the *Racial Discrimination Act, 1975.* They did not spell out the protection that *RDA* might provide to native title holders, but, as we saw earlier, in 1988 the High Court majority in the court's first *Mabo* decision invoked *RDA* as the basis for overturning Queensland's attempt to extinguish every bit of native title that might exist in the Torres Strait.[48] On that occasion, Brennan joined with Deane, Gaudron, and Toohey to form the majority. And the key to the majority's position was that *RDA* entitled the Murray Islanders to be treated according to the fundamental principles of human dignity and essential equality that underlie the international recognition of human rights. In 1988 the court had not yet determined what the Murray Islanders' land rights were, but, nonetheless, the majority was of the view that these rights must somehow encompass the universal right to own property alone and in association with others and to immunity from being 'arbitrarily deprived' of property. *RDA* might afford some compensation to native title holders who had lost their land through arbitrary dispossession since 1975, when the act came into force, but it would do nothing for the massive dispossession that occurred before 1975. It is disturbing that Brennan and the judges who concurred with him made no mention of the protection against the unjust taking of property that has been in Australia's Constitution since the country's founding. This protection, found in Section 51 (xxxi) of the Constitution, requires that 'just terms' apply to the taking of property by the Commonwealth from any state or person. Even though this constitutional right has no application to state legislatures, failure to mention it as binding on the Commonwealth suggests that the High Court majority did not look upon native title as conferring full-fledged rights of property ownership.

The demeaning, diminishing status accorded to common law native title by the High Court is based on a dubious understanding of common law rights. Brennan acknowledged that there is a presumption in common law that property rights founded on Crown grants are not to be interfered with by the Crown without clear statutory authority. But he thought that native title rights could not benefit from this presumption precisely because 'native title is not granted by the Crown.'[49] In other words, in Brennan's view, the exceptional vulnerability of native title rights stems from the fact that their source is an Aboriginal society. As McNeil has shown, there do not appear to be common law precedents for this position – and Brennan did not cite any.[50] McNeil cites English precedents that are quite to the contrary and give the same protection to land rights based on custom as to rights based on Crown grants. Besides, at least since Blackstone's time, it has been a well-established principle of the common law world that the Crown or the executive does not itself have legislative powers and cannot without clear and unambiguous legislative authority deprive subjects or citizens of their common law rights.[51] It is difficult to square Brennan's belief that native title holders from the beginning of British sovereignty were British subjects and held common law title to their lands with his view that the same common law permitted government officials, in the absence of any explicit legislative authorization, to extinguish native title without either consent or any obligation to provide compensation. One cannot help asking in what sense a right so easily denied really is a legal right.

Deane and Gaudron evinced a more robust understanding of the legal force of common law native title. Like Brennan, they accepted the dubious idea that common law native title was 'merely a personal right unsupported by any prior or presumed Crown grant of any estate or interest in the land'[52] and that, therefore, it was susceptible to being extinguished by a Crown grant that is inconsistent with native title. However, they were at pains to disassociate themselves from statements in some of the legal precedents set down at the high tide of imperialism which treated native title 'as no more than a permissive occupancy which the Crown was lawfully entitled to revoke or terminate at any time regardless of the wishes of those living on the land or using it for traditional purposes.'[53] Deane and Gaudron gave much more weight than Brennan to the British law and policy in relation to native peoples which operated during the late eighteenth and early nineteenth century. They recognized that under this relatively liberal brand of imperialism, the normal way of acquiring land subject to native title was through agreements with the native owners, not unilateral extinguishment. They cited with approval the following passage from the decision of the New Zealand judge, Chapman, made in 1847 in reference to the land rights recognized in the Treaty of Waitangi: 'Whatever may be the opinion of the jurists as to the strength or weakness of the Native Title ... it cannot be too solemnly asserted that it is entitled to be respected, that it cannot be extinguished (at least in times of peace) otherwise than by the free consent of the Native occupiers.'[54] And they noted that the instructions to Captain Cook and to Phillip, the first governor of New South Wales, manifested an intention to extend this respectful treatment to the native inhabitants of the colony. For this part of their judgment, Deane and Gaudron went beyond the submissions of the parties and drew extensively on the writings of scholars such as Henry Reynolds and R.J. King.[55]

But Deane and Gaudron also described how quickly and how drastically, despite colonial officials who knew better, the settler regime in New South Wales and, subsequently, in the other Australian colonies departed from this policy. Deane and Gaudron considered the massive process of coercive dispossession (which, according to Brennan, was sanctioned by the common law) a violation of the native title holders' rights. 'In theory, the native inhabitants were entitled to invoke the protection of the law in a local court,' though in practice, they conceded, 'there is an element of the absurd about the suggestion that it would have even occurred to the native inhabitants of a new British Colony that they should bring proceedings in a British Court against the British Crown to vindicate their rights under a common law of which they would be likely to know nothing.'[56] Over time, the denial of common law native title came to be sanctioned by administrators and judges operating on the erroneous belief that Australia was a *terra nullius*, in which the full and beneficial ownership of all land from the beginning of British sovereignty was vested in the Crown. The words with which Deane and Gaudron concluded this part of their judgment contain what is surely the starkest and most memorable indictment of this phase of Australian history: 'The acts and events by which that dispossession in legal theory was carried into practical effect constitute the darkest aspect of the history of this nation. The nation as a whole must remain diminished unless and until there is an acknowledgment of, and retreat from, those past injustices.'[57]

Oddly, Deane and Gaudron clung to their belief in 'the power of the Crown wrongfully to extinguish the native title by inconsistent grant.'[58] But they also insisted that the ordinary rules of statutory interpretation mean that clear and unambiguous words must be used before a legislature can be imputed to intend to expropriate or extinguish valuable rights relating to property without compensation. Nor did they have any doubt about the applicability of the 'just terms' clause of the Australian Constitution to native title. Common law native title rights 'are true legal rights which are recognized and protected by the law ... any legislative extinguishment of those rights would constitute an expropriation of property ... for the purposes of s.51 (xxxi).'[59] For these two judges, native title is not such a light legal burden on the settler regime. Native title rights, 'if wrongfully extinguished (e.g., by inconsistent grant) without clear and ambiguous statutory authorization, found proceedings for compensatory damages.'[60] Crown leases to missionaries and the operators of the sardine factory, in their view, pose the only possible extinguishment of the Murray Islanders' title to their lands. Deane and Gaudron did not come to any conclusion on the legal status and consequences of these leases because the parties involved were not before them. However, they stated that, even if the sardine factory lease was valid, it is unlikely that it extinguished native title because the lease itself 'recognized and protected usufructuary rights of the Murray Islanders, and was subsequently forfeited.'[61] Their stand (and difference with Brennan) on this issue has major implications for the survival of native title on those vast areas of Australia subject to pastoral leases.

Of the six High Court justices who rejected the validity of a *terra nullius* account of Australia, John Toohey put forward the firmest, most full-blooded account of native title. Toohey was the only member of the court who had an extensive professional background in the field of aboriginal law. His five years as aboriginal land commissioner in the Northern Territory gave him a great deal of first-hand experience with traditional owners of Aboriginal lands. Common law native title was simply one way of recognizing and protecting traditional title: 'Ultimately, traditional title has a common law existence because the common law recognizes the survival of traditional interests and operates to protect them.'[62] Toohey parted company with the other majority judges by rejecting any arguments to the effect that native title rights had an inferior status to other property rights of British subjects (or Australian citizens) that made them legally more vulnerable to extinguishment. Yes, traditional ownership was different from other kinds of land rights, but that difference did not equate with a lesser status in law. He approved of the view of native title articulated by the Canadian judge, Judson, in the 1973 *Calder* case: '[T]he fact is that when the settlers came, the Indians were there, organized in society and occupying the land as their forefathers had done for centuries. This is what Indian title means and it does not help one in the solution of this problem to call it a "personal or usufructuary right."'[63] He conceded that the Crown has the power to terminate native title, but he denied that this was a special power. It is the same power that the Crown has, 'subject to constitutional, statutory or common law restrictions,' to terminate any subject's title to property by compulsorily acquiring it.[64] One of the common law principles that applies to this power is that the Crown could not extinguish native title without being authorized to do so by legislation expressing a clear intent. Toohey concluded that the 'traditional title of the Meriam people to the land in the Islands has not been extinguished ... and may not be extinguished without the payment of compensation or damages to the traditional titleholders of the Islands.'[65]

At one point in his judgment, Toohey went further and came close to requiring consent as a condition for extinguishing native title. This point occurred in his discussion of the Crown's fiduciary obligation to Indigenous peoples. A fiduciary obligation is one that arises from a relationship that is based, at least in part, on trust. It has a long history in relations with North American native peoples, and began with small settler communities trusting in the good will of much more powerful Indian nations. When the power relations turned in favour of the settlers, the fiduciary obligation ran increasingly in the other direction.[66] An important aspect of this fiduciary relationship arose out of Britain's – and, subsequently, Canada's, the United States', and, at times, New Zealand's – insistence that native peoples could not sell their land to private persons or foreign nations but only to the Crown or its successor settler state. The quid pro quo of this restriction on the Indigenous peoples' control over their land – the 'inalienable' nature of their land ownership – is that the Crown (settler government) has an obligation to ensure that native peoples do not lose their land through fraudulent transactions or in a manner that is damaging to their interests.

Recognition of such a fiduciary obligation was the basis of an important 1984 decision of the Supreme Court of Canada in *Guerin*.[67] Toohey was the only High Court judge who gave serious consideration to the fiduciary aspects of settler-aboriginal relations.[68] He did not view a fiduciary obligation as arising from the inalienability of traditional title, because that restriction on native land ownership 'may itself be open to debate.'[69] But he viewed evidence of a long-standing Crown policy, not only in Australia but elsewhere in the British Empire, of protecting Aboriginal peoples from exploitation as giving rise to a trustlike obligation. He cited early Queensland legislation making the Murray Islands a reserve and the appointment of trustees as evidence of the Crown's assuming an obligation to protect the native inhabitants. Applying these thoughts to the case at hand, Justice Toohey stated: 'The obligation on the Crown in the present case is to ensure that traditional title is not impaired or destroyed without the consent of or otherwise contrary to the interests of the titleholders.'[70]

Toohey's approach is much more in accord with contemporary policy and law in other English settler countries, especially Canada and New Zealand, than that of the other majority judges. He sees the importance of consent in maintaining honourable relations with Indigenous peoples. But even Toohey wanted to assuage the fears of Australians, who are the beneficiaries of the Crown's dishonourable treatment of traditional land owners in the past. Nothing in his judgment, he wrote, 'should be taken to suggest that the titles of those to whom land has been alienated by the Crown may now be disturbed.'[71]

A Settler Bridge to Indigenous Law

Most of the judges' reasons in *Mabo (No. 2)* were concerned with establishing that native land ownership, as a matter of common law, survived the assertion of British sovereignty and then explaining how the settler state can extinguish common law native title. But the judges also gave some attention to the more positive task of elucidating what common law native title means. They did not attempt to provide an exhaustive account of native title. As Lisa Strelein observes, this economy of conceptualization is appropriate for 'judge-made law,' which develops on a case-by-case basis.[72] Indeed, many subsequent decisions of the High Court and other Australian tribunals will flesh out the meaning of Australian-style native title. And a huge piece of national legislation will set out conditions for exercising and for extinguishing native title rights, a statute that many Australians, unfortunately, will conflate with native title. This misunderstanding provides all the more reason to comprehend those features of native title that Australia's High Court laid down as the cornerstone of common law native title.

First and foremost, it is essential to understand that 'native title' as a concept in settler law is not itself a title to land ownership. It is a bridge, a legal connector, through which the law of the dominant society recognizes the traditional (long-established) connection of an Indigenous people to their land. In Justice Brennan's words: 'Native title, though recognized by the common law, is not an institution of the common law and is not alienable by common law.'[73] He went on to explain that 'the incidents of a particular native title' (by which he meant the detailed rules and practices of land ownership, inheritance, transfer, and other aspects of land use) are determined by 'the laws and customs of the

Indigenous inhabitants.'[74] Similarly, Deane and Gaudron stated: 'Since the title preserves entitlement to use or enjoyment under the traditional law or custom of the relevant territory or locality, the contents of the rights and the identity of those entitled to enjoy them must be ascertained by reference to that traditional law or custom.'[75] For Toohey, also, it was traditional title or ownership that common law native title recognizes. Common law title, in the eyes of these common law judges, may not be 'an institution of the common law,' but, as Noel Pearson comments, the High Court judges failed to acknowledge 'neither is native title an Aboriginal title.' It is not an Aboriginal title 'because patently Aboriginal law will recognize title where the common law will not.'[76] Pearson therefore characterizes native title as a 'recognition space.' We should note, however, that this space is very much controlled and shaped by the settler society's judiciary.

The second fundamental feature of native title follows logically from the first: its communal nature. Because native title is an instrument through which an Indigenous people's law is recognized, it inheres not in any individual but in the native society itself. The holder of native title is an Indigenous community. The traditional law of the title-holding community may recognize that individual families have exclusive or primary access to and responsibility for certain parts of the community's lands. That was clearly the case under Meriam law. Even if there were many disputes about who owned which plots of land, there was never any doubt that the Meriam people, as a people, had a long-established tradition of individual clan or family ownership of lands and waters. Indeed, that fact was at the very core of Mabo's confidence in the ultimate success of his case. We can see now how important it was for the plaintiffs to amend their claim to one of collective ownership.

The apparent uncertainty and flexibility of the Meriam property system was not a problem for the six High Court justices who recognized native title. They repudiated the idea that to merit recognition, the law of an Indigenous people must measure up to European standards of precision. This idea had been put forward in some of the Judicial Committee of the Privy Council decisions rendered when assumptions of Western superiority were at their zenith. Lack of precision in delineating land ownership within Meriam society had been a concern of Justice Moynihan in the fact-finding stage of the case and had made him reluctant to recognize the Meriam people's property arrangements as based on law. But the High Court justices did not share Moynihan's ethnocentric conception of law. As Justice Toohey put it: 'Because rights and duties inter se cannot be determined precisely, it does not follow that traditional rights are not to be recognized by the common law.'[77] Justice Brennan made the same point in commenting that disputes about land within the community 'may have to be settled by community consensus or in some other manner prescribed by custom,' but absence of precision or certainty was not a bar to recognizing native title.[78]

The only major exception to the High Court judges' rejection of testing the validity of Indigenous law by European legal standards is Brennan's statement that the Australian judiciary would have to withhold its sanction from native laws or customs that were 'repugnant to natural justice, equity and good conscience.'[79] He did not give any examples of the kind of practice he would view as violating this standard. The other majority judgments did not support the idea that Indigenous law must meet Australian judges' standards of natural justice in order to have their backing. Rather than trying to assimilate common law native title with other forms of property known to the common law, the High Court judges, like other judges in the common law world, stressed its distinctive – or to use the Latin of which they are so fond – sui generis, nature. This approach can be the basis of introducing a welcome element of pluralism into a settler country's legal system. But underlining the sui generis nature of native title can also be the basis for affording it significantly less legal protection than non-Indigenous property interests enjoy. We have already seen this negative implication in the judgments both of Brennan and of Deane and Gaudron.

These two judgments also agreed that there is one serious limitation on what owners of native title can do with their land: its reputed 'inalienability.' Both judgments were careful to acknowledge that land can be alienated (traded, sold, or surrendered) within and among native societies. But they supported the widely held view among common law judges and officials that, otherwise, native title lands can be alienated only to the Crown. On this point Brennan was a little narrower than Deane and Gaudron in stipulating that alienation other than to the Crown is confined to 'members of the Indigenous group to whom alienation is permitted by the traditional laws and customs.'[80] For Deane and Gaudron, native title rights 'are not assignable ... outside the overall native system.'[81] Toohey, as we have seen, had his doubts about these restrictions on the alienability of native title rights. Perhaps he sensed the strong connection between denying native peoples the right to have any land dealings with non-native persons or powers and the imposition of settler state sovereignty over Indigenous peoples. The right of pre-emption, of being the only agency that can directly acquire land from Indigenous owners, is a right claimed by state authorities in Canada, New Zealand, and the United States. Though this right may be a traditional feature of common law native title,[82] it is one that, as we saw earlier, caused the candid American chief justice Marshall some embarrassment when he enunciated it in 1823.[83]

The High Court judges who recognized the land rights of Indigenous peoples also recognized that, though the source of these rights is owner-ship of the land before settler sovereignty, title-holding peoples could continue to develop and modify their land law and practices after settler sovereignty. In the words of Deane and Gaudron, 'the traditional law or custom is not ... frozen at the moment of establishment of a Colony.'[84] For Brennan, too, 'so long as the people remain as an identifiable community ... living under its laws and customs,' the rights and interests in land of the members of that community are determined by the society's traditional law and customs 'as currently acknowledged and observed.'[85] Brennan did not accept the argument pushed so hard by Queensland that use of an island court, established under the aegis of colonial rule to settle land disputes among the Meriam, terminated their traditional system. A traditional Indigenous legal system like the com-mon law itself could evolve and adapt to changing societal circum-stances. Toohey made the same point more bluntly: 'An Indigenous society cannot, as it were, surrender its rights by modifying its way of life.'[86]

It is remarkable that these High Court judges did not acknowledge the *political* significance of an Indigenous people's right to maintain and develop their legal system. Granted, the laws and customs referred to are only those that deal with land use and ownership. But there is no matter of greater importance to an Indigenous people, no matter that is more central to its spiritual, social, and economic concerns – indeed, to its very identity – than its relationship to its traditional lands and waters. The right to preside over the development of laws and customs govern-ing these matters is surely a crucial element of self-government and political autonomy. Yet the High Court justices do not talk about native title in these political terms. Even if they thought about this implication of native title (and it is not clear that they did), they would surely have shied away from advertising the inherence of Indigenous self-govern-ment in common law native title. Telling Australians that their legal system recognized native ownership that preceded British sovereignty would be a big enough shock and a big enough political exposure for the

High Court. Telling them that inherent in this ownership and its continuation was an Indigenous right to self-government would have blown the lid off! Settler political culture in Australia was still too gripped by 'one nation' angst to be able to digest such a disclosure. Even so, this clear – and for Australians – radical implication of common law native title should not escape the reader's notice.

For the majority, the crucial defining feature of native title was an identifiable Indigenous community living on land governed by its own system of law at the time of colonization – and maintaining that connection ever since coming under British rule. An Indigenous people does not lose its title simply by changing its laws and customs, but its title would be extinguished if its members ceased to live on their traditional lands. This loss would occur whether or not their physical presence on traditional land was terminated voluntarily or involuntarily. Justice Brennan acknowledged that 'since European settlement of Australia, many clans or groups of Indigenous people have been physically separated from their land and have lost their connexion with it.'[87] This severance of physical presence on the land, no matter how it occurred, like the death of the last member of the group, extinguishes native title. And once extinguished, in Brennnan's view, beneficial ownership is taken over by the Crown and native title can never be restored. According to this conception of common law native title, once a native group is pushed out of the native title 'recognition space,' it can never get back in. Brennan also wrote about native title being lost 'when the tides of history have washed away any real acknowledgment of traditional law and any real observance of traditional customs.'[88] A few lines later he mentioned the 'abandonning of laws and customs based on tradition.' In these passages he seemed to be suggesting that members of an Indigenous society might continue to live on their traditional lands in an entirely non-traditional way and thereby lose native title. But he gave no examples, nor did he square this idea with his view that Indigenous people could change their laws and traditions without losing title.

On this point the judgments of Deane and Gaudron and of Toohey were more straightforward: for them it is continuous physical occupancy that must be maintained to avoid extinguishment of native title.[89] Only Toohey took care not to insist on a narrow conception of exclusive occupancy. Random or casual occupation of land could not be the basis for a valid claim to title, but a strict rule of exclusive use and occupancy would not fit the circumstances of Aboriginal societies on the Australian continent, where often a number of clans and groups shared the use of land.[90] That had certainly been the kind of situation considered by Justice Blackburn in *Milirrpum*. The situation in the Murray Islands, where the Meriam people asserted an exclusive right of occupancy, was entirely different.

Fortunately, none of the majority judgments in *Mabo (No. 2)* made exclusive occupancy a requirement of native title. Requiring continuous occupancy was tough enough. That requirement put native title out of reach of many Aboriginal groups that had been pushed off their lands by the advancing frontier of settlement. Moreover, the High Court majority ruled out any legal claim to receive compensation for such coercive dispossession. Despite the furore that arose after the *Mabo* case – the fear that urban Australians were about to lose their backyards – common law native title claims would be difficult, if not impossible, to support in those parts of Australia settled and occupied by non-Indigenous people.

In *Mabo (No. 2)*, the High Court had little to say about the requirements for proving legal title. In the case at hand, the plaintiffs had made out a very strong case that the Meriam people met the basic requirements of native title: they were a people with a firm sense of identity who had occupied their island homeland since well before British annexation and had continued to operate their own system of land law. All these facts had been amply made out before Justice Moynihan in the first stage of proceedings. But what about other Indigenous peoples who want Australian courts to recognize their native title? Would they have to go through a fact-finding process as rigorous, expensive, time-consuming, and often humiliating as Eddie Mabo and his fellow Murray Islanders had been put through? Canada's Supreme Court in the *Calder* case adopted a dictum from a 1921 Privy Council judgment: where a native group has established its original occupancy, native title 'must be presumed to have continued to exist unless the contrary is established by the context and circumstances.'[91] Under this approach, once a native group has established its occupancy of land at the time British sovereignty was asserted, the onus of proof shifts to those who wish to defeat claims of native title.[92] Adoption of this common law doctrine would have been of considerable assistance to native title claimants in Australia. But the High Court did not pronounce on the onus of proof in native title cases. As we will see, the Commonwealth Parliament, in enacting post-*Mabo* legislation, not the High Court, will be the first Australian legislator on these issues – ones that have such a vital bearing on accessibility to the native title 'recognition space.'

Limits of the Common Law

Common law is judge-made law. Judges do not 'make' the common law simply on the basis of whim or personal fancy. The stuff out of which judges find and adapt common law are previous judicial decisions and their understanding – assisted by the submissions of the parties and the writings of scholars – of the principles underlying those decisions and the social and political context in which they were made. We have seen all these factors in the judgments rendered by the High Court judges in *Mabo (No. 2)*. And we have seen how the judges' thinking about the requirements of justice influenced their assessment of the precedents in arriving at their decision. They fashioned their judgments not as Martians or super-humans totally uninfluenced by the normative discourse or the political issues of their times, but as judges seeking to formulate what they thought could be the common sense of justice of Australians in 1992. In the end, if they got it badly wrong – if the majority's position was out of phase with the needs and aspirations of most Australians – then there was, and is, a democratic corrective: the common law decisions of judges in all the common law democracies can be modified or countermanded by elected legislatures.

The judiciary's place in the political culture of common law democracies is such that elected legislatures do not casually or lightly overturn common law legal doctrines. When they do, more often than not, it is to overcome long-standing common law rules (for instance, on the status of women or the liability of manufacturers) that are perceived to have become anachronistic and out of phase with contemporary standards of justice. What makes the High Court's decision in the *Mabo* case so unusual is that it was discovering a principle of justice embedded in the common law for centuries but which Australia had not observed. The court's discovery, its cleansing of the common law, was now at the mercy of the majoritarian politics of the Australian democracy.[93]

In the Australian context, judicial recognition of common law native title, vulnerable though it is to settler politics, nevertheless has an exceptional importance. Recognition of Indigenous peoples' ownership of their traditional lands was an element in the founding of Canada, the United States, and New Zealand, the three other Anglo-American liberal democracies with which we have been comparing Australia's aboriginal relations. But these other settler societies' respect for native title in the early days of colonization was as much a matter of operative state policy as a principle of law. In all three of these countries, native title was recognized or reinforced by constitutional or quasi-constitutional provisions – in New Zealand by the Treaty of Waitangi; and in British North America by treaties, the Royal Proclamation of 1763, and subsequently by some recognition of Indigenous peoples in founding Constitutions. Very little of the limited success Indigenous peoples in these places have had in securing a measure of control over their lands and their lives has been made by claiming common law title in the courts. Australia, at the time of *Mabo*, was exceptional in placing so much reliance on judicial recognition of native title as an instrument for reforming relations with Indigenous peoples.

In New Zealand, the remarkable second article of the Treaty of Waitangi, as we noted earlier, recognized the Maori tribes' 'full exclusive and undisturbed possession' of their lands and resources and the exclusive right of the Crown to purchase land from them.[94] Kent McNeil says that the Waitangi Treaty 'probably did no more than affirm common law doctrine.'[95] However, the treaty itself has never been enforceable in the New Zealand courts, and Maori land rights have been regulated not by judicial decisions on common law native title but by the legislation issuing from New Zealand's Parliament and the Native (now Maori) Land Court it created. As we recounted in chapter 5, the statutory regime and Land Court during the most oppressive period of colonization, far from vindicating native title rights, served the settler state as instruments of massive dispossession and subversion of Maori law and custom. Even today, Maori land rights are shaped primarily by legislation rather than judicial determinations of common law native title. The authors of a recent overview of New Zealand's legal history write: 'The one basic principle which has dominated the situation is not the common law doctrine of aboriginal title, but, in fact, the principle of parliamentary supremacy.'[96]

A 1986 judicial decision in *Te Weehi*,[97] quashing a opinions for violating fishery regulations on the grounds that the accused had unextinguished common law fishing rights, showed that in the contemporary era there might be some scope for vindicating native title rights in New Zealand's courts. But judicial actions of this kind are exceptional. Maori decolonizing efforts have focused more on major structural reform of Maori/Pakeha relations. For some Maori nationalists, common law native title as a 'burden on the Crown' resonates too much with an affirmation of settler sovereignty. Much of the Maori political leadership is attracted to the vision of a country based on a Maori/Pakeha partnership. Claims of overriding sovereignty do not fit well with such a vision.[98] The resuscitation of the Treaty of Waitangi and recent jurisprudence of New Zealand's highest court have emphasized a partnership between the Crown and the Maori as a foundational constitutional principle in New Zealand. Certainly the most significant gains of Maori, at the time of *Mabo* and through the 1990s, in recovering control over land and resources have come through negotiations and legislation following reports of the Waitangi Tribunal. Maori rights may well have their base in the principle of justice that informs the doctrine of common law native title, but their assertion and vindication is much more a political than a litigious process.

Common law native title claims have been much more prominent in Canada. At several points in this book we have noted how the Supreme Court of Canada's 1973 decision in *Calder* was a catalytic event in changing Canadian Aboriginal policy. *Calder* was a successful claim of common law native title by the Nisga'a people of British Columbia. That province, in terms of Aboriginal relations, was in effect Canada's Australia. Since joining Canada in 1871, and even for a few years before, British Columbia's government, strongly supported by the settler population, denied that native title applied in that colony and province. The federal government, despite its exclusive constitutional authority for relations with Indians, did very little to prod British Columbia into respecting native title.[99] So *Calder* came as a wake-up call for Ottawa as well as the province. The Supreme Court ruled that British Columbia was not exempt from common law native title. Though the Indian nations'ownership of land was recognized by the Royal Proclamation of 1763, its source was not the proclamation but the Indigenous peoples' traditional ownership that pre-dates the assertion of sovereignty. Native title existed at common law wherever native people continued to live on land they occupied when British sovereignty was asserted – so long as they had not surrendered their title by treaty or had it clearly and plainly extinguished by competent settler authority.

The *Calder* case was not followed by a rush to the courts to lodge native title claims.[100] The Trudeau government admitted that it now had to take native title seriously, but through a process aimed at extinguishing native title rather than recognizing it. As we saw in chapter 6, the federal government viewed the uncertainty it associated with native title as a serious impediment to industrial development on Canada's resource frontier. It offered to negotiate with any eligible Aboriginal people (and the government would decide who was eligible) an agreement to extinguish native title in return for ownership in fee simple of a small parcel of their homelands and some economic benefits. A few Indigenous communities, especially those like the James Bay Cree who were confronted by imminent resource developments, entered into comprehensive claims agreements. But most of Canada's Indigenous peoples eschewed the comprehensive claims policy. Those who still occupied traditional homeland wished to assert native title rights, not barter them away. However, the time, cost, and uncertainty of outcome made resorting to the white man's courts an unattractive alternative. The Nisga'a litigation had taken many years, cost hundreds of thousands of dollars, and, even though successful at the level of principle, did not result in practical arrangements securing Nisga'a ownership. The Supreme Court held that the right to the Nisga'a native title had not been extinguished, but details of such matters as boundaries, compensation, governance, and legal modalities would still have to be worked out through a negotiated agreement with Canada. Litigating native title in Canada seemed, at best, a prelude to negotiating a political agreement.

At the pan-Canadian level, Aboriginal leadership concentrated on obtaining constitutional recognition of their peoples' rights. The upshot of this effort, as we have seen, was the insertion in the *Constitution Act, 1982*, of Section 35, recognizing and affirming 'the existing aboriginal and treaty rights of the aboriginal peoples of Canada.' It took eight more years for the Supreme Court of Canada in *Sparrow*[101] to declare that it was prepared to take this constitutionalization of Aboriginal rights seriously and give Section 35 rights a 'generous, liberal' interpretation. At the end of chapter 7, we noted that the Canadian Supreme Court rendered this important decision just as the *Mabo* case was coming before the Australian High Court.

The *Sparrow* case was referred to in several of the opinions in *Mabo*, but very little weight was given to the fact that native title rights in Canada had become constitutional rights.[102] Brennan cites it as one of his authorities for the rule that a clear and plain intention is a requirement for a legitimate act of extinguishment,[103] failing to note that once a common law right becomes a constitutional right, entrenched in the country's written constitution, old-fashioned extinguishment of the right is no longer acceptable. The Supreme Court judges in *Sparrow* were prepared to talk about the possibility of upholding *infringements* of a constitutional Aboriginal right, but not extinguishment of the right. Aboriginal rights, they reasoned, like other constitutional rights, must not trump all other constitutional values – they must be subject to some limits.

In effect, Canada's Supreme Court made constitutionally protected Aboriginal and treaty rights subject to the same kind of limits that the first section of the *Canadian Charter of Rights and Freedoms* (also added to Canada's Constitution in 1982) applies to all the rights and freedoms it enshrines. Legislation that infringes an 'existing Aboriginal right' could be upheld if it passes a judicially supervised test of justification. The first consideration in determining whether infringing legislation is justified is the 'special trust responsibility of the government vis-à-vis aboriginals.'[104] Government plans must treat Aboriginal peoples 'in a way ensuring that their rights are taken seriously,' and any infringement must interfere with their rights no more than is necessary. In *Sparrow*, the court said it would permit federal law to interfere with the Musqueam people's right to fish in a traditional manner only if the Musqueam were first consulted on their own conservation measures and given priority in any rationing scheme required do meet conservation objectives. Aboriginal leaders in Canada may not have been pleased to have their rights subjected to limits fashioned by Canadian judges, but nonetheless the solicitous judicial scrutiny of legislation interfering with their rights called for by the Canadian Supreme Court in *Sparrow* went well beyond the 'clear and plain intention' – which is all the High Court in *Mabo* required of legislation or executive acts that do not just infringe native title but totally extinguish it. Once common law rights are recognized as enforceable constitutional rights, they constitute a much heavier burden on the Crown.

After *Sparrow*, there was a lot more action in the Canadian courts based on claims of constitutionally protected Aboriginal and treaty rights. Some involved claims to ownership and control of traditional lands, based on the principles of common law native title. Others involved treaty rights and the freedom to carry on particular activities essential to the well-being of an Aboriginal community. In the 1990s, Aboriginal cases became a significant continuing component of the Supreme Court of Canada's docket. In chapter 11 we will see how the swerving trends in the Canadian court's Aboriginal rights jurisprudence parallels the Australian High Court's wavering interpretations of native title rights. Indigenous peoples in Canada were certainly not going to place all their bets on litigation as the means of obtaining political justice.

At the very time the High Court was deciding *Mabo (No. 2)*, pan-Canadian Aboriginal organizations were negotiating with the Canadian and provincial governments the terms of a more satisfactory definition of the status and rights of Aboriginal peoples in the Canadian Constitution.[105] The results, which included a clause recognizing 'that the Aboriginal peoples of Canada have the inherent right of self-government within Canada,' were incorporated in the Charlottetown accord, a grand resolution of all Canada's constitutional discontents which was put to the Canadian people in a referendum in October 1992.[106] Though the accord was rejected by a majority of the Canadian people, nevertheless the Government of Canada, and eventually most of the provinces, agreed to recognize the inherent right of self-government as a constitutional Aboriginal right. Later in the decade, self-government negotiations were rolled into the comprehensive land claims process. At the local level, the choice of whether to litigate or to negotiate – to claim Aboriginal or treaty rights in the courts or to negotiate a modern treaty – became a difficult strategic choice for many Indigenous peoples in Canada. There remained in Canada plenty of resistance to recognizing their 'peoplehood' – their right to survive and flourish as self-governing and self-sustaining peoples in traditional country. Though that right inheres in the policy and principle of common law native title, in Canada, at the time of *Mabo*, native title rights were part of a larger constitutional setting that provides opportunities for recognition which go well beyond claiming common law rights in the courts.

As for the United States, many times in this book we have noted how the treatment of Aboriginal land rights in that country is yet another example of American exceptionalism. Common law native title has never been a concept recognized by American jurists or legislators. In *Worcester*, the last of Marshall's famous trilogy of decisions on the rights of Indian nations, the chief justice adopted an understanding of Indian title that captures much of the principle underlying the doctrine of common law native title. As 'domestic sovereign nations,' Indian peoples were recognized as owners and rulers of their lands. That one limitation on Indian tribes' ownership was that only the United States could purchase land from them.[107] Three years later, in the 1835 case of *Mitchel v. U.S.*,[108] the Marshall Court in an opinion written by Justice Baldwin strengthened its recognition of Indian nations' original title by stating that their 'right of occupancy' was considered to be 'as sacred as the fee simple of the whites.'[109] But this recognition of original Indian title came with some major strings attached. Indian land ownership was at the mercy of the unbridled, plenary power of the United States. Not even in the minimal sense that Australian common law native title is a 'burden on the Crown' is original Indian title a burden on the U.S. Congress. The United States is considered 'to have the power to seize Indians lands within its territory by conquest.'[110] Moreover, the Supreme Court has classified as 'non-justiciable political matters' all challenges to Congress's treatment of lands held by original Indian title.[111] The court, as we have seen, delivered its *coup de grace* against original Indian title in the 1954 *Tee-Hit-Tons* case, when it denied that land owned under original native title qualified for the protection given property rights in the American Constitution.[112] For all these reasons, and other more technical factors, McNeil concludes that 'original Indian title does not correspond to common law aboriginal title.'[113]

Amerindians continue to resort to the white man's courts more than their counterparts in the other English-settler countries. But the matters they litigate have to do with such things as the scope of their own domestic sovereign jurisdiction, encroachments of the states, interpretation of Congressional legislation, and the fiduciary obligations of the United States – not native title. In the American courts, as in settler courts elsewhere, Indigenous peoples win some and lose some. Their relatively greater reliance in the United States on the judicial process as an arena for obtaining justice may, in part, stem from their imbibing the American tradition of vindicating rights in the courts. But to what other institutional processes can they turn? Since 1871 there has been no possibility of making treaties. Amending the great republic's Constitution is a heroic process for any cause, however popular it may be. For Amerindians constituting just 1 per cent of the population, constitutional amendment, even if it were viewed as a desirable means of redress, is totally inaccessible. Lobbying Congress and direct political action are the main alternatives to the courts, but their successful execution requires occupying a significant space in the political life of the country – a space that is just not there for Indigenous peoples in the United States. We can follow the US media for months without coming across a major story about native Americans. That certainly does not happen in Canada or New Zealand. And by the time of *Mabo*, it was much less likely to happen in Australia – even before the High Court's decision was released. Once news of *Mabo* blared out through the Australian media – and ever since – the 'aboriginal problem' would be a staple issue in the country's political life.

The High Court's finding that common law native title existed in Australia would now be exposed to the full and robust force of Australian politics. As a judicial revolution, it would arrive on the political stage with minimal protection from other institutions of Australia's constitutional democracy. A national *Racial Discrimination Act* in force since 1975 and binding on the states was its strongest bastion. But it could be swept aside by the Commonwealth – though not without a passionate political debate. There was also the Commonwealth's plenary jurisdiction to legislate with respect to Aborigines and Torres Strait Islanders which could be used – by a courageous government – to keep the states in line. Finally, a generation of pre-*Mabo* politics had produced land rights legislation, some of which was quite progressive – notably in the *Commonwealth Act* that applied to the Northern Territory and South Australia's legislation. However, for the settler state's legislature to enable Indigenous people to own land on the settlers' terms is one thing. To recognize that Aborigines and Torres Strait Islanders have rights whose existence does not depend on the settler state's government is a much more difficult pill to swallow. How that pill would go down with the Australian democracy we are now about to see.

CHAPTER 9

Consequences I:
Legislating Native Title

The High Court's decision in *Mabo (No. 2)* was undoubtedly a judicial revolution, but would it produce a real revolution in aboriginal relations in Australia? The answer to that question depends on the consequences of the decision – not simply the legal consequences but the broader political and societal consequences as well. As William Bogart has demonstrated, identifying the consequences of a change in the law is an extremely complex process.[1] That is certainly true of the change effected in Australian law by the High Court's decision in the *Mabo* case. Responses to the decision in the short term are readily marked, but longer-term consequences are still unfolding. In this chapter and the next we will look at how the High Court decision interacted with Australian politics and international influences over the decade that followed the decision. It is impossible in this account of post-*Mabo* Indigenous relations to unravel the effects of the *Mabo* decision itself from other forces shaping the context in which it was received. Of only two things can we be sure: first, that the real and experienced meaning of this remarkable law case will depend on how it is understood, acted upon, and resisted by those whose aspirations and interests it affects; and, second, that the High Court's decision will raise political interest in Indigenous affairs in Australia to an unprecedented level. The *Mabo* case was truly a catalytic political event.

First Responses: Shock and Surprise

On 4 June 1992, the day after the High Court rendered its decision, *Mabo* was the top news story across Australia. Media treatment of the case was typical coverage of a judicial decision deemed by editors to be of great public interest. Journalists are dispatched to get some pithy quotes from prominent people, usually leading politicians, on what they think of the case. Of course, the journalists' quarry have not had time to read the decision (all the more so, when as in *Mabo*, it is 217 pages long and contains four separate opinions) or be properly briefed by staff lawyers. Still, most of them have something to say about the decision – and the more flamboyant that something is, the more likely it is to be reported. Also, negative critical comments are at a premium. As the political scientist E.E. Schattsneider observed many years ago, in democracies the mass media cover the fights.[2] News editors are far more interested in hearing from those who promise to fight the case than those who wish to celebrate it. Such was the case with the first blast of news coverage of *Mabo (No. 2)*. A few frames of Trevor Graham's documentary *Mabo: Life of an Island Man* give the flavour of the comments that captured the headlines and made the evening news hour:

> 'The decision has the potential to destroy our society.'
> '80% of Western Australian could be claimed.'
> 'This is a day of shame for the Australian parliament.'
> 'Many mining projects are at risk.'

Mabo produced a major expansion in what John Hartley and Alan McKee refer to as the 'Indigenous public sphere,' but this sphere, as they point out, is not controlled by Indigenous people.[3] No journalist thought of interviewing Eddie Mabo's family or his people on Mer on their reactions. Bonita Mabo and members of her family were motoring to Sydney when they heard the news on the car radio. One of Mabo's daughters tells us that when she heard the news of her father's victory, she 'just cried' – with a mixture of joy and sorrow. She was very proud of her dad but sad that he wasn't there to share her joy in his victory.[4] But such reporting of positive reactions that there was – for instance, Pat Dodson's statement that the Council for Aboriginal Reconciliation received the decision 'in a spirit of joy and celebration,' and Lois O'Donoghue's statement on behalf of ATSIC welcoming *Mabo*'s help for those within its ambit and pointing to the need to assist the dispossessed who could not benefit from it[5] – was drowned out by those emphasizing the decision's problematic and disturbing implications.

The main source of concern and surprise was the possibility that native title claims could be successful on the Australian mainland. If the High Court majority had somehow contrived to limit their rejection of *terra nullius* to the Torres Strait, their decision in *Mabo (No. 2)* would have been much less alarming. The political attack on the decision was fuelled by comments of eminent members of the legal profession who claimed that the High Court had no business ruling on the native title rights of Aborigines on the Australian mainland in a case dealing with the claims of Torres Strait Islanders.[6] But consider the position the High Court judges would have had to take to limit the scope of their decision. The principal jurisprudential holding of six of the seven judges was that land rights of Indigenous occupiers survived the imposition of British sovereignty and, unless clearly extinguished by the Crown, continued for groups who had maintained their connection with traditional lands. The majority made no finding of native title outside the Murray Islands, but simply said, through Justice Brennan's judgment, 'there may be other areas of Australia' where native title had not been extinguished and an Aboriginal people had maintained its traditional connection with its lands.[7] The majority could deny the possibility of native title existing on the Australian continent only by adopting the racist evolutionary doctrine that, when the Europeans arrived, the Aborigines, as non-agriculturalists, were too primitive to be recognized as having societies with their own system of land law.

That, of course, was exactly the proposition which many of the court's critics wanted it to adopt and which Justice Blackburn had adopted as a proposition of law in *Milirrpum* – even though, as he acknowledged, it was not at all in accord with the factual evidence.[8] Jurisprudentially, it was possible for the High Court to distinguish Blackburn's decision and say that it did not apply to the Murray Islanders because they cultivated family-owned garden plots. But the justices of the High Court were unwilling to use the authority of Australia's highest court to encrust an ill-informed racial gradation of societies into Australian common law. Their unwillingness to do so, as the justices acknowledged, was based, at least in part, on considerations of moral philosophy. Most of their critics, it appeared, did not want Australia's common law cleansed of its earlier racist assumptions. Those Australians, politicians, lawyers, and scholars who advocated retaining an inferior human status for Aborigines belied Justice Brennan's optimism that the court's decision was in accord with the values of contemporary Australians.

Concern about the decision's potential application on the Australian mainland was much more than jurisprudential. Major economic and political interests were engaged – in particular the mining and pastoral industries, with a large stake in lands still used and occupied by Aborgines, and state governments accustomed to a plenary control over land and resource development. Representatives of these interests fired the first volley of shots against the decision and led the movement to blunt, if not entirely extinguish, common law native title on the Australian continent. But altogether aside from these material and political sources of concern and opposition, the High Court decision touched a deeper kind of anxiety. By recognizing that the first Australians were not Europeans but societies with long histories of their own and with legitimate claims to continue their collective existence, the High Court's decision in *Mabo*, as Jeremy Webber has argued, strengthened the basis on which Indigenous and non-Indigenous Australians could move beyond the settler state and share in building a deeply pluralist political community. But on 4 June 1992, that was very much the potential of *Mabo*. By casting a dark shadow over the beginning of British settlement in Australia and the conditions of its success, the decision's more immediate impact was to arouse a fierce outburst of settler nationalism. This reaction was fostered as much by the rhetoric of shame in some of the High Court judgments as by its basic holding. We can hear this deep sense of nationalist resentment in the statements of Hugh Morgan, the executive director of Western Mining and by far the fiercest and loudest of *Mabo*'s critics, that 'the free, prosperous and dynamic nation that our forebears built ... is irremediably tainted' and 'Mabo is a challenge to the legitimacy of Australia.'[9] It is the challenge posed to the traditional understanding of Australian history and nationhood that historian Bain Attwood argues gave rise to 'the sense of national crisis provoked by Mabo.'[10]

A real sense of national crisis did not come for quite some time. Historian Max Griffiths writes that 'the High Court Mabo decision exploded like a bombshell in the Australian community.'[11] But after the bomb went off on 3 June 1992, followed by a day or two of shouts and exclamations, there was a long lull of nearly nine months, lasting up to March 1993, before the political storm over native title came for a season to dominate Australian politics. It was as if the people who heard the blast held their breath and said, 'Well, this sounds pretty big, but what the hell does it mean and what will happen next?' We know from public opinion polling that in Western Australia, the hotbed of opposition to native title, 57 per cent of persons polled in January 1993 were unaware of *Mabo*.[12] That was before the response to *Mabo* had become a major political issue. By June 1993, when the political leaders of the country were engaged in an intense political battle over how to respond to the *Mabo* decision, a national survey would show public awareness had reached the 80 per cent level.[13]

In December 1991, six months before the release of the *Mabo* decision, Paul Keating had replaced Bob Hawke as prime minister and leader of the Labor Party. As treasurer in the Hawke government, Keating had been for many years a prominent figure in Australian politics, noted for his tough partisanship in jousting with his opponents in the Australian Parliament as well as with state premiers seeking to manage the Australian federation in a more cooperative manner. Though Keating had no background or previous involvement in aboriginal affairs, he immediately took charge of managing the Commonwealth government's response to the *Mabo* decision. As Don Watson, Keating's close adviser and speech-writer explains, responding positively to *Mabo* was, for Keating, the 'big chance to make a difference, a chance that Hawke had squibbed.'[14] On June 4 Prime Minister Keating had this statement for the House of Representatives – and the nation:

With the Mabo decision the Australian law has taken a major step away from this injustice and has finally entered the mainstream of world opinion. As a nation we are now far better prepared psychologically to proceed with the process of reconciliation. With this decision one more barrier – historically, perhaps the greatest barrier – has been effectively removed and the foundations of discrimination and prejudice have been kicked away. At least that is what all members of this House hope and want to see pursued in the next decade.[15]

We can see in this statement how anxious Keating was for *Mabo* not to become embroiled in partisan controversy. That was certainly the wish of his aboriginal affairs minister, Robert Tickner, and of the opposition's shadow minister of aboriginal affairs, Michael Wooldridge. It was perhaps inevitable that on an issue threatening major vested interests and calling for a significant change in public attitudes, partisanship would rear its noisy head. Such is the nature of democracy. But the national debate that erupted over *Mabo* might have been less divisive if the champion of the Commonwealth government's response had been a less partisan figure than Paul Keating. Non-partisanship was not Keating's forte.

Not that Keating's response to *Mabo* was particularly extreme or his support for it unqualified. While he wanted the decision to serve as a vehicle for recognizing the special status of Aborigines and Torres Strait Islanders as Australia's first peoples and for overcoming their dispossession, Keating was also sensitive to the importance investors attach to removing any legal uncertainty in relation to land they are considering for development. Labor historically has been a human rights party, but as we saw in chapter 6 with uranium mining in the Northern Territory, it has also been a party of economic development. In his memoir, Robert Tickner says: 'From the start Paul Keating's objective was to ensure what he saw as a balanced outcome advancing indigenous rights and providing certainty for industry and, ideally, one that was nationally negotiated with the support of state and territory governments.'[16] Given the historical opposition of the Western Australia, Queensland, and Northern Territory governments to Indigenous land rights, and the vitriolic attack on the decision by leaders of the mining industry, Tickner had reason to be sceptical about the merits of any deal negotiated with these parties.

The drive for legislation to remove uncertainties arising from *Mabo* was led by the mining industry. Hugh Morgan, the industry's most prominent spokesman, asserted that the law was in 'disarray'[17] and that 'all exploration leases are less secure today than they were prior to June 3 last.'[18] The focus of the miners' concern was the validity of mining rights granted since the coming into force of the *Racial Discrimination Act* in 1975. The High Court majority, it will be recalled, saw *RDA* as the only legal restraint on the power of the states to extinguish native title. Mining industry lawyers quickly identified *RDA*, a Commonwealth law with which the states must comply, as the one impediment to validating mining and other titles granted on lands subject to native title claims. There was a concern, which others disputed, that validating titles issued on public lands since 1975 would be found to be racially discriminatory. Hugh Morgan's solution was simple: the Commonwealth must either repeal or substantially amend the *Racial Discrimination Act*.[19]

The pastoral industry, the other economic interest group nervous about the implications of *Mabo*, was more muted in its call for action. In part this moderate response relied on the possibility held out in the High Court's decision that pastoral leases, from the time they were first issued, extinguished native title. There was such an implication in Justice Brennan's opinion that the sardine factory lease on Mer, if validly issued – even though given on condition that it not interfere with the traditional pursuits of the Meriam people – extinguished native title to the land on which the factory was located. Another factor was the leadership of Rick Farley, executive director of the National Farmers' Federation. Farley was no Hugh Morgan. His approach reflected his membership in the Council for Aboriginal Reconciliation. So, rather than launching a frontal attack on *Mabo*, Farley tried to take a constructive and pragmatic approach – though he, too, insisted that 'the considerable uncertainty about the validity of some land tenure' generated by the High Court's decision made it mandatory for the Commonwealth 'to deliver certainty.'[20] Farley's constituency, white rural Australia, would become much more agitated than he about the threat the High Court's recognition of Aboriginal title posed to their dominant position in the Australian 'outback.'

In the cities where the great majority of Australians live, concern was also being stirred up by what came to be known as 'ambit claims' – claims to stretches of valuable real estate in built-up areas of the country, including the land on which Sydney's Opera House sits and the entire downtown business district of Brisbane. Given the High Court's clearly expressed position that all grants of land in fee simple to private owners and any use of public lands inconsistent with traditional Indigenous activities extinguished native title, these claims were without any legal foundation. They represented more the frustration of dispossessed urban-dwelling Aborigines, who would get little direct benefit from *Mabo*. Nonetheless, these ambit claims were good fodder for the headline writers and for fear-mongering by those interested in making opposition to *Mabo* a popular cause. There was much loose talk about 'everyone's backyard' being at risk. Tickner says that the government was worried about these spurious claims stimulating a backlash against seeking 'a just outcome from Mabo.'[21] As minister of aboriginal affairs, he devoted considerable effort to explaining to the public that no privately owned land was at risk because of *Mabo*. Murray Goot's analysis of polling data shows that a year after the decision, 12 per cent of those surveyed thought that the land their homes was on was 'threatened by the *Mabo* judgment.'[22] While this figure suggests that not many Australians were taken in by the scare-mongering, still, as Goot writes, 'those who were misinformed may have been especially likely to develop a hostile response to land rights.'

Major aboriginal organizations, with their more democratic and accountable structures, took considerably longer than industry to register their position on *Mabo*. When they did, it was evident that they, too, wanted a legislative response from the Commonwealth. But the legislative response they sought was very different in nature from that called for by the miners and farmers. Early in 1993 the Central and Northern land councils in the Northern Territory, the Cape York Land Council in northern Queensland, and the Kimberly Land Council in the north of Western Australia wrote to Prime Minister Keating. Their letter requested legislation to preserve native title and to recognize it on lands such as national parks and vacant Crown land, so that once traditional owners were identified they could exercise their title without having to go through a complex process of litigation.[23]

By this time the Keating government was moving towards a legislative response to *Mabo*. Following a Cabinet discussion of an options paper on 27 October 1992, Keating announced that he would initiate a consultative process with state and territory governments, Indigenous organizations, and the mining and pastoral industries.[24] He followed this press release with a remarkable speech at Redfern Park on 10 December. Redfern is a district of Sydney with a large Aboriginal population. The occasion was the Australian launch of the UN International Year of the World's Indigenous People. Keating called on Australians to 'ignore the isolated outbreaks of hysteria and hostility of the past few months' and accept *Mabo* 'as an historic turning point, the basis of a new relationship between indigenous and non-Aboriginal Australians.'[25] In forging a new partnership, he said it might help if 'we non-Aboriginal Australians imagined ourselves dispossessed of land we had lived on for fifty thousand years – and then imagined ourselves told that it had never been ours.'[26] It was truly a landmark speech and, while it went down well with Keating's largely Aboriginal audience, it set off alarm bells for more conservative-minded Australians. On 18 January 1993 Keating announced his government's intention to implement *Mabo* through national legislation.[27] That was not the message state premiers and the mining industry were waiting for: the only Commonwealth legislation they wanted was a setting aside of the *Racial Discrimination Act*, leaving the states free to insulate their lands and resources from native title claims. Jeff Kennett, the premier of Victoria, called Keating's announcement 'inflammatory, unnecessary and divisive.'[28]

Still, in January 1993, the political dispute over *Mabo* was relatively muted. The decision and its implications continued to receive a great deal of media coverage, but discussion was not yet clearly focused on policy options. When *The Australian* on January 26 named Eddie Mabo, posthumously, Australian of the Year, it showed both how large the Indigenous public sphere was becoming and the respect for Mabo's achievement, whatever its implications.[29] It was becoming evident that *Mabo* and the response to it would not be a major issue in the federal election called for March 1993. The leader of the opposition, John Hewson, was clearly uncomfortable about *Mabo* and said that Keating was 'in hot water' because his proposed legislation raised the expectations of miners, pastoralists, and Aborigines beyond anything he could deliver.[30] Tim Fischer, leader of the National Party, the Liberals' coalition partner and the party that draws most of its strength from rural constituencies, was pledging that a Coalition government would legislate to overcome the uncertainties created by *Mabo*. But in Hewson's first media interview after the calling of the election, he defused the Indigenous rights issue by saying that 'the government had embarked on a negotiation now which runs I think through until September ... It's our view that that process should be allowed to run its course and hopefully it will resolve the problem.'[31] Hewson decided to fight the election on his proposal to introduce a tax on consumer spending, an issue on which the advantage clearly lay with Keating and Labor. A huge political battle over native title was simmering, but it would not come to the surface of politics until after the election.

The Fight to Legislate *Mabo*

On 13 March 1993 the Keating Labor government was returned to office. Prime Minister Keating quickly made it clear that implementing *Mabo* would be his government's top legislative priority. He was determined to get native title legislation through Parliament by the end of the year. From mid-March until three days before Christmas, when the Commonwealth Parliament passed the *Native Title Act*, the debate over the response to *Mabo* dominated Australian politics.

This nine-month-long Australian political struggle in many ways resembled the rounds of 'mega constitutional' politics that on several occasions have dominated Canadian politics. I coined that phrase to capture the exceptional nature of a political struggle in which what is at issue is not so much the merits of specific constitutional proposals as 'the very nature of the political community on which the constitution is based.'[32] Debates of this kind touch on fundamental issues of identity, political justice, and self-worth and, precisely because of these dimensions, engender a political struggle that is extraordinarily intense and emotional. When issues of this kind come to the surface of democratic politics, they tend to dwarf all other public concerns. That was certainly the case in Canada during the struggle over constitutional patriation and the abortive Meech Lake and Charlottetown accords. And it was very much the case with the 1993 Australian political battle over *Mabo* and native title legislation. Of course, in a formal sense the Australian debate was not about constitutional change. *Mabo No. 2* was a decision about the common law, and the responses receiving serious attention at this stage were ordinary legislation, not amendments to the Australian Constitution. But at the deepest level, constitutionalism is about the nature of the body politic – the political community and the people or peoples who constitute it – for which a constitution sets down the rules of government. Make no mistake about it – in that sense the 1993 native title debate in Australia was deeply constitutional.

The centrality of native title policy in the program of the new Keating government was evident when the prime minister announced on March 24 that responsibility for Aboriginal affairs was being moved to the Department of the prime minister and Cabinet.[33] The prime minister himself would chair a special committee of Cabinet, the Mabo Ministerial Committee, to coordinate the development of policy. Robert Tickner continued as minister for Aboriginal and Torres Strait Islander affairs, but he would now work in parallel with Frank Walker, who was appointed minister of state with a special responsibility for *Mabo*. Tickner reports that he had no difficulty working with Walker but admits that, under the new arrangements, two streams of advice flowed to the prime minister and that they often reflected significant differences within the Mabo Ministerial Committee.[34] ATSIC (the Aboriginal and Torres Strait Islander Commission) had been created in 1990 to maximize the input of Indigenous peoples on Commonwealth policy relating to them. With Lois O'Donoghue, a leading Aboriginal spokesperson as its chair, and elected Indigenous representatives on the commission and its regional councils, ATSIC would naturally favour a very liberal and generous approach to implementing *Mabo*. As ATSIC's minister, Tickner's input would reflect this orientation. It was also an approach that coincided with Tickner's own personal commitment to human rights. By way of contrast, the Office of Indigenous Affairs in the Prime Minister's Department was staffed by seasoned policy technicians with little background in aboriginal affairs. As time went on, it became increasingly clear that these officials were preoccupied with developing proposals that could win the support of the governments of the states and the Northern Territory. O'Donoghue came to refer to their office as the 'Office of Insidious Affairs.'[35] Eventually, Keating would have to choose between these two orientations within his own government, but for over six months he continued to harbour the hope that he could come up with a policy that satisfied both.

In developing its native title legislation, the Keating government engaged with players in four different corners of the political stage: Aboriginal and Torres Strait Islanders, the resource and pastoral industries, state and territorial governments, and opposition political parties. The first of these to engage directly with the Commonwealth government were Indigenous representatives. On April 27, a large delegation representing Aboriginal and Torres Strait organizations from all across the country and at the peak level in Canberra met with the Mabo Ministerial Committee in the Cabinet Room of Parliament House.[36] All the major land councils were represented, as were leading aboriginal legal service organizations. Torres Strait Islanders were represented by Getano Lui Jr, chair of the Torres Strait Regional Council, and the very experienced Islander leader George Mye. The delegation could not, of course, speak for all Australia's Indigenous people. Frank Brennan is right when he says that, at this time, 'most Aboriginal communities had heard nothing about the ramifications of *Mabo*.'[37] Moreover, Indigenous communities and leaders in Australia, as with Indigenous peoples in other settler countries, are never of one mind on how best to advance their people's interests. Nonetheless, the array of organizations and agencies represented at this meeting, all state-sponsored and -funded, shows how far Indigenous Australia had come in the last three decades in securing a hearing for the Indigenous voice in national affairs. The delegation's membership also demonstrated that Indigenous Australia had produced a remarkable group of political leaders with the skills of advocacy and negotiation which are prerequisites for influence in mainstream politics. The group – Lois O'Donoghue of ATSIC; Patrick Dodson, chair of the Council for Aboriginal Reconciliation, and his brother Mick Dodson, the first Aboriginal and Torres Strait Islander social justice commissioner; Galarrwuy Yunupingu and John Ah Kit from the Northern Land Council; David Ross, director of the Central Land Council; Noel Pearson representing the Cape York Land Council; Peter Yu, director of the Kimberley Land Council; and other Indigenous leaders – in terms of strength of character, intellect, and leadership ability, were more than a match for the team of Labor ministers sitting opposite them. The outstanding leadership in the Aboriginal and Torres Strait Islander corner would be a major factor in the political struggle that lay ahead.

The proposals the Aboriginal and Torres Strait Islander leaders presented to the Keating government on April 27 were contained in an 'Aboriginal Peace Plan' that had been drawn up at a meeting of aboriginal groups in Alice Springs.[38] The term 'peace plan' reflects the political dynamic of the moment. Up to this point, most of the pressure for legislation, as well as a discussion paper put out by Commonwealth bureaucrats, focused on overcoming uncertainties that *Mabo* was alleged to pose for the Australian economy. The aboriginal leaders agreed to support legislation meeting such concerns, providing there was some willingness to meet major concerns of Indigenous people. Their Peace Plan agreed to the validation of mineral rights granted to industry since 1975 that might be invalid because of the *Racial Discrimination Act*. But in return they wanted the resource companies benefiting from such validation to be required to negotiate agreements with native title holders on compensation, environmental protection, sacred sites, a share of revenues, and other matters. They insisted that Indigenous representatives be involved in drafting native title legislation and that such legislation provide certainty not only for holders of mineral rights but also for native title-holders by declaring their title in reserves and other defined lands and establishing a national tribunal to issue declarations of native title. Extinguishment of native title might occur, but only with the consent of the title-holders and not as an incidental consequence of a mineral title or a pastoral lease. Most important, an agreement producing peaceful and harmonious relations with Indigenous peoples must go beyond native title and provide some justice for those who had been dispossessed of their traditional lands. It must also lead to negotiations of formal constitutional recognition of Aboriginals' and Torres Strait Islanders' rights.

The Aboriginal Peace Plan was a much more coherent and plausible proposal than the vague ideas about a treaty, or makarrata, that an earlier generation of Indigenous leaders had brought forward. And it was presented in a context, created by the *Mabo* case, that put the Commonwealth government under more pressure than ever before to respond to Indigenous proposals. Bob Riley from Western Australian Legal Services told the ministers that 'there is a sense of history about this moment,' the possibility of 'the relationship between the indigenous people of this country and the Australian nation to take a quantum leap forward.'[39] The prime minister and his Cabinet colleagues mostly listened. It would be many months before Keating and Indigenous leaders negotiated in earnest. And then, although the negotiations produced legislation less unfavourable to Indigenous interests than would otherwise have been enacted, the final outcome was still a long way removed from the terms and the spirit of the Aboriginal Peace Plan.

From the opposite corner, the next protagonists to engage directly with the Cabinet were the industrial interests most directly affected by *Mabo*. The day after the meeting with the Indigenous delegation, the Mabo Ministerial Committee met with representatives of the Australian

Mining Industry Council (AMIC), the Australian Petroleum Association, and the National Farmers' Federation (NFF).[40] Their number one priority was validation of titles and leases, which their legal advisers believed were put at risk by *Mabo*. They also wanted to ensure that any compensation that might be owing to native title-holders be paid by government rather than by industry.

Business corporations did not rely on group meetings with Labor ministers to secure their interests. The mining industry in particular had been carrying on a high-powered media campaign since the day the High Court rendered its decision. Some of the mineral corporations who were promoting huge megaprojects in regions subject to native title claims were also doing their best to sound economic alarm bells about the urgent need to remove uncertainty. An agreement reached in January 1993 between the Jawoyn Association, representing the Indigenous community in the Mount Todd area of the Northern Territory, and the mining company Zapopan NL enabled a gold-mining venture to go forward on the basis of a negotiated agreement.[41] The agreement secured employment, title to certain lands, and other benefits to traditional owners. The Mount Todd Agreement was basically a success story and showed that, through negotiated agreements, economic development could go forward on native title lands. But it also had the effect of alarming the very development-minded Northern Territory government that other major resource projects might be held up or even cancelled because of the need to negotiate agreements with native title claimants. The most important project that was thought to be under immediate threat was Mount Isa Mines' $250 million lead-zinc-silver project at McArthur River in the Northern Territory. Northern Territory legislation ratifying the project and granting mineral leases to Mount Isa Mines had been passed at the end of 1992, but now there were worries that the *Racial Discrimination Act* might be an impediment to overcoming potential native title claims in the area. The Northern Territory government's determination to sweep away any native title impediments to this project became a vehicle for mobilizing support for a response to *Mabo* that made the validation of mineral titles and the extinguishment of native title the primary objectives.

Marshall Perron, the chief minister of the Northern Territory, was the one Australian politician who did try to inject the *Mabo* debate into the federal election campaign. On March 3, Perron, taunting other politicians in the country who thought that *Mabo* was too hot an issue to handle during the election and ignoring the protests of Lois O'Donoghue, introduced legislation that attempted to secure the validity of all titles issued since 1975. His legislation, he said, would be 'a toothless tiger' unless the Commonwealth enacted complementary legislation setting aside the *Racial Discrimination Act*.[42] The first weekend after the election, a large consortium of Australian business interests issued a public statement pressing for Perron-type legislation that would protect existing property rights. In May, Perron, under threat from the corporate partners to pull out of the McArthur River project unless certainty was provided by 1 July, introduced legislation to reissue the leases. This move brought the Commonwealth under direct pressure to say that it would deal with any problems the *Racial Discrimination Act* might pose to these leases. Keating succumbed to the pressure and, without consulting Robert Tickner, authorized his special minister of state, Frank Walker, to assure Perron that the Commonwealth would cooperate.[43] Keating's promise of support for the Northern Territory legislation came as a bombshell to the Indigenous leadership. They saw it as an act of betrayal.[44] Keating defended his action as politically necessary to avoid having 'the worst elements of conservative interests in this country up there blackguarding the Mabo decision and all it stands for.'[45] Nonetheless, at this stage in the struggle, it was hard to deny Garth Nettheim's impression that the Commonwealth government's 'priority concern is the uncertainty affecting commercial interests.'[46]

Marshall Perron's initiative was very much in line with the response to *Mabo* favoured by most of the state premiers. They, too, were most concerned about removing impediments to economic development and retaining control over land and resource management. From their perspective, Commonwealth legislation should be confined to relieving them of any problems posed by the *Racial Discrimination Act*. The politicians in the states and territorial corner played a much bigger role in the 1993 struggle over *Mabo* than the leaders of the official opposition in Canberra. John Hewson, the Liberal Party leader, remained committed to seeing whether a broad collaborative process could produce agreement by September. His National Party Coalition partner, Tim Fischer, was less muted and made speeches about *Mabo* having 'the potential to threaten the sovereignty of a great deal more land – and sea.'[47] But the Coalition was quite divided at this point on how to respond to *Mabo*. There were certainly those like Fischer (among Liberals as well as Nats) who took a very negative attitude to the decision, but others like Michael Wooldridge, the shadow aboriginal affairs minister, and Peter Nugent were more in the tradition of Malcolm Fraser and Fred Chaney and hoped that *Mabo* could be a positive basis for reconciliation. State premiers, in contrast, were much more aggressive and single-minded in voicing their concerns about *Mabo*, and none more so than Richard Court, the Western Australian Liberal leader who had defeated a Labor government in a state election just one month before Keating's election victory. Court's victory meant that Keating was confronted with a federal context in which four of Australia's six states and the Northern Territory were controlled by anti-Labor governments. That was quite different from the situation during Bob Hawke's time, when Labor predominated at the state as well as the federal level. The political pendulum in Australia, as elsewhere, was swinging to the right. It was to an unpromising gathering of state and territorial leaders that Paul Keating would unveil his government's legislative plan for responding to *Mabo*.

The occasion for Keating's first – and only – direct encounter with the other heads of government on the *Mabo* response was a meeting of COAG (the Council of Australian Governments) scheduled for 7–8 June 1993. COAG was an offshoot of Hawke's 'new federalism' reforms designed to bring about a more harmonious and coherent system of intergovernmental relations. Keating was inbued with Labor's traditional scepticism of any devolution of Canberra's social or fiscal powers to the states and owed his defeat of Hawke in the party caucus room partly to his opposition to Hawke's new federalism.[48] Still, in May 1992, he had presided over a Heads of Government meeting that established COAG,[49] and now, a year later, he sensed the need for a consensual response to *Mabo* that would strengthen the decision's capacity to serve as a instrument of reconciliation. But his relationships with the other level of government were never cordial and were not likely to improve, with most of the states and the Northern Territory led by Labor's political opponents. The COAG meeting would test Keating's ability to subordinate his partisanship to the need, in the circumstances, for statesmanship.

As a basis for discussion at the COAG meeting, Keating brought a statement of thirty-three principles that had been approved by his ministerial Cabinet committee on *Mabo*. The principles had been publicly released a few days earlier as an appendix to a discussion paper on *Mabo* prepared by Commonwealth officials. This statement of principles, though far from providing the basis for a consensual solution, turned out to be not far off the native title legislation that eventually was enacted. It will be useful to look at its principal features.[50]

In contrast to the bureaucrats' discussion paper, the thirty-three principles were framed in very positive language about *Mabo* and expressed a commitment to broader measures of reconciliation that went beyond immediate issues of land management. They included recognition of the need to deal with the consequences of past dispossession and to strengthen heritage protection legislation – but, notably, there was no mention of Indigenous interest in constitutional reform or a treaty. These points were the Keating government's main concession to the Aboriginal Peace Plan. The rest of the document focused on land management issues. It led off with proposing an 'accessible, informal, non-adversarial and expeditious method' of identifying native title ownership. The key to this system would be a special tribunal or tribunals. Here Keating made a major concession to the states and territories: they could set up their own tribunals for this purpose, providing they met national standards established by the Commonwealth. The 'integrity' of that all-important *Racial Discrimination Act* was to be maintained. But just how that could be done in a way that the states and Northern Territory could live with was, to say the least, a very tricky business. The approach tested here was to promise that native title 'should be treated no less favourably than other comparable titles,' but then quickly to add that this 'does not mean equating native title with other existing titles.' In this part of the statement the Commonwealth was clearly walking on egg shells. The participants in the native title debate could agree on respecting the principle of equality – but they held very different ideas on what that principle required in this context. If equality requires, as classical liberals insist, exactly the same rights for all, then native title holders' rights should mean no more (and no less) than any other property holder's rights. But if that view prevails and native title is reduced to equivalence, say, with the rights of a person who has recently purchased a piece of real estate or a corporation's right to prospect or extract minerals from some land, native title is drained of all its special meaning as the collective right of historic peoples to maintain their connection with lands that are integral to their being.

One point on which Keating's government was prepared to provide a dose of classical liberal equality that would be helpful to native title holders concerned the consequences of temporary grants. Brennan's majority judgment in *Mabo (No. 2)* had treated native title as an exceptionally fragile right of ownership – so weak that temporary use of native title lands for a sardine factory extinguished the native owners' rights for all time, an outcome that would not occur had the land been owned in fee simple. The Commonwealth now proposed to remedy this weakness in the High Court's conception of native title by legislating to promote a land regime in which native title could be preserved and co-exist to the maximum extent possible with other grants of land use. Principle 10 stated: 'Where possible, native title should revive at the expiry of a finite grant.' Here, too, Keating hedged his bets, promising that this principle might not as readily apply to pastoral leases as to mining grants.

In response to the immediate concern of mining companies, Keating (as he had signalled in his response to Marshall Perron) gave them most of what they wanted: validation of all post-1975 grants of interest in land up to 30 June 1993, and a promise to contribute to any compensation to be paid to native title holders. The statement denied any requirement for negotiations with the Indigenous peoples on the lands affected by this validation of titles – now, or in the future when grants were up for renewal. Here Keating's government totally rejected a central point of the Aboriginal Peace Plan. As for future grants of interest in lands subject to native title, Keating continued to walk on egg shells. The principle of non-discrimination requires that native title holders have 'a right of consent' where other 'comparable title holders' have such a right. The trouble is, of course, that other title-holders (for example, owners of land in fee simple) do not have a right of veto over whether a mining title can be granted on their land. So the statement added that, in recognition of Indigenous peoples' special attachment to their land, 'there could be additional rights of consent for native title holders in connection with actions affecting their lands.'

The COAG meeting, to borrow Frank Brennan's phrase, 'was a disaster.'[51] Far from pointing the way to consensus, the Commonwealth's thirty-three principles inflamed the parties on both sides. For the Indigenous leadership, it was further evidence that the Keating government, like the Hawke government before it, was caving in to industry and the states. They viewed the discussion paper and the thirty-three principles as a land-management scheme designed to assuage industry's fears about legal uncertainty and meet the state premiers' objections to Commonwealth encroachment on their jurisdiction. On the crucial issue of Indigenous consent to encroachments on their traditional lands, the Commonwealth was unwilling to grant any negotiating rights to past encroachments, and it appeared to be watering down Indigenous leverage on future encroachments to some vague 'rights of consent' that sounded weaker than the veto rights available under the 1976 *Aboriginal Land Rights (Northern Territory) Act.* No wonder Noel Pearson called the Commonwealth's statement a 'slimy useless document' and a 'bureaucratic real estate approach to an historic injustice.'[52]

On the other side, the state and territorial governments were not bought off by Keating's offer to help them with compensation for past encroachments. After the meeting, the four non-Labor premiers (New South Wales' John Fahey, Tasmania's Ray Groom, Victoria's Jeff Kennett, and Western Australia's Richard Court) announced that they would proceed with their own title-validating laws, without Commonwealth support.[53] Tickner reports that in the closed COAG meeting, Court refused to acknowledge the legitimacy of the High Court's decision, and proposals that he and other premiers put on the table would have eliminated any Indigenous rights to negotiate based on special attachment to the land. At a media conference after the COAG meeting, Ian MacLachlan, shadow minister for national development, accused Keating of 'Mabo failure' and, taking his cue from the premiers, commented: 'Native title has not yet been proved to exist on the mainland of Australia and it may be some time before the High Court is able to clarify these newly discovered Aboriginal rights which interfere with the long held belief that all Australians are equal under the law.'[54] Industry was equally negative. The front-page headline of the prestigious *Financial Review* on the weekend before COAG set the tone: 'Mabo: mining on hold.' Even the suggestion of some vague Indigenous consent rights, its lead article trumpeted, 'throws into doubt the ability of new mining projects to get underway without time-consuming delays.'[55]

If the COAG meeting was a disaster – and it was – the reason is clear. The principal parties to the issue were just too far apart to support Keating's effort at compromise. Over the next four months, as Keating gamely continued the effort to work out a consensual solution, it became increasingly clear that it would not be possible. Any solution acceptable to the states, the Northern Territory, industry, and the Coalition could not win the support of even a section of the Indigenous leadership. As is so often the case in these wrenching public debates over deeply emotional matters of identity and political justice, attitudes seemed to be polarizing, not coalescing around a compromise solution. A Newspoll survey published a week after COAG asking whether respondents were in favour of or against the High Court decision allowing native title claims on unalienated Crown land reported that 46 per cent said they were opposed, while 43 per cent were in favour.[56] Analysis of data from the June Newspoll survey shows that attitudes to *Mabo* were tending to divide along partisan lines: 56 per cent of Coalition supporters were on the negative side, with only 32 per cent in favour, whereas 52 per cent of Labor supporters were in favour and 39 per cent opposed.[57] As the struggle over native title ground on and on, the government's own polling showed that the majority of people 'thought the Prime Minister's efforts were more evidence that he was out of touch.'[58] However one assesses the final product of Paul Keating's effort to legislate native title, his absorption in the issue was patently not designed to maximize partisan political advantage.

Between June and November, when the Commonwealth's legislation was introduced in Parliament, the Keating government was in continual bilateral negotiations with all the parties and under constant public bombardment from all quarters over its native title proposal. One of the hot grenades tossed at it during these cool winter months provided a preview of the next major native title struggle that would erupt three years later. Early in July it was reported that the Wik peoples of Cape York in northern Queensland, with the assistance of the Cape York Land Council, were initiating a native title claim to 35,000 square kilometres of land and coastal waters. Some of Australia's major mining developments were located in the area subject to this claim. At Waipa, CRA, one of Australia's largest mining companies, had bauxite leases and plans for a major industrial development. Waipa was said to contain 15 per cent of the world's supply of bauxite.[59] In the 1950s, Queensland had forcibly removed Aboriginal people from Mapoon and issued a mining lease to Comalco. The Wik planned to challenge the validity of that lease on the grounds that, in issuing it, Queensland had breached its fiduciary obligation to them, and to negotiate with CRA the terms on which their mining operations could continue. In response, John Rolph, CRA's chief executive, said projects worth $1.75 billion would have to be scrapped unless the Wik claim were resolved. The Wik action propelled Queensland's premier, Wayne Goss, to centre stage in the struggle. Goss immediately began to pressure Keating for the same kind of help he had given the Northern Territory to ensure that the McArthur River project was not closed down. And Keating had to listen to Goss, as he was the one Labor premier with a good chance of re-election.[60]

Meantime Richard Court, the charged-up premier of Western Australia, was emerging as the politician making the most negative and populist attacks on *Mabo* on the national political stage. Western Australia was the only state on the Australian continent that had not enacted some kind of aboriginal, land rights legislation, and its newly elected premier took the most ideological position in rejecting *Mabo*. The Commonwealth's thirty-three principles, Court argued, were leading the country 'towards a form of apartheid where we are granting certain lands, certain rights to those lands to a group of people.'[61] Court claimed that 80 per cent of Western Australia was under the threat of native title claims and that Western Australia had much more at risk than any other state. Instead of cooperating with Canberra in a legislative scheme to implement *Mabo*, Court proposed a referendum to overturn the High Court's decision. The referendum proposal was not endorsed by John Hewson, the national Liberal leader, but that did not stop a Western Australia Liberal conference in July from supporting the proposal, along with another to give the Senate control over appointments to the High Court.[62] The referendum proposal had considerable purchase in Australia, where a populist tradition has deeper roots in the country's political culture than respect for minority rights. Later on, in November, when the country was reaching a state of exhaustion over *Mabo*, Newspoll found that 67 per cent of respondents supported a referendum to settle the native title issue.[63]

While state and industrial leaders were mobilizing support for a quick and dirty pro-development resolution of *Mabo* that would virtually drain the decision of any value, Indigenous leaders were not sitting idly by hoping for the best. On 3 August 1993, four hundred Indigenous people met at Eva Valley Station in the Northern Territory. This meeting was 'Aboriginal and Torres Strait Islander Peoples ... first historic National meeting to formulate a response to the High Court decision recognizing Native Title.'[64] It was certainly the largest country-wide gathering of Indigenous representatives in Australian history. The participation of members of organizations with no government funding or recognition, such as Michael Mansell and Geoff Clark of the Aboriginal Provisional Government, gave the Eva Valley meeting a more grassroots character than the meeting at Alice Springs which drew up the Aboriginal Peace Plan. And the message that came out of Eva Valley was a good deal less compromising than the Peace Plan. The Eva Valley Statement entirely rejected the approach the Commonwealth government was proposing for implementing *Mabo*. It called on the Commonwealth to honour its obligations under international human rights law and to recognize and protect the rights of Aboriginal and Torres Strait Islander peoples. The Commonwealth should go beyond the High Court and legislate to ensure that no grants of interest in land can extinguish native title or be made 'without the informed consent of all relevant title holders.' The assembly appointed a representative body to negotiate with the Commonwealth on the basis of this statement.

Prime Minister Keating, to put it mildly, was not pleased with the Eva

Valley meeting. He was bitter about how Aboriginal leaders whom he had consulted in private seemed to take a different stand in public.[65] In his view, Aboriginal leaders had a responsibility to promote compromise, and some had clearly been unwilling to do so. Eva Valley failed to lead to any fundamental change in process. Keating did not heed the Indigenous peoples' call for the Commonwealth to take full control of the *Mabo* process or to cease his government's efforts to placate the states and the industrial interests. But Eva Valley set down a marker: it demonstrated that the prime minister – and the country – would have to choose between honouring Keating's pledge at Redfern to build on *Mabo* as an instrument of reconciliation or collaborating with the states in clearing away native title as an obstacle to industrial development.

As the deadline for introducing legislation into Parliament came closer, it looked as though the Keating government was taking the latter choice and tailoring its proposal to win the support of at least a majority of the states and thereby secure the Coalition's support. The latter would ensure easy passage of the government's bill through the Senate, where, as is normally the case in Australian parliamentary politics, the governing party did not have a majority. The alternative would be to seek support from a handful of Greens and Democrats at the opposite end of the political spectrum who held the balance of power between Labor and the Coalition in the Senate.

In the middle of August, after several very difficult Cabinet meetings dealing with the Wik situation and Premier Goss's demands, Keating announced that his government was prepared to validate all non-Aboriginal title right back to 1788. As Keating put it, in his blunt style, his government was beginning to be 'spooked by the mining companies' into believing that all land-use titles ever granted, not just those issued since 1975, were at risk.[66] On September 2 the prime minister released a discussion paper setting out the core principles his government was preparing to incorporate in its native title legislation.[67] The paper suggested that the government was trying hard to win over the states and placate public concern about industrial development. The validation of all past grants of interest in land was to be ensured. The Commonwealth would accept state and territorial tribunals as the arbiters of native title claims – providing they met national standards. And state government interests, as well as the national interest, could be invoked to override tribunal decisions on native title. In dealings affecting their lands, native title holders would 'be afforded the same protections of fair process which apply to everyone else' – which is very little. An expedited process would be established for making decisions on mining leases (for example, exploration licences) regarded as having little impact on native title holders. The government was now talking about native title holders having their say and being consulted on developments on their lands, but not about 'consent rights,' let alone a veto. The whole approach was about land management. Gone was any reference to a land fund to address the needs of dispossessed Indigenous peoples or a social justice package. 'States win fight over Mabo,' announced the front-page headline of the 3 September issue of the *Financial Review*.[68] And, indeed, it did appear that the states had won.

But the struggle was far from over. The Cabinet allowed another month for consultations before introducing its bill in mid to late October in the House of Representatives. During this month, representatives of Indigenous peoples went into high gear. They were now working on two fronts. Within government, primarily through the efforts of Lois O'Donoghue, Keating was being pressed hard not to move even further than its thirty-three principles to accommodate state and industrial interests. Outside the corridors of power, Indigenous leaders were insisting on a more fundamental recognition of their peoples' rights. In the last week of September, seven hundred Aborigines and Islanders staged a protest outside Parliament House demanding that the Commonwealth abandon a legislative process which seemed aimed primarily at steam-rolling their rights.[69] But a coalition of leaders, including Lois O'Donoghue, land council representatives, and others who had been involved in the Aboriginal Peace Plan, came together to continue negotiating with the Keating government on the inside. Soon this group of Indigenous negotiators would be referred to as the 'A Team,' to be distinguished from the tougher and more radical 'B Team' of Indigenous protestors on the outside. At this point, rather than debating the details of the land-management issues, O'Donoghue and her colleagues focused their public attacks on the government's apparent intention to suspend the *Racial Discrimination Act* to validate non-aboriginal land interests. It was a point that had a strong symbolic resonance with much of the Australian electorate, the Labor back-benches, and the smaller parties in the Senate.

Keating's office remained open to O'Donoghue and others voicing Indigenous concerns, but the prime minister and his officials had become preoccupied with striking a deal with the states that were pressuring the Commonwealth to make even more concessions than those contained in the government's September paper. In Cabinet, Robert

Tickner found that he was now very isolated. By early October the Keating government was on the brink of negotiating a deal with the states and territories. And then, quite suddenly on Friday, October 8, the dynamics dramatically changed. On that day, which she would later dub 'Black Friday,' Lois O'Donoghue called a media conference at which she and other Aboriginal leaders expressed their profound disappointment with the point that the Commonwealth's response to *Mabo* had reached. O'Donoghue outlined the major concessions that Indigenous representatives had been willing to make. But apparently these were still not enough. Then came this ringing statement: 'At this vital juncture in the development of our nation the Prime Minister seems to have decided that 'States' rights' are more important than our human rights.'[70] She and her aboriginal colleagues would not walk away from the negotiating process, but they wanted Australians to know that, unless the Keating government changed its direction, the process was unlikely to fulfill the vision of the prime minister's Redfern Park speech. The moment of choice that Paul Keating had been trying for so long to avoid had now arrived.

Keating decided to try and salvage what he could of his pledge at Redfern to make Mabo 'the basis of a new relationship between indigenous and non-Aboriginal Australians.' For the next ten days he and members of his government engaged, day and night, in closed negotiations with the Indigenous A Team. On Tuesday, October 19, a day that was quickly dubbed 'Ruby Tuesday' after the year-old daughter of Marcia Langton, one of the key Aboriginal negotiators, the Keating government and the Indigenous leaders announced that they had made a deal. Much was made of the aboriginal breakthrough on Ruby Tuesday. The *Sydney Morning Herald* called it 'the day that changed history.'[71] The aboriginal side did recover some ground on 'Ruby Tuesday,' though we must bear in mind the thirty-three principles of the government's June paper had rejected much of the Aboriginal Peace Plan, and now the Indigenous negotiators agreed to concede even more.[72] There would be no compensation for impairment of native title before 1975. The interests of state governments, not just the national interest, could be invoked to approve development on native title lands. The states would be able to reassert their ownership of minerals and regulate aboriginal access to natural resources, including fish and timber. The states and territories were free to establish their own native title tribunals, but native title claimants would have the right to bring their claims before a national tribunal established and operated by the Commonwealth. That last point – the pre-eminence of the national tribunal – was a major win for the Aborigines and Islanders. They also secured a commitment to establish a land fund to acquire lands for the dispossessed and to make stronger provision for regional land agreements between governments. So some ground was recovered.

Two other points were crucial deal-makers. One was on the thorny issue of pastoral leases. At this time most lawyers, on the basis of Brennan's majority judgment in *Mabo*, believed that pastoral leases extinguished native title. But Rick Farley of the National Farmers' Federation, unlike the mining industry's representatives, kept in close touch with Aboriginal leaders. Farley agreed to their request (relayed to him late at night by the prime minister) that if Aboriginal people acquired a pastoral lease, their native title could be revived.[73] While agriculturalists could live with that, it was bad news for mining companies. It would enable people like the Wik to purchase pastoral leases on their traditional lands and thereby acquire any negotiating rights attached to native title – rights they could then use as leverage with mining companies planning developments on their land. The other crunch issue was the *Racial Discrimination Act*. Here the negotiators came up with another brilliant feat of legal magic. Instead of ensuring the validation of post-1975 land grants by suspending *RDA*, the *Native Title Act* would be deemed to be a 'Special Measure.' Section 7 of *RDA* allows for a 'Special Measure' that treats a particular group differently from the rest of society, but only for positive purposes. This meant, as Tim Rowse puts it, that 'the *Native Title Act* would have to contain more plums for Aborigines than it had so far looked like including.'[74]

After Ruby Tuesday, the die was cast – the Keating government now depended on the continuing support of Indigenous leaders and their political allies in the Senate to fulfill its aim of enacting legislation by the end of the year. On November 16, Keating introduced the legislation into the House of Representatives. The government had the numbers in the lower house, so it had no problem in securing passage of the *Native Title Act* through the House of Representatives by November 25. The bill now went to the Senate, where Labor did not have a majority. In September and October, Indigenous leaders had forged an alliance with the Australian Democrats and the Greens, who held the balance of power in the Senate. Two Western Australian Green senators, Christabel Chamarette and Dee Margetts, who had close links with members of the more radical Indigenous B Team, were highly critical of the government's legislation and began to press for changes to enhance the benefits for

Indigenous peoples. At one point when the bill was before the Senate's Standing Committee on Legal and Constitutional Affairs, they threatened to join with the Coalition in derailing the legislation by sending it to a select committee and an extensive process of public hearings. But this unholy alliance broke apart and, on Tuesday, December 14, the debate began in the full Senate.

The Senate debate went on for 111 hours and is said to be the longest in the Senate's history.[75] It was certainly one of the most acrimonious and intense ever conducted in a parliamentary chamber renowned for the liveliness and political prominence of its debates. By the end of the first week, 250 amendments had been moved. Many supported by the two Western Australian Green senators aimed at strengthening the protection of native title rights. Other amendments, some of which were introduced by the government, cut in the opposite direction and responded to policy concerns of the states and the pastoral and mining industries. Had the Coalition's leadership played its cards carefully, most of these amendments, in particular one providing more certainty for the mining industry in the renewing of grants, might have been adopted. But the Coalition decided to oppose all amendments – even those favoured by its policy allies, thereby abdicating the legislative initiative on the conservative side of politics to the state premiers. Richard Court showed the way for the latter by promising to introduce legislation in Western Australia that would totally extinguish native title and replace it with a qualified legislative recognition of 'the traditional use of the lands by Aboriginal peoples.'[76]

In the Senate, Gareth Evans, the government's house leader, took the key role in steering the bill through the shoal-filled waters it encountered. Evans spent many hours in the backrooms of Parliament House, negotiating with the Indigenous leadership (from both the A and B teams), the Western Australia Greens, the Democrats, and the independent Tasmanian senator, Brian Harradine, to broker a deal that could get the *Native Title Act* through Parliament before it adjourned for Christmas. In the end, with the help of a last-minute compromise on the coexistence of native title with pastoral leases worked out by Ron Castan (the lead barrister in the *Mabo* case) and Rick Farley, but without making any major changes in the government's bill, Evans was able to put together the numbers he needed to guillotine further debate a few days before Christmas.[77] In the early hours of Wednesday, December 22, with the public galleries packed, the Senate passed the *Native Title Act*. The House met next day to approve the amendments made in the Senate, and the governor general signed the act on Christmas Eve.

After the final vote in the Senate was taken, Robert Tickner, the minister of aboriginal and Torres Strait Islander affairs, who had worked so hard to salvage an act that could yield real benefits for Indigenous Australians, stood 'shoulder to shoulder with other Australians, both indigenous and non-indigenous, and gave a standing ovation for our country.' In Tickner's view, 'We had won.'[78] Certainly the legislation had the overwhelming approval of the Indigenous leadership. Lois O'Donoghue saluted it as 'the greatest proof yet of the probability of reconciliation.'[79] Even members of the B Team like Michael Mansell commended the aboriginal negotiators who had improved the bill.[80] This Indigenous approval was given even though the *Native Title Act* fell far short of what Indigenous leaders had set out to achieve, and they had conceded much to opponents who wanted to emasculate native title. In the next section we will take a closer look at the act, but, clearly, it was very much a compromise. And compromise is what we should expect in the resolution of an intense and sustained political debate on an issue that deeply divides a democratic country. But this was a compromise that was accepted by only one of the sides – the pro-Indigenous side – with grace and goodwill. Those who wanted to deflate or deny native title did not accept the act. The leader of the opposition said passage of the act was 'a day of shame for the Australian people' and vowed to make 'the Government's unjust, divisive and damaging Mabo legislation a major issue right up until the next election.'[81] Hewson, and his successor as Liberal Party leader, John Howard, would have no difficulty mobilizing support for that position at both the national and the state level.

So this first major consequence of *Mabo* – the *Native Title Act* (*NTA*) – was far from producing an accord between Indigenous and non-Indigenous Australians on how they might share their country. The act and the political struggle that produced it did forge a political alliance between the left side of politics and the Indigenous leadership – though the downside of that for Indigenous peoples was that the right was on the ascendance and dedicated to reducing, if not eliminating, the slight gains Indigenous peoples had secured in *NTA*. Still, the political aspirations and the leaders of Australia's Indigenous peoples gained a prominence during this period that is unmatched in any of the other English-settler countries. During the 1990s, Maori affairs in New Zealand and Aboriginal affairs in Canada were frequently front-page news and a continuing source of political interest and controversy. But neither New Zealand nor Canada, as modern democracies, have experienced anything like the 1993 season of post-*Mabo* politics in Australia, when for nearly a year issues concerning the rights and interests of Indigenous peoples dominated the political agenda. In the United States, observers would have to go back over a century and a half to the 1830s debate over the *Exclusion Act* to get anything even close to this experience in the American democracy. The cost of such prominence in Australia's political life is that the rights and status of Indigenous peoples became much more of a partisan issue than had ever been the case before in Australia, or has ever been the case in the other English-settler democracies. Partisanship is, after all, the organizing dynamic of democratic politics. But when partisanship infects – to the point of permeating – a settler country's efforts to deal with the rights and aspirations of the Indigenous peoples who reside within its borders, it makes consensual solutions much more difficult to achieve.

The Legal Fog of the *Native Title Act*

The principal product of the great political storm of 1993 was a legal fog – *The Native Title Act, 1993*. The broad purposes of the act were clear enough. On the one hand, it 'validated' the dispossession of Aborigines and Torres Strait Islanders that had taken place up until the coming into force of the act on 1 January 1994. On the other, it established a process whereby those who were not dispossessed could claim and exercise their native title rights. These two dimensions of the act embodied the fundamental compromise on which it was based. But the dense complexity of the act's 127 pages and 253 sections made it a very inaccessible instrument for those who are supposedly its primary beneficiaries – Australia's Indigenous peoples. ATSIC issued a twenty-page 'Plain English Introduction' to the act.[82] But even this brave attempt to help ordinary people – Indigenous and non-Indigenous – find their way through the act is a bewildering document.

Immediately after a short section recognizing common law native title and giving it 'the force of law of a law of the Commonwealth,'[83] the *Native Title Act* (*NTA*) gets down to the business of validating 'past acts.' The acts that are deemed in need of 'validation' are acts of government – executive acts, legislation, and grants of land – that occurred since the coming into force of the *Racial Discrimination Act* in 1975. Without such validation, any such acts that extinguished the rights of native title holders or encroached on their land interests without providing the due process of law available to other property owners might be a violation of *RDA*. The Commonwealth Parliament could have overridden *RDA*, as it was not constitutionally entrenched. But the Keating government, as we saw, was under strong pressure from pro-aboriginal groups not to do so and, instead, adopted the device of referring to the *NTA* in the act's Preamble as 'a special measure for the advancement and protection of Aboriginal peoples and Torres Strait Islanders.' Though the act's validation applies directly only to the Commonwealth's past acts, the *NTA* permits the states and territories to enact similar validating measures with regard to their past acts.[84]

Massive as the act's legitimatization of past dispossession was, it was not quite complete or without compensation. An intricate categorization of past acts enables native title to revive where a grant or lease ended before 1 January 1994.[85] Most important, existing mining leases are deemed only to 'suspend' but not extinguish native title. So the *NTA* did not give the mining industry the total certainty for which its representatives and political supporters had fought so hard. The pastoralists appear to have done considerably better, as their leases are in the highest 'A' category of past acts that could be considered to have an extinguishing effect. But the possibility was left open that pastoral leases with 'reservations' allowing Aborigines continued access to leased lands might not extinguish native title. This exception meant that, under *NTA*, a regime of coexistence might continue on pastoral lands, especially in Queensland and Western Australia where leases have reservations protecting Aboriginal interests.[86] This question would remain unresolved until the High Court's decision in the *Wik* case in 1996.

The act is much clearer than was the High Court in *Mabo (No. 2)* on native title holders' right to compensation for extinguishment or impairments of their land interests attributable to past acts of the Commonwealth, a state, or a territory.[87] Though the act itself did not set a cutoff date, the assumption has been that claims for compensation can go back only to 1975, when *RDA* was enacted, as *RDA* is the basis of the High Court's ruling in *Mabo (No. 1)* that Indigenous property rights must not be dealt with in a discriminatory manner.[88] The act promised the renewal of an earlier policy that would constitute an even larger measure of compensation – a land fund to acquire land for Aborigines and Torres Strait Islanders who have been dispossessed.[89] It would take until March 1995 for an amendment to the ATSIC act to establish and fund the Indigenous Land Corporation. The total funding commitment was for $1.5 billion over ten years.[90] This legislation, so crucial to fufilling the Act's promise of being a special measure for the advancement of Aborigines and Torres Strait Islanders, was the Keating government's last pro-Indigenous act and was supported by the Coalition only when threatened with a double dissolution of Parliament.[91]

For native owners still connected with their traditional lands, the *NTA* provides some protection against 'future acts' of state. The act, like the High Court's decision, affirms the Australian state's sovereign power over native title lands. Australia's non-Indigenous authorities – Commonwealth, state, and territorial – can, for public purposes or for the benefit of private interests, expropriate or encroach on native title lands. In this sense, native title owners are treated like private landowners or lease-holders and are similarly vulnerable to state power. The quid pro quo is that owners of land under native title must enjoy *at least* the due process of law accorded other property holders, such as the right to be notified and a right to fair compensation. Indeed, a fundamental objective of *NTA* is to ensure that, in the future, Aborigines and Torres Strait Islanders enjoy this much 'equality before the law.' But the act goes a little further and, 'in recognition of the special attachment that Aboriginal peoples and Torres Strait Islanders have to their land,'[92] establishes a special right for native title holders that other property owners do not enjoy. This is the right to negotiate before acts that have more than a 'minimal effect' on the native owners are taken. It is a right that relates essentially to the authorization of mining activities, but also to the compulsory acquisition of land for the purpose of making a grant to a third party, or 'any other act' approved by the Commonwealth minister.[93] The right applies only to an 'onshore place,' which means lands and waters within the boundaries of a state or territory. Here the act bore the consequences of the Murray Islanders' lawyers withdrawing Eddie Mabo's sea claims.

Though the right to negotiate goes beyond what state governments and the mining industry could tolerate, it falls well short of the right of veto available to traditional owners in the Northern Territory under the 1976 *Aboriginal Land Rights (Northern Territory) Act.* If the native owners and the party proposing to extinguish or infringe on their property rights fail to reach an agreement, either party can bring the matter before an 'arbitral body.'[94] When the future act at issue is being proposed by the Commonwealth, the arbitral body is the National Native Title Tribunal (NNTT), a new tribunal all of whose members are appointed by the Commonwealth government.[95] States and territories may establish their own arbitral bodies, but until they do, the NNTT also serves as the arbitral body for their future acts. In making decisions, arbitral bodies are to weigh the seriousness of the proposed development's interference with the society and interests of the native owners against the public interest in the proposed development and its importance to the economy. Even when the tribunal's decision favours the native owners, it can be overruled if the Commonwealth minister or a state or territorial minister consider doing so to be in the 'national interest' or 'in the interests of the State or Territory.'[96] The act also provides an 'expedited procedure' whereby 'the Government party' (which could be a state) can ignore native owners' right to negotiate if a registered native title holder fails to object within two months.[97] The right to negotiate, which aroused so much opposition from the act's opponents and is the main legal protection of native title, is a very soft right indeed.

To gain access to the benefits of the *NTA*, such as they are, native owners are required to establish their traditional ownership through a complex registration process. Here the highly litigious nature of the *NTA* process is manifest. To become registered as the holders of native title or to claim *NTA* rights (such as compensation or the right to negotiate), an Indigenous group must apply to the native title registrar operating under the aegis of the National Native Title Tribunal or to an approved state or territory arbitral body if one exists.[98] The act sets out an elaborate process for having applications for determinations of native title accepted. Besides providing evidence of their traditional 'connection' with the lands and waters they claim, native title claimants must by sworn affidavit state their belief that their native title has not been extinguished and set down all the information known to them about *other* interests in the their lands or waters. If and when an application is accepted, the Registrar is to notify 'all persons whose interests may be affected by a determination.'[99] This group would include all private owners and lease holders, public authorities (including local governments), as well as other Indigenous groups with interests in the area. If the application is contested, the tribunal is to try to mediate the claim, but if mediation fails, the matter is referred to the Federal Court.

The *NTA* does not take away the right of Aborigines and Torres Strait Islanders to emulate Eddie Mabo and the Murray Islanders and endeavour to vindicate their common law native title rights in the regular courts. But the act's drafters clearly hoped that most native title issues in the future would be settled in a less costly and less adversarial process. As originally enacted, the *NTA* gave the National Native Title Tribunal rather than the courts the primary role in its administration. Most of the tribunal's members are to be persons with special knowledge or experience, particularly in relation to Indigenous societies, land management, and dispute resolution. Only its president and any deputy presidents are required to be judges or former judges.[100]

Despite the Act's intentions, the procedures of the *NTA* have proved to be a formidable set of hurdles for native title claimants. The first successful resolution of a native title claim under the act did not occur until October 1996 – nearly three years after the act had come into force. It involved payment of $1 million compensation to the Dunghutti people in return for their allowing a residential development on a small parcel of land at Crescent Head near Kempsey on the New South Wales north coast.[101] The complex machinery of *NTA* is much more accessible to 'non-native claimants' than to the Indigenous peoples, who were, supposedly, its main beneficiaries. Non-native claimants could be governments or private interests who wish to find out whether native title exists in relation to certain lands or waters in which they are interested. Non-native claimants who encounter no opposition are free to go ahead with projects in the area in question. Researchers at the Australian Institute for Aboriginal and Torres Strait Islander Studies reported that, up to March 1995, as many non-native applications as native applications had been submitted to the tribunal.[102]

Right from the beginning, the machinery of the *Native Title Act* tended to be divisive and alienating for Indigenous peoples. This was so despite the intelligent and sensitive leadership of the tribunal's first president, Justice Robert French (from the Federal Court), and the excellent work of many of its Indigenous and non-Indigenous members. Aboriginal societies found it very difficult, indeed sometimes impossible, to fit into the bureaucratic grooves of the 'Representative Bodies' which the act contemplates as the organizational vehicles through which they would make their claims.[103] Often the funding needed for this organizational work was lacking. Having gained admission to the tribunal's mediation process, native claimants experienced a frustrating and unjust power imbalance. As Mick Dodson puts it: 'Most native claimants feel that the odds are stacked against them. The process works like this: Indigenous people have to prove that they have connection to land. Other parties don't have to justify their expropriation of Aboriginal land.'[104] And it was not only governments and corporate interests who engaged in these proceedings to oppose native title: very often a native group claiming ownership finds itself involved in an adversarial relationship with other native applicants.[105]

The suffocating legalism of the *NTA* got worse after a 1995 decision of the High Court ruled that decision-making powers of Australia's Human

Rights Commission breached the strict separation of judicial and executive powers which the judges read into the Australian Constitution.[106] This decision threw into jeopardy the power of the National Native Title Tribunal to make determinations of title even in uncontested cases. Proposals were made requiring that the Federal Court receive applications and make all determinations of native title. The tribunal would continue to carry out its mediation function, but under the Federal Court's control. In 1998, as part of the package of amendments provoked by the *Wik* case, these judicializing changes were adopted.[107]

For the most part, the *NTA* aims at setting out a system for incorporating property owned under native title into Australian land law. It is very much a technical scheme of real estate law rather than a program for working towards new, post-colonial, political arrangements with Indigenous peoples. In just one of the act's 253 sections, Section 21, is there even a whiff of broader political possibilities approaching those being worked out through New Zealand's Waitangi Tribunal or Canada's modern treaty process. Section 21 contemplates the possibility of native title holders entering into an agreement with the Commonwealth, a state, or a territory to surrender native title rights or to authorize future acts that affect their title in return for some consideration. It goes on to say that such agreements could be made 'on a regional or local basis.'[108] This provision is pretty thin gruel. The agreements contemplated seem designed mainly to remove native title as an impediment to state or private development. And no machinery is provided to follow through on the declaration in the act's Preamble that 'governments should, where appropriate, facilitate negotiation on a regional basis between the parties in relation to ... claims to land, or aspirations in relation to land, by Aboriginal peoples or Torres Strait Islanders.'[109] As Justice French would later explain, without a statutory mandate, the tribunal found it very difficult to bring about agreements on a local or regional basis.[110] Despite the tribunal's best efforts, the *NTA*, the most tangible legislative consequence of the *Mabo* case, would not readily serve as an instrument for restructuring the political relationship of Aborigines and Torres Strait Islanders with the Australian state.

One thing that the *Native Title Act* would do is keep a lot of lawyers, anthropologists, and administrators involved in the native title business very busy. Soon after the act came into force, applications of various kinds in rapidly increasing numbers flowed into the National Native Title Tribunal at its headquarters in Perth. After receiving only twenty-eight in its first year of operation, the tribunal reported that, by late 1996, it had received a total of 731 applications.[111]

Locating the National Native Title Tribunal in Western Australia's capital city, Perth, was a bold decision of the Keating government, for that state continued to be the heartland of resistance to the Commonwealth's native title regime. While some states exercised the option the *NTA* gave them of setting up their own arbital bodies,[112] Court's government in Western Australia remained in total denial of common law native title. The legislation enacted by Western Australia in December 1993, just as debate on the *NTA* was reaching its climax in Canberra, purported to replace common law native title rights with statutory 'rights of traditional usage.' The transformation of common law native title rights into the far more feeble rights of traditional usage was designed to ensure that any mining developments approved by the state could go ahead without interference.[113] The Court government continued to issue mining rights as if *Mabo* hadn't happened. It was banking on legal advice that the *NTA* was constitutionally invalid.

The advice was brash and doctrinaire, and turned out to be wrong. The Western Australian legislation clearly discriminated against Indigenous people in the state by giving their land interests less protection than other landowners. In March 1995 the High Court, invoking its decision in *Mabo (No. 1)*, ruled that the Western Australian legislation was inoperative because it was inconsistent with the Commonwealth's *Racial Discrimination Act*.[114] The court also rejected Western Australia's constitutional challenge to the *NTA* and found that, except for one section, it was valid under the Commonwealth's power in Section 51 (xxvi) 'to make laws with respect to the people of any race for whom it is deemed necessary to make laws.' The decision was made by the same seven justices who had decided *Mabo (No. 2)*. This time they were unanimous – Justice Dawson agreeing to accept the majority's jurisprudence in the two *Mabo* cases. The one exception was Section 12 which purported to give the common law in respect of native title 'the force of a law of the Commonwealth.' This wording implied that the Commonwealth Parliament was conferring legislative power on the judiciary. Taking its fetish about the separation of powers to new heights, the High Court said that no legislature can do that. However, the court also said that the invalidity of Section 12 did not affect the validity of any other provision of the act.[115] So the days of denial in Western Australia were now over. Common law native title lived there after all. The state's government and mining industry would have to comply with the Commonwealth's *NTA* regime. And so they did – in a most obstreperous way. The registrar reported in late 1996 that the tribunal had to deal with 5114 notices of 'future acts' – virtually all of them from the mining industry.[116]

By 1996 the legal fog of *NTA* was enveloping much of the field of Indigenous action concerned with defending and securing rights to water and land. This activity, most of it under the aegis of the tribunal, was highly localized and hardly visible politically. At the same time other consequences of the *Mabo* decision were occurring outside the *NTA* framework which brought larger issues of Indigenous relations back to the top of Australia's political agenda.

Koiki Mabo Comes Home

One such consequential event occurred three months after the High Court's decision disposing of Western Australia's challenge to the *Native Title Act*. It is an event that dramatically captures both the triumph and the tragedy of Eddie Mabo's victory.

On 3 June 1995, the third anniversary of the High Court's decision in *Mabo (No. 2)*, a tombstone at Koiki Mabo's grave in Townsville was unveiled. It was a day of great celebration. Following Mer Island tradition, the time of mourning was over. The time had come to celebrate Mabo's moving on to a better place where he could be with his ancestors. And there was more than that to celebrate. In the three years since his posthumous success in the High Court, Mabo's struggle and final victory had become a foundational story in Australia's history. Eddie Koiki Mabo, a Merian man of the Pladarim clan, pearler, long-time exile, cane-cutter, dock-worker, loving husband, father and grandfather, school founder, community activist, university groundsman, researcher and lecturer, champion of Indigenous culture, and a courageous, indefatigable but mortal litigator, had become an Australian hero. Mabo's story and its significance for his own people and for Indigenous people everywhere were now told in bold gold letters on a black marble headstone, with a three-dimensional bronze image of his smiling face fixed into the marble at the top of the stone. This handsome headstone would now replace the simple wooden cross on Mabo's grave in Townsville's Belgian Gardens cemetery.

The unveiling of the tombstone on that sparkling June day was a dignified and moving event.[117] It was done with all the trappings of

Meriam custom. Bonita Mabo, flanked by two of her twenty-seven grand-children, wept as relatives of her late husband unwrapped the tomb-stone from the cloth decorated with the symbols of the Meriam tribes. A colourful procession of Islanders and traditional dancers through Townsville's main street preceded the unveiling. Prominent leaders, including ATSIC chairman Lois O'Donoghue, Aboriginal Affairs Minister Robert Tickner, and the prime minister's wife, Annita Keating, joined a huge crowd at the City Mall to pay tribute to Eddie Mabo. In her speech, O'Donoghue said that Mabo's struggle and victory 'have changed Australia forever.'[118] In the evening a huge crowd attended a joyous and colourful Christian feast presided over by the great *agud*, Malo, in one of Townsville's largest hall. On this day, as filmmaker Trevor Graham put it, 'reconciliation seemed to be a possibility.'[119]

But the next day there was a rude awakening. A close friend of Mabo's went early to the cemetery to bid his friend a last farewell and discovered, to his horror, that the tombstone had been desecrated. Swastikas were sprayed in red paint all over the black marble, rude words painted across the bottom, and – most painful of all – Mabo's face had been pried off and removed from the headstone.[120] For Netta Mabo, her family and friends, the pain was nearly unbearable. Indeed, as Senator Margaret Reynolds, who had been so close to the Mabos throughout their struggles, said, it was an absolutely terrible moment 'for all fair-minded Australians'[121] – and I would add for fair-minded people everywhere. Mabo's immediate family now had a heart-wrenching decision to make. They dearly wanted Eddie to remain close to them, but they sensed that only on Mer would he truly rest in peace. And his stated wish had always been to be buried near his birthplace. So, reluctantly, the family agreed to have his body exhumed and transported to Mer for final burial.

The reburial on Mer was postponed until the school holidays in September, so that as many of Mabo's extended family as possible could participate. Prime Minister Keating provided a military aircraft (a Canadian Caribou) to ferry relatives to Mer. Many others came by commercial and charter flights. After the plane carrying Mabo's coffin landed on the grassy field that serves as an airstrip high in the centre of Mer Island, a procession led by Meriam elders carried it across the island to the village of Las, where Eddie had been born. As the bier moved slowly along the winding path, only the sound of weeping punctuated the solemn silence. At Las, on the far side of Mer from the main island settlement, Mabo's body lay in state for three days with the Meriam people's flag flying behind his coffin. In the funeral ceremony that followed, Netta Mabo unveiled the marble headstone with a new bronze image of Eddie's face affixed. The feast that took place that evening and the dancing, singing, and drumming that went on through the night were full of island ritual. In the words of historian Noel Loos, the ritual 'reached back past the missionaries and the other colonialist intruders to the time when Malo's law prevailed and unified the proud and independent clans of Mer.'[122] Eddie Mabo would surely have approved.

The great Indigenous challenger was home, but his political project was far from complete. Trevor Graham remembers Mabo saying that he hoped his law case would help unite Australia, not divide it.[123] The circumstances that brought his body home to his birthplace were a sign of the raw hatred in some sections of the Australian public against Indigenous people who are bold enough to assert their rights. The Townsville police pursued several lines of inquiry but have never been able to find evidence linking any person or group to the desecration of the Mabo headstone. Though that crime remains unsolved, evidence of a much more systemic resistance to Eddie Mabo's achievement was soon to surface on the national political stage.

CHAPTER 10

Consequences II:
Wik and a Country Deeply Divided

In the federal election held on 2 March 1996, the Keating Labor government was soundly defeated by the Liberal National Coalition. In his victory speech, John Howard, the new prime minister, emphasized national unity. 'I will focus on those things that bind us together,' he proclaimed.[1] Contrary to that undertaking, his first term would produce an Australia more divided than ever before in its history on the rights of Indigenous peoples.

The imminence of such division was not apparent at the time of the election. A year earlier, when the High Court rendered its decision rejecting Western Australia's challenge to the *Native Title Act*, Howard, as leader of the opposition, recognized the court's ruling as the final legal word on the *Mabo* legislation. 'The decision,' he said, 'confirms a significant shift of power to the Federal Government of matters previously within the direct authority of the states.'[2] At this time, Howard withdrew the Coalition's promise to repeal the act. The Coalition's election platform contained a commitment to amend the *Native Title Act* so as to 'ensure its workability,'[3] but aboriginal issues were not prominent in the election campaign. Neither Keating's defeat nor Howard's victory were attributed to *Mabo* and the debate over the *Native Title Act*. Two months after the election, the Howard government issued a discussion paper on an approach to amending the act, but it did not stir up much interest. The political scene with respect to Indigenous peoples was relatively quiescent until two days before Christmas 1996, when the High Court brought down its decision in *Wik*, in effect dropping the second shoe – and then all hell broke loose.

The High Court Decision in *Wik*

Wik Peoples v. Queensland[4] concerned a question about native title which was not definitively resolved in *Mabo (No. 2)* or by the *Native Title Act* – the question of whether the issuing of a pastoral lease automatically extinguished native title. Though it sounds very technical, this question had huge implications for Australia. The political economy of grazing alien livestock on the arid Australian outback meant that pastoralists held only leases, not full freehold ownership, to their grazing lands.[5] An analysis of Australian land tenure in 1980–1 showed that 52.6 per cent of Australia's total area, and 76.4 per cent of land held for private use, was under leasehold tenure.[6] While much of this land was still being used in varying degrees for grazing sheep and cattle, much of these pastoral lands continued to be lived on and used for various purposes by their traditional Aboriginal owners. It was also on these pastoral lands that the mining industry saw a huge potential for economic development, a potential that would be more difficult to realize if native title holders on pastoral lands had a right to negotiate before any mining project could go ahead. It is not without reason that the *Wik* case is referred to as the 'Mabo of the mainland.'[7]

In *Mabo (No. 2)*, two leases were involved – one in 1882 involving a two-acre plot on Mer to the London Missionary Society and the other over the islands of Dauer and Waier for a term of twenty years to two non-Islanders for the operation of a sardine factory. While Justice Brennan took the view that the very issuing of these leases was incompatible with the continuing existence of native title and therefore extinguished native title to the land covered by the leases, this position was not adopted by the other justices who wrote opinions, nor was Brennan's position part of the court's formal conclusions in the case. In the political struggle over the terms of the *Native Title Act*, the relative success of Rick Farley, the pastoralists' chief negotiator, as compared with the miners, created the impression that pastoralists had been totally protected from native title claims. In fact, Farley had secured only a clause including pastoral leases issued since 1975 among the past acts that could have the effect of extinguishing native title. The Keating government in effect decided that Aboriginal people on lands subject to pastoral leases 'were free to test their rights ... in the courts.'[8] And this they most certainly did.

The Wik were one of the first, if not the first, Indigenous people to attempt to assert native title rights in the courts after the *Mabo* case. In June 1993, well before passage of the *Native Title Act*, they applied to the

Federal Court for a declaration that they are the traditional owners of 28,000 square kilometres of land and waters on the western side of Cape York Peninsula in northern Queensland. A number of groups on the west coast of Cape York, and some further inland, identify themselves as the Wik people.[9] In their tenacity in defending their homeland, the Wik resemble the Meriam people. When Dutch explorers early in the 1600s landed on Wik territory, they encountered hundreds of armed warriors. Cape Keerweer (bearing the Dutch word for 'turn again') in the middle of the coastal Wik's country is as far south as the Dutch ever came.[10] In modern times, the Wik and other Aboriginal peoples of Cape York were less successful in resisting intrusions into their country and interference with their society. At Mapoon and Weipa they were forced to abandon coastal communities when rich deposits of bauxite were found where they were living. In 1957 Queensland gave Comalco (Commonwealth Aluminium Corporation) a mining lease over 5880 square kilometres along the west coast of Cape York.[11] Comalco built a port and processing plant at Weipa. The Aboriginal reserve in the area was reduced from 354,828 hectares to 142 hectares to accommodate Comalco's bauxite leases.[12] A challenge to the validity of this lease was part of the case the Wik brought to the Federal Court. Some of the Aborigines who had settled on the Weipa area were forced to move farther south to Aurukun, a largely Wik centre which, in the 1970s, had struggled vigorously against Bjelke-Peterson's government to assert its right to 'self-management.'[13] Part of the country to which the Wik claimed Aboriginal title was the Holroyd River Holding, an area of 2830 square kilometres in relation to which a pastoral lease had been issued in 1945. The lease had been surrendered in 1973 but renewed for thirty years in 1975.[14]

In September 1994 the Wik were joined in their legal action by another of Cape York's Aboriginal peoples, the Thayorre. Part of the land that was subject to the Wik claim overlapped an area of their country and had come under the Michellton Pastoral Lease, which had a short and vacuous history. The Michellton lease was first issued in 1915, forfeited in 1918, then reissued, and finally surrendered in 1922. During that short span, no pastoralist had entered the land and its traditional inhabitants continued to occupy it.[15] Since 1922 the land formerly subject to the Michellton leases had been reserved for the benefit of its Aboriginal occupants. Though the Holroyd leases covered many more years, the pastoral use of these lands was almost as slight as on those subject to the Michellton leases. No pastoralists lived on the Holdroyd Holding and no boundary fencing or buildings had been erected. A

1988 government inspector reported that only about one hundred feral cattle could be found on all this vast area.[16] As Justice Kirby was to comment, these particular circumstances, though by no means typical of all pastoral leases, gave 'an unreal quality' to pastoral leases, as giving their recipients 'exclusive possession' or 'exclusive occupation' of the lands to which they applied.[17]

Unreal as it may seem that a temporary lease of land for a very limited and special purpose could extinguish for all time the proprietorial interest of the people whose land it has been for centuries and who continue to use it and care for it, this was the view – the legal magic – that prevailed in the lower courts before *Wik* reached the High Court. The first judge to deal with the issue was Justice Robert French, the president of the Native Title Tribunal, when he was called upon to consider an application of the Waanyi people who lived in the far northwest region of Queensland. The land and water to which the Waanyi claimed native title was of great strategic economic importance. It formed a corridor over which the Rio-Tinto Zinc Corporation planned to build a pipeline for pumping zinc concentrates from the Century mine at Lawn Hill to port facilities at Karumba on the Gulf of Carpentaria. It was estimated that, when completed, the Century mine would produce 8 per cent of the Western world's zinc.[18] The Waanyi hoped to use their right to negotiate under the *Native Title Act* to gain some leverage on how this huge project proceeded and a share in its ownership. But the Century mineral leases at Lawn Hill were on lands that had been subject to a pastoral lease, and if a pastoral lease extinguished native title, the Waanyi would have no right to negotiate. Justice French applied the position Brennan had taken on leases in *Mabo (No. 2)* – that a lease once issued irrevocably extinguishes native title regardless of the current use of the land. Although French saw this position as 'a significant moral shortcoming in the principles by which Native Title is recognized,' he refused to register the Waanyi claim.[19]

Justice French's ruling was appealed to the full Federal Court, which upheld his decision in 1995.[20] Though the Wik and Thayorre peoples had argued their case before Justice Drummond in the Federal Court in September and October 1994, the judge did not render his decision until January 1996. At this time, Drummond considered he was bound by the full Federal Court's decision in the *Waanyi* case and ruled that pastoral leases extinguished native title.[21] When the *Waanyi* case was appealed to the High Court, the court allowed the appeal but on grounds that had nothing to do with the pastoral lease question.[22] The court applied its strict separation of powers doctrine and found that Justice French, as the head of a tribunal, had improperly exercised a judicial function in making his ruling. So it remained for the Wik and Thayorre peoples, who were now granted leave to appeal directly to the High Court from Justice Drummond's decision, to test whether a majority on Australia's highest court agreed with Justice Brennan and the lower court judges that the mere issuing of a lease extinguished for all time the native title of the land's traditional owners.

Two changes had taken place in the composition of the High Court since *Mabo (No. 2)*, and these changes were crucial in determining the outcome in *Wik*. Sir Gerard Brennan, who had succeeded Sir Anthony Mason as chief justice in 1995, stuck to his position and held that the issuing of a leasehold interest in land by the Crown irrevocably extinguished native title. He was joined in this decision by Justice McHugh, who had also concurred in Brennan's *Mabo (No. 2)* judgment, and by Justice Dawson, the lone dissenter in *Mabo (No. 2)*. But Brennan's position failed to win the support of a majority of the High Court judges. Justices Gaudron and Toohey, who in their *Mabo* judgments had not made any determination about the effects of Murray Island leases on native title, now rejected Brennan's categorical position on the extinguishing effect of leases. They were joined by the new appointees to the court, William Gummow, who filled the vacancy created by Mason's retirement, and Michael Kirby, who took Sir William Deane's place when Deane retired to become governor general in 1996. These four justices disagreed with Brennan that the Crown's issuing of a lease on lands traditionally owned by Indigenous people automatically and irrevocably, regardless of the conditions and terms of the lease or of its actual use, extinguished native title.

Given the tremendous furore that arose in response to the High Court's decision in *Wik*, it is important to understand the limited scope of the position taken by the majority. The majority judges did not uphold the native title claims of either the Wik or the Thayorre peoples. There was no clear tangible win here for the traditional owners the way there was for the Meriam people in *Mabo (No. 2)*. To gain recognition of title to any part of their traditional country, the Wik and Thayorre would have to go back to the Native Title Tribunal or the Federal Court to make out their claim. The four majority judges decided only that the issuing of leases for grazing cattle did not necessarily extinguish all native title rights that might otherwise exist.[23] Their judgment meant that a legal regime of coexistence between pastoral lease-holders and native title holders was possible – a pastoral lease did not automatically give its holder exclusive possession of the land in question. Whether coexistence was actually possible – in a legal sense – would depend on the terms and conditions attaching to any particular lease and the performance of those conditions.

The coexistence possible under the majority's position tilted very much against the Indigenous people's rights and interests. As Toohey put it in his judgment, if, in relation to any specific lease, the 'traditions, customs and practices of the aboriginal claiming the right' are inconsistent with the rights conferred on the grantee of the pastoral lease, 'to the extent of any inconsistency the latter prevail.'[24] In other words, in any conflict between the rights of pastoralists and the rights of native title holders, pastoralists prevail. Moreover, the majority agreed with Justice Brennan's rejection of the challenge to the validity of the 1957 Queensland statute that authorized establishing the bauxite mine at Weipa without any consideration of the interests of the Aboriginal people in the area. They also agreed with his rejection of the claim that Queensland's agreements with mining companies violated principles of natural justice and were a breach of the state's fiduciary obligations to the Wik people, whose interests were arbitrarily impaired. All seven judges remained firmly in support of the basic axiom of settler society justice: that clear exercises of settler legislative authority extinguishing or encroaching upon native rights are not to be questioned by the courts, however unilateral and unjust they may be.

The legal thinking of the majority in *Wik* is best described as nationalist, in contrast to Brennan's colonialist jurisprudence. The common denominator of the separate judgments written by the four majority justices – Toohey, Gaudron, Gummow, and Kirby – was their emphasis on the distinctive nature of land tenures in Australia. The word 'lease' in the colonial and post-colonial Australian statutes, including the *Land Act, 1910*, the Queensland act under which the Michellton and Holdroyd leases were first issued, had to be understood in terms of the legislation's economic and social objectives. The pastoral lease was created by Australian legislators as a device for giving pastoralists access to the immense tracks of land they needed for a decent return on their investment without giving them exclusive ownership and possession of areas – which, in Justice Kirby's words, could be 'as extensive as many a county in England and bigger than some nations.'[25] There was no evidence that the legislators intended holders of these limited-term leases to be in exclusive possession of the pastoral lands. Quite to the contrary, there was plenty of evidence that Aboriginal peoples would continue to live on these range lands. Many pastoral leases had reservation clauses reserving Aboriginal occupancy and use of the lands in question. Even where there were no such reservation clauses, as was generally the case in New South Wales and Queensland, there was no evidence that the legislature intended Aborigines to be removed from the land. On the basis of this historical background, the four majority judges all found they could not conclude that a necessary implication of a leasehold interest in land in the Australian pastoral context was exclusive possession. Even if a leasehold tenure in English law has been understood to give the grantee exclusive possession, '[It] is a mistake,' Kirby argued, 'to import into the peculiar Australian statutory creation, the pastoral lease, all of the features of leases in English leasehold tenures dating back to medieval times.'[26]

The chief justice, in contrast, felt compelled to interpret 'lease' in the Australian legislation according to its technical meaning in English law – unless the statute clearly indicated another meaning. The 1910 Queensland act did not indicate otherwise; therefore, reasoned Brennan, it must give lessees exclusive possession as 'that right is the leading characteristic of a leasehold estate, distinguishing the lease from a licence.'[27] For Brennan and the two justices who concurred with him, this necessary implication of the technical meaning of a leasehold tenure in English law was enough to meet the standard, set down in *Mabo (No. 2)*, of a 'clear and plain intention' to extinguish native title. Not only that, but the granting of an interest in land by the Crown, according to Brennan, converts the Crown's title to a full beneficial ownership, so that when the lease terminates, even if Aboriginal people are still vitally connected to the land, the Crown's title over it is no longer subject to the burden of native title. For the dissenting judges, the granting of a leasehold interest extinguishes native title for all time. For the majority judges, common law native title cannot be extinguished by the technical implications of land law. Justice Gummow, in quoting Lord Wilberforce's dictum that 'the task of the court is to do, and be seen to do be doing, justice between the parties,'[28] gave the best rationale for the majority's taking this approach to native title.

Howard, Hanson, and Bucketloads of Extinguishment

The political response to the High Court's decision in *Wik* was every bit as loud and intense as it had been to the court's decision in *Mabo (No. 2)* – except this time the political storm broke immediately. Even over the Christmas holiday period, the news media were full of stories and comments about the decision. As 1997 began, *Wik* continued to dominate the news and, for the rest of the year, aboriginal issues were once again at the top of Australia's national political agenda. The attention the country gave these issues did not seem to be leading towards a harmonious 'reconciliation.' Indeed, 1997 was truly an *annus horribilis* in Australian Indigenous affairs. By the end of the year, the country was on the brink of an election that would focus on a government proposal to roll back aboriginal rights.

Unlike the Keating government, which had aimed at providing some statutory protection for the aboriginal rights recognized by the High Court in *Mabo (No. 2)*, the Howard government came out quickly on the attack against the very modest bit of protection native title holders had won in *Wik*. The government was already working on a package of amendments to the *Native Title Act*. Now this package would be augmented by amendments designed to overcome the 'uncertainties' resulting from the High Court's ruling on pastoral leases. The great god 'certainty' had to be placated – certainty for those who want to 'develop' pastoral lands, but not certainty or security for the traditional owners of those lands. Mining industry spokesman howled about the 'horrifying' uncertainty they now faced in being dragged into time-consuming negotiations with holders of native title on pastoral lands.[29] Queensland premier Rob Borbidge began mobilizing state premiers to bring pressure on Canberra to extinguish native title. He advocated buying out native title claimants and inserting a 'sunset clause' in the *NTA* to put a terminal date on the uncertainty arising from native title claims.[30] Despite all the palaver about the grave threat the *Wik* decision posed to the mining industry, a few weeks after the decision, Pasminco, owner of the largest zinc and lead smelter in the world, purchased the Century mine at Lawn Hill, promising to make it the largest zinc mine in the world and, under the aegis of the National Native Tribunal, to continue negotiations with Aboriginal groups in the area.[31]

But it was partisanship and ideology, more than threats to material interests, that lay behind the attack on *Wik*. The Coalition government did not hesitate to make *Wik* a partisan issue. Prime Minister Howard accused the Keating Labor government of carrying 'a very heavy responsibility for having connived in misleading pastoralists ... when the Native Title Act was passed.'[32] Howard's response ensured the continuation and deepening of the partisan nature of Indigenous politics in Australia. The prime minister was pushed hard by the National Party wing of the Coalition to take a hard-line position against *Wik*. It was Tim Fischer,

leader of the National Party and deputy prime minister, who was the first
to come out swinging against the High Court's decision. The National
Party draws most of it strength from white rural Australia, where popular
resentment against the *Wik* decision – the decision as it was portrayed by
its political critics – was deepest. In early January 1997 Fischer toured
country towns in New South Wales and Queensland, promising 'that the
Government wasn't going to let them down in its response to the High
Court's ruling on the Wik case.'[33] Fischer lashed out at the High Court's
'activism,' suggesting that it pointed to the need to review how High
Court judges were appointed.[34] Many of those he encountered on his
tour were still unable to accept the High Court's *Mabo* decision, viewing
it as a denial of their rights rather than an affirmation of Aborigines'
common law rights. In these country towns, Fischer found himself being
pushed to deliver nothing less than 'legislation to fully and finally extinguish native title on pastoral leases.'[35]

There was a darker undercurrent of political disaffection that those
who wished to roll back the modest gains of Indigenous Australians
could draw upon. A mark of this undercurrent emerged in the desecration of Eddie Mabo's grave. Now it would find a dramatic vehicle for its
political expression in Pauline Hanson, whose brief, meteoric career
overlapped the struggle over *Wik*. In the 1996 election, Hanson won the
Queensland seat of Oxley. She had won pre-selection as the Liberal Party
candidate there and was designated as a Liberal on the ballot. But so
extreme was her anti-aboriginal, anti-immigrant campaign rhetoric that,
by the time of the election, the Liberals had disowned her.[36] Hanson's
maiden speech in the House of Representatives in September 1996 was a
populist appeal to Australians who resented the attention government
was giving to Aborigines and Torres Strait Islanders:

> Along with millions of Australians, I am fed up to the back teeth with the
> inequalities that are promoted by government and paid for by the taxpayer
> under the assumption that Aboriginals are the most disadvantaged people
> in Australia. I do not believe that the colour of one's skin determines
> whether you are disadvantaged.[37]

She went on to denounce those who support any kind of special administration of Indigenous affairs as separatists and to call for the rejection of
all Indigenous land claims.

Hanson's maiden speech was a huge media event. Her blunt statements rejecting multiculturalism and aboriginal rights had an outra-

geous simplicity that made them irresistible fodder for the media. Much of what she had to say – for instance, her questioning of ethnic pluralism and charging supporters of Indigenous peoples with intolerant 'political correctness' – echoed the ideas of the new prime minister. Only when Australia came under pressure from its Asian trading partners to repudiate the racist implications of Hanson's speech was Howard prepared to join with other party leaders and support a House of Representatives resolution affirming Australia's commitment to equality and to the process of reconciliation with Aborigines and Torres Strait Islanders.[38] That did not stop the pro-Hanson movement from rolling on and gathering enough strength to form the One Nation Party in April 1997. Hanson and One Nation were not key players in the *Wik* political battle – though, quite unintentionally, their temporary political success, as we shall see, helped secure some concessions from the government that somewhat softened its assault on native title. Nonetheless, the 'rightward shift in the policy "middle ground"'[39] that Hanson's movement reflects was undoubtedly a crucial factor in the political response to *Wik*.

The more mainstream political current pushing the Howard government towards a hard-line response to *Wik* was the organized voice of farmers. The agricultural lobby tapped into a more popular sense of uncertainty than the mining corporations could arouse. In March 1997 the National Farmers Federation placed a full-page advertisement in Australian newspapers calling on John Howard to defend the interests of 'thousands of farming families,' most of which have just 'managed to hang on by our fingernails through the long years of drought and low commodity prices,' but who now were 'worried sick' about this *Wik* decision and 'might not be strong enough to survive this uncertainty over our lives.'[40] The rhetoric was brilliant but misleading: brilliant because, politically, it called on 'city folk who might never meet an Aboriginal person' to support their hard-pressed countrymen in the outback; misleading in that it glossed over the extent of corporate and foreign control of pastoral properties and the many examples of co-operation and coexistence between pastoralists and Aborigines.

The '10-Point Plan' the Howard government unveiled in late April was primarily designed to assuage the hyped-up uncertainties of the pastoral and mining industries.[41] Only aficionados of the legal mysteries of the *Native Title Act* could understand the full implications of the amendments the 10-Point Plan proposed to make in the act. But there was no mistaking the plan's basic import: it would substantially reduce native title rights. Though it did not meet the demands of state premiers, like

Queensland's Borbidge, who called for total extinguishment of native title on pastoral lands, it went a long way towards delivering the 'bucketloads of extinguishment' Howard and Fischer promised. The *NTA* would be amended to validate all grants of land made since 1994, many of which would have an extinguishing effect.[42] All pre-1994 grants of freehold tenure and commercial, residential, and agricultural leases that could reasonably be thought to entail exclusive possession – including farmstay tourism – would extinguish native title. Pastoralists would be enabled to develop new forms of primary production with the effect of extinguishing native title rights in conflict with the new activities. Where native title rights survive, the 10-Point Plan would diminish their value by opening the way for states and territories to replace the right to negotiate with schemes affording substantially reduced due process rights. At the federal level, the Commonwealth minister could exclude from the right to negotiate exploration acts that are 'considered unlikely to have a significant impact on lands and waters.' The right to negotiate would not apply to the grant of exploration rights, nor to the renewal of mining rights. Any impediments that native title may pose to the provision of government services and the management of water resources would be removed.

Not only would the 10-Point Plan reduce the meaning of native title rights but it would also make these diminished rights more difficult to claim. The evidentiary burden that groups would have to meet to register claims would be significantly increased. Access to pastoral lands would be confined to members of native title groups who have maintained regular physical contact with these lands – thus excluding those who had been forcibly removed from their country. The *coup de grâce* in unburdening settler society from all the uncertainty flowing from *Mabo* and *Wik* was a six-year sunset clause on *all* native title claims. Whereas, after *Mabo (No. 2)*, Keating pledged to use the recognition of native title as the basis for establishing a new relationship with Indigenous peoples, Howard seemed determined to terminate the rights of Indigenous people and return Australia as quickly as possible to denying recognition of Aborigines or Torres Strait Islanders as distinct and enduring peoples.

Australia's Indigenous peoples did not take this assault on their rights lying down. One of the most important consequences of *Mabo* was enhancement of the capacity of Australia's Indigenous leadership to coalesce for political action in both the national and international arenas. This result was now evident in the Indigenous response to *Wik*. Since April 1996 Aboriginal and Torres Strait Islander organizations had been holding workshops on native title to consider constructive changes to the *Native Title Act*. The National Indigenous Working Group on Native Title (NIWG) developed out of these workshops. Its members came from the regionally based land councils as well as national institutions such as ATSIC and the Aboriginal and Torres Strait Islander Social Justice Commission. In late January 1997 Indigenous leaders met at Cairns in northern Queensland for a 'Wik summit' organized by the Cape York Land Council and its dynamic leader, Noel Pearson.[43] On the basis of positions developed at Cairns, NIWG members entered into talks with the prime minister and industrial representatives.[44]

It quickly became clear that there was no possibility of a meeting of minds on the legislative response to *Wik*. Indigenous leaders wanted amendments to the *NTA* to confirm the rights of both pastoralists and native title holders and improve the framework for working out negotiated agreements for regulating their coexistence on pastoral lands.[45] The 10-Point Plan contained a proposal to strengthen the enforceability of Indigenous Land Use Agreements as an alternative to the more formal native title machinery. However, the Howard government appeared to be so focused on resolving uncertainties by legislative extinguishment that its promise of one measure to enhance negotiated agreements was not enough to win Indigenous support for its legislative plan.

By the end of April, talks were over. Prime Minister Howard was determined to tough it out against the resistance of the Indigenous leadership and their supporters in Parliament – even if it meant forcing an election on the issue. On a Saturday afternoon in May, Howard addressed a large meeting of graziers and farmers who had come from all over Australian to Longreach in northwest Queensland to vent their anger at the 10-Point Plan's failure to deliver blanket extinguishment. At Longreach, Howard made what virtually amounted to a declaration of war on Indigenous peoples' rights. 'We have to get the balance right,' he said. 'The pendulum has swung too far in the direction of Aborigines in the argument.'[46]

Indigenous leaders were now mobilizing international as well as national support for their resistance to Howard's legislative plan. In March, Galarrwuy Yunupingu, chairman of the Northern Territory's Northern Land Council, was in Brussels urging the European Union to hold firm to the human rights clause in a trade and investment agreement with Australia.[47] On May 16 Senator Margaret Reynolds organized a press conference at Parliament House in Canberra on the international implications of Australia's proposed legislative response to the *Wik* decision.[48] A week later, National Indigenous Working Group representatives briefed diplomats from twenty-eight countries on the regressive human rights implications of the Commonwealth government's plan to roll back Indigenous rights.[49]

The 1997 Reconciliation Convention

It is ironic that positions were polarizing, as never before, at the very moment when the Council for Aboriginal Reconciliation was poised for its first major public effort to bring Australians together 'in shaping a more harmonious and united Australia.'[50] These were the words with which Patrick Dodson, the Reconciliation Council's chairperson, summed up the purpose of the Australian Reconciliation Convention held at Melbourne's Convention & Exhibition Centre from May 26 to 28. But by this time the Howard government's determination to swing back the pendulum and reduce native title rights had soured relations with Aborigines and Torres Strait Islanders too much for anyone to believe that the Reconciliation Convention could be a decisive step towards a consensual settlement with Indigenous Australia. Three days before the convention opened in Melbourne, members of Indigenous communities and organizations whose involvement in Australian aboriginal politics went back to the 1967 referendum campaign and the 1972 Tent Embassy struggle assembled in Canberra for a conference on Aboriginal Nations and the Australian Constitution. The Howard government's hard line on *Wik* was pulling Indigenous Australians back to an insistence on constitutional protection of their rights. The conference concluded with a statement 'that the process of Reconciliation cannot proceed unless it is based on principles of justice and equity for Sovereign Aboriginal and Torres Strait Islander Peoples.'[51] Many who attended the Canberra conference saw no point in going on to the Reconciliation Convention in Melbourne. Those who did go to Melbourne went with a sinking feeling about the futility of the entire reconciliation effort.

Though the shadow of the *Wik* conflict hung over the Reconciliation Convention, another development dominated the event. On the opening day of the convention, *Bringing Them Home*, the report of the Human Rights and Equal Opportunity Commission, was tabled in Parliament. *Bringing Them Home* was the result of a national inquiry into the 'stolen generations' – the separation of Indigenous children from their families and communities. The inquiry was led by Sir Ronald Wilson, the former High Court justice who had been one of the dissenting judges in *Mabo (No. 1)* and was now president of the Human Rights Commission, and Mick Dodson, the Aboriginal and Torres Strait Islander social justice commissioner. Their report estimated that, from approximately 1910 to 1970, between one in three and one in ten Indigenous children had been forcibly taken from their black parents and extended families to be raised in a white environment.[52] The hundreds of interviews of those who had been removed disclosed, in Sir Ronald Wilson's words, 'that many of our fellow Australians are still suffering from the wounds inflicted by past laws, practices and politics which, notwithstanding that they may have been devised with the best will in the world, were ill-conceived and led to gross violations of human rights.'[53] The presentation of the report to the Reconciliation Convention elicited moving addresses of sorrow and apology from the governor general, Sir William Deane, Lady Deane, and the leaders of the opposition parties, Labor's Kim Beazely and the Democrats' Cheryl Kernot. But the main political story was Prime Minister Howard's response.

In his speech to the convention, Howard expressed his personal sorrow for the 'injustices suffered under the practices of past generations towards indigenous people' and said he was 'sorry for the hurt and trauma many people here today may continue to feel as a consequence of those practices.'[54] Despite his hostility to what he dubbed 'black armband' history, Howard came close to the sentiments of the High Court majority in *Mabo* in acknowledging 'that the treatment accorded to many indigenous Australians over a significant period of European settlement, represents the most blemished chapter in our history.' But he refused to move beyond a personal apology and offer an official Australian apology. Why? Because, he explained, 'Australians of this generation should not be required to accept guilt and blame for past actions and policies over which they had no control.' Howard's refusal to make his apology on behalf of his government or the Australian people may have been calculated to avoid incurring any legal liability to compensate the thousands of living victims of past policies, but it was not well calculated to win the hearts or the minds of his audience.

Howard coupled the stiffness of his apology with a reaffirmation of his 10-Point Plan. It was, he said, the 'only basis' for a 'fair and equitable solution' to *Wik*. He told the convention that, for his government, aboriginal reconciliation was primarily 'a shared commitment to raise living standards and broaden the opportunities available to the most disadvantaged group in Australian society – and that is indigenous Australians.' Entirely missing from that vision is any commitment to Aborigines and Torres Strait Islanders as peoples with the right to flourish on their traditional lands and waters. In many ways the Howard government's approach resembles that of the first Trudeau government, which offered Canada's Indigenous peoples all the rights and opportunities of Canadian citizens providing they would surrender their special rights and treaties and, indeed, their very identity with their traditional societies. The reconciliation Howard proposed would be as firmly rejected as Trudeau's was. As Pat Dodson succinctly put it, 'On someone else's terms, reconciliation can not be progressed.'[55] Indigenous peoples in Australia and Canada, as elsewhere in the world, are all for improvements in their living conditions and for greater economic security and opportunity, but not at the price of surrendering their right to survive and develop as distinct societies in traditional country. In the context of *Wik*, there could be no reconciliation without coexistence.

The effect of the Reconciliation Convention, despite its sponsors' good intentions, was to leave Australia more divided than ever on aboriginal issues. As the prime minister spoke, many in the convention hall, Indigenous and non-Indigenous, rose and stood with their backs to him. The scene, viewed by a very large television audience, dramatized the division in the country. Many 'white Australians' were willing to go no further than Howard in seeking reconciliation with 'black Australians' and were offended by the rudeness shown to him by convention participants. But just about everyone in the Melbourne Convention Centre, those who stood in defiance of Howard and those who remained seated, black as well as white, knew that what was on offer as 'reconciliation' from this Australian government failed to engage with the structural and mental reshaping of Australia that true reconciliation requires. The mood of the convention was captured in the prolonged standing ovation for Noel Pearson's concluding words: 'There is a need for a moral and philosophical lobotomy or heart transplant on the part of our national leadership.'[56]

Senator Harradine to the Rescue

Australia was now reeling towards a national election on the rights of Indigenous peoples. By November, another massive bank of Australian legal fog, the 400-page *Native Title Amendment Act* (*NTAA*) incorporating Howard's 10-Point Plan, engulfed the federal Parliament, plunging the country into a political storm much like that which had raged around the original *Native Title Act* four years earlier. The government's bill passed easily through the House of Representatives, where the government had a comfortable majority. But in the Senate, the Coalition was one vote shy of a majority. That one crucial vote was held by a Tasmanian senator, Brian Harradine, a devout Catholic who had been expelled from the Labor Party in 1975 for accusing his party opponents of being 'friends of the Communists' and who, since then, had sat in the Senate as an independent.[57] The opposition parties in the Senate – Labor, the Democrats, and the Greens – in the second-longest debate in Australia's parliamentary history, moved hundreds of amendments to the government's bill, including some that would reject much of the 10-Point Plan. But none of their amendments could be passed without senator Harradine's support. For a while Harradine kept his own counsel. Finally, in early December, he declared his intention to support key opposition amendments that, among other things, would maintain the right of native title holders to negotiate over new developments on pastoral lands and require that the legislation be subject to the *Racial Discrimination Act*.[58]

Howard was determined to stand firm and get his 10-Point Plan through intact. The only way to do that was to bring on a double dissolution of Parliament and an election.[59] Under Section 57 of the Australian Constitution, if the Senate rejects a bill that the House of Representatives has passed, the House can pass it again three months later and, if the Senate again rejects it, the governor general can be asked to dissolve both Houses of Parliament. After the election, a majority of both houses meeting in a joint session decides the fate of the legislation. The deadlock procedure had been used on only five previous occasions. The sixth now loomed as an ominous probability. Unless Senator Harradine changed his mind, an election as early as July seemed likely.

With the three months ticking away before the *Native Title Amendment Act* could be reintroduced in Parliament, neither Howard nor his parliamentary opponents showed any signs of backing down. Howard continued to claim that a reduction of native title rights was essential for the Australian economy, while the Labor Party at its annual convention in January 1998 unanimously supported Kim Beazley's determination to block the government's bill.[60] At the end of March, as the critical parliamentary moment approached, a delegation of Wik people made their way to Canberra to make sure the senators understood that 'the

Wik are a people whose culture has survived until now, but that survival must be brought into question if the 10–point plan comes through and they lose access to their traditional country.'[61]

Judicial politics now swirled into this political vortex. At the beginning of April the High Court of Australia upheld a Howard government law banning Aboriginal people from using heritage protection legislation to stop the building of a bridge to Hindmarsh Island off the coast of South Australia over waters of deep spiritual significance to Ngarrundjeri women.[62] The argument against the legislation was that the Commonwealth's jurisdiction in relation to Aborigines and Torres Strait Islanders – authority it had obtained through the 1967 amendment to the 'race power' – could not be used to the detriment of Indigenous peoples but only for their benefit. The five-judge majority that upheld the legislation did so primarily on the grounds that it was amending the *Heritage Protection Act*, and Parliament had the power to amend any legislation it had passed. Only Justice Kirby categorically ruled out any legislation that is detrimental to or discriminates against people on the basis of their race. But two of the majority judges, Gummow and Hayne, indicated that there could well be some constitutional limits on the negative use of the Commonwealth's power if it amounted to a 'manifest abuse,' and Justice Gaudron found it 'difficult to conceive of any circumstances in which a law presently operating to the disadvantage of a racial minority would be valid.'[63]

Howard and his legal advisers saw the High Court's decision in the Hindmarsh Bridge case as clearing away any constitutional roadblocks to the *Wik* legislation.[64] For Indigenous people, the case was a further demonstration that the Australian Constitution, and the High Court that interprets it, provide a slender line of defence for their rights. That was especially so now that a Coalition government was appointing its judges. The Howard government's first appointment to the High Court, Kenneth Hayne, a Victorian judge, was relatively moderate. But its second, Ian Callinan, a prominent Queensland QC, was forced to withdraw from the Hindmarsh Bridge case when, despite his earlier denial, it was disclosed that before his appointment he had given legal advice on the matter to Howard's aboriginal affairs minister, John Herron.[65] Justice Callinan was expected to provide strong judicial support for the Howard government's project of reversing the swing of the pendulum on native title rights.

When the *Wik* legislation came back to the Senate, once again, it all came down to one man, Brian Harradine. Through three days of intensive debates and negotiations, Harradine was at the centre of efforts to soften the government's bill enough to get it through the Senate and avoid a 'race election.' The pressure on him was so great that, at one point, he fled from Parliament House to nap in a bus shelter.[66] After some flipping and flopping, Senator Harradine stood firm with Labor, the Democrats, and the Greens on four crucial points.[67] First, native title holders' rights to negotiate over new developments must not be reduced to rights generally available under state mining and property laws. This was, and is, a crucial point ideologically, for it recognizes that equitable treatment of Indigenous peoples does not mean treating their interests in their homelands as identical with private land rights. Second, the requirement that native title claimants have a physical connection with their traditional country was unacceptable because it denied the reality of a spiritual connection and was unjust to those who were forcibly excluded – including members of the stolen generations. Third, the six-year sunset clause, treating Indigenous peoples' interests in their home-lands as nothing more than a temporary burden on the Crown, was utterly unacceptable. Finally, the legislation must be subject to the *Racial Discrimination Act*, Australia's quasi-constitutional protection against racist legislation. Senate amendments based on these four points were promptly rejected by the House of Representatives. The starting gun for a double dissolution and a 'race election' was now loaded and cocked.[68]

The trigger on this gun was never pulled. Australia had a federal election in October 1998, but it was not a double dissolution triggered by a second Senate rejection of the government's *Wik* legislation. In July, Prime Minister Howard agreed to almost all of Senator Harradine's sticking points, and the amended *Native Title Amendment Act* was passed by both Houses of Parliament. What caused Howard and his Coalition partners to 'blink' was not a change of heart but a sudden change in their political prospects. And – irony of ironies – the source of this change that led to a slight softening of the Coalition's legislative assault on Indigenous rights was none other than Pauline Hanson, the most strident opponent of Indigenous rights in the country.

In the Queensland state election of June 1998, Hanson's One Nation Party was enjoying its one brief moment of political success. With the polls showing support for One Nation candidates at 14 per cent and rising, Queensland's Coalition parties, with the acquiescence of Howard's Coalition government in Canberra, instructed their supporters to place Hanson's party ahead of Labor in ordering their preferences. This move backfired – spectacularly. One Nation didn't need second preferences to register a stunning electoral breakthrough. Nearly one out of four Queensland voters cast first-preference votes for Hanson's party. The main victims of One Nation's breakthrough were National Party candidates in the party's rural heartland who were conservative, but not quite conservative enough, and Liberal candidates in the cities and suburbs who were punished for encouraging voters to prefer the far right One Nation over Labor.[69] The Labor Party was the chief beneficiary of the Coalition's cynical electoral strategy. Though its vote was down from the previous election, the party still managed to win just enough seats to throw out Rob Borbidge's Coalition government and form a Labor government under Peter Beattie.[70]

Suddenly, the Howard government's chances in an election forced by a double dissolution and fought on the issue of rolling back native title rights did not look very good. If Hanson's success in Queensland carried over into a federal election occasioned by a double dissolution, in which all twelve Senate seats in each state are contested, she might do very well. In such an election it would take only one-twelfth of the statewide vote to elect a senator. Hanson could easily end up holding the balance of power in the Senate, and the moderate, centrist part of the electorate might be angry enough with the Coalition to give Kim Beazley and Labor a majority in the House of Representatives. Howard was now ready to make a deal on the *Wik* legislation.

Late on July 1, after an intense day of discussions devoted to winning the support of Western Australia premier Richard Court, the Northern Territory's chief minister, Shane Stone, the Coalition Cabinet, and party room, the prime minister announced that he had struck a deal with Senator Harradine.[71] It was a deal in which the government gave most of the ground. The six-year sunset clause on making native title claims would be scrapped. The stolen generations and Aborigines locked out of their lands by pastoralists would not be denied recognition of their title by a requirement of continuing physical contact with traditional lands. The amending legislation would be subject to the *Racial Discrimination Act*. The one point on which Senator Harradine backed down was the possibility that the right to negotiate which the *Native Title Act* provided with respect to future acts on Indigenous lands could give way to state- or territorial-based regimes governing mining leases on pastoral lands. At first blush, this last point would seem to be a serious backdown by Harradine. However, it should be noted that any state or territorial alternative to the right to negotiate in the *NTA* would have to be approved by the Commonwealth minister applying a list of procedural requirements designed to protect the interests of native-title holders. Moreover, a positive determination by the minister could be disallowed by either House of the Commonwealth Parliament.[72]

A week after the Howard-Harradine deal, the Senate voted 33 to 31 to support the government's bill incorporating the changes negotiated with Senator Harradine. Even with those changes, Labor, Democrats, and the Greens remained opposed to the *Native Title Amendment Act 1998*. Though Indigenous leaders like Noel Pearson welcomed the changes Harradine negotiated, they still saw the act as a major setback. The original *NTA* of 1993, as we have seen, involved a massive extinguishment of rights that had been recognized in *Mabo (No. 2)*, and now the amended version of the act would seriously diminish the value of the rights that remained. Lois O'Donoghue poignantly suggested that it should have been titled the 'Colonial Title Amendment Act.' Though it recognized the possibility of negotiated Indigenous land use agreements, its emphasis was on arming governments and corporate interests with legal rights that would minimize the claims of native title holders. ATSIC's summary statement on the legislation's overall effect seems apt: 'The Bill as a whole reduces the ability of Indigenous people to have a meaningful say in what happens on their traditional country but not as much as the Government wanted to.'[73]

The process in which Aborigines and Torres Strait Islanders watched from the outside as white legislators wheeled and dealed over their rights was as colonial, and as objectionable, as the substance of the act. This way of dealing with the rights of Indigenous peoples, as Henry Reynolds observed, represented the still widely held view in conservative circles 'that Aborigines really don't have legitimacy, that they are to be given things and dealt with but not treated as serious negotiating partners in big decision making.'[74] From this point on, Indigenous political leaders in Australia would look for treaty-like agreements as the appropriate means of advancing their right to self-determination. And, increasingly, they would seek encouragement and models for this approach from outside Australia.

CHAPTER 11

International Dimensions
and Reconciliation

By the 1990s the struggle for Indigenous self-determination had become a major international human rights movement. Recognition as political societies (rather than cultural or ethnic minorities) with freedom to determine their political status was the common political aspiration of Indigenous peoples around the world. Such recognition is fundamental to the principle of self-determination enshrined in Article 3 of the *United Nations Draft Declaration of the Rights of Indigenous Peoples* that, by 1994, was formally before the UN's Human Rights Committee. Article 3 states: 'Indigenous peoples have the right of self-determination. This means that they can choose their political status and the way they want to develop.'[1] Consensual agreements or treaties, rather than state-imposed arrangements (including those imposed after 'consultation' with native peoples), would seem the only appropriate way of complying with that principle. For that reason, a 'special rapporteur' was authorized by the UN Working Group on Indigenous Populations to conduct a study of treaties between Indigenous peoples and states.[2] Nervousness about national sovereignty would make it difficult for all the UN member states with Indigenous peoples within their borders to accept the right of self-determination in the UN Draft Declaration. This was the case even for the three English-settler countries – Canada, New Zealand, and the United States – with a history of treaty-making. All three of these countries continued to find it easier to make Indigenous policy through top-down legislated solutions rather than agreements negotiated under conditions with sufficient freedom and fairness to be dignified as 'treaties.' Settler governments find it difficult to relinquish the control they have exercised for so long over Indigenous peoples.

Indigenous Self-determination in Canada, New Zealand, and the United States

By the 1990s the struggle for Indigenous self-determination in Canada, New Zealand, and the United States was encountering ideological resistance similar to that which underlies the Howard government's attack on Aboriginal rights in Australia. In these countries, as in Australia, it was much easier to win popular support for treating Indigenous people simply as disadvantaged citizens rather than members of political communities with distinctive historical rights. Even in Canada, where the English-speaking majority's accommodation of Quebec nationalism created a more promising milieu for the recognition of Indigenous nations, a multinational understanding of the country is a perspective held mostly by a small group of intellectuals.[3] In recent years the influence of that group has been countered by public intellectuals who challenge the principle of Indigenous self-determination. In 2001 the winner of the Canadian Political Science Association's prestigious Smiley Prize was Tom Flanagan's *First Nations? Second Thoughts*, calling into question the 'fiction of aboriginal sovereignty' and nationhood.[4] Another widely acclaimed book, Alan Cairns's *Citizens Plus*, argues that a nation-to-nation approach to restructuring Aboriginal relations threatens to undermine the integration of Aboriginal citizens into the Canadian state.[5] By the turn of the century, these ideas were beginning to be reflected in federal government policy that increasingly focused on reforming Canada's imperialist *Indian Act* rather than negotiating or renewing treaty relationships with Aboriginal peoples.[6]

In New Zealand, the National Party defeated Labor in 1990 and came to power with a commitment to 'mainstreaming' Maori policy and quickly repealed the *Runanga Iwi Act* conferring governmental authority on iwi structures.[7] Maori organizations could take on service delivery functions, but mainly by participating in contracting out and competitive programs that are part and parcel of neo-conservative reforms. In the United States, where 'self-determination' is treated as something 'which Congress might bestow on Indians,'[8] there was pressure on self-administering Indian tribes – notably, amendments to the *Indian Child Welfare Act* – to have their laws conform with other federal legislation.[9]

But there is a fundamental difference between Australia and these three other English-settler countries. In Canada, New Zealand, and the United States, assimilating colonialist impulses run up against not only

Indigenous resistance (of which, as we have seen, there is also plenty in Eddie Mabo's Australia) but a foundation of law and practice embedded in the very fabric of the country. The historical legacy of recognition and treaty-making – the absence of a long *terra nullius* period – provides much stronger re-enforcement for Indigenous resistance than Mabo's judicial victory can provide in Australia. Thus we find that the Bolger government in New Zealand, despite its desire to 'mainstream' Maori policy, accepted the Waitangi Treaty as a founding document of New Zealand and continued to implement restorative recommendations of the Waitangi Tribunal – albeit under a tight fiscal cap.[10] And in Canada the Chrétien government, while trying to impose much tighter management constraints on Indian bands, at the same time recognized the inherent right of Aboriginal peoples to govern themselves as a constitutional right on terms agreed to through negotiated agreements. In the United States the existence of many old treaties and the recognition of Indian nationhood in the nineteenth-century Marshall jurisprudence gave Indigenous peoples a purchase in the settler legal system for mounting their own efforts to recover treaty entitlements and control over their own societies.

Overcoming Third World living conditions in Indigenous communities and improving economic opportunities for individuals of native ancestry were common themes of government rhetoric in all the English-settler states. But Howard's Coalition government is exceptional in striving so ardently – so ideologically – to make this welfare-state approach the single dimension of its aboriginal policy. The wrongheadedness of this approach is borne out by growing evidence from experience outside Australia that there is a positive correlation between Indigenous peoples resuming responsibility for their societies (including their societies' natural resources) and the well-being of the members of those societies. Joseph Kalt, an American researcher, told Canada's Royal Commission on Aboriginal Peoples (RCAP):

> One of the interesting phenomena we see in the United States is that those tribes who have broken out economically and really begun to sustain economic development are uniformly marked by an assertion of sovereignty that pushes the Bureau of Indian Affairs into a purely advisory role rather than a decision making-role.[11]

Stephen Cornell, who with Kalt has co-directed the Harvard Project on Indian Economic Development, writes:

After years of research, we have yet to find a single case of an American Indian nation demonstrating sustained, positive economic performance in which somebody other than the Indian nation itself is making the major decisions about resource allocation, project funding, development strategy, governmental organization and related matters.[12]

The need to connect reforms aimed at improving social and economic conditions with Aboriginal nation-building is a theme running through the recommendations of Canada's commission. The RCAP is yet another example of the crucial role of determined Indigenous resistance in pushing settler states to modify colonialist policies. The commission, as we saw in chapter 7, had been established by the Conservative Mulroney government in response to the 1990 Oka crisis, when for an entire summer Mohawks on two reserves on the outskirts of Montreal maintained an armed standoff with Quebec police and the Canadian Army in resisting the plans to extend a golf course onto a sacred Mohawk burial ground.[13] Its terms of reference could not have been more comprehensive:

The Commission of inquiry should investigate the evolution of the relationship among aboriginal peoples (Indian, Inuit and Métis), the Canadian government and Canadian society as a whole. It should propose specific solutions, rooted in domestic and international experience to the problems that have plagued those relationships and which confront aboriginal peoples today.[14]

Seven commissioners were appointed: four widely respected Aboriginal persons – George Erasmus (co-chair), Viola Robinson, Paul Chartrand, and Mary Sillett – drawn from the four main components of Canada's Indigenous population, status and non-status Indians, Métis, and Inuit, as well as René Dussault (co-chair), Bertha Wilson, and Allan Blakeney, a distinguished Quebec jurist, a former Supreme Court of Canada justice, and a former provincial premier, respectively. The same bicultural balance was maintained in the commission's administration and research.[15] Canada's royal commission was likely the most extensive inquiry into Indigenous relations ever conducted on a partnership basis in a settler society. Its five-volume report documented how much Aboriginal peoples' living standards remained below those of other Canadians – lower life expectancy, poorer health, inferior housing, inadequate water and sanitation, more family violence, more alcohol abuse, fewer graduates from high school, more unemployment, and more time in jails and prisons – and made many recommendations aimed at ameliorating these conditions.[16] However, the means of achieving this kind of 'practical reconciliation' (to use the language of the Howard government) was not to be top-down, government handouts to individuals but negotiated agreements with Aboriginal communities 'that would permit them to fashion their own institutions and work out their own solutions to social, economic and political problems.'[17]

By the time the commission filed its report in 1996, the Mulroney Conservative government had been replaced by a Chrétien Liberal government, and while there was no philosophical divide between Conservatives and Liberals on Aboriginal policy, the Liberals felt no sense of ownership towards the royal commission. Nonetheless, the government's written response to RCAP, a document entitled *Gathering Strength*, was an 'Aboriginal Action Plan' building on the principles of mutual respect, and mutual recognition, and mutual responsibility and sharing identified as fundamental by the commission. *Gathering Strength*, was accompanied by a 'Statement of Reconciliation' in which the government acknowledged that, 'as a country, we are burdened by past actions that resulted in weakening the identity of Aboriginal peoples,' and that these actions stemmed from attitudes of 'racial and cultural superiority.'[18] In particular, to those who had suffered from the break-up of families, removal of children, and devaluing of culture that were part of Canada's residential school system, the Government of Canada said, 'We are deeply sorry.' It backed up these words with a commitment to establish a 'Healing Fund' of $350 million to be administered by a commission headed by George Erasmus. The contrast with John Howard's tepid response to *Bringing Them Home* could hardly be stronger. Nor was there any trace of rolling back Aboriginal rights in the Action Plan's commitment to 'strengthening the partnership between Aboriginal and non-Aboriginal Canadians' and its affirmation that 'a vision for the future must build on recognition of the rights of Aboriginal people and on the treaty relationship.'[19]

But the old adage that 'actions speak louder than words' was borne out in the implementation of Canada's new Aboriginal Action Plan. The government did not commit itself to the commission's fiscal plan of investing an additional $1.5 to $2 billion annually in spending on Aboriginal communities to reduce the growing dependency of their members on government welfare.[20] Direct federal expenditures targeting Aboriginal people continued to grow from the 1996 level of $7.5 billion, but not at the rate needed to improve their living conditions significantly or to help them build self-sustaining communities. And the Chrétien government showed no inclination to replace the huge and bureaucratic Department of Indian Affairs and Northern Development with a minister for aboriginal relations. This was the key organizational step recommended by the commission for restructuring government to move from a colonial relationship to a partnership relationship with Aboriginal peoples. Though in 1995 the federal government announced a policy framework for 'implementing the inherent right of self-government' and established a process for negotiating self-government agreements with Aboriginal peoples, it continued to conduct its relations with Aboriginal peoples primarily through the top-down, imperialist machinery of the *Indian Act*.[21]

The most significant breakthroughs in Canada in moving to relationships based on consent came not from any new governmental initiatives but from agreements negotiated with very resolute Indigenous peoples over a great many years. These two events were the establishment of Nunavut in the Eastern Arctic and the Nisga'a Agreement in British Columbia. Nunavut is a self-governing territory that had been part of the Northwest Territories. It encompasses nearly a quarter of Canada's land mass and is based on a 1993 agreement between Canada and representatives of the 22,000 Inuit people who constitute 85 per cent of the population of this vast region.[22] The agreement vests ownership of approximately 350,000 square kilometres, just under 20 per cent of the territorial lands (including mineral rights over some of the most promising geological formations), in an Inuit land corporation and presaged an Act of Parliament giving province-like responsibilities over the territory to a democratically elected Nunavut government.

Inuit negotiators were more concerned about practical benefits than fussing about the legal formalities of their agreement with Canada. They consented to give up all claims to native title in exchange for ownership in fee simple of the Inuit-owned portion of Nunavut, priority harvesting rights throughout the territory, a 5 per cent share of royalties on Crown lands, various measures to increase Inuit employment, a fund of $1.148 billion for economic development, a $13 million training fund, and other benefits. Constitutional purists and anthropological purists might be troubled by the fact that the Inuit would exercise their right to self-government through European-type institutions, such as an elected legislature, responsible Cabinet, and prime minister, all of which were provided for in an act of the Canadian Parliament. But the Inuit, who had no tradition of structured political authority, seemed not to be concerned. They would, like other formerly colonized peoples, put their own stamp on the practice of parliamentary democracy in the High Arctic in a number of ways, including the official status of their own language, Inuktituk, the absence of political parties, and an emphasis on decentralizing administration to small hamlets. Large majorities of Inuit ratified the agreement in all three of Nunavut's regions. Nunavut comes closer to satisfying the meaning of the Indigenous right to self-determination as spelled out in the Draft UN Declaration on the Rights of Indigenous Peoples than any other arrangement up to this time in Canada.

With the Nisga'a agreement, we return to an Indigenous people whose struggle to gain recognition of their rights, as has been noted several times in this book, played a crucial role in the *Mabo* case.[23] The Nisga'a people's persistence in claiming their rights led to the Supreme Court of Canada's 1973 decision in *Calder* that resuscitated common law native title in Canada. In the wake of that decision, the Government of Canada conceded that the Nisga'a people's title to their homeland in the Nass Valley of British Columbia had not been extinguished. Since then, the Nisga'a had been endeavouring to negotiate a comprehensive agreement with Canada which included land and self-government. Such an agreement did not become possible until the 1990s, when the governments of both Canada and British Columbia made important policy changes: Canada agreed to include land and self-government in a modern treaty having formal constitutional status, and British Columbia, the part of Canada most like Australia in its denial of Aboriginal rights,[24] finally abandoned its policy of *terra nullius* and accepted the need to negotiate settlements with the many Indigenous peoples still living on traditional lands within its borders.[25]

Although the Final Agreement the Nisga'a people's representatives signed with British Columbia and Canada in 1998 gives them ownership in fee simple only of 8 to 9 per cent of the lands they claimed, the area covered is the heart of their homeland where their villages have traditionally been located and where they carry on the fishing, forestry, and farming activities that have become the basis of their modern economy.[26] Other First Nations have as yet unsettled, overlapping claims over much of the remainder. The agreement recognizes the authority of the Nisga'a government over a wide range of matters, including public order, environmental protection, education, health, and social welfare. The Nisga'a government's authority applies to all residents of the Nisga'a territory and to Nisga'a citizens who reside elsewhere in Canada.[27] On most of these matters, federal and provincial laws prevail if they are in conflict with Nisga'a law. But in matters essential to their collective life, including management of their lands, their constitution, rules governing citizenship in the Nisga'a nation, language, and culture, Nisga'a laws prevail over federal or provincial laws. In effect, the agreement recognizes the Nisga'a as having a share of sovereign law-making authority in Canada.

The ratification of the Nisga'a Agreement by the people and institutions to which the signatories were accountable was an extremely difficult process. To reach an agreement, negotiators on all sides had to make concessions on points of vital importance to their constituents. Selling such an agreement to the political leaders and public whose assent is legally – and democratically – necessary is a high political art. It was not easy for the Nisga'a to accept an agreement in which they abandoned claims to much of their traditional country as well as many elements of their sovereignty and to regard the agreement as 'the full and final settlement in respect of the aboriginal rights, including aboriginal title, in Canada of the Nisga'a Nation.'[28] It should not be surprising that in the Nisga'a referendum that took place later in 1998, the agreement was approved by only 51 per cent of the 2384 eligible Nisga'a voters.[29] In the ratification debates that took place in the British Columbia legislature and the Canadian Parliament, the agreement came under fierce attack from the opposite direction – for being too generous to the Nisga'a people. Many in British Columbia resented not having a provincial referendum, even though the province has bound itself to have a referendum before its legislature acts on any constitutional proposal. The polls showed that a province-wide poll would likely result in the overwhelming rejection of the Nisga'a Agreement. The left-of-centre New Democratic government had to invoke closure to overcome the opposition Liberals' efforts to obstruct ratification in the BC legislature. Ratification was completed in the federal Parliament early in 2000, but not without anxious examination of the agreement's implications for Canadian sovereignty by the Liberal government's supporters in the Senate. Gordon Campbell, leader of the BC Liberals, with the assistance of two former justices of the Supreme Court of Canada, also challenged the agreement in the courts on the grounds that it unconstitutionally recognized Nisga'a sovereignty. In July 2000 Justice Williamson of British Columbia's Supreme Court rejected the challenge and held that the forming of Canada in 1867 did not extinguish the right of Aboriginal peoples to govern their own societies.[30] In May 2001 Campbell's Liberals scored a landslide victory over the NDP and promised a BC referendum on the whole treaty process.[31]

The Nisga'a Agreement is undoubtedly a landmark constitutional development for Canada and a significant world achievement in Indigenous self-determination. But the bitter rancour accompanying its ratification makes it a doubtful instrument of settler-Aboriginal 'reconciliation.' For many Aboriginal peoples in Canada and for the many non-Aboriginal Canadians – and for opposite reasons – it is not seen as an attractive model to emulate.

In Canada, as we noted at the end of chapter 9, the courts had become an important alternative site for the advancement of Aboriginal claims. The decade of the 1990s would show that judicial decisions can sometimes be obtained more quickly than negotiated settlements but that their outcome is extremely uncertain. After its very liberal interpretation of Aboriginal rights in the 1990 *Sparrow* case, the Supreme Court performed like the legendary trickster.[32] In 1996, in the so-called *Van der Peet* trilogy of cases,[33] the court's majority adhered to a 'frozen rights' doctrine that threatened to reduce the Aboriginal rights recognized in Canada's Constitution to the bundle of activities that judges view as integral to the distinctive culture of an Aboriginal people at the time of first contact with Europeans. In *Badger*, decided that same year, the court seemed to drain much of the meaning out of the Crown's fiduciary obligation and weakened treaty rights by not questioning the federal government's unilateral extinguishment of historical treaty rights.[34] But soon after these decisions, the judicial roller-coaster was on the rise again. In its 1997 Delgamuukw[35] decision, Canada's Supreme Court rendered the broadest, most liberal interpretation of native title the common law world has yet seen.

Unlike the *Van der Peet* trilogy, where the rights claimed were to carry on specific activities (commercial fishing and high-stakes gambling), in *Delgamuukw* the Gitksan and Wet'suwet'en peoples claimed a more fundamental and comprehensive Aboriginal right – Aboriginal title to their traditional lands in northern British Columbia on which they still lived. When the case reached the Supreme Court, because of flaws in the trial judge's handling of the case (including a dismissive treatment of oral history) and changes to the claim made by the plaintiffs after trial, the Supreme Court decided that a new trial would be required if the parties could not reach a negotiated settlement of the matters in dispute. So, instead of deciding the specific issues in dispute, the court used the case to flesh out the scope and nature of Aboriginal title as a constitutional right in Canada. The key point in the Canadian Supreme Court's view of Aboriginal title is that it is a recognition of full property ownership, except that it is a communal, rather than an individual, kind of ownership. 'What aboriginal title confers,' states Chief Justice Lamer, 'is the right to the land itself.'[36] The chief justice, speaking for the majority, was now willing to step away from the 'frozen rights' approach so far as native title is concerned:

> Aboriginal title is a right in land and, as such, is more than the right to engage in specific activities which may be themselves aboriginal rights. Rather, it confers the right to use land for a variety of activities, not all of which need be aspects of practices, customs and traditions which are integral to the distinctive cultures of aboriginal societies.[37]

But a tinge of 'frozen rights' remains: holders of native title have the right to develop their lands, including exploitation of subsurface minerals in non-traditional ways – providing that nothing they do is irreconcilable with their historical attachments to those lands (for example, strip-mining a hunting ground or paving over a burial ground). Lamer was also anxious to reconcile Aboriginal title with his understanding of Canadian sovereignty: 'Because ... distinctive aboriginal societies exist within, and are part of, a broader social, political and economic community, over which the Crown is sovereign, there are circumstances in which, in order to pursue objectives of compelling and substantial importance to that community as a whole ... some limitation on those rights will be justifiable.'[38]

The Canadian chief justice's view of developments sufficiently compelling to justify infringements on Aboriginal title owners' rights was very broad indeed. It includes 'the general development of the interior of British Columbia ... the building of infrastructure and the settlement of foreign populations to support those aims.' The 'burden' of native title on Crown sovereignty seems to be getting as light in Canada as in Australia under *Mabo (No. 2)* – except that Lamer throws in the Crown's fiduciary duty (denied by the Australian High Court), which means that serious infringements are justifiable only if native title interests are given priority and that 'some cases may require the full consent of an aboriginal nation.'[39] In performing its balancing act, Canada's highest court may be trying to encourage negotiated political settlements over litigation, but by arming each side with such verbally powerful markers, it may well have the opposite effect.

Canada's Supreme Court under its new chief justice, Beverley McLachlin, also shows signs of swaying with the political winds. In 1999, in *Marshall (No. 1)*, the court found that federal fishing regulations contravened rights of the Maliseet and Mi'kmaq peoples secured in eighteenth-century treaties with the Crown.[40] The decision provoked communal violence between native and non-native fishers and angry attacks on the court in the right-wing national press, already stirred up in opposition to the Nisga'a Agreement. When organizations representing non-native fishers asked for a rehearing of the case, the Supreme Court, instead of simply saying no, it never rehears cases, issued an eighteen-page opinion, *Marshall (No. 2)*, re-explaining its decision and laying particular emphasis on its view that the federal government has an overarching sovereign power to set justifiable limits on all Aboriginal rights, including treaty rights.[41] It is difficult to disagree with Mi'kmaq chief Lawrence Paul's verdict, when the second *Marshall* decision was rendered, that, as an impartial arbiter of Aboriginal rights, the court 'hurt its credibility today.'[42] Backlash in Canada, though not as strong as during the Howard years in Australia, was beginning to slow down the advancement of Aboriginal rights in Canadian courts as well as through negotiated settlements.

New Zealand, too, had its Indigenous rights breakthroughs in the 1990s which significantly increased Maori control over resources. The largest and most dramatic of these was the 1992 Sealord fishing agreement, through which Maori have acquired ownership of 50 per cent of New Zealand's commercial sea-fisheries. This arrangement is of extraordinary importance to a people for whom the sea and its resources have been at least as important as land resources. But like Nunavut and the Nisga'a Agreement in Canada, the fisheries 'deal' in New Zealand shows that advancing Indigenous self-determination through treaty-like agreements is a heavily compromised process, with results that are always problematic. The most difficult questions arising in the New Zealand case concern the identity of the Indigenous 'self' that should be the bearer and beneficiary of Indigenous rights.

An amalgam of court-based litigation and Waitangi Treaty claims led to what is, in effect, the first modern treaty between Maori and the New Zealand state. The High Court's 1986 decision in *Te Weehi*, citing Canadian native title jurisprudence and recognizing unextinguished Maori fishing rights based on pre-settlement activities, came at the very time New Zealand was introducing a national quota-based system to prevent overfishing. The Muriwhenua of the North Island and the Ngai Tahu of the South Island, as well as the Maori Council, successfully applied for injunctive relief in the courts to prevent the loss of vital fishing interests secured through the second article of the Treaty of Waitangi.[43] Maori and government leaders then began to work on a negotiated settlement. The Maori position was strengthened by the Waitangi Trubunal's *Muriwhenua Fishing Report* in 1988.[44] A national *hui* (meeting) mandated the Maori negotiators to settle for no less than 50 per cent of the quota.[45] The 10 per cent of quota offered in the 1989 *Maori Fisheries Act* fell far short of that share.

The possibility of a more satisfactory settlement arose in 1992 with the opportunity of purchasing Sealord products that held 26 per cent of the quota. Another intensive round of bargaining took place – and once again the Maori position was fortified by a Waitangi Commission report, this time documenting encroachments on the Ngai Tahu sea fisheries. In September 1992 *The Fisheries Settlement, 1992* ('a deed of agreement') was signed by seventy-five tribal representatives[46] and, in December 1992, was given legal effect in the *Treaty of Waitangi (Fisheries Claim) Settlement Act.* The nub of the settlement was that the New Zealand government purchased the Sealord interest for the Maori in return for the Maori surrendering all future claims on the commercial sea fishery. The statute also protected traditional fishing for private consumption. With the 23 per cent of commercial quota acquired from Sealord, the 20 per cent of quota for new species, and aggressive management by the Maori Fisheries Commission, the Maori soon had the 50 per cent of commercial sea fisheries they claimed. Even though a number of tribes opposed the settlement and tried unsuccessfully to block it in the courts, the 1992 act made it clear that 'the Crown would have no further obligations to Maori regarding commercial fishing, and all fishing claims before the Waitangi Tribunal would be deemed to be discharged.'[47]

Implementing the Sealord fishing settlement raised difficult issues of self-government and distribution. Responsibility for administering the fishing rights acquired through the settlement was handed over to the Maori Fishing Tribunal (Te Ohu Kaimoana), comprised largely of representatives of iwi with large coastlines. Important though this commission surely was for Maori self-government, appointment of the first commissioners, in 1993, 'was a government decision made behind closed doors.'[48] There was considerably more consultation when new appointments were made in 1996. Delegates at a 1997 conference on 'The Treaty of Waitangi and Political Representation' passed a motion calling for appointments in the future to be made by Maori rather than the Crown.[49]

Major issues of distributive justice arise in deciding who should represent the Maori for this or any other all-Maori purpose. The sea-fisheries settlement was for 'all Maori.' But, as Andrew Sharp points out, the ethnic or racial group 'Maori' cannot act.[50] Traditionally, Maori identify with a tribe or iwi. Tribal chiefs signed the Treaty of Waitangi, and its second article (in the Maori version) recognizes *hapu*, the local subunits of the iwi, as having *rangatiratanga* (control and possession) of lands, forests, fisheries, and other properties. And yet, 22 per cent of those who identified as Maori in the 1992 census could not name the iwi with which they were connected.[51] These, mostly urban-based Maori, seemed to get a boost from a ruling of New Zealand's Court of Appeal that the benefits of the fisheries settlement 'were for iwi (i.e., Maori people) including those who did not have or were unable to establish specific tribal affiliations.'[52] But then the Judicial Committee of the Privy Council, flexing the last residue of imperial judicial muscle that still applied to New Zealand, quashed the Court of Appeal's decision on the grounds that, without proper evidence, the Court of Appeal should not have been considering what constitutes iwi.[53] The matter then went back to Ke Ohu Kaimoana (the Maori Fishing Commission), which allocated the inshore quotas on the basis of tribal coastlines and divided the deepwater quota on the basis of 60 per cent for tribal coastline and 40 per cent for tribal population. The commission subsequently provided a toll-free phone service to help urban iwi trace their tribal ancestry.[54]

In Sealord and the fishing agreement we can see that Indigenous decolonization in New Zealand is a distinctive and somewhat incoherent exercise in restorative justice. The justification for reform always comes back to the Treaty of Waitangi and the failure of the New Zealand state to comply with obligations that contemporary Maori believe were the reasonable expectations of their forebears who signed the treaty.[55] While the justification for recovering ownership and power over land and resources is always backward looking, the remedies are forward looking and pragmatic, designed more to restore to Maori in different parts of Aotearoa the capacity to shape the terms on which their communities participate in a modern industrialized society than to compensate for past injustice. Such a process is bound to produce heavily compromised results – much too much for many newcomers to New Zealand who do not share the Maori understanding of the Treaty of Waitangi and for Pakeha who do not wish to see conservation lands returned to Maori control, and much too little for some Maori who view the settlements as betrayals of their societies' historical entitlements. Nevertheless, the process continues to be used and to produce results. Mason Durie reports that, by 1997, 600 claims had been registered with the Treaty of Waitangi Tribunal and approximately one-third had been cleared.[56] Of course, 'cleared' does not mean satisfactorily resolved. As we saw earlier, in most instances the tribunal has no power to render legally binding settlements. But some of its reports have led to very large negotiated settlements[57] – notably the 1994 Tainui settlement for the massive confiscation of Maori lands along the Waikato River, and the 1997 Ngai Tahu settlement of what may well be 'the longest running land claim by any indigenous people in the world'[58] for dispossession that took place through land sales and inadequate reserves in the South Island.

That the Tainu and Ngai Tahu settlements were each valued at $170 million, the exact amount of the sea-fisheries settlement, is not a coincidence. It is the result of the National government's decision to contain settlements within a fiscal envelope of $1 billion spread over ten years. Douglas Graham, the minister in charge of Treaty of Waitangi negotiations, explained that the envelope was aimed at ensuring some finite end to the settlement process.[59] Even in a country founded on a treaty relationship, settler government showed its overriding interest in securing a final and certain solution rather than being party to an on-going and open-ended relationship. On Waitangi Day, 1995, the Maori staged an angry protest against the fiscal cap. The three big settlements quickly ate up over half the funds available, leaving very little for the many claims not yet settled, let alone the hundreds waiting to be heard. This protest bore some fruit when New Zealand's new mixed-member proportional (MMP) electoral system led to the formation of a coalition government in late 1996. The Bolger/Shipley government, in which Winston Peters, a Maori and leader of the New Zealand First Party, served as deputy prime minister, dropped the fiscal envelope as official policy – although fiscal constraints continue to be a major factor in the Crown's approach to settlements.[60]

No settler state's history shows as clearly as New Zealand's the multidimensional and evolving nature of Indigenous self-determination. Maori have come to participate in the governing institutions of the settler state much more than their counterparts elsewhere. Though the special seats reserved for Maori in New Zealand's Parliament in 1867 were to last for only five years, representation of Maori as a distinct part of the body politic has become a permanent feature of parliamentary democracy in New Zealand.[61] Since 1975, Maori have had the option of voting in Maori electorates or as general voters. In the 1990s the number of Maori electorate seats became proportional to the number of electors on the Maori roll and has increased from four to six. The new electoral system has also increased Maori participation in Parliament. Seven of the sixteen Maori elected in 1999 to the 120-seat New Zealand Parliament were from party lists, three were elected from single-member constituencies based on the general roll, and six were elected by Maori electorates. With 13.3 per cent of the seats, Maori representation is closely in line with their proportion of the country's population. In terms of partisan politics, the New Zealand First Party captured all the Maori seats in 1996, thus ending Labor's domination of these electorates. Mason Durie writes, 'The more obvious fact was that Maori were affiliated to a wide range of mainstream parties.'[62] Through their participation in Parliament, Maori have also gained a more powerful presence in Cabinet than ever before, holding important portfolios such as treasurer and Maori affairs.

The extent of Maori participation in New Zealand's governing institutions should not be viewed as abandoning the cause of Indigenous self-determination. This kind of participation is something that a great many Maori, over time, have chosen as a means of developing their political status. When there has been talk about giving up special Maori seats, Maori leaders have made it clear that they wish to retain them. Participation in mainstream New Zealand politics has been freely chosen by the majority of Maori citizens. In response to a claim supported by the three pan-Maori organizations, the Waitangi Tribunal found that effective Maori political representation is essential to realizing the promise in the Waitangi Treaty's third article to extend to Maori 'all the rights and privileges of British Subjects.'[63] Certainly it gives Maori much more direct influence on programs directed at giving them access to the full benefits of New Zealand's welfare state than is available to Indigenous peoples in Australia, Canada, or the United States – including, in the Australian case, the influence available through ATSIC. At the same time, a strong presence in Parliament and Cabinet gives Maori some leverage on how well the New Zealand state supports Maori aspirations for autonomy and for recovery of lands and resources – witness the softening of the fiscal limitations on agreements with iwi after the 1996 election. Participation in the governance of the New Zealand state is not an alternative to the autonomy side of decolonization. Nor does it require Maori acceptance of the sovereignty of the New Zealand state.[64] The struggle of Maori iwi and hapu through negotiated agreements to recover and assert their authority over the development of their communities remains an on-going work in progress that, despite Pakeha longings for closure, is likely to require a treaty tribunal as a permanent feature of New Zealand life. At the same time, the strong and visible Maori presence in New Zealand government and politics has made New Zealand less of a 'settler state.'

The Maori's demographic strength – 14 per cent of the population, versus the roughly 1, 2, and 3 per cent of Indigenous peoples in the United States, Australia, and Canada, respectively – their relative homogeneity of culture and language, and a long and distinct political tradition may explain why the Maori have put far more stock in this dimension of self-determination than have Indigenous peoples in other English-settler states.[65] In 1991 a Canadian Royal Commission on Electoral Reform put forward a proposal for establishing up to eight seats in the House of Commons to be based on Aboriginal electorates,[66] but Aboriginal organizations in the country showed no interest in the proposal. Such an arrangement does not sit well with the nation-to-nation relationship that First Nations wish to have with Canada. The Royal Commission on Aboriginal Peoples considered it 'in the interests of all Canadians that Aboriginal peoples be represented more adequately and participate more fully in the institutions of Canadian federalism,' but favoured the idea of a third chamber of Parliament, a House of First Peoples, directly elected by Aboriginal voters.[67] The commissioners envisioned that such a chamber, unlike the Sami parliaments of Scandinavia, would have power to initiate and approve legislation affecting Aboriginal interests. Lack of Aboriginal interest and constitutional exhaustion in Canada have meant that this idea has not been pursued.

In Australia, watching from the outside as the Commonwealth Parliament legislated their rights has been an alienating experience for Aborigines and Torres Strait Islanders. When Aden Ridgeway won a seat in the Senate for the Democrats in the October 1998 election, he became just the second Indigenous person to be elected to the federal Parliament in its ninety-seven-year history. But the only flicker of interest in institutional change to secure a stronger Indigenous presence in parliamentary institutions has been at the state level. A parliamentary committee in Queensland has put out an issues paper on ways of enhancing Indigenous participation in Queensland's democratic process.[68] Similarly, in the United States, it would seem that it is only in Maine, whose state legislature since the early 1800s has provided for two non-voting delegates of the largest Indian First Nations in the state, that there is any provision for distinct Indigenous representation in legislative bodies.[69]

In the United States, in the contemporary period, there have been no dramatic developments of a progressive or reactionary character in the politics of Indigenous self-determination. In the 1990s, Congress and presidents sputtered away with various declarations, trying to sound benignly anti-colonial. However, US governments have showed no inclination to implement the first recommendation of the 1987 Senate Select Committee on Indian Affairs, chaired by Hawaii Senator Daniel Inouye, that 'the federal government must relinquish its current paternalistic controls over tribal affairs.'[70] Indian nations in the United States, like many in Canada, continue to work on forms of self-government that, in varying degrees, enable them to recover their own traditions of governance. Though Congress terminated formal treaty-making with Indian nations in 1871, the federal government continues to make settlement agreements with Indian tribes. Contemporary agreements most often aim at settling local land, resource, and governance issues 'related to tribal self-determination.'[71]

The most notable recent effort of an Indigenous people to reverse its colonization by the United States has come from native Hawaiians. When the United States connived in the overthrow of traditional Hawaiian authorities and annexed Hawaii in 1896, native Hawaiians were not granted even the domesticated form of sovereignty that American jurisprudence conceded to Indian nations.[72] Indigenous dispossession took place rapidly through an internal process of assimilation to private land ownership.[73] Today, fuelled by the influence of Indigenous internationalism, the Hawaiian Kingdom government is leading efforts to expose Hawaii's colonization and achieve some measure of restorative justice for native Hawaiians.[74] In 1993 President Clinton signed Public Law 103-150, which begins by confirming that 'the indigenous Hawaiian people never directly relinquished their claims to their inherent sovereignty as a people or over their national lands.'[75] As for a remedy, the legislation offers only an apology and the mushy idea of reconciliation. Like the Howard version of reconciliation in Australia, reconciliation without justice cannot provide the basis for a less colonial and truly consensual relationship with Indigenous peoples in the United States.

International Pressures and Standards

The Howard government's commitment to rolling back the rights of Aborigines and Torres Strait Islanders brought Australia under intense international scrutiny, especially at the United Nations. Since this change in policy, no other settler country has received as much critical attention from the international community for its treatment of Indigenous peoples as Australia. This, too, is a consequence of *Mabo*. States founded by English-speaking settler societies aspire to be seen as holding to the highest standards of human rights. Other states – for instance, Russia, China, Japan, and a number of Latin American countries – may be far more barbarous in their treatment of Indigenous peoples, some like China even denying their existence, but less seems to be expected of them. In the past, as we have seen, all the English-settler states imposed harsh imperial measures on Indigenous peoples within their borders, and lingering elements of settler-society control over Indigenous peoples and their lands certainly remain intact. In all four of the English-settler countries, the colonial regime in relation to Indigenous peoples has been softened but not abandoned. Nonetheless, in Canada, New Zealand, and the United States, Indigenous policy for the last thirty years or so has moved steadily, albeit slowly, in the direction of greater recognition of the rights of first peoples. The High Court's decision in *Mabo (No. 2)* and the Keating government's response to it seemed to place Australia firmly on the same track. Then the Howard government, in responding to *Wik*, decided to reverse direction and roll back the rights so recently recognized in *Mabo* as well as to back away from that decision's sense of moral purpose. In an era when global attention to human rights issues was never greater, there was no chance that such a change in policy would fail to attract a good deal of critical international notice.

The sharp change in the Australian government's position soon became evident in the working group set up by the UN's Committee on Human Rights (CHRWG) to consider the Draft Declaration on the Rights of Indigenous Peoples. In chapter 7 we saw how representatives of Indigenous peoples from all around the world had developed this declaration. The submission of the Draft Declaration to the UN Human Rights Commission in 1994 launched the Decade of Indigenous Peoples, which was to culminate with the adoption of the declaration by the UN in 2004. Work on the draft at the UN now became highly political. Indigenous representatives wanted to see the draft they had developed adopted without changes. However, representatives of states with significant Indigenous populations, even those generally supportive of the draft, had many concerns about the wording of its forty-five articles. And none caused them more anxiety than article 3, recognizing that Indigenous peoples have the right to self-determination. At the CHRWG's second meeting in 1996, Canada agreed to accept 'a right of self-determination for Indigenous peoples which respects the political, constitutional and territorial integrity of democratic states.'[76] Australia – which, under Keating had worked closely with Canada on these issues at the UN – had gone this far the previous year when its representative stated that 'self-determination for Australia's indigenous peoples has been Government policy since 1972.' But the statement quickly added the usual jittery caveat that acceptance was 'on the basis that the principle of the territorial sovereignty of states is sufficiently enshrined internationally that a reference to self-determination in the Draft Declaration would not imply a right of secession.'[77] Even though this qualified acceptance of Indigenous peoples' right to self-determination would not, as a matter of principle, be acceptable to Indigenous representatives at Geneva, it did seem a positive step for Australia and Canada, two of the most active and respected UN states on Indigenous issues, to be willing to go this far in recognizing Indigenous peoples as political societies with a right to shape their own form of government, albeit within each country's borders.

But at the CHRWG's third session in 1997, the Howard government parted company with states like Canada, New Zealand, Denmark, and Norway, which were working to gain acceptance for as much of the draft as possible. Sarah Pritchard reports that many of the delegations – both Indigenous and non-Indigenous – observed that the Australian government's approach to the draft had 'hardened significantly' and that Australia was 'no longer seen as a constructive and sympathetic advocate of the declaration.'[78] Indigenous self-determination, even when defined to rule out secession, was too much for an Australia led by John Howard. In August 1998 Foreign Minister Alexander Downer confirmed that Australia would now be urging the UN to water down Indigenous self-determination to self-management. At the UN, Australia had joined the ranks of states that 'challenge fundamental principles underlying the Declaration.' Interestingly, besides Australia, the other states active at the CHRWG included in this category are Japan, the United Kingdom, and the United States.[79]

It was not its government's repudiation of Indigenous self-determination which put Australia in the UN spotlight, but the Wik legislation's reduction of native title rights. Early in 1999 the UN's Committee on the Elimination of Racial Discrimination grilled Australia's attorney general, Daryl Williams, on the amendments the Commonwealth Parliament had made to the *Native Title Act*. The committee found that the amendments appeared to 'wind back' Indigenous rights, to subordinate the property interests of Indigenous peoples to concerns of government and third parties for legal certainty, and to be made without sufficient consultation with Indigenous communities. For all these reasons, the committee concluded that the amendments violated the UN Convention on the Elimination of All Forms of Racial Discrimination.[80] It urged the government to suspend implementation of the 1998 amending act and to reopen discussions with Aboriginal and Torres Strait Islander representatives.[81] Even though the CERD Committee's finding was in keeping with advice given privately to the government by the Australian Law Reform Commission,[82] the Commonwealth government continued to maintain that the *Wik* amendments were not discriminatory. The UN Committee vowed to continue its 'early warning' watch on Australia's treatment of Indigenous peoples.[83]

In 2000 UN human rights scrutiny of Australia intensified. The death of Johnno Warramarden by suicide in a Darwin prison quickly became a national and international *cause célèbre*. Johnno had been brought 800 kilometres from his home in Groote Eylandt to serve a twenty-eight-day prison term in Darwin for taking some pens and pencils from a school near his home. Under recently enacted Northern Territory legislation, a juvenile convicted of a second offence – no matter how trivial – was subject to a mandatory term of imprisonment. Similar legislation existed in Western Australia, but the Commonwealth Parliament had no jurisdiction to interfere with state legislation, whereas it could overturn or force amendments in territorial legislation. Howard was immediately pressured not only by the opposition but by members of his own caucus to rescind the Northern Territory's mandatory imprisonment law. Much to Howard's annoyance, opposition leader Kim Beazley and Labor's foreign affairs spokesman, Laurie Bereton, made sure that Howard also came under UN pressure by referring the issue to UN Secretary-General Kofi Annan, who was visiting Australia at this time to thank the country for the constructive role it was playing in East Timor as well as for its fifty-five years of model UN membership. Annan undertook to refer Australia's mandatory sentencing laws to the UN high commissioner for human rights, Mary Robinson.[84]

Now the fat was truly in the fire! For the next few months there was virtually open warfare between the Australian government and the human rights section of the United Nations. In 1997, well before mandatory sentencing had become a headline issue, the UN Committee on the Rights of the Child had condemned Australia for the disproportionately high number of aboriginal children in its juvenile justice system. Following the reference to Robinson, mandatory sentencing laws were critically examined by the committee monitoring compliance with the International Covenant on Civil and Political Rights, as well as CERD. The latter continued to express concern about the *Wik* legislation. UN committee reprimands of Australia were not confined to Indigenous issues: Australia was also hauled over the coals for discrimination against women and for its treatment of refugees.[85] On the premise that the best defence is an offence, the Howard government faught back. It accused the UN Human Rights Committee of intruding unreasonably in domestic Australian affairs. Foreign Minister Downer said that UN committees would not be allowed to visit Australia and threatened to boycott the UN Human Rights committees until the system was overhauled.[86] In September, on the eve of opening the Olympics Games in Sydney, Howard took his attack on the UN human rights committee system to New York as his contribution to the UN's Millennium Summit.[87]

As an exercise in 'the politics of shame,' the resort of Australian Indigenous leaders to UN human rights committees had mixed results. Condemnation of Australia by UN committees, many of whose members represent countries with atrocious human rights records, can be portrayed as hypocritical foreign interference in Australian affairs. John Howard and his colleagues, as well as a number of media commentators, tapped into this nationalist sentiment in rejecting the UN committees' condemnation. There were others, however, in politics and in the media who reminded Australians of their aspiration to be judged by the highest standards and of Australia's exceptional use of international treaties and covenants to advance its national interests. The federal government in Australia has used adhesion to international agreements – most famously in the Tasmania Dam case[88] – as a basis for defending its jurisdiction in matters normally reserved to the states. Earlier we saw how Australia's adherence to the UN Convention on the Elimination of all Forms of Racial Discrimination was used as a basis for defending the validity of the *Racial Discrimination Act*.[89] John Howard, himself, invoked Australia's participation in the International Narcotics Convention as grounds for attacking New South Wales' planned trial of heroin injecting rooms.[90] Australia is hardly in a position to thumb its nose at the commitments its has taken on as a party to international agreements when they are at odds with the government's political agenda. In this respect its position is very different from that of the United States, the other English-settler state whose government's position in modern times most resembles Australia's. The United States, as the world's only reigning superpower, does not care much about how the world judges its human rights record and can easily shrug off international criticism.

For representatives of Australia's Indigenous organizations and communities, the objective in taking their cause to UN was not to shame Australia but to achieve justice for their own people. The remedies available to Aboriginal and Torres Strait Island peoples in Australia were proving to be considerably weaker than those available to their counterparts in other English-settler states. The Marshallian jurisprudence in the United States, Canada's constitutional recognition of Aboriginal and treaty rights, and the Waitangi Treaty process in New Zealand all provide stronger foundations for seeking justice through local remedies than anything available to Indigenous peoples in Australia. *Mabo (No. 2)* had the potential for providing something equivalent in Australia. But the Howard government's determination to wind back what was being built on the *Mabo* base (including appointing High Court justices who are unsympathetic to aboriginal rights) was bound to quicken the interest of Australia's Indigenous leadership in seeking justice outside the country. On the issues that triggered UN committee reviews of Australian policy, aside from securing international validation of their grievances, Indigenous Australians gained very little relief. It is possible that international disapprobation was a factor in persuading the Howard government to offer the Northern Territory $5 million to modify its draconian sentencing law and provide some diversionary alternatives to mandatory imprisonment.[91] But the government did not show the slightest inclination to comply with the UN committee's view that it should reopen the *Native Title Amendment Act* – though international condemnation of the legislation may have stiffened the resolve of the opposition in the Senate to be rigorous in reviewing state alternatives to the National Native Title Tribunal.

The real import of international criticism of Australia's treatment of Indigenous peoples is that it serves as a warning to the country that there will be serious consequences for its standing in the international community if there is a sustained effort to reverse the direction of reforms which had been building up since the early 1970s and that took such a significant leap forward in *Mabo*. The success of the 2000 Olympics shows how important fair treatment of Aboriginals and Torres Strait Islanders is to Australia's international image. Governor General Deane's receiving the Olympic torch from Aboriginal runners to begin its progress around the country was a moment full of symbolic meaning. Deane, one of the most popular representatives of the Crown in the country's history, was one of the justices who fashioned the High Court's decision in *Mabo (No. 2)*. The torch began its journey at the red centre of Australia near Uluru and Kata Tjuta. Fifteen years earlier these lands had been returned to their traditional owners – much to the chagrin of the Coalition politicians then in opposition. Aboriginal athletes and performers, led by the magnificent sprinter Cathy Freeman, who participated so prominently in the Olympic Games, temporarily set aside their peoples' struggle for recognition and respect so the country they share with all Australians could secure international respect.[92] The global audience that watched and welcomed the symbolic recognition of aboriginality as central to the Australian identity was, for the most part, unaware that Australia's national government was committed to reducing the rights and status of Australia's aboriginal peoples. While the triumphs made for a very successful Olympics, they were not a harbinger of true reconciliation.

Reconciliation?

The 1997 Referendum Convention made it abundantly clear that unless the Howard government fundamentally changed its policy, there was virtually no chance of realizing the Reconciliation Council's objective of reaching a broad consensual agreement on relationships with Aborigines and Torres Strait Islanders by the end of the century. As the government pushed through its *Wik* legislation and toughed it out at the UN, it was very clear that this administration was not about to change its position and become better disposed towards recognizing Indigenous peoples and respecting their rights. Over the last two years of the century, as the Council for Australian Reconciliation struggled to conclude its decade-long mandate with some significant product or event, there was plenty of talk about reconciliation. Most of it took the form of tortuous efforts in prose and poetry to find some verbal formulation that everyone could agree to, would make everyone feel good, but would not commit anyone to anything.

The first of these efforts took the form of a proposed constitutional preamble to be part of Australia's transformation from a constitutional monarchy to a republic. The idea of drafting a new constitutional preamble was taken up by the Constitutional Convention held in February 1998. The convention's principal mandate was to consider whether Australia should become a republic. It concluded by calling for a referendum in which Australians would be asked to decide whether Australia should become a republic, with the Queen and the governor general being replaced by a president elected by two-thirds of the members of the Commonwealth Parliament. Towards the end of the convention, the delegates were persuaded that in the referendum on the republic, the people should be asked to vote on a second item – a new constitutional preamble that, among other things, would acknowledge 'the original occupancy and custodianship of Australia by Aboriginal peoples and Torres Strait Islanders.'[93]

The prime minister did not follow the Constitutional Convention's direction on the preamble. Instead, he enlisted the services of a well-known Australian poet, Les Murray, to help him draft his own version of a suitable constitutional preamble. The Howard-Murray draft aimed at a positive celebration of one-nation nationalism in which Australia was heralded as 'a nation woven together from many ancestries and arrivals.' The bit on Indigenous peoples dropped the word 'custodianship,' with its implication of ownership and land rights, and instead offered the following: 'Since time immemorial our land has been inhabited by Aborigines and Torres Strait Islanders, who are honoured for their ancient and continuing cultures.'[94] A reference to 'mateship' as a defining Australian value made the prime minister's effort at constitutional poetry as alienating to Australian women as its timid reference to Indigenous peoples was to Aborigines and Torres Strait Islanders. The opposition parties in the Senate refused to support Howard's draft unless it contained some acknowledgment of Aborigines relationship with the land. Eventually, Howard negotiated some modifications with Aboriginal senator Aden Ridgeway. The proposed preamble would now speak of Aborigines' and Torres Strait Islanders' 'deep kinship with their lands,' and the reference to 'mateship' would be dropped. This was enough to get the proposed preamble through the Senate in time to be included in the November 6 referendum.

The proposal presented to the Australian people in the referendum read as follows:

With hope in God, the Commonwealth of Australia is constituted as a democracy with a federal system of government to serve the common good.

We the Australian people commit ourselves to this Constitution proud that our national unity has been forged by Australians from many ancestries;

upholding freedom, tolerance, individual dignity and the rule of law;

honouring Aborigines and Torres Strait Islanders, the nation's first people, for their deep kinship with their lands and for their ancient and continuing cultures which enrich the life of our country;

recognizing the nation-building contributions of immigrants mindful of our responsibility to protect our unique natural environment;

supportive of achievement as well as equality of opportunity for all;

and valuing independence as dearly as the national spirit which bind us together in both adversity and success.[95]

To ensure that this syrupy addition to the Australian Constitution would have no legal consequences, a clause would be inserted in the Constitution stating that the courts would not be able to use the preamble in constitutional interpretation. Needless to say, this legally castrated token of recognition had little appeal to Indigenous people. Nearly all their leaders rejected it, as did virtually all aboriginal rights groups.[96] Nor did it win the approval of the majority of Australian voters: 60 per cent of the voters turned it down, 6 per cent more than rejected the proposal on the republic.[97]

Corroboree 2000 was to be the culmination of the Reconciliation Council's work. The last week of May would be considered Reconciliation Week, with events building up to the Corroboree itself, 'a ceremonial gathering of Australians to exchange commitments, make agreements and share in cultural performances for reconciliation.'[98] The Corroboree would take place in Australia's most renowned public building, the Sydney Opera House, on Saturday, May 27.

Corroboree 2000 was too big an event – too hyped up politically – for Prime Minister Howard to ignore it. So he began to scramble about trying to work out some way in which he could be part of a harmonious, happy outcome. Instead of considering a significant change of policy, he tried to negotiate a verbal formulation that would cover enough common ground with the Indigenous leadership to serve as the basis for 'an agreement' to which he could commit his government at the Corroboree. To this end, he invited the entire ATSIC Board, led by its fiery chairman, Geoff Clark, to dine with him at his official residence, The Lodge.[99] The prime minister's drafts were getting close to what the Reconciliation Council's chair and deputy chair, Evelyn Scott and Gustav Nossal, considered an acceptable 'aspirational document' for the Corroboree.[100] But the cleverest of word-smithing could not paper over the cracks separating Howard from the Indigenous leadership and from other Australians working for adequate recognition and just treatment of Aborigines and Torres Strait Islanders.

The crucial points of difference can be boiled down to two words –

'sorry' and 'treaty.' Howard could express regret for the treatment of Aborigines and Torres Strait Islanders in the past in any number of ways, but the word 'sorry' stuck in his throat. He would die before that word fell from his lips. Nor could he admit to any injustice or mistreatment of Indigenous Australians during his own time in politics, including his *Wik* legislation rolling back native title rights. On the biggest 'sorry issue' of the day, the Stolen Generation, Howard even hardened his position. He gave his full support to the statement of his aboriginal affairs minister, John Herron, that it was not a whole generation but just 10 per cent of aboriginal families whose children had been forcibly removed,[101] and his attorney general vigorously fought against the first claim for damages to be brought to court by victims of the forced removal policy.[102] The prime minister's refusal to say sorry came down to a matter of political and personal pride. Uttering that word is something he had refused to do, and that is precisely why 'blacks' and 'whites' turned their backs on him in the Melbourne Convention Centre in 1997 and why they would do so again in the Sydney Opera House on 27 May 2000. A true statesman could have risen to the occasion.

The treaty issue raised a much bigger and more fundamental question of policy and ideology. Underlying the desire for a treaty type of agreement as the essential instrument of reconciliation is the principle of self-determination. The advocates of a treaty relationship who pushed the idea within the Reconciliation Council, with Howard and the Commonwealth government, and with the Australian public were vague about what such a treaty or treaties might entail – what form it would take, who would be the parties, and what would be the contents. In this sense, treaty talk had not really advanced beyond where it had been in the late 1970s and the 1980s. There was still much work to be done within the Indigenous community in working out the terms of 'a treaty.' But the rationale of the need for a treaty relationship was clear: if the relationship of Aborigines and Torres Strait Islanders with the Australian state is to be post-colonial, it must be based on the 'informed consent' of the Indigenous peoples. The alternative to a treaty relationship is an imposed legislative regulation of the rights and status of Indigenous peoples. Even if such legislation is accompanied by much 'consultation' and the consent of some individual members of Indigenous communities, it is still a relationship that does not recognize the right of Aboriginal and Torres Strait Islander peoples to determine their relationship with the Australian state. An imposed legislated relationship can, at best, be a more liberal version of a colonized relationship. As Patrick Dodson, the former chair of the Reconciliation Council, put it in his Lingiari Lecture:

'The sovereign position that Aboriginal peoples assert has never been ceded. Recognition starts from the premise that *terra nullius* and its consequences were imposed upon the Aboriginal peoples, and certainly there was never any choice given to the Aboriginal peoples concerning the Constitution or the rule of law.'[103] In Dodson's view, if Australia's original peoples and those Australians who came later are to share the country on just terms, it must be through agreement on the terms of that sharing. That is the nub of the matter and the basic rationale for insisting on 'a treaty' or, to use Dodson's language, 'a comprehensive framework agreement' as the key to reconciliation.

Admittedly, relations with Indigenous peoples in the other English-settler states could not be said to have reached a post-colonial condition. But the national governments in Canada and New Zealand for some time have been working through treaty processes to settle major issues of land, resources, and governance. In both countries, these processes are painfully slow and the agreements they produce, as we have seen, are pragmatic compromises. They are not a grand resolution – a reconciliation – of differences between native peoples and the settler state in which they are participating. But in both countries, these efforts at resolving differences by negotiated agreements entail recognition of the Indigenous societies as political communities and a desire to resolve questions concerning the political status and collective rights of Indigenous peoples by mutual agreement rather than by the blunt exercise of the majority's legislative power. The position of the US government in the contemporary period has been much closer to that of John Howard's Australian government. Still, a legacy of recognizing the sovereignty of Indian tribes and of treaty-making remains imbedded in American constitutional law and in the historical experience of its native peoples. Though Australia and the United States were now lining up together at the UN, the American door was not shut tight against recognizing some measure of Indigenous self-determination – and the American government was not engaged in a high-profile political effort at reconciliation with its Indigenous peoples. But John Howard was, and he would not endorse any reconciliation document that even promised to look into what a treaty relationship might mean. Aboriginal reconciliation for Howard could not go beyond a commitment to work at raising the living standards and economic opportunities of Aborigines and Torres Strait Islanders so that, in effect, they would disappear as disadvantaged minorities and Australia's national union would be complete. No matter how much he might sugar coat that position with soothing words, it would not do as the basis for a reconciliation agreement.

As it became evident that, on the big ticket issues, the prime minister wouldn't budge, several of the most prominent Aboriginal leaders decided not to participate in the Corroboree. They included Patrick Dodson, the founding chairman of the Reconciliation Council; Peter Yu of the Kimberley Land Council; Galarrwuy Yunupingu, chairman of the Northern Land Council; and Charles Perkins, the former senior Commonwealth official and, at this time, a member of the ATSIC Board.[104] Others, including Mick Dodson, Lois O'Donaghue, and Geoff Clark, the past and present chairs of ATSIC; Terry Waia, chairman of the Torres Strait Regional Authority; and Senator Aden Ridgeway, decided to attend. They would work with Evelyn Scott, the chairman of the Reconciliation Council, and her colleagues to wring what they could out of what would be the most comprehensive gathering of political and social leaders in Australia's history.

The show that took place in the Sydney Opera House on 27 May 2000 was an extraordinary event.[105] It was indeed 'a show' – with great showbusiness values. A huge television audience watched a warrior outrigger from the Torres Strait arrive at the steps of the Opera House with the 'Reconciliation Documents.' Glen Kelly, an Aboriginal boxer body-painted in traditional style, brought them into the Opera House. The symbolic delivery of the documents seemed far more important than their contents. Inside the Opera House, the first people to come on stage were elders of the Eora, Biripi, Darug, Ngarrinjerri/Barkindji, Tharwal, and Wiradjuri peoples, all of whom have traditional links with the Sydney area. The program that then unfolded wove together music and dance, traditional and contemporary, with all kinds of ceremony interspersed with speeches from many of the notables on hand. Among the notables present were leaders of the Commonwealth, state, territorial, and local governments; major Aboriginal and Torres Strait Island institutions; and business, labour, and religious organizations. And introduced to the audience, along with former prime ministers Whitlam, Fraser, and Hawke, was Eddie Mabo's widow, Bonita – an indication of the primacy that *Mabo* had assumed in Australian life.

Three of the most eloquent speeches were those given by Evelyn Scott, the Aboriginal woman who now chaired the Reconciliation Council; Bob Carr, the host premier of New South Wales; and Governor General Deane. But the oratory that was much more important politically and that so starkly displayed the barrier to true reconciliation was Prime Minister Howard's address, sandwiched between the contributions of Geoff Clark and Mick Dodson. Clark, ATSIC's first elected president, did not mince words: for Aborigines and Torres Strait Islanders, reconciliation must provide constitutional protection for their rights. 'This country of 19 million,' he said, 'consists of two nations – Indigenous and non-Indigenous.' Reconciliation between the two nations requires 'a commitment from government to negotiate a treaty.'[106] Howard got up to speak next – looking distinctly uncomfortable. He lavished praise on the members of the Council for Aboriginal Reconciliation for their hard work and expressed his hope that the reconciliation process would continue. He acknowledged 'the 60,000 years of human habitation which has produced the cultures of the Indigenous people has so much to offer to all of us,' and then went on to express 'regret for the mistakes and injustices of the past.'[107] He referred to Indigenous people (in the singular) as 'the most profoundly disadvantaged within our communities.' His government's commitment to reconciliation was to 'adopt practical measures to address that disadvantage.' Throughout his speech, members of the audience shouted 'Say sorry!' When he finished, about half the audience were standing with their backs turned to him.

Then it was Mick Dodson's turn. He began by comparing his own life with that of John Howard, pointing out the discrimination and harsh government policy experienced by Indigenous people of his generation. Wistfully he recalled the Whitlam government's commitment to Indigenous self-determination. Though not much happened after that recognition of Indigenous rights, still he welcomed it and expressed sadness at how much 'we have slipped.' Dodson concluded on a rousing and positive note. He summoned Australians – Indigenous and non-Indigenous – to join together in a national task 'too great to be derailed by pettiness and denial ... Let us rejoice in our diversity ... Listen to those whispers in our hearts and let them bellow out for a better future – a future steeped in the spirit of reconciliation.'[108] That better future, he said, might well have to wait for a new prime minister, and it is a future for which 'we must have a treaty.'

On Sunday, May 28, in a massive display of support for reconciliation, thousands of Australians walked over the Sydney Harbour Bridge.[109] Above the walkers, a sky-writer scrawled 'Sorry' across the sky. In the following days, similar 'walks for reconciliation' took place in virtually all Australia's major cities, as well as some smaller towns.[110] The participants in these walks were not bound together by a common idea of what true reconciliation requires. Some of the walkers would be happy with Howard's program of practical reconciliation, while others were protesting the inadequacy of Howard's approach. The high level of public participation and interest in the Corroboree 2000 events was not a sign that a happy, harmonious moment of reconciliation was at hand but that the Australian body politic was deeply engaged in working towards a satisfactory relationship between Indigenous and non-Indigenous Australians. Indeed, that political project was now Australia's most fundamental issue of political justice.[111] Getting the Indigenous/non-Indigenous relationship right was now as important politically in Australia as French-English relations have been historically in Canada, as the position of the Maori is in New Zealand and as the civil rights of black Americans have been in the United States.

For the promise of *Mabo* to be realized in a way that enables Indigenous and non-Indigenous Australians to share a common sense of nationhood, Australia would have to be redefined. At the heart of the majority judgments in *Mabo (No. 2)* is recognition of the Merriam as a law-making political society that had existed and evolved for many centuries before the arrival of European settlers and the imposition of British sovereignty. The court saw no reason to deny that other Torres Strait Island communities or the many Aboriginal peoples of Australia could validly make the same claim. True, the High Court judges set down an exacting and insulting test for other Indigenous communities to establish such a claim. And they allowed for the continuation of the colonial subjugation of Aborigines and Torres Strait Islanders by recognizing the right of Australian governments to extinguish, unilaterally, any of their rights that might be recognized by Australian courts. But the High Court did not call for a continuation of settler imperialism. The spirit of its decision was to invoke among non-Indigenous Australians a sense of regret for the dispossession and brutalities of the past and to engender a desire to build a more honourable and respectful relationship with Indigenous peoples in the future. Such a relationship can only be established through consensual agreement – treaties, if you like – not imposed legislation. Such treaty-type relationships are incompatible with a strongly held, one-nation understanding of Australia. That is why John Howard could not go near this idea. For reconciliation to advance in the direction promised by the spirit of *Mabo (No. 2)*, Australia's non-Indigenous leadership – on both left and right – would have to be reconciled with thinking of Australia as a complex country in which Aborigines and Torres Strait Islanders form distinct political communities – and with the freedom to negotiate their political relationships with the state.

Corroboree 2000 exhausted the formal reconciliation process. The Council on Aboriginal Reconciliation would be succeeded institutionally by a government-seeded foundation, Reconciliation Australia Ltd, that would not figure prominently in the country's political life. The Coroboree documents, including the council's *Roadmap for Reconciliation*, recognized that reconciliation was not something that could be accomplished in a decade. If it were to occur, it would require recognition by the Australian state and its people of the rights of Indigenous peoples to sustain and direct their societies and enjoy economic security in traditional lands and waters. Its *Final Report*, released in December 2000, acknowledged the imperative of consensual agreements and recommended that 'each government and parliament recognize that this land and its waters were settled as colonies without treaty or consent and that to advance reconciliation it would be desirable if there were agreements or treaties.'[112]

A post-Coroboree Newspoll disclosed that supporters of a treaty with Aboriginal peoples outnumbered opponents 45 per cent to 37 per cent. Not too much weight should be attached to snapshots of this kind. Public opinion on such matters is volatile and largely incohate – 18 per cent of those asked about a treaty had no opinion. But at least this report suggests that the one-nation ideological opposition to basing relationships with Indigenous peoples on consent and agreements at this point in Australian history was not an insurmountable obstacle to the kind of reconciliation sought by most Indigenous leaders.

Looking back on Corroboree 2000, it is difficult to take issue with Ravi de Costa's verdict that, 'for those who were intoxicated by the "magic anniversary syndrome," it was selfish to tie the question of improving indigenous lives and relations with settlers to the anniversary of the settler state.'[113] Indigenous reconciliation in Australia, as elsewhere, is still very much a work in progress. The decade-long effort of the Council on Aboriginal Reconciliation had shown that, for reconciliation to occur with justice, non-Indigenous Australians must become reconciled to recognizing Aborigines and Torres Strait Islanders as constituent peoples of Australia with distinctive and fundamental rights. In the meantime, in the words of Larissa Behrendt: 'Indigenous Australia remains the unreconciled, unattended aspect of Australia's past and present and, until this relationship has been attended to and reconciled, it will continue to divide Australians.'[114]

CHAPTER 12

The Limits of Judicial Power

The long-term importance of Eddie Mabo's judicial triumph depends much more on its broad political effect in helping to build a climate of opinion more conducive to respectful and just relations with Indigenous peoples than its usefulness as a legal basis for recovering *terra nullius*. In chapters 9–11 we saw that, while the *Mabo* case was undoubtedly a catalyst in moving Australia in that direction, there is still a very long way to go. This concluding chapter will look more closely at the tangible payoffs of the case in terms of Indigenous Australians regaining control and ownership of land. From this perspective, it is important to bear in mind that *Mabo* is part of a land rights movement that began in the 1970s. In quantitative terms, increases in Indigenous land ownership and control which can be directly attributed to *Mabo* and the native title land claims process resulting from it are modest compared to gains made through other instruments and processes. Most of those gains – and in terms of the amount of land returned to some form of Indigenous ownership and control, the gains are impressive – were made before *Mabo*. As a basis for recovering *terra nullius* through the courts and the formal claims process, *Mabo* still has much work to do. But as we watch the High Court abandon its leadership role in vindicating the rights of Indigenous peoples and observe Aboriginal and Torres Strait Islanders turning to less litigious and more political ways of securing their interests in traditional lands and waters, it becomes clear that in terms of making major gains in overcoming their colonized status, Australia's Indigenous peoples are running up against the limits of judicial power.

Practical Gains

By the end of June 2000, only nine Indigenous communities had been to able to follow the Meriam people in gaining some recognition of their original ownership – their native title – of their lands and waters.[1] The first 'determination' of native title, as was noted in chapter 9, did not occur until late 1996 and concerned a small parcel of land of the Dunghutti people in Kempsey, NSW. In the late 1990s the Hopevale Aboriginal community near Cooktown on Queensland's Cape York and the Western Yalanji near Cairns in Queensland achieved similar 'consent determinations' through the National Native Title Tribunal's mediation process. The areas involved, though not vast, were considerably larger than the Dunghutti's – 110 square kilometres and 25,122 hectares, respectively. In 1999 the peoples of Moa and Saibai in the Torres Strait secured recognition of title to their island homes in the Torres Strait. In 2000 the Bangarra people in the Kimberley region of Western Australia secured a consent determination to 15,000 square kilometres – by far the largest recognition of native title to date. In addition to these six 'consent determinations,' three Northern Territory peoples – the Arrente around Alice Springs, the Miruwung-Gajerrong in the northwest corner of the territory, and the people of Croker Island – had some limited success to gaining recognition of their native title through litigation.

These successful, or partially successful, claims represent only a small proportion of native title's full potential. Hundreds of other native title claims have been lodged and are at some point in the complex claims system. The Commonwealth government has asserted that 78 per cent of the area of Australia is available for claim.[2] But it may well turn out that little more than the tip of the native title iceberg will ever surface to provide legal protection of Indigenous ownership. The complexity, uncertainty and alienating nature of the process set out in the *Native Title Act* for claiming native title has already been noted. Moreover, the value of native title – the power and protection it yields to its holders – has been so diminished by the *Wik* amendments to the act and (as will soon be noted) by the post-*Wik* High Court that alternative ways of securing Indigenous land ownership have been and are likely to remain more accessible and more fruitful.

Since the land rights movement was launched three decades ago, Indigenous groups have secured ownership of a considerable portion of the Australian territory. Very little of this Indigenous ownership has been secured through the recognition of native title made possible by *Mabo.* Data reported by the Indigenous Land Corporation in 1996 showed that 1,162,400 square kilometres, constituting 15.1 per cent of the Australian land mass, was recognized as 'owned' by Indigenous groups or organizations.[3] Most of this land had been brought under Aboriginal ownership through Commonwealth and state legislative schemes that pre-date the *Native Title Act* by many years. D.P. Pollack estimates that between 1996 and 30 June 2000, Indigenous landholdings increased by just under 36,000 square kilometres, making it 'reasonable to suggest that the amount of land held by Indigenous interests in Australia is at least 16 per cent of the area of Australia.'[4] Though the increase since 1996 is small, most of it has come about through the *Native Title Act*, including its provisions for Indigenous Land Use Agreements. The amount of control and security of tenure over the lands conveyed to Indigenous owners by these various statutory schemes varies considerably and generally falls far short of the full political law-making responsibility recognized by the High Court in *Mabo (No. 2)*. The ownership rights established by these schemes are statutory creations lacking any constitutional protection. Some of the land involved is not traditional country. Most of it is in the remotest areas of the country. Nonetheless, in purely quantitative terms, the proportion of Indigenous land ownership recognized by the Australian state at the end of the twentieth century is impressive.

By far the greatest recoveries of *terra nullius* by Indigenous peoples in Australia have been obtained through the *Aboriginal Land Rights (Northern Territory) Act, 1976 (ALRA)* and by South Australian legislation. Over half of the lands – 584,000 square kilometres – reported to be under Indigenous ownership in 1996 was in the Northern Territory, and nearly all was secured through the *ALRA*. Though 1987 amendments to *ALRA* included a 'sunset clause' that cut off new claims, in June 2000 over one hundred claims lodged before that, covering 10 per cent of the Northern Territory, remained to be dealt with. As we saw earlier, South Australia's *Aboriginal Lands Trust Act, 1966*, was the first Australian land rights legislation.[5] By 1989 the trust established by that act controlled 5400 square miles of South Australia. The really large accretions of Indigenous-owned lands in South Australia came not through its Lands Trust legislation but through legislation transferring inalienable freehold title to specific Aboriginal groups. In 1981 the *Pitjantjatjara Land Rights Act* transferred 102,650 square kilometres of South Australia, covering much of the northwest area of the state, to a corporate body representing the traditional owners of the country. Three years later the *Maralinga Tjarutja Land Act* similarly transferred ownership of 81,373 square kilometres of land to the Maralinga people, whose country is just to the south of the Pitjantjatjara lands. Together, these areas constitute 18 per cent of South Australia.

The distinctive Australian federalization of jurisdiction in relation to

Indigenous peoples surely has had its most benign consequences in South Australia. The other states, with the single exception of Western Australia, have enacted Indigenous land rights legislation, but none that comes close to either South Australia's or the Commonwealth's Northern Territory land rights acts.[6] Under its *Aboriginal Land Rights Act*, New South Wales has been operating a land claims process in the state since 1983. Lands previously held by the New South Wales Land Trust (about 46 square kilometres) were handed over to land councils in the state. The number of claims lodged (6266) and the number that have been successful (1815) under the state's land claims process are impressive. But the claims are mostly to small parcels of land to be used for residential or commercial development. New South Wales has also combined with the Commonwealth to return many of the state's nature reserves and much of its parkland to Aboriginal ownership and joint management.

In 1991, a year before the *Mabo* case was decided, Queensland became the second state to have a land claims process. Under the legislation introduced by the Goss Labor government, the lands that could be claimed were designated in advance by the state. Claimable land includes reserve lands that previously could be brought under the DOGIT (Deed of Grant in Trust) scheme, which had so offended Eddie Mabo and the Murray Islanders.[7] As with the New South Wales scheme, successful claims have been for relatively small parcels of land. By mid-2000, ownership of eighty parcels of land with a total area of 540,287 hectares had been transferred to Indigenous ownership. Instead of setting up a state-operated claims process, Victoria and Tasmania have enacted legislation granting Aboriginal communities or organizations ownership of specific plots of land. In Victoria this transfer has been done through six separate statutes. Tasmania's *Aboriginal Lands Act, 1995* vested ownership of twelve areas of culturally significant land (including six islands in the Bass Strait) in the Aboriginal Land Council of Tasmania.

Western Australia, whose government spear-headed the political attack on the commonwealth's native title legislation, remains the one state not to have introduced some form of land rights legislation. State governments, Labor as well as Liberal, showed no inclination to establish the land claims process recommended in 1983 by the Seaman inquiry.[8] Instead, a state-appointed Aboriginal Lands Trust for many years has had a mandate to acquire and manage lands reserved for Aborigines. In 1996, showing some sensitivity to post-*Mabo* political pressure to move towards Aboriginal ownership, Western Australia asked Neville Bonner, the first Aboriginal member of the Commonwealth Parliament, to review these trust lands. Bonner recommended that, over the next ten years, the area under review, constituting 12 per cent of the state, be transferred to Aboriginal corporations. In 1999 the first of these handovers took place. As Australia's largest state, with so much Crown land (36 per cent of the state) lived on solely by its traditional Aboriginal owners and no land claims process of its own, Western Australia is where the native title process has its greatest potential. It is also the location of nearly half the land purchased for Aboriginal peoples by the Commonwealth's Indigenous Land Corporation (ILC).

The ILC, it will be recalled, was one of the Keating Labor government's final efforts to support Indigenous Australians in recovering *terra nullius*.[9] Funding the purchase of land for the dispossessed was a crucial part of the Aboriginal Peace Plan that Indigenous leaders brought forward after the High Court's decision in *Mabo (No. 2)*. Unlike the Aboriginal Land Fund established by the Whitlam government in 1994, the Indigenous Land Corporation, though very modestly funded, is set up in a way that makes it less vulnerable to a change of government. And despite the controversy over the *Mabo* case and the political struggle over the *Native Title Act*, state governments in post-*Mabo* Australia are not inclined – as at least Queensland was in the 1970s – to resist this kind of Commonwealth intervention to acquire state lands for Aborigines and Torres Strait Islanders. The ILC fund, which by 2006 is to be self-sustaining, yields $45 million a year for the acquisition and management of land.[10]

Under the leadership of David Ross, formerly director of the Central Land Council in the Northern Territory, the ILC, in buying land, has given more weight to cultural attachment than commercial possibilities. It simply does not have the funds needed to be a major vehicle for Indigenous economic development. Nonetheless, many of the 4,799,356 hectares that the ILC had purchased by June 30, 2000, have great meaning for the descendants of original owners who had been forced off traditional lands and would likely find it difficult, if not impossible, to be successful in claiming native title. Land has also been purchased for Aborigines and Torres Strait Islanders, on a much smaller scale, through other Commonwealth programs, notably ATSIC's Regional Land Fund and the Aboriginal and Torres Strait Islander Commercial Development Corporation. The most common uses of properties so acquired have been to provide office space for Indigenous organizations and hostels in urban settings.[11]

Negotiated Agreements

The practical importance of the *Mabo* case in enabling Indigenous Australians to gain more control over traditional country goes beyond the few successful 'determinations' of native title reached through the tortuous procedures of the *Native Title Act* and lands purchased for the dispossessed by the Indigenous Land Corporation. The case and the legislation it led to has also had some effect in increasing the leverage – the political opportunities – of traditional owners to protect and advance their interests through negotiated agreements outside of the formal, litigious native title process. As we noted earlier, the preamble to the *Native Title Act* makes a slight gesture towards a more Canadian or New Zealand type of process for negotiating land claims on a regional or local basis.[12] But the 1993 act provided no machinery or guidelines for such negotiations and no statutory basis for agreements reached. Moreover, its provisions for settlement by agreement anticipated that governments would be involved primarily where native title holders surrendered their title in return for other benefits. This faint and, for native title holders, unattractive provision for a more political, less litigious process came to very little.[13]

One of the few progressive aspects of the 1998 *Wik* amendments to the *Native Title Act* were detailed provisions for Indigenous Land Use Agreements (ILUAs).[14] ILUAs give native title holders opportunities to by-pass the cumbersome process of obtaining a determination of their title and reap some immediate benefits from acknowledgment of their ownership. But, as Patricia Lane notes, they are also attractive to non-Indigenous parties 'because they bind all native title holders, and cap compensation entitlements.'[15] Up to 30 June 2000, only six ILUAs had been registered with the National Native Title Tribunal. These agreements deal with 'future acts' on small parcels or corridors of land where corporate interests are willing to grant limited benefits in order to overcome the uncertainty and delays of the formal claims process. The largest, a gold-mining project in New South Wales, accounts for all but 37 of the 8542 square kilometres affected by the first batch of ILUAs.[16] The agreement included some provision for protecting Aboriginal heritage, but much of the land had been subject to 'prior extinguishing events,' and the extent to which it enables native title holders to participate in land management is unclear.[17]

The ILUA process is a product of the legal gnomes of Canberra, accountable to a government with not the slightest interest in assisting Aborigines and Torres Strait Islanders in recovering control over their traditional lands. The twenty-six pages of the revised *Native Title Act* that are taken up with spelling out every conceivable aspect and implication of these agreements are a monument to the hair-splitting finesse of the white man's legal culture in Australia – at its worst. This attitude means that the agreement process authorized by the Commonwealth Parliament for traditional owners is a largely inaccessible and inappropriate mechanism for securing their interests. Much more promising for the recovery of *terra nullius* are agreements reached through processes in whose design and operation Aboriginal communities directly affected by a development have played a major role. Because Cape York Peninsula in Queensland has been the site of many such agreements, these arrangements are sometimes referred to as the 'Cape York Model.'[18] Similar agreements have been negotiated in the Kimberley Region of Western Australia[19] and in the Northern Territory,[20] and in other parts of the country where Aborigines are the predominant people on the land and have developed a capacity and a tolerance for protecting their country through political negotiations with business corporations that wish to exploit resources on their lands.

Up to now, agreements reached through what Mary Edmunds, in her overview of regional agreements, calls 'the organic approach'[21] have tended to be development driven and project specific. This approach has enabled Indigenous communities to have some influence on the conditions under which an industrial project takes place on the lands they own, or with which they have a historical association, and to gain some benefits from such projects. In this sense they are not unlike Canada's comprehensive land claims agreements, which have so often been triggered by the prospects of a major non-renewable resource development. But unlike Canada, the parties to these Australian agreements are the Indigenous groups and business interests involved, not governments. State or Commonwealth governments may come in at the end of the negotiating process, but only if needed to implement some aspect of the agreement. And though these agreements are not comprehensive in the Canadian sense of being a settlement of all Indigenous people's claims, they can cover a wide range of Indigenous interests, including (virtually always) sacred site protection, employment and training, a share in royalties, a say in environmental protection, and improvements in government services. Though the first generation of agreements have been very localized and focus on the conditions for proceeding with a specific project (typically mining), they have the potential for serving as 'the building blocks for larger regional agreements – or what might be called "nested agreements."'[22]

The lukewarm interest of government has been a serious obstacle to moving forward with a more organic, less top-down, process of agreements with Indigenous peoples. But even if governments were more enthusiastic about this way of sharing the country, finding willing, legitimate, and able bodies to represent the Indigenous side would still be an enormous challenge. Commenting on the prospects for a broad agreement in the Kimberley region, Patrick Sullivan writes that 'the main problem' is not the willingness of the state to come to the table but 'the ability of the Aboriginal groups to respond.'[23] It is a constitutional principle of Aboriginal society that 'no Indigenous person can speak for another's country.' It is often extremely difficult to identify the members of the group who belong to a given section of land and are entitled to speak for them. The Janus-like quality of native title adds to the difficulty. Native title often provides the leverage for initiating negotiations, but, as Jon Altman observes, situations in which it is difficult to clearly demarcate the native title parties may 'result in heightened disputation in the Indigenous domain about the distribution of benefits.'[24] When the scale of negotiations extends to larger regions, the problems of structuring an appropriate Aboriginal negotiating party – a legitimate Native Title Representative Body, to use the language of the *Native Title Act* – are compounded. The cosmology and sociology of Aboriginal culture do not fit readily into structures required for making binding agreements with corporate and government bodies grounded in European traditions and operating on the basis of an imposed and alien law. Across the top of Australia, regional land councils, in particular the Cape York Land Council in Queensland and the Kimberley Land Council in Western Australia, have provided the most effective leadership in this process of political organization. But they are still a long way from establishing a legitimate basis for agreements covering the country and interests of numerous Aboriginal groups.

The most ambitious effort in building a larger and more comprehensive negotiating framework is in South Australia. Since 1999 the Aboriginal Land Rights Movement (ALRM) in South Australia has been building an alliance of Aboriginal groups from all parts of the state to work towards establishing a process for negotiating agreements that would be statewide and capable of dealing with issues of legislative and constitutional reform extending well beyond a narrow focus on native title.[25]

ALRM's emphasis is on 'empowerment, building governance and equipping claimant groups for the negotiation of agreements and for their implementation' and on a process 'that is accountable to traditional owners and through them to The Dreaming.' The Government of South Australia, even under the Liberals who had fought against native title in the courts and bitterly resisted recognition of Aboriginal heritage in the Hindmarsh Bridge affair,[26] agreed to work with the ALRM in developing a statewide process. The Labor government that came to power in February 2002 has gladly continued state government participation. Peak industrial bodies representing farmers and miners have also agreed to participate. Since October 2000, organizations representing twenty-two groups of native title claimants have been working at establishing a South Australian Aboriginal Congress to be their forum in statewide negotiations. It is much too early to assess whether such a congress can serve 'as an effective agent of Aboriginal self-determination and governance in Australia.'[27] The first test will be to see if it can deliver some immediate practical benefits and build the protocols needed to ensure that no one speaks for another's country.

Even when the negotiating takes place through procedures that are more sensitive to the interests and capacities of Indigenous peoples, there are many pitfalls and shortcomings. Where the agreement is tied to a resource development project, the Indigenous party negotiates under duress, and, though agreements may provide jobs that reduce dependence on welfare, they may neglect the development of renewable resources vital for long-term economic security. It is usually difficult to find independent funding adequate to ensure that negotiations are truly accountable to the people who have so much at stake. There is always a serious risk that benefits negotiated on paper will not materialize in practice, especially when government is a passive partner to the agreement. And though agreements will have the legal force of contracts, they lack any constitutional status that would protect them from unilateral change by governments claiming sovereign power over Indigenous peoples and their lands. But even with all these faults, these resource project and regional agreements with Indigenous peoples in the Australian hinterland should be seen as an important step towards more consensual, less colonial ways of sharing country. The *Mabo* case has been a major catalytic event in stimulating this development. The extent to which these agreements can serve as instruments of Indigenous self-determination depends primarily on the political development of Indigenous Australia – on the willingess and capacity of Aborigines and Torres

Strait Islanders to use new forms of political organization to secure traditional interests.

Nowhere are the opportunities for Indigenous self-determination greater than in Eddie Mabo's 'homeland' – the Torres Strait Islands. In 1997 a committee of the Commonwealth Parliament issued a report calling for greater autonomy for the Torres Strait Islanders.[28] Three years earlier, the Torres Strait Island Authority, elected by Islanders, took over responsibilities formerly administered through ATSIC. The committee envisaged the next step being the establishment of a Torres Strait Regional Assembly, with responsibility for a wide range of governmental tasks. For this to happen, Queensland must agree to having the functions of the Island Coordinating Council, which organizes the delivery of state policies in the region, taken over by a single government elected by all the people resident in the Islands. Such a development calls for an unprecedented feat of intergovernmental cooperation. But it might well happen if rivalries between Islanders holding leading positions in the Commonwealth and state authorities now operating in the region can be overcome[29] and a Torres Strait Island political allegiance comes to be at least as strong as Islanders' identity with their own home islands. A Torres Strait regional government, accountable to the people of the region, that becomes responsible for designing and implementing public policies in many areas formerly under federal and state authorities would, in many ways, parallel the establishment of Nunavut in Canada's Eastern Arctic. Though such a development would not be as far along the road to independence as the nationalist firebrand, Eddie Mabo, wished to go, it may well satisfy the aspirations of the current generation of Islanders.

The End of the High Court's Leadership

Eddie Mabo's and the Meriam people's resort to the courts in 1981 was an attempt to do politics by other means. By going to court and winning two cases in the country's highest court, they gained a good deal. One decision protected them from a state government's attempt to extinguish all their rights, and the other gained some settler-state recognition not only of their rights but of the rights of all of Australia's Indigenous peoples. But in the aftermath of these court victories, it quickly became clear that their value to Indigenous people would very much depend on what happened in the regular avenues of politics. The High Court continued to be involved in adjudicating disputes about native title but was no longer the site of the main developments in Indigenous relations. That moment passed with the High Court's decision in *Mabo (No. 2)*. In *Wik*, the majority held that native title and pastoral leases could coexist on the same land, but that the native title holders must not interfere with the conduct of the pastoralists' business. That even this very moderate support for native title carried a bare majority of the court, and raised a huge political storm, was a sign that judicial leadership in the recovery of *terra nullius* was on the wane. Contrary to what the mainstream of Australia's legal profession would have you believe, courts are not immune to changes in the political climate.

Although I end my account of recovering *terra nullius* at the end of the twentieth century, I will add just a few words about more recent High Court decisions on native title to show the very limited support Aborigines and Torres Strait Islanders can expect to receive from the High Court in the foreseeable future. It is not that the current High Court repudiates the court's 1992 decision recognizing native title but that it follows the more limiting potentialities of that decision and seems anxious to pass on to the legislature the primary responsibility for defining its meaning. Claimants of native title rights have had some success in the High Court, but the rights upheld by the court's majority have been limited to carrying on some very specific traditional activities. For example, in *Yanner v. Eaton*,[30] decided in October 1999, the court's majority upheld the right of Murrandoo Yanner (a prominent Aboriginal leader) to hunt crocodiles with a traditional harpoon on his clan's traditional country even though he lacked the licence required by Queensland law.

A much more significant decision came in 2001, when the court dealt with sea rights, an important dimension of native title that it had not been required to consider in *Mabo (No. 2)*. The issue was brought to court by Aboriginal peoples in the Croker Island area off the north coast of the Northern Territory who had secured ownership of their island homes through the *Aboriginal Land Rights (Northern Territory) Act, 1976*.[31] These Aboriginal islanders now claimed, as Eddie Mabo had done, that their traditional country embraced the sea and parts of the seabed around their islands. The court's majority, in a five-to-two decision, overturned the lower courts and upheld the claimants' right to traditional use of the seas and the seabed in the waters surrounding their island homes – but not on an exclusive basis. In effect, the court's majority allowed for a regime of coexistence in coastal waters similar to that it endorsed in *Wik*. From the perspective of most non-Indigenous Australians, this win was very significant for Indigenous peoples. But from the Indigenous perspective, except for Justice Kirby's decision, it was a total repudiation of the continuity of land and water in traditional understandings in favour of the relatively modern common law doctrine that the seas must be a commons.[32]

Though these High Court decisions yielded some positive results for native title holders, there is no echo in them of the majority's declaration at the end of *Mabo (No. 2)* 'that the Meriam people are entitled as against the whole world to possession, occupation use and enjoyment of the island of Mer.'[33] The Australian judges seem to be whittling native title down to 'a bundle of rights' – rights to carry on specific traditional activities – rather than a controlling interest in their traditional country. A majority of judges in the Federal Court in *Western Australia v. Ward* took this approach.[34] The case arose out of an application for a determination of native title by the Mirriuwung, Gajerrong, and Balangarra peoples in relation to an area covering 8000 square kilometres, mostly in the East Kimberley area of Western Australia but extending over into the northwest corner of the Northern Territory. Major economic developments had taken place in the region – notably, the Argyle Diamond Mine and the Ord River Irrigation project, designed to facilitate citrus fruit farming and other forms of agriculture in the region. The immediate issue in the case was the extent to which native title was extinguished by these and other developments. But as the case moved on appeal to the High Court, it was seen as a test of whether the court would subscribe to the 'bundle of rights approach' developing in Australia's lower courts, rather than the understanding of native title as full and exclusive ownership of land which the Canadian Supreme Court had articulated in *Delgamuukw*.

The High Court's decision in the *Ward* case, rendered on 8 August 2002, reached new heights (or depths) of prolixity and opaqueness. Its four hundred pages of opinions contained some good news for the claimants: five of the seven justices held that their native title had not been entirely extinguished by all the projects and leases authorized on their lands by settler governments. In effect, the majority, as in *Wik*, endorsed a regime of coexistence between native title holders and others granted rights by the state. But all the justices took a very limited view of native title. They showed no interest in the Supreme Court of Canada's approach in *Delgamuukw* which recognized native title as a full right of property ownership, including the right to develop the land in non-traditional ways.[35] Their guide to fleshing out the meaning of native title was not to be their own decisions or those of other common law courts but section 223(1) of the *Native Title Act*, which makes the rights and interests possessed under traditional laws and custom the touch-stone of native title. This 'frozen rights' approach, among other things, led to the conclusion that the claimants' native title does not include minerals or petroleum – because there is no evidence of any Aboriginal law, custom, or use relating to these substances.[36]

On the nature and conditions of extinguishment, the court insists that here, too, it must be guided by the act and its implications rather than anything that its members may have said on the subject. Thus it confirms that an Aboriginal people's title to its homeland is extinguished to the extent that any rights granted to other interests are incompatible with the continued exercise of native title rights. In a region like East Kimberley, where so many other interests have been granted leases and permits, this approach removes the possibility of native title amounting to a right of exclusive possession or control. In areas where there are no competing interests or acts of partial extinguishment, native title might amount to more than 'a bundle of rights,' and the Aboriginal principle that only the traditional owners have a right to speak for country may be recognized. However, as Lisa Strelein observes, 'the occurrence of such areas may be limited.'[37] Indeed, to Justice McHugh, who had supported Brennan's opinion in *Mabo (No. 2)*, it was becoming increasingly clear that redress for the dispossession of the Aboriginal peoples, which 'was a great wrong ... can not be achieved by a system that depends on evaluating the competing legal rights of landholders and native-title holders. The deck is stacked against the native-title whose fragile rights must give way to the superior rights of the landholders.'[38] McHugh suggested it might be better to move to 'an arbitral system that declares what the rights of the parties ought to be according to the justice and circumstances of the case.'[39] These concluding words of McHugh's opinion were virtually a letter of judicial resignation from the 'administration of justice' for Australia's Indigenous peoples.

In December 2002 the High Court rendered a decision that was the toughest blow yet to common law native title. The case involved the Yorta Yorta, the very first Aboriginal community to apply to the National Native Title Tribunal for a determination of native title, in 1994. The Yorta Yorta's historical lands were in northern Victoria and southern New South Wales. The opening up of the area in the nineteenth century to agriculture, forestry, commercial fishing, and substantial white settlement meant that the Yorta Yorta had experienced a great deal of forced dispossession. But many of them had continued to live on or near their country. The area of about 200 square kilometres on both sides of the

Murray River they now claimed was said to be public lands and waters. The Yorta Yorta claim was vigorously contested by both Victoria and New South Wales in 114 days of proceedings extending over two years before Justice Howard Olney of the Federal Court. At the end of 1998, Justice Olney delivered his verdict and it was extremely negative: any rights that the Yorta Yorta had to their land had been 'washed away by the tides of history.'[40] Olney's verdict was upheld on appeal to the full court of the Federal Court. It was now the High Court's turn.

The High Court, five judges to two, upheld the lower courts' verdict. Two points stand out in the judgment. The first is the vigorous way in which the majority nails down the frozen rights approach and denies any continuing life for Aboriginal sovereignty. The majority rejected the Yorta Yorta's argument that though they had changed and adapted the laws and customs governing their relation to their lands, that did not sever their connection with those lands. Chief Justice Gleeson and Justices Gummow and Hayne, writing the main majority judgment, said that the Yorta Yorta could not adapt their traditional laws and customs to their changing circumstances because, after the white man moved in, they lost any independent law-making power: '... what the assertion of sovereignty by the British Crown necessarily entailed was that there could thereafter be no parallel law-making system in the territory over which it asserted sovereignty.'[41] According to this view of Australian constitutionalism, while it is possible under Australia's federal system for the Commonwealth and the states to share sovereign law-making power, there is no room in this sovereign federal house for a share of aboriginal sovereignty. These judges added that 'one of the uncontestable consequences of the change in sovereignty was that the only native title rights or interests in relation to lands or waters which the new sovereign recognized were those that existed at the time of change in sovereignty.'[42] Native title remains as a bridge to recognizing an aboriginal regime of law and custom, but a regime which, according to these judges, atrophied in 1788.

The second point that was hammered home in this decision was killing the common law foundation of native title. In the lower courts, some weight had been given to the fact that the definition of native title in Section 223 of the *Native Title Act* gives, as one of the criteria of native title, that 'the rights and interests are recognized by the common law of Australia.' But this criterion is now firmly subordinated by the High Court majority to the other criteria calling for a continuing connection based on traditional laws. Gleeson, Gummow, and Hayne leave no doubt that, in their view, native title is now entirely a creature of statutes passed by a majority in the Commonwealth: 'To speak of the "common law requirements" of native title is to invite fundamental error. Native title is not a creature of the common law, whether the Imperial common law as that existed at the time of sovereignty and first settlement, or the Australian common law as it exists today. Native title, for present purposes is what is defined and described in s.223 (1) of the *Native Title Act*.'[43] Justice McHugh, who agreed with most of the majority judgment, had trouble swallowing this point. He acknowledged the excision of Section 12 of the *Native Title Act, 1993*, which had stated that 'Subject to this Act, the common law of Australia in respect of native title has, after 30 June 1993, the force of law of the Commonwealth.' But, even so, McHugh notes that when Senator Minchin was defending his government's amendments to the *Native Title Act* in 1997, he told the Senate that 'our Act preserves the fact of common law: who holds native title, what it consists of, is entirely a matter for the courts of Australia. It is a common law right.'[44]

The High Court's retreat on native title is only partly explained by changes in its personnel. The three judges who wrote the majority judgment in *Yorta Yorta* – Gleeson, Gummow, and Hayne – were also part of the majority in *Yanner, Croker Island,* and *Ward.* None of them was on the court that decided *Mabo (No. 2).* But two of them, the chief justice and Gummow, were appointed by the Keating government, and in all but *Yorta Yorta,* Justice Mary Gaudron, co-author of one of the most liberal opinions in *Mabo (No. 2),* joined them. Of the post-*Mabo* appointees on the court, only Kirby, a Keating appointee, and Callinan, a Howard appointee, have consistently taken distinctive positions on native title. Kirby and Callinan cancel each other out. Kirby has been on the majority side in the decisions that have been at least moderately supportive of the native title claim, but in each case he has written his own opinion advancing a more robust and sympathetic treatment of native title than other members of the majority. In *Yorta Yorta,* he joined Gaudron in a short but strongly worded dissent. Callinan, as one would expect from the circumstances surrounding his appointment, has been at the other extreme. He has dissented even when support for native title is moderate. Only in *Yorta Yorta* has he been on the majority side. McHugh, who supported the most conservative of the *Mabo* judgments, has slid over to Callinan's side, supporting him in all his dissents from the moderate middle.

More important than personnel changes has been the judges' sense of a change in the political climate. The political row over *Mabo (No. 2)* and the row over *Wik* – in which the court's activism was even more heavily targeted – have given most members of the court a sense that their political mandate to be pace-makers on the rights of Indigenous people has run out. In a constitutional democracy, we should not be shocked or surprised that judges' assessment of the boundaries of their political legitimacy should be a factor in their decision-making.

But a judicial retreat, however explicable in terms of the pressures of majoritarian democracy, can never be good news for the minority, whose rights judicial activism was protecting. This is certainly true of the Aborigines and Torres Strait Islanders in Australia. But though these peoples constitute a minority of Australians in a statistical sense, they are a minority in no other sense. They are members of historical societies that have never given up their own laws and their continuing and sovereign responsibility for their lives and their lands. In the resort to the white man's courts that Eddie Mabo inspired, they hoped to improve their chances for establishing a just relationship with the much more powerful society that has colonized them. In that case, they did achieve a measure of justice. That is about all Indigenous peoples can expect from these courts. As I have written elsewhere, as a person whose ancestral ties are with the colonizing English-speaking people: 'At their best, my people's courts can prod, provoke, and, yes, on their *very* best days, inspire my people and our political leaders to work for a just relationship with the peoples we have colonized. But justice will only come through the political agreements my people and Indigenous peoples in freedom construct together.'[45]

I hope Eddie Mabo would say 'Amen' to that.

Notes

Introduction

1 I was planning to write a book comparing Australia's and Canada's frustrations in attempting major constitutional reform, building on two articles I had published: 'The Politics of Frustration: The Pursuit of Formal Constitutional Change in Australia and Canada,' and 'The Politics of Frustration II: Constitutional Politics in Canada and Australia since 1987.' For a more popular version of the main thesis of these articles, see Russell, 'Mega Constitutional Politics: Canada's Agony, Australia's Warning.'

2 In Canada, 'Aboriginal' is written in the upper case to refer to all of Canada's Indigenous peoples – various Amerindian nations, the Inuit peoples, the Métis nation, and other Métis peoples. In Australia, 'Aborigines,' written in the upper case, refers to the Indigenous people of the Australian mainland and Tasmania, but not the Torres Strait Islanders. Therefore, in the Australian context, 'aboriginal' is written in the lower case to refer to all of Australia's Indigenous peoples – the Aborigines and the Torres Strait Islanders. If the reference applies only to the Indigenous people of the mainland, however, Aboriginal is written in the upper case.

3 Bickel, *The Least Dangerous Branch.*

4 For my exposition of this thesis, see Russell, 'Canada's Megaconstitutional Politics in Comparative Perspective.'

5 In United Nations documents, 'Indigenous' is written in the upper case to connote peoples with a distinct political status. The working definition of Indigenous used at the UN is as follows: 'Indigenous communities, peoples and nations are those which, having a historical continuity with pre-invasion and pre-colonial societies that developed on their territories, consider themselves distinct from other sectors of societies now prevailing in those

territories, or parts of them. They form at present non-dominant sectors of society and are determined to preserve, develop and transmit to future generations their ancestral territories and their ethnic identity, as the basis of their continued existence as peoples, in accordance with their own cultural patterns, institutions and legal systems.' See Irons, 'Indigenous Peoples and Self Determination,' 199.

6 See Watkins, *Dene Nation.*

7 For an account of this encounter, see Russell, 'Doing Aboriginal Politics.'

Chapter 1: Preparation of an Indigenous Challenger

1 For an account of Mabo's life, see Loos and Mabo, *Edward Koiki Mabo.* Parts One and Three are biographical essays by historian Noel Loos; Part Two is 'Koiki Mabo's Story' as told by him.

2 For interpretations of the history and culture of the Torres Strait Islanders, see Beckett, *Torres Strait Islanders:* Sharp, *Stars of Tagai*; and Singe, *The Torres Strait.*

3 Loos and Mabo, *Edward Koiki Mabo*, 29.

4 Ibid., xx–xxi.

5 Beckett, *Torres Strait Islanders*, 54.

6 Sharp, *Stars of Tagai*, 24.

7 Ibid., 30.

8 The missionaries actually reached Darnley on May 30, 1871. The celebration of July 1 was instituted by the Church of England. See Beckett, *Torres Strait Islanders*, 87.

9 Loos and Mabo, *Edward Koiki Mabo*, 105.

10 Sharp, *No Ordinary Judgment*, 156.

11 For Mabo's account of this episode, see Loos and Mabo, *Edward Koiki Mabo*, 68.

12 Beckett, *Torres Strait Islanders*, 127.

13 Ibid., 180.

14 Torres Strait Island Regional Authority, *Corporate Plan 1994–95*, 4.

15 For historical accounts of this period of aboriginal politics in Australia, see Goodall, *Invasion to Embassy*, Part Six; Bennett, *Aborigines and Political Power*, ch. 1; and Griffiths, *Aboriginal Affairs*, chs. 9 and 10.

16 Loos and Mabo, *Edward Koiki Mabo*, 51.

17 Haddon, ed., *Reports of the Cambridge Anthropological Expedition to Torres Straits.*

18 Loos and Mabo, *Edward Koiki Mabo*, 11.

19 In a 1981 interview with Nonie Sharp, these are the words Eddie recalled saying. See Mabo Papers, Series 2. See also Loos and Mabo, *Edward Koiki Mabo*, 11.

20 Mabo Papers, Series 2, folio 1.
21 This timeframe is as close as Loos can identify the date of the conversation. For the fullest published account, see his interview with Ryan, 'Tribute to the Mabo Title Fight.' In conversation with the author, Reynolds recalls the conversation taking place around 1973–4.

Chapter 2: Western Imperialism and Its Legal Magic

1 Said, *Culture and Imperialism*, 10.
2 Williams Jr., *The American Indian in Western Legal Thought*, 6.
3 McNeil, *Common Law Aboriginal Title*, 110.
4 *Johnson and Graham's Lessee v. McIntosh*, 21 U.S. (8 Wheat) 534 (1823) at 588.
5 It may seem anomalous to include 'treaties' as part of domestic law. Though Aboriginal parties to these treaties have usually regarded treaties with imperial powers and their successor states as international, the legal and political authorities of the colonizing countries have not accorded them that status.
6 For accounts, see Williams, *The American Indian in Western Legal Thought*, 78–81; and Green, 'Claims to Territory in Colonial America,' in *The Law of Nations and the New World*, 4–7.
7 See Lindley, *The Acquisition and Government of Backward Territories in International Law*, ch. 2.
8 Ibid., 10–11.
9 Hanke, *The Spanish Struggle for Justice in the Conquest of America*, 33.
10 Hanke, *Aristotle and the American Indians*, 12–13.
11 Dickason, 'Concepts of Sovereignty at the Time of First Contact,' 184.
12 For a summary of the lectures, see Williams, *The American Indian in Western Legal Thought*, 96–103.
13 Quoted in Henderson, *The Mi'kmaw Concordat*, 61.
14 Ibid., 63.
15 Quoted in Williams, *The American Indian in Western Legal Thought*, 103.
16 Hanke, *The Spanish Struggle for Justice in the Conquest of America*, 21.
17 McNutt, *Bartholomew de Las Casas*, 212.
18 Quoted in Hanke, *The Spanish Struggle for Justice*, 125.
19 Hanke, *The Spanish Struggle for Justice*, 74.
20 Henderson, *The Mi'kmaw Concordat*, 70.
21 St Leger, *The 'Etiamsi Daremus' of Hugo Grotius*, 14–15.
22 Lindley, *The Acquisition and Government of Backward Territories in International Law*, 27.
23 Crawford, *The Original Status of Aboriginal Peoples in North America*, 8.
24 Hughes, *The Fatal Shore*, 55.

25 Vattel, *The Law of Nations*, 164.
26 A number of contemporary legal scholars have exposed the confusion engendered by the classic distinction. See, for instance, Slattery, *The Land Rights of Indigenous Canadian Peoples as Affected by the Crown's Acquisition of Their Territories*, 34–5.
27 Lindley, *The Acquisition and Government of Backward Territory in International Law*, 26–8.
28 Locke, *The Second Treatise of Government*, 20.
29 Lindley, *The Acquisition and Government of Backward Territory in International Law*, 40.
30 Beaglehole, ed., *The Voyage of the Endeavour, 1768–1771*, ccixxxiii.
31 Harlow, *The Founding of the Second British Empire, 1763–1793*, 1: 37–8.
32 Williams, *The American Indian in Western Legal Thought*, 206.
33 Washburn, *Red Man's Land/White Man's Law*, 34–5.
34 Williams, *The American Indian in Western Legal Thought*, 207.
35 Nies, *Native American History*, 129–30.
36 In the 1600s the French also entered into agreements with several North American peoples. These agreements dealt mainly with trade and military matters, not land rights. See Canada, Royal Commission on Aboriginal People, *Report*, 1: 122–3.
37 Jones, *License for Empire*, 16.
38 Lloyd, *The British Empire, 1558–1995*, 29.
39 Williams, *The American Indian in Western Legal Thought*, 302.
40 Blackstone, *Commentaries on the Laws of England*, 105.
41 Slattery, *The Land Rights of Indigenous Canadian Peoples*, 44.
42 The Royal Proclamation can be found in many collections of Canadian constitutional documents. A recent collection is *Canada 125: Its Constitutions, 1763–1982*, where the proclamation is reproduced at 85–8.
43 Dickason, *Canada's First Nations*, 183.
44 Borrows, 'Wampum at Niagara,' 161–5.
45 For accounts, see Williams Jr, 'The Algebra of Federal Indian Law,' and Tully, *Strange Multiplicity*, 127–8.
46 For an account of this continuity, see Clark, *Native Liberty, Crown Sovereignty*.
47 Canada, *Constitution Act, 1982*, Schedule B, Part 1, Section 25.
48 Williams, *The American Indian in Western Legal Thought*, 229.

Chapter 3: Eddie Mabo's Project and Its Obstacles

1 Bennett, *Aborigines and Political Power*, 24.
2 *Racial Discrimination Act 1975*, s. 9(1).

3 Quoted in Maddock, *Your Land Is Our Land*, 26.

4 Loos and Mabo, *Edward Koiki Mabo*, 51.

5 Ibid., xxiv.

6 Ibid.

7 See Mabo Papers, Series 6.

8 For Bonita (Netta) Mabo's reflections on her husband, see her interview with Sykes, 'After Eddie,' 70.

9 Trevor Graham (co-producer/director), *Mabo: Life of an Island Man*, Australian Film Board, 1997.

10 This thesis is more fully developed in Russell, 'Aboriginal Nationalism,' 57.

11 Loos and Mabo, *Edward Koiki Mabo*, 56.

12 Griffin, 'A Background Paper to the Torres Strait Border Issue,' xiii.

13 Lui, 'A Perspective from the Torres Strait,' 32.

14 Ibid., 31.

15 Ibid., 35.

16 Ibid.

17 Griffin, 'A Background Paper to the Torres Strait Border Issue,'121.

18 Treaty between Australia and the Independent State of Papua New Guinea concerning Sovereignty and Maritime Boundaries in the Area between the Two Countries, including the Area Known as Torres Strait, and Related Matters (Sydney, 18 December 1978), Treaty Series 1985, No. 4. Note that the treaty did not come into force until 1985.

19 For an analysis, see Stanford. 'The Torres Strait Treaty,' 572.

20 Article 12 of the treaty.

21 Statement of Facts submitted to High Court of Australia, November 1984, Mabo Papers, Series 8, 23–4.

22 Telegram from chairman of Murray Island Council to Eddie Mabo, 17 October 1974, Mabo Papers, Series 2, folio 1.

23 Graham, *Mabo*.

24 Sykes, 'After Eddie,' 73.

25 Beckett, *Torres Strait Islanders*, ch. 7.

26 Graham, *Mabo*. 1997.

27 In 1991 the Murray Island Council clerk ruled that Mabo was ineligible to stand for election to the council because he had not resided on the island continuously for the previous twenty four months. In an affidavit supporting his challenge to this ruling, Mabo stated that, since 1977, he had returned to the island 'two or three times a year.' Mabo Papers, Series 11.

28 Ibid., Series 2, folio 1.

29 Ibid., Series 8, folder 4.

30 Patapan, 'The Liberal Politics of Rights.'

31 See Australia, Council for Aboriginal Reconciliation, *The Position of Indigenous People in National Constitutions.*
32 The High Court did not become supreme until 1986, when appeals from state courts to the Judicial Committee of the Privy Council were abolished. Appeals from the High Court to the Privy Council were abolished in 1975.
33 For a good account, see Galligan, *Politics of the High Court.*
34 The court struck the law down not as a violation of civil liberties but as exceeding the Commonwealth's defence power.
35 See Sexton and Maher, *The Legal Mystique.*
36 See Hocking, *Lionel Murphy.*
37 *Milirrpum and Others v. Nabalco Pty Ltd and the Commonwealth of Australia* (1970), 17 F.L.R. 141.
38 Yunupingu, 'Introduction,' in *Our Land Is Our Life*, 4.
39 *Milirrpum*, 151–2.
40 Ibid., 242.
41 *Cooper v. Stuart* (1889), 14 App. Cas. 286 at 291.
42 *Milirrpum*, 267.
43 Ibid., 244.
44 Ibid., 212.
45 *Tee-Hit-Ton Indians v. United States*, (348 U.S. 272, 1955).
46 *Calder v. Attorney General of British Columbia*, (1970) D.L.R. (3d) 64.
47 Ibid., 222.

Chapter 4: The Distinctive Foundations of Australian Colonialism

1 Hughes, *The Fatal Shore*, 54.
2 Ibid., 57, and O'Brien, *Joseph Banks*, 126–7.
3 The aboriginal population in 1788 is estimated to have been 314,500. Horton, ed., *The Encyclopaedia of Aboriginal Australia*, 1299.
4 According to Manning Clark, between 26 January 1788 and 20 November 1823, 37,606 convicts embarked for New South Wales. Clark, *A History of Australia*, 90.
5 Walker, *Ka Whawhai Tonu Matou*, ch. 5.
6 King, *Nga Iwi O Te Motu*, ch. 1.
7 Orange, *The Treaty of Waitangi*, ch. 3.
8 See Ossen, 'Mr Wakefield and New Zealand as an Experiment in Post-Enlightenment Experimental Practice,' 197–218.
9 Ibid., 31.
10 This is the English text, and it is printed along with a Maori text as appendix 1 in Orange, *The Treaty of Waitangi.*

11 Kawharu, ed., *Waitangi*.
12 Spiller, Finn, and Boast, *A New Zealand Legal History*, 139.
13 This phrase was used by Chief Justice James Prendergast in *Wi Parata v. Bishop of Wellington*, [1877] 3 NZ Jur (NS)SC 72.
14 See Clarke, 'Indigenous People in Australian Constitutional law,' 18.
15 Clark, *A History of Australia*, 151.
16 Blainey, *A Shorter History of Australia*, 51.
17 Horton, *Encyclopaedia of Aboriginal Australia*, 1299.
18 Clark, *A History of Australia*, 80.
19 Ibid., 115.
20 Atkinson, *The Europeans in Australia*, 1: 158.
21 See, for instance, Emmett, *Fleeting Encounters*.
22 Reynolds, *The Other Side of the Frontier*, 31.
23 Hughes, *The Fatal Shore*, 91.
24 Day, *Claiming a Continent*, 65.
25 Quoted in Day, *Claiming a Continent*, 65–6.
26 Watson, *Frontier Lands and Pioneer Legends*.
27 Stanner, *White Man Got No Dreaming*, 32–3.
28 See Broome, *Aboriginal Australians*, ch. 1.
29 Blainey, *Triumph of the Nomads*, 77.
30 Sutton, *Country*, 70.
31 Young, 'Aboriginal Frontiers and Boundaries,' 88.
32 Reynolds, *The Other Side of the Frontier*, 66.
33 Ibid., 61.
34 Murray, 'What Really Happened to the Kooris?' 19.
35 David Ritter, 'The "Rejection of Terra Nullius,"' 9.
36 Reynolds, *The Law of the Land*, 61.
37 Day, *Claiming a Continent*, 111.
38 Castles, *An Australian Legal History*, 30–1.
39 Reynolds, *Law of the Land*, 110.
40 Ibid., 107.
41 For an account of a similar development in colonial British Columbia, see Harris, *Marking Native Space*, ch. 3.
42 McGrath, 'Tasmania: 1,' 320.
43 Reynolds, *Fate of a Free People*, 118.
44 Ibid., 4.
45 McGrath, 'Tasmania: 1,' 323.
46 Reynolds, *Fate of a Free People*, 133. Before being moved to Flinders Island, Aboriginal families were moved to the Bruny Island mission south of Hobart and then to Gun Carriage (or Vansittart) Island in Bass Strait.

47 Reynolds, *Fate of a Free People*, 122.
48 Maykutenner, 'Tasmania: 2,' 354–5.
49 *Cooper v. Stuart* (1889), 14 App. Cas. 286 at 291.
50 Castles, *Australian Legal History*, 521.
51 Atkinson, *The Europeans in Australia*, 165.
52 Clark, *History of Australia*, 3: 149.
53 Reynolds, *Aboriginal Sovereignty*, 62.
54 Hookey, 'Settlement and Sovereignty,' 3.
55 Ibid., 4.
56 *Cherokee Nation v. Georgia*, 30 U.S. (5 Pet.) 1 (1831) at 17.
57 *Worcester v. State of Georgia*, 31 U.S. (6 Pet.) 515 at 547.
58 Ibid., 559.
59 For accounts of *R. v. Bon Jon*, see Hookey, 'Settlement and Sovereignty';
    Reynolds, *Aboriginal Sovereignty*; and Strelein, 'Indigenous Self-determination
    Claims and the Common Law in Australia' (thesis).
60 Reynolds, *Aboriginal Sovereignty*, 119.
61 Ibid., 115.
62 Ibid., 120.
63 Ibid., 121.
64 Hookey, *Settlement and Sovereignty*, 9.
65 See Denoon, *Settler Capitalism*; and Weaver, 'Beyond the Fatal Shore,' 981–
    1007.
66 On the strength of this belief in colonial Australia, see Clark, *A History of
    Australia*, 3: 150, and Frost, *Botany Bay Mirages*, ch. 9.
67 Reynolds, *With the White People*, 117.
68 Goodall, *Invasion to Embassy*, 59.
69 Ibid., 65.
70 See chapters on Queensland, South Australia, Western Australia, and the
    Northern Territory in McGrath, *Contested Ground.*
71 This is the term used by Goodall. See *Invasion to Embassy*, ch. 5.
72 *The Wik Peoples v. Queensland* (1996), 187 C.L.R. 1 at 217.
73 Ibid., 8.
74 See Innis, *The Fur Trade in Canada.*
75 Ann McGrath, 'History, Wik and Relations Between Aborigines and
    Pastoralists,' in *Sharing Country: Land Rights, Human Rights, and Reconciliation
    after Wik*, 89.
76 Quoted in Foster, 'The Origin of the Protection of Aboriginal Rights in
    South Australian Pastoral Leases.'
77 Quoted in Goodall, *Invasion to Embassy*, 49.
78 Goodall, *Invasion to Embassy*, 53.

79 Quoted in Foster, 'The Origin of the Protection of Aboriginal Rights,' 6.
80 Reynolds, *The Law of the Land*, 143–4.
81 See Holmes, 'Land Tenures in the Australian Pastoral Zone,' 44.
82 Reynolds, *Law of the Land*, 144.
83 Goodall, *Invasion to Embassy*, 49.
84 Ibid., 49–50.
85 Brock, 'South Australia,' 222.
86 Goodall, *Invasion to Embassy*, 56.
87 Reynolds, *Law of the Land*, 131.
88 Goodall, *Invasion to Embassy*, 78.
89 Reynolds, *Law of the Land*, 132–3.
90 *Attorney-General (N.S.W.) v. Brown*, [1847] 1 Legge 312 at 318.
91 Todd, *Parliamentary Government in the British Colonies*, ch. 2.
92 House of Commons, *Report from the Select Committee on Aborigines (British Settlements)*, 26 June 1837, 77.
93 Hasluck, *Black Australians*, 62.
94 Ferguson, *Empire*, 111.
95 Canada's Royal Commission on Aboriginal Peoples refers to it as the Crown/colony/Aboriginal tripartite imperial system. *Report of the Royal Commission on Aboriginal Peoples*, 1: 273.
96 Quoted in Harring, *White Man's Law*, 21.
97 Mill, *Considerations on Representative Government*, ch. 18.
98 For a penetrating analysis of the United States' abandonment of British practice in relations with Indigenous peoples, see Hall, *The American Empire and the Fourth World*.
99 Washburn, *Red Man's Land/White Man's Law*, 53.
100 The turning point was the defeat of the Indians at the Battle of Fallen Timbers in 1794. See Nies, *Native American History*, 216.
101 10 U.S. (6 Cranch) 87.
102 For a discussion of the confusing implications of this case, see Barsh and Henderson, *The Road*, 37–9.
103 *Johnson v. McIntosh*, 21 U.S. (8 Wheat.) 543 (1823) at 274.
104 Ibid., 584.
105 Ibid., 585.
106 Ibid., 588.
107 Ibid., 591–2.
108 30 U.S. (5 Peters) 1 (1831).
109 Ibid., 18.
110 Ibid., 16–17
111 31 U.S. (6 Peters) 515 (1832).

112 Ibid., 547.
113 Ibid., 559.
114 Ibid., 559–60.
115 Ibid., 544.
116 Beveridge, *The Life of John Marshall*, 4: 551.
117 Satz, *American Indian Policy in the Jacksonian Era*, 6–10.
118 Wright, *Stolen Continents*, 220–1.
119 On the significance of this event in world history, see Wilmer, *The Indigenous Voice in World Politics*, 75–7.
120 Justices Deane and Gaudron make the same observation in the *Mabo* case and add: 'There is an element of the absurd about the suggestion that it would have even occurred to the native inhabitants of a new British Colony that they should bring proceedings in a British court against the British Crown to vindicate rights under a common law of which they would be likely to know nothing.' *Mabo v. Queensland (No. 2)* (1992), 175 C.L.R. 1 at 93–4.
121 Barsh and Henderson, *The Road*, 54.
122 McNeil, *Common Law Aboriginal Title*, 248–9.
123 See Justice Brennan's opinion in *Mabo v. Queensland (No. 2)*, 60, and Justice Dawson's dissenting judgment at 135–6.
124 This thesis is more fully articulated and defended in Russell, 'High Courts and the Rights of Aboriginal Peoples.'
125 Wilson, *The Earth Shall Weep*, 158.
126 Mankiller, *Mankiller*, 83.
127 Quoted in Wilson, *The Earth Shall Weep*, 163.
128 For a useful chronology and analysis of settler relations with Indigenous peoples in Australia, Canada, and New Zealand, see Havemann, ed., *Indigenous Peoples' Rights in Australia, Canada, and New Zealand*.
129 Sinclair, *A History of New Zealand*, ch. 5.
130 For an account of Maori social structures, see Walker, *Ka Whawhai Tonu Matou*, ch. 4.
131 Cox, *Kotahitanga*, ch. 4.
132 Sinclair, *A History of New Zealand*, ch. 6.
133 Orange, *The Treaty of Waitangi*, 184.
134 Sinclair, *A History of New Zealand*, 103.
135 Orange, *The Treaty of Waitangi*, 179–81.
136 Fleras, 'From Social Control towards Political Self-Determination?' 557.
137 For a discussion of such possibilities, see Mulgan, *Maori, Pakeha and Democracy*; and Fleras, 'Politicizing Indigeneity,' 123.
138 *Constitution Act, 1867*, Section 91(24). The Inuit people (whom Europeans

at this time referred to as Eskimos) were not mentioned because the northern lands they inhabited were not part of Canada at this time. A 1939 decision of the Supreme Court of Canada ruled that, for constitutional purposes, Eskimos are covered by Section 91(24). In 1982 the *British North America Act* was renamed the *Constitution Act, 1867*.

139 This phrase is the title of the 1993 commentary of the Royal Commission on Aboriginal Peoples.

140 *Constitution Act, 1867*, Section 129.

141 For example, this 'boiler-plate' language is found in Treaty 8, which covered hundreds of thousands of square miles in northern Alberta, northeast British Columbia, and the Northwest Territories. See Fumoleau, *As Long as This Land Shall Last*, 71. (The capitalized words were upper case in the original of all these treaties.)

142 See Canada, Royal Commission on Aboriginal Peoples, *Report*, 1: 271–3.

143 See chapter 2.

144 Quoted in Milloy, *A National Crime*, 6.

145 Ibid., 277.

146 *Statutes of Canada, 1894*, Ch. 32, Section 11.

147 See Royal Commission on Aboriginal Peoples, *Report*, 1: ch. 10.

148 For brief accounts, see Royal Commission on Aboriginal Peoples, *Report*, 4: ch. 5; and Purich, *The Metis*. Some other communities of mixed native/ non-native heritage in other parts of Canada now see themselves Métis. But these communities are not part of the Métis Nation, whose members are descendants of the Red River Métis who took part in the Riel rebellions.

149 For an overview, see Royal Commission on Aboriginal Peoples, *Report*, 4: ch. 5.

150 Royal Commission on Aboriginal Peoples, *The High Arctic Relocation*.

151 See Royal Commission on Aboriginal Peoples, *Report*, 4: ch. 2.

152 For an account of the struggle to remove this provision and the consequences of the 1985 legislation, see ibid., 31–50.

153 Hasluck, *Black Australians*, 121.

154 Reynolds and May, 'Queensland,' 172.

155 Brock, 'South Australia,' 228.

156 Broome, 'Victoria,' 135–42.

157 Quoted in Chesterton and Galligan, *Citizens without Rights*, 18.

158 For a full account of the doomed-race theory, see McGregor, *Imagined Destinies*.

159 Goodall, *Invasion to Embassy*, 97.

160 Goodall, 'New South Wales,' 80.

161 Goodall, *Invasion to Embassy*, 127.

162 Ibid., 96–137.
163 Wood, 'Nineteenth-Century Bureaucratic Constructions of Indigenous Identities in New South Wales,' 49.
164 Section 70 of the *Constitution Act, 1889*, set the amount at £5000 a year, or 1 per cent of the colony's revenues, whichever was greater, but the Western Australian Parliament did not feel bound by this clause. See Hasluck, *Black Australians*, 118–20.
165 The words used by geographer D.S. Davidson, as quoted in Loos, *Invasion and Resistance*, 3.
166 Loos, *Invasion and Resistance*.
167 For an account of the motives and methods of Aboriginal resistance, see Reynolds, *The Other Side of the Frontier*, chs. 3 and 4.
168 On the native police, see Broome, *Aboriginal Australians*, 45–7, and Elder, *Blood on the Wattle*, ch. 8.
169 Reynolds and May, 'Queensland,' 178.
170 Murray, 'What *Really* Happened to the Kooris?' 19.
171 Elder, *Blood on the Wattle*, chs. 11 and 12.
172 Read, 'Northern Territory,' 273–5.
173 Pedersen and Woorunnmurra, *Janadamarra and the Bunuba Resistance*, 19.
174 Loos, *Invasion and Resistance*, 5.
175 Kidd, *The Way We Civilise*, 73–5.
176 Reynolds and May, 'Queensland,' 182.
177 Toussaint, 'Western Australia,' 252–3.
178 Read, 'Northern Territory,' 276.
179 Reynolds and May, 'Queensland,' 183.
180 Rowley, *The Remote Aborigines*, 6.
181 See, for instance, Sharp, *Footprints along the Cape York Sandbeaches*, 4.
182 Shnukal, 'Locals, Immigrants and Outsiders.'
183 Beckett, *Torres Strait Islanders*, 57.
184 Ibid., 58.
185 See the description in the 1907 report of Queensland's Chief Protector of Aboriginals, as quoted by Justice Brennan in his opinion in *Mabo v. Queensland (No. 2)*, 23.
186 *Mabo v. Queensland (No. 2)*, 24.
187 Beckett, *Torres Strait Islanders*, 45.
188 Ibid., 55.
189 Rowley, *The Remote Aborigines*, 7.
190 See Hobsbawm, *The Age of Empire, 1875–1914*.
191 Ibid., 70.
192 Seeley, *The Expansion of England*, 54.

193 Ibid., 55–6.
194 *Cooper v. Stuart*, [1889] App. Cas. 286 at 291.
195 *Re Southern Rhodesia*, [1919] A.C. 211 at 233–4.
196 See Bell and Asch, 'Challenging Assumptions,' 64.
197 *St. Catherine's Milling and Lumber Company v. The Queen* (1889), 14 A.C. 46 at 54.
198 See Tennant, *Aboriginal Peoples and Politics*; and Harris, *Making Native Space*.
199 See, for example, the battle fought by the Nlaka'pamux people with invading gold-miners in the Fraser Canyon, in Laforest and York, *Spuzzum*, 51–2.
200 Royal Commission on Aboriginal Peoples, *Report*, 1: 296.
201 See Barsh and Henderson, *The Road*, 68–9.
202 *Ex Parte Crow Dog*, 109 U.S. 556 (1883). For a discussion, see Frickey, 'Congressional Intent, Practical Reasoning, and the Dynamic of Federal Indian Law,' 1189–93.
203 Wunder, '*Retained by the People*,' 36.
204 Wilson, *The Earth Shall Weep*, 299.
205 Nies, *Native American History*, 295.
206 For an account, see Brown, *Bury My Heart at Wounded Knee*.
207 *Elk v. Wilkins*, 112 U.S. 94.
208 Under the original *Allotment Act*, allottees automatically became citizens. In 1906 this process was changed, so only those whose land was no longer held in trust became citizens.
209 *U.S. v. Sandoval*, 231 U.S. 28 (1913) at 39, 46.
210 King, *Nga Iwi O Te Motu*, 49–50.
211 Horton, *Encyclopaedia of Aboriginal Australia*, 1299; and Royal Commission on Aboriginal Peoples, *Report*, 1: 14.
212 Siffarm with Lane Jr, 'The Demography of Native North America,' 36.
213 See Sorrenson, 'The Settlement of New Zealand from 1835,' 172–3.
214 King, *Nga Iwi O Te Motu*, 60
215 Quoted in Day, *Claiming a Continent*, 186.
216 Ibid., 189–90.

Chapter 5: Colonialism Contested

1 The classic account is La Nauze, *The Making of the Australian Constitution*.
2 This thesis is elaborated by Chesterton and Galligan in their *Citizens without Rights*. See especially chapter 4 (written in association with Tom Clarke) for a discussion of the exclusionary legislation.
3 Day, *Claiming a Continent*, 210.

4 Ibid.
5 See Chesterton and Galligan, *Citizens without Rights*, 67–73.
6 La Nauze, *The Making of the Australian Constitution*, 67.
7 See Fletcher, *Aboriginal Politics*.
8 *Katinyeri v. The Commonwealth* (1998), 72 ALJR 722. For a comment on this case, see Nettheim, 'The Hindmarsh Bridge Act Case.'
9 McGregor, *Imagined Destinies*, 161–80.
10 Stokes, 'Citizenship and Aboriginality,' 170.
11 Chesterton and Galligan, *Citizens without Rights*, 71.
12 Ibid., 78.
13 Ibid., 82.
14 Reynolds and May, 'Queensland,' 200.
15 Kidd, *The Way We Civilise*, ch. 4.
16 Quoted in Beckett, *Torres Strait Islanders*, 59.
17 Goodall, *Invasion to Embassy*, ch. 15.
18 Barsh and Henderson, *The Road*, ch. 9.
19 Quoted in Partington, *Hasluck versus Coombs*, 37.
20 See Hasluck, *Shades of Darkness*, 67.
21 McGregor, *Imagined Destinies*, ch. 5.
22 Gray, 'From Nomadism to Citizenship,' 66–7.
23 Ibid., 59.
24 Quoted in McGregor, *Imagined Destinies*, 208.
25 McGregor, *Imagined Destinies*, 123.
26 See Miller, *Skyscrapers Hide the Heavens*, ch. 12.
27 See Cornell, *The Return of the Native*.
28 Goodall, *Invasion to Embassy*, 130.
29 Russell, 'Aboriginal Nationalism,' 60.
30 For a discussion of this process in the Canadian context, see Borrows, *Recovering Canada*.
31 Goodall, *Invasion to Embassy*, 129–30.
32 Cowlishaw, 'The Materials for Identity Construction,' 94.
33 Goodall, *Invasion to Embassy*, 149–56.
34 Ibid., 156.
35 Ibid., 163–4.
36 Ibid., 168.
37 Bourke, 'Australia's First Peoples,' 40.
38 Day, *Claiming a Continent*, 283.
39 Ibid., 284.
40 Anaya, *Indigenous Peoples in International Law*, 4.
41 Goodall, *Invasion to Embassy*, 158–9.

42 Quoted in Bennett, *Aborigines and Political Power*, 5.
43 For a discussion of differing views of Aboriginality, see Beckett, *Past and Present*, especially Beckett's own introduction and concluding essay.
44 Emerson, *From Empire to Nation*.
45 Tully, *Strange Multiplicity*.
46 Beckett, *Past and Present*, 212.
47 Anaya, *Indigenous Peoples in International Law*, ch. 1.
48 See discussion in chapter 4.
49 See Alston, 'Individual Complaints,' ch. 7.
50 Williams Jr, 'Encounters on the Frontiers of International Human Rights Law,' 669.
51 United Nations Charter, Article 1(2).
52 Ibid., Article 2(1),(4),(7).
53 Cassese, *Self-Determination of Peoples*, 40.
54 United Nations Charter, Article 2(7).
55 Wilmer, *The Indigenous Voice in World Politics*, 24.
56 Westlake, *Chapters on the Principles of International Law*, 141–3.
57 United Nations Charter, XI (73).
58 Quoted in Anaya, *Indigenous Peoples in International Law*, 60 note 26.
59 Iorns, 'Indigenous Peoples and Self-Determination,' 253.
60 Ibid., 250–1.
61 Ibid., 43.
62 Wilmer, *The Indigenous Voice in World Politics*, 63.
63 Quoted in Wilmer, *The Indigenous Voice in World Politics*, 87.
64 Barsh, 'Indigenous Peoples,' 370.
65 For an account, see Sanders, 'The Re-emergence of Indigenous Questions in International Law,' 19–20.
66 See ibid.
67 Barsh, 'Indigenous Peoples,' 370.
68 For the text and a discussion of the articles, see Iorns, 'Indigenous Peoples and Self-Determination,' 256–7.
69 For an elaboration of this point, see Kymlicka, 'Human Rights and Ethno-cultural Justice,' 4–17.
70 Pritchard, 'The Significance of International Law,' 14.
71 See Sniderman, Fletcher, Russell, and Tetlock, *Clash of Rights*.
72 See Williams, *A Bill of Rights for Australia*.
73 Nettheim, 'The Relevance of International Law,' 56–7.
74 See Moss, 'Indigenous Self-Government in Canada and Sexual Equality under the Indian Act.
75 Conference on Australia's signing the Optional Protocol.

76 Chesterton and Galligan, *Citizens without Rights*, 185–6.
77 See ibid.
78 For a discussion of these conflicting myths about the 1967 referendum, see Attwood and Markus, 'Representation Matters.'
79 Quoted in Chesterton and Galligan, *Citizens without Rights*, 186.
80 See Markus, *Australian Race Relations, 1788–1993*.
81 Quoted in Day, *Claiming a Continent*, 416.
82 Quoted in Chesterton and Galligan, *Citizens without Rights*, 185.
83 Attwood and Markus, 'Representation Matters,' 124.
84 Russell, 'The Politics of Frustration,' 3–32.
85 Bennett, *Aborigines and Political Power*, 9.
86 Goodall, *Invasion to Embassy*, 320.
87 Quoted in Bennett, *Aborigines and Political Power*, 11.
88 Goodall, *Invasion to Embassy*, 277.
89 Ibid., 312.
90 See discussion in chapter 3.
91 Chesterton and Galligan, *Citizens without Rights*, 157–62.
92 Ibid., 166.

Chapter 6: The Land Rights Movement

1 See Henry Reynolds, 14–15.
2 See chapter 2.
3 See chapter 5.
4 See Read, 'Northern Territory,' 291–3.
5 See Maddock, *Your Land Is Our Land*, ch. 2.
6 See Goodall, *Invasion to Embassy*, 324–5.
7 Rowse, *Obliged to Be Difficult*, 57.
8 Stanner, *White Man Got No Dreaming*, 241.
9 Rowse, *Obliged to Be Difficult*, 54.
10 Ibid., 67.
11 Goodall, *Invasion to Embassy*, 339.
12 For a detailed account of the embassy, see Robinson, 'The Aboriginal Embassy,' 49–63.
13 Rowse, *Obliged to Be Difficult*, 97.
14 Robinson, *The Aboriginal Embassy*, 55.
15 Bennett, *White Politics and Black Australians*, 61.
16 Australia, House of Representatives, *Debates*, 1972, vol. 76, 128, 135.
17 Dunston, 'Aboriginal Land Title and Employment in South Australia.'
18 Ibid., 317–18.

19 Broome, 'Victoria,' 54.
20 Goodall, 'New South Wales,' 111.
21 Quoted in Bennett, *White Politics and Black Australians*, 104.
22 House of Representatives, *Hansard*, vol. 82, February 27, 1973, 14.
23 Aboriginal Land Rights Commission, *Second Report*, 1.
24 House of Representatives, *Hansard*, vol. 82, February 27, 1973, 540.
25 Ibid., 14.
26 Lawrence, *Kakadu*, 32.
27 Griffiths, *Aboriginal Affairs*, ch. 12.
28 Berger, *Village Journey*, 23–4.
29 Dickason, *Canada's First Nations*, 405–6.
30 Canada, Task Force to Review Comprehensive Claims Policy, *Living Treaties: Lasting Agreements*, 9.
31 Washburn, *Red Man's Land/White Man's Law*, Part III, ch. 3.
32 See Richardson, *Strangers Devour the Land*.
33 Dickason, *Canada's First Nations*, 404.
34 Berger, *Village Journey*, 24–6.
35 Berger, *Northern Frontier, Northern Homeland*, vol. 1. The difference between Berger's and the American approach is clearly developed in *Village Journey*, Berger's critical review of the Alaskan settlement cited above.
36 Berger, *Northern Frontier, Northern Homeland*, 196.
37 For an assessment, see Feit, 'James Bay Cree Self-Government and Land Management,' 68–98; and Scott, ed., *Aboriginal Autonomy in Northern Quebec and Labrador*, esp. ch. 1.
38 Maddock, *Your Land Is Our Land*, 52–3.
39 See Watkins, ed., *The Dene*.
40 See Eames, 'The Central Land Council.'
41 Rowse, *Obliged to Be Difficult*, 144.
42 Aboriginal Land Rights Commission, *Second Report*, 5.
43 Maddock, *Your Land Is Our Land*, 64.
44 Aboriginal Land Rights Commission, *Second Report*, 129.
45 See Churchill, *Since Predator Came*,' 115–17.
46 Ibid., 10.
47 Ibid., 11.
48 Quoted in Griffiths, *Aboriginal Affairs*, 135.
49 Senate, *Hansard*, February 20, 1975.
50 House of Representatives, *Hansard*, vol. 102, November 17, 1976, 2783.
51 *Aboriginal Land Rights (Northern Territory) Act, 1976*, s. 73.
52 Eames, 'The Central Land Council,' 269–70.
53 Maddock, *Your Land Is Our Land*, 65.

54 Ibid., 69.
55 *Aboriginal Land Rights (Northern Territory) Act 1976*, s. 23.
56 Ibid., s. 40. Section 42 requires that a proclamation be laid before both houses of Parliament, and each House has fifteen days to pass a motion of disapproval.
57 *Aboriginal Land Rights (Northern Territory) Act, 1976*, s. 45.
58 Rowse, *Obliged to Be Difficult*, 151.
59 *Aboriginal Land Rights (Northern Territory) Act, 1976*, ss. 63–4.
60 Quoted in Lawrence, *Kakadu*, 87.
61 Mining permits granted before June 4, 1976, and land known as the Eastern Areas on Groote Eylandt were also exempted from the requirement of land council consent. *Aboriginal Land Rights (Northern Territory) Act, 1976*, s. 40, subsections (3) to (7).
62 *Aboriginal Land Rights (Northern Territory) Act, 1976*, s. 23(3)(a). For details of the negotiations, see Rowse, *Obliged to Be Difficult*, ch. 8.
63 House of Representatives, *Hansard*, 16 October 1975, 2223.
64 Loos and Mabo, *Edward Koiki Mabo*, 169–70.
65 This is all in Section 3, the interpretation section of the act.
66 Hocking, 'Is Might Right?'
67 Yunupingu, 'From Bark Petition to Native Title,' 10.
68 Ibid., 11.
69 Rowley, *Recovery*, 76.
70 See Durie, *Te Mana, Te Kawanatanga*, ch. 5.
71 King, *Nga Iwi O Te Motu*, 96.
72 Orange, *The Treaty of Waitangi*, 246–7.
73 Quoted in Asch, *Home and Native Land*, 9.
74 Canada, Task Force to Review Comprehensive Claims Policy, *Living Treaties: Lasting Agreements*.
75 Canada, Minister of Indian Affairs and Northern Development, *In All Fairness*, 12.
76 The policy is set out in another glossy federal pamphlet, *Outstanding Business*.
77 For a review of federal claims policies and an analysis of their inadequacies, see Royal Commission on Aboriginal Peoples, *Report*, vol. 2, Part Two, ch. 5.
78 Ibid., 422.
79 See chapter 4.
80 *Tee-Hit-Ton Indians v. United States*, 348 US 273 (1955) at 279.
81 Ibid.
82 Ibid., 282.
83 187 U.S. 533 (1903).

84 Wunder, '*Retained by the People*, 40–1.
85 Cornell, *The Return of the Native*, 190.
86 See Means, with Wolf, *Where White Men Fear to Tread*, 228–30.
87 Churchill, 'The Earth Is Our Mother,' 167.
88 Means, with Wolf, *Where White Men Fear to Tread*, 293.
89 Wilson, *The Earth Shall Weep*,' 405.
90 *Joint Council of the Passamaquoddy Tribe v. Morton et al.*, 528 F. 2d 370 (1975). For a discussion, see Wunder, *'Retained by the People,'* 167–9.
91 See Wilmer, *The Indigenous Voice in World Politics*, 136.
92 Hall, *The American Empire and the Fourth World*, xxv.
93 See Kleivan, 'The Arctic Peoples' Conference in Copenhagen, November 22–25, 1973,' 227–36; Jull, 'Them Eskimo Mob.'
94 For an account, see Sanders, *The Formation of the World Council of Indigenous Peoples*, IWGIA Document no. 29.
95 Manuel and Posluns, *The Fourth World*, 236.
96 Ibid., 6–7.
97 Ibid., 245.
98 Ibid., 236–7.
99 Russell, 'The Global Dimensions of Aboriginal Politics,' 105.
100 Anaya, *Indigenous Peoples in International Law*, 46.
101 Ibid., 51.
102 Quoted in Nettheim, *Victims of the Law*, 134.
103 Nettheim, *Victims of the Law*, 134–5.
104 Ibid., 4.
105 For a brief account, see Harris, *It's Coming Yet*.
106 *Coe v. The Commonwealth of Australia and the United Kingdom* (1979), 53 A.L.J.R. 334.
107 See Russell, 'High Courts and the Rights of Aboriginal Peoples,' 247–76.
108 See *Campbell v. British Columbia* (2000), 189 D.L.R. (4th) 333.
109 *Coe v. Commonwealth of Australia*, 408 412.
110 Ibid., 412.
111 See essays on this movement written by Coombs in his *Aboriginal Autonomy*, chs. 2 and 14.
112 Rowley, *Recovery*, 73.
113 Horton, ed. , *The Encyclopaedia of Aboriginal Australia*, 1299.
114 Nettheim, *Victims of the Law*, 9.
115 *Aboriginal and Torres Strait Islander (Queensland Reserves and Communities) Self-Management Act, 1978*.
116 Nettheim, *Victims of the Law*, 11–12.
117 Quoted in Coper, *Encounters with the Australian Constitution*, 28.

118 Brennan, *Land Rights Queensland Style*, 1.
119 *Koowarta v. Bjelke-Petersen* (1982), 153 C.L.R. 168.
120 Rowse, *Obliged to Be Difficult*, 174.
121 Ibid., 176.
122 Wright, *We Call for a Treaty*, 116–17.
123 Horton, *The Encyclopaedia of Aboriginal Australia*, 643.
124 Rowse, *Obliged to Be Difficult*, 179.
125 See Tatz, 'Aborigines and the Day of Atonement,' 291–306.
126 See chapter 1.
127 See chapter 3.
128 Loos and Mabo, *Edward Koiki Mabo*, xxiv.
129 For a chronological list of all these activities and references to papers concerning them, see *Guide to the Papers of Edward Koiki Mabo*.
130 In replying to a challenge to his eligibility to run for the Murray Island Community Council, Mabo said that, since 1977, he had returned to the island 'two or three time a year.' Mabo Papers, Series 11, letter of 22 February 1991.
131 Sykes, 'After Eddie,' 72.
132 Keon-Cohen, 'The *Mabo* Litigation,' 8.
133 Mabo, 'Land Rights in the Torres Strait,'147.
134 See Sorenson, 'Law in Norfolk,' 634–43.
135 Mabo, 'Land Rights in the Torres Strait,' 167.
136 Sharp, *No Ordinary Judgment*, 23.
137 Based on the author's interview with Barbara Hocking, Melbourne, 8 May 1998.
138 Hocking, 'Does Aboriginal Law Now Run in Australia?'
139 Ibid., 186.
140 Hocking, 'Is Might Right?' 207–22.
141 Based on interview with Greg McIntyre, Perth, 20 March 1997.
142 Obrei, *Black Australians*, 223.
143 Based on interview with Noel Loos, Townsville, 9 May 1997.

Chapter 7: Ten Long Years of Litigation

1 For this interpretation of the *Mabo* case, I am much indebted to the writings of Jeremy Webber in 'Beyond Regret: Mabo's Implications for Australian Constitutionalism.'
2 For a classic work on this theme, see Otto Kirchheimer, *Political Justice: The Use of Legal Procedures for Political Ends.*
3 See chapter 4.

4 For a discussion of the limited value of Aboriginal victories in settler courts, see Russell, 'My People's Courts as Agents of Indigenous Decolonization.'
5 See chapter 3.
6 See chapter 6.
7 Section 75(iii).
8 Keon-Cohen, 'The *Mabo* Litigation: A Personal and Procedural Account.'
9 The Murray Islands are a cluster of three islands – Mer, Dauar, and Waier. Today, only Mer has permanent residents.
10 Sharp, *No Ordinary Judgment*, 27.
11 Sharp, *No Ordinary Judgment*, 27.
12 A summary of the original statement of claim and relief sought is given by Chief Justice Gibbs in *Mabo and Others v. the State of Queensland and Another* (1986), 64 ALR 1.
13 For a discussion of this concern, see Sharp, *No Ordinary Judgment*, ch. 1.
14 Koen-Cohen, 'The *Mabo* Litigation,' 27.
15 The seminal article is Galanter, 'Why the Haves Come Out Ahead.'
16 Interview with Barbara Hocking, Melbourne, 8 May 1998.
17 Ron Castan died on October 21, 1999. For a tribute to his life and commitment, see Mick Dodson and David Allen, 'Ron Castan, 1940–1999,' *The Age*, October 23, 1999; and Farrant, 'Under grey skies, they honour the lawyer who fought racism.'
18 See chapter 6.
19 Keon-Cohen, 'The *Mabo* Litigation,' 8.
20 Interview with Ron Castan, 28 February 1997.
21 Beckett, *Torres Strait Islanders*, 194.
22 Quoted in Sharp, *No Ordinary Judgment*, 31.
23 Keon-Cohen, 'The *Mabo* Litigation,' 15–16.
24 Ibid., 17.
25 Sharp, *No Ordinary Judgment*, 8.
26 Ibid., 27–9.
27 According to Keon-Cohen, members of the legal team did not make this discovery until their second trip to Mer in March 1983.
28 Keon-Cohen, 'The *Mabo* Litigation,' 16.
29 Ibid., note 189.
30 Sharp, *No Ordinary Judgment*, 36.
31 *Ibid.*, 38.
32 Keon-Cohen, 'The *Mabo* Litigation,' 17.
33 *Mabo and Others v. the State of Queensland and Another* (1986), 64 A.L.R. 1.
34 Ibid., 4.
35 Keon-Cohen, 'The *Mabo* Litigation,' 19.

36 Sharp, *No Ordinary Judgment*, 70.
37 Quoted in Keon-Cohen, 'The *Mabo* Litigation,' 20.
38 Keon-Cohen, 'The *Mabo* Litigation,' 25.
39 The only other witness heard during this period was Robert Pitt, an elderly Islander called by the plaintiffs. Ibid., note 211.
40 Brennan, *Land Rights Queensland Style*, 57–71.
41 Sharp, *No Ordinary Judgment*, 34–5.
42 Keon-Cohen, 'The *Mabo* Litigation,' 22.
43 Ibid.
44 Ibid., 23. Ron Castan and Bryan Keon-Cohen both took their law degrees at the University of Melbourne.
45 *Mabo v. Queensland* (1988), 166 C.L.R., 186, 211.
46 See ibid., 193–5, for a summary of the parties' arguments.
47 For a discussion of the U.S. Supreme Court's denial of Indian property rights, see chapter 6.
48 Solomon, *The Political High Court*, 33.
49 *Gerhardy v. Brown* (1984/85), 159 C.L.R. 70 at 136.
50 See chapter 5.
51 *Mabo v. Queensland* (1988), 216.
52 Ibid., 229.
53 Ibid., 206.
54 Michael Ignatieff, *The Rights Revolution* (Toronto: Anansi, 2000).
55 *Mabo v. Queensland* (1988), 220.
56 On this point, see especially Sharp, *No Ordinary Judgment*, 46–53.
57 *Transcript of Proceedings in the Mabo Case*, vol. 3, 1038.
58 Ibid., 123.
59 Trevor Graham, *Mabo: Life of an Island Man*, Australian Film Board, 1997.
60 *Transcript of Proceedings in the Mabo Case*, vol. 3, 120.
61 Ibid., 130–1.
62 Keon-Cohen, 'The *Mabo* Litigation,' 27.
63 Sharp, *No Ordinary Judgment*, 149.
64 *Mabo v. Queensland: Determination of Facts*, 1: 197.
65 Ibid., 184–5.
66 Ibid., 221.
67 Ibid., 212.
68 Ibid., 157–72.
69 For a discussion of this issue, see Sharp, *No Ordinary Judgment*, 158–64.
70 *Mabo v. Queensland: Determination of Facts*, 227.
71 Ibid., 156.
72 Sharp, *No Ordinary Judgment*, 149

73 Graham, *Mabo.*
74 Ibid.
75 Keon-Cohen, 'The Mabo Litigation,' 24.
76 Jennett, 'Aboriginal Politics,' in *The Australian People*, edited by James Jupp, 124.
77 Tickner, *Taking a Stand*, 21.
78 Bennett, *White Politics and Black Australians*, 33.
79 Jennett, 'Aboriginal Politics,' 124.
80 See chapter 6, and note that the veto can be bypassed by a government proclamation declaring 'the national interest' requires the granting of a concession.
81 Bennett, *White Politics and Black Australians*, 45.
82 Quoted in Brennan, *Sharing the Country*, 72.
83 Maddock, *Your Land Is Our Land*, 114–15.
84 Horton, ed., *Encyclopaedia of Aboriginal Australia*, 657.
85 Goodall, *Invasion to Embassy*, 356–7.
86 Horton, *Encyclopaedia of Aboriginal Australia*, 1113.
87 Tickner, *Taking a Stand*, 23 and 255.
88 Brennan, *Sharing the Country*, 64.
89 Ibid., 74.
90 Ibid., 79.
91 For the spirit of this protest, see Gilbert, *Breath of Life*, 49.
92 For papers on the movement and Mabo's role in it, see Mabo Papers, Series 14, folders 4–6. See also Singer, 'Torres Islanders deadly serious.'
93 Tickner, *Taking a Stand*, 25.
94 Quoted in Brennan, *Sharing the Country*, 83.
95 Brennan, *Sharing the Country*, 84.
96 Ibid., 82.
97 The statement is included as Appendix 5, in Yunupingu, ed., *Our Land Is Our Life.*
98 Australia, Constitutional Commission, *Final Report – Summary*, 55.
99 This was the Advisory Committee on the Distribution of Powers. For an account of the Constitutional Commission, see Russell, 'The Politics of Frustration II,' 64–7.
100 *Aboriginal and Torres Strait Commission Act, 1989.*
101 Horton, *Encyclopaedia of Aboriginal Australia*, 71.
102 *Aboriginal and Torres Strait Island Commission Act 1989*, Section 3.
103 See Fleras and Elliott, *The Nations Within.*
104 Ward and Hayward, 'Tino Rangatiratanga,' 396.
105 Fleras and Elliott, *The Nations Within*, 191.

106 Tickner, *Taking a Stand*, 51.
107 Sullivan, 'All Things to All People,' 122.
108 Coombs, *Aboriginal Autonomy*, 184.
109 Tickner, *Taking a Stand*, 51.
110 Lui, *Planning Our Future*, 3.
111 On this possibility, see Rowse, 'The Political Identity of Regional Council-lors,' 42–69.
112 Sanders, Taylor, and Ross, 'Participation and Representation in ATSIC Elections,' 493–513.
113 Australia, Royal Commission into Aboriginal Deaths in Custody, *National Report*.
114 Tickner, *Taking a Stand*, 54.
115 Bennett, *White Politics and Black Australians*, 64–5.
116 Tickner, *Taking a Stand*, 29.
117 *Council for Aboriginal Reconciliation Act, 1991*, Section 5.
118 Ibid., Section 6(1)(g).
119 Tickner, *Taking a Stand*, 38.
120 See chapter 6.
121 See Sanders, 'The UN Working Group on Indigenous Populations,' 406–33.
122 Ibid., 408.
123 Anaya, *Indigenous Peoples in International Law*, 5.
124 Goehring, *Indigenous Peoples of the World*, 6.
125 Sanders, 'The UN Working Group on Indigenous Populations,' 415.
126 Quoted in Anaya, *Indigenous Peoples in International Law*, 64.
127 For a full discussion of these issues, see Irons, 'Indigenous Peoples and Self-Determination.'
128 A 'plain language' version of the UN Draft Declaration on the Rights of Indigenous Peoples is available from the Aboriginal and Torres Strait Islander Commission, Canberra.
129 See chapter 5.
130 The Convention is included in the appendix section of Anaya, *Indigenous Peoples in International Law*, 193–204. The disclaimer that use of the word 'peoples' has any implications in international law is in Article 1(3).
131 Anaya, *Indigenous Peoples in International Law*, 50.
132 This informal forum at Geneva should not be confused with the New York–based Permanent Forum on Indigenous Issues established by UNESCO in 2002.
133 Brennan, *Sharing the Country*, 118.
134 Ibid., 119.

135 See Anaya, *Indigenous Peoples in International Law*, 49–58.
136 Dodson, 'Linking International Standards with Contemporary Concerns of Aboriginal and Torres Strait Islander Peoples,' 22.
137 For a discussion of the use of the Optional Protocol by Indigenous peoples, see Australia, Aboriginal and Torres Strait Islander Social Justice Commission, *First Report*, 91–100.
138 For an account of this development, see Mulgan, *Maori, Pakeha and Democracy*.
139 See chapter 6.
140 Durie, *Te Mana, Te Kawanatanga*, 186. In 1998, six of the tribunal members were Maori and nine were Pakeha.
141 Oliver, *Claims to the Waitangi Tribunal*, 15.
142 For a penetrating analysis of the tribunal's work before and after 1985, see Sharp, *Justice and the Maori*, Part Two.
143 Durie, *Te Mana, Te Kawanatanga*, 185–6.
144 See Fleras and Elliott, *The Nations Within*, 190–1.
145 *New Zealand Maori Council v. Attorney General*, [1987] 1 N.Z.L.R. 641.
146 *State-Owned Enterprises Act 1986* (NZ), No. 124 of 1986, s. 9.
147 Durie, *Te Mana, Te Kawanatanga*, 671.
148 Ibid., 664.
149 Ibid., 668.
150 See chapter 5.
151 Sharp, *Justice and the Maori*, 274.
152 Geoffrey Palmer, *New Zealand's Constitution in Crisis: Reforming our Political System* (Dunedin, 1992), 92–3.
153 For an account, see Durie, *Te Mana, Te Kawanatanga*, ch. 6.
154 Wilkinson, *American Indians, Time, and the Law*, 25.
155 Ibid., 2.
156 For an account, see Russell, *Constitutional Odyssey*, 2nd ed.
157 The *Canada Act* (UK), 1982, c. 11, gave legal effect to this change. The substantive changes are set out in *The Constitution Act, 1982*, which is Schedule B of the *Canada Act*.
158 *Constitution Act, 1982*, Section 35 (1). Section 35(2) stated that 'aboriginal peoples of Canada' includes the Indian, Inuit and Métis peoples of Canada.
159 *Constitution Act, 1982*, Section 25.
160 Ibid., Section 35.1.
161 *The Australian Constitution*, Section 51 (xxvi.).
162 For an account, see Sanders, 'The Indian Lobby,' 301–32.
163 For an account of the conferences, see Hawkes, *Aboriginal Peoples and Constitutional Reform*.

164 For a collection of Aboriginal views on self-government, see Little Bear, Boldt, and Long, eds., *Pathways to Self-Determination.*

165 Unlike Indians and Métis, Canadian Inuit refer to their societies as peoples rather than nations.

166 Canada, Parliament, *Report of the Special Parliamentary Committee on Indian Self-Government.*

167 *Constitutional Amendment Proclamation, 1983.*

168 See above, chapters 3 and 6.

169 See above, chapter 6.

170 For a summary of this agreement, see Royal Commission on Aboriginal Peoples, *Report,* vol. 2, Part Two, 723–4.

171 See Parker, *Native American Estate.*

172 Churchill, 'The Earth is Our Mother,' 147.

173 For an overview of some leading examples, see ibid.

174 See, Russell, 'My People's Courts as Agents of Indigenous Decolonization?' 50–61.

175 *Brendale v. Confederated Tribes and Bands of Yakima Indian Nation,* 492 U.S. 492 (1989) 408.

176 *Employment Division, Dept. of Human Resources of Oregon et al. v. Alfred L. Smith et al.* (1990).

177 Frickey, 'Congressional Intent, Practical Reasoning, and the Dynamic Nature of Federal Indian Law,' 1205.

178 For an account, see York and Pindera, *People of the Pines.*

179 *Sparrow v. The Queen,* [1990] 1 S.C.R. 1075 at 1106.

180 Reynolds, *The Law of the Land.*

181 Graham, *Mabo.*

182 Nonetheless, Mabo was listed as the first plaintiff in the case and was represented by Greg McIntyre, who adopted the submissions made on behalf of David Passi and James Rice.

183 Keon-Cohen, 'The Mabo Litigation,' 26.

184 Mabo Papers, Series 1, folder 8.

185 Loos and Mabo, *Edward Koiki Mabo,* 171.

186 This part of the diary is quoted ibid., 175.

187 Graham, *Mabo.*

Chapter 8: The High Court's Decision

1 *Mabo and Others v. the State of Queensland (No. 2)* (1992), 175 C.L.R. 1 at 70.

2 Ibid., 31.

3 Bartlett, 'Mabo: Another Triumph for the Common Law.'

4 See chapter 4.

5 *Johnson v. McIntosh*, 21 U.S. (8 Wheat) 543 (1823) at 591–2.

6 *Mabo (No. 2)* at 63.

7 Hunter, 'Native Title: Acts of State and the Rule of Law.'

8 I first developed this theme in Russell, 'High Courts and the Rights of Aboriginal Peoples.'

9 See Nettheim, 'The Consent of the Natives.'

10 *Mabo (No. 2)* at 43.

11 Ibid., 145.

12 The phrase is from Llewellyn, *The Common Law Tradition.*

13 See chapter 2, and Patapan, *Judging Democracy.*

14 *Mabo (No. 2)* at 45.

15 Ibid., 48–9.

16 Ibid., 51.

17 *In re Southern Rhodesia*, [1919] A.C. 211 at 233.

18 *Amodu Tijani v. Secretary Southern Nigeria*, [1921] A.C. 399 at 407.

19 *Adeyinka Oyekan v. Musendiku Adele*, [1957] All E.R. 785 at 788.

20 McNeil, *Common Law Aboriginal Title.* See especially chapter 4.

21 *Mabo (No. 2)* at 127.

22 Ibid., 144.

23 Ibid., 55.

24 Ibid., 131. Note how Dawson seems to get his centuries mixed up when he downplays Lord Denning's 1957 'guiding principle dictum as expressing "sentiments which had emerged by the mid-nineteenth century,"' 126–7.

25 *Mabo (No. 2)* at 29.

26 Ibid., 57.

27 *Guerin v. the Queen*, [1984] 2 S.C.R. 335.

28 See chapter 2.

29 *Mabo (No. 2)* at 83.

30 See chapter 4.

31 [1847] 1 Legge 312.

32 (1913), 16 C.L.R. 404.

33 (1959), 102 C.L.R. 54.

34 [1919] A.C. 211 at 233–4.

35 (1975), 1 C.J.R.

36 *Mabo (No. 2)* at 42.

37 Pearson, '204 Years of Invisible Title.'

38 *Mabo (No. 2)* at 38.

39 Bayne, 'Mabo and the Basis of Acquisition of the Colonies of Australia.'

40 *Mabo (No. 2)* at 52.

41 Bartlett, *The Mabo Decision*, xx.
42 *Ibid.*, 64.
43 Ibid., 69.
44 Ibid., 68–9.
45 Ibid., 69.
46 Ibid., 73.
47 Ibid., 15.
48 See chapter 7.
49 *Mabo (No. 2)* at 64.
50 McNeil, 'Racial Discrimination and Unilateral Extinguishment of Native Title.'
51 Ibid., 187.
52 *Mabo (No. 2)* at 89.
53 Ibid., 90.
54 Ibid., 92. The New Zealand decision was rendered in *Reg v. Symonds*, [1847] N.Z.P.C.C. 387.
55 *Mabo (No. 2)* at 120.
56 Ibid., 93.
57 Ibid., 109.
58 Ibid., 111.
59 Ibid.
60 Ibid., 119.
61 Ibid., 117.
62 Ibid., 187.
63 Ibid., 195.
64 Ibid., 194.
65 Ibid., 216. Note that Toohey did not rule on effect of the missionaries' or the sardine factory leases.
66 For a full account and analysis of the fiduciary relationship, see Rotman, *Parallel Paths*.
67 *Guerin v. The Queen*, [1984] 2 S.C.R. 335.
68 Brennan thought that a fiduciary duty might arise in relation to a native group that had surrendered its native title on the expectation that the Crown would grant members another kind of tenure. *Mabo (No. 2)*, at 60.
69 Ibid., 194.
70 Ibid., 204.
71 Ibid., 196.
72 Strelein, 'Conceptualizing Native Title,' 96.
73 *Mabo (No. 2)* at 59.

74 Ibid., 61.
75 Ibid., 110.
76 Pearson, 'Concept of Native Title at Common Law.'
77 *Mabo (No. 2)* at 191.
78 Ibid., 62.
79 Ibid., 61.
80 Ibid., 70.
81 Ibid., 110.
82 For a critical examination of the acceptance of this idea by common law judges, see McNeil, *Common Law Aboriginal Title*, 221–35.
83 See chapter 4.
84 *Mabo (No. 2)* at 110.
85 Ibid., 61.
86 Ibid., 192.
87 Ibid., 59.
88 Ibid., 60.
89 Ibid., 110.
90 Ibid., 190.
91 *Calder v. British Columbia*, [1973] S.C.R. 313 at 402.
92 For a critical examination of common law courts' treatment of this issue, see McNeil, 'The Onus of Proof of Aboriginal Title,' 775–803.
93 For a penetrating analysis of the legal and political implications of the High Court's cleansing operation, see Patapan, *Judging Democracy*, ch. 5.
94 See chapter 4.
95 McNeil, *Common Law Aboriginal Title*, 189.
96 Spiller, Finn, and Boast, *A New Zealand Legal History*, 172–3.
97 *Te Weehi v. Regional Fisheries Officer*, [1986] 1 N.Z.L.R. 680.
98 For an analysis, see McHugh, 'From Sovereignty Talk to Settlement Time.'
99 For details, see Harris, *Making Native Space*, especially chapters 4–8.
100 For a discussion of the political consequences of the *Calder* case, see Tennant, *Aboriginal Peoples and Politics*, ch. 16.
101 *Sparrow v. The Queen*, [1990] 1 S.C.R. 1075.
102 Dawson's dissenting judgment notes that government's fiduciary obligation to Indigenous peoples in Canada is reflected in giving constitutional status to their rights and gives that as a reason for not recognizing the fiduciary obligation in Australia. *Mabo (No. 2)* at 166.
103 *Mabo (No. 2)* at 64.
104 *Sparrow v. The Queen*.
105 See, Russell, *Constitutional Odyssey*, ch. 11.

106 Part IV of the accord dealt with Aboriginal peoples. The words quoted were in Section 41, the first Section of Part IV. Russell, *Constitutional Odyssey*, Appendix, 255.
107 See chapter 4.
108 (1835) 9 Peters 711.
109 Ibid., 746.
110 See McNeil, *Common Law Aboriginal Title*, 249 note 21.
111 Ibid.
112 See chapter 6.
113 McNeil, *Common Law Aboriginal Title*, 267.

Chapter 9: Consequences I: Legislating Native Title

1 Bogart, *Consequences*.
2 Schattsneider, *The Semi-Sovereign People*.
3 Hartley and McKee, *The Indigenous Public Sphere*, 3.
4 Trevor Graham, *Mabo: Life of an Island Man*, Australian Film Board, 1997.
5 Quoted in Tickner, *Taking a Stand*, 90.
6 See, for example, Lumb, 'The Mabo Case'; Cooray, 'The High Court in Mabo.'
7 See chapter 8.
8 See chapter 3.
9 Quoted in Attwood, ed., *In the Age of Mabo*, 104–5.
10 Attwood, 'Mabo, Australia and the End of History,' 100.
11 Griffiths, *Aboriginal Affairs*, 248.
12 Goot, 'Polls as Science, Polls as Spin,' 135.
13 Ibid., 136.
14 Don Watson, *Recollections of a Bleeding Heart: A Portrait of Paul Keating, PM* (Sydney: Knopf, 2002), 381.
15 *House of Representatives Debates*, June 4, 1992, 3586.
16 Tickner, *Taking a Stand*, 93.
17 Ibid., 90.
18 Quoted in Brennan, *One Land, One Nation*, 39.
19 Tickner, *Taking a Stand*, 91.
20 Farley, 'The Mabo Spiral,' 167.
21 Tickner, *Taking a Stand*, 97.
22 Goot, 'Polls as Science, Polls as Spin,' 136.
23 Tickner, *Taking a Stand*, 97.
24 Ibid., 92.

25 'Speech by the Honorable Prime Minister, P.J. Keating MP, Australian Launch of the International Year for the World's Indigenous Peoples,' 5.
26 Ibid.
27 Barker and Ormonde, 'Keating to put Mabo into law.'
28 Ibid.
29 Walker, 'Eddie Mabo – Australian of the Year.'
30 Barker and Ormonde, 'Keating to put Mabo into law.'
31 Quoted in Tickner, *Taking a Stand*, 104.
32 Russell, *Constitutional Odyssey*, 75.
33 Easterbrook, 'Keating move boosts profile of Aborigines.'
34 Tickner, *Taking a Stand*, 107.
35 Ibid., 109.
36 Ibid., 112–14.
37 Brennan, *One Land, One Nation*, 43.
38 'The Aboriginal Peace Plan,' 8 (document).
39 Quoted in Tickner, *Taking a Stand*, 114.
40 Ibid., 114–15.
41 Rowse, 'How We Got a Native Title Act,' 112.
42 Nason, 'Perron ignores Aboriginal protests on anti-Mabo Bill.'
43 Ibid., 118–22.
44 Alcorn and Chamberlin, 'Blacks accuse PM of betrayal.'
45 Quoted in Tickner, *Taking a Stand*, 120.
46 Nettheim, 'McArthur River and the Mabo Response,'16.
47 Quoted in Tickner, *Taking a Stand*, 110.
48 See Russell, 'The Politics of Frustration II,' 72–3.
49 Brown, *Market Rules*, 182.
50 Australia, Commonwealth Government, '*Mabo*: The High Court Decision on Native Title, Discussion Paper, June 1993, Extracts,' 8–10.
51 Brennan, *One Land, One Nation*, 49.
52 Quoted in Rowse, 'How We Got a Native Title Act,' 114.
53 Ibid., 115.
54 Quoted in Tickner, *Taking a Stand*, 129.
55 Gill, 'Mabo: Mining on hold.'
56 Milne, 'Community divided on native title but most oppose compensation.'
57 Marks and McDonald, 'The Mabo Debate and Public Opinion on Native Title' (unpublished paper).
58 Watson, *Recollections of a Bleeding Heart*, 382.
59 Tickner, *Taking a Stand*, 138.
60 Brennan, *One Land, One Nation*, 58.
61 Quoted in Tickner, *Taking a Stand*, 123.

62 Ibid., 143.
63 Rowse, 'How We Got a Native Title Act,' 123.
64 These are the words used in the account of the Eva Valley Meeting and the introduction to the Eva Valley Statement in *Aboriginal Law Bulletin* 3 (August 1993): 2.
65 Willox, 'Relations sour as PM rejects black critics.'
66 Quoted in Rowse, 'How We Got a Native Title Act,' 121.
67 The paper is set out in Tickner, *Taking a Stand*, 169–71.
68 Gill, 'States win title fight over Mabo.'
69 Brennan, *One Land, One Nation*, 61–3.
70 Quoted in Tickner, *Taking a Stand*, 188.
71 Chamberlin, 'The day that changed history.'
72 Frank Brennan cites nine demands they gave up. See his *One Land, One Nation*, 67.
73 Ibid.
74 Rowse, 'How We Got a Native Title Act,' 127.
75 Brennan, *One Land, One Nation*, 77.
76 Tickner, *Taking a Stand*, 202.
77 Ibid., 217–18.
78 Ibid., 219.
79 Ibid., 220.
80 Brennan, *One Land, One Nation*, 79.
81 Taylor, 'Mabo win for PM.'
82 Australia, Aboriginal and Torres Strait Islander Commission, *The Native Title Act 1993*.
83 *NTA*, s. 12.
84 Ibid., s. 19.
85 Ibid., ss. 228–32.
86 See, Stephenson, 'Pastoral Leases and Reservations Clauses.'
87 NTA, ss. 17–18.
88 See Stephenson, 'Compensation and Valuation of Native Title.'
89 *NTA*, s. 201.
90 Commonwealth of Australia, *Aboriginal and Torres Strait Islander Land Fund: An act of good faith.*
91 Tickner, *Taking a Stand*, ch. 11.
92 'Commentary' in *Native Title Act: legislation with commentary by the Attorney-General's Legal Practice*, C17.
93 *NTA*, s. 26.
94 *NTA*, s. 27.
95 *NTA*, s. 111.

96 *NTA*, s. 42(1)(2).

97 *NTA*, s. 32.

98 As of 2000, only South Australia's Environment Resources and Development Court and Supreme Court were so recognized. See, Bartlett, *Native Title in Australia*, 139.

99 *NTA*, s. 66 (2).

100 *NTA*, s. 110.

101 'Landmark native title decision to pay $1m,' *Brisbane Courier-Mail*, 10 October 1996.

102 Altman and Smith, 'Funding Aboriginal and Torres Strait Islander Representative Bodies under the *Native Title Act 1993*.'

103 *NTA*, s. 202. Note that the act does not require people claiming native title to use a Representative Body. But Representative Bodies are the principal means of obtaining funds and it is the minister who decides whether they are representative.

104 Dodson, 'Power and Cultural Difference in Native Title Mediation,' 9.

105 Edmunds, 'Conflict in Native Title Claims.'

106 *Brandy v. Human Rights and Equal Opportunity Commission* (1995), 183 C.L.R. 245.

107 Bartlett, *Native Title in Australia*, 140.

108 *NTA*, s. 21(4).

109 *NTA*, Preamble, 3.

110 French, 'Local and Regional Agreements.'

111 *1995/96 Annual Report* (Perth: Native Title Tribunal), 12.

112 In 1994, New South Wales and Queensland passed native title legislation designating their own arbital bodies, but their legislation was not put into operation and South Australia's tribunals remain the only recognized equivalent bodies. See, Neatte, 'Alternative State and Territorial Schemes,' 47.

113 See Brennan, *One Land, One Nation*, 105–9.

114 *Western Australia v. Commonwealth of Australia* (1995), 183 C.L.R. 373.

115 Ibid., 484–8.

116 *1995/1996 Annual Report*, 1.

117 For a full account, see Loos and Mabo, *Edward Koiki Mabo*, 177–80.

118 Graham, *Mabo: Life of an Island Man* (film).

119 Ibid.

120 Wells and Martin, 'Racist Outrage.'

121 Graham, *Mabo: Life of an Island Man*.

122 Loos and Mabo, *Edward Koiki Mabo*, 183.

123 Graham, *Mabo: Life of an Island Man*.

Chapter 10: Consequences II: *Wik* and a Country Deeply Divided

1 Quoted in Larkin, 'Libs Landslide.'
2 Boreham and Wilcox, 'Howard softens line on Mabo.'
3 See Bartlett, 'Native Title in Australia,' 423.
4 *Wik Peoples v. Queensland* (1996), 187 C.L.R. 1.
5 See chapter 4.
6 Holmes, 'Land Tenure in the Australian Pastoral Zone,' table 1, 44.
7 See Woodley, 'Mabo of the mainland.'
8 Tickner, *Taking a Stand*, 201.
9 *Encyclopaedia of Aboriginal Australia*, 1179. The encyclopaedia suggests that the Wik 'are better considered as a nation than a tribe.'
10 For a full account, see Sutton, '*Wik*' (thesis).
11 Kauffman, *Wik, Mining and Aborigines*, 38.
12 Brennan, *Land Rights Queensland Style*, 8.
13 See chapter 6.
14 Hunter, 'The Wik Decision,' 11.
15 Bottoms, 'Thayorre People v. Queensland,' 19.
16 See Justice Kirby's judgment in *Wik Peoples v. Queensland* at 203–5.
17 Ibid., 205.
18 Kauffman, *Wik, Mining and Aborigines*, 132–5.
19 *Re Waanyi People's Native Title Application* (1995), 129 ALR 118 at 166.
20 *North Ganalanja Aboriginal Corporation v. Queensland* (1995), 61 FCR 1.
21 *Wik Peoples v. Queensland* (1996), 134 ALR 637.
22 *North Ganalanja Aboriginal Corporation v. Queensland* (1996), 185 CLR 595.
23 For a succinct analysis of the decision in *Wik*, see Hiley, ed., *The Wik Case*, 1–5.
24 *Wik Peoples v. Queensland* (1996), 187 CLR 75.
25 Ibid., 217.
26 Ibid.
27 Ibid., 20.
28 Ibid., 146.
29 See, for example, Dowling, 'Mining dismay at Wik decision.'
30 Lehmann, 'Borbidge promises Wik cash.'
31 Wilson, 'Pasminco makes deal of the century.'
32 Quoted in Bennett, *White Politics and Black Australians*, 54.
33 Johnstone, 'Heart of the matter.'
34 See Patapan, *Judging Democracy*, 141.
35 Ibid., note 153.
36 For an account of the Hanson phenomenon, see Leach, Stokes, and Ward, eds., *The Rise and Fall of One Nation*.

37 Quoted in Jull, 'Hansonism and Aborigines and Torres Strait Islanders,' 208.
38 Short, 'Leaders unite for tolerance.'
39 Leach, Stokes, and Ward, eds., *The Rise and Fall of One Nation*, 12.
40 The Farmers of Australia, 'Dear John.'
41 Short, 'The PM locks in tough Wik plan.'
42 My account of the plan is based on 'Amended Wik 10 Point Plan,' Prime Minister's news release of May 8, 1997. For a detailed analysis of the plan, see Bartlett, *Native Title in Australia*, ch. 5.
43 For an account of the conference, see Woodford and Millett, 'Title Fight.'
44 Short and Windsor, 'Minds fail to meet on Wik.'
45 For a full statement of NWIG's position, see National Indigenous Working Group on Native Title, *Coexistence*.
46 Campbell, 'PM hits blacks' sway on Wik.'
47 'Rebuff Australia on rights bid, EU told,' *The West Australian*, March 26, 1997.
48 The author spoke at this conference on Canada's experience with and its government's participation in negotiated agreements to regulate coexistence on Indigenous lands. The other speakers were Father Frank Brennan and Janet Hunt, executive director of the Australian Council for Overseas Aid.
49 McPhedran, 'Diplomats voice concern over race debate, Wik response.'
50 'Message from Patrick Dodson,' *Program of Australian Reconciliation Council*, Melbourne Convention and Exhibition Centre, May 26–28, 1997, 1.
51 Australia, University of Canberra, 'Aboriginal Nations and the Australian Constitution Conference,' 3.
52 Australia, Human Rights and Equal Opportunity Commission, *Bringing Them Home*.
53 Wilson, 'Preface,' xv.
54 John Howard, 'I am an optimist, but this optimism cannot be blind' (edited text of Mr. Howard's speech to the Reconciliation Convention), *The Australian*, May 27, 1997, 4.
55 Quoted in Forbes, 'Coming Together.'
56 Forbes, 'Council in quest of moral solution.'
57 Montgomery, 'Power of one holds nation in the balance.'
58 Short, 'Harradine sets Senate on path for Wik conflict.'
59 Gratton, 'Election '98.'
60 Kingston, 'Beazley.'
61 Meryment, Aldred, and Collie, 'All roads lead to Canberra for Wik showdown.'
62 *Kartinyeri v. Commonwealth* (1998), 152 ALR 540.

63 Ibid., 544.

64 Kingston, 'Ban on Aborigines "valid".' See also the article by David Bennett, Commonwealth solicitor general, 'Native Title and the Constitution.'

65 McCabe, 'Judge quits High Court bridge case.'

66 Kingston, 'Brian takes shelter as Aborigines nearly miss the bus.'

67 Windsor, 'Harradine holds firm in Senate's Wik endgame.'

68 Tingle and Kingston, 'Howard's pledge to voters.'

69 For an analysis of the Queensland election, see Reynolds, 'One Nation's Electoral Support.'

70 McGregor and Emerson, 'Hanson ruins PM's poll plan.'

71 Kingston, Woodward, and Seccombe, 'Wik deal scuttles race poll.'

72 *Native Title Act 1993* (consolidated to include the *Native Title Amendment Act 1998*), Section 43. For a full account, see Neatte, 'Alternative State and Territory Schemes.'

73 'ATSIC on the Howard/Harradine compromise,' in *Native Title Newsletter*, AIATSIS, No. 4/98, 12.

74 Kingston, 'Native Title.'

Chapter 11: International Dimensions and Reconciliation

1 Draft Declaration as Agreed upon by the Members of the Working Group at Its Eleventh Session, UNESCO, E/CNR/Sub2/1994/Add 1, 20 April 1994.

2 Anaya, *Indigenous Peoples in International Law*, 51.

3 See Russell, 'Canada – A Pioneer in the Management of Constitutional Politics in a Multi-national Society.'

4 Flanagan, *First Nations? Second Thoughts?*

5 Cairns, *Citzens Plus*.

6 For commentaries on *Indian Act* reform, see papers presented at the Queen's University Conference on Reconfiguring Aboriginal-State Relations, Nov. 1–2, 2002, http://qsilver.queensu.ca/iigr/conferences/state/conference_agenda.html.

7 Fleras and Spoonley, *Recalling Aotearoa*, 128–9.

8 Deloria Jr and Lytle, *The Nations Within*, 231.

9 Ekstedt, 'International Perspectives on Aboriginal Self-Government,' 52.

10 See Graham, *Trick or Treaty?*

11 Royal Commission on Aboriginal Peoples (RCAP), *Report*, 2, part two: 834.

12 Cornell, 'Nation-Building and the Treaty Process,' 7.

13 For an account, see York and Pindera, *Peoples of the Pines*.

14 RCAP, *Report*.

15 See Russell, 'The Research Program of the Royal Commission on Aboriginal Peoples.'
16 For a short summary, see RCAP, *People to People, Nation to Nation.*
17 Ibid., 18–20.
18 Canada, Minister of Indian Affairs and Northern Development, *Gathering Strength – Canada's Aboriginal Action Plan.* The words quoted are from the one-page 'Statement of Reconciliation' distributed with this publication.
19 Ibid., 10.
20 For the commission's fiscal plan, see *Report,* 5: chs. 2 and 3.
21 For an account that focuses on practical problems in implementing self-government arrangements, see Hylton, ed., *Aboriginal Self-Government in Canada.*
22 For a full account, see Dahl, Hicks, and Jull, eds., *Nunavut.*
23 See especially chapters 3 and 8.
24 See Tennant, *Aboriginal Peoples and Politics.*
25 See McKee, *Treaty Talks in British Columbia.*
26 *Nisga'a Final Agreement.* For an account of the negotiation and ratification of the Nisga'a treaty by the chief federal negotiator, see Molloy, *The World Is Our Witness.*
27 Nisga'a governmental authority is exercise through both a central (Lisims) government and village governments. The agreement (ch. 11, s. 20) provides that residents who are not Nisga'a may participate in a Nisga'a public institution whose activities significantly affect them.
28 *Nisga'a Final Agreement,* ch. 2, s. 22.
29 Molloy, *The World Is Our Witness,* 154.
30 *Campbell et al. v. British Columbia* (1997), 153 DLR (4th), 193.
31 See Kajlich, 'The British Columbia Treaty Referendum.'
32 See Borrows, 'The Trickster'
33 *R. v. Van der Peet,* [1996]) 2 S.C.R. 507; *R. v. Gladstone,* [1996] 2 S.C.R. 723; *R. v. Pamajewon,* [1996] 2 S.C.R. 821. For a critical assessment, see Christie, 'Judicial Justification of Recent Developments in Aboriginal Law.'
34 *R. v. Badger,* [1996] 1 S.C.R. 771. For a critical appraisal, see Bell, '*R. v. Badger.*'
35 *Delgamuukw v. British Columbia,* [1997] 3 SCR 1010.
36 Ibid., 252
37 Ibid., 240–1.
38 Ibid., 261.
39 Ibid., 263–4.
40 *R. v. Marshall (No. 1),* [1999] 3 S.C.R. 456.

41 *R. v. Marshall (No. 2)*, [1999] 3 S.C.R. 533.

42 Quoted in Roach, *The Supreme Court on Trial*, 91. For a discussion of the *Marshall* cases, see Issac, *Aboriginal and Treaty Rights in the Maritimes*.

43 *Te Ruanga o Muriwhenua Inc. v. Attornet-General and Others*, High Court, Wellington, CP 553/87, October 1987, Greig J.

44 Ward, *An Unsettled History*, 46.

45 Durie, *Te Mana, Te Kawanatanga*, 154.

46 Ward, *An Unsettled History*, 47. Durie, in *Te Mana, Te Kawanatanga*, states that there were forty-seven signatories representing seventeen different iwi.

47 Durie, *Te Mana, Te Kawanatanga*, 159.

48 Ibid., 161.

49 Ibid., 169.

50 Sharp, 'Blood, Custom, and Consent,' 18.

51 Durie, *Te Mana, Te Kawanatanga*, 166.

52 Ibid.

53 *Treaty Tribes Coalition, Te Runanga o Ngati Porou and Tainui Maori Trust Board v. Urban Maori Authorities, Treaty of Waitangi Fisheries Commission and Ors*, [1997] 1 N.Z.L.R. 513 (PC). On how unsatisfactory it is for such matters to be decided by a non-Indigenous court, see Gover and Baird, 'Identifying the Maori Treaty Partner.'

54 Durie, *Te Mana, Te Kawanatanga*, 169.

55 On the problems of historiography around this issue, see Oliver, 'The Future Behind Us.'

56 Ibid. 185.

57 For a good summary, see Ward, *An Unsettled History*, ch. 3.

58 Fleras and Spooney, *Recalling Aotearoa*, 133.

59 Graham, *Trick or Treaty?* 58–60.

60 Ward, *An Unsettled History*, 67.

61 For an account, see Magallanes, 'Indigenous Political Representation.'

62 Durie, *Te Mana, Te Kawanatanga*, 102.

63 Ibid., 99.

64 For a discussion of the emerging possibility of a shared sovereignty, see McHugh, 'A History of Crown Sovereignty in New Zealand.'

65 For a discussion of various ways of strengthening Aboriginal and Torres Strait Islander participation in Queensland governance, see Struthers, 'Hands on Parliament.'

66 Royal Commission on Electoral Reform and Party Financing, *Reforming Electoral Democracy*, vol. 2.

67 Royal Commission on Aboriginal Peoples, *Report*, 2, Part One: 377–8.

68 Struthers, 'Hands on Parliament.'

69 For an account, see Magallanes, 'Indigenous Political Representation,'
    135–6.
70 See Robbins, 'Self-Determination and Subordination,' 109–12.
71 Utter, *American Indians*, 90.
72 See Trask, *From a Native Daughter.*
73 See Parker, *Native American Estate.*
74 See the Hawaiian Kingdom website, www.hawaiiankingdom.org.
75 Quoted in Di Alto, 'Frame wars' (unpublished paper).
76 Quoted in Pritchard, 'The United Nations and the Making of a Declaration
    on Indigenous Rights,' 8.
77 Quoted in Dodson and Pritchard, 'Recent Developments in Indigenous
    Policy, '6.
78 Pritchard, 'Commission on Human Rights (CHRWG),' 11.
79 International Work Group for Indigenous Affairs, *The Indigenous World,
    2000–2001*, 444.
80 Schürmann-Zeggel, 'UN CERD Committee,' 20.
81 Saunders, 'Native title laws breach UN race rules.'
82 Kingston, 'Discrimination?'
83 Martin, 'Australia faces UN race inquiry over Wik.'
84 Daley, 'UN to vet jailing laws.'
85 Arndt, 'Conventional behaviour.'
86 Associated Press, 'Australia Will Restrict U.N. Access'; and Staff Reporters,
    'Backtrack on rights tragic.'
87 Grattan, 'Howard left in the diplomatic shade.'
88 See Coper, *The Franklin Dam Case.*
89 See chapter 6.
90 Arndt, 'Conventional behaviour.'
91 McGurik, 'Jail deal silences MPs on reforms.'
92 This cooperation was particularly evident in the Games' opening ceremony.
    See, for example, Editorial, 'Truly a night to remember.'
93 Australia, *Report of the Constitutional Convention* (Canberra: Commonwealth
    of Australia, 1998). For an account of the Preamble, see Williams, 'Why
    Australians Kept the Queen.'
94 AAP, 'Draft Preamble to the Constitution.'
95 Australia, Constitutional Centenary Foundation, *1999 Referendum – A New
    Preamble.*
96 Kingston, 'ALP predicts preamble doom.'
97 Williams, 'Why Australians Kept the Queen,' 495.
98 Official letter of invitation from Evelyn Scott, chairperson of the Council for
    Aboriginal Reconciliation.

 99 Grattan, 'Reconciliation Rescue Mission.'
100 Kerr, 'Council plays down Prime Minister's negative stance.'
101 Garran, 'PM backs Herron's hard line.'
102 See *Cubillo and Gunner v. Commonwealth of Australia* (2000), 174 A.L.R. 97.
103 Dodson, 'Lingiari – Until the Chains Are Broken' (lecture).
104 Taylor, 'Indigenous leaders hit by rift.'
105 The account that follows is based on the author's own observations
    and *Corroboree 2000*, a booklet published by the Council for Aboriginal
    .Reconciliation in its *Walking Together* series (No. 29, August 2000).
106 *Corroboree 2000*, 15.
107 Ibid., 16.
108 Ibid., 20–1.
109 O'Rourke, '100,000 for historic walk.'
110 *Corroboree 2000*, 6–7.
111 This perspective is more fully developed in Russell, 'Corroboree 2000 – A
    Nation Defining Event.'
112 Australia, Council on Aboriginal Reconciliation, *Annual Report 2000*,
    chapter 10, recommendation 5.
113 Ravinda Noel John de Costa, 'New Relationships, Old Certainties' (thesis).
114 Behrendt, *Achieving Social Justice*, 8.

Chapter 12: The Limits of Judicial Power

 1 The account that follows is based on data presented in Pollack, 'Indigenous
   land in Australia,' table 6.
 2 Ibid., 1.
 3 Ibid., table 1.
 4 Ibid., 30.
 5 See chapter 6.
 6 For details of these state land right schemes, see Pollack, 'Indigenous Land
   in Australia,' 20–8.
 7 See chapter 7.
 8 Toussaint, 'Western Australia,' 262.
 9 See chapter 9.
10 Pollack, 'Indigenous Land in Australia,' 13.
11 Ibid., 14–15.
12 See chapter 9.
13 See Bartlett, 'Only an Interim Regime.'
14 *Native Title Act, 1993* (Consolidated to include the *Native Title Amendment
   Act, 1998*), Section 24, subdivisions B to E.

15 Lane, 'A Quick Guide to ILUAs,' 331.
16 Pollack, 'Indigenous Land in Australia,' Table 7.
17 Kee, 'Indigenous Land Use Agreements,' 348.
18 See O'Faircheallaigh, 'Negotiating Major Project Agreements.'
19 Irving, 'The Kimberley Region Native Title and Heritage Protection Memorandum of Understanding and the Native Title and Heritage Protection Model Agreement.'
20 See, for instance, the discussion of the Mt Todd Agreement and the McArthur River Agreement in O'Faircheallaigh, 'Mineral Development Agreements Negotiated by Aboriginal Communities in the 1990s,' 5–10.
21 Edmunds, 'Key Issues for the Development of Regional Agreements.'
22 Ibid., 7.
23 Sullivan, 'The Kimberley,' 54.
24 Altman, 'Economic Development of the Indigenous Economy and the Potential Leverage of Native Title,' 114.
25 Agius et al., 'Negotiating Comprehensive Settlement of Native Title Issues.'
26 For an account, see Simons, *The Meeting of the Waters.*
27 *Supra.*, note 331, 10.
28 Australia, House of Representatives Standing Committee on Aboriginal and Torres Strait Islander Affairs, *Torres Strait Islanders.*
29 For an account of recent political difficulties among Islander politicians, see Prior, 'Dire Straits.'
30 *Yanner v. Eaton*, [1999] H.C.A. 53.
31 *Commonwealth of Australia v. Yarmir*, [2001] H.C.A. 56.
32 See Sharp, *Saltwater People.*
33 See chapter 8.
34 *Western Australia v. Ward* (2002), 191 ALR 1.
35 See chapter 11.
36 Ibid.
37 Strelein, '*Western Australia v. Ward on Behalf of Miriuwung Gajerrong*,' 4.
38 *Western Australia v. Ward*, 561.
39 Ibid.
40 *Members of the Yorta Yorta Aboriginal Community v. The State of Victoria* (1998), FCA 1606.
41 *Members of the Yorta Yorta Aboriginal Community v. Victoria*, [2002] H.C.A. 58 at 44.
42 Ibid., 55.
43 Ibid., 75.
44 Ibid., 130.
45 Russell, 'My People's Courts as Agents of Indigenous Decolonization?' 60–1.

Bibliography

Unpublished Sources

De Costa, Ravinda Noel John. '*Australia's Reconciliation and Treaty-Making in British Columbia.*' PhD thesis, Swinburne University of Technology, Melbourne, 2002.

Di Alto, Stephen. 'Frame Wars: The case of "Reconciliation" with Native Hawaiians and Native Americans.' Paper delivered at the annual meeting of the American Political Science Association, Boston, August 29–September 1, 2002.

Dodson, Patrick. 'Langiari – Until the Chains Are Broken.' Annual Vincent Lingiari Memorial Lecture, Darwin, 27 August 1999.

Kymlicka, Will. 'Human Rights and Ethno-cultural Justice.' Sixth J.C. Rees Memorial Lecture. Cardiff: Department of Political Theory and Government, University of Wales.

Mabo Papers. Australian National Library, Canberra.

Marks, Gary N., and Paula McDonald. 'The Mabo Debate and Public Opinion on Native Title.' Paper presented at Research School of Social Sciences, Australian National University, 17 June 1994.

Patapan, Haig. 'The Liberal Politics of Rights: Changing Constitutionalism and the Bill of Rights Debate in Australia and Canada.' PhD thesis, University of Toronto, 1997.

Shnukal, Anna. 'Locals, Immigrants and Outsiders: Refiguring Identity in the Torres Strait.' Paper presented to Fulbright Symposium on Indigenous Cultures in an Interconnected World, Darwin, July 1997.

Strelein, Lisa Mary. 'Indigenous Self-Determination Claims and the Common Law in Australia.' PhD thesis, Australia National University, 1998.

Sutton, Peter J. 'Wik: Aboriginal Society, Territory and Language at Cape Keerweer, Cape York Peninsula.' PhD thesis, University of Queensland, 1978.

Books and Journals

Agius, Parry, et al. 'Negotiating Comprehensive Settlement of Native Title Issues: Building a New Scale of Justice in South Australia.' *Native Title Research Unit: Issues Paper No. 20.* Canberra: Australian Institute of Aboriginal and Torres Strait Islanders Studies, December 2002.

Altman, Jon. 'Economic Development of the Indigenous Economy and the Potential Leverage of Native Title.' In *Native Title in the New Millennium,* edited by Bryan Keon-Cohen, 105–15.

Altman, Jon, and Dianne Smith. 'Funding Aboriginal and Torres Strait Islander Representative Bodies under the *Native Title Act 1993.*' *Native Title Research Unit: Issues Paper No. 8.* Canberra: Australian Institute of Aboriginal and Torres Strait Islanders Studies, April 1995.

Alston, Philip. 'Individual Complaints: Historical Perspectives and the International Convention on Economic, Social and Cultural Rights.' In *Indigenous Peoples, the United Nations and Human Rights,* edited by Sarah Pritchard, 130–4.

Anaya, S. James. *Indigenous Peoples in International Law.* New York: Oxford University Press, 1996.

Asch, Michael. *Home and Native Land: Aboriginal Rights and the Canadian Constitution.* Toronto: Methuen, 1984.

– ed., *Aboriginal and Treaty Rights in Canada: Essays on Law, Equality and Respect for Difference.* Vancouver: UBC Press, 1997.

Atkinson, Alan. *The Europeans in Australia: A History,* Vol. 1. Melbourne: Oxford University Press, 1997.

Attwood, Bain. 'Mabo, Australia and the End of History.' In *In the Age of Mabo: History, Aborigines and Australia,* edited by Bain Attwood, 100–16.

– ed. *In the Age of Mabo: History, Aborigines and Australia.* St Leonards, NSW: Allen & Unwin, 1996.

Attwood, Bain, and Andrew Markus. 'Representation Matters: The 1967 Referendum and Citizenship.' In *Citizenship and Indigenous Australians: Changing Conceptions and Possibilities,* edited by Nicolas Peterson and Will Sanders, 118–40.

Barsh, Russel Lawrence. 'Indigenous Peoples: An Emerging Object of International Law.' *American Journal of International Law* 80 (1986), 370–85.

Barsh, Russel Lawrence, and James Youngblood Henderson. *The Road: Indian Tribes and Political Liberty.* Berkeley: University of California Press, 1980.

Bartlett, Richard. 'Mabo: Another Triumph for the Common Law.' In *Essays on the Mabo Decision,* 58–66. Sydney: The Law Book Company, 1993. Special issue of the *Sydney Law Review* 1993.

– *The Mabo Decision.* Sydney: Butterworths, 1993.

- *Native Title in Australia.* Sydney: Butterworths, 2000.
- 'Native Title in Australia: Denial, Recognition and Dispossesion.' In *Indigenous Peoples' Rights in Australia, Canada and New Zealand,* edited by Paul Havemann, 408–27.
- 'Only an Interim Regime: The Need for a Long Term Settlement Process.' In *Indigenous Social Justice,* Vol. 2: Regional Agreements, edited by Mick Dodson, Aboriginal Social Justice Commissioner, 105–20. Sydney: Human Rights Australia, April 1995.

Bayne, Peter. 'Mabo and the Basis of Acquisition of the Colonies of Australia.' In *The Australian People: An Encyclopedia of the Nation, Its People and Their Origins,* edited by James Jupp, 115–21. Cambridge: Cambridge University Press, 2001.

Beaglehole, J.C., ed. *The Journals of Captain James Cook on His Voyage of Discovery: The Voyage of the Endeavour, 1768–1771.* Cambridge: Cambridge University Press, 1955.

Beckett, Jeremy. *Torres Strait Islanders: Custom and Colonialism.* Cambridge: Cambridge University Press, 1987.
- ed. *Past and Present: The Construction of Aboriginality.* Canberra: Aboriginal Studies Press, 1988.

Behrendt, Larissa. *Achieving Social Justice: Indigenous Rights and Australia's Future.* Sydney: The Federation Press, 2003.

Bell, Catherine. '*R. v. Badger.* One Step Forward and Two Steps Back?' *Constitutional Forum* 8 (xxxx), 21–??.

Bell, Catherine, and Michael Asch. 'Challenging Assumptions: The Impact of Precedent in Aboriginal Rights Litigation.' In Michael Asch, ed., *Aboriginal and Treaty Rights in Canada: Essays on Law, Equality, and Respect for Difference,* 38–74.

Bennett, David. 'Native Title and the Constitution.' In *Native Title in the New Millennium,* edited by Bryan Keon-Cohen, 3–19. 2001.

Bennett, Scott. *Aborigines and Political Power.* Sydney: Allen & Unwin, 1989.
- *White Politics and Black Australians.* Sydney: Allen & Unwin, 1999.

Berger, Thomas. *Village Journey: The Report of the Alaska Native Review Commission.* New York: Hill and Wang, 1985.

Beveridge, A.J. *The Life of John Marshall.* Boston: Houghton Mifflin, 1919.

Bickel, Alexander. *The Least Dangerous Branch: The Supreme Court at the Bar of Politics.* New York: Bobbs-Merrill, 1962.

Blackstone, William. *Commentaries on the Laws of England.* Facsimile of the First Edition. Chicago: University of Chicago Press, 2002.

Blainey, Geoffrey. *A Shorter History of Australia.* Milsons Point, NSW: Mandarin Books, 1997.

Bogart, William. *Consequences: The Impact of Law and Its Complexity*. Toronto: University of Toronto Press, 2001.

Borrows, John. 'Wampum at Niagara: The Royal Proclamation, Canadian Legal History and Self-Government.' In *Aboriginal and Treaty Rights in Canada: Essays on Law, Equality and Respect for Difference*, edited by Michael Asch, 155–72.

Bottoms, John. 'Thayorre People v. Queensland.' In *The Wik Case: Issues and Implications*, edited by Graham Hiley, 19–22.

Bourke, Eleanor. 'Australia's First Peoples: Identity and Population.' In *Aboriginal Australia: An Introductory Reader in Aboriginal Studies*, edited by Colin Bourke, Eleanor Bourke, and Bill Edwards, 35–48. St Lucia: University of Queensland Press, 1994.

Brennan, Frank. *Land Rights Queensland Style: The Struggle for Aboriginal Self-Management*. St Lucia: University of Queensland Press, 1992.

– *One Land, One Nation: Mabo – towards 2001*. St Lucia: University of Queensland Press, 1995.

– *Sharing the Country: The Case for Agreement between Black and White Australians*. Ringwood: Penguin Books, 1991.

Brock, Peggy. 'South Australia.' In *Contested Ground*, edited by Ann McGrath, 208–39.

Brown, Douglas M. *Market Rules: Economic Union Reform and Intergovernmental Policy-Making in Australia and Canada*. Montreal and Kingston: McGill-Queen's University Press, 2002.

Broome, Richard. *Aboriginal Australians*. Sydney: Allen & Unwin, 1982.

– 'Victoria.' In *Contested Ground*, edited by Ann McGrath, 121–67.

Cairns, Alan C. *Citizens Plus: Aboriginal Peoples and the Canadian State*. Vancouver: UBC Press, 2000.

Cassese, Antonio. *Self-Determination of Peoples: A Legal Reappriasal*. Cambridge: Cambridge University Press, 1995.

Castles, Alex C. *An Australian Legal History*. Sydney: The Law Book Company, 1982.

Chesterton, John, and Brian Galligan. *Citizens without Rights: Aborigines and Australian Citizenship*. Cambridge: Cambridge University Press, 1997.

Christie, Gordon. 'Judicial Justification of Recent Developments in Aboriginal Law.' *Canadian Journal of Law and Society* 17, 2 (2002), 41–71.

Churchill, Ward. 'The Earth Is Our Mother: Struggles for American Indian Land and Liberation in the Contemporary United States.' In *The State of Native America: Genocide, Colonization, and Resistance*, edited by M. Annette Jaimes, 139–88.

– *Since Predator Came: Notes from the Struggle for American Indian Liberation*. Littleon, Colorado: Aigis Press, 1995.

Clark, Bruce. *Native Liberty, Crown Sovereignty: The Existing Aboriginal Right of Self-government in Canada.* Montreal & Kingston: McGill-Queen's University Press, 1990.

Clark, C.M.H. *A History of Australia.* 6 vols. Melbourne: Melbourne University Press, 1962.

Clark, Jennifer. 'Indigenous Peoples in Australian Constitutional Law.' In *Australian Constitutional Law,* edited by Peter Hanks et al.

Coombs, H.C. *Aboriginal Autonomy: Issues and Strategies.* Cambridge: Cambridge University Press, 1994.

Cooray, L.J.M. 'The High Court in Mabo: Legalist or l'Egotiste.' In *Make a Better Offer: The Politics of Mabo,* edited by Murray Goot and Tim Rouse, 82–96.

Coper, Michael. *Encounters with the Australian Constitution.* Sydney: CCH Australia, 1987.

– *The Franklin Dam Case.* Sydney: Butterworths, 1983.

Cornell, Stephen. 'Nation-Building and the Treaty Process.' *Indigenous Law Bulletin* 5, 17 (2002), 7–10.

– *The Return of the Native: American Indian Political Resurgence.* New York: Oxford University Press, 1988.

Cowlishaw, Gillian K., 'The Materials for Identity Construction.' In *Past and Present: The Construction of Aboriginalty,* edited by Jeremy Beckett, 87–107.

Crawford, James. *The Original Status of Aboriginal Peoples in North America: A Critique of L.C. Green and O.P. Dickason, The Law of Nations and the New World.* Manitoba Inquiry into the Administration of Justice and Aborginal People. Winnipeg, 1989.

Dahl, Jens, Jack Hicks, and Peter Jull, eds. *Nunavut: Inuit Regain Control of Their Lands and Their Lives.* Copenhagen: International Work Group for Indigenous Affairs, 2000.

Day, David. *Claiming a Continent.* Sydney: Angus & Robertson, 1996.

Deloria, Vine, and Clifford M. Lyttle. *The Nations Within: The Past and Future of American Indian Sovereignty.* Austin: University of Texas Press, 1998.

Denoon, Donald. *Settler Capitalism: The Dynamics of Dependent Development in the Southern Hemisphere.* Oxford: Clarendon Press, 1983.

Dickason, Olive P. *Canada's First Nations: A History of Founding Peoples from Earliest Times.* Toronto: McClelland & Stewart, 1992.

– 'Concepts of Sovereignty at the Time of First Contact.' In *The Law of Nations and the New World,* edited by L.C. Green and Olive P. Dickason. Edmonton: University of Alberta Press, 1989.

Dodson, Mick. 'Linking International Standards with Contemporary Concerns of Aboriginal and Torres Strait Islander Peoples.' In *Indigenous Peoples, the United Nations and Human Rights,* edited by Sarah Pritchard, 18–29.

- 'Power and Cultural Difference in Native Title Mediation.' *Aboriginal Law Bulletin* 3, 84 (1996), 8–11.
- 'Ron Castan, 1940–1999.' *Indigenous Law Bulletin* 4, 24 (October 1999), 23.
Dodson, Mick, and Sarah Pritchard. 'Recent Developments in Indigenous Policy: The Abandonment of Self-Determination.' *Indigenous Law Bulletin* 4, 10 (1998), 4–11.
Dodson, Patrick. 'Message from Patrick Dodson.' In *Program of Australian Reconciliation Council.* Melbourne Convention and Exhibition Centre, 26–28 May, 1997.
Dunston, D.A. 'Aboriginal Land Title and Employment in South Australia.' In *Aborigines in the Economy: Employment, Wages and Training*, edited by Ian G. Sharp and Colin M. Tatz, 314–26. Brisbane: Jacaranda Press, 1966.
Durie, Mason. *Te Mana, Te Kawanatanga: The Politics of Maori Self-Determination.* Auckland: Oxford University Press, 1998.
Edmunds, Mary. 'Conflict in Native Title Claims.' *Native Title Research Unit: Issues Paper No. 7*, Canberra: Australian Institute of Aboriginal and Torres Strait Islander Studies, February 1995.
- 'Key Issues for the Development of Regional Agreements.' In *Regional Agreements in Australia*, Vol. 1, edited by Mary Edmunds, 6–18.
Edmunds, Mary, ed. *Regional Agreements in Australia.* Canberra: Australian Institute of Aboriginal and Torres Strait Islanders Studies, 1998.
Ekstedt, John W. 'International Perspectives on Aboriginal Self-Government.' In *Aboriginal Self-Government in Canada*, 2nd ed., edited by John H. Hylton, 45–58.
Elder, Bruce. *Blood on the Wattle: Massacres and Maltreatment of Australian Aborigines since 1788.* Brookvale, NSW: National Book Distributors, 1988.
Emerson, Rupert. *From Empire to Nation: The Rise to Self-Assertion of Asian and African Peoples.* Boston: Beacon Press, 1960.
Emmet, Peter. *Fleeting Encounters: Pictures and Chronicles of the First Fleet.* Sydney: Museum of Sydney Gallery, 1995.
Farley, Rick. 'The Mabo Spiral: A Farm Sector Perspective.' In *Make a Better Offer: The Politics of Mabo*, edited by Murray Goot and Tim Rouse, 167–78.
Feit, Harvey. 'James Bay Cree Self-Government and Land Management.' In *We Are Here: Politics of Aboriginal Land Tenure*, edited by E. Wilmsen, 68–98. Berkeley: University of California Press, 1988.
- 'Self-Management and State-Management: Negotiating Recognition of Aboriginal Rights: History, Strategies and Reactions to the James Bay and Northern Quebec Agreement.' In *Traditional Knowledge and Renewable Resource Management*, edited by M. Freeman and L. Carbyn. Edmonton: Boreal Institute for Northern Studies, 1988.
Ferguson, Niall. *Empire: The Rise and Demise of the British World Order and the Lessons for Global Power.* London: Basic Books, 2002.

Flanagan, Tom. *First Nations? Second Thoughts?* Montreal and Kingston: McGill-Queen's University Press, 2000.

Fleras, Augie. 'From Social Control towards Political Self-Determination? Maori Seats and the Politics of Separate Maori Representation in New Zealand.' *Canadian Journal of Political Science* 18, 3 (1985), 551–76.

– 'Politicizing Indigeneity: Ethno-politics in White Settler Dominions.' In *Indigenous People's Rights in Australia, New Zealand and Canada*, edited by Paul Havemann, 187–234.

Fleras, Augie, and Jean Leonard Elliott. *The Nations Within: Aboriginal State Relations in Canada, the United States and New Zealand*. Toronto: Oxford University Press, 1996.

Fleras, Augie, and Paul Spoonley. *Recalling Aotearoa: Indigenous Politics and Ethnic Relations in New Zealand*. Auckland: Oxford University Press, 1999.

Fletcher, Christine. *Aboriginal Politics: Intergovernmental Relations*. Carleton, Victoria: Melbourne University Press, 1992.

Foster, Robert. 'The Origin of the Protection of Aboriginal Rights in South Australian Pastoral Leases.' *Native Title Research Unit: Issues Paper No. 24*. Canberra: Australian Institute of Aboriginal and Torres Strait Islander Studies, August 1998.

Frickey, Philip P. 'Congressional Intent, Practical Reasoning, and the Dynamic Nature of Federal Indian Law.' *California Law Review* 78 (1990), 1137–1240.

Frost, Alan. *Botany Bay Mirages*. Carlton, Victoria: Melbourne University Press, 1994.

Fumoleau, Rene. *As Long as This Land Shall Last: A History of Treaty 8 and Treaty 11, 1870–1939*. Toronto: McClelland and Stewart, 1973.

Galanter, Marc. 'Why the Haves Come Out Ahead.' *Law and Society Review* 9 (1974), 95–160.

Galligan, Brian. *Politics of the High Court: A Study of the Judicial Branch of Government in Australia*. St Lucia: University of Queensland Press, 1987.

Gilbert, Kevin. *Breath of Life: Moments in Transit towards Aboriginal Sovereignty*. Canberra: Canberra Contemporary Art Space, 1996.

Goehring, Brian. *Indigenous Peoples of the World*. Saskatoon: Purich, 1993.

Goodall, Heather. *Invasion to Embassy: Land in Aboriginal Politics in New South Wales, 1770–1972*. Sydney: Allen and Unwin, 1996.

Goodall, Heather. 'New South Wales.' In *Contested Ground*, edited by Ann McGrath, 55–120.

Goot, Murray. 'Polls as Science, Polls as Spin: Mabo and the Miners.' In *Make a Better Offer: The Politics of Mabo*, edited by Murray Goot and Tim Rowse, 132–56.

Goot, Murray, and Tim Rowse. *Make a Better Offer: The Politics of Mabo*. Leichhardt, NSW: Pluto Press, 1994.

Gover, Kirsty, and Natalie Baird. 'Identifying the Maori Treaty Partner.' *University of Toronto Law Journal* 52, 1 (2002), 39–68.

Graham, Douglas. *Trick or Treaty?* Wellington: Institute of Policy Studies, Victoria University, 1997.

Gray, Geoffrey. 'From Nomadism to Citizenship: A.P. Elkin and Aboriginal Achievement.' In *Citizenship and Indigenous Australians*, edited by Nicolas Peterson and Will Saunders, 55–76.

Green, L.C. 'Claims to Territory in Colonial America.' In *The Law of Nations and the New World*, edited by L.C. Green and Olive P. Dickason. Edmonton: University of Alberta Press, 1989.

Griffin, James. 'A Background Paper to the Torres Strait Border Issue.' In *The Torres Strait Border Issue*, edited by James Griffin, xiii–xxxi.

– ed. *The Torres Strait Border Issue: Consolidation, Conflict or Compromise.* Townsville: College of Advanced Education, 1976.

Griffiths, Max. *Aboriginal Affairs: A Short History.* Kenthurst: Kangaroo Press, 1995.

Haddon, A.C., ed. *Reports of the Cambridge Anthropological Expedition to Torres Strait.* Cambridge: Cambridge University Press, 1901–3.

Hall, Anthony J. *The American Empire and the Fourth World.* Montreal and Kingston: McGill-Queen's University Press, 2003.

Hanke, Lewis. *Aristotle and the American Indians: A Study in Race Prejudice in the Modern World.* Bloomington: Indiana University Press, 1959.

– *The Spanish Struggle for Justice in the Conquest of America.* Philadelphia: University of Pennsylvania Press, 1949.

Hanks, Peter, and Bryan Keon-Cohen, eds. *Aborigine and the Law.* Sydney: Allen and Unwin, 1997.

Hanks, Peter, et al., eds. *Australian Constitutional Law*, 6th ed. Holmes Beach, FL: Gaunt Inc., 1999.

Harlow, Vincent Todd. *The Founding of the Second British Empire, 1763–1793.* Vol. 1. London: Longmans, Green, 1952.

Harring, Sidney L. *White Man's Law: Native People in Nineteenth-Century Canadian Jurisprudence.* Toronto: University of Toronto Press, 1998.

Harris, Cole. *Making Native Space: Colonialism, Resistance, and Reserves in British Columbia.* Vancouver: UBC Press, 2002.

Harris, Stewart. *It's Coming Yet ...: An Aboriginal Treaty within Australia between Australians.* Canberra: Aboriginal Treaty Committee, 1979.

Hartley, John, and Alan McKee. *The Indigenous Public Sphere: The Reporting and Reception of Indigenous Issues in the Australian Media, 1994–1997.* Oxford: Oxford University Press, 2000.

Hasluck, Paul. *Black Australians: A Survey of Native Policy in Western Australia, 1829–1897.* Carlton, Victoria: Melbourne University Press, 1942.

- *Shades of Darkness: Aboriginal Affairs, 1925–65*. Melbourne: Melbourne University Press, 1988.

Havemann, Paul, ed. *Indigenous Peoples' Rights in Australia, Canada and New Zealand*. Auckland: Oxford University Press, 1999.

Hawkes, David. *Aboriginal Peoples and Constitutional Reform: What Have We Learned?* Kingston, ON: Institute of Intergovernmental Relations, Queen's University, 1989.

Henderson, James (Sakej) Youngblood. *The Mi'kmaw Concordat*. Halifax: Fernwood, 1997.

Hiley, Graham, ed. *The Wik Decision: Issues and Implications*. Sydney: Butterworths, 1997.

Hobsbawm, Eric. *The Age of Empire, 1875–1914*, New York: Vintage Books, 1989.

Hocking, Barbara. 'Does Aboriginal Law Now Run in Australia?' *Federal Law Review* 10 (1979), 161–87.

- 'Is Might Right? An Aargument for the Recognition of Traditional Aboriginal Title to Land in the Australian Courts.' In *Black Australians: The Prospects for Change*, edited by Erik Obrei, 207–21.

Hocking, Jenny. *Lionel Murphy: A Political Biography*. Cambridge: Cambridge University Press, 1997.

Holmes, John. 'Land Tenure in the Australian Pastoral Zone: A Critical Appraisal.' In *North Australian Research: Some Past Themes and New Directions*, edited by Ian Mofatt and Ann Webb. Darwin: North Australia Research Unit, Australian National University, 1991.

Hookey, John. 'Settlement and Sovereignty.' In *Aborigines and the Law*, edited by Peter Hanks and Bryan Keon-Cohen, 3–17.

Horton, David, ed. *Encyclopaedia of Aboriginal Australia*. Canberra: Aboriginal Studies Press, 1994.

Hughes, Robert. *The Fatal Shore*. New York: Pan Books, 1987.

Hunter, Ian. 'Native Title: Acts of State and the Rule of Law.' In *Make a Better Offer: The Politics of Mabo*, edited by Murray Goot and Tim Rowse, 97–109.

Hunter, Phillip. 'The *Wik* Decision: Unnecessary Extinguishment.' In *The Wik Case: Issues and Implications*, edited by Graham Hiley, 6–18.

Hylton, John H. *Aboriginal Self-Government in Canada*, 2nd ed. Saskatoon: Purich, 1999.

Innis, Harold A. *The Fur Trade in Canada*. New Haven: Yale University Press, 1930.

Irons, Catherine J. 'Indigenous Peoples and Self-Determination: Challenging State Sovereignty.' *Case Western Reserve Journal of International Law* 24 (1992), 199–348.

Irving, George. 'The Kimberley Region Native Title and Heritage Protection

Memorandum of Understanding and the Native Title and Heritage Protection Model Agreement.' In *Native Title in the New Milenniumm*, edited by Bryan Keon-Cohen, 163–7.

Issac, Thomas. *Aboriginal and Treaty Rights in the Maritimes*. Saskatoon: Purich, 2001.

Ivison, Duncan, Paul Patten, and Will Sanders, eds. *Political Theory and the Rights of Indigenous Peoples*. Cambridge: Cambridge University Press, 2000.

Jaimes, M. Annette, ed. *The State of Native America: Genocide, Colonization and Resistance*. Boston: South End Press, 1992.

Jennett, Christine. 'Aboriginal Politics' and 'The Movement for Indigenous Peoples' Rights: Land Rights and Self-Determination.' In *The Australian People: An Encyclopedia of the Nation, Its People and Their Origins*, edited by James Jupp. Cambridge: Cambridge University Press, 2001.

Jones, Dorothy V. *License for Empire: Colonialism by Treat in Early America*. Chicago: University of Chicago Press, 1982.

Jull, Peter. 'Hansonism and Aborigines and Torres Strait Islanders.' In *The Rise and Fall of One Nation*, edited by Michael Leach, Geoffrey Stokes, and Ian Ward, 206–19.

– 'Them Eskimo Mob: International Implications of Nunavut,' Rev. 2nd ed. Research Study for Royal Commission on Aboriginal People, 1996.

Kajlich, Helena. 'The British Columbia Treaty Referendum: An Appropriate Democratic Exercise?' *Indigenous Law Bulletin* 5, 17 (2002), 11–14.

Kauffman, Paul. *Wik, Mining and Aborigines*. St Leonard's, NSW: Allen and Unwin, 1998.

Kawaharu, I. H., ed. *Waitangi: Maori and Pakeha Perspectives of the Treaty of Waitangi*, Auckland: Oxford University Press, 1989.

Keating, Paul. 'Speech on the Australian Launch of the International Year for the World's Indigenous Peoples.' [Redfern Speech]. *Aboriginal Law Bulletin* 3, 61 (1993), 4–5.

Kee, Sue. 'Indigenous Land Use Agreements: Which, Why and Where?' In *Native Title in the New Millennium*, edited by Bryan Keon-Cohen, 345–51.

Keon-Cohen, Bryan A. 'The *Mabo* Litigation: A Personal and Procedural Account.' *Melbourne University Law Review* 24 (2000), 2–66.

Keon-Cohen, Bryan A. ed. *Native Title in the New Millennium*. Canberra: Aboriginal Studies, Press, 2001.

Kidd, Roslyn. *The Way We Civilize: Aboriginal Affairs – The Untold Story*. St Lucia: University of Queensland Press, 1997.

King, Michael. *Nga Iwi O Te Motu: 1000 Years of Maori History*. Auckland: Reed Books, 1997.

Kirchheimer, Otto. *Political Justice: The Use of Legal Procedures for Political Ends*. Princeton: Princeton University Press, 1961.

Kleivan, I. 'The Arctic Peoples' Conference in Copenhagen, November 22–25, 1973.' *Études Inuit Studies* 16 (1992), 227–36.

Laforest, Andrea, and Annie York. *Spuzzum: Fraser Canyon Histories, 1808–1939.* Vancouver: UBC Press, 2002.

La Nauze. *The Making of the Australian Constitution.* Melbourne: Melbourne University Press, 1972.

Lane, Patricia. 'A Quick Guide to ILUAs.' In *Native Title in the New Millennium,* edited by Bryan Keon-Cohen, 331–9.

Lawrence, David. *Kakadu: The Making of a National Park.* Melbourne: Melbourne University Press, 2000.

Leach, Michael, Geoffrey Stokes, and Ian Ward, eds. *The Rise and Fall of One Nation.* St Lucia: University of Queensland Press, 2000.

Little Bear, Leroy, Menno Boldt, and J. Anthony Long, eds. *Pathways to Self-Determination: Canadian Indians in the Canadian State.* Toronto: University of Toronto Press, 1984.

Lindley, M.F. *The Acquisition and Government of Backward Territories in International Law.* London: Longmans, 1928.

Llewellyn, Karl N. *The Common Law Tradition: Deciding Appeals,* Boston: Little Brown, 1960.

Lloyd, T.O. *The British Empire, 1558–1995.* 2nd ed. Oxford: Oxford University Press, 1996.

Locke, John. *The Second Treatise of Government.* New York: Liberal Arts Press, 1952.

Loos, Noel. *Invasion and Resistance: Aboriginal-European Relations on the North Queensland Frontier.* Canberra: Australian National University Press, 1982.

Loos, Noel, and Koiki Mabo. *Edward Koiki Mabo: His Life and Struggle for Land Rights.* St Lucia: University of Queensland Press, 1996.

Lui, Gaetano. 'A Perspective from the Torres Strait.' In *The Torres Strait Border Issue: Consolidation, Conflict or Compromise,* edited by James Griffin, 31–3.

Lui, Getano. *Planning Our Future: Corporate Plan, 1994–95.* Thursday Island: Torres Strait Regional Authority, 1995.

Lumb, R.D. 'The Mabo Case: Public Law Aspects.' In *Mabo: A Judicial Revolution,* edited by Margaret Stephenson and Suri Ratnapala, 1–23.

Mabo, Eddie Koiki. 'Land Rights in the Torres Strait.' In *Black Australians: The Prospects for Change,* edited by Erik Obrei, 143–7.

Maddock, Kenneth. *Your Land Is Our Land: Aboriginal Land Rights.* Ringwood, Victoria Penguin Books, 1983.

Magnallanes, Catherine J. Iorns. 'Inidgenous Political Representation: Separate Parliamentary Seats as a Form of Indigenous Self-Determination.' In *Unfinished Constitutional Business? Re-thinking Indigenous Self-Determination,* edited by Barbara Ann Hocking, forthcoming, 2004.

Mankiller, Wilma. *Mankiller: A Chief and Her People*. New York: St Martin's Press, 1993.

Manuel, George, and Michael Posluns. *The Fourth World*. Toronto: Collier-Macmillan, 1974.

McGrath, Ann. 'Tasmania: 1.' In *Contested Ground*, edited by Ann McGrath, 306–37.

– ed. *Contested Ground: Australian Aboriginals under the British Crown*. Sydney: Allen and Unwin, 1995.

McGregor, Russell. *Imagined Destinies: Aboriginal Australians and the Doomed Race Theory, 1880–1939*. Melbourne: Melbourne University Press, 1997.

McHugh, P.G. 'From Sovereignty Talk to Settlement Time.' In *Indigenous Peoples' Rights in Australia, Canada, and New Zealand*, edited by Paul Havemann, 447–67.

– 'A History of Crown Sovereignty in New Zealand.' In *Histories, Power and Loss: Uses of the Past – A New Zealand Commentary*, edited by Andrew Sharp and Paul McHugh, 189–211.

McKee, Christopher. *Treaty Talks in British Columbia: Negotiating a Mutually Beneficial Future*. Vancouver UBC Press, 1996.

McNeil, Kent. *Common Law Aboriginal Title*. Oxford: Clarendon Press, 1989.

– 'The Onus of Proof of Aboriginal Title.' *Osgoode Hall Law Journal* 37, 4 (1999), 775–803.

– 'Racial Discrimination and Unilateral Extinguishment of Native Title.' *Australian Indigenous Law Reporter* 1, 2 (1996), 181–222.

McNutt, Francis Augustus. *Bartholomew de Las Casas: His Life, Apostolate and Writings*. Cleveland: Arthur Clark, 1909.

Means, Russell, with Marvin J. Wolf. *Where White Men Fear to Tread: The Autobiography of Russell Means*. New York: St Martin's Press, 1995.

Mill, John Stuart. *Considerations on Representative Government*. Oxford World's Classics, 1998.

Miller, J.R. *Skyscrapers Hide the Heavens: A History of Indian-White Relations in Canada*. Toronto: University of Toronto Press, 1989.

Milloy, John S. *A National Crime: The Canadian Government and the Residential School System, 1879–1986*. Winnipeg: University of Manitoba Press, 1999.

Molloy, Tom. *The World Is Our Witness: The Historic Journey of the Nisga'a into Canada*. Calgary: Fifth House, 2000.

Mulgan, Richard. *Maori, Pakeha and Democracy*. Auckland: Oxford University Press, 1989.

Murray, Robert. 'What Really Happened to the Kooris?' *Quadrant*, November 1996, 10–21.

Mykutenner. 'Tasmania: 2.' In *Contested Ground*, edited by Ann McGrath, 338–58.

Neatte, Graeme. 'Alternative State and Territorial Schemes: A National Overview.' In *Native Title in the New Millennium* edited by Bryan Keon-Cohen, 33–65.

Nettheim, Garth. 'The Consent of the Natives: Mabo and Indigenous Political Rights.' In *Essays on the Mabo Decision*, 103–26. Sydney: The Law Book Company, 1993.

– 'The Hindmarsh Bridge Act Case.' *Indigenous Law Bulletin* 4, 12 (1998), 17.

– 'McArthur River and the Mabo Response.' *Aboriginal Law Bulletin* 3, 62 (1993), 15–16.

– 'The Relevance of International Law.' In *Aborigines and the Law*, edited by Peter Hanks and Bryan Keon-Cohen, 50–72.

– *Victims of the Law: Black Queenslanders Today*. North Sydney: Allen and Unwin, 1981.

Nies, Judith. *Native American History*. New York: Ballentine Books, 1996.

Obrei, Erik, ed. *Black Australians: The Prospects for Change*. Townsville: Students Union, James Cook University, 1982.

O'Faircheallaugh, Ciaran. 'Mineral Development Agreements Negotiated by Aboriginal Communities in the 1990s.' *Discussion Paper No. 85*. Canberra: Centre for Aboriginal Economic Policy, Australian National University, 1995.

– 'Negotiating Major Project Agreements: The "Cape York Model."' *Research Discussion Paper No. 11*. Canberra: Australian Institute for Aboriginal and Torres Strait Islanders Studies, 2000.

Oliver, W.H. *Claims to the Waitangi Tribunal*. Wellington: Department of Justice, 1991.

– 'The Future Behind Us.' In *Histories, Power and Loss: Uses of the Past – A New Zealand Commentary*, edited by Andrew Sharp and Paul McHugh, 9–29.

Orange, Claudia. *The Treaty of Waitangi*. Wellington: Allen and Unwin, 1987.

Ossen, Erik. 'Mr. Wakefield and New Zealand as an Experiment in Post Enlightenment Experimental Practice.' *New Zealand Journal of History* 31 (1997), 197–218.

Parker, Linda S. *Native American Estate: The Struggle over Indian and Hawaiian Lands*. Honolulu: University of Hawai'i Press, 1996.

Partington, Geoffrey. *Hasluck versud Coombs: White Politics and Australia's Aborigines*. Sydney: Quakers Hill Press, 1996.

Patapan, Haig. *Judging Democracy: The New Politics of the High Court of Australia*. Cambridge: Cambridge University Press, 2000.

Pearson, Noel. '204 Years of Invisible Title.' In *Mabo: A Judicial Revolution*, edited by M.A. Stephenson and Suri Ratnapala, 75–95. St Lucia: University of Queensland Press, 1993.

– 'Concept of Native Title at Common Law.' In *Our Land Is Our Life: Land Rights Past, Present and Future*, edited by Galarrwuy Yunupinga, 150–62.

Pederson, Howard, and Banjo Woorunnmurra. *Jandamarra and the Bunuba Resistance.* Broome: Magabala Books, 1995.

Peterson, Nicolas, and Will Sanders, eds. *Citizenship and Indigenous Australians: Changing Conceptions and Possibilities.* Cambridge: Cambridge University Press, 1998.

Pollack, D.P. 'Indigenous Land in Australia: A Quantitative Assessment of Indigenous Landholdings.' *Discussion Paper No. 221.* Canberra: Centre for Aboriginal Economic Policy Research, Australian National University, 2001.

Pritchard, Sarah. 'Commission on Human Rights (CHRWG): Third Session, 27 October–7 November 1997.' *Indigenous Law Bulletin* 4, 10 (1998), 4–11.

– 'The Significance of International Law.' In *Indigenous Peoples, the United Nations and Human Rights*, edited by Sarah Pritchard, 2–17. Leichhardt, NSW: Federation Press, 1998.

– 'The United Nations and the Making of the Declaration on Indigenous Rights.' *Indigenous Law Bulletin* 4, 10 (1998), 4–9.

– ed. *Indigenous Peoples, the United Nations and Human Rights.* Leichhardt, NSW: Federation Press, 1998.

Purich, Donald. *The Metis.* Toronto: James Lorimer, 1988.

Read, Peter. 'Northern Territory.' In *Contested Ground*, edited by Ann McGrath, 269–305.

Reynolds, Henry. *Aboriginal Sovereignty: Reflections on Race, State and Nation.* St Leonards, NSW: Allen and Unwin, 1996.

– *Dispossession: Black Australians and White Invaders.* St Leonards, NSW: Allen and Unwin, 1989.

– *Fate of a Free People: A Radical Re-examination of the Tasmanian Wars.* Ringwood, NSW: Penguin Books, 1995.

– *The Law of the Land.* Ringwood, NSW: Penguin Books, 1988.

– *The Other Side of the Frontier: Aboriginal Resistance to the European Invasion of Australia.* Ringwood, NSW: Penguin Books, 1982.

– *With the White People: The Crucial Role of Aborigines in the Exploration and Development of Australia.* Ringwood, NSW: Penguin Books, 1990.

Reynolds, Henry, and Dawn May. 'Queensland.' In *Contested Ground*, edited by Ann McGrath, 168–207.

Reynolds, Paul. 'One Nation's Electoral Support: The State and Federal Elections Compared.' In *The Rise and Fall of One Nation*, edited by Michael Leach, Geoffrey Stokes, and Ian Ward, 153–69.

Richardson, Boyce. *Strangers Devour the Land: The Cree Hunters of the James Bay Area versus Premier Bourassa and the James Bay Development Corporation.* Toronto: Macmillan of Canada, 1975.

Ritter, David. 'The Rejection of Terra Nullius.' *Sydney Law Review* 18, 5 (1996), 6–33.

Roach, Kent. *The Supreme Court on Trial: Judicial Activism or Democratic Dialogue.* Toronto: Irwin Law, 2001.

Robbins, Rebecca L. 'Self-Determination and Subordination: The Past, Present and Future of American Indian Government.' In *The State of Native America,* edited by M. Annette Jaimes, 87–122.

Robinson, Scott. 'The Aboriginal Embassy: An Account of the Protests.' *Aboriginal History* 18, 1 (1994), 49–63.

Rotman, Leonard Ian. *Parallel Paths: Fiducuiary Doctrine and the Crown-Native Relationship in Canada.* Toronto: University of Toronto Press, 1996.

Rowse, Tim. 'How We Got a Native Title Act.' In *Make a Better Offer: The Politics of Mabo,* edited by Murray Goot and Tim Rowse, 111–32.

– *Obliged to Be Difficult: Nugget Coombs' Legacy in Indigenous Affairs.* Cambridge: Cambridge University Press, 2000.

– 'The Political Identity of Regional Councillors.' In *Shooting the Banker,* edited by Patrick Sullivan, 42–69.

Rowley. C.S. *Recovery: The Politics of Aboriginal Reform.* Ringwood, NSW: Penguin Books, 1986.

– *The Remote Aborigines.* Ringwood, NSW: Penguin Books, 1972.

Russell, Peter H. 'Aboriginal Nationalism: Prospects for Decolonization.' *Pacifica Review,* November 1996, 57–67.

– 'Canada – A Pioneer in the Management of Constitutional Politics in a Multi-national Society.' In *The Politics of Constitutional Reform in North America,* edited by Rainer-Olaf Schultze and Roland Strum, 227–34. Druck, Germany: Leske and Budrich, 2000.

– 'Canada's Megaconstitutional Politics in Comparative Perspective.' In *Managing Constitutional Change,* edited by Bertus de Villiers and Jabu Sindane, 69–96. Pretoria: HSRC Publishers, 1996.

– *Constitutional Odyssey: Can the Canadians Become a Sovereign People?* 2nd ed. Toronto: University of Toronto Press, 1993.

– 'Corroboree 2000 – A Nation Defining Event.' *ARENA Journal,* new series, no. 15 (2000), 25–38.

– 'Doing Aboriginal Politics.' *Canadian Political Science Association Bulletin* 30, 2 (2001), 7–11.

– 'The Global Dimensions of Aboriginal Politics.' In *Education for Australia's International Future,* edited by Rodney Sullivan et al., 104–11. Townsville: School of History and Politics, James Cook University, 1998.

– 'High Courts and the Rights of Aboriginal Peoples: The Limits of Judicial Independence.' *Saskatchewan Law Review* 61, 1 (1998), 247–76.

- 'Mega Constitutional Politics: Canada's Agony, Australia's Warning.' *Quadrant* 38, 10 (1994), 15–21.
- 'My People's Courts as Agents of Indigenous Decolonization?' *Law in Context* 18, 1 (2001), 1–11.
- 'The Politics of Frustration: The Pursuit of Formal Constitutional Change in Australia and Canada.' *Australian-Canadian Studies* 6, 1 (1988), 3–32.
- 'The Politics of Frustration II: Constitutional Politics in Australia and Canada since 1987.' *Australian-Canadian Studies* 10, 2 (1992), 57–85.
- 'The Research Program of the Royal Commission on Aboriginal Peoples.' *International Journal of Canadian Studies* 12 (1995), 277–83.

Ryan, Mary-Ellen. 'Tribute to the Mabo Title Fight.' *Campus Review* (James Cook University), 7, 25, 1997.

Said, Edward. *Culture and Imperialism.* New York: Vintage Books, 1994.

St Leger, James. *The 'Etiamsi Daremus' of Hugo Grotius: A Study in the Origins of International Law.* Rome: Pontificium Athenaeum Internationale 'Angelicum,' 1962.

Sanders, Douglas. 'The Indian Lobby.' In *And No One Cheered: Federalism, Democracy and the Constitution Act,* edited by Keith Banting and Richard Simeon, 301–32. Methuen: Toronto, 1983.
- 'The Remergence of Indigenous Questions in International Law.' *Canadian Human Rights Year Book,* 1 (1983), 3–30.
- 'The UN Working Group on Indigenous Populations.' *Human Rights Quarterly* 11 (1989), 406–33.

Sanders, Will, John Taylor, and Kate Ross. 'Participation and Representation in ATSIC Elections: A-10 Year Perspective.' *Australian Journal of Political Science* 35 (2000), 493–513.

Satz, R.N. *American Indian Policy in the Jacksonian Era.* Lincoln: University of Nebraska Press, 1975.

Schattsneider, E.E. *The Semi-Sovereign People: A Realist's View of Democracy in America.* New York: Holt, Rinehart and Winston, 1960.

Schürmann-Zeggel, Heinz. 'UN CERD Committee.' *Indigenous Law Bulletin* 4, 20 (1999), 20.

Scott, Colin, ed. *Aboriginal Autonomy and Development in Northern Quebec and Labrador.* Vancouver UBC Press, 2001.

Seeley, Sir J.R. *The Expansion of England.* London: Macmillan, 1906.

Sexton, Michael, and Laurence V. Maher. *The Legal Mystique: The Role of Lawyers in Australian Society.* Sydney: Angus and Robertson, 1982.

Sharp, Andrew. 'Blood, Custom, and Consent.' *University of Toronto Law Journal* 52, 1 (2002), 9–37.
- *Justice and the Maori: The Philosophy and Practice of Maori Claims in New Zealand since the 1970s,* 2nd ed. Auckland: Oxford University Press, 1997.

Sharp, Andrew, and Paul McHugh, eds. *Histories, Power and Loss: Uses of the Past.* Wellington: Bridget Williams, 2001.

Sharp, Ian G., and Colin M. Tatz, eds. *Aborigines in the Economy, Employment, Wages and Training.* Bisbane: Jacaranda Press, 1966.

Sharp, Nonie. *Footprints Along the Cape York Sandbeaches.* Canberra: Aboriginal Studies Press, 1992.

– *No Ordinary Judgment.* Canberra: Aboriginal Studies Press, 1996.

– *Saltwater People: The Waves of Memory.* Toronto: University of Toronto Press, 2002.

– *Stars of Tagai: The Torres Strait Islanders.* Canberra: Aboriginal Studies Press, 1993.

Siffarm, Lenore A., and Phil Lane Jr. 'The Demography of Native North America: A Question of American Indian Survival.' In *The State of Native America,* edited by M. Annette Jaimes, 23–53.

Simons, Margaret. *The Meeting of the Waters: The Hindmarsh Island Affair.* Sydney: Hodder, 2003.

Sinclair, Keith. *A History of New Zealand.* Wellington: Oxford University Press, 1961.

Singe, John. *The Torres Strait: People and History.* St Lucia: University of Queensland Press, 1989.

Slattery, Brian. *The Land Rights of Indigenous Canadian Peoples as Affected by the Crown's Acquistion of Their Territories.* Saskatoon: Native Law Centre, University of Saskatchewan, 1979.

Sniderman, Paul. Joseph Fletcher, Peter Russell, and Philip Tetlock. *Clash of Rights: Liberty, Equality and Legitimacy in Pluralist Democracy.* New Haven: Yale University Press, 1997.

Solomon, David. *The Political High Court: How the High Court Shapes Politics.* St Leonards, NSW: Allen and Unwin, 1999.

Sorenson, D.K. 'Law in Norfolk: The De Facto Position.' *Commonwealth Law Bulletin* (1990), 634–43.

Spiller, Peter, Jeremy Finn, and Richard Boast. *A New Zealand Legal History.* Wellington: Brookers, 1995.

Stanford, P.S.B. 'The Torres Strait Treaty.' *Australian Foreign Affairs Review,* December 1978, 572–77.

Stanner, W.E.H. *White Man Got No Dreaming: Essays, 1938–1973.* Canberra: Australian National University Press, 1979.

Stephenson, Margaret A. 'Compensation and Valuation of Native Title.' In *Mabo: The Native Title Legislation,* edited by Margaret A. Stephenson, 135–54.

– 'Pastoral Leases and Reservation Clauses.' In *Mabo: The Native Title Legislation,* edited by Margaret A. Stephenson, 104–19.

Stephenson, M.A., ed. *Mabo: The Native Title Legislation: A Legislative Response to the High Court's Decision.* St Lucia: University of Queensland Press, 1995.

Stephenson, M.A., and Suri Ratnapala, eds. *Mabo: A Judicial Revolution. The Aboriginal Land Rights Decision and Its Impact on Australian Law.* St Lucia: University of Queensland Press, 1993.

Stokes, Geoffrey. 'Citizenship and Aboriginality: Two Conceptions of Identity in Aboriginal Political Thought.' In *The Politics of Identity in Australia*, edited by Geoffrey Stokes, 158–171.

– ed. *The Politics of Identity in Australia.* Cambridge: Cambridge University Press, 1997.

Strelein, Lisa. 'Conceptualizing Native Title.' *Sydney Law Review* 23, 1 (2001), 95–124.

– '*Western Australia v. Ward on Behalf of Miriuwung Gajerrong*, High Court of Australia 8 August 2002: Summary of Judgment.' *Native Title Research Unit: Issues Paper No. 17.* Canberra: Australian Institute of Aboriginal and Torres Strait Islanders Studies, 2002.

Struthurs, Karen. 'Hands on Parliament: A Parliamentary Inquiry into Aboriginal and Torres Strait Islander Peoples.' *Indigenous Law Bulletin* 5, 22 (2003), 6.

Sullivan, Patrick. 'All Things to All People: ATSIC and Australia's International Obligation to Uphold Indigenous Self-determination.' In *Shooting the Banker*, edited by Patrick Sullivan, 105–29.

– 'The Kimberley.' In *Regional Agreements in Australia*, edited by Mary Edmunds, 52–6.

Sullivan, Patrick, ed. *Shooting the Banker: Essays on ATSIC and Self-Determination.* Darwin: North Australia Research Unit, Australian National University, 1996.

Sutton, Peter. *Country: Aboriginal Boundaries and Land Ownership in Australia.* Canberra: Aboriginal History Inc., 1995.

Sykes, Roberta B. 'After Eddie.' *HQ Magazine*, March/April 1995, 70–2.

Tennant, Paul. *Aboriginal Peoples and Politics: The Indian Land Question in British Columbia, 1849–1989.* Vancouver: UBC Press, 1990.

Tickner, Robert. *Taking a Stand: Land Rights to Reconciliation.* Crows Nest, NSW: Allen and Unwin, 2001.

Todd, Alpheus. *Parliamentary Government in the British Colonies.* Boston: Little and Brown, 1880.

Touissant, Sandy. 'Western Australia.' In *Contested Ground*, edited by Ann McGrath, 240–68.

Trask, Havanni-Kay. *From a Native Daughter: Colonialism and Sovereignty in Hawai'i.* Monroe, ME: Common Courage Press, 1993.

Tully, James. *Strange Multiplicity: Constitutionalism in an Age of Diversity.* Cambridge: University of Cambridge Press, 1995.

Utter, Jack. *American Indians: Answers to Today's Questions*, 2nd ed. Norman: University of Oklahoma Press, 2001.

Vattel, Emmerich de. *The Law of Nations, or Principles of the Law of Nature Applied to the Conduct and Affairs of Nations and Sovereigns.* 3 vols., 1760. Washington: Carnegie Institute, 1916.

Walker, Ranginui. *Ka Whawhai Tonu Matou: Struggle without End.* Auckland: Penguin Books, 1990.

Washburn, Wilcomb E. *Red Man's Land/White Man's Law.* 2nd ed. Norman: University of Oklahoma Press, 1995.

Ward, Alan. *An Unsettled History: Treaty Claims in New Zealand Today.* Wellington: Bridget Williams, 1999.

Ward, Alan, and Janine Hayward. 'Tino Rangatiratanga: Maori in the Political and Administrative System.' In *Indigenous Peoples' Rights in Australia, Canada and New Zealand,* edited by Paul Havemann, 378–99.

Watkins, Mel. *Dene Nation: The Colony Within.* Toronto: University of Toronto Press, 1977.

Watson, Pamela Lukin. *Frontier Lands and Pioneer Legends: How Pastoralists Gained Karuali Land.* Sydney: Allen and Unwin, 1999.

Weaver, John C. 'Beyond the Fatal Shore: Pastoral Squatting and the Occupation of Australia, 1826 to 1852.' *The American Historical Review* 101, 4 (1996), 980–1007.

Webber, Jeremy. 'Beyond Regret: Mabo's Implications for Australian Constitutionalism.' In *Political Theory and the Rights of Indigenous Peoples,* edited by Duncan Ivison, Paul Patton, and Will Sanders, 60–88. Cambridge: Cambridge University Press, 2000.

Westlake, John. *Chapters on the Principles of International Law.* Cambridge: Cambridge University Press, 1894.

Wilkinson, Charles F. *American Indians, Time, and the Law.* New Haven: Yale University Press, 1987.

Williams, George. *A Bill of Rights for Australia.* Sydney: University of New South Wales Press, 2000.

Williams, Robert A., Jr. 'The Algebra of Federal Indian, Law: The Hard Trail of Decolonizing and Americanizing the White Man's Indian Jurisprudence.' *Wisconsin Law Review* 1 (1968), 219–99.

– *The American Indian in Western Legal Thought: The Discourses of Conquest.* New York: Oxford University Press, 1990.

– 'Encounters on the Frontiers of International Human Rights Law: Redefining the Terms of Indigenous Peoples' Survival in the World.' *Duke Law Journal* (1990), 660–705.

Wilmer, Franke. *The Indigenous Voice in World Politics.* Newbury Park, CA: Sage, 1993.

Wilson, James. *The Earth Shall Weep: A History of Native America.* New York: Atlantic Monthly Press, 1998.

Wilson, Sir Ronald. 'Preface.' In *The Stolen Children: Their Stories*, edited by
    Carmel Bird, Sydney: Random House Australia, 1998.
Wood, Marilyn. 'Nineteenth-Century Bureaucratic Constructions of Indigenous
    Identities in New South Wales.' In *Citizenship and Indigenous Australians:
    Changing Conceptions and Possibilities*, edited by Nicolas Peterson and Will
    Sanders, 35–54.
Wright, Judith. *We Call for a Treaty*. Sydney: Collins/Fontana, 1985.
Wright, Ronald. *Stolen Continents: The 'New World' through Indian Eyes*. Toronto:
    Penguin Books, 1993.
Wunder, John R. *'Retained by the People': A History of American Indians and the Bill
    of Rights*. New York: Oxford University Press, 1994.
York, Geoffrey, and Loreen Pindera. *People of the Pines: The Warriors and the Legacy
    of Oka*. Boston: Little Brown, 1991.
Young, Elspeth. 'Aboriginal Frontiers and Boundaries.' In *Country: Aboriginal
    Boundaries and Land Ownership in Australia*, edited by Peter Sutton, Appen-
    dix 1.
Yunupingu, Galarrwuy. 'Introduction.' In *Our Land Is Our Lifes*, edited by
    Galarrwuy Yunupingu, 1–17.
– ed. *Our Land Is Our Lifes: Land Rights, Past, Present and Future*. St Lucia: Univer-
    sity of Queensland Press, 1997.

Newspaper Articles

AAP, 'Draft Preamble to the Constitution.' *The Age*, 23 March 1999.
Alcorn, Gay, and Paul Chamberlin. 'Blacks accuse PM of betrayal.' *The Austra-
    lian*, 28 May 1993.
Arndt, Bettina. 'Conventional behaviour.' *Sydney Morning Herald*, 3 March 2000
    (News Review).
Associated Press. 'Australia will restrict UN access.' *New York Times*, 30 August
    2000.
Barker, Geoffrey, and Tom Ormonde. 'Keating to put Mabo into law.' *The Age*
    (Melbourne), 19 January 1993.
Boreham, Gareth, and Innes Wilcox. 'Howard softens line on Mabo.' *The Age*,
    17 March 1995.
Campbell, Roderick. 'PM hits blacks' sway on Wik.' *Canberra Times*, 19 May 1997.
Chamberlin, Paul. 'The day that changed history.' *Sydney Morning Herald*,
    20 October 1993.
Daley, Paul. 'UN to vet jailing laws.' *The Age*, 22 February 2000.
Dowling, Joseph. 'Mining Dismay at Wik decision.' *Brisbane Courier Mail*,
    24 December 1996.

Easterbrook, Margaret. 'Keating move boosts profile of Aborigines.' *The Age*, 25 March 1993.

Editorial, 'Truly a night to remember.' *The Age*, 18 September 2000.

Farrant, Darrin. 'Under grey skies, they honour the lawyer who fought racism.' *The Age*, 23 October 1999.

Forbes, Cameron. 'Coming Together.' *The Australian*, 26 May 1997, 11.

– 'Council in quest of moral solution.' *The Australian*, 29 May 1997.

Garron, Robert. 'PM backs Herron's hard line.' *The Australian*, 3 April 2000.

Gill, Peter. 'Mabo: Mining on hold.' *Financial Review*, 4 June 1993.

– 'States win fight over Mabo.' *Financial Review*, 3 September 1993.

Gratton, Michelle. 'Election '98: Howard risks it all.' *Financial Review*, 6/7 December 1997.

– 'Howard left in diplomatic shade.' *Sydney Morning Herald*, 8 September 2000.

– 'Reconciliation Rescue Mission.' *Sydney Morning Herald*, 14 April 2000.

Howard, John. 'I am an optimist, but this optimism cannot be bind.' *The Australian*, 27 May 1997, 4.

Johnstone, Craig. 'Heart of the matter.' *Courier Mail*, 18 January 1997.

Kerr, Joseph. 'Council plays down Prime Minister's negative stance.' *Sydney Morning Herald*, 12 May 2000.

Kingston, Margo. 'ALP predicts preamble doom.' *Sydney Morning Herald*, 1 November 1999.

– 'Ban on Aborigines "valid."' *Sydney Morning Herald*, 2 April 1998.

– 'Beazley: We'll fight race poll if we have to.' *Sydney Morning Herald*, 22 January 1998.

– 'Brian takes shelter as Aborigines nearly miss bus.' *Sydney Morning Herald*, 9 April 1998.

– 'Discrimination? I don't see any, says Honest John.' *Sydney Morning Herald*, 18 August 1999.

– 'Native Title: The dust settles – A painful journey to heal.' *Sydney Morning Herald*, 4 July 1998.

Kingston, Margo, James Woodward, and Michael Seccombe. 'Wik deal scuttles race poll.' *Sydney Morning Herald*, 15 June 1998.

Larkin, John. 'Libs landslide: Our mandate is emphatic.' (Melbourne) *Sunday Telegraph*, 3 March 1996.

Lehmann. John. 'Borbidge promises Wik cash.' *Courier Mail*, 20 January 1997.

Martin, Lauren. 'Australia faces UN race inquiry over Wik.' *Sidney Morning Herald*, 18 August 1999.

McCabe, Helen. 'Judge quits High Court bridge case.' *Brisbane Courier Mail*, 26 February 1998.

McGregor, Richard, and Scott Emerson. 'Hanson ruins PM's poll plan.' *The Australian*, 15 June 1998.

McGurik, Rod. 'Jail deal silences PM on reforms.' *The Age*, 12 April 2000.

McPhedran, Ian. 'Diplomats voice concern over race debate.' *Canberra Times*, 22 May 1997.

Merryment, Elizabeth, Debra Aldred, and Gordon Collie. 'All roads lead to Canberra for Wik showdown.' *Brisbane Courier Mail*, 30 March 1998.

Milne, Glenn. 'Community divided in native title but most oppose compensation.' *The Australian*, 17 June 1993.

Montgomery, Bruce. 'Power of one holds nation in balance.' *The Weekend Australian*, 6/7 December 1997.

Nason, David. 'Perron ignores Aboriginal protests on anti-Mabo Bill.' *The Australian*, 3 March 1993.

O'Rourke, Jim. '100,000 for historic walk.' *Sydney Sun-Herald*, 28 May 2000.

Prior, Cathy. 'Dire Straits.' *The Weekend Australian*, 15/16 April 2000.

Saunders, Megan. 'Native title laws breach UN race rules.' *The Weekend Australian*, 20/21 March 1999.

Short, John. 'Harradine sets Senate on path for Wik conflict.' *The Australian*, 5 December 1997.

– 'Leaders unite for tolerance: Asian backlash prompts vote against racism.' *The Australian*, 31 October 1996.

– 'The PM locks in tough Wik plans.' *The Australian*, 24 April 1997.

Short, John, and Georgina Windsor. 'Minds fail to meet on Wik.' *The Weekend Australian*, 15/16 February 1997.

Singer, Errol. 'Torres Islanders deadly serious.' *The Weekend Australian*, 30/31 January 1988.

Staff Reporters. 'Backtrack on rights tragic.' *Sidney Morning Herald*, 30 August 2000.

The Farmers of Australia. 'Dear John.' *West Australian* (Perth), 24 March 1997, 21.

Taylor, Kerry. 'Indigenous leaders hit by rift.' *The Age*, 4 May 2000.

Taylor, Lenore. 'Mabo win for PM.' *The Age*, 22 December 1993.

Tingle, Laura, and Margo Kingston. 'Howard's pledge to voters: "It won't be a race election,"' *Sydney Morning Herald*, 10 April 1998.

Walker, Jamie. 'Eddie Mabo – Australian of the Year.' *The Australian*, 26 January 1993.

Wells, Jill, and Jill Martin. 'Racist Outrage: Desecration Condemned by PM and Opposition.' *Townsville Bulletin*, 5 June 1995.

Willox, Innes. 'Relations sour as PM rejects black critics.' *The Age*, 7 August 1993.

Wilson, Bob. 'Pasminco makes deal of the century.' *Brisbane Courier Mail*, 20 January 1997.

Windsor, Georgina. 'Harradine holds firm in Senate's Wik endgame.' *The Australian*, 11 April 1998.

Woodford, James, and Micahel Millett. 'Title Fight.' *Sydney Morning Herald*, 25 January 1997.

Woodley, John. 'Mabo of the mainland.' *Brisbane Courier Mail*, 23 December 1997.

Government Reports and Public Documents

'The Aboriginal Peace Plan.' *Aboriginal Law Bulletin* 3, 62 (1993), 8.

Australia. Aboriginal and Torres Strait Islander Social Justice Commissioner. *First Report*. Sydney, 1993.

– *The Native Title Act: A Plain English Introduction*. Canberra: Australian Government Publishing Service, 1994.

Australia. Commonwealth Government. 'Commentary.' In *Native Title Act: Legislation with Commentary by the Attorney General's Legal Practice*. Canberra: Australian Government Publishing Service, 1994.

– '*Mabo*: The High Court Decision on Native Title, Discussion Paper.' *Aboriginal Law Bulletin* 3, 62 (1993), 8–10.

Australia. Constitutional Centenary Foundation. *1999 Referendum – A New Preamble*. Melbourne, 1999.

Australia. Constitutional Commission. *Final Report*. Canberra: Australia Government Publishing Service, 1988.

Australia. Council on Aboriginal Reconciliation. *Annual Report, 2000*.

– *Corroboree 2000*. August 2000.

– *The Position of Indigenous Peoples in National Constitutions*. Canberra, 1993.

Australia. House of Representatives Standing Committee on Aboriginal and Torres Strait Islanders Affairs. *A New Deal: A Report on Greater Autonomy for Torres Strait Islanders*. Canberra: Parliament of the Commonwealth of Australia, August 1997.

Australia. Human Rights and Equal Opportunity Commission. *Bringing Them Home: National Inquiry into Separation of Aboriginal and Torres Strait Islander Children from Their Families*. Sydney, 1997.

Australia. *Mabo v. Queensland: Determination of Facts*. Supreme Court of Queensland, Moynihan J., 16 November 1990.

Australia. National Native Title Tribunal. *1995/96 Annual Report*. Perth, 1996.

Australia. Royal Commission into Aboriginal Deaths in Custody. *National Report:*

Overview of Recommendations. Canberra: Australia Government Publishing Service, 1991.

Australia. National Indigenous Working Group on Native Title. *Coexistence – Negotiation and Certainty: Indigenous Position on the Wik Decision and the Government's Proposed Amendments to the Native Title Act, 1993*. Canberra, April 1997.

Australia. *Transcript of Proceedings in the Mabo Case*. 9 volumes.

Australia. University of Canberra. *Final Report of Aboriginal Nations and the Australian Constitution Conference*. Canberra, 24 May 1997.

Canada 125: Its Constitutions, 1763–1982. Edited by J. Ferdinand Tanguay. Ottawa: Canada Communication Group, 1992.

Canada. Federal Treaty Negotiation Office. *Nisga'a Final Agreement*. Ottawa, 1998.

Canada. Minister of Indian Affairs and Northern Development. *Gathering Strength – Canada's Aboriginal Action Plan*. Ottawa, 1997.

– *In All Fairness: A Native Claims Policy*. Ottawa, 1981.

– *Outstanding Business*. Ottawa, 1982.

Canada. Parliament. *Report of the Special Parliamentary Committee on Indian Self-Government* (Penner Report). Ottawa, 1983.

Canada. Royal Commission on Aboriginal Peoples. *The High Arctic Relocation*. Ottawa: Canada Communications Group, 1994.

– *People to People, Nation to Nation* (Summary of Report). Ottawa: Canada Communications Group, 1996.

– *Report*. 5 vols. Ottawa: Canada Communication Group, 1996.

Canada. Royal Commission on Electoral Reform and Party Financing. *Reforming Electoral Democracy*. Ottawa: Supply and Services, 1991.

Canada. Royal Commission on the Mackenzie Valley Pipeline. *Northern Frontier, Northern Homeland*. (Berger Inquiry). Ottawa: Minister of Supply and Services Canada, 1977.

Canada. Task Force to Review Comprehensive Claims Policy. *Living Treaties: Lasting Agreements*. Ottawa: Department on Indian Affairs and Northern Development, 1985.

Great Britain. House of Commons. *Report from the Select Committee on Aborigines (British Settlements)*, 26, June 1837.

Hawaiian Kingdom. Website, www.hawaiiankingdom.org.

International Work Group for Indigenous Affairs. *The Indigenous World, 2000–2001*. Copenhagen, 2001.

United Nations. *Draft Declaration of the Rights of Indigenous Peoples*. As Agreed upon by the Members of the Working Group at its Eleventh Session, UNESCO, E/CNR/1944/Add 1, 20 April 1994.

Law Cases

Adeyinka Oyekan v. Musendiku Adele, [1957] All E.R. 785.

Amodu Tijani v. Secretary Southern Nigeria, [1921] A.C. 399.

Attorney General (N.S.W.) v. Brown, [1847] 1 Legge 312.

Brandy v. Human Rights and Opportunity Commission (1995), 183 C.L.R. 245.

Brendale v. Confederated Tribes and Bands of Yakima Indian Nations, 109B S. Ct. 2994 (1989).

Calder v. Attorney General of British Columbia (1973), 34 D.L.R. (3rd) 145.

Campbell v. British Columbia (2000), 189 D.L.R. (4th) 333.

Campbell v. Hall, 1 Cowp. 204 (1774).

Cherokee Nation v. Georgia, 30 US (5 Pet.) 1 (1831).

Coe v. Commonwealth of Australia and the United Kingdom (1979), 53 A.L.J.R. 334.

Commonwealth of Australia v. Yarmir, [2001] H.C.A. 56.

Cooper v. Stewart (1889), 14 App. Cas. 286.

Cubillo and Gunner v. Commonwealth of Australia (2000), 174 A.L.R. 97.

Delgamuukw v. British Columbia, [1997], 3 S.C.R. 1010.

Elk v. Wilkins, 112 U.S. 94 (1884).

Employment Division, Dept. of Human Resources of Oregon et al. v. Alfred L. Smith et al., 494 U.S. 872 (1990).

Gerhardy v. Brown (1984/5), 159 C.L.R. 74.

Guerin v. The Queen, [1984] 2 S.C.R. 335.

Lone Wolf v. Hitchcock, 187 U.S. 553 (1903).

Johnson and Graham's Lessee v. McIntosh, 21 U.S. (8 Wheat) 543 (1823).

Joint Council of Passamaquoddy Tribe v. Morton et al., 528 F. 2d 370 (1975).

Kartinyeri v. The Commonwealth, [1997] A.L.J.R. 722.

Koowarta v. Bjelke-Peterson (1982), 153 C.L.R. 168.

Mabo v. Queensland (1988), 166 C.L.R. 186.

Mabo v. Queensland (No. 2) (1992), 175 C.L.R. 1.

Members of the Yorta Yorta Aboriginal Commnity v. The State of Victoria, [1998] F.C.A. 1606

Members of the Yorta Yorta Aboriginal Community v. Victoria, [2002] H.C.A. 58.

Milirrpum and Others v. Nabalco Pty Ltd and the Commonwealth of Australia (1970), 17 F.L.R. 141.

Mitchell v. U.S. (1835), 9 Peters 711.

New Zealand Maori Council v. Attorney General, [1987] 1 N.Z.L.R. 641.

North Ganalanja Aboriginal Corporation v. Queensland (1996), 61 F.L.R. 1.

R. v. Badger, [1996] 1 S.C.R. 771.

R. v. Gladstone, [1996] 2 S.C.R. 723.

R. v. Marshall (No. 1), [1999] 3 S.C.R. 456.

R. v. Marshall (No. 2), [1999] 3 S.C.R. 533.

R. v. Pamejewon, [1996] 2 S.C.R. 821.

R. v. Van der Peet, [1996] 2 S.C.R. 507.

Reg. v. Symonds, [1847] N.Z.P.C.C. 387.

St. Catherine's Milling and Lumber Company v. The Queen (1889), 14 A.C. 46.

Southern Rhodesia [1919] A.C. 211.

Sparrow v. The Queen, [1990] 1 S.C.R. 1075.

Tee-Hit-Tom Indians v. United States, 348 U.S. 272 (1995).

Te Ruanga o Muriwhenua Inc. v. Attorney General and Others, High Court, Wellington, CP 533/87, October 1987, Greig J.

Te Weehi v. Regional Fisheries Officer, [1986] 1 N.Z L.R. 680.

Treaty Tribes Coalition, Te Runanga o Ngati Porou and Tainui Maori Trust Board v. Urban Maori Authoirites, Treaty of Waitangi Fisheries Commission and Ors, [1977] 1 N.Z.L.R. 513.

U.S. v. Sandover, 231 U.S. (1913) 39.

Waanyi People's Native Title Application, Re (1995), 129 A.L.R. 118.

Western Australia v. Commonwealth of Australia (1995), 183 C.L.R. 373.

Western Australia v. Ward (2002), 191 A.L.R. 1.

Wi Parata v. Bishop of Wellington, [1877] 3 N.Z. Jur (NS) SC 72.

Wik Peoples v. Queensland (1996), 187 C.L.R. 1.

Worcester v. State of Georgia, 31 U.S. (6 Pet.) 515.

Yanner v. Eaton, [1999] H.C.A. 53.

Index

13, 122, 124, 152, 175, 188–9, 199–
218, 220, 284–5, 297, 316–21, 322–
3, 331–3, 367, 369, 376; *Aboriginal
Protection and Restoration of the Sale of
Opium Act, 1897,* 111–13; attempt
to stop the *Mabo* case, 207–13;
*Community Services (Torres Strait Act)
1984,* 207; Deeds of Grant in Trust
(DOGIT), 207, 369; Indigenous
population, 108, 188, 220; involvement in *Mabo* case, 11, 199–218;
involvement in post-*Mabo* politics,
284, 297, 299; involvement in post-
Wik politics, 322–3, 332–3; Island
Co-ordinating Council, 375; Labor
Party, 332–3; National Party, 333;
native title determinations, 367;
North Queensland Land Council,
190–1; pastoral leases, 87, 316–21;
*Queensland Coastal Islands Declara-
tory Act,* 207–8; resistance to Commonwealth purchasing of lands for
Aboriginal communities, 175, 188–
9, 370; settler administration of
Indigenous affairs, 108–13; Su-
preme Court, 205, 331; Torres
Strait Island administration, 24–5,
55–6, 58–9, 111–13; *Torres Strait
Islanders Act, 1939,* 113; Torres
Strait Treaty, 55–8. *See also* Bjelke-
Petersen; *Wik Peoples v. Queensland*

R. v. Badger (1996), 343
R. v. Gladstone (1996), 419n.33
R. v. Marshall (No. 1) (1999), 345
R. v. Marshall (No. 2) (1999), 345
R. v. Pamejewon (1996), 419n.33
R. v. Van der Peet (1996), 343
race, racism, 11, 30–1, 51, 105–8, 111,
114–15, 117, 119, 122–4, 128–30,

133–4, 138, 140, 145, 147–8, 230–1,
281
Racial Discrimnation Act, 1973, 52,
54,62, 123, 184–5, 188–9, 201, 208–
9, 213, 260, 277, 284, 286, 290–2,
302, 305, 311, 330, 332–3, 355
Raglan Golf Course, 176
Randwick Corporation v. Rutledge, 252
Ranger Uranium Inquiry, 172–3
reconciliation, 12, 223, 226–7, 283,
293, 299, 324, 327–9, 351, 357–65;
Council for Australian Reconcilia-
tion, 226–7, 280, 284, 359–60;
Melbourne Conference (1997),
327–9; Reconciliation Australia
Limited, 365; Sydney Conference
(2000), 359–63
Redfern, 286, 299, 301
Reed, Justice Stanley, 178
Reg. v. Symonds (1847), 261
Rehnquist, Chief Justice William, 241
Reynolds, Henry, 18, 28, 76–7, 79–80,
84, 87–9, 109, 191, 196, 243, 252,
262, 334
Reynolds, Margaret, 227, 313, 326
Rice, James, 199, 214, 216–18, 243
Richardson, Sir Ivor, 235
Ridgeway, Aden, 350, 358, 362
Riel, Louis, 104, 109
Riley, Bob, 290
Rio-Tinto Corporation, 318
Ritter, David, 78
Robinson, George Augustus, 80–1,
89
Robinson, Mary, 354
Robinson, Viola, 338
Ross, David, 289, 370
Roth, W.E., 111
Rowley, C.S., 111,158, 175, 189
Rowse, Tim, 160, 302